A BIRDER'S GUIDE TO METROPOLITAN AREAS OF NORTH AMERICA

PAUL LEHMAN
EDITOR

 American Birding Association, Inc.

Library of Congress Control Number: 2001096956
ISBN Number: 1-878788-15-9
First Edition
    1   2   3   4   5   6   7   8
Printed in the United States of America

Publisher
    American Birding Association, Inc.
Production Editor
    Virginia Maynard
Copy Editor
    Hugh Willoughby
Layout and Typography
    Virginia Maynard; using CorelVENTURA, Windows version 5.0
Maps
    Virginia Maynard; using CorelDRAW version 5.0
Photography
    front cover: *Olive-sided Flycatcher;* Alan Hopkins
Illustrations
    Mountain Plover; Shawneen Finnegan
    Cerulean Warbler; Dan Lane
    Purple Sandpiper; Michael O'Brien
    Iceland Gull; Michael O'Brien
    Long-billed Dowitcher; Terry O'Nele
    Swainson's Hawk; Louise Zemaitis
    Broad-winged Hawks; David Sibley
    Black-headed Gull; Shawneen Finnegan
    Swainson's Warbler; Shawneen Finnegan
    Le Conte's Thrasher; Dan Lane
    Northern Hawk Owl; Louise Zemaitis
Distributed by
    American Birding Association Sales
    PO Box 6599
    Colorado Springs, Colorado 80934-6599 USA
    Tel: (800) 634-7736 or (719) 578-0607
    fax: (800) 590-2473 or (719) 578-9705
    email: abasales@abasales.com
    www.americanbirding.org

TABLE OF CONTENTS

INTRODUCTION

Perhaps it is inevitable that on thinking about birding in metropolitan regions we might envision making outings through highway gridlock to reach sewage-treatment plants or large landfills. Or we see ourselves peering at waterbirds as they scurry between discarded shopping carts and used tires. Such stereotypes, while unfortunately true in a few instances, do not apply to a vast number of excellent birding destinations in and around North America's major cities. We hope to show that these human population centers provide some of the best birding on the continent and how you can use your birding time here to best advantage.

An unfortunate, but birder-positive, result of urbanization is the creation of habitat oases—patches of green or blue surrounded by large expanses of concrete and suburbia that act as magnets to migrants, both waterbirds and landbirds. In fact, many of North America's best migrant traps are located in urban settings. These include such well-known sites as Central Park in New York City, Mount Auburn Cemetery near Boston, several lakefront parks near downtown Chicago, and Point Loma in San Diego. Add to this list many superb migrant traps that are little known to birders living outside the region: Kennesaw Mountain near Atlanta or Corn Creek near Las Vegas, for example. Every city covered in this guide supports such oases, and a number of these migrant hot-spots are discussed in each chapter.

The sizable number of birders living in metropolitan regions, coupled with the intensive coverage which they give many of the local sites, means that information on the best places to visit and on the status and distribution of species throughout the year is relatively well known. It also means that local and regional rarities are found on a regular basis, and news of their occurrence is usually readily available.

This guide is intended for the birder planning a trip to any of the 33 metropolitan regions covered in this guide. It is designed to assist both "layover" birders—those with only a few hours to spend during a business junket or a family trip—and "destination" birders—those with the luxury of several days to get out and prospect. For each city, the authors have selected prime birding spots that support a fine variety of species and an interesting cross-section of habitats, making sure to provide attractive options for any time of the year. The book treats not only destinations that are in and close to the urban core, but also one or more that are as far as a two-hour drive from downtown. Thus, travelers with a free day can leave the old shopping carts and tires behind and experience some of the continent's most picturesque natural areas. Head out from Calgary to the Canadian Rockies, from Houston or New Orleans to some of the best migrant stopovers on the Gulf Coast, or from Denver to miles and miles of shortgrass prairie or to ptarmigan-infested alpine tundra. Or perhaps wander away from Miami into endless sawgrass marshes of the Everglades, head outside Albuquerque to montane conifer forests, or explore rugged coastlines near Seattle, San Francisco, or Halifax. Every city treated in this book has rural gems close by that most birders will want to visit.

Unlike most birdfinding guides, which treat just one region in detail, this guide covers scattered areas across almost the entire width and breadth of the United States and Canada, including virtually all of the continent's major habitat types. The number of species mentioned exceeds 600. Further, a large majority of the most sought-after species found in the ABA Area are treated: from Three-toed to Red-cockaded Woodpeckers, Snail Kite to Gyrfalcon, Great Gray and Northern Hawk Owls to Swainson's and Red-faced Warblers, from Atlantic Puffin to Rock Sandpiper, Spruce Grouse to Baird's Sparrow, California Gnatcatcher to Saltmarsh Sharp-tailed Sparrow, Yellow-billed Magpie to Bicknell's Thrush, and Yellow Rail to Le Conte's Thrasher...to name just a few.

THE PLAN OF THE BOOK

The cities are organized alphabetically. During the book's planning stages, two categories of cities were identified: those receiving detailed treatment, and those to be covered somewhat more briefly. The former class includes major urban centers not previously covered by ABA/Lane birdfinding guides. The latter category includes large cities already served by ABA/Lane guides (e.g., Boston, Denver, Los Angeles, Miami, San Diego), smaller cities that receive a relatively large number of visitors, major airline hubs, and cities found in regions that otherwise would have gone unrepresented. In a perfect world, every deserving city on the continent would have been included, and the amount of detail given to each metropolitan area would have been greater. Space, as usual, was the limiting factor—and the final product still turned out to be this 512-page behemoth.

Despite these limitations, every attempt has been made to include a selection of diverse sites for each chapter. Such a diversity of habitats results, of course, in a greater number of species that might be found. Such a treatment also provides the reader with a greater appreciation of the ecological diversity found in and around each city. Armed with the ability to recognize major habitat types, micro-habitats, habitat edges, and the characteristic and special birdlife found in each metropolitan region, the birder will become a better bird-finder. Rather than becoming dependent on birdfinding guides for tracking down sought-after species, let these books whet your appetite to explore further the well-known, and the not-so-well-known, nooks and crannies of North America.

Each of these 33 chapters starts with background introductory material normally found at the beginning of an ABA/Lane birdfinding guide. This section includes discussions on hotels and car rentals, traffic, climate, insects and other perils, the birding seasons, Rare Bird Alerts (RBAs) and web sites, other resources, and non-birding destinations. Because each chapter was authored by one or more local experts, potential existed for the diversity of writing-styles to match that of the subject matter. Although the editorial staff endeavored from the beginning to establish a certain level of standardization and consistency, we simultaneously tried to allow authors ample flexibility within these constraints and the reality of word counts.

Use this guide in conjunction with good maps of the applicable area (e.g., DeLorme, AAA, Rand McNally). The detailed directions in the text and the book's many maps will get you to all the principal sites covered, but having an additional good map along facilitates additional exploring on your own. *Note that Canada is on the metric system; rental cars there will have a speedometer based on kilometers. One kilometer is 0.624 mile.*

Other suggestions to improve your birdfinding success include keeping current on weather forecasts—particularly during migration—and contacting local birders (e.g., those listed in the ABA membership directory) before reaching a destination. There is no substitute for tapping local expertise.

In each chapter note that some places—typically the most interesting and productive—are **bold-faced**. To help you decide where and when to visit, most locations include important information on avian specialties and seasonal status.

No birdfinding guide can stay fully up-to-date for long. The sites themselves, access to some properties, route numbers, RBA phone numbers, and (especially) the addresses of web sites all change over time. The American Birding Association keeps an active file of updates and corrections to their birdfinding guides. Please submit needed text or map changes to ABA so that they can be used in possible future editions.

SAFETY

Sadly, any birdfinding guide used in today's world must address issues of personal security. Worthwhile birding sites that are known to be unsafe are excluded from this book. Some other locations, such as the less traveled sections of some large city parks, are included with precautions. To provide an extra level of safety, birders—particularly lone females—should consider visiting such areas with a friend or with a group. Away from the sites that caution single birders, you should be as safe as you are virtually anywhere in North America. Nonetheless, as a birder, you are likely to habitually visit relatively remote areas while carrying expensive optical equipment, and this combination may increase your attractiveness as a target of theft. We urge all readers to be vigilant to their surroundings, and to practice common sense in regard to their personal safety and property. While in the field, if you see, hear, or otherwise sense something that is not quite right, go somewhere else. As a general rule, we recommend birding with others in most urban and some suburban settings. These days, many birders carry cell phones, also.

BIRDER BEHAVIOR

The American Birding Association *Code of Birding Ethics* appears near the end of this book. In addition to personal safety, safe driving behavior while birding in traffic is an additional concern for birders visiting metropolitan areas. Respecting the rights of landowners is also extremely important. Never enter private property without permission of the owner. Many will grant permission if asked, but few take kindly to unannounced visitors, and trespassing birders give us all a bad name. Please do not be the next birder whose lack of courtesy leads to closure of a productive spot.

ACKNOWLEDGMENTS

I thank all the many authors of the accounts in this guide for their excellent contributions. Without their incredible local knowledge and hard work, this book would not have been possible. There were also many, many people who helped these authors to assemble their treatises. We acknowledge them all at the end of the appropriate chapter. Each completed chapter also was reviewed by a local expert; they are listed on page 6.

The work of artists Shawneen Finnegan, Dan Lane, Michael O'Brien, Terry O'Nele, David Sibley, and Louise Zemaitis adds greatly to the appearance of this book. The San Francisco chapter author, Alan Hopkins, performed double duty, having also contributed our cover photo.

Several individuals were of assistance to me and to the editorial team in providing advice, information, or other comments on a variety of draft material, on early project organization, or with many other little things; they include Paul Baicich, Larry Balch, Bob Berman, Shawneen Finnegan, Daphne Gemmill, Robb Hamilton, Victoria Irwin, Cindy Lippincott, and Brad Schram. The entire manuscript was reviewed by the eagle eyes of Hugh Willoughby.

Most of all, I wish to thank Virginia Maynard, who was a true co-editor of this guide. She prepared all the countless fine maps and the overall layout, assisted with editing, coordinated the book's production, and basically kept things running when I was away (which was often). She deserves much of the credit for this product as well.

Paul Lehman
Cape May, New Jersey
October 2001

Listed here are the authors for each of the chapters, without whose dedication and volunteer work this book would not have been possible.

Albuquerque – John Parmeter
Atlanta – Giff Beaton
Boston – Robert H. Stymiest, Marjorie Rines, and Ron Lockwood
Buffalo and Niagara – Willie D'Anna and Kayo Roy
Calgary – Calgary Field Naturalists' Society
Chicago – Lynne Carpenter and David B. Johnson
Cleveland – Larry Rosche, Paula Lozana, and Bob Finkelstein
Dallas/Fort Worth – Martin Reid and Matt White
Denver – Tony Leukering and Christopher L. Wood
Detroit – Karl Overman
Halifax – Blake Maybank
Houston – David Sarkozi
Kansas City – Chris Hobbs
Las Vegas – Marian and Jim Cressman
Los Angeles – Jean Brandt and Kimball Garrett
Memphis – Jeff R. Wilson
Miami – Larry Manfredi and Mickey Wheeler
Minneapolis/St. Paul – Paul Budde and Mark Ochs
Montréal – Pierre Bannon and Richard Yank
New Orleans – Dan Purrington
New York – Peter Joost
Philadelphia – John Harding
Phoenix – Richard Ditch
Portland – Jeff Gilligan and Owen Schmidt
Saint Louis – Bill Rowe and Randy Korotev
Salt Lake City – Ella Sorensen, Georgene Bond, and Robert Bond
San Diego – Richard Webster
San Francisco – Alan Hopkins
Seattle – Steve Mlodinow and Kevin Aanerud
Toronto – Hugh Currie
Vancouver – Wayne Weber
Washington, D.C. – Ottavio Janni and Rob Hilton
Winnipeg – Rudolf Koes and Peter Taylor

We wish also to thank the following local experts who reviewed and checked the chapters listed below. Their insights were crucial in helping to ensure accuracy.

Albuquerque – Jerry Oldenettel
Atlanta – Pierre Howard
Boston – Wayne Petersen
Buffalo/Niagara Falls – John Black and Mike Morgante
Calgary – Ian Halladay
Chicago – Steve Mlodinow
Cleveland – Rob Harlan
Dallas/Fort Worth – Jim Peterson
Denver – Joey Kellner
Detroit – Mike Mencotti
Halifax – Ian McLaren
Houston – Matt White
Kansas City – Robert Fisher and Mick McHugh
Las Vegas – Ted Floyd
Los Angeles – Mike San Miguel, Sr.
Memphis – Bob Foehring
Miami – Wally George
Minneapolis/St. Paul – Anthony Hertzel
New Orleans – Dave Muth
New York City – Tom Burke and Angus Wilson
Philadelphia – Nick Pulcinella
Phoenix – Steve Ganley and Roy Jones
Portland – Ray Korpi
Salt Lake City – Terry Sadler
San Diego – Guy McCaskie
San Francisco – Joseph Morlan
Seattle – Hal Opperman
Toronto – Dave Milsom
Vancouver – Larry Cowan
Washington, D.C. – Dave Czaplak
Winnipeg – Larry DeMarch and Gene Walz

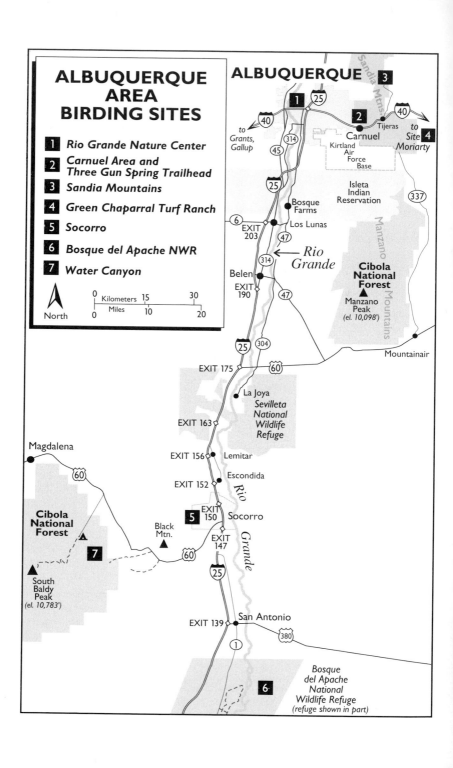

ALBUQUERQUE AREA BIRDING SITES

1 Rio Grande Nature Center
2 Carnuel Area and Three Gun Spring Trailhead
3 Sandia Mountains
4 Green Chaparral Turf Ranch
5 Socorro
6 Bosque del Apache NWR
7 Water Canyon

North

Kilometers 0 15 30
Miles 0 10 20

ALBUQUERQUE

3

1 25
40 2 40
to Grants, Gallup 314 Carnuel Tijeras to Site Moriarty 4
Kirtland Air Force Base
45
25 Isleta Indian Reservation 337
Bosque Farms
6 EXIT 203 Los Lunas
47
314 ← Rio Grande Cibola National Forest
Belen Manzano Peak (el. 10,098')
EXIT 190
47
25 304
EXIT 175 60
Mountainair
La Joya
Sevilleta National Wildlife Refuge
EXIT 163
Magdalena EXIT 156 Lemitar
60 Escondida
EXIT 152 Rio Grande
Cibola National Forest
7 Black Mtn.
EXIT 150 Socorro
5
EXIT 147
South Baldy Peak (el. 10,783') 60
25
EXIT 139 San Antonio
380
1
Bosque del Apache National Wildlife Refuge (refuge shown in part)
6

ALBUQUERQUE, NEW MEXICO

John Parmeter

The city of Albuquerque lies at an elevation of 5,000 to 6,000 feet between the Rio Grande to the west and the Sandia Mountains to the east. With a population of 500,000, it is New Mexico's largest city, offering a wide variety of motels and restaurants.

The area offers varied birding all year. Important habitats within a one-hour drive of the city include the bosque (cottonwood riparian woodlands) along the Rio Grande, desert washes, pinyon-juniper woodlands, montane chaparral in the Sandia foothills, and the mixed and coniferous forests of the Sandias, which rise to over 10,000 feet. Slightly farther away, but still within a one-hour drive, is a sod farm that hosts several interesting grassland species. Less than 100 miles and two hours south of the city there are two other highly productive birding areas. The first is the famous Bosque del Apache National Wildlife Refuge south of Socorro, which is by far the area's best spot for waterbirds. The second is Water Canyon in the Magdalena Mountains, less than thirty minutes west of Socorro. This spot offers good birding especially in spring and summer, with a few southwestern species that do not range north to the Sandias.

ESSENTIAL INFORMATION

Getting Around: It is essential to have a vehicle when birding the area because public transportation is almost non-existent. Rental cars from several companies are available at the Albuquerque International Sunport (i.e., Airport). Traffic in Albuquerque is generally not bad for a large city, although there can be some rush-hour congestion on weekdays on both I-25 and I-40 within the city limits.

Climate: Albuquerque is dry all year. Summers are hot with low humidity, and temperatures are typically in the 90s Fahrenheit. It rarely gets hotter, because of the high elevation. Winters are moderately cold (you will need warm clothing), but daily highs are almost always well above freezing. Winter storms are occasional, but snow rarely sticks at elevations below 7,000 feet. It is advisable to check weather and road conditions if you plan to travel above that elevation between November and March. The transition from winter to summer can occur quite rapidly between mid-March and mid-May. Spring is often very windy, especially during the month of March. The period from mid-September to early November usually features mild weather, and is perhaps the most pleasant time of year.

Natural Hazards: Biting insects are rarely a problem in New Mexico (except for possible mosquitoes at Bosque del Apache). Rattlesnakes are rarely encountered, but they can occur almost anywhere away from the highest mountains, so watch where you step. Remember that this area is at high elevation; the lowest-elevation spot covered, Bosque del Apache NWR, lies at 4,500 feet. It is thus important to avoid excessive physical exertion if you are coming from sea level, especially when in the mountains above 7,000 feet. The near-constant sunshine and high altitude make sunscreen and a hat essential, especially in summer.

Safety: The birding localities mentioned in this chapter are generally safe, but it is probably advisable to have at least two people if going forth nocturnally to look for owls. When leaving a parked car for a long period, do not leave valuables visible in the car. Break-ins have been known to occur at the Three Gun Spring Trailhead.

Other Resources: Highly recommended is the latest edition of the New Mexico Ornithological Society's (NMOS) *New Mexico Bird Finding Guide* (see the NMOS home page at *http//mvar.nmsu.edu/nmos*). This guide covers all of the spots in this chapter in greater detail, as well as many others. The birdfinding guide, as well as a field checklist of New Mexico birds, can be ordered from NMOS, P.O. Box 3068, Albuquerque, NM 87190-3068. These materials are also usually sold at both the Rio Grande Nature Center and Bosque del Apache NWR. Visitors may also want to call the New Mexico Rare Bird Alert at (505) 323-9323. Note, however, that this tape usually focuses on birds that are rarities in New Mexico, and not on the local specialties that may be of interest to a visiting birder.

THE BIRDING YEAR

Spring migration begins in late February with flocks of Sandhill Cranes and Snow and Ross's Geese flying north up the Rio Grande Valley. By the end of March, all of the cranes and most of the white geese have departed, along with other wintering species, such as Bald Eagles and longspurs. Several early spring migrants arrive in March, including Cinnamon Teal, Mountain Plover and a few other shorebirds, and several swallows. Migration increases through April, with the peak passage occurring from approximately 20 April to 15 May for migrant landbirds, such as *Empidonax* flycatchers, vireos, and warblers. Shorebird migration peaks about a week earlier. The months of May through July offer excellent opportunities for montane birding in the Sandia and Magdalena Mountains, including a few southwestern species, such as Virginia's, Grace's, and Red-faced Warblers. This is also a good time to seek summering Flammulated Owls in the mountains, as well as the resident but locally rare Northern Pygmy-Owl. Fall shorebird migration can be good from late July through September, while southbound passerine migration is best from mid-August to mid-October. October and November see the arrival of most wintering birds, including those species listed above as departing in March. Rarely, winter can bring Pine Grosbeaks and rosy-finches to the Sandia Mountains (November to March). A variety of foothill and desert species can be found year round, including Scaled and Gambel's Quail, Greater Roadrunner, Ladder-backed Woodpecker, Pinyon Jay, Chihuahuan Raven, Curve-billed and Crissal Thrashers, and Black-throated Sparrow. Neotropic Cormorant is normally present year round at Bosque del Apache.

RIO GRANDE NATURE CENTER

One to three hours; year round

The best place to visit the Rio Grande bosque is at the **Rio Grande Nature Center**, on the east side of the river, north of downtown Albuquerque. From the junction of Interstates 25 and 40, head west on I-40 for about 2 miles and exit north onto Rio Grande Boulevard (Exit 157). Go north on Rio Grande for 1.4 miles, and turn left at a stoplight onto Candelaria Road. In a few blocks Candelaria ends, and a right turn leads into the nature-center parking lot, from where one can continue on foot. The center and the parking lot are open daily (except holidays) from 10:00AM to 5:00PM ($1 fee requested). If the center is closed, park near the end of Candelaria and walk west along a bike trail to access the bosque.

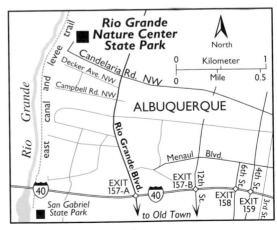

Either of these approaches will lead to a bridge across a drainage channel west of the center; after crossing the bridge, one can work the edge of the bosque along a north-south dike, or walk the two trails running through the bosque to the river.

Resident birds in this area include Cooper's Hawk, Ring-necked Pheasant, Gambel's Quail, Greater Roadrunner (uncommon), Downy Woodpecker, Black Phoebe (near water), Black-capped Chickadee, White-breasted Nuthatch, Bewick's Wren, and Great-tailed Grackle. Western Screech-Owl is also resident and may be heard at night. Summering species include Green Heron, Yellow-billed Cuckoo (uncommon), Common Nighthawk, Black-chinned Hummingbird, Western Wood-Pewee, Western Kingbird, Yellow-breasted Chat, Summer Tanager, Black-headed and Blue Grosbeaks, Common Grackle, Bullock's Oriole, and Lesser Goldfinch. In winter look for Mountain Chickadee (sporadic), Hermit Thrush, "Audubon's" Yellow-rumped Warbler, Spotted Towhee, and several sparrows, including an occasional White-throated. Many other species can be found during migration, mainly from late April to mid-May and late August through September. Frequently encountered are Willow, Dusky, Gray, and Ash-throated Flycatchers, Cassin's (fall) and Plumbeous (mainly spring) Vireos, Violet-green Swallow, Virginia's, Townsend's (fall), and MacGillivray's Warblers, Western Tanager, and Green-tailed Towhee. A number of rare landbirds have been banded here in migration, including Canada Warbler and Scarlet Tanager.

If the nature center is open, check the pond just north of the headquarters building. It hosts numerous waterfowl in migration and winter. Canada Geese are resident, and Wood Ducks are often present. In spring, Blue-winged and Cinnamon Teal occur. Rare species such as Greater White-fronted Goose and Eurasian Wigeon have been found here in recent winters.

Carnuel and Three Gun Spring Trailhead

One to three hours; year round

The best area for a diversity of desert and foothill species is near the community of **Carnuel**, located north of I-40 just east of Albuquerque. Head east on I-40 to the Carnuel exit (Exit 170). Exit the freeway and turn

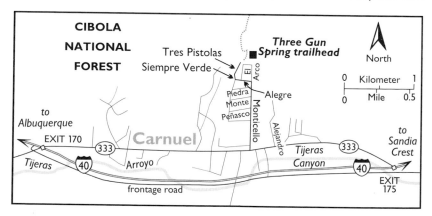

left (east) at the stop sign, continuing east 1.75 miles on NM-333. A housing development is uphill to the left. Turn left onto Monticello Drive, go 0.5 mile and turn left onto Alegre Road, and in 0.1 mile turn right onto Siempre Verde. Almost immediately, bear right onto Tres Pistolas, and continue uphill 0.2 mile to the parking area at the **Three Gun Spring Trailhead** (do not leave valuables in car). Walking uphill along the first mile of the trail allows access to desert scrub, rocky hillsides, and juniper woodlands.

Resident birds here include Scaled Quail, Ladder-backed Woodpecker, Western Scrub-Jay, Pinyon Jay, Juniper Titmouse, Bushtit, Rock, Canyon, and Bewick's Wrens, Western Bluebird, Curve-billed and Crissal Thrashers, Canyon Towhee, and Rufous-crowned Sparrow. In winter, Townsend's Solitaires are often present, and flocks of White-crowned Sparrows sometimes contain local rarities such as "Slate-colored" Fox Sparrow or Golden-crowned Sparrow. From late April to August, Black-chinned Sparrow and Scott's Oriole are present. For both species, it helps to know their songs. Common Poorwills are easily heard on warm evenings (April to August).

SANDIA MOUNTAINS

Several hours to half day; year round

To bird the **Sandia Mountains**, head east past Carnuel on I-40 to Exit 175. Turn left (north) under the freeway toward Cedar Crest on NM-14, and continue about six miles. Here NM-536 goes left, continuing 14 miles to Sandia Crest at 10,678 feet. The best montane birding is above the turn-off to **Capulin Spring** (near mile 8), with several parking lots ($3 fee) and trailheads providing access. (This road may be closed or require chains in winter.) The parking lot at the crest offers spectacular views of the city.

Resident species of the high coniferous forests include Hairy and Three-toed (rare) Woodpeckers, Steller's Jay, Clark's Nutcracker (near

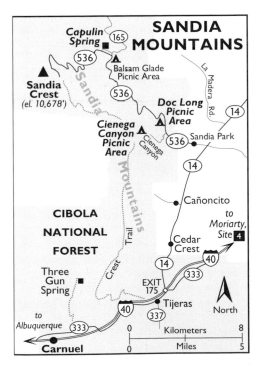

the crest), Common Raven, Mountain Chickadee, Red-breasted Nuthatch, Brown Creeper, Golden-crowned Kinglet, and Red Crossbill (sporadic). Other species such as Williamson's and Red-naped Sapsuckers (both uncommon), Townsend's Solitaire, "Gray-headed" Dark-eyed Junco, Cassin's Finch, Pine Siskin, and Evening Grosbeak may be present year round but tend to disperse to lower elevations in winter. Additional summering birds include Band-tailed Pigeon, White-throated Swift, Broad-tailed Hummingbird, Olive-sided, Dusky, and Cordilleran Flycatchers, Violet-green Swallow, House Wren, Ruby-crowned Kinglet, Hermit Thrush, Orange-crowned and "Audubon's" Yellow-rumped Warblers, Western Tanager, and Green-tailed Towhee. From mid-July to September, look also for Rufous and Calliope Hummingbirds around meadows. From mid-November to March, Pine Grosbeaks and flocks of rosy-finches containing all three species are encountered—although rarely— at the crest. Rosy-finches are perhaps most likely to be found a few days after a severe storm, when there is plenty of snow but when enough melt-off has occurred to expose a few rocky areas at the highest elevations. The relative abundance of the three species varies greatly. (Those birders with a strong desire to see rosy-finches should consult local birders about a trip to the Taos Ski Village, some three hours north of Albuquerque.) Along the lower part of NM-536, a stop at the Cienega Canyon or Doc Long picnic areas in summer may reveal a few species not found at higher elevations, including Plumbeous Vireo and Virginia's and Grace's Warblers. Owling above Capulin Spring can produce Northern Saw-whet Owl year round and Flammulated Owl from May to July.

GREEN CHAPARRAL TURF RANCH, MORIARTY

Several hours; spring, fall, and winter

Excellent grassland birding can be had at the **Green Chaparral Turf Ranch**, a sod farm about 40 miles east of Albuquerque. From Albuquerque, head east on I-40. Take Exit 196, marked for NM-41, and turn north, crossing over the freeway. Go east for 5.2 miles on the frontage road, and then turn left into the turf ranch. A grid of dirt roads offers access; it is normally best to drive along the central north-south road and explore the side roads on foot. *This is private property, so stay on the roads at all times.* Do not bird this site after heavy rains; the roads can become impassably muddy.

The ranch is a well-known site for longspurs, which are often present in large flocks, sometimes with Horned Larks. A scope is essential for viewing these birds, and knowledge of calls is helpful (as is a lack of wind). McCown's is present from late October to March, and hundreds may spend the winter. Chestnut-collared can be present from late September to March; it is usually most numerous in migration. Rarely, one or two Laplands are present from November to March. Another attraction here is Mountain Plover, which can be found from March through September, though it is often scarce in spring.

Mountain Plover
Shawneen Finnegan

It is most regular and sometimes common from July to September. Other shorebirds may be found in migration, including Long-billed Curlew and Baird's Sandpiper (fall). The brushy edges of the sod farm attract migrant sparrows, including Chipping, Clay-colored (fall), Brewer's, Vesper, Lark, Savannah, and Lark Bunting (mainly fall). Interesting raptors, including Ferruginous Hawk and Merlin, are sometimes noted in winter and migration, and both ravens can sometimes be found. An added attraction here is a small pond surrounded by trees near the owner's residence. This area is located at the north end of the central road, and as of this writing, birders are welcome to walk on the dike around this pond. The trees here can harbor many migrants from mid-April to May and August to October. Vagrants have included Sulphur-bellied Flycatcher and Kentucky Warbler.

SOCORRO

Several hours; spring and fall

The city of **Socorro**, located about 75 miles south of Albuquerque on I-25, provides a convenient base for birding Bosque del Apache and the Magdalena Mountains, although birding these spots on day trips from Albuquerque is also possible. Residential areas host resident White-winged and Inca Doves, and Bronzed Cowbird can sometimes be found in summer on the golf course east of the New Mexico Tech campus. Turtle Bay, a group of tree-lined ponds on the east edge of the golf course behind the university's Macey Center, is an excellent spot for migrant landbirds.

BOSQUE DEL APACHE
NATIONAL WILDLIFE REFUGE
Half to full day; year round

To reach **Bosque del Apache**, continue south from Socorro on I-25 for 9 miles to the turn-off for US-380 (Exit 139). Go east less than one mile, and then turn south onto NM-1. Proceed about 8 miles to the refuge headquarters on the right. Here one can obtain information on birding the 15-mile tour loop ($3 fee required) and news of recent sightings. The brush around the headquarters has resident Gambel's Quail and an occasional wintering Pyrrhuloxia. Verdin and Black-throated Sparrow are resident in the adjacent desert scrub, and Phainopeplas are often present in summer.

The refuge tour loop offers a variety of waterbirds at any season, especially in migration and winter. A short summary such as the one given here can scarcely do this locality justice. From October to mid-March, thousands of Sandhill Cranes and Snow Geese are present, and careful study of the Snows will almost always produce a few Ross's Geese. A variety of ducks is always present, and in April and May and from late July to September 10 to 15 species of shorebirds are not unlikely. Neotropic Cormorant is present year round, usually outnumbering Double-crested and generally easy to find. Franklin's

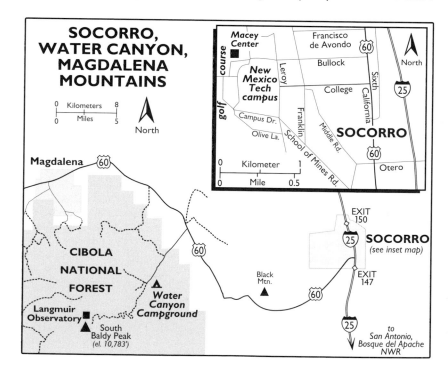

SOCORRO, WATER CANYON, MAGDALENA MOUNTAINS

0 Kilometers 8
0 Miles 5

North

Macey Center
Francisco de Avondo 60
North

golf course

New Mexico Tech campus
Leroy
Bullock
25

College
California
Sixth

Campus Dr.
Franklin
Middle Rd.
SOCORRO
60

Olive La.
School of Mines Rd.

0 Kilometer 1
0 Mile 0.5

Otero

Magdalena 60

CIBOLA
NATIONAL
FOREST
60

Langmuir Observatory
South Baldy Peak (el. 10,783')
Water Canyon Campground

Black Mtn.

60

EXIT 150

25 **SOCORRO**
(see inset map)

EXIT 147

25
to San Antonio, Bosque del Apache NWR

Gull is a fairly common spring migrant, and White-faced Ibis can be common in spring and fall. A variety of herons and egrets occurs in summer, including the locally rare Little Blue Heron and Least Bittern. Common Moorhen is another locally scarce summering bird. A variety of raptors winter, including 10–20 Bald Eagles; Peregrine Falcon is a frequent migrant. Landbirds are generally similar to those at the Rio Grande Nature Center in Albuquerque. Greater Roadrunner is often encountered. In summer, be alert for Lesser Nighthawk, Vermilion Flycatcher, and Lucy's Warbler, all locally scarce and near the northern limits of their ranges.

WATER CANYON

Several hours; spring and early summer

To reach Water Canyon in the Magdalena Mountains, head west from Socorro on US-60. After going about 16 miles, turn left onto a paved road marked for **Water Canyon** (just past mile marker 124). From here, pavement continues 6 miles to Water Canyon Campground, passing through desert grasslands and pinyon-juniper woodlands. At the campground, there is extensive riparian forest and the lower limit of Ponderosa Pine. Beyond the campground, the road becomes dirt and continues several miles to the Langmuir Observatory at over 10,000 feet. Driving to the top may require a high-clearance vehicle and can be impossible in winter, but from April to September the first two miles above the campground can usually be driven in any vehicle. There is a camping fee here, but no day-use fee. A spring day that combines a morning here with an afternoon at Bosque del Apache may produce over 100 species. Water Canyon becomes somewhat less productive in late summer and fall, when summering birds stop singing and begin to head south.

Many species mentioned for Carnuel and the Sandia Mountains are also found in Water Canyon. A specialty here that does not reach the Sandias is Red-faced Warbler, which can be found from late April to August in fir trees one to two miles above the campground. Look also for summering Hepatic Tanagers in this area. Summering Virginia's, Black-throated Gray, and Grace's Warblers are easily found at or just above the campground, and a few Acorn Woodpeckers are resident. Magnificent Hummingbird makes rare appearances at campground feeders. In recent summers, a few Olive Warblers have been found near the observatory. Water Canyon also offers excellent nocturnal birding. Western Screech-Owl is resident in the campground area, and the rare Northern Pygmy-Owl occurs at higher elevations. From late April to at least July, Flammulated Owl, Whip-poor-will, and Common Poorwill may also be found, with the owl often present right in the campground. Spotted and Elf Owls are rare in the canyon.

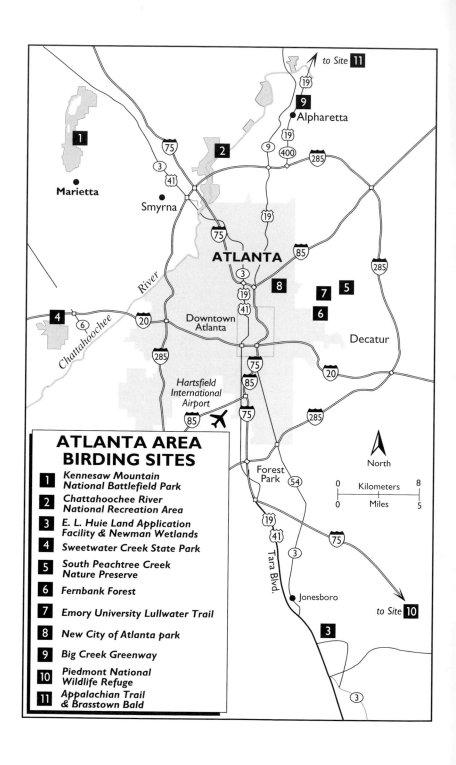

**ATLANTA AREA
BIRDING SITES**

1. Kennesaw Mountain
National Battlefield Park
2. Chattahoochee River
National Recreation Area
3. E. L. Huie Land Application
Facility & Newman Wetlands
4. Sweetwater Creek State Park
5. South Peachtree Creek
Nature Preserve
6. Fernbank Forest
7. Emory University Lullwater Trail
8. New City of Atlanta park
9. Big Creek Greenway
10. Piedmont National
Wildlife Refuge
11. Appalachian Trail
& Brasstown Bald

ATLANTA, GEORGIA

Giff Beaton

Although it is a large city, Atlanta has several top birding sites and enjoys not only excellent birding during spring and fall migrations but also is situated far enough south to have access to some southern specialties. There are a number of easily accessible parks and nature reserves in the metro area that are good not only for passerine migrants but also for winter residents such as waterfowl and sparrows. Additionally, almost any area of green space can harbor at least a few interesting residents or migrants. Atlanta also has a great deal to offer the non-birder, from museums and shopping to a number of historic sites.

ESSENTIAL INFORMATION

Getting Around: Almost all birding will require your own transportation. The rail system in Atlanta does not go to any of the good birding areas, and a bus will get you close to only the smaller areas included in northeast Atlanta. Because Atlanta is a major tourist and business destination, all of the car-rental companies are represented at the airport.

The traffic in Atlanta is bad and getting worse. Try to avoid traveling during rush hour times, or you will spend all of your "birding time" in the car. The times to avoid are approximately 7:00 to 9:00AM and 4:00 to 7:00PM. Interstate 285 on the north end of town is atrocious, eastbound in the morning and westbound in the afternoon. Expect the other interstates to be bad inbound in the morning and outbound in the late afternoon.

Climate: The Atlanta area is fairly hot from April through October, and mild during most of the winter, with just a few really cold days. Temperatures during spring and fall migration range in the 40s Fahrenheit at night to the 60s or 70s in the daytime during early spring and late fall, and from the 70s at night to the 90s during the day in late spring and early fall. Summer can be very hot and muggy, with both temperatures and humidity in the 90s. Rain can occur at any time in any season, so rain-gear is useful.

Natural Hazards: Atlanta has its share of biting insects, mostly during the warmer months. Mosquitoes and flies will be found at all locations, especially those near water. Areas with tall grass may have chiggers, more irritating than actually harmful, but if you don't sit, lie down, or stand for long periods in grass you can usually avoid them. Ticks are very common, so take the normal precautions. There are a few snakes found in this area, but most are harmless, and few if any are likely to be encountered at any of the Atlanta locations. On the other hand, Poison-Ivy is very common and likely to be found at all of these locations.

Safety: All of the areas listed in this section are safe for birding at any time. There are a few other parks or green spaces in the Atlanta area that can have good birding but which are in questionable areas, and thus have not been included.

Other Resources: Very detailed directions for birding all of these and other sites (with the exception of the four northeast Atlanta sites) can be found in *Birding Georgia* by Giff Beaton (2000, Falcon Publishing). The Atlanta Audubon Society (AAS) has an excellent web site, *www.atlantaaudubon.org*, and offers local birding trips. All recurring trips are also mentioned in the text. The Georgia Ornithological Society (GOS) also has an excellent web site, *www.gos.org*, with an index to all recent RBA transcripts, and maintains a telephone hotline covering the state, (770) 493-8862. A great source of information about lodging is the official Georgia guidebook, *Georgia On My Mind*, available free by calling (800) 847-4842, or from *www.gomm.com*.

Other Destinations: Probably the most interesting locations for the visiting natural-history buff are the Fernbank Museum (close to Fernbank Forest) and Zoo Atlanta, 800 Cherokee Avenue SE, (404) 624-5600.

THE BIRDING YEAR

Atlanta's spring migration actually starts in February with the northward movement of Sandhill Cranes overhead and continues with waterfowl moving through during March and April. Passerine migration cranks up at the very end of March and peaks from 20 April through early to mid-May, depending on species. Most of the species represented here are trans-Gulf migrants, with warblers leading the way and cuckoos and flycatchers bringing up the rear. Late April to mid-May is also the best time for shorebirds at the E. L. Huie site. Summer is June and July, with emphasis on breeding species, including the Peregrine Falcons at the Sun Trust building downtown, but fall migration actually starts in July with species such as Cerulean and Black-throated Green Warblers and Louisiana Waterthrush. This is also the beginning of the southbound shorebird migration. August brings in a few more shorebirds and passerines, and is the best month for Cerulean and Worm-eating Warblers, but the peak numbers of vireos, warblers, and tanagers pass through September and early October. Toward the end of October attention shifts to waterfowl and sparrows again, and the last birds moving through involve the tail-end of the waterfowl flight and Sandhill Cranes again, in November and early December.

BIRDING DESTINATIONS

This chapter covers three distinct types of locations. The first four are major Atlanta metro birding sites, which among them provide good birding potential during the entire year. They are Kennesaw Mountain, the Chattahoochee River, the E. L. Huie Land Application Facility, and Sweetwater Creek State Park. The next four sites are smaller in size, are in northeast Atlanta, and are good for a couple of hours of birding, but they are not as productive as the first set of prime locations. Another small site, Big Creek Greenway, is north of the city. Last are two full-day trips, one south to Piedmont National Wildlife Refuge for specialties such as Red-cockaded Woodpecker and Bachman's Sparrow, and one north to Neel's Gap, Lake Winfield Scott, and nearby Brasstown Bald for mountain-region breeding specialties. Although they are not covered in this chapter, Stone Mountain Park, Panola Mountain State Park, and Lake Lanier are also worth a visit.

KENNESAW MOUNTAIN NATIONAL BATTLEFIELD PARK

Half-day; spring and fall for the mountain; winter for the marsh

Kennesaw Mountain offers the best inland birding for migrant vireos, warblers, and other landbirds In Georgia, if not the entire Southeast. Warbler counts of over 20 species in a morning are not uncommon during peak migration, and this Is one of the best spots in the East to see a migrant Cerulean Warbler. Hawk migration is scattered, but ten or more raptor species will be seen over the course of a season. All six Georgia vireos have been seen here, and all but Warbling are regular (Philadelphia is toughest to find but is seen in small numbers during September). Both eastern tanagers pass through commonly and breed in smaller numbers, and Rose-breasted Grosbeak is found in both spring and fall. It is very easy to bird here — just walk up a paved road for 1.5 miles to the summit at your own pace, and you may find birds anywhere along the road. The birds tend to move across the mountain in feeding flocks, and if you are lucky you get them on the downhill side where you can view them at eye level. The road gets a little steep in places, but you can simply slow down if you feel tired.

To reach Kennesaw Mountain, take I-75 to Exit 269, which is Barrett Parkway. Go west 2.1 miles (follow the signs for the park) to Old Route 41, and turn left at the light. Go 1.3 miles, passing the park entrance sign, and turn right on Stilesboro Road. Immediately turn left into the Visitor Center parking lot. The park is open dawn to dusk, but note that this gate is opened

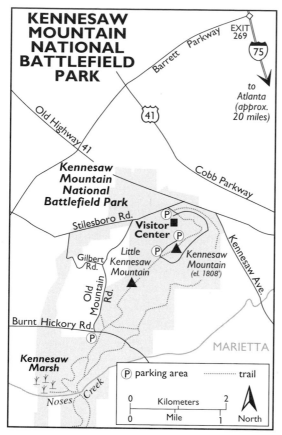

KENNESAW MOUNTAIN NATIONAL BATTLEFIELD PARK

at irregular hours (usually around 7:00AM). If the gate is not open, you can park along Old Route 41 in the designated areas and walk in. The best way to see as many birds as possible is to walk up and then back down the mountain, although on weekdays you may drive. The Visitor Center, (770) 427-4686, has restrooms (locked until 8:30AM), maps of the park, and bird checklists. The Atlanta Audubon Society offers bird walks here, and the Visitor Center has a schedule of upcoming trips (usually during April and September).

Basic strategies to use here include birding sunny areas on cooler days, listening for flocks that may include vocal residents such as Carolina Chickadees, and birding out of the wind. It is worth making a loop around the parking lot before you go up the mountain, especially very early in spring or later in fall. At the lower part of the parking lot is a picnic area, very good for thrushes, especially in fall when they tend to linger a few days among the Dogwood trees. There are also several trees along the edge of the parking lot, especially a large Black Gum at the steps to the picnic area, which host lots of vireos, thrushes, and tanagers. From here start walking up the mountain road. The gate here is not opened until around 8:00AM, but you can walk on the road at any time. In about 0.4 mile you will reach a trail that crosses the road. Most of the avian action will be found above this area. Look especially in areas where the forest thins out or opens up into shrubby areas, and check all the forest edges. The next trail across the road is at the "Saddle" to Little Kennesaw, and here and at the very top are the best views for raptors, swallows, and other aerial species. Unless it's mid-day, you may see just as many species on your way down as on the way up.

Cerulean Warbler
Dan Lane

There are many other parts of the park worth birding, mostly for summer breeding species. Probably the best of these is the trail that goes to **Kennesaw Marsh,** which has possibilities for migrants and is a great place to bird in late fall and winter. The marsh area and the field it is in may be very wet, so bring appropriate footwear. To get there, turn left out of the lot at the Visitor Center onto Stilesboro Road for 0.5 mile and turn left onto Old Mountain Road. It dead-ends in 1.4 miles at Burnt Hickory Road, where you can park in the spaces provided. Walk down the good dirt trail away from Old Mountain Road. At the bottom of the first small hill is an open area of scrub, good for migrants in spring and fall. Kentucky and Hooded Warblers breed here. In winter, this area is good for sparrows and other landbirds, such as Ruby-crowned Kinglet. Climb the hill away from here; at the top (about 0.3 mile from Burnt Hickory) there is a trail off to the right. An area of large, mostly hardwood trees about 100 yards down this trail is good in late fall and winter for Brown Creeper. Return to the main trail and go right 0.4 mile to a larger stream (Noses Creek). Turn right before the bridge and follow the small trail along the side of the creek. When you get to a point where the trail makes a sharp turn to the right uphill (only about 100–200 yards), look for a small trail that goes straight ahead along the creek. There is a large downed tree here, and the trail goes around it. The park does not maintain this trail, and it may be somewhat overgrown, but follow it only 100 feet or so into a large overgrown field. This field is excellent for sparrows in fall and winter. The brushy areas along the edge are good for White-throated Sparrow; Song and Swamp Sparrows are generally found out in the more-open areas. In late October and early November, this field has produced several Lincoln's Sparrow records, which makes it as reliable as any Georgia site for this rare and elusive species. This is also a good spot for wrens; House Wren can be found along the edges of the field in winter, and Winter Wren can be anywhere along the creek or near the field. Also, the marsh has a small wintering population of Sedge Wrens. In summer, White-eyed Vireo, Gray Catbird, and Indigo Bunting breed here. At the very bottom of this field, look over the marsh to an area of dead trees. Watch for raptors perched here as well as for the many woodpeckers that frequent this area, including Red-headed, which nests here. In any season, this is a great place to bird.

CHATTAHOOCHEE RIVER NATIONAL RECREATION AREA

Half day; year round, best spring through late fall

The **Chattahoochee River National Recreation Area** (CRNRA) consists of a series of distinct sections along the Chattahoochee River near Atlanta. Though you may have to share space with joggers, bike riders, pets, and who knows what else, some parts are much less heavily used and offer good birding close to metro Atlanta. Given that all rivers in Georgia are used as migration pathways, and that this is one of the larger ones, both spring and fall migrations here can be spectacular. The best sections for birding are the Johnson Ferry North and South Units, the Cochran Shoals Unit, and the Paces Ferry/Palisades Units, although just about anywhere you can access the river could offer good birding. Early in the day is best in summer. In more heavily used areas such as Cochran Shoals, you may have to get away from the crowds to find birds, especially on the first sunny spring days when it seems that the entire city turns out. There is a $2.00 fee to park in any of these areas; use the pay boxes provided at all the parking lots (annual pass available for $20.00). The river is second only to Kennesaw Mountain for migrants, and it is better for a few species, such as Yellow and Prothonotary Warblers and both waterthrushes, and, in fall, Philadelphia Vireo. Raptors and waterfowl also use the river during migration, and just about all of the hardwood floodplain breeding species occur along the river. Brown-headed Nuthatch and Pine Warbler are both common in the mature pines, and there are many woodpeckers all along the river. Many of these areas also have open fields or scrub for Gray Catbird, Yellow-breasted Chat, and Indigo Bunting.

To get to the **Johnson Ferry Units**, go north on Roswell Road from I-285 (Exit 25) to Johnson Ferry Road, and turn left . These two units are immediately north of the river. The Johnson Ferry North Unit is on your right, with a large field bordered by woods along the river and more trails. On your left is the Johnson Ferry South Unit. Turn left onto Columns Drive and choose either of the two parking areas. Both offer good birding for sparrows in winter in the brush and for migrant passerines along the river. At the end of Columns Drive is the Cochran Shoals Unit, which has access at both ends of a long loop trail (see map).

To get to the main access point for the **Cochran Shoals Unit**, take Exit 22 from I-285, which is signed for New Northside Drive, Northside Drive, and Powers Ferry Road. If westbound, turn right onto New Northside Drive for 0.2 mile to the traffic light and go straight across onto Interstate Parkway North. If eastbound, turn left on Northside Drive to cross I-285 and turn left at the first light for Interstate Parkway North (0.1 mile). Once on Interstate Parkway North, drive 0.8 mile to the Cochran Shoals entrance (after you cross the river) and turn right into the parking lot. This unit is the most popular with birders; you can find birds along any of the trails here, especially the smaller paths that go off into the woods or along the river. The Atlanta Audubon Society offers field trips here every Saturday morning at 7:30AM during spring and fall migration seasons.

The last section is the **Paces Mill/Palisades Units**. Get on I-75 just south of I-285, and take Exit 256 for Mt. Paran Drive. Go just slightly west

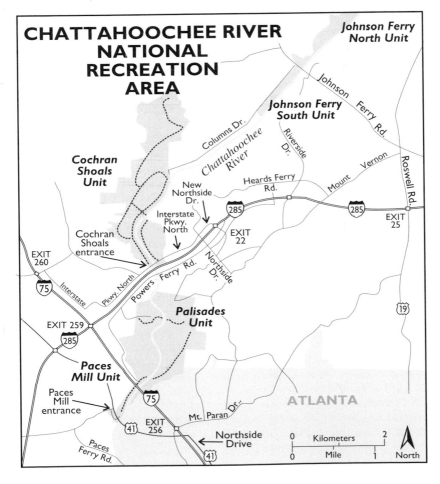

(0.1 mile) to US-41 (Northside Drive) and turn right, cross the Chattahoochee River in 1.1 miles, and turn left at the sign for the Paces Mill Unit. Follow this curving road 0.4 mile as it comes back under US-41 to the parking lot. Check the trail-map sign and park in the back part of the lot. There are restrooms here, and a concession stand which is open in summer only. There is another trail here that follows the west bank of the river under I-75 and connects with the West Palisades Unit and its trail system. The total length of trail along the riverbank is about 1.3 miles, and the migrant birding is as good here as at Cochran Shoals, but with a fraction of the pedestrian traffic. There isn't as much wetland habitat here for breeders, though, and this Unit is not as good in winter.

The **Chattahoochee Nature Center** is along the river north of these areas on Willeo Road, just west of GA-400. Hours are 9:00AM to 5:00PM Monday–Saturday, and 12:00PM to 5:00PM on Sunday; admission is $5 for adults, $3 for seniors and children. The birding is great all year, with several ponds and trails, including a river boardwalk trail along the Chattahoochee . There are a nature store, an interpretive center, guided walks, and other programs; telephone (770) 992-2055. A map of the entire Recreation Area is available from the National Park Service, (770) 399-8070. The map shows areas not covered in this chapter. Virtually any of these sections can be good birding, so try them all!

E. L. HUIE LAND APPLICATION FACILITY AND THE NEWMAN WETLANDS CENTER

Half day, year round

The **E. L. Huie Land Application** Facility, a 4,000-acre wastewater-treatment site about 20 miles south of downtown Atlanta, is a must-visit location during the entire year. Featuring a series of ponds that can be excellent in migration for shorebirds and equally good for ducks in winter, and a nearby boardwalk trail and several other birdable areas, "E. L. Huie" has also built up an impressive list of rarities over the years. There are a total of five ponds, four roughly square ones of more or less equal size, and a much larger one on the south end of the complex. Because these holding-ponds are part of the wastewater-treatment process and are not specifically managed for bird habitat, the ponds range in depth at any given time from full to bone-dry. Fortunately, there is usually at least one which is low enough to provide good shorebird habitat in spring and fall. In winter, most of the ponds remain full and house a good population of waterfowl species. In general, E. L. Huie is great for any waterfowl during migration and for some species all winter, such as Ring-necked Duck, Lesser Scaup, Bufflehead, and Ruddy Duck. During shorebird migration, there are always a few species here, but obviously more are present when there is more available habitat. Just about every shorebird species that has been seen inland in Georgia has been recorded here. Swallows are plentiful during migration, with Purple Martins and Tree Swallows nesting. In late summer there can be impressive numbers of herons, and it's always worth checking overhead for raptors. There is a road system along the dikes that allows birders to drive all the way around each of the five ponds.

Take I-75 south to Exit 235, which is US-19/41, also named Tara Boulevard. At the end of the exit ramp go straight through the traffic light onto Tara Boulevard and go 7.9 miles to Freeman Road (on the left). Turn on Freeman. This turn can be missed, but when the multi-lane, multi-business road becomes a less-developed two-lane road each way, you are getting close. The best landmark is the new Water Authority building on the corner (your left), which is a huge modern-looking structure with lots of glass. (There are no other buildings like it near there.) Go down Freeman for 0.2 mile, passing the E. L. Huie Land Application Facility building on your right, and turn left onto Dixon Industrial Boulevard. Shortly thereafter, turn left into the pond area. Yield to all Water Authority vehicles, and stay on the roads. The pond area is open during daylight hours daily (closing time varies). Exercise caution when the dirt roads are wet. The Atlanta Audubon Society has field trips at the E. L. Huie ponds every Sunday at 8:00AM during migration season.

When you are finished here, it's worth heading over to the **Newman Wetlands Center**, an area of swampy woods with a very nice half-mile combination boardwalk and trail, as well as an interpretive nature center. Go back to Freeman Road, turn left, and drive 2.0 miles to the Wetlands Center on the right. The building is open daily except Sunday (also closed Saturday in winter) from 8:30AM to 5:00PM and has restrooms along with lots of interesting exhibits, (770) 603-5606. The entire center, including the parking lot and the trail, is open daily from 8:30AM to 5:00PM. The trail

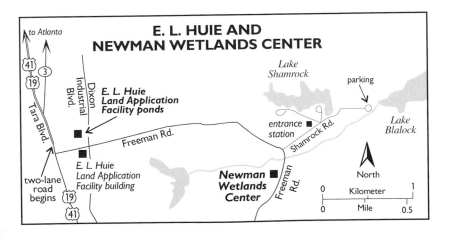

E. L. HUIE AND NEWMAN WETLANDS CENTER

to Atlanta

E. L. Huie Land Application Facility ponds

Lake Shamrock

parking

Dixon Industrial Blvd.

Tara Blvd.

Freeman Rd.

entrance station

Shamrock Rd.

Lake Blalock

two-lane road begins

E. L. Huie Land Application Facility building

Newman Wetlands Center

Freeman Rd.

North

0 Kilometer 1

0 Mile 0.5

starts on the far side of the parking lot and is about 0.5 mile long. It travels through mostly swampy woods on a nice boardwalk and finishes with a dirt trail along the forest edge. In spring, the boardwalk area is generally the first place in Atlanta with Louisiana Waterthrush and Prothonotary Warbler, both of which breed here; it is also good for all passerine migrants. In winter the boardwalk is worthwhile for woodland winter birds such as Brown Creeper and Winter Wren. Check out the feeders around the center for finches (House and rarely Purple) in winter, and Ruby-throated Hummingbirds in summer. The tall mature pines around the center are also a good place to look for Brown-headed Nuthatch. A small flock of Wild Turkeys is resident here, and a few of them are frequently seen casually strolling around the grounds near the parking lot.

There are also two nearby lakes that can be checked for waterfowl in winter. **Lakes Shamrock and Blalock** are next to each other and very close to the Newman Wetlands Center. Go back to Freeman Road, turn left and immediately turn right on Shamrock Road. This area is operated as a fee fishing-lake by the water authority, which charges a $5.00 admission. Birders may enter for free but can stay only 20 minutes. If you wish to bird longer, you must pay the fee. Lake Shamrock has nice birding around its edges and a fairly dependable Red-headed Woodpecker colony to the right and downhill from the entrance. The larger lake at the bottom of the hill is Lake Blalock. Ospreys sometimes nest here, and in summer there are frequently Bald Eagles in the area. Great Blue Herons have nested in recent years, along with dozens of Double-crested Cormorants. In migration this is another good spot for swallows. Both lakes usually have some ducks in winter. The Shamrock Lake and Blalock Lake area is open during daylight hours, year round.

SWEETWATER CREEK STATE PARK
Half day, fall through spring

Sweetwater Creek is a large and fairly deep lake that attracts more diving birds than do the shallower lakes. Good access for viewing is available for almost the entire lake. There are several trails along Sweetwater Creek itself which are productive for migrants during spring and fall.

Follow I-20 west to Exit 44, which accesses Thornton Road and Georgia Route 6. Turn south (left) onto Thornton for 0.4 mile, and turn right onto Blairs Bridge Road. Drive 2.1 miles and turn left onto Mount Vernon Road. In 0.5 mile you will see a sign for **Sweetwater Creek State Park**, followed by a small parking lot on the left. Scan the lake from any spot where you can see water, although the best viewing of the main lake is from the Boat Ramp in another 0.5 mile. You have to pay the daily state park fee of $2.00 to use this park, and you may pay either at any of the small fee boxes located in the parking lots or at the office found near the ramp, (770) 732-5871. Lesser Scaup, Bufflehead, and Ruddy Duck are very reliable here, and, rarely, other divers such as Canvasback, Redhead, and Common Goldeneye are present. Almost every species of duck and a few gulls and terns are seen every year. There is a flock of American Coots and Mallards of dubious lineage that frequent the ramp area, and if you see a child approaching with a piece of bread, hide quickly lest you be trampled in the ensuing melee.

Return to Mount Vernon, turn left, and proceed for 0.3 mile, then turn left again onto Factory Shoals Road. From here you can scan any areas on your left. Continue 0.4 mile to where the road forks, and take the left fork until it dead-ends in another 0.4 mile. Here you can scan the last small corner of the lake. A gated, paved road leads into the woods. Take this road to a dirt road leading off to the right for the "Yellow Trail." This path runs down to the creek, and if you turn left you can walk along Sweetwater Creek until you reach a large bridge. A left turn before the bridge will take you along a smaller creek all the way to the bottom of the dam. The entire walk is good for wintering passerines, such as Blue-headed Vireo, Winter Wren, and both kinglets. During migration, any area along either stream is worth checking for migrant vireos and warblers. When you reach the dam, you can either go back the way you came or walk up to the top of the dam and follow a fisherman's trail heading left back to the parking lot.

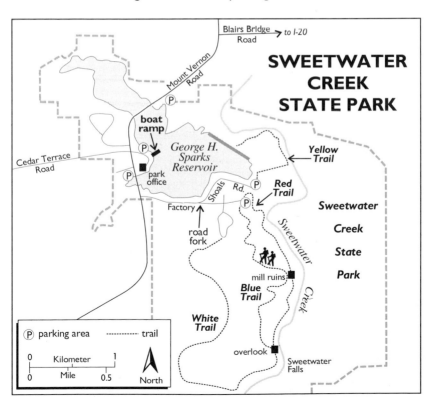

When finished, go back to the fork, and turn left 0.3 mile to the end in a small parking lot. Here the "Red Trail" goes down along Sweetwater Creek itself and is very good for migrants. The first 0.6 mile, until you get to some mill ruins, is easy walking. From there, the trail follows along the stream and is a little more difficult. This trail ends in another 0.5 mile at an overlook, and it is a picturesque walk in any season. If you go all the way to the overlook, you may take either of two trails back (or return the way you came). The "Blue Trail," marked by blue paint at frequent intervals, is about 1.5 easy miles back to the parking lot. The "White Trail," marked by white paint, is a more difficult and longer trail of about 3 miles in length. Both trails meander through hardwood forest with typical Piedmont bird species.

Northeast Atlanta Sites

Two hours per site; spring through fall

South Peachtree Creek Nature Reserve is a small, 38-acre park on the northeast side of Atlanta that has been a good place recently for migrant passerines and a few scrub-habitat breeding species. It has two trails and a short boardwalk. From I-285, take US-78 west (Exit 39A). From where the exit ramp joins US-78, go 1.5 miles to Orion Drive. Continue on US-78, but take your next right on Harrington Drive and follow it 1.1 miles through several right-hand turns to Pine Bluff Drive and the preserve.

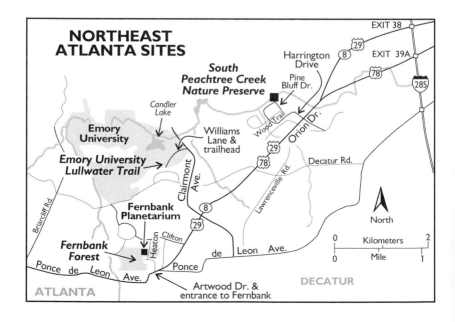

Close to Peachtree Creek is **Fernbank Forest**, a nice 65-acre block of forest adjacent to the Fernbank Science Center. This is another good place for migrant passerines, with typical Piedmont breeders as well. Hours are limited, so you might consider combining this with a trip to Peachtree Creek first. The forest is open from 2:00PM to 5:00PM Sunday–Friday and 1:00PM to 5:00PM Saturday. There are guided bird walks here on Saturdays during migration at 8:00AM. From Peachtree Creek, go back to US-29/78 and follow it toward the city (turn right off Harrington) for about 3 miles to Artwood Drive (just past Ponce de Leon) and turn right. Take your next right on Heaton Park Drive and park in the lot on your left. Watch for signs to the Science Center, where there are exhibits and maps available; the telephone number is (404) 378-4311.

Also in this same general area is the **Lullwater Trail at Emory University**. Take Clairmont Avenue to the north from US-29/78 (between Peachtree Creek and Fernbank) for 1.0 mile to Williams Drive, turn left, and follow the road as it curves right. The trail is on your right as you go up the hill. It offers more open areas than the two previous spots, plus a small lake. You can find a few migrants here during spring and fall, and a few sparrows in winter.

A new 75-acre city park (not named at press time and not shown on the map) can be reached from I-85 southbound at Exit 88. Take Cheshire Bridge Road south for 0.7 mile to Woodland Avenue, turn left, and take an immediate right onto Lenox Road for 0.9 mile to Wildwood Road. Go right for 0.4 mile to Woodcliff Terrace and turn right to the end. (If northbound on I-85, exit to Lenox directly from Cheshire Bridge.) There are over 50 acres of great floodplain forest here on the South Fork of Peachtree Creek, with trails to check for migrants and breeding species; there is some upland habitat as well. This park is closer to the center of Atlanta than the three previous sites.

BIG CREEK GREENWAY
Two hours; spring and fall

Big Creek Greenway is a small park with good migrant possibilities, located in the town of Alpharetta, about 20 miles north of downtown Atlanta. There is some decent forest along Big Creek itself, as well as a marsh and a trail system (which will be about six miles long when completed). Head north from Atlanta on GA-400 and take Exit 8, Mansell Road; turn right, and then left at the first stoplight onto Northpoint Parkway. The entrance is easy to miss; look for Center Bridge Road in 0.6 mile and continue past the next building on the right (currently Homelife Furniture). Look for the small greenway sign on your right (0.8 mile from Mansell), leading to a parking lot, trail, and restrooms.

PIEDMONT NATIONAL WILDLIFE REFUGE
Full day; year round, best spring through fall

Piedmont **National Wildlife Refuge** is about a 90-minute drive south of Atlanta, and is the closest place to find Red-cockaded Woodpecker and Bachman's Sparrow, along with a host of other interesting breeding species, including Acadian Flycatcher, Yellow-throated Vireo, and Prairie and Kentucky Warblers. The woodpeckers are easiest to find during late May and June when they are feeding nestlings, although they can be found during most of the year, particularly if you are willing to be at one of the breeding clusters at dawn or dusk. The sparrows can be found readily only when they are singing, usually from March to July. There are also numerous ponds here as well, with a few ducks found during the winter and lots of excellent sparrow habitat. There are trails to explore as well. Keep in mind that this refuge is lousy with ticks! To get here, go south on I-75 to Juliette Road, Exit 186. Turn left, drive 17.4 miles to the refuge sign, and turn left. The Visitor Center, 0.8 mile down this road, has maps, exhibits, and information. The staff can also tell you which woodpecker clusters are being used. The hours are 8:00AM to 4:30PM weekdays and 9:00AM to 5:30PM weekends, (912) 986-5441.

APPALACHIAN TRAIL AND BRASSTOWN BALD
Full day; late spring through fall

Some 90 minutes north of Atlanta is **Brasstown Bald**, Georgia's tallest mountain, where there is great birding for passerines during summer and migration. Take GA-400 north from Atlanta, and continue on US-19 on as the expressway ends; stay on US-19 through Dahlonega. About 12 miles past town you will reach US-129; turn left for 7 miles to Neel's Gap. Park at Byron Herbert Reece Park on the left; you can access the **Appalachian Trail** from here. At this elevation in May and June you can expect higher-elevation breeders such as Broad-winged Hawk, Blue-headed Vireo, Chestnut-sided, Black-throated Blue, Black-throated Green, and Blackburnian Warblers, and Ovenbird. If you wish to do some serious hiking, the Walasi-Yi Center, located just before the park on US-129, offers trail maps and other information. About 2 miles past Reece Park turn left onto GA-180 West and go 3 miles to **Sosebee Cove**, which features several loop trails. Here you will find the same species mix as at Neel's Gap. Another 3.7 miles farther on GA-180 brings you to **Lake Winfield Scott**, a good place for several of the same species as well as American Redstart. Any of these spots can also be good during migration. In May and June stop a few miles farther on at the intersection of GA-180 and Kennedy Bridge Road (on the left) for Least Flycatchers that call from the White Pines; the birds have been seen only in the last two years (2000 and 2001).

Brasstown Bald is Georgia's highest mountain (el. 4,784 feet), and it has the same breeding species as well as Veery, Canada Warbler, and Rose-breasted Grosbeak, along with resident Ruffed Grouse and Common Raven. To get there, go back to US-129 and continue north 2.3 miles to Georgia Route 180 East, and turn right for 7.2 miles to Georgia Route 180 Spur. Turn left 2.5 miles to the parking area ($2.00). Bird the edges of the parking area or walk one of the 0.5-mile trails up to the

Visitor Center. For ravens scan the sky or listen, but to find Ruffed Grouse you will need to do some hiking. Trails to try are the Arkaqua and Jack's Knob Trails from the parking lot. Details are available at the Visitor Center, (706) 745-6928.

ACKNOWLEDGMENTS

Thanks to Mark Davis, Malcolm Hodges, Carol Lambert, Mark Oberle, and Georgann Schmalz for their suggestions on locations to include and for their editing help.

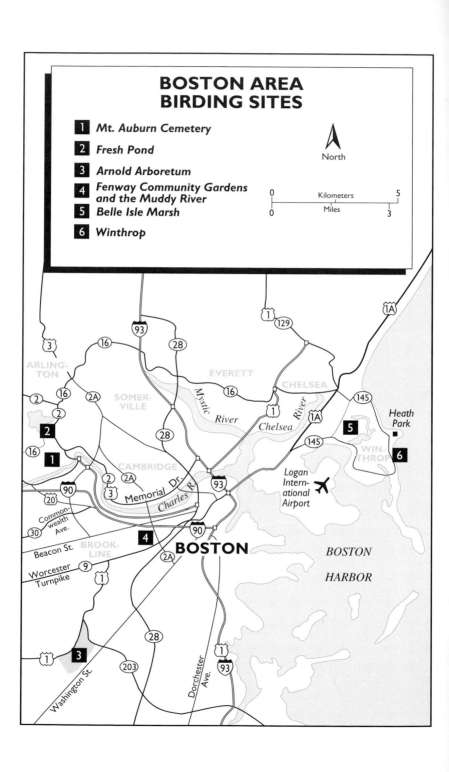

BOSTON AREA BIRDING SITES

1 Mt. Auburn Cemetery

2 Fresh Pond

3 Arnold Arboretum

4 Fenway Community Gardens and the Muddy River

5 Belle Isle Marsh

6 Winthrop

North

| 0 | Kilometers | 5 |
| 0 | Miles | 3 |

ARLINGTON

EVERETT

CHELSEA

SOMERVILLE

Mystic River

Chelsea River

Heath Park

WINTHROP

CAMBRIDGE

Memorial Dr.

Charles R.

Logan International Airport

Commonwealth Ave.

Beacon St.

BROOKLINE

Worcester Turnpike

BOSTON

BOSTON HARBOR

Washington St.

Dorchester Ave.

BOSTON, MASSACHUSETTS

Robert H. Stymeist, Marjorie Rines, and Ron Lockwood

The city of Boston offers opportunities to observe a diverse avifauna despite the heavily urbanized environment. Spring and fall migrations yield a wide variety of waterfowl, shorebirds, and songbirds, and the winter season can be very productive for certain seabirds and gulls. Summer birding is less diverse but can still be rewarding, especially for herons and terns. Your time in Boston will be well spent whether you have only a few hours or a couple of days to bird. Additionally, the visiting birder might want to tour some of the numerous historical and cultural sites in and around the city. The Museum of Science, the New England Aquarium, and the Harvard Museum of Natural History have extensive natural-history exhibits.

ESSENTIAL INFORMATION

Getting Around: The birder visiting eastern Massachusetts in general, and Boston in particular, will encounter a bewildering system of roads that are often poorly marked. If you choose to bird an area that requires an automobile, be sure to purchase a detailed map. Fortunately, Boston has a safe system of public transportation that can get you to some of the best birding areas. Traffic is generally heavy, so leave a generous amount of time for travel when you plan your birding day.

Climate: The weather in New England is highly variable and usually defies prediction. Be sure to bring layers of clothing to keep warm, as days can be rather cool well into May, and some winter days are truly brutal with low temperatures and high winds. Fall is a particularly pleasant time of year, but even on nice days the mornings can be brisk. Be sure to bring waterproof and warm footwear. The Boston office of the National Weather Service has a helpful web site at *www.nws.noaa.gov/er/box* that contains forecasts and a tide table.

Safety: Boston is probably typical of most urban areas: if you exercise common sense, you can usually feel safe. Most of the places described herein are frequented by other people enjoying the outdoors, and where there are many other people, there is generally better personal safety. The Fenway Gardens is one of the few locations where it is wise to exercise extra caution, either by birding in a group or staying close to high-traffic pedestrian areas. Theft is another issue; no matter how innocuous a location may seem, you should hide any valuables that you leave in a locked vehicle.

Birding Resources: In addition to this guide, ABA publishes *A Birder's Guide to Eastern Massachusetts* (1994). That guide provides detailed instructions to a variety of birding locations, including such well-known hot-spots as the Parker River National Wildlife Refuge (Plum Island) and Newburyport. The visiting birder should also check *www.massbird.org* on the Internet for a variety of links and to determine if the very active Brookline Bird Club is leading any local trips during your stay. The Massachusetts Audubon Society also leads trips in the area and maintains the local rare bird alert, (888) 224-6444, which is updated every Monday and Friday. Their office number is (781) 259-9500. The Greater Boston Chamber of Commerce is a good source for lodging and travel information and can be reached at One Beacon Street, 4th Floor, Boston, MA 02108, (617) 227-4500, *www.gbcc.org*.

THE BIRDING YEAR

B irding the Boston area can be very rewarding at any time of year. Winter is the best time to look for a variety of gulls. The "white-winged" gulls, particularly Iceland, are present in small numbers, and Black-headed, although less common than in years past, is still present. Rarer gulls, such as the European subspecies of Mew and Lesser Black-backed Gulls, are also a possibility. Common Loon, Horned and Red-necked Grebes, Brant, Common Eider, and the three scoters are easily observed, and the more unusual sea ducks, such as King Eider and Barrow's Goldeneye, should be looked for as well. Rocky areas along the shore and rocky islets in Massachusetts Bay are frequented by Great Cormorant and Purple Sandpiper. Snowy Owl, although it can be difficult to observe because of access limitations, is usually present at Logan Airport from mid-November until April and rarely into May.

Spring migration begins with waterfowl in late March and April and reaches its peak with shorebirds and songbirds during May. Look for Yellow-bellied Flycatcher, "gray-cheeked" thrushes, and Mourning Warbler in late May. Mid-summer is the slowest birding time, although terns can be found along the coast, and herons are present in appropriate habitats.

The protracted fall migration begins in late June with shorebirds, which pass through Massachusetts in two waves. The first wave peaks in late July and early August and is composed of adults. The second wave is comprised mostly of juveniles, and peaks from late August to mid-September. It is also during late August and early September that the greatest variety of shorebird species can be observed. Songbirds, including flycatchers, vireos, and warblers, migrate in late August and September, whereas sparrow migration peaks in early October. Look for Philadelphia Vireo, Connecticut Warbler, and Mourning Warbler in September, and Orange-crowned Warbler and Lincoln's Sparrow in late September and October. Seabird migration is in full swing by mid-October. Large numbers of Red-throated Loons and Northern Gannets, as well as scoters and other sea ducks, are on the move and easy to find by late October and early November.

MOUNT AUBURN CEMETERY

Several hours; spring and fall

Birders come from all over New England to experience spring migration at Mount Auburn. The cemetery is a large patch of green that beckons to migrants flying over Boston. Its popularity with birders ensures that few rarities pass through undetected. Over the years some of the more unusual species have been Hermit and Townsend's Warblers and Golden-crowned Sparrow. Other occasional visitors have included Yellow-throated, Prothonotary, and Kentucky Warblers, Summer Tanager, and Blue Grosbeak. Birding can also be good in fall, although the birds are harder to find and to see. Recent fall rarities have included Ash-throated Flycatcher and Black-throated Gray Warbler. Winter birding can occasionally yield crossbills.

Birding aside, Mount Auburn is a garden showpiece, filled in spring with flowers, trees, and shrubs in enough variety to dizzy the senses. It was, in fact, the first garden cemetery in the country, founded in 1831, and is the resting-place of many ornithological luminaries, including Glover Allen, Thomas Barbour, Thomas Mayo Brewer, William Brewster, Ludlow Griscom, and Charles W. Townsend. A pamphlet entitled *Ornithologists and Benefactors of Birds at Mount Auburn* is available from the Friends of Mount Auburn at the cemetery office.

To get to **Mount Auburn** by automobile from downtown Boston, take Storrow Drive along the Charles River west to the Harvard Square/Cambridge exit (some 5 miles from I-93); turn right onto the small bridge over the Charles River, then left at the other side of the bridge onto Memorial Drive. (The street sign may be missing here!) At the next major intersection with a stoplight (0.9 mile), bear right onto Fresh Pond Parkway (past the sign to Routes 2 and 3 to Arlington), but stay in the left lane, and bear left at the fork onto Mt. Auburn Street (following the sign to Route 16 to Watertown and Waltham, 0.2 mile). This last part can be confusing for someone unfamiliar with the area, so look for the overhead trolley cables and follow them to the left.

The cemetery appears almost immediately on your left; the gated entrance is obvious (0.4 mile). Mount Auburn doesn't officially open until 8:00AM, but

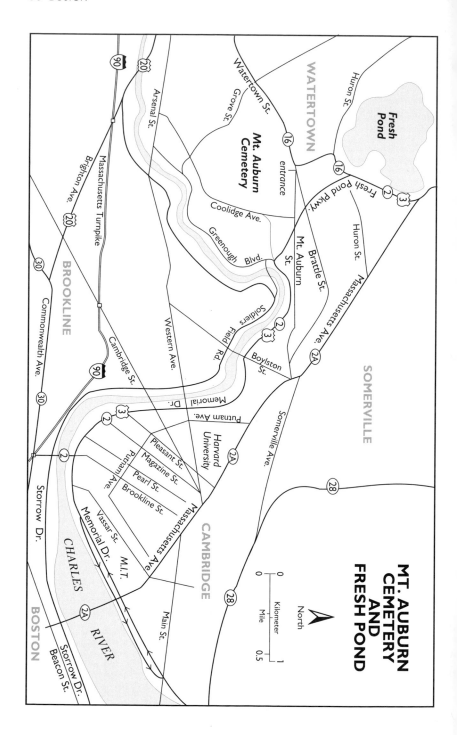

MT. AUBURN
CEMETERY
AND
FRESH POND

on weekdays the gates are often open at 7:00AM. When the cemetery gates are open, you may drive a vehicle through the cemetery and park by the side of the road (please don't park on the grass). Bird walks are conducted almost daily in the spring by the Brookline Bird Club, and usually begin at 6:00AM. Club officials have a key to the gate, so if you are eager for an early start, be there promptly at 6:00AM. (You take your chances if it is one of the rare days when there is no organized walk.)

To get to the cemetery gate by public transportation, take the Red Line subway (the "T") to Harvard Square, where you go to the underground bus pick-up/drop-off area. Ride either Bus 71 (Watertown) or Bus 73 (Waverly) to Mount Auburn Cemetery, which is only a 10-minute ride from Harvard Square. At the gatehouse you can purchase a map of the cemetery (highly recommended if you plan on going unescorted); you should also check the well-maintained blackboard for news of recent bird sightings. The cemetery's paved roads make it easily accessible for wheelchair birding.

FRESH POND

Several hours; fall

Fall migration at **Fresh Pond** in Cambridge is as productive as spring migration is at nearby Mount Auburn Cemetery. From late September until cold weather freezes the pond, a multitude of waterfowl can be seen at very close range. The area is also wonderful for migrant passerines, especially sparrows.

From Mount Auburn Cemetery, turn right as you leave the main gate and quickly get into the left lane. Bear left immediately at the wedge-shaped building (a few hundred feet) onto Brattle Street (no sign). Turn left at the stoplight (0.2 mile) onto Fresh Pond Parkway and follow signs for Routes 2 and 3. You will come to a rotary (0.9 mile) intersecting Concord Avenue (no sign). Turn left at the rotary, then right at the next rotary (0.1 mile), again following Routes 2 and 3 signs. A shopping center, the Fresh Pond Mall, will appear on your right. Park here, and use the pedestrian crosswalk to cross busy Routes 2/3; then turn left. After about 200 yards, you can cross Concord Avenue to a path that takes you to Fresh Pond. Alternatively, access by public transportation is easy: from Harvard Square take Bus 74 (Belmont) to Fresh Pond, only a 10-minute ride.

The path leads into a soccer field with a number of fruit trees where hundreds of American Robins and Cedar Waxwings may be found until November and early December. The adjacent thickets and weedy fields are good for sparrows and other songbirds. Like Mount Auburn Cemetery, Fresh Pond has a long history of birdwatching, particularly for waterfowl. William Brewster chronicled the hunting of the earlier days when upwards of 50 Ruddy Ducks were shot in a single day. Today Canvasbacks and Ring-necked

Ducks are the most numerous, sometimes reaching several hundred individuals each. Both scaup species as well as Ruddy Duck and American Coot are also usually seen. Less common are all three scoters, Long-tailed Duck, Bufflehead, Common Goldeneye, and a variety of dabbling ducks. In all, 30 species of waterfowl have been recorded, in addition to Red-throated and Common Loons, and Pied-billed, Horned, and Red-necked Grebes. Occasionally a real rarity shows up. On several occasions following major easterly storms, Leach's Storm-Petrel and Dovekie have been recorded. In the fall of 1989 an immature Purple Gallinule remained here for nearly a month.

ARNOLD ARBORETUM

Several hours; year round

The 265 acres of the **Arnold Arboretum** are under lease for a thousand years to Harvard University, which supervises the botanical research there. Like Mount Auburn Cemetery, the Arboretum offers an expanse of green attractive to migrants, but unlike Mount Auburn, most of the area is not intensively landscaped and therefore provides plenty of habitat for breeding and wintering birds. Most of the trees and shrubs have been planted in groups by family, thereby offering contiguous areas of habitat. You must park outside the arboretum and walk in, but for handicap access a car permit is generally available; call to check at (617) 524-1717. Located in the Jamaica Plain section of Boston, Arnold Arboretum is only about a 15-minute drive from downtown. Getting there is half the fun; there are a few places en route to the arboretum where the directions are confusing (offering opportunities to get lost), as well as a few possible detours on the way back offering good birding (and more opportunities to get lost). A good map will be helpful; directions to the suggested detours are not described in detail because they change frequently.

From I-93 in downtown Boston, take the Storrow Drive exit (Exit 26). Follow Storrow Drive west to the Fenway/Route 1 exit (1.8 miles). At the end of the exit, bear right to the stoplight, following signs for Boylston Street Outbound. At the next light (less than 0.1 mile), go straight. Three stoplights later (0.5 mile) bear right (no signs), and at the next light (less than 0.1 mile) bear left (a shallow left, not a hard left), following signs to Fenway and Providence/Points South. This turn will put you on the Riverway, with the Muddy River on your right. Relax; that was the worst part. Now you have a leisurely drive until you reach a rotary just beyond Jamaica Pond (2.7 miles). Drive two-thirds of the way around the rotary until you reach the 203 East exit, which is the first right after the Route 1 exit. After exiting the rotary onto Route 203, follow the signs for the Arboretum on the right. The main entrance to Arnold Arboretum is immediately after the rotary (0.2 mile), where there is parking by the side of the road. It can get crowded on weekends, but birders getting an early start should have no problem. The

Hunnewell Visitor Center is inside the main gate, and maps are available there. Access by public transportation is easy via the Orange Line to the Forest Hills station. Cross the street, and walk north up South Street about one-quarter mile, where there is a back entrance on the right side at 383 South Street. The other entrances to the Arboretum also afford parking, so you can explore by car if you prefer. Drive past the main gate on Route 203, and just keep making right turns wherever possible.

FENWAY COMMUNITY GARDENS AND THE MUDDY RIVER

Several hours; fall and winter

Return to Route 1, and continue into the city to the Boston Museum of Fine Arts on the Fenway. Parking here is at a premium, and you may have to pay at the Museum lot (this is a great museum to visit). Across the street from the back of the Museum is the Muddy River and the Kelleher Rose Garden (more than 800 bushes), part of the Emerald Necklace, the largest and oldest park system in the country and designed by Frederick Law Olmsted starting in 1878. The river here rarely freezes, and a variety of puddle ducks and both Great Blue Herons and Black-crowned Night-Herons find refuge among the grasses that line the river. Walk across the bridge to explore the community gardens, which can be very good in late fall and into the winter for sparrows and other songbirds. In late fall as many as three Orange-crowned Warblers and two Yellow-breasted Chats have been recorded on a single day. In 1999 the gardens hosted a month-long visit by a MacGillivray's Warbler.

BOSTON HARBOR NORTH

Half to full day; year round

From downtown Boston north to nearby Revere there are numerous opportunities to observe ducks and shorebirds. Travelers who are on a business trip to Boston, or who have a long stopover at Logan Airport, can see a wide variety of birds within just a few minutes of the airport.

Boston Harbor itself hosts rafts of wintering sea ducks, breeding herons in summer, and great numbers of migrant shorebirds from July to October. Most places with good views of the harbor can be reached easily by car. Public transportation is possible to some of the areas, but that method requires a bit more effort and a lot of walking.

Some of Boston's most interesting birds can be seen at **Belle Isle Marsh** in East Boston. To reach Belle Isle by car from downtown Boston, follow signs to the Callahan Tunnel and Logan Airport. Upon emerging from the tunnel, stay left and drive north on Route 1A. (The airport exit goes off to the right.) Take the next exit for Chelsea, Winthrop, and Route 145 (0.7 mile). Stay straight at the bottom of the ramp, and you will merge onto Bennington Street (Route 145). Soon Route 145 branches off to the right (1.1 miles); stay straight ahead on Bennington past the Orient Heights T (subway) station. A short distance ahead (0.5 mile) you should see the New England Casket Company on your right on the corner of Palmero Street.

Clear views of the marsh are available from Palmero Street (a poorly-maintained side road), but the area behind the casket company and railroad yard give a close-up view of both the marsh and a small pond where shorebirds often congregate. This is private property, but birders are tolerated. Drive behind the casket company, keeping the chain-link fence to your left, where you can get good views of the marsh and "**Rosie's Puddle**," both particularly good at high tide.

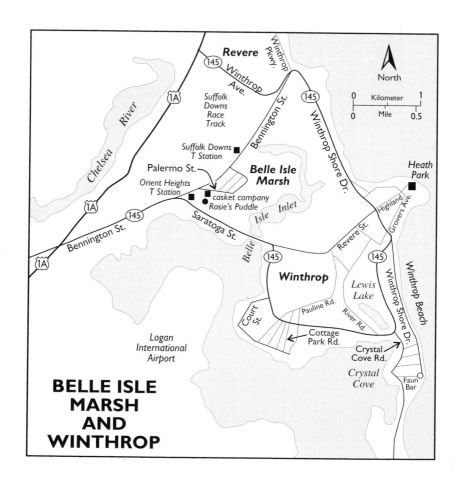

BELLE ISLE MARSH AND WINTHROP

Long-billed Dowitchers and both Hudsonian and Marbled (rare) Godwits can linger into November, and Long-billed Dowitcher has been recorded here twice on Christmas Bird Counts. Willets, Whimbrels, and occasionally Wilson's Phalaropes show up along with the more-abundant yellowlegs, peeps, and dowitchers. A variety of herons are also visible here at high tide.

To explore another section of the marsh, return to Bennington Street and turn right. The main entrance to the **Belle Isle Marsh Reservation** (including a parking lot) is 0.5 mile down on your right and is well marked by a wooden sign. If you walk all the way through on the paved paths, you will discover a deck built into the marsh from which you can view the shorebirds that come to roost at high tide.

Both Rosie's Puddle and the main section of Belle Isle Marsh are within reasonable walking distance of the subway line that runs to Logan Airport (the Blue Line). The Orient Heights station is about a half-mile walk from Rosie's. Just before the main entrance to Belle Isle is the Suffolk Downs station.

Only a few minutes away, **Winthrop** can be a winter birding bonanza as well as a good spot to look for migrant shorebirds. Retrace your steps on Bennington Street to the stoplight (0.8 mile) and turn left onto Saratoga Street (Route 145). The road crosses Belle Isle Inlet (0.8 mile) and takes a sharp right. Take your first right onto Court Street (0.4 mile), which runs along the edge of the water. After a mile, you can duck down a side street to view Logan Airport across the harbor. Logan Airport's wintering Snowy Owls can sometimes be seen perching near the edge of the water.

Return to Route 145 by turning left onto Cottage Park Road (1.2 miles), and then turn right (0.3 mile) onto Route 145. When you see the Elks Hall on your right (0.7 mile), look immediately for a small pond on your left, and pull into the parking lot on the right. The pond is **Lewis Lake,** where many birders come to seek Black-headed Gulls. In some years there have been impressive numbers, with as many as 35 tallied on a Christmas Bird Count, although recent counts have been considerably lower. Recently the city of Boston has performed a major clean-up of the harbor, resulting in the transport of sewage far out to sea. Since then it has become much more difficult to find Black-headed Gull.

Look for the Black-headeds roosting on the ice among the more numerous Bonaparte's and Ring-billeds, usually from October through March. On several occasions a Mew (Common) Gull has also been spotted among this flock. If the gulls are not here, they are likely to be on Winthrop Beach. Follow Route 145, which makes a sharp right turn to Crystal Cove Avenue (five very short blocks on the left). Take a left on Faun Bar Avenue to the rotary at the start of Winthrop Shore Drive (recently changed to a one-way road). Try walking down the seawall beyond the rotary to scan the ocean for large rafts of ducks, or just look from the rotary.

Purple Sandpiper
Michael O'Brien

Continue north along Winthrop Shore Drive. Winter parking is easy anywhere along the seawall, and it's worth making several stops. In addition to the gulls, Purple Sandpipers are a specialty here; check the large stone breakwaters that parallel the beach (the Five Sisters), or for a closer look try the several rock ledges that jut into the ocean farther along the seawall. In spring and from late summer through fall, the beach (at low tide) and breakwaters (at high tide) may host Black-bellied Plover, Ruddy Turnstone, Red Knot, Sanderling, and Dunlin.

There can be a wide variety of waterbirds offshore from the beach. Red-throated and Common Loons and Horned and Red-necked Grebes, as well as large rafts of diving ducks, are usually visible. King Eider, Harlequin Duck, and Barrow's Goldeneye are possible, and Western Grebe has been spotted several times.

After you pass the beach, take your first right onto Grovers Avenue (1.1 mile from the rotary). Take your second right (0.3 mile) onto the extension of Highland (currently no sign), and go straight to the wall (0.1 mile). Turn right into **Heath Park** for a spectacular view of the harbor. (The park may not have a sign.) Among the raft of Common Eiders often present offshore, look for an occasional King Eider at the outer edges of the feeding flock. In some winters, Horned Grebes assemble here in large rafts at dusk.

PELAGIC BIRDING

Pelagic birding can be excellent no matter what the season. The New England Aquarium offers bay tours and whalewatches daily during the summer months and sporadically during the rest of year. During the summer it is possible to see Greater, Sooty, and Manx Shearwaters as well as Wilson's Storm-Petrel on a single trip. Cory's Shearwater is also a possibility, but numbers are highly variable from year to year. Fall and winter bring Northern Gannet, Black-legged Kittiwake, Razorbill, and Black Guillemot. Parasitic Jaeger is present during late summer and early fall, and Pomarine Jaeger is uncommon in September and October. If you are particularly lucky, in the late fall and early winter you could see Dovekie, Common or Thick-billed Murre, or Atlantic Puffin, but don't hold your breath. Check the Aquarium's web page at *www.neaq.org* or call **(617) 973-5281** for trip times and reservations.

EXTRA EFFORT

In addition to the areas described above, there are many excellent locations that are within a two-hour drive of the Boston metropolitan area. The **Parker River National Wildlife Refuge (Plum Island)** and **Newburyport**, which are about an hour's drive north of Boston, offer excellent birding year round. **Cape Ann** is worthwhile at any season but can be particularly rewarding during the winter, when five species of alcids have been observed. **Great Meadows National Wildlife Refuge** in Concord can be very good during migration, particularly in the fall, when good numbers of shorebirds may be present. In central Massachusetts, the **Quabbin Reservoir** area has a diverse population of breeding birds that include Common Loon, Bald Eagle, Acadian Flycatcher, 19 warbler species including Cerulean, and Evening Grosbeak. Additionally, during the winter, both Bald and Golden (rare) Eagles are present, and, depending upon the year, there can be Pine Siskins, Common Redpolls, and, less frequently, Pine Grosbeaks. Finally, fall shorebird migration at **South Beach** and **Monomoy National Wildlife Refuge** just south of Chatham on Cape Cod can be truly spectacular. For precise directions to these and other locations (including maps), please consult ABA's *A Birder's Guide to Eastern Massachusetts*.

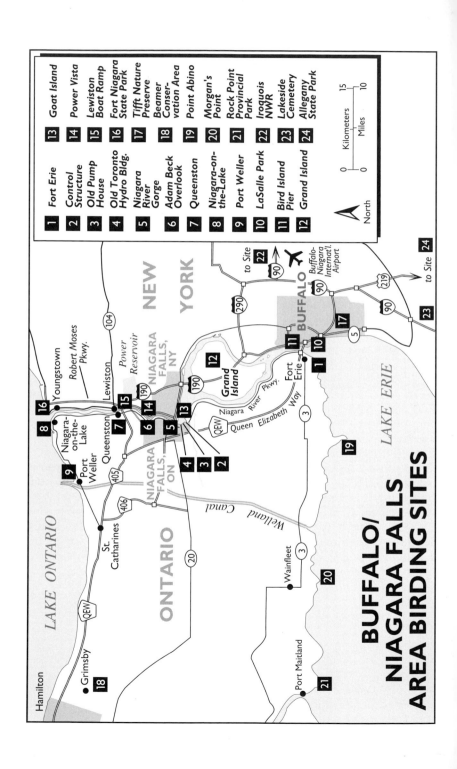

1	Fort Erie	
2	Control Structure	
3	Old Pump House	
4	Old Toronto Hydro Bldg.	
5	Niagara River Gorge	
6	Adam Beck Overlook	
7	Queenston	
8	Niagara-on-the-Lake	
9	Port Weller	
10	LaSalle Park	
11	Bird Island Pier	
12	Grand Island	
13	Goat Island	
14	Power Vista	
15	Lewiston Boat Ramp	
16	Fort Niagara State Park	
17	Tifft Nature Preserve	
18	Beamer Conservation Area	
19	Point Abino	
20	Morgan's Point	
21	Rock Point Provincial Park	
22	Iroquois NWR	
23	Lakeside Cemetery	
24	Allegany State Park	

Kilometers 0 — 15
Miles 0 — 10

North

**BUFFALO/
NIAGARA FALLS
AREA BIRDING SITES**

Buffalo, New York, and Niagara Falls, Ontario

Kayo J. Roy and Willie D'Anna

Mention Buffalo and Niagara Falls, and most knowledgeable birders will think of gulls in late fall and winter. But travelers to this picturesque area straddling the border between Canada and the United States can be rewarded at other seasons as well: interesting waterfowl, shorebirds, songbirds, and northern specialties may be found.

The region around Buffalo, situated on the Niagara River and on Lake Erie, has a long and rich ornithological history, from the visits of John James Audubon and Alexander Wilson in the 1800s to today's attention from birding organizations and tours. The payoff, of course, is the amazing late-fall and early-winter concentration of gulls on the Niagara River, which flows 35 miles from Lake Erie to Lake Ontario. Dubbed the "Gull Capital of the World," this region has recorded 19 gull species. Midway between the two lakes is Niagara Falls, the preferred central location for gull aficionados during peak season, which occurs mid-November through late January. The geography of the area dominates the birdlife. The elevation change from Lake Erie to Lake Ontario is 326 feet, most obvious and dramatic at Niagara Falls. The proximity of these two large bodies of water and the presence of the Niagara Escarpment constitute major influences on the weather and migration.

Essential Information

Getting Around: Many travelers arrive in Buffalo at the Buffalo-Niagara International Airport. Airport limousine service to the town of Niagara Falls, Ontario, can be arranged through Niagara Airbus, (905) 374-8111; visitors can also be picked up at several downtown hotels. Rail services to the area are provided by Via Rail in Canada, (800) 361-1235, and Amtrak in the United States, (800) 561-3949. All major car-rental companies have outlets at the airport and in downtown Buffalo and Niagara Falls. It is possible to bird a portion of the Niagara River on the Canadian side by public buses. For information and bus schedules, call Niagara Transit, (905) 356-1179.

Climate: Average daytime high temperatures are 77°F (25°C) in summer, 54°F (12°C) in fall, 34°F (1°C) in winter, and 66°F (18°C) in spring. But wind chill and snowfall can make the winter months uncomfortable. Because the best concentrations of gulls usually occur during the cold, windy conditions which follow the passage of cold fronts, birders need to be prepared with layers of warm clothing, hat, boots, and a full thermos. A lot of standing time is needed to study the large numbers of gulls, and a spotting scope with a sturdy tripod is a necessity. Birders stalking gulls are also advised to bring a range of field guides to study various plumages (preferably in the warmth of a hotel room beforehand).

Other Resources: Two Rare Bird Alert numbers cover the area. In Ontario, the Hamilton number is (905) 381-0329; in the United States, the Buffalo number is (716) 896-1271. Buffalo is a major business and education center in upstate New York and has a wide range of hotels both downtown and near the airport. Niagara Falls (Ontario and New York) has approximately 180 hotels/motels covering all price ranges. During the peak tourist periods at the Falls in summer, reservations must be made well in advance.

Other Destinations: Non-gull birding in Niagara Falls, Ontario, is enjoyable at the Niagara Parks Botanical Gardens, located on the Niagara River Parkway just south of the Hydro generating-station (5.6 miles north of the Falls). Anyone with an interest in flowers and trees will also enjoy this 100-acre garden housing the Niagara Parks School of Horticulture. Birding here may provide a surprise or two as well. Also located on the grounds of the Botanical Gardens is a glass-enclosed, 990-square-meter butterfly conservatory. Open year round, this conservatory has over 2,000 free-flying butterflies from around the world flitting in a tropical rain-forest setting.

THE BIRDING YEAR

Peak numbers of gulls are present along the Niagara River from November to January. Although gull numbers begin to decline after mid-January, the opportunity to find a variety of gulls and many species of waterfowl remains excellent along the Niagara River. The Niagara Falls area hot-spots are still the places to view a good number of gull species, with the waterfowl being found primarily in the southern third of the river and along the Fort Erie riverfront. The spring waterfowl migration commences in late February and peaks around the end of March. The Tifft Nature Preserve in Buffalo, and especially the Iroquois National Wildlife Refuge near Alabama, New York, are the choicest spots at this time. The raptor migration starts in March, with two local sites providing fine viewing of numbers of these birds: Beamer Conservation Area atop the escarpment in Grimsby, Ontario, and Lakeside Cemetery in Hamburg, New York. Songbird migration begins slowly in March and peaks with some 30 species of warblers in mid-May. Although there are numerous areas to look for migrants, birders most often trek to Goat Island and Tifft Nature Preserve on the New York side of the River and to Port Weller, Morgan's Point, Point Abino, and Rock Point Provincial Park in Ontario. It is easy to rack up an impressive list in mid- to late May, but only Iroquois NWR offers the habitat diversity necessary to tally over 100 species without going anywhere else.

The summer breeding season offers limited diversity in the near-vicinity of the Niagara River. However, Iroquois NWR is a fine place (insect repellent is often necessary), and Allegany State Park, 1.5 hours south of Buffalo, is a jewel. The latter offers over 20 species of breeding warblers.

Fall shorebirding, starting in early July, is pleasant along Ontario's north shore of Lake Erie, particularly at Rock Point. Area sewage ponds can be rewarding as well. Fall songbird migrants start returning in mid-to-late August and generally peak in mid-September. The fall waterfowl migration is sometimes spectacular on the Great Lakes. After the onset of sustained winter weather, the abundant gulls on the Niagara River are joined by exceptional numbers of many species of ducks. Northern Shrike, Snow Bunting, and, in some years, Snowy Owl, Bohemian Waxwing, and Common Redpoll can be observed near the shores of Lake Ontario and Lake Erie. Several species of owls are present in the area during most winters.

BIRDING SITES

Birding the entire length of the Niagara River can be rewarding, especially in late fall and early winter, when it is one of the very best areas in North America to view large numbers and a great variety of gulls. (On one occasion, keen observers found 14 gull species in a single day.) In addition to the common species (Bonaparte's, Ring-billed, Herring, and Great Black-backed),

Iceland Gull
Michael O'Brien

MOB '00

Little, Thayer's, Iceland, Lesser Black-backed, and Glaucous Gulls can be found on most days. Franklin's and Sabine's Gulls arrive earlier, usually between early September and early November. Throughout the late fall and winter period, Black-headed Gull and Black-legged Kittiwake make brief, occasional visits, and California Gull has become annual. There are four records of Ivory Gull. In 1992, both Mew Gull and Slaty-backed Gull (first Ontario and New York records) were observed. A very pink Ross's Gull was found in 1995. The 19th gull species recorded at Niagara—Laughing Gull—is a rare visitor during the warmer months.

The Canadian side is the preferred route for birders. Ontario has much more public access to the river than does New York, and, more importantly, the lighting is better on the Canadian side most of the day. *Be aware, however, that parking may be difficult at some sites (e.g., the Gorge) after early morning on weekends.*

NIAGARA RIVER, CANADIAN SIDE

Full day (or half day if a partial itinerary is followed);
late fall and early winter

From Buffalo, take the Peace Bridge (toll) to **Fort Erie, Ontario**. Turn south toward Old Fort Erie (see map on page 53). Starting at Jaeger Rocks just south of Old Fort Erie and backtracking toward the Peace Bridge to Gilmore Road, carefully check all gulls in the river, as well as those resting on grassy areas. September and October are best for Franklin's and Sabine's Gulls. In December and January, Little Gull and (with luck) Black-legged Kittiwake can be found. In winter the area south of the Peace Bridge holds several thousand diving ducks. Rarities have included Tufted Duck, King Eider, Harlequin Duck, and Barrow's Goldeneye.

Proceed north on the Niagara River Parkway (see map on opposite page). The drive from Fort Erie to Niagara Falls will allow close views of many duck species. There are plenty of turn-outs where birders can safely park and view the waterfowl. American Black Duck, Mallard, Canvasback, Redhead, Greater Scaup, Bufflehead, Common Goldeneye, and Common Merganser should be evident in large numbers. Tundra Swans have been regular in recent winters.

As you approach the Falls, the road bears left along Chippewa Creek. Turn right in the town of Chippewa and cross the bridge. Then turn right again after crossing the bridge, and you will come to two large gates. Just past the gates is the **Control Structure**, a weir that stretches halfway across the Niagara River; park south of the weir. This is an outstanding area for gulls, where any species is possible. Large numbers of diving ducks feed in the rapids. A keen observer may find Purple Sandpipers as they feed out on the small rock islands. Large numbers of gulls also rest on the breakwall on

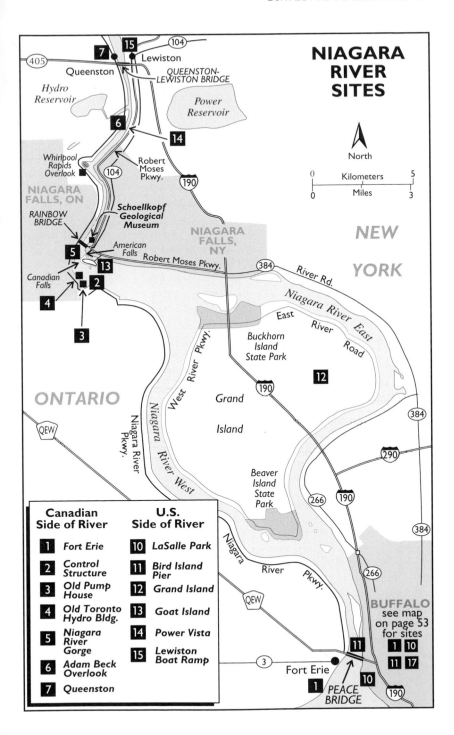

NIAGARA RIVER SITES

North

0   Kilometers   5
0   Miles   3

104

15 Lewiston

7 Queenston

QUEENSTON-LEWISTON BRIDGE

405

Hydro Reservoir

Power Reservoir

6

14

Whirlpool Rapids Overlook

Robert Moses Pkwy.

104

190

NIAGARA FALLS, ON

Schoellkopf Geological Museum

RAINBOW BRIDGE

American Falls

NIAGARA FALLS, NY

Robert Moses Pkwy.

384 River Rd.

5

13

Canadian Falls

2

4

3

Niagara River East

East River Road

Buckhorn Island State Park

NEW YORK

West River Pkwy.

12

190

ONTARIO

Grand Island

384

Niagara River Pkwy.

Niagara River West

290

QEW

Beaver Island State Park

266

190

384

Canadian Side of River

1 Fort Erie

2 Control Structure

3 Old Pump House

4 Old Toronto Hydro Bldg.

5 Niagara River Gorge

6 Adam Beck Overlook

7 Queenston

U.S. Side of River

10 LaSalle Park

11 Bird Island Pier

12 Grand Island

13 Goat Island

14 Power Vista

15 Lewiston Boat Ramp

Niagara River Pkwy.

QEW

266

BUFFALO
see map on page 53 for sites

11

1 **10**

11 **17**

3 Fort Erie

1 PEACE BRIDGE

11

10

190

the south side of the control structure. Beyond the breakwall, scaup and Canvasback feed, often joined by Redhead and Ring-necked Duck. Snowy Owls can sometimes be found on the control structure. Continue north to the **Old Pump House Building**. The overlook behind this small building just south of the Old Toronto Hydro Building (see below) is the best location on the Canadian side to look for Purple Sandpiper. Look for several species of ducks, including Gadwall, in the quieter waters close to shore. The **Old Toronto Hydro Building** is located above the falls opposite the Horticulture Greenhouse (restrooms; fee parking). Little, Lesser Black-backed, and various "white- winged" gulls often can be found feeding or resting in the rapids here. Look carefully—such rarities as Eurasian Wigeon, Harlequin Duck, Barrow's Goldeneye, and Red-necked and Red Phalaropes have been observed.

Continuing north on the Parkway, the **Niagara River Gorge** between the Canadian Horseshoe Falls and Rainbow Bridge is striking—as well as a good spot to find ducks and gulls as they feed on materials swept up in the rapids and deposited in quieter eddies. Common Loon and Double-crested Cormorant are often present, and a Pacific Loon made a brief visit in 1995. The Whirlpool Rapids Overlook at the Spanish Aerocar is worth a stop for the view alone, and there may be a rarity among the many Bonaparte's Gulls.

The **Adam Beck Hydro Overlook** is located directly above the generating-stations, and one can look straight down into the gorge. This is the best place on the river to look for "white-winged" gulls. Lesser Black-backed and occasionally Franklin's and California Gulls are found here as well, and the very rare Mew Gull has been spotted. A birder's skills are put to the test at this location, as one must identify the gulls from above by mantle color and wing-tip and tail patterns as the birds forage over the river. Be sure to scope the rocks and the Power Vista across the river for roosting gulls.

Continue north to **Queenston**. The boat-launching ramp, accessed off Princess Street at the end of Dumfries Street, is a good place from which to observe gulls feeding over the river. Park at the upper lot and walk down the path to the boat ramp. Here, at water level, is the best area to find Little Gull among the thousands of Bonaparte's. Other small gulls such as Franklin's, Black-headed, and Sabine's are also possible. Bald Eagles are often seen here in winter. Return to the upper lot and walk the path heading south along the River. About halfway to the visible Queenston-Lewiston Bridge, you will arrive at a clearing between the path and the river. Be on the lookout for anything unusual; for example, an immature Northern Gannet was present in December 1990.

The final destination is **Niagara-on-the-Lake**, where **Queen's Royal Park**, located at Ricardo and Regent Streets, offers an excellent view of Lake Ontario and the mouth of the Niagara River. Hundreds of Long-tailed Ducks usually can be seen in winter, as well as other ducks, loons, grebes, scoters, gulls, and occasionally jaegers. King Eiders have been observed here, and single Razorbills created considerable excitement in 1982 and 1985. From

November to April at the river mouth at sunset, there is a fly-past of gulls heading out to roost on the lake for the night. At peak times, especially with northerly winds, thousands of Bonaparte's Gulls pass by fairly low over the water, challenging the birder to spot other gull species in the flocks. The best viewing is from behind the **Pump House Art Centre** on Collingwood Street, or from the parking lot of **Navy House** on the Niagara River Parkway, opposite Old Fort George.

At all seasons, there are interesting birds to be found on **Shakespeare Avenue** and roads running off it. Look for Red-bellied Woodpecker, Tufted Titmouse, Carolina Wren, and, in winter, Pine Siskin and other northern species. During spring and fall migration this area can be very rewarding. The **Niagara Shores Conservation Area** is located along Lakeshore Road about one-half mile west of Shakespeare Avenue. Red-bellied Woodpecker, Red-headed Woodpecker, and Tufted Titmouse can often be found here.

A 20-minute drive farther west is **Port Weller** and the Welland Canal. This is the north end of the canal through which Great Lakes and ocean-going freighters pass between Lake Ontario and Lake Erie. Two long, tree-lined piers extend out into Lake Ontario, forming a natural attraction for grebes, herons, gulls, and migrant landbirds. Interesting finds range from a Rock Wren in December 1964 to an Ancient Murrelet in November 1994 to two Ross's Gulls in the winter of 1994-1995. Some 34 species of warblers have been found in spring, including such locally rare species as Prairie, Prothonotary, Worm-eating, Kentucky, Connecticut, and Hooded. The fall migration can also be rewarding. In late fall and winter, a walk out to the tip

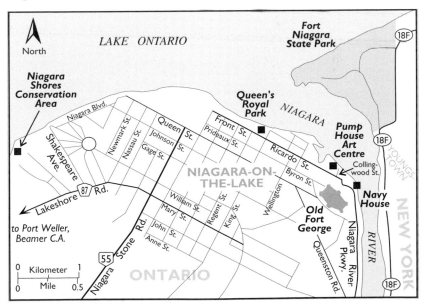

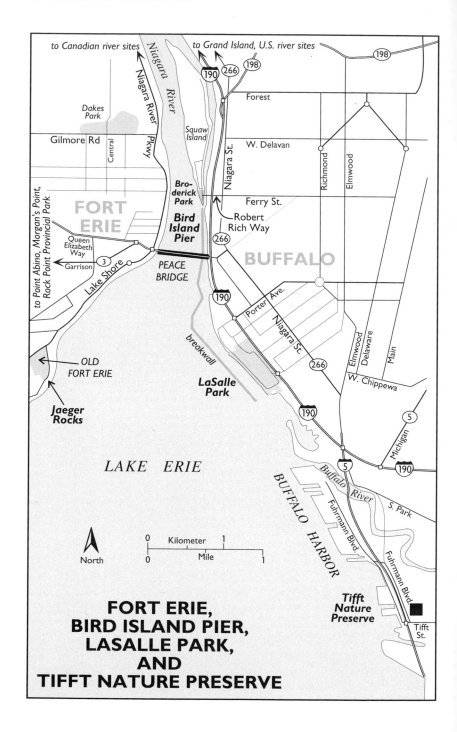

to Canadian river sites

to Grand Island, U.S. river sites

Niagara River

Niagara River Pkwy

198

190 266 198

Dakes Park

Gilmore Rd

Central

Squaw Island

Forest

W. Delavan

Richmond

Elmwood

Niagara St.

FORT ERIE

Bro-derick Park

Bird Island Pier

Ferry St.

Robert Rich Way

266

BUFFALO

Queen Elizabeth Way

Garrison

3

Lake Shore

PEACE BRIDGE

190

Porter Ave.

to Point Abino, Morgan's Point, Rock Point Provincial Park

breakwall

OLD FORT ERIE

LaSalle Park

Niagara St.

266

W. Chippewa

Elmwood

Delaware

Main

Jaeger Rocks

190

5

Michigan

LAKE ERIE

5

190

Buffalo River

BUFFALO HARBOR

Fuhrmann Blvd.

S. Park

North

0   Kilometer   1

0   Mile   1

Fuhrmann Blvd.

Tifft Nature Preserve

Tifft St.

FORT ERIE, BIRD ISLAND PIER, LASALLE PARK, AND TIFFT NATURE PRESERVE

of the east pier may produce Tundra Swan, Brant, Purple Sandpiper, Snowy Owl, American Pipit, Lapland Longspur, or Snow Bunting. The east pier is open to the public, but access to the west pier is open only as far as the Canadian Coast Guard gate. At the south end of the west pier is **Mary Malcolmson Park**, an area also worth birding during spring migration.

NIAGARA RIVER, U. S. SIDE

Half or full day; fall, winter, and spring

Begin the day at **LaSalle Park** in Buffalo (best in winter), at the west end of Porter Avenue, accessed from I-190 or Niagara Street (Route 266) about one mile south of Ferry Street. Drive the one-mile loop, checking for waterfowl inside the breakwall. The loop is closed in mid-winter, but one can still view the water from the foot of Porter Avenue. Many dabblers, diving ducks, and rarities, such as Brant, Harlequin Duck, and even a Brown Pelican, have been seen here. Check the gulls that occasionally roost on the grass in the park. Common Terns are likely from spring to fall.

Continue to **Bird Island Pier** (also best in fall and winter). This 1.5-mile long breakwall parallels the Buffalo shore and can be accessed from its north end at Broderick Park on Squaw Island. Turn west onto Robert Rich Way (opposite Ferry Street) from Niagara Street (Route 266), cross the bridge, and turn left to reach the pier. The river here is a good place for Bonaparte's Gull and rare small gulls, such as Little, Franklin's, Sabine's, and Black-legged Kittiwake. Late September to early November is the best time for Sabine's Gull, which has also been seen north of the pier along the bike path. A stiff west to southwest wind off Lake Erie produces the best birding. Look for all three scoters, jaegers, and the occasional shorebird, including Red-necked and Red Phalaropes, particularly when the wind is strong off the lake.

For birding along the Niagara River, return to Route 266 and head north to the Ontario Street ramp onto I-190 northbound. (See map on page 50.) The first stop will be **Grand Island**, excellent for waterfowl, particularly diving ducks in winter. The state parks at the north end (**Buckhorn Island**) and the south end (**Beaver Island**, fee in summer) are recommended. Loons, grebes, and Tundra Swan are often seen from both sites. Check the river off the southeast corner of Beaver Island, where waterfowl numbers can be particularly impressive. Keep an eye out for Iceland and Glaucous Gulls as well as Bald Eagles. A time-saving route would visit the state parks and drive only the West River Parkway between them. (Note: if the parkway is not plowed, you can use the adjacent service road.)

Continue north on I-190 and take the Robert Moses Parkway, the first exit after crossing the Grand Island bridge, to **Goat Island**, situated between the brinks of the American and Canadian falls. Park in the large lot (fee in summer) on the west end and check the gorge from the northwest and southwest corners of the island. Most of Niagara's gulls have been seen from here. In recent years the small woodland east of this parking lot has been one of the best warbler spots in the region. Up to 23 species have been found here in one day. Rarities have included Varied Thrush and Prairie, Prothonotary, Worm-eating, Kentucky, and Connecticut Warblers. The shallows above Three Sisters Islands, located off the middle of the south side of Goat Island, often provide better views of Purple Sandpiper than can be had from the Canadian side. Look for this specialty from November to mid-May.

The **Schoellkopf Geological Museum** provides an overlook into the gorge, where Bonaparte's Gulls and occasionally rarer small gulls, as well as an assortment of waterfowl, are seen. Access is from the Robert Moses Parkway near its entrance from Route 104. Continue to the **Power Vista,** located along Route 104 about one-half mile (0.8 kilometer) south of the Lewiston-Queenston bridge. The entrance is on the east side of Route 104, immediately north of Niagara University. Operated by the New York State Power Authority, the Power Vista provides an overlook of the outflow from the Adam Beck Hydro and Robert Moses power plants. There is usually an abundance of gulls here from early November well into January. Most of Niagara's gulls have been observed here, including Mew, California, Slaty-backed, Ross's, and all of the regularly occurring species. Gull enthusiasts will enjoy the opportunity to study the upper side of these birds in flight.

The **Lewiston Boat Ramp** at the foot of Center Street in the Village of Lewiston, accessed via Route 104 and Route 18F, is probably the best place to see Little Gull on either the American or the Canadian sides of the river.

Continue north to the mouth of the Niagara River at **Fort Niagara State Park**. Many rarities have been found in fall and winter near the breakwall at the Coast Guard station, including Northern Gannet, King Eider,

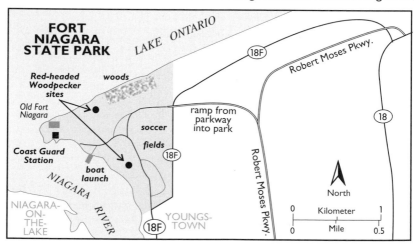

Purple Sandpiper, Red Phalarope, and Razorbill; many gulls are also present. Listen and watch for Snow Bunting and Common Redpoll overhead. Snowy Owls are occasionally seen around the fort and on the breakwall at the river mouth. Starting in late November, Long-tailed Duck is common. The evening gull "fly-past" can be viewed from the park, but the sun may be in your eyes (surveying from the Canadian side is preferable). If the sky is overcast, try viewing from the boat-launch area a little south of the fort. The woods next to Lake Ontario at the northeast corner of the park can be excellent for warblers and other songbird migrants. The open oak grove next to these woods, or the grove across from the soccer fields, often harbors a wintering Red-headed Woodpecker or two. Check the berry and crabapple trees in winter for irregular Bohemian Waxwings. To visit the Coast Guard station, park in the lot next to the old fort (fee required in summer) and walk the road to the breakwall at the Niagara River mouth. Before looking, let the station personnel know of your presence.

TIFFT NATURE PRESERVE, BUFFALO

Half-day; spring and fall

This "oasis" in the city of Buffalo attracts an impressive variety of migrants in spring and fall. March, April, October, and November bring numbers of marsh-loving waterfowl. Mid-April through May and late August through early October are best for songbird migrants; 20 or more species of warblers have been found on several dates. Shorebirds are usually seen in May, August, and September, though they—and the water levels—are somewhat irregular. Among the rarities found here are Little Blue and Tricolored Herons, Yellow-crowned Night-Heron, Glossy Ibis, Eurasian Wigeon, Gyrfalcon, Marbled Godwit, Boreal Owl, and Yellow-headed and Brewer's Blackbirds. Least and American Bitterns are regular breeders. Stop at the visitor center, (716) 825-6397, and get a trail map of the preserve, which can be thoroughly birded in half a day. The most productive trails are those bordering the cattail marsh. The preserve is located on Fuhrmann Boulevard, very near Lake Erie, and can be reached from Route 5 by taking the Tifft Street exit and following the signs to the preserve (see map on page 53).

EXTRA EFFORT

The **Iroquois National Wildlife Refuge** in Alabama, New York, is a worthwhile trip for seeing marsh-loving birds, and its extensive fields and woods provide habitat for many other species as well. It is most productive from March through November. Thousands of waterfowl are present in March/April and October. Breeding species include Osprey, Bald Eagle, and many warblers (including Golden-winged, Cerulean, and Hooded). The refuge is located along Routes 77 and 63 about 35 miles northeast of Buffalo.

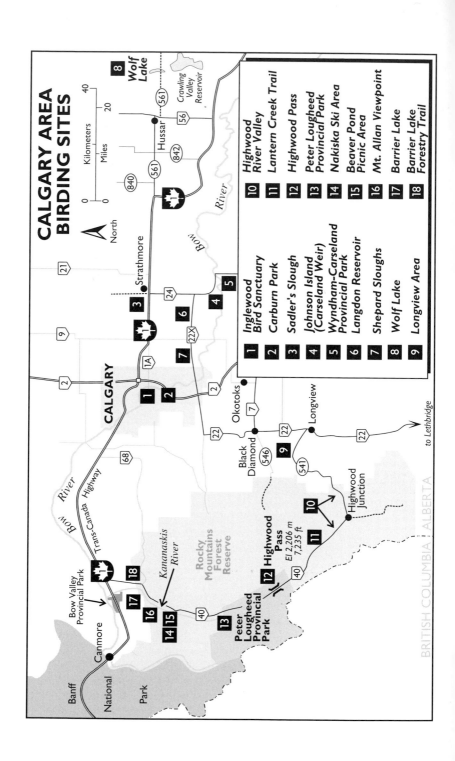

CALGARY, ALBERTA

Calgary Field Naturalists' Society

The city of Calgary is located in southern Alberta, straddling the Bow River as it emerges from the foothills of the Rocky Mountains on the northwestern edge of the Great Plains. With its proximity to Banff National Park, and as the center of Canada's energy industry, Calgary is a popular destination for both pleasure and business.

The area around Calgary contains more varied bird habitats than almost any other location in Canada. Within a day's drive it is possible to visit alpine, subalpine, and foothills habitats, boreal forest, muskeg, aspen parkland, riverine forest, natural grasslands, eroded badlands, seasonal sloughs, wetlands, and lakes. This great diversity of natural environments, coupled with the region's location in the overlap zone between western and eastern breeding species, ensures that Calgary has much to offer visiting birders.

ESSENTIAL INFORMATION

Getting Around: Within the city there is a good public-transit service; call (403) 262-1000 for information, 6:00AM to 11:00PM weekdays, 8:00AM to 9:30PM weekends and holidays. There is a Light Rail Transit system that is free to users in the downtown core. Nevertheless, most visitors interested in birding will find renting a car essential. All major rental companies are represented in the city. Driving around the city is generally easy, but traffic at rush hour (7:00 to 9:00AM and 4:00 to 6:00PM) can be heavy. Expect delays on the major routes at these times.

Climate: Because Calgary is located at an elevation of around 1,000 meters (3,500 feet) and at a latitude of almost 51°, the climate is typical of mountainous regions. The intense sun can burn unprotected skin rather quickly, temperatues cool quickly in the evenings, and sudden changes in weather can occur. It is important to be prepared when going into the mountains, because the pleasant sunny weather in Calgary may not be the same at your destination 100 kilometers away and several hours later. Snow may occur until mid-May, and frosts are possible until late May. Summer (mid-June through late August) is generally warm, with temperatures in the mid-to-high 20s Centigrade (75 to 85°F). By September autumn arrives, although warm weather can continue well into October. Winter arrives sometime in October or November. Although temperatures can fall to as low as -40°C, it is usually much warmer, and given the prevailing low humidity, most people find that birding even at -15°C (5°F) is not unpleasant.

Dress: Warm, layered clothing, including warm head-gear, is advisable at any time of the year. Even in July, mornings can be cool, particularly near the river. During winter, thermal underwear is usually required.

Natural Hazards: Bugs are not as much of a problem as in many other North American cities, but mosquitoes can be troublesome from June to August.

Other Resources: The Calgary Rare Bird Alert number is (403) 237-8821. The official Alberta Road Map published by Alberta Tourism can be obtained from any Travel Alberta Information Centre or by writing to Alberta Tourism, Box 2500, Edmonton, AB T5J 2Z4, (800) 661-8888, or at its web site www.visitor.calgary.ab.ca. The preferred topographic maps for southern Alberta are the 1:250,000 series published by Alberta Forestry, Lands, and Wildlife, since these are the most up-to-date. A Birdfinding Guide to the Calgary Region, prepared by the Calgary Field Naturalists' Society, is a good source of detailed information. Unfortunately, the book is currently out of print, although plans are afoot to have a revision available in the near future.

Tourist information on Calgary can be obtained from the Calgary Convention and Visitors Bureau at (800) 661-1678 (toll-free in North America), or (403) 263-8510 (elsewhere), or on the Internet at www.visitor.calgary.ab.ca.

THE BIRDING YEAR

The spring waterfowl and raptor migration starts in late March. Shorebirds begin to arrive in late April and peak in May, whereas passerines do not appear in good numbers until approximately mid-May. Spring migration is essentially over by the beginning of June. Of the approximately 300 species seen regularly in the Calgary area, some 200 remain to nest.

Returning shorebirds begin to appear by early July, with good numbers of juveniles present beginning in early August. Mid-August to mid-September is the peak of the warbler and shorebird migrations, with most waterfowl and raptors following in October.

After freeze-up, which usually occurs in early November, over 60 species overwinter in the Calgary area. These include a variety of waterfowl that remain north of their usual winter ranges because parts of the Bow River remain open within the city.

INGLEWOOD BIRD SANCTUARY

Half day; spring, late summer, and fall

The **Inglewood Bird Sanctuary** is a city park that has been designated a natural area and a federal migratory-bird sanctuary. It consists of approximately 34 hectares of riverine woodland. This area usually produces the city's finest concentrations of warblers during fall migration; also, it is the best location in Calgary for finding uncommon species of gulls in spring and late fall.

To reach the sanctuary from the Deerfoot Trail, take the Blackfoot Trail exit westbound, cross the bridge, and turn left onto 19 Street S.E.; turn left onto 9 Avenue S.E. Drive east on 9 Avenue S.E. almost to the end and turn right into the parking lot at the Visitor Center. (From downtown Calgary drive east on 9 Avenue to the sanctuary.) The sanctuary is open from dawn to dusk every day of the year and is accessed by way of the gate to the right of the Visitor Center, which is staffed between 8:00AM and 4:00PM in summer.

Species that may be seen at the sanctuary vary dramatically from season to season. In May, small numbers of eastern and western warblers can be observed, together with summer residents such as American Kestrel, Northern Flicker, Western Wood-Pewee, Least Flycatcher, Eastern Kingbird, and Baltimore Oriole. Of the warblers, only Yellow nests regularly. By far the most opportune time to watch for migrant songbirds is from the middle of August until the end of September. On exceptionally good days up to 20 species of warblers may be found. Warblers to watch for include Tennessee, Orange-crowned, Chestnut-sided, Magnolia, Cape May, Yellow-rumped, Townsend's, Black-throated Green, Palm, Bay-breasted, Blackpoll, Black-and-white, American Redstart, MacGillivray's, Wilson's, and Canada. Vagrant warblers include Nashville, Northern Parula, Black-throated Blue, Black-throated Gray, and Yellow-breasted Chat. Other species to watch for at this time include flycatchers, Warbling and Red-eyed Vireos, nuthatches, and kinglets. Accipiters, especially Sharp-shinneds, are attracted by these flocks of migrant passerines.

In early spring and late fall the Bow River at Inglewood is a good location for migrant gulls. The most-productive area is the series of gravel bars toward the northern end. Rarities recorded here include Mew, Iceland, Lesser Black-backed, Glaucous-winged, Glaucous, Slaty-backed, and Sabine's. Interesting ducks to watch for include Harlequin, Common and Barrow's Goldeneyes, and all three mergansers. Descendants of a small introduced population of Wood Ducks nest in the old Balsam Poplars, one of the few places in southern Alberta where this species can be found reliably.

CARBURN PARK

Half day; winter

In Calgary, sections of the Bow River remain open throughout the coldest part of winter and attract a good variety of waterfowl. The **Carburn Park** area has usually been one of the most reliable locations. From the Glenmore Trail and Deerfoot Trail intersection, head east on Glenmore Trail to 18 Street S.E. Turn right (south) onto 18 Street S.E., then right onto Rivervalley Drive, and then left onto Riverview Drive. From the parking lot, walk along the paved trail around the north side of the lagoon to the river.

Large numbers of Canada Geese and Mallards are usually to be found, together with good numbers of Buffleheads, Common Goldeneyes, and Common Mergansers. Small numbers of Barrow's Goldeneyes also occur regularly. A variety of other dabbling and diving ducks have been seen occasionally on this stretch of the river in winter. A telescope is useful for examining inlets on the far side of the river, where some of the waterfowl may be feeding. At least one Bald Eagle should be present in this vicinity, while other possible raptors are Rough-legged and Red-tailed Hawks and Merlin. Other birds that may be seen include Ring-necked Pheasant, Killdeer, Belted Kingfisher, Downy and Hairy Woodpeckers, Northern Flicker, White-breasted Nuthatch, American Robin, American Tree Sparrow, Rusty Black-bird, and Common Redpoll.

Follow the riverbank southward for about 300 meters to a stretch where it runs almost due east between tall trees on both banks. Bald Eagles often perch in these trees. A Great Horned Owl might be found in the woods, as well as a Northern Saw-whet Owl, if you are very lucky. From the eastern end of this stretch a short walk through the woods will bring you back to the parking lot.

Another access to the north end of Carburn Park, near the Glenmore Trail bridge, is reached by turning north on 18 Street S.E. and then left on 76 Avenue at the first lights. Continue to the escarpment and park along Ogden Drive, close to the Bow River Pathway sign. Follow the paved trail down to the bridge. The fast-flowing water around the gravel bars on both sides of the bridge is a fairly reliable location for Harlequin Duck. From the bridge, the path to the south enters Carburn Park, whereas to the north it soon reaches a sweeping bend in the river. A large raft of geese and ducks concentrates at this bend; Gadwall, Northern Pintail, Redhead, Lesser Scaup, Bufflehead, Barrow's Goldeneye, and Hooded Merganser might be found here.

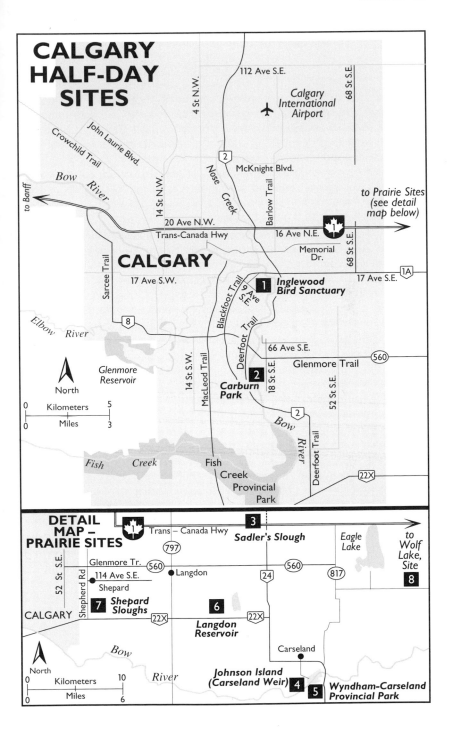

CALGARY
HALF-DAY
SITES

112 Ave S.E.

4 St N.W.

68 St S.E.

Calgary
International
Airport

John Laurie Blvd.

Crowchild Trail

2

McKnight Blvd.

Nose Creek

Barlow Trail

Bow River

to Banff

14 St N.W.

to Prairie Sites
(see detail
map below)

1

20 Ave N.W.

Trans-Canada Hwy

16 Ave N.E.

68 St S.E.

CALGARY

Memorial
Dr.

17 Ave S.W.

17 Ave S.E.

1A

Sarcee Trail

Blackfoot Trail

9 Ave S.E.

1 Inglewood
Bird Sanctuary

8

Deerfoot Trail

Elbow River

66 Ave S.E.

Glenmore Trail

560

Glenmore
Reservoir

14 St S.W.

MacLeod Trail

18 St S.E.

52 St S.E.

North

2 Carburn
Park

0 Kilometers 5

0 Miles 3

Bow River

2

Deerfoot Trail

Fish Creek

Fish
Creek
Provincial
Park

22X

DETAIL
MAP –
PRAIRIE SITES

1

Trans – Canada Hwy

3

Sadler's Slough

Eagle
Lake

to
Wolf
Lake,
Site

797

52 St S.E.

Shepherd Rd

Glenmore Tr.

560

Langdon

560

817

8

114 Ave S.E.

Shepard

24

CALGARY

7 Shepard
Sloughs

22X

6

Langdon
Reservoir

22X

Carseland

0 Kilometers 10

North

Bow River

Johnson Island
(Carseland Weir)

4

5 Wyndham-Carseland
Provincial Park

0 Miles 6

PRAIRIE BIRDING

Half day; spring, summer, and fall

S adler's Slough, Wyndham-Carseland Provincial Park, and Langdon Reservoir: This is a prairie birding trip concentrating on a variety of wetlands and a good riverine woodland. It is most rewarding during migration when large numbers of waterfowl and shorebirds should be found, together with good numbers of raptors, but it can also be rewarding during the June and early July breeding season. At least five hours are needed to cover the 120-kilometer round-trip to Johnson's Island. During the peak fall migration period, Langdon Reservoir and the Carseland Weir area may each require that amount of time to bird thoroughly.

From the traffic light at the junction of the Trans-Canada Highway (16 Avenue N.E.) and 84 Street N.E. in Calgary at the city limits, proceed east for 28.5 kilometers and watch for the sign on the right indicating Highway 24 to Lethbridge. Turn left (north) at this intersection onto the unnumbered gravel road. The **Sadler's Slough** wetland area begins at this intersection, and consists of a series of small, interconnected sloughs and creeks (part of a Ducks Unlimited conservation project) on both sides of the road.

During the migration seasons, the entire two kilometers from the Trans-Canada north to the first farm should be driven slowly as you observe carefully on both sides. Because the habitat is so close to the road—much of it no more than 50 meters away—this location offers an outstanding opportunity for viewing many kinds of shorebirds and surface-feeding ducks at very close range. A telescope on a window-mount is a great help for viewing the birds closely without disturbing them.

Semipalmated, Least, and Baird's Sandpipers (the three common peeps of the Calgary Region) are usually present during this period, often in good numbers. Western and White-rumped Sandpipers turn up in very small numbers from time to time. Other migrant shorebirds that may be expected are Black-bellied and Semipalmated Plovers, Greater and Lesser Yellowlegs, Solitary Sandpiper, Sanderling, Pectoral and Stilt Sandpipers, and both Long-billed and Short-billed Dowitchers. More unusual species such as Hudsonian Godwit and Dunlin might occur. In the second half of May there may be American Golden-Plovers in the plowed fields immediately beyond the wetlands.

There also will be several species of surface-feeding ducks present, including Cinnamon Teal, and possibly five species of grebes: Pied-billed, Horned, Red-necked, Eared, and Western. The most northerly slough on the right-hand side is larger than the others and may contain Double-crested Cormorant, some diving ducks, and, in the second half of May, Red-necked Phalarope. At this time, too, there may be the occasional Greater White-fronted Goose among the numerous Canada Geese.

By the time the fall shorebird migration gets underway in earnest around the middle of July, only the larger sloughs usually contain water, and most of the muddy edges will have dried up. At this time the productive habitat is restricted to the two small sloughs by the Trans-Canada Highway and the two larger ones at the northern end of the complex. The location is still worth visiting, however, as any of the migrants may turn up again, though in smaller numbers; a Ruff was seen here in September 1996. Late July is a good time to look for Short-billed Dowitcher, as this species usually passes through before most of the more-numerous Long-billeds arrive.

From Sadler's Slough, cross the Trans-Canada Highway and proceed south on Highway 24 for 21 kilometers. Turn left (east), following Highway 24. The village of Carseland is now visible ahead on the left. (Gas and food are available here.) At 26.2 kilometers from the Trans-Canada, turn right (south) onto a gravel road marked *Johnson's Island* (**Carseland Weir**). This road is the entrance to a reliable migrant trap for waterfowl, shorebirds, and passerines. About 2.4 kilometers south of the highway, the gravel road turns sharply left and proceeds 0.8 kilometer eastward along the edge of the escarpment, with spectacular views of the Bow River Valley. It then makes a hairpin turn to the right and descends to the valley bottom by means of switchbacks. At the bottom of the hill, follow the right fork to the parking area by the river's edge. This 9-kilometer round-trip from the highway is not recommended after a heavy rain or a snowfall, when the switchback portion may not be passable by automobiles.

Long-billed Dowitcher
Terry O'Nele

The reservoir formed in the Bow River by the weir is one of the first places in the Calgary Region to become ice-free in spring, and it usually has a good assortment of waterfowl present before the end of March. In the past few years, a flock of over 100 American White Pelicans has been present above the weir from late July to October.

North of the parking area, along the bottom of the escarpment, is a backwater channel. The mudflats here can be very productive for shorebirds in both spring and fall. The trail that heads east along the shore of the backwater reaches the river downstream from the weir; the gravel bars here are used for resting by several species of waterfowl and gulls. Between the gravel bars and the shore are more mudflats. This is the best location in the immediate vicinity for shorebirds. The trail may be followed southward along the river's edge to the weir and along the top of the levee back to your vehicle.

Drive back up the escarpment and turn right (east) onto Highway 24. Highway 24 soon turns south and crosses the Bow River; 0.3 kilometer after the bridge turn right into the entrance to **Wyndham-Carseland Provincial Park**. The park is closed to vehicles from early October until mid-April, but may be entered on foot. The access road forks immediately; take the left fork through open farmland for 1.6 kilometers to a parking area at the south end of the weir and good views of waterbirds.

Returning to the fork, continue into the park (day use is free) and turn left immediately on entering the campground, situated in a large tract of riparian woodland. Continue westward for about 2 kilometers through the campground into a parking and picnic area by the river, opposite the gravel bars. A trail runs along the riverbank through dogwood and willow shrubbery, and a stroll along here can turn up a wide variety of warblers and other small woodland birds. Watch for raptors along the escarpment at any season. Upstream toward the weir, the trail passes through a lawn area with scattered bushes that can be rewarding for sparrows. There are pit toilets at the picnic area (open year-round) and throughout the campground.

From the campground, turn left (north) back onto Highway 24 and retrace your route north and then west on Highway 24 past Carseland to the four-way stop. Turn right, proceed 6.5 kilometers north on Highway 24, and watch for a sign at a four-way stop indicating Highway 22X. Turn left (west) here and drive 5 kilometers to a gravel road to the right (north) just before a power line. This road is one of the most-consistent locations in the Calgary area for Upland Sandpiper (May to August). After 1.8 kilometers, turn around at the T-intersection and return to Highway 22X. Turn right (west) and proceed about 2 kilometers, watching for a sign on the right-hand side and above a fence about 50 meters from the road, indicating the **Langdon Reservoir Wetland Conservation Project**. (On older maps this area is named Dalemead Lake.) You can park here and walk across the shallow ditch, or drive 0.6 kilometer past the sign, turn right onto a dirt track, and then right again (east), parallel to the fence, and back to the sign. *If the track looks at all muddy, park and walk, since the prairie gumbo here has mired the vehicles of several unwary birders.*

A narrow passage through the fence at the sign provides access to Langdon Reservoir, a large irrigation-storage reservoir that is usually full of water in spring and early summer, but has a reduced water level in late summer and fall. Consequently, there is an abundance of waterfowl present during spring migration, but usually few shorebirds. During fall migration, however, large numbers of many shorebird species are present. In recent years this has been one of the best locations for fall shorebirds in the Calgary region. Rarities reported have included Spotted Redshank, Wandering Tattler, Black Turnstone, Sharp-tailed Sandpiper, and Ruff. The area most commonly birded is the southern one-third of the shoreline. If sufficient time is available, it would probably be worthwhile walking north along the eastern and western shorelines. The area behind the shoreline consists of rough grassland and weedy areas with cultivated fields beyond, so there is virtually no cover present. Upland Sandpiper has been seen in the weedy areas in late May and Chestnut-collared Longspur during the summer.

From the dirt track at the west end of Langdon Reservoir, proceed about 19 kilometers west on Highway 22X to **Shepard Road** (88 Street S.E.). Soras can often be heard in the small sloughs at this intersection. Turn onto Shepard Road and proceed north for 1 kilometer to a shallow slough on the left, just before a bend in the road. In dry summers this is usually just a dry alkali bowl, but if the slough contains water, it can be excellent for shorebirds during migration. In August 1986 a Red-necked Stint was observed here, together with many other shorebirds. The road at this point has no shoulder, so park on one of the nearby side roads.

Proceeding north to the village of Shepard, watch the fields on both sides of the road for dry-land shorebirds such as American Golden-Plover and Long-billed Curlew. Short-eared Owls and, in winter, Snowy Owls may be found in this vicinity. Just before the community hall in Shepard, turn right (east) onto Beaulah Vesta Road and drive east for about 2 kilometers. A semi-permanent slough on both sides of the road is often good for shorebirds and puddle ducks. Since 1989, in years of adequate water levels, Black-necked Stilts have nested here. In late April and early May, Hudsonian Godwit has often been present. Turn around at the first farm driveway and return to the intersection in Shepard; then turn right (north) for 3 kilometers to the junction with Glenmore Trail. Turn left (west) back to Calgary.

Caution: During the fall waterfowl-hunting season, which runs from mid-September to early December, locations such as Langdon Reservoir and Carseland Weir can be heavily shot-over. Birding during this period will be more enjoyable if you restrict your visits to Sundays, when shooting is not permitted.

WOLF LAKE

Half to full day; late spring and summer

Grassland specialties such as Sprague's Pipit, Baird's Sparrow, and McCown's and Chestnut-collared Longspurs can all be found in the Calgary area, but good locations for each can vary from year to year. A dependable place to try is the eastern side of **Wolf Lake**, which is a large, shallow slough located about 110 kilometers east of Calgary on SR-561. In years with little rainfall Wolf Lake is often dry in summer. *Caution: this trip should be attempted only if the weather and the roads are dry; the roads will be extremely slippery when wet.*

To reach Wolf Lake from Calgary, drive east on the Trans-Canada Highway (Highway 1) and turn left onto SR-561. This intersection is about 22 kilometers east of the town of Strathmore. Continue east on SR-561 for 27 kilometers to Hussar. About 2 kilometers east of Hussar turn right (south) on Hwy 56 for 3.3 kilometers, then left (east) onto SR-561 again. From this point the road is gravel-surfaced and can be dusty when dry and very slippery when wet. Wolf Lake is reached after an additional 23 kilometers. Watch for Merlin and Loggerhead Shrike in or near shelter-belts along this section. Wolf Lake stretches on both sides of the road, and it is worthwhile scoping the shore and water from here, particularly during May, late July, August, and September, when migrant shorebirds are present. The eastern shore of the lake is accessed by continuing 1.6 kilometers east and then turning north on a gravel track, which leads to a gravel pit. Public access is permitted to these grasslands.

A spring or summer walk through the grasslands along this road and north of the gravel pit can produce Long-billed Curlew, Burrowing Owl, Sprague's Pipit, and McCown's and Chestnut-collared (common) Longspurs. Watch overhead for Northern Harrier, Swainson's Hawk, Ferruginous Hawk, Golden Eagle, and Prairie Falcon. Baird's Sparrow may also be present.

Returning to Calgary by the same route, this trip takes a half day to complete.

LONGVIEW TO HIGHWOOD PASS

Full day; summer and fall

The 230-kilometer drive from Calgary to Longview, over Highwood Pass to the Kananaskis Valley, and back to Calgary, is one of the most beautiful drives in southern Alberta. It starts on the prairies and goes over the highest drivable pass (2,206 meters, 7,225 feet) in Canada. The road is an excellent paved highway with picnic areas, campgrounds, and hiking trails giving access to a wide variety of foothill, subalpine, and alpine habitats.

To reach the start of this route, head south from Calgary on Highway 2 and take the Highway 2A exit for Okotoks. Continue on Highway 2A for 11.5 kilometers to the junction with Highway 7. Turn right (west) on Highway 7 and drive for 19.5 kilometers to Black Diamond, then turn left (south) on Highway 22 for 17 kilometers to the junction with Secondary Road (SR) 541 (Highwood Trail) in Longview.

Turn right (west) on SR-541 (kilometer 0.0). All distances are given from here to the access points and do not include side-trips. Between 6.5 and 9 kilometers a low ridge parallels the highway to the north. This is an excellent location for migrant raptors, particularly from late March to early May. Swainson's, Red-tailed, and Rough-legged Hawks, both Bald and Golden Eagles, and Prairie Falcon can all be expected. In some years Golden Eagles summer in the area, and it is worthwhile stopping to check the ridge, as they often may be seen resting on the ground.

In this area the valley and rolling hills are a mosaic of open pastures and aspen woodland. Mountain Bluebird is an early migrant and may be seen along the highway by the end of March. Lewis's Woodpeckers have been observed in this part of the valley. Good stopping points along the highway are at **Sullivan Creek** (14.8 kilometers), **Trap Creek** (21.3 kilometers), and **Green Ford Campground** (24 kilometers). Species to watch for at these locations include Western Wood-Pewee, Alder, Least, and Pacific-slope Flycatchers, Eastern Phoebe, Eastern Kingbird, American Dipper, Warbling Vireo, Tennessee and Yellow Warblers, Chipping, Clay-colored, Vesper, Savannah, Song, Lincoln's, and White-crowned Sparrows, Brewer's Blackbird, Baltimore Oriole, Pine Siskin, and American Goldfinch. Check all sapsuckers carefully; they may be either Yellow-bellied or Red-naped, with Red-naped and hybrids predominating.

At 34 kilometers the Kananaskis Country sign marks the boundary of the **Forest Reserve**; this is public land with free access. The area is home to Mule Deer, Elk, Bighorn Sheep, Cougar, Coyote, and both Black and Grizzly Bears. Birders should be aware that, although the chances are remote, the possibility of encountering a bear does exist. Birders hiking in this area should also be aware that the hunting season for large game extends from the beginning of April to mid-May and from the last week of August to the end of November; shooting is not permitted within 365 meters of the highway.

The stretch between the Kananaskis Country boundary and Highwood Junction travels between grassy hillsides dotted with clumps of aspen on the north side of the road and scrubland with Balsam Poplars and some spruce stands along the valley floor to the south. MacGillivray's Warbler and Lazuli

Bunting frequent the aspen clumps, while Rufous Hummingbird, Dusky Flycatcher, Warbling Vireo, and White-crowned Sparrow can be found in the poplars and scrub. The spruce stands may contain Sharp-shinned Hawk, Yellow-rumped Warbler, Northern Waterthrush, and Wilson's Warbler, while Harlequin Duck, Common Merganser, Spotted Sandpiper, and American Dipper may be seen along the river. Several picnic areas with parking places and toilets are located along this stretch, providing convenient access points. The **Highwood River Group Camp and Picnic Area** (34.2 kilometers) immediately after the Kananaskis Country sign is a good location for Lazuli Bunting, the best time for finding this species being late June. A

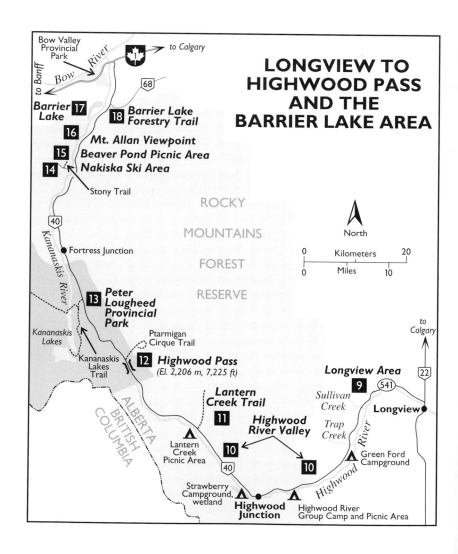

LONGVIEW TO HIGHWOOD PASS AND THE BARRIER LAKE AREA

walk into the Group Camp should turn up many of the species mentioned above.

At Highwood Junction (43.4 kilometers) the road becomes the Kananaskis Trail (Highway 40). The convenience store at **Highwood House** usually has active hummingbird feeders that may be visited by both Calliope and Rufous Hummingbirds, with the latter being the more numerous. A large colony of Cliff Swallows nests beneath the road bridge just south of the junction, and Willow Flycatcher can occur along the riverbank. Listen, too, for Pileated Woodpecker.

There is an extensive wetland complex, formed by the action of Beavers, on the left as the road climbs a hill (47.8 kilometers) just after **Strawberry Campground**. This is a good spot for Common Snipe, Calliope Hummingbird, Willow Flycatcher, Northern Waterthrush, MacGillivray's and Wilson's Warblers, and Lincoln's Sparrow.

The highway continues north, still in the Highwood Valley, with the magnificent peaks of the Continental Divide to the west and the Highwood Range to the east. There are several day-use areas and campgrounds, and from these one can hike trails to the river and longer ones into the mountains. The first kilometer of the **Lantern Creek Trail** (60.6 kilometers) can be rewarding in late June. In addition to the common montane passerines, watch for Northern Goshawk, Golden Eagle, Spruce Grouse, Ruffed Grouse, Olive-sided Flycatcher, Clark's Nutcracker, and, irregularly, both Red and White-winged Crossbills.

After about 70 kilometers the road starts to climb to **Highwood Pass**, which is reached at 81 kilometers. Varied Thrush and Chipping, "Timberline" Brewer's, "Slate-colored" Fox, and White-crowned Sparrows can sometimes be seen along the interpretive trail at the parking area. Follow this trail across the road to **Ptarmigan Cirque**, a 2.5-kilometer hike that climbs 230 meters into the alpine zone. The height is gained in the first kilometer, the trail then emerging from the trees into an alpine valley with superb views; in July and August it is filled with flowers. Species to watch for on this hike include White-tailed Ptarmigan (elusive; most easily located in fall after the first snows when their tracks may be followed), Clark's Nutcracker, Mountain Chickadee, American Pipit, and Gray-crowned Rosy-Finch.

From Highwood Pass, continue on for 17.4 kilometers to Kananaskis Lakes Trail, which is reached at 98.4 kilometers, and which gives access to **Peter Lougheed Provincial Park**. Park maps and information can be obtained at the Visitor Information Centre (3.6 kilometers from Highway 40). Good birding locations within the park include Pocaterra Trail and marsh, Kananaskis Canyon Interpretive Trail, and Boulton Creek Interpretative Trail. The Kananaskis Lakes are worth checking in late fall for loons, grebes, and scoters. American Dipper may be seen along the fast-flowing creeks.

Additional sites along Highway 40, for those with a little extra time, include the **Nakiska Ski Area road** (125.5 kilometers), which provides access to a good birding area in the vicinity of **Mt. Lorette**. Follow the Nakiska road across the Kananaskis River, continue for another kilometer, and park in the Stoney Trailhead parking area. It can be worthwhile following this equestrian trail for 3 or 4 kilometers to Mt. Lorette Creek. Species to watch and listen for in appropriate habitat include Harlequin Duck, Alder, Willow, Least, Dusky (the most widespread *Empid* in this area), and Pacific-slope Flycatchers, Winter Wren, Fox Sparrow, and Cassin's Finch (rare). Black Swifts occur regularly in the area, with flocks of up to five to ten birds being present until early September.

A stroll along the footpaths at the **Beaver Pond Picnic Area** (127.5 kilometers) can be rewarding, especially in the early morning or the evening. Watch for the trail sign to the bridge, halfway along the parking lot. Species of note include Varied Thrush and Townsend's Warbler.

During spring and fall, Golden Eagles migrate across the Kananaskis Valley between Mt. Lorette and the Fisher Range. The **Mt. Allan Viewpoint** (127.6 kilometers) is a good location for viewing this migration. The birds will be at mountain-top height, so a telescope will be an asset. Migration peaks are mid-to-late March and late September to early October. Up to 500 raptors a day have been observed at those times, mainly Golden Eagles but also including Bald Eagle, Sharp-shinned Hawk, and Northern Goshawk.

At about 135 kilometers, the southern end of **Barrier Lake** will be seen to your left. This cold, deep reservoir is lacking in nutrients and does not attract many waterfowl. In October, however, it should be checked for loons (Pacific is fairly regular, and Yellow-billed has occurred) and Surf Scoter. Black Scoter has been recorded in the vicinity of the dam. At 137.3 kilometers the boat-launch access road is reached on the left. Follow this road, taking the right-hand turn down the hill to the parking area. A short walk south along a path provides good views of the lake.

Continuing on for another 2 kilometers, there is an access road to the dam at 139.3 kilometers. Opposite this road is the University of Calgary Field Station. Here, the 2.3-kilometer **Barrier Lake Forestry Trail** can be worth walking. Spruce Grouse and Three-toed Woodpecker are elusive residents of the area; it can also be good for Red Crossbill when there is an abundant cone crop. Boreal and Mountain Chickadees may be common. Inquire at the buildings for the location of any feeders, especially in early summer for hummingbirds.

At 150 kilometers, Highway 1, the Trans-Canada Highway, is reached. Turning right (east) will return you to Calgary in about 80 kilometers. Turning left (west) takes you to Banff in about 55 kilometers.

Gas can be obtained in Longview and at the Fortress Junction Service Centre. Highwood House has a Park Ranger Office and Information Centre, (403) 558-2151, a seasonal gas station, and a convenience store; these are open only from mid-May to early October. Snacks can also be obtained at Fortress Junction Service Centre, and meals are available at the restaurants at the Kananaskis Village hotels. It should be noted that Highway 40 (Kananaskis Trail) is closed between Highwood Junction and Peter Lougheed Provincial Park (north of Highwood Pass) from 1 December to 15 June.

ACKNOWLEDGMENTS

Work on this manuscript was provided by Malcolm McDonald, Andrew Slater, and William J. F. Wilson.

Swainson's Hawk
Louise Zemaitis

CHICAGO AREA BIRDING SITES

1. The Magic Hedge
2. Lincoln Park Bird Sanctuary
3. Navy Pier & Olive Park
4. Meigs Field
5. McCormick Place
6. Jackson Park
7. Waukegan Harbor and Beach
8. Illinois Beach State Park
9. North Point Marina
10. Chicago Botanic Gardens
11. Lake Calumet Area
12. Indiana Dunes National Lakeshore
13. Indiana Dunes State Park
14. The Migrant Trap
15. Goose Lake Prairie State Park

CHICAGO, ILLINOIS

Lynne Carpenter and David B. Johnson

The "Windy City" is located at the junction of the Great Lakes and the prairie. The waters of Lake Michigan, its rivers, and the prairie soil form a rich mosaic that has always attracted vast numbers of birds. The region's marshes, savannas, forests, and glacial lakes provide abundant food and cover for a wide variety of wildlife. Although agriculture, industry, and population eliminated much habitat, important stretches of land have been protected which benefit both the public and the region's wildlife. When the city incorporated, early commissioners declared that Chicago's lakefront should be "forever open, clear, and free," and the result is one of the world's most-accessible city waterfronts. Twenty-five of its 29 miles are accessible to the public along Lake Michigan's beaches, harbors, and pathways. Inland, a crescent of parks and boulevards are linked in a chain around the city.

ESSENTIAL INFORMATION

Getting Around: Conventioneers and other tourists in Chicago's Loop or at McCormick Place can easily enjoy birding along Lake Michigan, but for all other locations, a car is needed. Rush-hour traffic is heavy in all directions, and summer weekend traffic is particularly heavy on Friday and Sunday afternoons. Lake Shore Drive south of the Loop should be avoided when there are Bears' football games or other events at Soldier Field.

Climate: Chicago is known for its icy winters and strong winds, but for much of the year the weather is mild enough to require only a rain jacket. The peak birding month of May can produce anything from a freak snowfall to temperatures in the 90s Fahreinheit, and conditions can change dramatically within minutes. Temperatures near Lake Michigan can be much cooler then, and winds off the lake can drive birds and birders inland to warmer and more-protected areas. During the transition from winter to spring, it is best to be prepared with warm clothing and rain-gear. Summer weather is good for birding, but temperature and humidity can be high.

Natural Hazards: Mosquitoes do not usually appear until June and can be bothersome through August in wooded areas. Ticks are prevalent in forest preserves and grasslands, but Lyme disease is not yet a problem.

Safety: Most of the birding locations described are popular year round and can be visited with the same precautions needed in any urban area. The sites near Lake Calumet and sections of Jackson Park and the Indiana Dunes are somewhat isolated and should be visited with other birders familiar with those areas. Hunting is allowed at the Des Plaines Conservation Area, and recreational use can make other locations unattractive for birding beyond the early-morning hours.

Other Resources: Two recent guides have directions and maps for these and other sites in the area. *A Birder's Guide to the Chicago Region* by Lynne Carpenter and Joel Greenberg (1999, Northern Illinois University Press) describes 250 sites in the 19 counties surrounding Chicago, including those found in Illinois, Indiana, Wisconsin, and Michigan. *Birding Illinois* by Sheryl DeVore (2000, Falcon Press) covers the entire state.

The Chicago Rare Bird Alert number is (847) 265-2118 ; Indiana's hotline is (317) 767-4727. The listserve IBET (Illinois Birders Exchanging Thoughts) has recent postings at *www.birdingonthe.net*. Birding organizations in the region include Chicago Audubon Society, *www.audubon.org/chapter/il/chicago*; Chicago Ornithological Society, *www.chicagobirder.org/index.html*; Evanston North Shore Bird Club, *www.members.aol.com/ensbc/index.html*; DuPage Birding Club, *www.home.xnet.com/~ugeiser/Birds/BirdClub.html*; and the Illinois Ornithological Society, *www.chias.org/ios/*.

General information on the City of Chicago is available at *www.ci.chi.il.us*. The Field Museum, *www.fieldmuseum.org*, has a fine collection of bird skins and maintains a database on birds that collide with lakefront structures.

CHICAGO LAKEFRONT TOUR

Half day; winter, spring, fall

This tour begins at the most well-known and well-birded site in Chicago, the **Magic Hedge** in Lincoln Park. If only one site can be visited during the months of April/May and September/October/November, this is it! Migrants follow the western shore of Lake Michigan each spring and fall, and nocturnal migrants can stray or be blown out over the lake; in the morning hordes of passerines "zing" in off the lake, hitting the first available patch of vegetation. Diurnal migrants also concentrate at the shore to avoid the lake.

To get to the Magic Hedge and Montrose Harbor, exit Lake Shore Drive eastbound at Montrose Avenue (4400N); go toward the lake and turn right at the bait shop. The small rise with trees on the north side of the road is the Magic Hedge. Early morning is most productive. The Chicago Park District has recognized the importance of this promontory as a migratory stopover for birds and has a sign dedicating the area. After birding every nook and cranny of the Hedge, bird the beach, the fisherman's pier, and the jetty for shorebirds and gulls. If the wind is from the east, you'll do better at inland birding locations for passerines, except in fall when those same winds bring jaegers and other waterbirds close to shore. Stay a bit out of the wind at the beach house north of the Hedge. Scopes are a necessity for seawatching along the lake.

THE MAGIC HEDGE, LINCOLN PARK BIRD SANCTUARY

Nearly all of the expected passerines, as well as the occasional rarity, can be found here during spring and fall. One can easily run up a 75-plus species list on a good day. Rarities recorded here (but not to be expected) include Brown Pelican, Reddish Egret, Yellow and Black Rails, Mew, California, and Ivory Gulls, Royal Tern, Groove-billed Ani, Rock Wren, Kirtland's Warbler, Lark Bunting, and Golden-crowned Sparrow. The Hedge, as well as the other lakefront parks described here, is good for such scarce migrants as Yellow-bellied and Alder Flycatchers, Philadelphia Vireo, Gray-cheeked Thrush, Mourning and Connecticut Warblers, and Le Conte's and Nelson's Sharp-tailed Sparrows. During an invasion winter as many as five Snowy Owls have been seen in the Montrose Harbor area. Look on the star-floats in the harbor, on the beach, and out on the fishing-pier jetty. Gulls eat hand-outs on the harbor drive that goes out to the harbor inlet to the south. Lesser Black-backed Gull recently has been a regular here—but usually on the beach—in late fall and early winter. Bring your "Wonder Bread" hand-out in winter—who knows what you'll attract! A Peregrine Falcon (from a recent re-introduction program to city skyscrapers) often sits on the tower at the east end of the beach.

As you leave the Montrose Harbor area, turn south on Lake Shore Drive to the exit at Irving Park Road (4000N, Route 19) for the **Lincoln Park Bird Sanctuary**, also known as the Addison Street Bird Sanctuary. Go east and take the drive to the south for about one-half mile until you see a totem pole to the east. Park just south of here—or wherever you can find parking—

and walk to the sanctuary just east of the totem pole. This wooded four-acre sanctuary is surrounded by a chain-link fence and has several ponds and a small marsh. The site is an excellent migrant trap, as long as you don't mind peering through a fence into the woods. Birds can be "pished-in," and warblers and sparrows often dot the ground just outside the fence. Hummingbirds usually visit the jewelweed in fall, and rails and water-thrushes can be seen in the wet spots. In winter, bird seed is often put just outside the fence for sparrows.

Return to Lake Shore Drive and turn south. At Fullerton you may want to exit and bird the **Lincoln Park Zoo**. Passerines are often seen in and about the zoo. The ponds both north and south of Fullerton often have waterbirds. Owls such as Barn, Long-eared, and Northern Saw-whet have been found in the ev-

ergreens that dot the zoo enclosures, though they're not normally expected. Farther south, the **North Avenue beach** is a good area for gulls in winter.

Although primarily a tourist attraction, **Navy Pier and Olive Park** off Lake Shore Drive are good birding locations. After parking in the (expensive) lot at the end of the pier, walk out and scan the jetties and water for loons, sea ducks, and Snowy and Short-eared Owls from late October through March. Loons, grebes, and other waterfowl, including wintering Long-tailed Ducks, can be fairly close. The old pier pilings south of the Navy Pier building and the rocky jetties to the east occasionally harbor a Snowy Owl in winter. Close to Navy Pier, on the west side of the Chicago Water Filtration Plant, **Olive Park** is an unassuming little park that often harbors many migrant passerines. The hawthorn trees near the wall of the filtration plant attract thrushes and sparrows.

Meigs Field Airport is east of the Field Museum of Natural History and the Shedd Aquarium. Take McFetridge Drive east from Lake Shore Drive and turn north to Planetarium Drive, then east to the lakefront airport, where you can park on either side of the terminal building. Bring a scope. Walk up the stairs on the outside of the terminal building to a platform look-out on the second story. It is from here that most Chicago birders have seen their first Snowy Owl in winter. In fact, during non-invasion years, this is the most likely location in Illinois to see this bird. Mobbing crows often clue in a birder to an owl's location. Often the owls sit by the rocks on the east side of the runway. Dawn and dusk are the best times. Short-eared Owls, Horned Larks, and Snow Buntings can also be seen on or near the airport runways.

McCormick Place, visible from Meigs Field, is a large Chicago convention center. From Lake Shore Drive exit at 31st Street and drive back north to the convention center. Parking is difficult. You must pay to park in the convention center or get permission from the guard at the shack to park nearby; otherwise, you must walk at least a mile from 31st Street north to the center. Birds abound during migration, and ornithologists from the Field Museum collect dead bird specimens from window and building strikes each spring and fall. Birders often look for scarce sparrows such as Grasshopper, Henslow's, Le Conte's, and Nelson's Sharp-tailed along the grassy areas by the rocks. The bushes and trees immediately south of the McCormick building host a variety of passerines during migration.

A few miles south of McCormick Place, the excellent migrant trap **Jackson Park** is located immediately south of the Museum of Science and Industry. Exit Lake Shore Drive at 57th Street and park just southeast of the museum. Walk west to **Wooded Isle** (the Paul Douglas Nature Preserve) and cross the bridge south to the preserve. Birders should visit this site only with others. Guided bird walks are held each Wednesday and Saturday morning by the Chicago Audubon Society.

NORTHERN LAKEFRONT

Half to full day; spring, fall, and winter

This tour begins at **Waukegan Harbor**, approximately one hour north of downtown Chicago. Take Route 41 or I-94/I-294 north and exit east on Route 120 (Belvedere Street) to downtown Waukegan. When Route 120 ends, turn north on Pershing Road to the south harbor entrance to the east. Go through the gates and south through the parking lot until you reach the jetty at the south end of the marina. Look along the 50-yard sandy beach

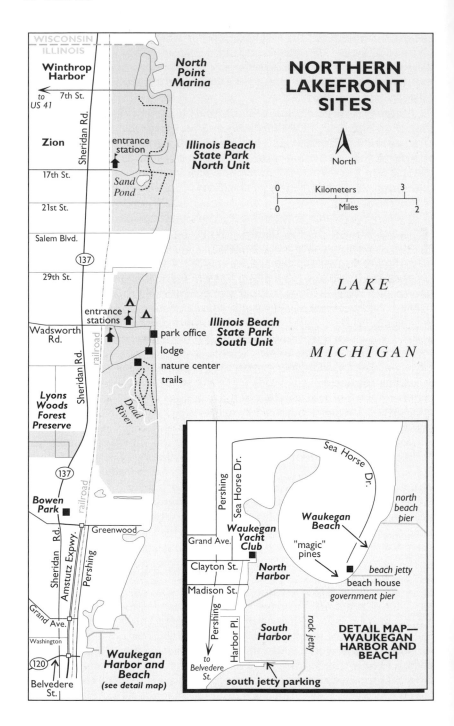

NORTHERN LAKEFRONT SITES

WISCONSIN
ILLINOIS

Winthrop Harbor

North Point Marina

to US 41

7th St.

Zion

Sheridan Rd.

entrance station

Illinois Beach State Park North Unit

17th St.

Sand Pond

21st St.

Salem Blvd.

137

29th St.

entrance stations

park office

lodge

nature center

trails

Illinois Beach State Park South Unit

Wadsworth Rd.

Sheridan Rd.

railroad

Lyons Woods Forest Preserve

Dead River

137

railroad

Bowen Park

Greenwood

Sheridan Rd.

Amstutz Expwy.

Pershing

Grand Ave.

Washington

120

Belvedere St.

Waukegan Harbor and Beach
(see detail map)

North

0 — Kilometers — 3

0 — Miles — 2

LAKE

MICHIGAN

DETAIL MAP—WAUKEGAN HARBOR AND BEACH

Sea Horse Dr.

Pershing

Sea Horse Dr.

Waukegan Yacht Club

Grand Ave.

Clayton St.

North Harbor

Madison St.

Pershing

Harbor Pl.

to Belvedere St.

South Harbor

rock jetty

south jetty parking

Waukegan Beach

"magic" pines

north beach pier

beach jetty

beach house

government pier

along the parking lot; if seaweed and other gunk is washed up on the beach, this can be a good place for ducks, shorebirds, or gulls. From here one can often see scaup, Bufflehead, and other diving ducks in late fall and winter. This is also a good location to chum for gulls with bread during the winter. Thayer's, Iceland, and Glaucous Gulls are unusual but do occur.

You can also bird the old harbor by going north and parking at the Yacht Club at the end of Clayton. This is a good place for wintering Hooded Mergansers and Greater Scaup, and comparisons with Lesser Scaup can often be made. Between the yacht club and the concrete jetty to the south that bisects the north and south harbors, water stays open all winter. It is not uncommon to encounter a Wood Duck or an American Wigeon looking for a hand-out.

From the Yacht Club, drive west on Clayton Street to Sea Horse Drive (just east of Mathon's Restaurant). Take Sea Horse north and east to the **Waukegan Beach** and beach house, as well as the famous north beach pier, where many Illinois birders have tallied their first Purple Sandpiper in November (although it is rare and not to be expected). If your time is limited, scan the beach between the two jetties and bird the "magic pines" behind the beach house. The pines are a migrant trap for passerines, and the municipal beach often has groups of shorebirds, gulls, and terns to look over. Scoters and Long-tailed Ducks are often seen off the harbor mouth in winter, and Snowy Owls have roosted on the jetties during invasion years. From Memorial Day to Labor Day a fee is required to park and walk the beach, which extends about one mile to the north; it is worth the cost because there are often many shorebirds and gulls along the way. During migration check the cottonwood trees along the beach for birds, including occasional Black-crowned Night-Herons. This stretch of beach is perhaps the best place in Illinois to look for the rare Piping Plover in spring and fall, and Ruddy Turnstones and Sanderlings are often present. American Avocet, Whimbrel, Red Knot, and Laughing and Franklin's Gulls are rare but regular during migration.

Return to Clayton Street and go west to Pershing Road. Take Pershing north to Grand Avenue, and then west on Grand to the Melvin E. Amstutz Expressway. Take it north for 1.0 mile and turn west on Greenwood Avenue to Sheridan Road. Go north on Sheridan Road and turn into **Bowen Park**, a wooded ravine good for migrant passerines in both spring and fall. One-and-a-half miles farther north on the west side of Sheridan Road, **Lyons Woods** includes a stand of conifers that often attracts such irruptive winter finches as Pine Siskin, White-winged Crossbill, and Evening Grosbeak; an occasional Long-eared Owl can be found roosting in the conifers. Golden-crowned Kinglets are suspected of nesting. As the trail winds out of the coniferous woods into fields, look for Northern Shrike in winter. In summer, Blue-winged Warbler and Yellow-breasted Chat can be found, as well as the occasional Chestnut-sided or Hooded Warbler in the deciduous woods. The latter two are found about one mile to the west under the power-lines. One hour could be spent birding here and another hour at Bowen Park.

Continue north on Sheridan Road to Wadsworth Road and turn east into **Illinois Beach State Park**. Bird the deciduous woods just south and east of the railroad tracks near the entrance guard shack. The woods often host a large number of migrant passerines. Follow the road south and east to the nature center; check with the park naturalist to find out what birds are around. The Dead River trail is worth a walk at any season. The hawk observation tower at the mouth of the Dead River near Lake Michigan can be good in fall for migrating raptors, particularly falcons. A Northern Shrike occasionally winters near the mouth of the Dead River. North of the nature center, a lodge with a restaurant and gift shop is located on the beach. The park office, beach, and campground are farther north. Sea ducks can be observed offshore, and Red-throated and Pacific Loons have been seen here and near the nuclear power plant to the north.

The pines and prairie to the south are worth the long walk, but a permit is required to enter this area. Check in at the park headquarters and ask for a special day-use permit for birding. The almost century-old Austrian Pines harbor Pine Warblers during late September and early October, and Red Crossbills and other winter finches irregularly in late fall and winter. Wet swales and prairie to the south have supported nesting Upland Sandpipers, Grasshopper Sparrows, Brewer's Blackbirds, and Western Meadowlarks. During migration, Yellow Rails and Le Conte's and Nelson's Sharp-tailed Sparrows have been found in the wet swales, though they are difficult to see.

Back on Sheridan Road, head north. Turn east onto 17th Street in Zion to the Camp Logan part of the **North Unit of Illinois Beach State Park**. Sand Lake pond is often good for ducks; the prairies and swales are worth checking in migration. A Northern Shrike winters here in most years. Just to the south, American Woodcocks, Common Snipe (both in spring), and Whip-poor-wills can be heard after dark.

Return to Sheridan Road and go north to the last town in Illinois, Winthrop Harbor. Take Seventh Street east to **North Point Marina**, which is particularly good for bay and sea ducks in winter. Common Goldeneye and Bufflehead are common, and all three scoters have occurred. Rarities have included Barrow's Goldeneye and Harlequin Duck. Large groups of gulls gather here, and the marina area is a good place for Lesser Black-backed and Glaucous Gulls in winter. Snow Buntings are often seen in November, and Snowy Owl is occasional in winter. American Woodcocks, Sedge Wrens, and Yellow-breasted Chats are usually found during spring and summer in the wet swales to the west of the harbor in Spring Bluff Forest Preserve.

Common Snipe, American Woodcocks, and Whip-poor-wills can all be heard to the south along the sand ridges and swales of the park during evening hours in spring, and Least Bittern, King Rail, and Virginia Rail nest in the wetter areas. Return to the Chicago area by driving west to Highway 41 south.

The **Chicago Botanic Gardens** can be visited on the way back to Chicago by exiting Route 41 at Lake Cook Road eastbound. Non-members must pay a $7.00 fee to park; maps and a checklist are available at the entrance gate and the visitor center. A wide variety of habitats include man-made lagoons, islands planted with fruiting trees, and prairies. Waterfowl are plentiful, with late March/earlyApril and October and November having the most variety. Spring migration can be spectacular, beginning with raptors in early to mid-March. Sparrows and grassland birds are found in the prairie and along the west side of the garden, and rails have been seen along the boardwalk on Marsh Island. Warblers can be numerous along the northern perimeter, in McDonald Woods, at the waterfalls, in the Sensory Garden, and along the eastern fence-line. Black-crowned Night-Heron, Wood Duck, Willow Flycatcher, Orchard Oriole, and Brewer's Blackbird are among the species that have nested.

LAKE CALUMET

Half day; year round

The **Lake Calumet** area on Chicago's far southeast side was once known as the grand Calumet Marsh, and hosted the first nesting record of Black Rail known to science, as well as nesting Le Conte's Sparrows. Today, only remnants of this landscape remain, with wetlands and rookeries of endangered birds surrounded by aged industrial plants, dump sites, giant landfills, and sewage-treatment lagoons. Birds still come, though, and so do the birders, particularly when a rarity is reported. This location is considered by some to be an industrial nightmare, but it has hosted many stellar rarities and continues to lure birders. It is best to bird with others and to avoid the area during hunting season.

This tour begins at Lake Calumet, about 20 minutes south of Chicago's loop via Interstate 94 (the Dan Ryan Expressway). Exit eastbound on 130th Street and turn north on the frontage road immediately east of I-94. Follow the frontage road 1.75 miles and park at the gate to Medusa Cement Company. On weekdays, one may obtain permission to drive into the Lake Calumet area via the numerous access roads from the cement company, but don't bet on it; walking is best, anyway. This is the best place in the Chicago area to look for Great Black-backed and Glaucous Gulls in winter. Hundreds of Common Goldeneyes and Common Mergansers also use the lake. If you leave your car at this area, make sure that it is safely locked and that all your birding optics and valuables are with you or out of view. Several birders have had scopes stolen near this location, so beware.

Return to 130th Street and go east to the **Thomas J. O'Brien Lock and Dam** by turning south on the road just west of the bridge over the Calumet River. Follow the road to the east and south to the Lock and Dam parking lot. This is one of the best areas in the Chicago area to study gulls as they congregate in the river and on the grassy area above the lock and dam. Iceland, Glaucous, and Great and Lesser Black-backed Gulls are uncommon but regular in winter. Not-to-be-expected rarities have included Glaucous-winged and California Gulls. From May to October you may want to skip this location and go directly to one of the marshes.

Return to 130th Street and take it east to Torrence Avenue. Go south for about a half block and look for the gated road on the west side of the road. Walk west to the **Hegewisch Marsh**, which can be excellent for

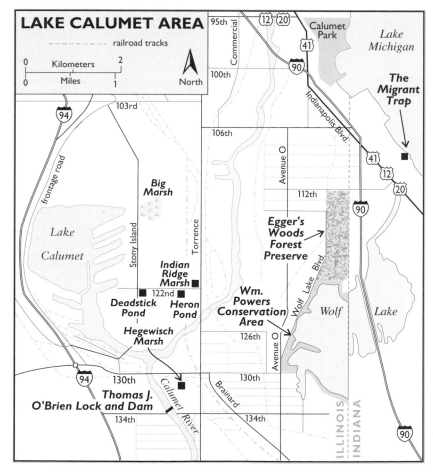

LAKE CALUMET AREA

wetland birds. Yellow-headed Blackbirds nest sporadically, and Redheads and Ruddy Ducks nested once. Pied-billed Grebe, Blue-winged Teal, Common Moorhen, and American Coot nest regularly.

Go north on Torrence to 122nd Street and turn west. The marsh on the north side of the road east of the railroad tracks is called **Indian Ridge Marsh**. Egrets and Black-crowned Night-Herons have nested in the cottonwood trees when the marsh had higher levels of water. Shorebirds may be present in July and August if water levels are low. In winter, thousands of blackbirds and starlings roost at this location and marshes nearby. Continue west to Heron Pond on the south side of 122nd Street for nesting Yellow-headed Blackbirds. One of the best areas to view fall shorebirds is **Deadstick Pond** at the southeast corner of 122nd Street and Stony Island Avenue. July through September are the best months, although lingering juvenile Long-billed Dowitchers have been seen in November. Stilt Sandpiper occurs regularly. Snowy Egrets and Little Blue Herons have appeared in late summer, and Common Moorhens and Yellow-headed Blackbirds have nested.

For **Big Marsh**, go north 1.0 mile from the intersection of 122nd Street on Stony Island Avenue until you see the large marsh on the east side of Stony Island. Access can be restricted, and you may be permitted to view the marsh only from Stony Island Avenue. Egrets and herons abound, and Black-crowned Night-Heron and Least Bittern nest.

For **Wolf Lake**, return to Torrence and drive south to 130th Street. Turn east and south immediately on Brainard Avenue. At 134th Street, turn east and then turn north on Avenue O. The entrance to Wolf Lake and the William Powers Conservation Area is on the east side of the road. A large flock of Mute Swans winters, and a Tundra Swan might be observed. It can be good in fall and spring for ducks. North of Wolf Lake, **Egger's Woods Forest Preserve** has a large marsh with nesting Yellow-headed Blackbirds. Take Avenue O north to 112th Street and turn east to the entrance for Egger's Woods on the south side of the road. The woodlands and nearby grassy area can be excellent in spring and fall for migrant passerines.

Conclude this tour by going north on Avenue O to 106th Street, where you turn west. At Torrence Avenue, turn north to 103rd Street and follow it to the west to enter Interstate 94 back to Chicago. To extend the tour, drive into Indiana and bird The Migrant Trap (see next section).

INDIANA DUNES

Full day; spring, summer, and fall

East of Chicago, the area between Gary and Michigan City, Indiana, is known as the Indiana Dunes. Many of the original dunes have been obliterated to make way for steel mills, but 12,000 acres are protected in a patchwork of sites known as the **Indiana Dunes National Lakeshore**, and another 2,200 acres are preserved in the **Indiana Dunes State Park**. Many migrants stream through the area; in spring the northbound migrants find themselves facing the expanse of Lake Michigan and may pause before continuing up the eastern or western shore of the lake. Birding highlights are the hawk flights in April, the southern birds that nest (White-eyed Vireo, Wood Thrush, Cerulean Warbler, Prairie Warbler, Louisiana Waterthrush, and Hooded Warbler), the northern species that nest (Veery, Chestnut-sided Warbler, and Canada Warbler), and the migrant waterfowl that pause on the shallow lakes in the western part of the National Lakeshore.

Indiana Dunes State Park is just over one hour east of Chicago. From Chicago, drive east on Interstate 90 and the Indiana Toll Road to Interstate 94. Take I-94 east for 10 miles to Indiana Highway 49. Turn north and follow Highway 49 directly into the Indiana Dunes State Park. Be sure to get a map at the gate house. The climax forest, wooded swamp, and sand dunes are particularly attractive in spring and summer for migrants and nesting species.

Take the park road east to the Wilson Shelter. A walk along Trail #2 should turn up breeding Acadian Flycatcher, Veery, Blue-winged Warbler, Cerulean Warbler, Ovenbird, and Louisiana Waterthrush. Red-shouldered and Broad-winged Hawks, Barred Owls, and Hooded Warblers are also often seen. Trail #10 is particularly good for migrants on cool spring days when warblers drop down into the bushes near the water to forage on insects in the lee of the dunes. Look for nesting Cerulean, Prothonotary, and Canada Warblers from the footbridge over the marsh. Trail #9 takes you up steep, wooded dunes to open areas where Prairie Warblers and Field Sparrows may be found.

Drive 2 miles east of the state park on SR-12 to the Dorothy Buell Visitor Center for the **Indiana Dunes National Lakeshore** on Kemil Road. Park maps and interpretive materials are available here, and Kenneth Brock's excellent book, *Birds of the Indiana Dunes*, is one of the many books available. Good birding can be had north of SR-12 on Kemil Road. From the visitor center walk north or drive to the parking lot near Lake Michigan. From this location, it is easy to check the lake and to walk back along Kemil Road. Prairie Warblers nest west of the road in the State Park and are sometimes observed from the road. Acadian Flycatchers and Cerulean Warblers have nested in the dense woodlands near the road, and the inter-dune marsh along Beverly Drive east of Kemil Road supports nesting Willow and (possibly) Alder Flycatchers, White-eyed Vireos, Yellow-breasted Chats, Indigo Buntings, and Swamp Sparrows. Parking restrictions are strictly enforced here, so park only in designated lots.

One mile west of the state park, **Johnson Beach** (also called Waverly Beach) has a high sand dune overlooking Lake Michigan and is a good vantage point for seeing migrating raptors. From Route 12, turn north on Waverly

Road, the first street west of SR-49. Follow the road toward the lake and park. Walk away from the lake and up the dune. The best time for the northbound hawk flights is March and April on days with moderate to strong southerly winds. The peak numbers of Broad-winged Hawks are usually seen around the third week in April. Fall flights are less impressive, but can be rewarding, particularly when easterly winds force raptors to follow the shoreline.

Two miles west of Indiana Dunes State Park, **Cowles Bog** has nesting Sora, Virginia Rail, American Woodcock, White-eyed Vireo, Marsh and Sedge Wrens, Yellow-breasted Chat, and Swamp Sparrow. Drive north of SR-12 on Mineral Springs Road. Park in the lot at the railroad tracks or at the north end of the road near the guard station for the community of Dune Acres. Birding can

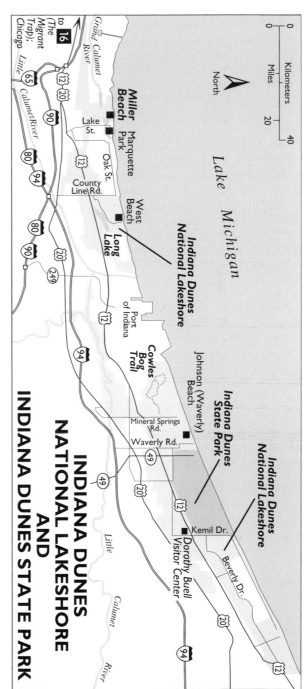

be good along the road; walk west from either parking spot.

Return to SR-12, drive 7 miles west to County Line Road, and turn north. Turn right (after crossing the railroad tracks) for West Beach. **Long Lake**, a large pond and marsh, is just past the entrance kiosk. During migration, a variety of waterfowl can be seen, and passerines are attracted to the the trees and shrubs along the northern edge of the lake. Long Lake Trail on the dune at the west end of the lake affords good afternoon views.

West of this point, **Miller Beach** marks the southernmost point of Lake Michigan. In fall, birds following the shores of Lake Michigan during migration are funneled here. The birding is best on days with brisk northwest winds, which seem to stimulate the movement of birds along the lakefront. From Long Lake, drive north on County Line Road toward Lake Michigan and turn left onto Oak Street. Stop at Marquette Park, where there is a nice view of Lake Michigan; a concession stand here offers shelter from the wind. Continue through the park and turn west onto Hemlock Avenue. At Lake Street turn north and park in the lot for Miller Beach. More jaegers have been seen here than at any other place in the Midwest. Pomarine, Parasitic, and Long-tailed Jaegers, Sabine's Gull, and Black-legged Kittiwake are some of the rarities which have been recorded from September through November. These birds are infrequent; they are usually seen only during strong northwest winds. Loons and grebes are present in October and November, and rafts of other waterfowl, including all three scoters and various gulls, can be seen during these months and into December. (Parking fees are required at Miller and West Beaches in summer.)

Return to Highway 12 by driving south on Lake Street. Turn west for two miles and take Interstate 90 (the Indiana Toll Road) back to Chicago, or continue west on Highway 12 to visit **The Migrant Trap**. Turn off at the exit for the Hammond Marina and Empress Casino and park at the end of the overflow parking lot to bird the narrow strip of trees along the lake known as The Migrant Trap. The only good cover for miles, the trap is particularly attractive to birds from mid-August through October. Impressive build-ups also occur in May. Remarkable concentrations of passerines and an occasional Sora, Virginia Rail, American Woodcock, Short-eared Owl, or Whip-poor-will seek cover here. Winter Wrens are frequently found under and around the rocks. In winter, rarities such as scoters, Glaucous and Great Black-backed Gulls, Black-legged Kittiwake, and Snowy Owl have been seen.

PRAIRIES AND GRASSLANDS

Full day; year round

The largest native tallgrass prairie east of the Mississippi River is located just 40 miles southwest of Chicago. **Goose Lake Prairie State Park** is the highlight of this trip, but additional grasslands, riparian woodlands, and a rookery along the way provide interest and add to the bird list for the trip.

From Chicago, drive southwest on Interstate 55. Soon after crossing the Des Plaines River, turn off on Lorenzo/Pine Bluff Road (Exit 240). Drive west for 7.0 miles and turn right on Jugtown Road to Goose Lake Prairie State Park, (815) 942-2899. The interpretive center opens at 10:00AM, except for winter weekends, when it is closed. The Tallgrass Nature Trail and Marsh Loop trails east of the visitor center total 4 miles and pass through prairie and pot-holes. Sedge Wrens and Henslow's Sparrows can be found in the tall, dense grasses, and marsh species may be found near the pond. Beyond the marsh loop, the Sagashka Trail (photo blind) has good habitat for herons. Loggerhead Shrikes have nested near the picnic area near the entrance to the park, and Northern Mockingbirds and Orchard Orioles are present in some years. Other nesting species include Northern Harrier, Northern Bobwhite, Common Snipe, American Woodcock, Bell's Vireo, Yellow-breasted Chat, Grasshopper Sparrow, and Field Sparrow. In winter, Northern Harrier, Cooper's Hawk, Rough-legged Hawk, and Short-eared Owl are possible.

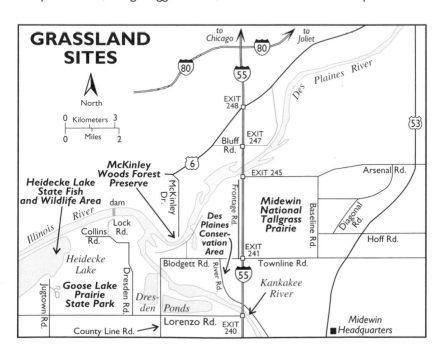

From the entrance to the park, turn right (north) to **Heidecke Lake State Fish and Wildlife Area**, (815) 942-6352. An 1,800-acre cooling-lake for the nearby power station, Heidecke Lake has been leased by the Illinois Department of Conservation for fishing and hunting. Shorebirds probe along the rocky dikes in the fall, and a good variety of waterfowl and gulls frequent the lake in winter. Another view can be had from the eastern edge of the lake. Return to Lorenzo/Pine Bluff Road and turn east. Turn north onto Dresden/Collins Road and follow it north and west to the parking lot, where it is possible to bird from your car.

From Collins Road, a short detour north on Lock Road leads to **Dresden Lock and Dam** on the Illinois River, an excellent location for waterfowl and gulls in the winter and terns in the spring. Birds are frequently seen below the dam, where the water stays open. In spring and summer, Loggerhead Shrikes and Northern Mockingbirds may be found along Lock Road, and Bell's Vireos, White-eyed Vireos, and Yellow-breasted Chats are found in shrubby areas along Dresden/Collins Road to the south. Farther south, marsh birds nest near the ditch along the road. Back at Lorenzo Road, turn north onto County Line Road and cross over the Dresden Ponds, cooling-lakes for the Dresden Nuclear Station. Ring-billed Gulls nest on a dike east of County Line Road. The gull colony can be seen from Lorenzo Road or Cottage Road on the north and east side of the pond. The water stays ice-free all winter, and a variety of waterfowl is present from November to April.

Continue north on County Line Road, cross the Kankakee River, and turn east for the **Des Plaines Conservation Area**, a 5,080-acre area of open fields, thickets, woods, and sloughs between the Des Plaines and Kankakee Rivers. Turn east on Blodgett Road and pass through the Grant Creek cut-off, where waterfowl may be seen in season. Continue to Frontage Road. The pond at Blodgett Road and Frontage Road is good for herons, ducks, and shorebirds, and American Redstarts are frequently found nearby where Grant Creek crosses the road. Farther north, turn west into an area of grassland and thickets with nesting Bell's and White-eyed Vireos, Blue-winged Warblers, Yellow-breasted Chats, and Grasshopper Sparrows. Return to Blodgett Road and go west to River Road. Turn south to the park headquarters. Much of the area is managed for hunting, so inquire at the headquarters before venturing forth. South of headquarters, look for Northern Bobwhite along the road and nesting Dickcissels, Grasshopper Sparrows, Bobolinks, and Orchard Orioles in the fields. After crossing I-55, turn north to Grant Creek Prairie, a 78-acre wet prairie on the east side of Des Plaines Conservation Area, (815) 423-5326, where Upland Sandpipers, Sedge Wrens, Grasshopper Sparrows, and Bobolinks have nested. Return to River Road and continue south to Boathouse Road. Yellow-breasted Chats and Orchard Orioles nest across the road from the Field Trial headquarters and Stable Trails.

Continue east to Highway 53 and turn north to the **Midewin National Tallgrass Prairie**, where 19,000 acres of the former Joliet Arsenal are being preserved as a vast area of open fields, wetlands, and woods. Trails are being developed at this time. The U.S. Forest Service Headquarters is located in a house at 30071 South Route 53, one mile north of River Road; call to see if any tours are scheduled, (815) 423-6370. This large grassland supports a wide variety of species, including the largest population of Upland Sandpipers in Illinois and the largest concentrations in northern Illinois of Loggerhead Shrikes. Nesting species include Northern Harrier, Bell's Vireo, Northern Mockingbird, Dickcissel, Grasshopper Sparrow, Bobolink, and Western Meadowlark. Wintering birds may include Northern Harrier, Rough-legged Hawk, Short-eared and Long-eared Owls, and Western Meadowlark.

Drive 1.25 miles north on US-53, and turn west to the parking lot and interpretive sign. The Henslow Trail is a 1.5-mile loop where Henslow's Sparrows, Bobolinks, and other grassland birds nest. West of the fence, Upland Sandpipers and Loggerhead Shrikes might be seen. At Arsenal Road, turn west to return to I-55. Drive north to the next exit (Bluff Road) and turn west. At US-6, turn southwest for 2 miles and make a sharp left onto Bridge Street. Turn immediately south onto McKinley Drive to the **McKinley Woods Forest Preserve**, (815) 727-8700, and park in the lower parking lot. This 473-acre wooded forest preserve is on the Des Plaines River, and the 60-mile-long I & M Canal State Trail is accessible here. This is an excellent spot to see warblers in migration. Nesting species include Broad-winged Hawk, Brown Creeper, Prothonotary Warbler, Ovenbird, and Kentucky Warbler.

Return to I-55 northbound, and exit at US-30 toward Aurora. Turn right at Renwick Road for the visitor center for the Lake Renwick Heron Rookery Nature Preserve, (815) 727-8700, or park along US-30 north of Renwick Road. From May through August, the visitor center is open on Saturdays from 8:00AM to noon, and for Wednesday tours at 10:00AM. This 320-acre abandoned gravel pit is now filled with water and islands that have nesting Double-crested Cormorants, Great Blue Herons, Great Egrets, Black-crowned Night-Herons, and Cattle Egrets. The lake has also attracted migrant waterfowl, gulls, and terns in spring and fall. Waterfowl are present until the water freezes.

ACKNOWLEDGMENTS

William Glass, Joel Greenberg, Kanae Hirabayashi, Robert Hughes, James Landing, Walter Marcisz, Joe Milosevich, John Purcell, and Al Stokie provided assistance, and we appreciate the use of Kenneth Brock's book, *Birds of the Indiana Dunes,* and Lynne Carpenter and Joel Greenberg's book, *A Birder's Guide to the Chicago Region.*

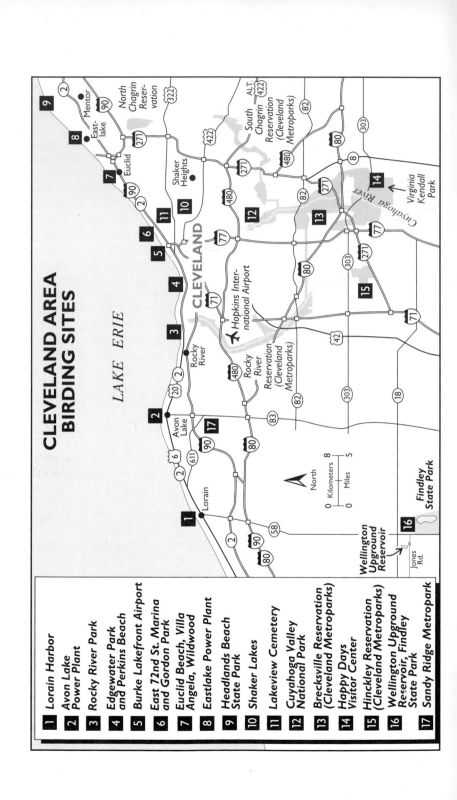

CLEVELAND AREA BIRDING SITES

LAKE ERIE

CLEVELAND

1 Lorain Harbor
2 Avon Lake Power Plant
3 Rocky River Park
4 Edgewater Park and Perkins Beach
5 Burke Lakefront Airport
6 East 72nd St. Marina and Gordon Park
7 Euclid Beach, Villa Angela, Wildwood
8 Eastlake Power Plant
9 Headlands Beach State Park
10 Shaker Lakes
11 Lakeview Cemetery
12 Cuyahoga Valley National Park
13 Brecksville Reservation (Cleveland Metroparks)
14 Happy Days Visitor Center
15 Hinckley Reservation (Cleveland Metroparks)
16 Wellington Upground Reservoir, Findley State Park
17 Sandy Ridge Metropark

North
0 Kilometers 8
0 Miles 5

CLEVELAND, OHIO

Larry Rosche, Paula Lozano, and Bob Finkelstein

Cleveland, a cosmopolitan city located at the mouth of the Cuyahoga River on the south shore of Lake Erie, has become a popular tourist destination in the Great Lakes region. Visitors come to enjoy a wide variety of attractions, including its museums, symphony orchestra, theaters, and recreational areas. They also come for various business reasons and to use the excellent medical facilities. If you're in Cleveland for any reason and have time to look for birds, a number of excellent opportunities await you!

The Cleveland region is defined as an area inclusive of the following northern Ohio counties: Cuyahoga, Geauga, Lake, Lorain, Medina, Portage, and Summit. The region encompasses 2,938 square miles and five major watersheds: the Black, Chagrin, Cuyahoga, Grand, and Rocky Rivers. Measured by its influence on migration patterns, Lake Erie—with over 100 miles of shoreline—is by far the most important physiographic feature in the region, serving as a barrier to northward movement in spring and turning the Ohio shoreline into a landfall for southbound birds in autumn. For thousands of birds it is the natural pathway of flight. Also, the discharge of warm water by electric generating plants maintains ice-free sections of the lake in winter that attract waterfowl and thousands of gulls. An average of 279 species has been recorded annually in the Cleveland region during the period 1989–2000.

ESSENTIAL INFORMATION

Getting Around: Most visitors arrive at Cleveland Hopkins International Airport, which is 10 miles southwest of Downtown's Public Square. All of the major car-rental agencies, taxis, limousines, and a rapid-transit train are available at the airport. Although some birding sites can be reached by public transportation, a car offers the visiting birder maximum flexibility in deciding where to go. Cleveland is also served by Amtrak, (800) 872-7295, and by Greyhound Bus Lines, (800) 231-2222. For additional information, contact the Convention and Visitors Bureau of Greater Cleveland, (216) 621-5555, or check their web site at *www.travelcleveland.com*.

Climate: Cleveland's weather follows Midwest seasonal patterns and is moderated by Lake Erie; however, wind chill is always a factor to be reckoned with from late fall to early spring. The lake's waters are slow to warm in spring and slow to cool in fall. In spring, the effect is often a steep drop in air temperature as the birder approaches the shoreline. It may be a balmy 65°F in the southern suburbs, but the birding sites adjacent to the lakefront can be a chilly 45°F. Cleveland-area roads can be icy and snow-covered from late fall to early spring. Road conditions are posted between 1 November and 31 March by AAA Ohio Motorists' Association at (216) 606-6423.

Safety: As in other large metropolitan areas, crime is a fact of life in northeast Ohio. Birding areas are generally safe, but one should always be cautious, especially when birding alone in isolated areas. To date, theft from cars has not been a general problem for birders, but there is always a need for preventive measures.

Other Resources: A Rare Bird Alert covering the area is sponsored by the Kirtland Bird Club, (330) 467-1930. Also check the web site *www.aves.net* for current sightings throughout the region and the state. Web sites for the many area park systems follow:

Cleveland Metroparks *www.clemetparks.com*
Cleveland Lakefront State Park *www.dnr.state.oh.us/odor/parks*
Cuyahoga Valley National Park *www.222.nps.gov.cuva*
Geauga Park District *www.geaugalink.com*
Lake Metroparks *www.lakemetroparks.com*
Lorain County Metroparks *www.loraincountymetroparks.com*
Medina County Park District *www.medinacountyparks.com*
Summit County Metroparks *www.neo.lrun.com/MetroParks*

The birder visiting Cleveland in spring may want to join one of the morning bird walks conducted the last three Sundays of April and the first three Sundays of May by the Audubon Society of Greater Cleveland, (216) 861-5093; the Cleveland Museum of Natural History, (216) 321-4600; the Cleveland Metroparks, (216) 351-6300; the Lake County Metroparks, (440) 256-1404; the Geauga County Metroparks, (440) 286-9504; and the Nature Center at Shaker Lakes, (216) 321-5935. For further information and detailed directions call one of these sponsoring organizations.

THE BIRDING YEAR

A s early as mid-February, the northward movement of waterfowl may be evident. The formation of large leads in the ice on Lake Erie provides resting and foraging areas for a variety of ducks. As Skunk Cabbages emerge through the snow, and ice melts on inland lakes, elegant Northern Pintails and snappy-looking Ring-necked Ducks begin to descend on the region. They may be joined later by many other species during peak waterfowl migration from mid-March into April. Gull-watching can be remarkable through March as lingering winter visitors are often joined by early migrants. Seeing 10 species of larids in a day's outing is not out of the question. By mid-April, though, most of the wintering gulls have pulled out of their Lake Erie haunts.

American Woodcock and Common Snipe also appear in fair numbers by mid-March. The first noticeable movement of landbirds will invariably include Eastern Phoebes, Tree Swallows, Fox Sparrows, and Eastern Meadowlarks. By mid-April Pine Warblers, Louisiana Waterthrushes, and many sparrows are on territory, and, depending on weather patterns, early flights of several warbler species may be found during the last third of the month.

Locally, passerine migration peaks in the middle third of May and tapers off afterward. A good day should produce 20 or more species of warblers along the Lake Erie shoreline. Inland, migration is not as noticeable, but many species are returning nesters. Indeed, it is far easier to find such birds as Alder Flycatcher and Yellow-breasted Chat inland than it is to find them along Lake Erie. The last third of May is the best time to find Mourning and Connecticut Warblers, as well as the uncommon Olive-sided and Yellow-bellied Flycatchers.

The number of nesting species is impressive. In recent years over 150 species have summered locally, including 25 species of warblers. Hikes along the Black, Chagrin, Cuyahoga, and Grand Rivers can produce an impressive day list even on the warmest days of June and July. Half-day trips to Brecksville, Hinckley, or North Chagrin Metroparks should reward birders with chances to see many interesting nesters. The hemlock gorges of Geauga and Lake Counties provide habitat for many northern breeders. Enthusiastic birders have often said that it is entirely possible to find over 100 species in the Cleveland region on any given day from May to September.

The migration of shorebirds has been well-documented in *The Cleveland Bird Calendar* since 1905. In the past two decades, 39 species have been found in the region. Unfortunately, at the time of this writing, little shorebird habitat is available along Lake Erie due in part to the vagaries of the lake level and the filling of dredge-spoil sites in Lorain (east of the mouth of the Black River) and in Cleveland (near East 72nd Street). When suitable habitat exists, however, a good number and variety of shorebirds will be present.

As summer ends, passerine migration heats up again. Along the shore of Lake Erie, swallows gather in the beginning of August. Common Nighthawks often migrate through the river valleys in impressive numbers at the end of the month. Both Blue-winged and Green-winged Teal gather at preferred locations along the major rivers and streams throughout the region. A noticeable southward passage of Red-breasted Nuthatches is often an indication of future movements of northern finches.

The first half of September is a good time to look for the rare Piping Plover and Buff-breasted Sandpiper. September can bring many warblers, including the more uncommon and rare species. At this time of year, most lakefront birding sites harbor birds for longer periods of time than in the spring. As in spring, inland migration is more subdued, but many areas still produce an excellent variety of flycatchers, vireos, warblers, and sparrows.

Major flights of sparrows occur in early October, and the second week of October has long been noted as "sparrow time" in the Cleveland region. This is the time to look for rare Clay-colored, Le Conte's, and Nelson's Sharp-tailed Sparrows. On inland lakes and reservoirs, Ring-necked and Ruddy Ducks gather. If it is to be an invasion year, Purple Finches and Pine Siskins will be widespread.

As November arrives, Snowy Owls may appear along Lake Erie. For the exceptionally hardy birder, being at the right place at the right time along the shore of Lake Erie during a "witch of November" can be rewarding. These strong northwesterly winds can bring in large flights of loons and swans. Thousands of Bonaparte's Gulls are often found at the various river mouths. These gatherings provide larophiles the opportunity to ferret out rare Little, Black-headed, or Sabine's Gulls. Pomarine Jaegers are prone to show up at this time. American Tree, White-throated, White-crowned, and Swamp Sparrows will be settled into their favored winter residences by month's end.

As December progresses, gull numbers continue to increase along the lakefront, and this is probably the best time to look for rare loons and grebes. Inland, waterfowl gather on reservoirs, lakes, ponds, and marshes for their last feedings before freeze-up. Local Christmas Bird Counts usually record between 60 and 85 species. Winter generally has the region fully within its grip by mid-January. As ice forms on Lake Erie, Bonaparte's Gulls depart and larger gulls move into the warm-water outlets. Gull enthusiasts closely watch Avon Lake, East 72nd Street, and Eastlake for uncommon and rare species amid the throngs of Ring-billeds, Herrings, and Great Black-backeds. American Black Duck, scaup, Common Goldeneye, and Common and Red-breasted Mergansers are the dominant waterfowl species. A drive through the rural areas of Geauga, Lorain, Medina, or Portage Counties could reward observers with large flocks of Horned Larks and Snow Buntings. Other finds might include Lapland Longspurs, as well as an occasional Rough-legged Hawk or Short-eared Owl.

BIRDING SITES

Most local counties have excellent facilities and preserves that provide suitable nest-sites for many of the 150-plus nesting birds of the Cleveland region. The steep valleys associated with the Chagrin and Grand Rivers are renowned for the numbers of relic populations of Canadian Zone species. The gently-flowing Upper Cuyahoga River provides numerous nesting spots for Prothonotary Warblers and Northern Waterthrushes. The Middle Cuyahoga River is the local stronghold of Yellow-throated Warbler. It is difficult to recommend one park over another, and birders are encouraged to contact local park systems for information on trails and avifauna. We have separated this chapter into Lake Erie sites (which are covered west to east) and inland sites. In most cases, directions to a site originate in downtown Cleveland.

LAKE ERIE SITES

Lorain Harbor (Lorain County) has been a remarkable birding site over the years. From I-90 west exit at SR-611 and proceed north (west). When SR-611 turns left, continue straight ahead on Colorado Avenue, cross US-6 (Erie Avenue), turn left on Lakeside Avenue, and then immediately right into the Spitzer Marina. Park along the western edge of the lot and walk out on the pier to bird the marina area, the western half of the river mouth, and the dredge-spoil site inside the fenced area. Return to Erie Street and, after crossing the bridge over the Black River, turn right and right again along the eastern edge of the power plant to bird the western side of the harbor. The list of rarities is long, and, although the power plant rarely provides open-water areas in mid-winter, this site is always worth a stop. Gull numbers can be simply staggering. It is not uncommon to have 5,000 Bonaparte's Gulls fishing the harbor and river. Chances for Laughing, Franklin's, Little, Black-headed, Sabine's, California, Thayer's, Iceland, and Lesser Black-backed Gulls and Black-legged Kittiwake are as good here as anywhere else in Ohio. This site provided Ohio's first Royal Tern record and the unprecedented summering of a Sabine's Gull. The grassy areas and trees offer birders a chance to view passerine migrants, including rarer species such as Le Conte's and Nelson's Sharp-tailed Sparrows.

Avon Lake Power Plant (Lorain County) is a good place to search for rare ducks and gulls from late fall through winter. From I-90 west, exit at SR-611 and proceed north (west) to the first light. Turn right onto Miller Road and follow it to its end at US-6 (Lake Road). Turn right and watch for the parking areas on your left; a small one is along Lake Road, and a larger one is on the west side of the power plant. The bluff overlooking the lake and boat launch area offers an excellent place to view the waterfowl and the gulls. There is a fishing pier, but it may not be open in winter. Birders must be prepared to be chilled to the bone on a breezy winter day, but the opportunity to find several "white-winged" gulls, Harlequin Duck, Barrow's Goldeneye, or King Eider lessens the effect of the wind and cold. Purple Sandpipers have been seen on the breakwall.

Rocky River Park (Cuyahoga County) is a small lakefront park. Take the Cleveland Memorial Shoreway West (US-6, US-20, and OH-2) to its western terminus. Continue west on Clifton Boulevard through Cleveland and Lakewood and onto US-6 (Lake Road) into Rocky River. Turn right (north) onto either Cornwall or Kensington Roads, left (west) onto Beach Cliff Boulevard, and right at the park entrance opposite the northern end of Falmouth Drive. This is a reliable site to study waterfowl in late fall through

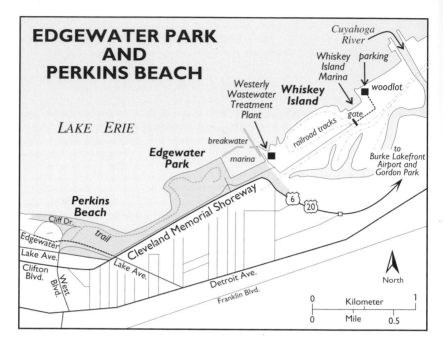

**EDGEWATER PARK
AND
PERKINS BEACH**

*Cuyahoga
River*

Whiskey
Island
Marina

parking

Westerly
Wastewater
Treatment
Plant

**Whiskey
Island**

woodlot

LAKE ERIE

railroad tracks

gate

breakwater

**Edgewater
Park**

marina

*to
Burke Lakefront
Airport and
Gordon Park*

**Perkins
Beach**

Cliff Dr.

Cleveland Memorial Shoreway

6 20

Edgewater

trail

Lake Ave.

Lake Ave.

Clifton
Blvd.

West Blvd.

Detroit Ave.

Franklin Blvd.

North

0   Kilometer   1

0   Mile   0.5

early spring when there is open water. The main attractions are flocks of scaup, the regular occurrence of scoters, and the possibility of finding rarities.

Cleveland Lakefront State Park: Edgewater Park and Perkins Beach areas (Cuyahoga County) are urban parks abutting the lakeshore on the near west side of Cleveland. From downtown take the Cleveland Memorial Shoreway West to the Edgewater Drive exit. At the stop sign at West Boulevard, turn right. Park in the first area on the left, which is sometimes referred to as Perkins Beach. The bluffs provide an excellent place to view the waters below, which often have large gatherings of waterfowl and gulls during late fall and winter, depending on ice conditions. Check the beach areas to the east of the bluffs for shorebirds, including plovers in late fall, and gulls any time. In spring, hawks and vultures can be seen migrating along the shore in good numbers; keep an eye out for the local Peregrine Falcons. The trees and grassy areas are good for migrants, and this has been one of the top sites in the region for Red-headed Woodpecker. An additional site for viewing the lake and harbor is the breakwater at the northwest corner of the Westerly Wastewater Treatment Plant at the east end of the lower park.

A trip to this area would be incomplete without visiting the Whiskey Island Marina on the west side of the mouth of the Cuyahoga River. From the Edgewater exit off the Shoreway, follow the signs for the marina. There is a gate at the entrance which is not always open. If this is the case, press the call button and identify yourself as a birder. Once through the gate, follow the gravel road east and then north to a parking area close to the harbor entrance. On a wave day, birding can be very satisfying in the woodlot that is wedged between the harbor, river, and railroad tracks. There is always a chance of seeing a rare bird, such as the five Pomarine Jaegers that frequented the harbor entrance in April-May 1998.

Burke Lakefront Airport and **Cleveland Lakefront State Park, East 55th Street** (Cuyahoga County): Burke Airport has long been known as the place to see Snowy Owls in winter and grass-loving sandpipers in migration. The airport lies along the North Marginal Road between East 9th and East 55th Streets. From outside the fence, look for plovers and sandpipers from August to mid-October, and Snowy Owls, Horned Larks, Lapland Longspurs, and Snow Buntings in the winter. At the east end of the North Marginal Road check near the East 55th Street Marina for gulls and other waterbirds.

Cleveland Lakefront State Park, East 72nd Street Marina and **Gordon Park** areas (Cuyahoga County) offer more lake-watching opportunities, and are reached by exiting Cleveland Memorial Shoreway East (I-90) at Martin Luther King Jr. Drive. The marina area has hosted some remarkable birds over the years and is always worth checking. Thse power plant no longer puts out much warm water, but when it does, the adjacent waters of Lake Erie can provide thrilling birding. Rarities have included Black-headed Gull, the only Sabine's Gull known to have wintered in the ABA Area, Ivory Gull, and Black Guillemot.

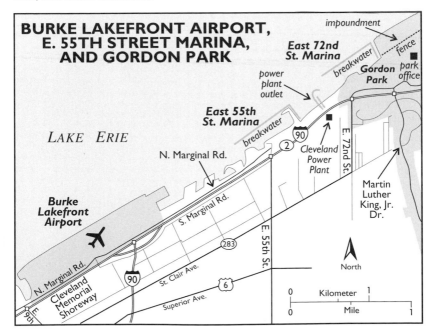

BURKE LAKEFRONT AIRPORT, E. 55TH STREET MARINA, AND GORDON PARK

At the present time, the area inside the fence at Gordon Park is closed to public access, but over the years the impoundment has hosted a large number of species, including such goodies as Sharp-tailed and Curlew Sandpipers, Ruff, Least Tern, and Smith's Longspur. Few shorebirds use the area at present because of habitat change; however, the area still offers excellent landbird possibilities. Migrant and wintering Northern Saw-whet Owls can occasionally be found in the pines. Rough-legged Hawks and Short-eared Owls can sometimes be seen hunting the areas beyond the fence in fall and winter. This is a fairly reliable area for Northern Shrike from late October through mid-March. Northern Mockingbird is resident. During migration, check the conifers near the headquarters building for Yellow-bellied Sapsuckers and Pine Warblers, and in winter for the occasional Long-eared Owl. Migrant sparrows number in the hundreds from mid-October to December.

Cleveland Lakefront State Park: Euclid Beach, Villa Angela, and **Wildwood** (Cuyahoga County) can provide some top-notch migrant watching for the birder with only a little time. The areas can be reached from the Cleveland Memorial Shoreway East (I-90, SR-2). Exit the Shoreway at 185th Street and head north. Turn left on Neff Road and left again at Lakeshore Drive. Turn right at the park entrance and follow the drive to the Wildwood Marina parking lot. Before exploring areas to the west, check the marina and the mouth of Euclid Creek. Numerous migrant loons, grebes, ducks, and gulls can be seen here in spring, fall, and early winter, as long as there's open water. Small gulls sometimes stage in impressive numbers. Don't forget to scan the breakwaters; one might find a stray Purple Sandpiper in fall or early winter.

To reach the Villa Angela and Euclid Beach areas, walk back across the

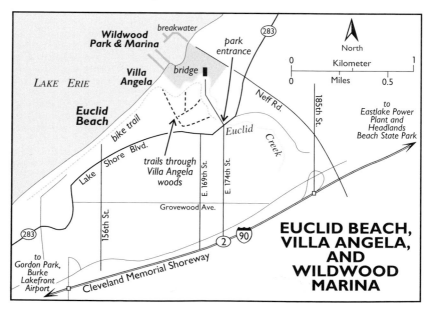

bridge over Euclid Creek and continue on the path that goes north and then west. There is a variety of habitats, including areas of grass, weeds, woods, and beach. By walking the trails through the woodlot during the spring and fall, birders can expect to see a variety of migrants and a satisfying number of warblers, perhaps even a rare Connecticut Warbler. Fox Sparrows are fairly reliable in early spring. Also, scan the beach and lake as you continue west on the path to the Euclid Beach area.

Eastlake Power Plant (Lake County). This location offers prime access for close viewing of waterfowl and gulls. To reach the power plant, take SR-2 east from Cleveland to the SR-91 exit in Eastlake. Go left (north) onto SR-91 until it ends at Lakeshore Boulevard. Turn right (east) onto Lakeshore Boulevard; at the first traffic signal turn left (north) onto Erie Street and continue to its end at a parking area. (In very cold weather the parking lot may be closed.) This area is excellent for migrant and wintering waterfowl and gulls. The number of Red-breasted Mergansers and Bonaparte's Gulls that feed in the hot-water outlet is sometimes staggering, and Lesser Black-backed Gulls are also frequent. Over the years, 16 species of gulls have been seen at Eastlake.

Headlands Beach State Park (Lake County) offers some of the best birding along the south shore of Lake Erie. Take I-90 east from Cleveland, then eastbound SR-2 to the SR-44 exit (Heisley Road). Turn left (north) onto SR-44 and follow it to the park entrance. The main park gate opens at 8:00AM; early-arriving birders use what is known as the fishermen's parking lot. To reach this area, turn right at the stop sign at the corner of SR-44 and Headlands Road. Immediately turn left and follow the access road for the U.S. Coast Guard station. After passing the Morton Salt Company, watch for a small sign indicating the fishermen's entrance, the first left. Turn right onto the park road and follow it to the parking lot. The entrance to Headlands Dunes State Nature Preserve is at the north end of the lot.

The nature preserve has proven to be an excellent migrant trap. On a wave day in May the number of migrants can be very impressive, with over 100 species possible. A walk through the dune area, the woodlots adjacent to the Coast Guard station, and along the road leading to the station can be productive during both spring and fall. From mid-September through early October passerines are numerous throughout the goldenrod-laden stretches of the park. In late fall, the breakwaters offer good vantage points for lake-watching, with the possibility of seeing a rare Northern Gannet, a Purple Sandpiper, a Red Phalarope, or a jaeger. *Hunting is allowed along the breakwater during November and December, so caution is advised.*

Gull-watching can be as spectacular in the Headlands area as at any other site in Ohio. Fall and spring build-ups of Bonaparte's Gulls reach well into the thousands, with the chance for rarer larid species. Although no two years are alike, a build-up of gulls at Headlands at some time during both spring and fall is a dependable event. In late February and early March as many as 28 Little Gulls have been noted. In 1998, on a nasty November day, over 30 birders were treated to a Ross's Gull in a flock of Bonaparte's off the beach. This same spot hosted Ohio's first Snowy Plover. Long-tailed Jaegers have been observed here on at least four occasions; each observation of this highly prized state bird came on a September day that felt like January.

On the south side of Headlands Road and west of the park entrance is a parking area for the Zimmerman Trail in the Mentor Marsh State Nature Preserve. The trail is a circular route that winds south and west, exiting on Headlands Road. Cuckoos and flycatchers prefer the areas along the trail rather than those immediately adjacent to Lake Erie.

I f enthusiasm still persists, a trip to **Fairport Harbor** is recommended. A Mew Gull was such a hit with state listers that many call the Fairport Harbor marina that it frequented "Mew Gull Marina." The fields at a former Superfund site on both sides of SR-535 (Fairport Nursery Road) may yield nesting Bobolinks, Savannah and Grasshopper Sparrows, and Eastern Meadowlarks. In fall and winter look for rare Rough-legged Hawks, Merlins, Snowy and Short-eared Owls, and Northern Shrikes. Upland Sandpipers are found regularly in migration and have nested here on several occasions.

INLAND SITES

The **Shaker Lakes** (Cuyahoga County) have long figured in the annals of Cleveland birdwatching. The Shaker Lakes Nature Center can be accessed by taking the Green Line of the Shaker Rapid to the South Park station and walking north on South Park Boulevard approximately one-quarter mile. To reach the nature center by car, exit the Cleveland Memorial Shoreway East at Martin Luther King Jr. Drive, which you stay on for nearly 3 miles. After crossing Chester Avenue, follow the signs for Fairhill (Stokes Boulevard). Where Stokes ends, turn left on Coventry Road and right at the next light on North Park Boulevard. The first road on the right is a parking area for Lower Shaker Lake. To reach the Shaker Lakes Nature Center, continue on North Park Boulevard and, at the next light, bear right on South Park Boulevard and watch for the entrance on the right.

First, explore the trails around the nature center, including the boardwalk that provides a view of the marsh at the inlet of Lower Shaker Lake. Scan any mudflats on both sides of the bridge over the inlet for the occasional shorebird. Also, scan the lake for Pied-billed Grebes and waterfowl. There is an unmarked trail around Lower Shaker Lake, which often produces good numbers of Yellow-bellied Sapsuckers, vireos, Brown Creepers, thrushes, warblers, and sparrows. The stand of conifers and adjacent trees and bushes on the south side of the lake are fairly reliable for Pine Warblers in late April and early May. Although Lower Shaker Lake seems to get more attention from birdwatchers than Horseshoe Lake, don't overlook the latter. To reach Horseshoe Lake from the Shaker Lakes Nature Center, turn right onto South

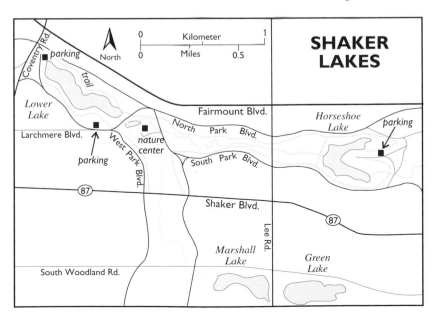

Park Boulevard. A short distance from the entrance drive you will come to a Y in the road. Bear left. After crossing Lee Road, watch for Horseshoe Lake on the left. Take the first left (Park Road) and the next left. Park here and walk around the locked gate.

Lakeview Cemetery (Cuyahoga County) is east of University Circle, an area where there are many cultural institutions, including Severance Concert Hall, the Cleveland Museum of Art, and the Cleveland Museum of Natural History. The main entrance to the circle is on Euclid Avenue (US-6/20) near East 123rd Street. There is also an entrance on Mayfield Road (US-322) about a half-mile west of the intersection with Coventry Road. Lakeview Cemetery is the final resting-place of many famous Clevelanders, as well as some internationally known people, such as John D. Rockefeller. A monument to President James A. Garfield is located here; the monument's second-floor balcony looks north to Lake Erie and is an excellent place to watch for migrating hawks as they skim the Portage Escarpment, which passes through the cemetery. The many plantings provide an arboretum-like setting, which is good for birding year round. Dick and Jean Hoffman have studied this area extensively and maintain detailed directions and a bird list at *www.pwl.netcom.com/~djhoff/lvc/breeding.html*.

Cuyahoga Valley National Park (Cuyahoga and Summit Counties) is a large area with varied habitats supporting a good diversity of birds. Take I-77 south to the Rockside Road exit (approximately 12 miles). Turn left (east) onto Rockside, and take it to Canal Road. Turn right (south) on Canal Road and follow the signs to the Canal Road Visitor Center. Detailed maps of the areas can be picked up there, or may be downloaded at *www.gov/carto/CUVA.html*. The wooded swamp north along the railroad tracks from the Station Road parking lot in the Pinery Narrows area provides excellent birding opportunities. This area is the site of a heron colony, and Red-headed Woodpeckers and Prothonotary Warblers have nested here. It is fairly reliable for nesting Hooded Mergansers, Yellow-billed Cuckoos, Pileated Woodpeckers, Brown Creepers, Eastern Bluebirds, and Baltimore Orioles. In summer, Cerulean Warblers are forced to share top billing with Yellow-throated Warblers in this sector of the park.

Brecksville Reservation (Cleveland Metroparks; Cuyahoga County) is another outstanding birding site for summering species. The area is immediately west of the Cuyahoga Valley National Park and south of SR-82, and it offers more of the same summer birding opportunities as the previous site. The Plateau Picnic Area has had nesting Cooper's Hawks and Northern Parulas. Broad-winged Hawks sometimes nest in the Oak Grove picnic area. Near the stables you can find Red-shouldered Hawks. Along the Buckeye Trail at the south side of the park, Sharp-shinned Hawks have nested in recent years. Hikes along this trail should produce many looks at Yellow-throated Vireo, Veery, Wood Thrush, Ovenbird, and Hooded Warbler.

The **Happy Days Visitor Center** (part of Cuyahoga Valley National Park; Summit County) is one of the best-monitored and well-studied summer bird areas in the region. The center is located on SR-303 one mile west of SR-8, and provides a point of access as well for Virginia Kendall Park. In addition to the many regular woodland species, Blue-headed Vireo, Winter Wren, Hermit Thrush, and Magnolia and Canada Warblers have been found nesting in the visitor center area.

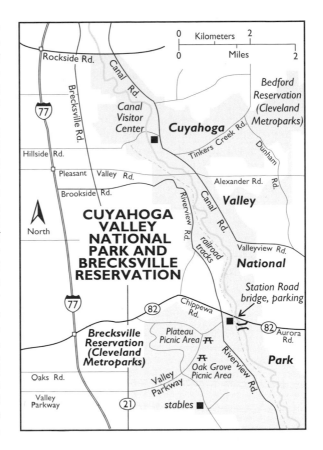

H**inckley Metropark** (Cleveland Metroparks; Medina County) may well be the best summer birding area in the region. Its beautiful woodlands have yet to be adversely affected by the burgeoning Whitetail Deer population, and it is a good place to look for some of the region's rarer nesting species. The park is approximately 30 miles south of Cleveland and southeast of the town of Hinckley. Take I-71 south to SR-303. Go east on 303 to SR-606. Turn right onto 606 to Bellus Road, and then go left (east). Continue on Bellus to reach the Whipp's Ledges area, or turn right onto West Drive to reach the Johnson Picnic Area. Both areas are excellent for breeders. Hikes along the many trails winding their way through this beautiful park can be rigorous, and proper footwear is recommended. Species recently found nesting here include Black-billed and Yellow-billed Cuckoos, Golden-crowned Kinglet, White-eyed, Blue-headed, and Yellow-throated Vireos, Blue-winged, Chestnut-sided, Magnolia, Black-throated Green, Pine, Kentucky, and Hooded Warblers, American Redstart, and Louisiana Waterthrush.

Coniferous areas near the boat house (near the intersection of West Drive and State Road) and near the Kiwanis Cabin off Kellogg Road harbor many "northern" species, including Red-breasted Nuthatch.

Wellington Upground Reservoir and **Findley State Park** (Lorain County) offer more birding opportunities for birders visiting the west side of Cleveland. Both areas are to be found off of SR-58 south of the city of Wellington. Take I-71 south, I-480 west, and US-20 west to SR-58 south. For access to the reservoir turn right (west) onto Jones Road to the entrance. Large numbers of diving ducks can be found here during migration. All three species of scoters and Long-tailed Duck have been seen regularly. Continue south on SR-58 about 2 miles to Findley State Park. The large areas of conifers in the park can be good for a variety of wintering birds, including Brown Creeper and Golden-crowned Kinglet. When there is a winter-finch invasion, these same woodlands may host Pine Siskin and Common Redpoll. Crossbills have also been found during some invasion years, but they are rare.

Sandy Ridge Metropark (Lorain County) is a well-designed and well-managed wetland-mitigation project in the city of North Ridgeville. Take I-90 west to SR-611 south, which ends at SR-254 (Detroit Road). Turn right (west) onto Detroit Road and left (south) onto Case Road. Turn left (east) onto Otten Road and watch for the park entrance on the right. With more than 100 acres of wetlands, this park has become the best site in the Cleveland region to see marshland birds. In some years American and Least Bitterns can be seen and heard with relative ease between May and late July. Virginia Rail, Sora, Common Moorhen, American Coot, and Marsh Wren are conspicuous.

FARTHER AFIELD

B irders with enough time can visit sites at a greater distance from Cleveland. These include Conneaut Harbor in Ashtabula County, Magee Marsh Wildlife Area and Ottawa National Wildlife Refuge in Ottawa and Lucas Counties, and Woodbury Wildlife Area in Coshocton County.

Conneaut Harbor, on the north side of Conneaut, Ohio, is approximately 70 miles east of Cleveland. From I-90, exit at SR-7 and follow it north through town. Where SR-7 ends at SR-531, continue straight ahead on Broad Street to the harbor area. The western end of the harbor has a postage-stamp-sized wetland and sandy stretches where shorebirds, gulls, and terns rest and feed. Shorebirds are the main attraction in the fall, but spring can be good, too. In addition to the common migrants, American Avocet, Red Knot, and White-rumped, Baird's and Buff-breasted Sandpipers are sometimes seen. The harbor is also a reliable site for finding gulls (winter) and terns (spring and fall). Caspian Terns can be found here, along with smaller numbers of Common and Forster's Terns.

The vicinity of **Magee Marsh State Wildlife Area** and **Crane Creek State Park** is one of the most important birding areas in Ohio. The wildlife area is about 90 miles from Cleveland and 2 miles west of the intersection of SR-19 with SR-2. A large sign marks the entrance to the area, and there is a visitor center. The Magee Marsh Bird Trail, sandwiched between the marsh on the south and an expanse of Lake Erie beach on the north, is arguably the best migrant trap in the state. The entrances to the Bird Trail are at the north end of the preserve road. The trail is actually a 0.6-mile-long boardwalk that winds and loops through a narrow stand of trees bordering the marsh. In May the trail is generally thronged with people. The area in general, and the trail specifically, rival Point Pelee for the number of migrants that can be seen on a wave-day in May. On such a day, it is not unusual to see 20–25 warbler species plus numerous other species. Southwest winds in late April and early May can bring southern overshoots, such as Worm-eating and Kentucky Warblers and Summer Tanager. Mid-to-late May is the time to search for Mourning and Connecticut Warblers. Soras, Virginia, and, sometimes, King Rails may be found at the edge of the marsh bordering the wildlife-area road. May is also the time to look for Ruddy Turnstones along the beach. No birder with enough time for the trip should pass up the opportunity to experience a wave-day on the Bird Trail. A detailed description of this area can be found in "Crane Creek, Ohio" by Eric Durbin in *Winging It*, May 1997.

Ottawa National Wildlife Refuge, one mile west of Magee Marsh, is also on the north side of SR-2. Ottawa is much like Magee Marsh but without the Bird Trail. However, it has an extensive network of dike-top walking trails, and large numbers of herons, waterfowl, and shorebirds can be found in its impoundments in migration. The refuge has recently been discovered to be a resting and molting area for a large number of Long-billed Dowitchers in late summer and fall—if refuge-management practices have provided suitable habitat for shorebirds in general.

Woodbury Wildlife Area is approximately two hours south of Cleveland and is an excellent place to look for grassland species in summer. Take I-77 south to the Newcomerstown exit (US-36), head west to Coshocton, and take SR-541 west, which will cross the wildlife area. Woodbury is approximately ten minutes west of Coshocton. A walk along the dirt roads in the grassland areas should produce numerous Grasshopper and Henslow's Sparrows. Henslow's Sparrows sing at most times of the day and can be viewed consistently from May through July (early and late in the day are best as the season progresses). Other species seen here include Northern Bobwhite, Prairie Warbler, Yellow-breasted Chat, Dickcissel, and Bobolink. Birders are forewarned of the numerous ticks that infest this productive area.

ACKNOWLEDGMENTS

Thanks to Dwight and Ann Chasar for their knowledge of the Cuyahoga Valley National Park and its birds. Also, special thanks to Dick and Jean Hoffman for their help and to Haans Petruschke for his invaluable map resources.

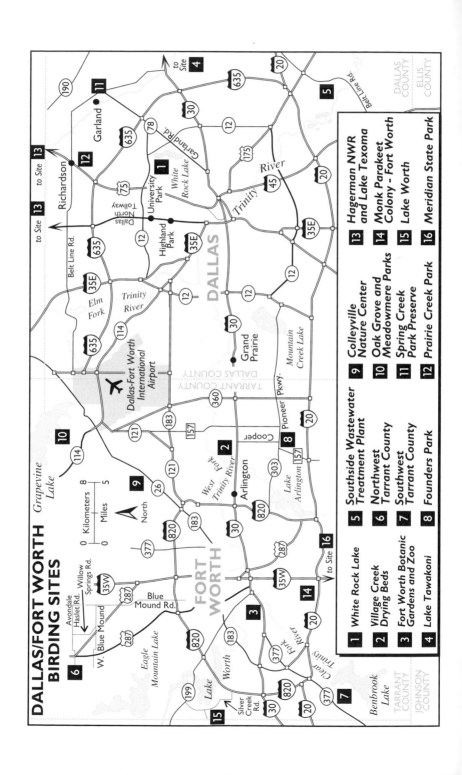

DALLAS/FORT WORTH BIRDING SITES

1 White Rock Lake	**5** Southside Wastewater Treatment Plant	**9** Colleyville Nature Center	**13** Hagerman NWR and Lake Texoma
2 Village Creek Drying Beds	**6** Northwest Tarrant County	**10** Oak Grove and Meadowmere Parks	**14** Monk Parakeet Colony - Fort Worth
3 Fort Worth Botanic Gardens and Zoo	**7** Southwest Tarrant County	**11** Spring Creek Park Preserve	**15** Lake Worth
4 Lake Tawakoni	**8** Founders Park	**12** Prairie Creek Park	**16** Meridian State Park

DALLAS/FORT WORTH, TEXAS

Martin Reid and Matt White

When birders think of Texas, their thoughts inevitably turn to images of Colima Warblers and Lucifer Hummingbirds in Big Bend, Black-capped Vireos and Golden-cheeked Warblers in the Hill Country, an array of Tamaulipan specialties in the Lower Rio Grande Valley, or those wonderful migrant fall-outs at High Island. As most of us who live here know, there is far more to birding in the Lone Star State, and the Dallas/Fort Worth Metroplex (henceforth the Metroplex) is a great place to start.

The Metroplex is one of America's largest population centers, and it is where East meets West. Nowhere is this encounter more evident than in the culture of the two main cities, only thirty miles apart: Dallas is a fast-paced, lively, sophisticated place that would remind visitors of any large southeastern city; Fort Worth is a laid-back, friendly, "country" place, home to Billy-Bob's, the world's largest Honky-Tonk saloon (complete with its own bull-riding ring!). The "East meets West" theme is just as appropriate for birds, for this is where you can see Glossy and White-faced Ibises, Eastern and Spotted Towhees, Indigo and Lazuli Buntings, and Rusty and Yellow-headed Blackbirds. The terrain is mostly flat and wooded, with a few low escarpments, while to the west there is some remnant rolling prairie. Numerous lakes surround the urban centers, and although suburban sprawl is rampant, there are still many parks and nature centers protecting vital habitat. Although north-central Texas is far from the coast and has no local specialties, the region nonetheless has much to offer. More than 370 species have been seen locally, including six "firsts" for Texas. Thus, anyone dropping in for a day or two will see plenty of birds and perhaps even something unexpected.

ESSENTIAL INFORMATION

Getting Around: Dallas and Fort Worth have reasonable public transportation (Dallas has a local train system; otherwise, there is bus service), including to and from DFW Airport, located halfway between the two cities.

For Fort Worth contact the T at (817) 215-8600; for Dallas contact DART at (214) 979-1111. Few other cities in the Metroplex have public-transport services, and generally you will have to travel by private vehicle or taxi to reach most of the birding locations, although White Rock Lake in Dallas and the Botanic Gardens in Fort Worth are exceptions. The rush-hour times in Dallas (and to a lesser extent in Fort Worth and the Mid-Cities) can seriously impact your drive times; avoid cutting across Dallas or traveling between Fort Worth and Dallas in the periods 7:00 to 9:00AM and 4:00 to 6:45PM on weekdays.

Climate: Winter temperatures are usually mild, but the area is subject to sudden changes in temperature (drops of 40 degrees in a couple of hours can occur), and if an Arctic blast arrives, the temperature may drop into the low teens, with the wind chill much lower. Mid-June to early September sees highs between 95° and 105°F every day, and the sun is harsh, so plan accordingly, and try to bird either very early or late in the day.

Natural Hazards: Texas is blessed with lots of things that might bite you! Expect any natural grassy area to have chiggers from late March until the first frost (often late November). There are few biting flies, but mosquitoes will be found near any standing water from late March through November. Fire Ants are everywhere, so look down before you stand still, or you may be ripping off your pants in a hurry. There is a healthy population and a good variety of snakes, and while most are non-poisonous, Cottonmouths and Copperheads are always possible near water.

Other Considerations: In Texas more than 95 percent of the land is privately owned. Texans are a pretty friendly bunch, and a polite request to the landowner or tenant will usually gain you access, but they do not take kindly to finding unannounced strangers on their property.

Safety: As in most metropolitan areas, there are some places that are not safe; check with your hotel concierge if unsure. Virtually all of the good birding sites are in safer neighborhoods. One exception might be the fish hatchery below the dam at White Rock Lake in Dallas, which may not be suitable for the unaccompanied birder (male or female).

Other Resources: The regional Rare Bird Alert is available only electronically through the TEXBirds chat group (archived at *www.birding onthe.net/mailinglists/TEXS.html*). There are two statewide birdfinding guides that cover some of these sites (plus other sites just beyond the scope of this chapter): *Birding Texas* by Ro Wauer and Mark Elwonger (1998, Falcon Press), and *Birder's Guide to Texas (2nd Edition)* by Edward Kutac (1998, Lone Star Books). The standard reference for birds in this area is *The Birds of North Central Texas* by Warren M. Pulich (1988, Texas A&M University Press); it remains a fairly accurate resource, but some of the species stated as being absent do indeed occur as rare visitors (Pulich is working on a second edition). Fort Worth Audubon Society publishes a *Bar Graph Checklist for the Birds of Tarrant County*, updated in January 2000. This small booklet shows abundance by month for every species recorded in the Fort Worth area; it is available for $3.99 from the Fort Worth Nature Center, 9601 Fossil Ridge Road, Fort Worth, TX 76135, (817) 237-1111; you must include a stamped, self-addressed, 9½-inch envelope with your order. You can find some very helpful information on local birding at Derek Hill's web site, *www.members.home.net/kinglet32.* The Dallas Audubon Society posts details of their activities at *www.dcas.homepage.com.* Fort Worth Audubon Society has an extensive site at *www.fwas.org,* including recent sightings and an excellent article on local birding sites created by Carl Haynie (from which we have borrowed shamelessly!). A helpful new web site, North-Central Texas Birds, *www.nctexas-birds.com,* has checklists, information on area sightings, and useful links.

Other Destinations: Dallas and Fort Worth both have excellent zoos, which are also good places to bird for woodland species in winter and spring. The Fort Worth Museum of Science and History has a variety of interesting exhibits, including a small display of local birds—worth a visit since it is close to the Botanic Gardens and the Kimball and Amon Carter Museums (the latter is the repository for Eliot Porter's 1950s collection of groundbreaking photographs of birds).

THE BIRDING YEAR

At this latitude spring birding starts in late February with the first reports of Purple Martins and northbound geese, soon followed by Sandhill Cranes, while in early March come the first herons from the coast. Gulls (Bonaparte's, Ring-billed, a few Herring) start to thin out, except for increasing numbers of Franklin's. Mid-March sees the first Swainson's Hawks and Scissor-tailed Flycatchers arriving on territory; before month's end they are joined by White-eyed Vireos, swallows, and Chipping Sparrows; most wintering waterfowl have departed. April is a heady month, with large numbers of ibises, dabbling ducks, shorebirds, rails, Yellow-billed Cuckoos, goatsuckers, Chimney Swifts, hummingbirds, kingbirds, vireos, wrens, Swainson's Thrushes, 20-plus species of warblers, Clay-colored Sparrows, and the early buntings and orioles. Most of our wintering creepers, kinglets, towhees, and sparrows depart in April. May is slower, but it is the month when most rarities appear. Late migrants that peak in May include Hudsonian Godwit, White-rumped (continues well into June) and Buff-breasted Sandpipers, Black Tern, Black-billed Cuckoo (rare), most flycatchers, Magnolia, Blackburnian, and Bay-breasted Warblers (all uncommon), Mourning and Wilson's Warblers, and Indigo, Painted, and a small scattering of Lazuli Buntings.

Summer is Hot. That's almost all there is to say. Noteworthy breeding species include Neotropic Cormorant (rare), Black-bellied Whistling-Duck (now a regular breeder at a couple of sites), Mottled Duck (only two regular sites), Mississippi Kite, the Fuertes' form of Red-tailed Hawk, Swainson's Hawk, Least Tern (rare and local), Scissor-tailed Flycatcher, Western and

Eastern (uncommon) Kingbirds, Loggerhead Shrike (fairly common), White-eyed, Warbling, Red-eyed, and Bell's (rare and rapidly declining) Vireos, Northern Parula (scarce), Yellow-throated (scarce) and Prothonotary Warblers, Yellow-breasted Chat (scarce), Summer Tanager, Cassin's (scarce), Grasshopper, and Lark Sparrows, Indigo and Painted Buntings, and Blue Grosbeak. Late July sees some post-breeding dispersal that brings White and White-faced Ibises, plus a few Wood Storks and the odd Roseate Spoonbill up from the Gulf of Mexico.

Fall migration starts in July for shorebirds, and landbirds begin to arrive from the north in mid-August. The same species that graced us in spring can be expected, except for Hudsonian Godwits and White-rumped Sandpipers. The usual woodland migrants peak in early-to-mid-September, whereas shorebirds are at their highest numbers and diversity in late August/early September. Hummingbirds start to build up in August, peak in early September, and mostly depart by mid-October. Wintering sparrows (including Fox and lots of Harris's) start to arrive in mid-to-late October, with diving ducks about one month later.

Winter is difficult to characterize, as cold weather is usually sporadic (interspersed with mild, spring-like periods), occurring mainly between mid-December and mid-February. Wintering hawks are present by late November and include every kind of Red-tail there is (with many Harlan's), the odd Ferruginous, occasionally a Rough-legged, a scattering of Bald Eagles, lots of Northern Harriers, increasing numbers of Sharp-shinneds and Cooper's, a handful of Merlins, and the occasional Peregrine and Prairie Falcons. Longspurs are generally uncommon; McCown's and Chestnut-collared arrive mostly in late November and depart in early March, while Lapland and the rare Smith's can be expected only from mid-December to early February (and may be absent during mild winters). American Woodcocks are best found from December to February, when they can be seen at a few traditional sites.

WHITE ROCK LAKE

Half day; year round

White Rock Lake is Dallas's Central Park. Located in the heart of the city, the lake is surrounded by extensive parks and green space. Biking trails and roads ring the entire lake, making it particularly accessible to birders who have only an hour or so to bird. To reach the lake from downtown, take South Garland Road northeast to Winstead Drive; go left onto Winstead to enter the park. Alternatively, take Mockingbird to either East or West Lawther Drive. East Lawther will take you along the eastern side of the lake, and West Lawther will take you to the western side. There are a number of pull-outs and parking lots from which you can scan the lake and walk to the wooded areas. For an urban park surrounded by development, White Rock has a remarkably diverse birdlife. Barred Owls and Red-shouldered Hawks haunt the remnants of mature riparian woodlands of White Rock Creek, located below the dam. For passerines, the **Old Fish Hatchery** is one of the best places in the Metroplex during spring and fall migrations, but may not be suitable for a lone birder. Prairie, Palm, Cerulean, and Hooded Warblers have been seen here recently. To bird here, use the parking lot on Winstead just north of Garland Road. An extensive network of trails winds through this maze of levees and shallow ponds (mostly dry but varies from year to year) choked with trees and vines. Although the area was abandoned years, efforts are planned are to make the area even more bird-friendly by

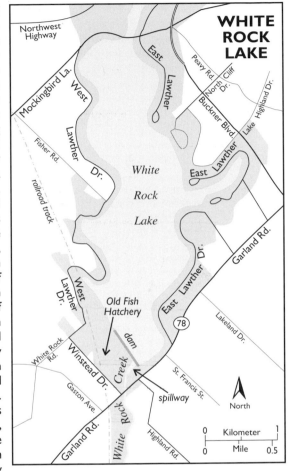

refilling the ponds at different seasons. White-winged Doves are now commonplace; look for them on the western side near the tall electrical lines. A long-established Monk Parakeet communal nest is on the transformers near the electrical substation a hundred yards or so west of the red-brick water-works building; look for the tall smoke-stack.

From fall through spring, hundreds of birds are usually in evidence on White Rock Lake itself, including American White Pelicans, cormorants, ducks, gulls, and terns. Little Gulls are almost annual in winter among the hundreds of Bonaparte's and Ring-billed Gulls. Rarities such as Parasitic Jaeger, Mew Gull, and Black-legged Kittiwake have also been seen; searching through the flocks may well turn up a surprise. Many gulls often roost on the spillway, along with an assortment of shorebirds during migration.

Though you can bird here year round, fall, winter, and spring are best. In summer, Warbling Vireo and Northern Parula nest at the Old Fish Hatchery. Generally rare in the Metroplex, White-breasted Nuthatches have recently nested in the mature Pecans and Chinquapin Oaks on the east side of the lake. Louisiana Waterthrush has not been found nesting, though summer sightings below the dam are strongly suggestive.

VILLAGE CREEK DRYING-BEDS AND RIVER LEGACY PARK

Half or full day; year round

The **Village Creek Drying-Beds** (VCDB) has a most diverse avifauna, given its small size. It includes numerous ponds, weedy fields, and overgrown shrubby patches, and it is bordered by a wooded swamp and a large area of old-growth wooded bottomland. In early May, more than a hundred species can be found in a morning. Directions: From DFW head west on TX-183, then south on FM-157 (also called Collins Street); after crossing the Trinity River, turn right at the light (Green Oaks Boulevard) and continue through four lights (past River Legacy Park at second light); after 400 yards turn right into the entrance. This property is operated by the Fort Worth Water Department and is not open to the public, but birders have permission to enter. If the gate is locked (usually it is open), call the telephone number on the gate, (817) 277-7591, and someone will come to let you in.

The drying-beds comprise 48 old settling-ponds surrounded by a levee. Within this small (264 acres) site more than 285 species have been recorded; a seasonal abundance checklist is available from the Water Department or

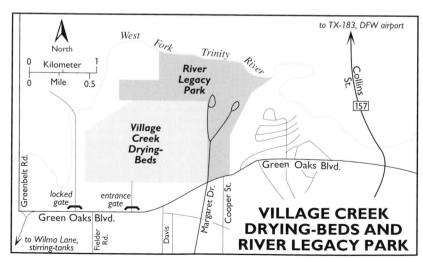

Fort Worth Audubon Society. When dry, the perimeter levee is drivable, as are the internal dirt roads, but after heavy rain the only section that is passable with two-wheel-drive is the eastern half of the perimeter levee. Birding is often excellent after a rain, but we advise visitors to walk it (bring appropriate footwear).

VCDB can be fabulous for shorebirds, but it is subject to the vagaries of recent rainfall. With normal water levels, a late April/early May day might yield more than a thousand shorebirds of 18-plus species, often including Upland Sandpiper, Hudsonian Godwit, and White-rumped and Buff-breasted Sandpipers, plus the occasional Red-necked Phalarope. Fall migration can be equally rewarding but is more protracted, with lower numbers on any given day. State rarities found here have included Sharp-tailed Sandpiper, Ruff, and Red Phalarope.

Winter sees large numbers of smaller gulls and dabbling ducks plus small numbers of Lesser Scaup and Buffleheads. Rarities found here include American Black Duck, "Eurasian" Green-winged Teal, and Barrow's Gold-eneye. The weedy, damp ponds harbor large numbers of wintering sparrows, usually including a few Le Conte's, Swamp, and Harris's. In winter the stirring-tanks at the nearby Water Department headquarters attract smaller gulls that can be studied/photographed at very close range. Regular checking has produced rarities such as Black-headed, Mew, California, and Thayer's, plus the occasional Herring and wintering Franklin's (which is common on migration in March/April and October/November). Directions from VCDB: go right (west) onto Green Oaks Boulevard, straight through two lights, as the road heads southwest and then west again; turn right (north) at the next road (Wilma Lane; about 1.5 miles from the VCDB entrance); sign-in at the office, then drive around the lower six stirring-tanks to study the gulls.

River Legacy Park is immediately east of VCDB and has many trails through dense wooded riverine bottomland. This park has an impressive list of species, with Summer Tanager and Painted Bunting both common breeders. Ask for a map and checklist at the Living Science Center east of the main park entrance. Weekends can get very crowded with skaters, bicyclists, joggers, and picnickers; some of the best birding is found on the secluded northern trails where the park borders the Trinity River.

FORT WORTH BOTANIC GARDENS
AND THE ZOO
Half day (early or late); spring, fall, winter

The Trinity River forms a riparian corridor through the middle of Fort Worth, and west of downtown this corridor widens to form the core element of the **Botanic Gardens**. From the I-35 interchange in downtown Fort Worth go west on I-30 for 2.8 miles, exit at N. University Drive, and then drive north for about 600 yards. The main (north) entrance offers plentiful parking and access to the buildings, which include a walk-in tropical plant/butterfly exhibit. The best birding is south of here. You can park along the side of the south entrance road (coming from I-30, turn left 200 yards before the main entrance). The habitat is mostly tall mixed woodland with lots of natural understory, plus a few small, modified "gardens," and there are surfaced trails through these areas. Birding can be excellent during migration, especially along the natural-looking pumped stream that meanders through the southernmost woodlands. In winter the understory and thickets are home to many Hermit Thrushes and sparrows, as well as the occasional Eastern Towhee among the common Spotted Towhees. The canopy harbors mixed-species flocks that often contain a few Brown Creepers, the occasional Golden-crowned Kinglet, and sometimes a wintering Blue-gray Gnatcatcher or Pine Warbler.

The Zoo (privately owned) is a mile south of the Botanic Gardens. At I-30 go south onto University Drive, over the Trinity River, then left at the light onto Colonial Parkway, and follow the signs for the Zoo's main parking lot. The Zoo itself has a walk-in aviary with a good variety of birds, and the raptor exhibit includes Andean Condors and Harpy Eagles. The wooded stands and thickets around the zoo offer excellent migrant birding, and in winter many seed-eaters are drawn to the spilt animal foods in the zoo; Green-tailed Towhee (extremely rare) has been recorded there on the Christmas Bird Count. *Note: there have been thefts from unattended vehicles at both the Botanic Gardens and the Zoo* .

LAKE TAWAKONI

Half to full day; year round

One of the state's premier inland reservoirs is only an hour or so east of Dallas. In addition to being the best place in the state to find Smith's Longspur, **Lake Tawakoni** has earned a reputation as an excellent vagrant trap. Some of the rarest have been Harlequin Duck, Long-tailed Jaeger, and Snow Bunting. Of course these species are more than long shots, but Lake Tawakoni does consistently reward the careful observer.

In winter the short grassy fields near the Sabine River Authority Head-quarters harbor Smith's Longspurs and one or two Sprague's Pipits. From FM-47 north of Flats turn left on Rains County Road 1480. The office is a short distance down this road, and during weekdays (8:00AM to 4:30PM) birders need to sign a liability waiver in the office before they may proceed onto Authority property. Rock Wrens sometimes winter on the dam nearby, and Crested Caracaras occur regularly. Birders are allowed to walk along the top of the dam, a great place to view the dozens of wintering Common Loons. Careful scrutiny often reveals that a few Pacific and Red-throated Loons are present also. The loons can also be viewed from the parking lot

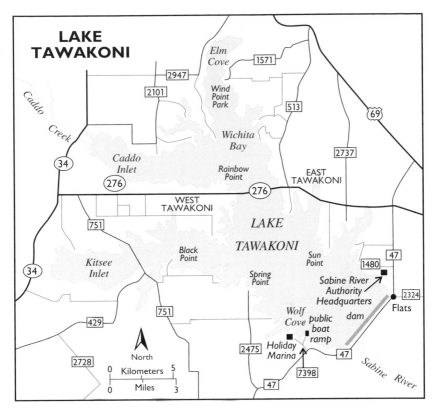

at the public boat ramp on the western end of the dam. From FM-47 take PR-7398 (look for an old Coca-Cola sign and a worn Holiday Marina sign); to reach the Holiday Marina continue straight at the fork; to reach the Public Boat Ramp turn right at the fork. Although the Holiday Marina is private property, birders have been allowed to enter, but the owners ask that you stop in at the store to say hello and that you strictly follow the 5-mph speed limit. This is also a good place to look for gulls and terns. From spring through fall Neotropic Cormorants are often seen resting on the pilings offshore.

In summer, Cave Swallows are found in the Cliff Swallow colony under the bridge below the spillway. Black-and-white, Prothonotary, and Kentucky Warblers, as well as Northern Parula, breed in the woods around the spillway parking lot. Fish Crows have recently taken up summer residence.

SOUTHSIDE WASTEWATER TREATMENT PLANT

Half day; year round

The **Southside Wastewater Treatment Plant** is one of the area's premier birding locales. Its large size (over one square mile) and habitat diversity—including plowed fields, several small reservoirs, sewage drying-beds, grassy fields, and wooded bottomland hardwoods—all make it attractive to an equally diverse array of birds. The area can be good all year, though summer is often slow until early July when southbound migrants begin to appear. The gates are usually open on weekdays 7:30AM to 4:30PM. Weekend access is variable, but birders can press any of the call buttons at the entrance to have the gate opened. Visitors must register at the desk on the third floor of the headquarters (the tallest building in the facility). Some areas are off-limits, so you may be given a map detailing areas to avoid. Please follow posted speed limits and traffic rules and stay clear of the heavy machinery. To reach Southside, take US-175 east to Belt Line Road and turn right. Southside is 1.8 miles on the right; look for 10011 Log Cabin Road. If an attendant is at the entrance, you may be asked to sign in at the gate, and again at the main office. Southside is easily birded from your vehicle from the network of roads. The best shorebird areas vary depending on water levels, though generally the most productive are the sewer ponds located just south of the main office.

In summer several dozen pairs of Black-necked Stilts breed here, and Ruddy Ducks and Common Moorhens lurk in the marshy vegetation. Look for Scissor-tailed Flycatchers and Western Kingbirds on the utility wires; Dickcissel may be the most common songbird in summer. Since 1991 endangered "interior" Least Terns have nested here, and the managers have worked closely with Dallas County Audubon Society to protect them. From May through August these dainty terns are present and usually are not hard to find; indeed, the staff will usually steer you in the right direction. Late summer and early fall bring an annual influx of Tricolored Herons, White Ibises, Roseate Spoonbills, and Wood Storks (often well over 100 birds). Late summer is also the season of the peak shorebird migration. Long-billed Curlew and Red-necked Phalarope are rare but regular, and Red Phalarope has been recorded. As you enter, the plowed fields on both sides of the road are good for Buff-breasted Sandpiper, fairly common during spring and fall migration. A large pond on the left usually harbors American White Pelicans. Black-bellied Whistling-Ducks and Mottled Ducks are most likely in summer. Thousands of gulls congregate in winter; recent vagrants have included Little and Thayer's. Ducks of a dozen species or more are often packed so tightly into the ponds that you must look carefully to be certain that you are not overlooking something. Sprague's Pipits sometimes overwinter in the short grass, and Le Conte's Sparrows are regularly found in overgrown fields.

NORTHWEST TARRANT COUNTY

Half day; winter

The west side of **Tarrant County** is a transition from oak-dominated woodland to rolling prairie, and the northwest sector has many large crop fields, patches of native prairie, hedge-lined lanes, and a few small lakes—great habitat for wintering ducks, hawks, sparrows, and longspurs. The most reliable Metroplex location for McCown's Longspur is in northwest Tarrant, at Willow Springs Golf Course. Go north on I-35W (from downtown Fort Worth), passing I-820, then exiting onto US-287 toward Decatur. Exit US-287 at W. Blue Mound and Willow Springs (after the Hicks Road exit; be aware that there is another Blue Mound Road exit before Hicks Road). After exiting, stay on the access road parallel to US-287, northwest to Willow Springs Road, and turn right (north). After 1.7 miles the road ends at a T-junction at Avondale Haslet Road; park off the road here and scan the golf driving range to the north for Horned Lark, McCown's Longspur, and sometimes Lapland Longspur. Almost any side road in this area could turn up a "Harlan's" Hawk, a Merlin, or an occasional Ferruginous Hawk.

SOUTHWEST TARRANT COUNTY LOOP

Half day; mainly winter and early spring

This loop starts and ends in the city of Benbrook, southwest of Fort Worth. From the junction of US-377 and I-820/I-20 go southwest through Benbrook on US-377 toward Granbury. At the FM-2871 light (2.3 miles) turn right; after the railroad tracks (1.5 miles) immediately turn left onto Aledo Road. As you pass a gated community on the right, check the ponds for ducks drawn in by a few tame (and noncountable) Mute Swans. The hedgerows harbor wintering sparrows, including "Red" Fox and Harris's; soon you will enter rolling grassland prairie where abundant Savannah and Vesper Sparrows are joined by a few Grasshopper and Lark Sparrows and an occasional Le Conte's. At 2.5 miles the road crosses the railroad tracks. Pull over and scan to the north for raptors; on winter evenings Short-eared Owls can sometimes be seen among the numerous Northern Harriers. Continue to FM-1187 (2.5 miles); turn left and thence back to US-377 (3.5 miles), through mixed woodland and pastures good for wintering sparrows.

At US-377 turn left (northeast); within 100 yards turn right onto South Lakeview (signed for Holiday Park). At the entrance booth (1.8 miles) tell the attendant that you are birding in order to enter with no charge (Monday–Thursday only; you might be asked to pay the hefty fee on other days). *Note:* lighting is best in the late afternoon, and in winter large rafts of ducks roost just beyond the line of flooded trees; thus, this is a great place to check about two hours before darkness. In late summer look for post-breeding

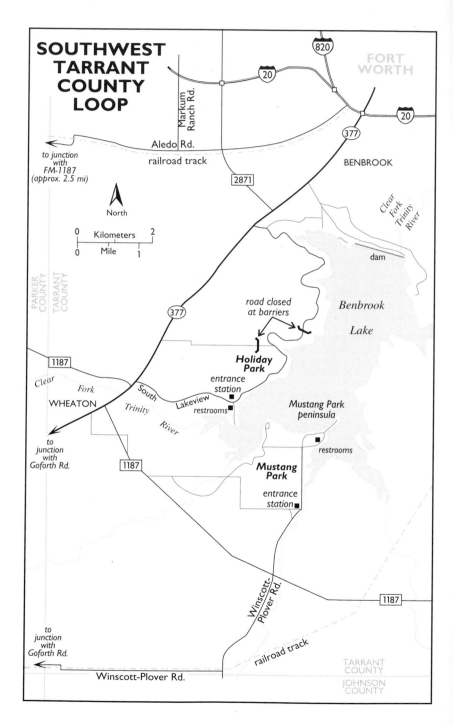

SOUTHWEST TARRANT COUNTY LOOP

Markum Ranch Rd.

820

20

FORT WORTH

20

377

BENBROOK

Aledo Rd.

railroad track

2871

to junction with FM-1187 (approx. 2.5 mi)

North

0 ——— Kilometers ——— 2

0 ——— Mile ——— 1

PARKER COUNTY

TARRANT COUNTY

377

Clear Fork Trinity River

dam

Benbrook Lake

road closed at barriers

Holiday Park

1187

Clear Fork

WHEATON

South Trinity River

entrance station

Lakeview

restrooms

Mustang Park peninsula

restrooms

to junction with Goforth Rd.

1187

Mustang Park

entrance station

1187

Winscott-Plover Rd.

to junction with Goforth Rd.

railroad track

Winscott-Plover Rd.

TARRANT COUNTY

JOHNSON COUNTY

wandering waterbirds; the shallows around the creek mouth (turn right after the booth and drive past the restrooms to the end of the road) have produced Roseate Spoonbill and Caspian Tern. The woods abound with breeding Indigo and Painted Buntings, and the many dead trees can harbor Red-headed Woodpecker (scarce), plus thousands of staging Purple Martins in late July.

Return to US-377 and turn left (southwest); at the Chevron station in Wheaton (0.8 mile) turn left onto FM-1187. At Winscott-Plover Road (4.2 miles) turn left (north), and after 1.1 miles bear right at the fork and approach the booth for **Mustang Park**. The park is free (unstaffed) from October through March; from April to October there is a camping fee, but birdwatchers are not charged (this situation may vary on weekends). The area of woodland/parkland on both sides of the road about 200 yards after the booth is a good spot to find Fox and Harris's Sparrows in winter. Slowly drive the 1.5 miles to the Mustang Park peninsula (turning right at the stop sign after 1.2 miles), checking the sparrow flocks. At the peninsula, drive past the unstaffed booth and turn left after the restrooms; continue to the covered picnic site on the lakeshore. This is a wonderful spot from which to scan the lake for waterbirds, especially in the early morning when the sun is behind you. The large roost of wintering waterfowl will be lingering far out to the left. Mid-November has produced numerous rare species, including the smaller loons, larger grebes, sea ducks, and a Little Gull. Drive the rest of the peninsula, checking the scattered trees for Ladder-backed Woodpeckers and the distant snags for Osprey and perhaps Bald Eagle.

Retrace your route to FM-1187 and cross over it, remaining on Winscott-Plover Road. The rolling prairie is home to a few breeding Cassin's Sparrows, and in winter the area can be excellent for raptors, with records of White-tailed Kite, Prairie Falcon, and even Golden Eagle (very rare). Go south on Winscott-Plover Road to the railway-crossing (1.7 miles), then continue south for 70 yards to where the tall grassland abuts both sides of the road; flocks of Chestnut-collared Longspurs often cross the road here, but seeing them in the long grass can be tough. Go back to just before the railway crossing and turn left (west) back onto Winscott-Plover Road. The next 2.7 miles parallel the railway, through excellent tallgrass prairie where raptors abound and flocks of grassland sparrows and Chestnut-collared Longspurs dance over the road. In late March/April and October/November look and listen for Sprague's Pipit (American Pipit is common when the ground is wet). In March/April look for American Golden-Plovers and Upland Sandpipers.

After crossing over the railway the road becomes unpaved; 3.5 miles farther on turn right onto the unpaved Goforth Road. This road winds around for 3.5 to 4 miles to US-377. It cuts through a variety of different habitats, including (in the first mile) scattered oak/juniper scrub— rare habitat this far north of the Hill Country—where rarities such as Mountain Bluebird, Sage Thrasher, and Baird's Sparrow have been seen. Back at US-377 turn right (northeast) and return through Wheaton and Benbrook to I-820 and I-20.

MIGRANT-TRAP PARKS

Each good for a few hours in spring or fall

Founders Park: From I-30 in North Arlington go south on Cooper Street for 3.4 miles to a fork where Cooper bears right and Matlock continues straight; stay on Matlock, cross Pioneer Parkway, then turn left onto Arkansas Lane. Founders Park starts on the south side of Arkansas Lane, at the creek crossing just a few yards from Matlock; parking is just beyond the creek on the right (south). This riparian corridor along Village Creek is a magnet for migrants, with many local rarities having been found here, including Vermilion Flycatcher, Cerulean Warbler, and Black-headed Grosbeak.

Colleyville Nature Center: Starting at North Richland Hills go north on Northeast Loop I-820 and stay in the westbound lanes toward Haltom City; very soon after the airport split, take the Grapevine Highway/Davis exit, and at the intersection turn right onto Grapevine Highway. Continue northeast on Grapevine Highway for 5 miles to Glade Road; turn left (west) onto Glade and go 0.7 mile to Mill Creek Drive; turn left (south) onto this road and continue until it dead-ends at the Nature Center (0.3 mile). This park is comprised mostly of riparian woodland and attracts concentrations of migrants, including rarities such as Great Kiskadee and Golden-winged and Black-throated Blue Warblers.

Oak Grove and **Meadowmere Park**s, **Lake Grapevine**: From the north exit of DFW Airport at TX-114, turn left (west) and continue 2.5 miles to the Main Street exit; go north on Main for 1.2 miles to the T-junction with Business 114. Turn left (west) and go 0.6 mile to Dove Road; turn right (north) and continue for almost 1 mile until you cross the creek, then right at the turn signed for Oak Grove Park. Drive around the lake, checking for migrants in the trees and waterbirds along the shore. After about 1 mile turn right on Kimball; after exploring farther northward, return to this junction and go west on Kimball 1.1 miles to Snakey Road on the right (just before Kimball makes a sharp turn to the left); turn right (north) onto Snakey to explore Meadowmere Park. These two parks offer woodland and scrub birding, plus waterbirds on the lake; a number of rare gulls and terns have been found here, and in recent years Sabine's Gull has become almost annual in late September. To return to the freeway system, go south on Kimball until you cross TX-114, then follow the signs for TX-114 South.

Garland/**Richardson Parks**: North of Dallas there are numerous small parks with riparian habitat that can be excellent for migrants; visit Derek Hill's fine web site for more details (see *Other Resources* in the Introduction). Two of the best sites are discussed here. **Spring Creek Park Preserve**

has produced rarities such as Cerulean Warbler, American Tree Sparrow, and Smith's Longspur. From Dallas go north on I-75 (Central Expressway) then east on TX-190 (Northeast Parkway) in Plano; after about 4.5 miles turn south on Holford Road; the park extends on both sides of the road at the creek. **Prairie Creek Park** has a list of 21 warbler species; from Dallas go north on I-75 into Richardson and turn west on Campbell Road; after 0.4 mile turn right onto Collins Boulevard for access to the park.

OTHER POSSIBILITIES

Hagerman National Wildlife Refuge and Lake Texoma: Hagerman NWR, an hour or so north of Dallas, is a spectacular birding area. Over the last 50 years more than 350 species have been recorded at this 11,000-acre refuge. In winter Ross's Geese may number over 100, and Brant has been recorded. Shorebirds are a highlight, and this is one of the best places in the area to see Whimbrel and Red Knot (both rare inland) during migration. Winter sparrows are also found in good numbers here, and include Fox, Song, Harris's, and White-crowned. From Dallas go north on I-75 to US-82 north of Sherman, and turn west; from Fort Worth go north on I-35 to Gainesville and go east on US-82. Hagerman NWR has a signed exit to the north, half way between Sherman and Whitesboro.

Monk Parakeet Colony (Fort Worth): Like several other major metropolitan areas in Texas, Fort Worth has its colony of countable Monk Parakeets. Look for the tree full of their nests at the southeast corner of 6th Avenue and Boyce Street in south Fort Worth, just south of the Southwest Baptist Theological Seminary. This colony has been present since about 1987.

American Woodcock: Western Oaks on the west side of Lake Worth is a traditional location to see American Woodcock from mid-December to mid-February. From I-30 west of Fort Worth go north on I-820 and exit on Silver Creek Road (2.3 miles). At Silver Creek turn left; it winds west and then north for 2.5 miles to Western Oaks (a left turn only, soon after crossing a small bridge). Drive to the end of Western Oaks (1 mile) and park (do not block the private ranch access), then walk back 100 yards to the low point of the road (at a stream crossing) and wait. As darkness falls, woodcocks should be heard calling, then seen in display over the road (calm moonlit evenings are best).

Meridian State Park: The nearest location for **Golden-cheeked Warblers**, Meridian is about 1.5 hours from DFW. Go south on I-35 to Hillsboro, then west on TX-22 through Whitney (the lake has wintering Bald Eagles that may linger into spring) to Meridian. Stay on TX-22, and about 3 miles outside of town you will find the park on the right. Look for the warbler in the mature Ashe Juniper growth in the northwest part of the park above the lake, and note that Black-capped Vireo is sometimes found here in the thick clumps of oak. For information on access check the web site at *www.bb35.tpwd.state.tx.us/park/meridian/meridian.htm*.

DENVER AREA BIRDING SITES

1 *Barr Lake*

2 *Lower Latham Reservoir*

3 *Pawnee National Grassland*

4 *Wheat Ridge Greenbelt*

5 *Red Rocks Amphitheater*

6 *Genesee Mountain Park*

7 *Georgetown and Guanella Pass*

8 *Loveland Area Sites: Larimer County Landfill Lake Loveland Horseshoe Lake*

9 *Pueblo*

North

| 0 | Kilometers | 16 |
| 0 | Miles | 10 |

Pawnee National Grassland

287

25

85

Cache la Poudre River

Fort Collins

14

Ault

14

Briggs-dale **3**

392

Estes Park

34

8

34

263

37

Greeley

Riverside Reservoir

Rocky Mountain National Park

Loveland

25

2

34

36

85

Long-mont

287

Boulder

S. Platte River

Fort Lupton

52

52

76

40

25

1

79

under con-struction

Denver International Airport

Idaho Springs

Golden

58

70

6

6

6

4

70

70

George-town

70

7

285

5

DENVER

Cherry Creek Reservoir

Guanella Pass (el. 11,669')

Mt. Evans (el. 14,264')

Evergreen

470

470

(470 is a toll road east of I-25)

83

285

Chatfield Reservoir

25

285

to Site **9**

DENVER, COLORADO

Tony Leukering and Christopher L. Wood

Denver lies at or near the meeting points of a variety of avifaunas: eastern, western, montane, and southwestern. This mix has produced an incredible list of 470 species in Colorado, a state that is over 550 miles from an ocean. Additionally, of the 470 species, at least 280 have bred in the state at least once. The variety of breeding species within 100 miles of the capitol building is exciting and includes such disparate birds as Greater Roadrunner, Boreal Owl, Red-headed Woodpecker, and Green-tailed Towhee.

In addition to widespread species whose ranges reach their limits in Colorado, the state is also host to a number of species that are specific to the Rocky Mountains and/or adjacent Great Plains (e.g., White-tailed Ptarmigan, Mountain Plover, and Brown-capped Rosy-Finch). The Denver area provides the birder with an excellent chance of seeing these sought-after specialties. Combine this avian diversity with the cross-country travel hub that is Denver International Airport, and you have a great, easy-to-reach birding destination, good for both short and extended stays.

This site guide is aimed at those birders who have limited time in the area and describes a few of the best sites close to downtown and the airport, as well as a few more-distant ones. The excellent ABA/Lane guide, *A Birder's Guide to Colorado* (Holt 1997), has more detailed directions to all of these locations except the Loveland area.

ESSENTIAL INFORMATION

Getting Around: Most travelers arrive in Denver at the Denver International Airport (DIA). There is abundant cab and limousine service to downtown Denver and shuttles to most of the national hotel and car-rental chains. Amtrak also services Denver, (800) 561-3949. Driving on I-70 within 5 or 10 miles of I-25 and on I-25 from I-70 south to C-470 is usually very congested during both rush hours; it is advisable to take alternate routes, or better yet, avoid those areas at rush hour. Extensive construction on the I-25 corridor from 2001 to 2008 will certainly exacerbate this congestion.

We strongly suggest obtaining a copy of either of the two excellent Colorado road atlases (the DeLorme *Colorado Atlas and Gazeteer* and Shearer Publications' *Roads of Colorado*).

Climate: Average daytime high (and low) temperatures, in degrees Fahrenheit, are 88 (52) in summer, 68 (32) in fall, 47 (17) in winter, and 65 (32) in spring. Surprising to most easterners, Denver-area winters are often mild; many days are in the 50s with warm sunshine. Because Denver lies in the rain shadow of the great Rocky Mountains, weather can be quite unpredictable and changeable, but it is usually sunny, with most precipitation falling during the spring and in the summer monsoon season (frequent afternoon thunderstorms). In comparison to the Denver area, Chicago's moniker ought to be "The Somewhat Breezy City." In other words, be prepared for wind, and if you plan to visit varied elevations, prepare for a variety of weather conditions, including snow in any month of the year.

Natural Hazards: Except in very localized places, annoying insects are few, even in the warmest of times. But don't forget the sunscreen, and always have plenty of water, particularly if you visit the prairie or alpine tundra.

Safety: All sites in this chapter are safe, with little or no history of vandalism or theft from people and/or cars. Some sites, however, are in or very close to this major metropolitan area, so use common sense.

Other Resources: There is a statewide Rare Bird Alert, (303) 424-2144, which is updated at least weekly, but more frequently during migration. There is also a Colorado Listserve (COBirds) that can provide up-to-the-minute news on rarities and bird events (subscribe by sending an e-mail with the words "subscribe cobirds" and your name to *listproc@lists.colorado.edu*). Many birding organizations in the Denver area sponsor field trips. The most active of these groups is the Denver Field Ornithologists, which runs a field trip on most weekend days. Monthly trip information is available at *www.geocities.com/dfobirders*. Other birding groups include the Boulder Bird Club, the Audubon Society of Greater Denver, and the Colorado Field Ornithologists (*www.cfo.-link.org*).

Other Destinations: Non-birding opportunities in and around Denver are numerous and include the Denver Museum of Nature and Science, Denver Zoo, and Denver Botanic Gardens. Consult the official web site of Denver Tourism (*www.milehighcity.com*), the Northeastern Colorado web site (*www.northeasterncolorado.com/tourism.htm*), or Cybertourist (*www.cybertourist.com/coloradotl.cfm*).

THE BIRDING YEAR

Spring migration kicks off in mid-to-late February, and continues through March and April with large movements of waterfowl and gulls; this flight can be noticeable on most of the numerous reservoirs along the urban corridor and includes such early migrants as Cinnamon Teal and interesting gull species such as Thayer's and Glaucous. The passerine migration, though light and sporadic until May, can be interesting at some of the more wooded sites, with an eclectic mix of eastern and western species. The spring migration peak for most groups of landbirds falls in mid-to-late May.

Summer is a wonderful season in the Denver area, with a wide variety of breeding species and, as a result of elevation differences, temperatures that should make cold-blooded and warm-blooded birders equally happy. This season provides about the only opportunity to bird in the alpine tundra, an incredibly beautiful habitat that should not be missed. The wildflower show in mid-summer is itself worth the trip. Summer also brings an array of butterflies and dragonflies into prominence, featuring such beauties as Colorado Hairstreak, Phoebus Parnassian, and Variegated Meadowhawk. So bring your other field guides with you, as well.

Autumn is a protracted season, bird-wise, in most parts of North America, but possibly nowhere more so than in Colorado. The season can be wonderfully clement and long in duration. Fall migration starts in late June with the arrival of the first adult shorebirds, highlighted by gobs of Wilson's Phalaropes and Long-billed Dowitchers. When the variety really picks up in July, Baird's Sandpipers will dominate the flight for most of the rest of the season. Though passerine migration probably starts in July, it really picks up in earnest in late August with the first of the hordes of Wilson's Warblers arriving at nearly all suitable patches of habitat. Another highlight of the autumn is the migration of various waterbirds (loons, waterfowl, gulls) from mid-September to December. Interesting species seen with some regularity (and some in numbers) include Pacific Loon, Barrow's Goldeneye, and Lesser Black-backed and Sabine's Gulls.

Winter is a very dynamic time to bird the Denver area, as there is still much movement into and through the state by waterbirds, and the numerous reservoirs provide habitat for a good number and assortment of waterfowl and gulls. Away from the Pacific Coast, Colorado is the most reliable place in the Lower 48 to find Yellow-billed Loon, with at least one seen during most winters. There are also usually a few odd landbirds, e.g., Varied Thrush or Golden-crowned Sparrow, that attempt to winter. One of the more popular features of winter landbirds in Colorado is rosy-finches: all three species (plus Hepburn's form) visit many sites west of Denver, though in highly variable numbers.

BARR LAKE AND VICINITY

Half day; year round

Barr Lake can be reached by a 25-minute drive from DIA. This spot can be interesting at any time of year. (Refer to Holt's ABA guide for more specific information.) From DIA, take Peña Boulevard west to the Tower

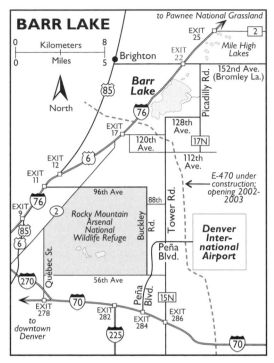

BARR LAKE

to Pawnee National Grassland

EXIT 25

EXIT 22 — Brighton

Mile High Lakes

152nd Ave. (Bromley La.)

0 — Kilometers — 8

0 — Miles — 5

North

Barr Lake

128th Ave.

120th Ave.

112th Ave.

E-470 under construction; opening 2002-2003

EXIT 17

EXIT 12

EXIT 11

96th Ave

88th

Rocky Mountain Arsenal National Wildlife Refuge

Tower Rd.

Buckley Rd.

Peña Blvd.

Denver International Airport

56th Ave

Quebec St.

Peña Blvd.

EXIT 278 to downtown Denver

EXIT 282

EXIT 284

EXIT 286

Picadilly Rd.

Road exit and turn north (right) off the ramp. Proceed north on Tower to W. 128th, where Tower Road bends to the east (right) and is now named 128th. At the first stop sign, Picadilly Road, turn north (left) and travel to the entrance to Barr Lake State Park (1.1 miles). One can hire a taxi, but the expense makes it cheaper to rent a small car for several hours. Highlights of the area include such breeders as Swainson's Hawk, Burrowing Owl, Western Wood-Pewee, Western and Eastern Kingbirds, and Yellow- headed Blackbird. Interesting wintering birds include a large number of raptor species: both eagles, Red-tailed, Ferrugi- nous, and Rough-legged Hawks, Merlin, and Prairie Falcon, with the latter two usually attending the large wintering flocks of Horned Larks. Check for Lapland Longspur among the larks. The best part of the raptor show is the variety of Red-tailed Hawks (black, rufous, eastern, western, and, best of all, "Harlan's"). In spring and fall, a wide variety of passerine migrants has turned up in the gallery forest around the lake, including an impressive list of rarities. During migration, the lake usually hosts a large number of waterbirds, including Eared and Western Grebes, American White Pelican, and a good assortment of ducks.

PAWNEE NATIONAL GRASSLAND

Half or full day; spring, summer, fall

Pawnee National Grassland is a favorite destination of birders from Colorado and elsewhere. To reach it from DIA, follow the directions above for Barr Lake, but continue on Picadilly Road past the park entrance to W. 152nd and turn west (left) to I-76. (When the toll road E-470 is completed to I-76, simply take Peña Boulevard west to E-470 north to I-76.) Go east (right) on I-76 to Exit 34. Turn north (left) off the exit ramp onto 49 Road, travel north to 48 Road, and turn west (left). Drive roughly 1.5

miles to the south end of **Lower Latham Reservoir,** where American Bittern, Franklin's and California Gulls, and "Western" Marsh Wren, as well as all of the expected marsh-nesting Icterids (including Great-tailed Grackle), may be found. There is no public access to the reservoir so it can be difficult to see the birds on the lake. However, there are often pools on both sides of 48 Road between 47 and 43 Roads that are good for shorebirds, with specialties being Black-necked Stilt, American Avocet, and Wilson's Phalarope. Also check Beebe Draw, on the north side of 42 Road between 45 and 47 Roads, for ducks and shorebirds.

If you are pressed for time and wish to skip the reservoir, simply continue north on 49 Road to US-34 and turn east (right). Go two miles to 53 Road (Highway 37) at Kersey and turn north (left). Stay with Highway 37 as it turns east at its junction with Highway 263 and then back north on 55 Road. At the intersection with Highway 392 (approximately 4.5 miles beyond Highway 263), turn east

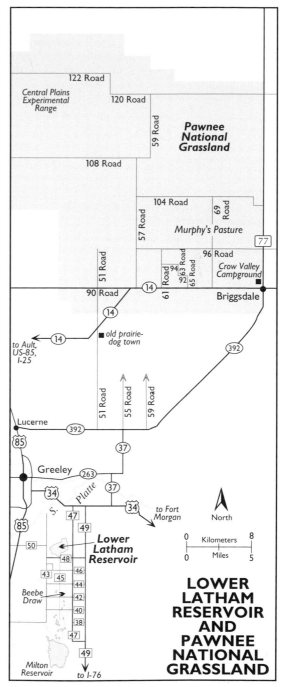

LOWER LATHAM RESERVOIR AND PAWNEE NATIONAL GRASSLAND

(right) onto 392 and follow it to the hamlet of Briggsdale and Highway 14. On the way, watch for Burrowing Owls and Mountain Plovers (April through August or September) in and around prairie-dog towns. Lark Buntings are usually numerous along this route in late spring and summer. Pick up Holt's Pawnee route at the intersection of Highway 14 and CR-77 by going straight (north) across Highway 14 from Briggsdale. *Note: Since the publication of the Holt ABA guide in 1997, CR-77 has been re-routed at its southern end to intersect Highways 14 and 392 at Briggsdale, rather than west of town.*

In the breeding season, this trip may produce Ferruginous (uncommon and local on the Grassland, almost non-existent in agricultural areas) and Swainson's Hawks (common and widespread), Cassin's (variable numbers on the Grassland) and Grasshopper Sparrows, and McCown's and Chestnut-collared Longspurs. The single best spot for the two longspurs is usually along 96 Road in Murphy's Pasture (described well in Holt). If you don't find Chestnut-collared here (McCown's is the much more common of the two), continue on 96 Road west to 61 Road and turn south. The roads on the Pawnee are mostly dirt and can quickly become impassable with any precipitation; use common sense and avoid driving these roads when they are muddy. If you do not find Mountain Plover on the Pawnee, carefully check the prairie-dog town at the southeast corner of the intersection of Highway 14 and 51 Road (and nearby areas), about 13.5 miles west of Briggsdale.

JEFFERSON AND CLEAR CREEK COUNTIES

Half or full day; year round

The following locations lie within a few miles of I-70, and each can be reached from DIA within 1.5 hours. The sites provide an excellent introduction to birds of the foothill and mountain habitats. Birders can combine these spots in any order for a half-day or a full-day trip, depending upon season, time, and interests.

One of the best Denver-area woodland spots, the **Wheat Ridge Greenbelt,** is also a good waterbird spot in winter. From DIA, take Peña Boulevard to I-70, and go west on I-70 to Exit 267 (Kipling Street). Turn south (left) off the ramp and go to W. 44th Avenue and turn west (right) for 0.8 mile to the entrance to Prospect Park on the left. Eastern Screech-Owl is a year-round resident, and the site can be excellent in May and September for migrants. A number of very rare birds for Colorado have been recorded here, including the state's only record of Red-faced Warbler.

Long known as the site closest to Denver to find rosy-finches in winter, **Red Rocks Park** is also good for a variety of lower-foothills birds. Although the rosy-finches aren't as reliable here as they once were, the location is still good at all seasons for Golden Eagle, Prairie Falcon, Western Scrub-Jay, Canyon Wren, and Spotted Towhee. These species are joined in summer by breeding White-throated Swift, Virginia's Warbler, and Lesser Goldfinch. In

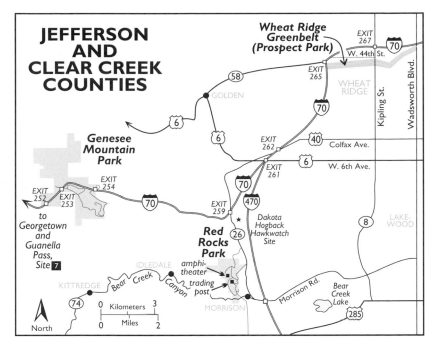

JEFFERSON AND CLEAR CREEK COUNTIES

winter, check the feeders behind the trading post, which often host a rarity or two (e.g., "Red" Fox Sparrow, Golden-crowned Sparrow). To reach Red Rocks, head west out of Denver on I-70. At Exit 259, turn south (left) onto Colorado 26, and travel 1.5 miles to the signed entrance on the right.

Nearby **Genesee Mountain Park** is one of the best Ponderosa Pine areas near Denver for Williamson's Sapsucker, Plumbeous Vireo, Western and Mountain Bluebirds, and Green-tailed Towhee (all in the breeding season only) and for such "permanent" residents as all three Colorado nuthatch species and Red Crossbill ("type 2"). To reach the park head west along I-70 to Exit 254. After exiting, turn left, cross over I-70 to Genesee Mountain Road, turn right, and follow it to the top of the mountain, stopping frequently to look for birds. Williamson's Sapsuckers and Red Crossbills are most often found in the vicinity of the sheltered picnic area.

Georgetown and **Guanella Pass** are well known as the most convenient places in winter (specifically January to early April) to see rosy-finches and White-tailed Ptarmigan, respectively. Your best bet is to bird Georgetown on your way to Guanella Pass, because the ptarmigan often roost under snow until late morning. Currently, the most reliable place in town to view rosy-finches (and Mountain Chickadee and Pine Grosbeak) is at the intersection of Rose and 2nd on the west side of town just as the route to Guanella Pass starts uphill. If you have time, look for other active feeders in town (particularly from Main to Biddle between 11th and 9th). The road up to Guanella Pass can be excellent year round for high-elevation birds such as

Three-toed Woodpecker (particularly at or near the Guanella Pass campground), Gray Jay, Clark's Nutcracker, Golden-crowned Kinglet, Brown Creeper, Pine Grosbeak, Cassin's Finch, and Red Crossbill ("type 5"). These birds are joined in summer by Red-naped Sapsucker, Hammond's, Dusky, and Cordilleran Flycatchers, MacGillivray's Warbler, Western Tanager, and "Slate-colored" Fox Sparrow. White-tailed Ptarmigan are most easily found near the large parking area at the top of the pass. Walk or drive a short way beyond the parking area and scan the hillside to the west of the parking area and south of the road. The birds often can be found sheltering in a small stand of conifers here. If you are here in winter and you don't find the birds, be prepared to walk (with showshoes) through deep snow to search for ptarmigan.

LOVELAND

Half or full day; winter to early spring

In recent years, the **Loveland area** has become *the* hot-spot for gulls in the state. In winter and spring, the reservoirs and the nearby landfill have hosted such rarities as Mew, Lesser Black-backed, Glaucous-winged, and Great Black-backed Gulls, as well as the first state record of Slaty-backed Gull. This trip could be combined with nearby sites mentioned in Holt's book. The large gulls usually spend the morning hours foraging at the **Larimer County landfill** and/or at various reservoirs. They pass much of

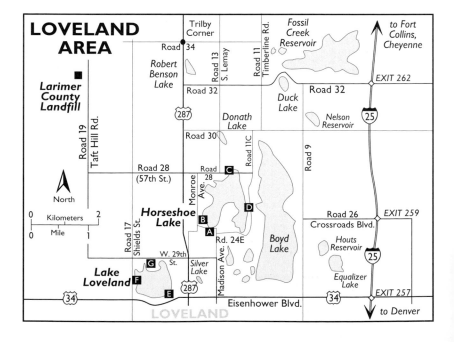

the afternoon loafing at favored reservoirs, particularly **Horseshoe Lake** (sites A-D) if open, and roosting on **Lake Loveland** (sites E-G) if not frozen. If you have only a morning, start *very* early at Lake Loveland (site G) and then head to the landfill and the other reservoirs. If you have only an afternoon, start at Horseshoe Lake and follow the birds to Lake Loveland (sites E or F) at dusk. These sites are variably good from September through April, but are best from December to March. In addition to gulls, the lakes can host good numbers of waterfowl, with rarities including Long-tailed Duck, scoters, and Barrow's Goldeneye. Horseshoe Lake and the property around it are private; do not trespass. There are numerous other reservoirs around Loveland, many of which have hosted interesting gulls. *A scope is useful, even necessary, at all of these locations.*

The **Larimer County landfill** is open from 8:00AM to 4:30PM, Monday–Saturday, and 9:00AM to 4:00PM Sunday. At this writing, landfill personnel have been very cooperative and have permitted access to the landfill and its attendant gulls. Please keep this relationship healthy by following all rules and directions from landfill personnel. Once past the entrance kiosk, where you ask permission to look at the gulls, go straight to the T-intersection and turn right. Find some place out of the way to park and scan through the myriad gulls. Check the wastewater ponds beyond the recycling center (which is signed) before leaving.

PUEBLO

Full day; year round

This is arguably the best all-around birding destination in Colorado. The combination of a large, productive reservoir, an excellent stretch of riparian forest on the Arkansas River, some cholla grasslands, and the surrounding foothills clothed in oak brush and pinyon-juniper woodland provide habitat for a large variety of birds. This area, just a bit over a two-hour drive from DIA, is well worth the effort for those with the time and inclination, no matter the season. Please refer to Holt's guide for an excellent account of birding opportunities in the area.

ACKNOWLEDGMENTS

We acknowledge the work of the late Jim Lane and the late Harold Holt in producing seminal site guides to Colorado, references that all of us use and from which some of the material in this chapter is drawn. We also thank the Larimer County birders who have discovered most of the good gull-viewing opportunities in the Loveland area, particularly Steve Dinsmore, Nick Komar, and Dave Leatherman.

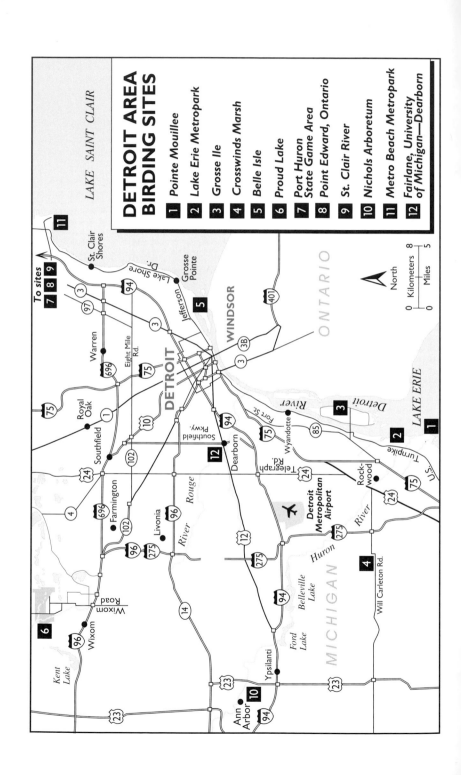

DETROIT AREA BIRDING SITES

1 Pointe Mouillee
2 Lake Erie Metropark
3 Grosse Ile
4 Crosswinds Marsh
5 Belle Isle
6 Proud Lake
7 Port Huron State Game Area
8 Point Edward, Ontario
9 St. Clair River
10 Nichols Arboretum
11 Metro Beach Metropark
12 Fairlane, University of Michigan—Dearborn

North

0 Kilometers 8
0 Miles 5

LAKE SAINT CLAIR

ONTARIO

LAKE ERIE

MICHIGAN

To sites 7 8 9

St. Clair Shores

Lake Shore Dr.

Grosse Pointe

Jefferson

WINDSOR

DETROIT

Warren

Eight Mile Rd.

Royal Oak

Southfield

Farmington

Livonia

Dearborn

Southfield Pkwy.

River Rouge

Telegraph Rd.

Fort St.

Wyandotte

Rock-wood

Detroit River

Detroit Metropolitan Airport

Huron River

Belleville Lake

Ford Lake

Ypsilanti

Ann Arbor

Wixom Road

Wixom

Kent Lake

Will Carleton Rd.

DETROIT, MICHIGAN

Karl Overman

Here you had hoped that the convention would be booked in Las Vegas again, but someone at the top decided to be innovative and have it in Detroit instead. For some folks, that might lead to much wailing and gnashing of teeth, but for you as a birder, count yourself lucky—you won't lose as much money, and the birding can be exciting any time of the year, with a number of species that are difficult to get elsewhere. The geography of Michigan is shaped (mittens, of course) by the Great Lakes, and it is the Great Lakes and its connecting waterways that have a profound impact on birding in Michigan. Waterfowl migrate through the region en masse, with thousands staying to winter. When water levels are right, shorebirds concentrate in the area with a diversity of species that is hard to match anywhere. Most raptors do their best to skirt the Great Lakes in migration, and in the process pile up by the thousands at hawkwatch locales in the area. In a similar vein, many passerines are loath to cross the Great Lakes, and such nearby migrant traps as Point Pelee, Ontario, and Crane Creek, Ohio, are justly famous as birding destinations.

ESSENTIAL INFORMATION

Getting Around: As would be expected for the motor capital of the world, public transportation is minimal and not a real option for a visiting birder. There is city bus service to Belle Isle in Detroit, and, at least in summer, both Lake Erie Metropark and Metrobeach Metropark can be reached by SMART buses, (313) 962-5515. Car rental is by far your best option if you plan on birding in the Detroit area. Detroit Metropolitan Airport is located 25 miles west of downtown Detroit and can be reached by shuttle bus or taxi. The demographic and economic reality is that most birders visiting Detroit will not be staying downtown but somewhere in suburbia, and bus service would be impractical.

Safety: Detroit has the reputation of being a dangerous city, but the only birding destination within the city for visiting birders is Belle Isle, and that area is safe if reasonable precautions are taken. The place where crime is a more serious consideration is Pointe Mouillee, and the problem there is vehicle break-ins.

Natural Hazards: Although Michigan probably cannot compete with South Florida or Alaska, mosquitoes can be ferocious here in summer. Deer Flies also can make birding in the summer unpleasant. Chiggers should not be a factor. Poison-Ivy is plentiful in many areas.

Other Resources: There is an ABA birdfinding guide for Michigan in the works that will be available within a year or two. Both the Detroit Rare Bird Alert, (248) 477-1360, and the Michigan Rare Bird Alert, (617) 471-4919, cover the Detroit area. The Detroit Audubon Society has at least 20 field trips per year, and visitors are welcome; contact them at 320 N. Campbell, Royal Oak, MI 48067, (248) 545-2929, e-mail *detas@bignet.net*.

THE BIRDING YEAR

Michigan's birds are overwhelmingly eastern in affinity, with only a few western components to the local avifauna. Michigan may be a northern border state, but to see most of the truly boreal birds and winter specialties, you'll have to drive north six hours to the Upper Peninsula. See for example K. Overman, "Winter Birding at the Soo," *Winging It,* November 1992.

What you will see on a visit to the Detroit area depends on when you visit, so here is one version of a Detroit birding calendar:

January: Happy New Year! Time to start a new list, hopefully with something other than House Sparrow. Stop by Westcroft Gardens on Grosse Ile in the lower Detroit River for semi-hardy birds such as Hermit Thrush and Yellow-rumped Warbler, and hope for a finch flight bringing in crossbills. Bundle up and check the St. Clair River for wintering waterfowl and "white-winged" gulls.

February: Forget about the Vernal Equinox; spring has sprung, with Tundra Swans and Sandhill Cranes arriving by the middle of the month and most waterfowl species arriving by the end of the month.

March: Some birders view this as their least favorite month to bird, but what do they know? Waterfowl migration peaks. Anyone seen a Eurasian Wigeon lately? American Woodcocks are back and displaying, and shorebird migration begins around 20–25 March with the arrival of yellowlegs and Pectoral Sandpipers at places such as the Erie Marsh Preserve and Pointe Mouillee in Monroe County. Eastern Phoebes and Tree Swallows can show up any time after 20 March.

April: Often a cruel month, as birders are thinking spring and are too often handed another round of winter. Forster's and Caspian Terns can be back by 10 April. This is the month for sparrow migration, with the likes of American Tree Sparrows and juncos exiting and Savannah Sparrows and Vesper Sparrows arriving. Upland Sandpipers are back at Willow Run Airport in Wayne County after 25 April. For the raptor aficionados, look for the hawk flight along the Lake Huron shoreline north of Port Huron.

May: In these parts, this is the month birders live for. Often at the beginning of the month there is little to look at in the woods other than chickadees, but birders know that any day the floodgates will open and the woods will be filled with migrants: flycatchers, vireos, thrushes, warblers—you name it. Be at the Arboretum in Ann Arbor around 22 May to look for Connecticut Warbler. Where do you look for May migrants? Do what most Detroit birders do—leave the state. Journey to the nearby famous migrant traps of Point Pelee, Ontario (40 minutes from Detroit's Ambassador Bridge), or Crane Creek/Magee Marsh, Ohio (a two-hour drive from most of metro Detroit). If you want to look for migrants in southeast Michigan, try the Arboretum in Ann Arbor, Metrobeach in Macomb County, Fairlane at the University of Michigan–Dearborn campus, or Belle Isle.

June: Time to slap on the bug-juice and start looking for breeding birds. The Port Huron State Game Area is hard to beat, with a fine mix of northern and southern species. The last of the spring migrants, say, White-rumped Sandpipers, leave around 10 June, and the first of the fall migrants, usually Least Sandpipers, are back around 24 June (okay, maybe the 25th).

July: After the 4th of July, breeding-bird song greatly diminishes, so finding birds gets progressively more difficult. If Dickcissels show up at all, this is a good month to find them. If water levels are low, take your kid's bike and go to Pointe Mouillee for a smorgasbord of waterbirds. If water levels are high, might as well go over your "Honey-do" list and stay home.

August: It can be the "Dog Days of Birding" unless there is good shorebird habitat present. Warblers start migrating through around 25 August, though most birders don't seem to notice.

September: Look up: the Broad-wings are coming. Try to be at Lake Erie Metropark around 17 September when the wind has a northern component, and you should be rewarded with a sky full of thousands of Broad-winged Hawks. Warbler migration peaks early in the month before most birders are mentally in gear for things autumnal. By the end of the month, waterfowl and sparrows are moving (though not in mixed flocks), and the sound of the Golden-crowned Kinglet is heard throughout the land, at least for those birders who can still hear it.

October: A great month to be a birder. Almost anything is possible: warblers are still migrating early in the month, waterfowl are moving in good numbers, and shorebirds can be very good if there is habitat (a good time to find Hudsonian Godwits in Monroe County). Bonaparte's Gull numbers start to build, so it is time to sort through them looking for rarer species such as Little and Franklin's. When a wintry blast is predicted, head up to Port Huron/Sarnia in hopes of pelagic goodies such as jaegers, Sabine's Gull, and Black-legged Kittiwake. By mid-month, scoters are to be expected in the same area. At the hawkwatches, Red-shouldered Hawks start appearing, and by the end of the month, with favorable winds, you should find . . .

November: Golden Eagles! Again, Lake Erie Metropark is the place, and early November is a great time to find them.   If it is going to be a winter-finch year or a Snowy Owl year, we should know by sometime during this month. Waterfowl migration is a dominant feature, including the arrival of Tundra Swans.

December: December is an excellent month for gulls along the Great Lakes and at landfills inland. Fall migration comes to a close with the departure of Tundra Swans and Sandhill Cranes. Best of all, you should end the birding year with the camaraderie of the Christmas Bird Counts.

POINTE MOUILLEE

Full day; spring, summer, and winter

This location is about a half-hour drive from Detroit Metropolitan Airport. From the airport, go east 3.8 miles on I-94 to US 24 (Telegraph Road). Go south 4.8 miles to a stop light at Eureka Road. Continue through the light, bearing left, which will take you onto I-75 south. Once on I-75 proper, continue south for 7.8 miles to the Rockwood exit (# 27). Turn left onto Huron River Drive. Follow Huron River Drive 2.3 miles to W. Jefferson. Turn right and follow W. Jefferson (which becomes U. S. Turnpike) 2.1 miles to Sigler Road. Turn left and go to the gravel parking lot at the end of the road. This is the most northerly of three access points, all off U.S. Turnpike and each with a gravel parking lot. Be sure to lock up and don't leave valuables in sight, as some birders have had their vehicles broken into here.

When water levels are right, **Pointe Mouillee** is one of the premier inland locations for waterbirds in North America. There are some logistical considerations to address before setting out to bird Pointe Mouillee. First, how does one physically get around the miles of dikes there? Alas, the road system on the dikes is not available to private vehicles. That leaves you with two options: walking or biking. I strongly recommend the latter. Given the scale of the place, a scope is required equipment. Be prepared for long spells in the sun, as there is no shade on the dikes.   Keep an eye out for thunderstorms, as you are likely to be the tallest object around.

Early spring, after the break-up of ice, can be very profitable for both diving and dabbling ducks, especially in the Vermet Unit. Good numbers of Tundra Swans are seen in late February and early March. Greater White-fronted Geese were found there from mid-February to mid-March in at least five years during the 1990s. After waterfowl migration starts to wane in early April, Pointe Mouillee is not generally viewed as a productive stop in spring unless it is the unusual year in which water levels are low enough to attract

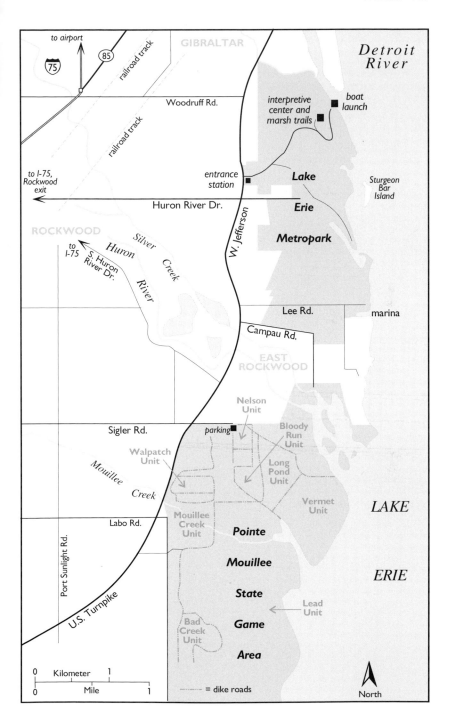

to airport

75

85

railroad track

GIBRALTAR

Detroit River

Woodruff Rd.

interpretive center and marsh trails

boat launch

to I-75, Rockwood exit

entrance station

Lake

Sturgeon Bar Island

Huron River Dr.

Erie

ROCKWOOD

Silver Creek

W. Jefferson

Metropark

to I-75

S. Huron River Dr.

Huron River

Lee Rd.

marina

Campau Rd.

EAST ROCKWOOD

Nelson Unit

Sigler Rd.

parking

Bloody Run Unit

Walpatch Unit

Long Pond Unit

Mouillee Creek

Vermet Unit

LAKE

Mouillee Creek Unit

Labo Rd.

Pointe

Port Sunlight Rd.

Mouillee

ERIE

State

Lead Unit

U.S. Turnpike

Bad Creek Unit

Game

Area

0   Kilometer   1

0   Mile   1

----- = dike roads

North

shorebirds. An exception to this rule is that it is an excellent place to witness migrant Whimbrel between 15 May and 1 June.

Breeding birds at Pointe Mouillee run the gamut of expected marsh birds—such as Pied-billed Grebe, Common Moorhen, Marsh Wren, and Swamp Sparrow—plus more-sought-after birds including American (rare) and Least Bitterns, King Rail (unreported since 1996), and Yellow-headed Blackbird (a few present most years since late 1980s). It is a very good spot for loitering ducks in the summer, with Canvasback, Redhead (breeding), Lesser Scaup, and even Greater Scaup all being regular.

Late summer can be a magical time at Pointe Mouillee. Shorebird migration starts with the appearance of both yellowlegs, Least Sandpipers, and Short-billed Dowitchers around 1 July. If water levels are low in the Vermet Unit, shorebird numbers can quickly build up to the thousands by late July. When shorebird diversity peaks in early August, a proficient observer can find up to 25 species of shorebirds in a day. It is a great place for finding rare shorebirds. Curlew Sandpiper showed up during seven years between 1988 and 1998; Ruff appeared in four years over the same period. American Avocets are annual visitors. Buff-breasted Sandpipers are frequently found on either the dikes or the dry fringes of the impoundments. A Snowy Plover spent over a month here in 1994. Shorebirds are not the only group generating rarities at Pointe Mouillee in late summer. Rare herons and ibises are found with regularity, including Snowy Egret (present most years), Little Blue Heron, Tricolored Heron, Reddish Egret (1993), Cattle Egret (less common or even absent in recent years), Yellow-crowned Night-Heron, Glossy Ibis, and White-faced Ibis (1994). American White Pelicans have shown up in summer six of the last seven years. Pointe Mouillee has a number of summer Arctic Tern records, with birds reported between 18 June and 14 July in four summers since 1989. Don't overlook the gulls in mid-summer, for both Little and Black-headed have turned up.

During the fall, Pointe Mouillee is off-limits because of hunting, roughly from 15 September through 1 December. In early December, Purple Sandpipers have been found on the rocky perimeter of Pointe Mouillee. In mid-winter the impoundments are typically frozen over, but Lake Erie may still be open for those willing to walk the extra mile. Exceptionally, both Harlequin Duck and Barrow's Goldeneye have been found in mid-winter. Pointe Mouillee is also a good place for Short-eared Owl (it sometimes breeds there, as well), and Snowy Owl. Snow Buntings and, not infrequently, Northern Shrikes are present in winter, but there are easier places to get those birds.

Broad-winged Hawks
David Sibley
courtesy of New Jersey Audubon Society

LAKE ERIE METROPARK

Half day; spring, fall, and winter

From Metro Airport, follow the same directions as to Pointe Mouillee until Huron River Drive meets West Jefferson. There, turn north and drive 0.2 mile to the entrance to the park on the east side of West Jefferson; there is an entrance fee. This park is one of a chain of suburban parks run by the Huron-Clinton Metropolitan Authority. **Lake Erie Metropark** is primarily oriented toward mass entertainment for visitors, with large public swimming pools, a golf course, and wide swaths of lawn punctuated with picnic facilities. Summer here is like a day at the beach, which it is, with throngs of people and no birds, and thus to be avoided. Spring in the park is normally only marginally productive, though rarities such as Black Vulture and White-faced Ibis have appeared. But come fall and winter, this is a must-stop on Michigan's birding circuit.

Lake Erie Metropark is Michigan's premier fall hawkwatching location. Southeastern Raptor Research runs the hawkwatch from 1 September through 30 November. The hawkwatchers are in constant radio contact with the well-known Ontario hawkwatch location of Holiday Beach, eight miles across Lake Erie as the Broad-wing won't fly. There is a Hawkfest at Lake Erie Metropark that is timed to coincide with the peak of the Broad-winged Hawk flight, which can be any time from 14 September to 25 September. The numbers of Broad-wings can be staggering. In 1999, for example, the total count during the period 4 September–11 October was 102,623, with a peak count of 69,676 on 17 September. In recent years a few Swainson's Hawks have been found in with the Broad-wings. The park is also well-known for its Golden Eagle flight, which typically runs from mid-October through the end of November and peaks in late October or early November. Where to view the hawks changes depending on the wind direction, but a good starting point is the boat-launch area at the north end of the park.

Lake Erie Metropark is located where the Detroit River empties into Lake Erie, and there is always open water here in winter. Hundreds of coots can be found wintering here, with dozens of American Wigeon hanging around them trying to steal their hard-earned vegetarian food. In the winter of 1993 a Eurasian Wigeon was present. This is the best place in the region to find Tundra Swans wintering, which they do annually (as do numerous Mute Swans). A wide range of diving and puddle ducks can be found here, as well, in fall and winter. The marshy slough that runs the length of the park can be productive in some years for shorebirds, including an occasional Hudsonian Godwit. There is a loop nature trail starting near the Interpretive Center that can be productive for migrants and wintering birds including Hermit Thrush and Yellow-rumped Warbler. Long-eared Owls are sometimes found along the trail in winter.

GROSSE ILE

Half day; winter

To reach **Grosse Ile** from Lake Erie Metropark, head north on West Jefferson for 4.3 miles to the light at Grosse Ile Parkway. Cross over the bridge to the island.

This large island in the lower Detroit River is upscale suburbia and has undergone massive development during the last 20 years. Fortunately, the island residents have had the foresight to preserve some extensive woodlands on the island, and there are many pockets of thickets that can harbor both migrants and winter residents. There are roads around the perimeter of the island, making it easy to look for wintering waterfowl. Parking is always a problem on the island, though, and you may have to be innovative.

On the east side of Grosse Ile, overlooking marshy Stony Island, there is a lovely observation deck from which to scan the river below for waterfowl. A few Tundra Swans can usually be found here in winter. Good numbers of Canvasbacks, Redheads, and Common Goldeneyes winter around Grosse Ile, and occasionally rarer diving ducks are found as well, such as Harlequin Duck, Long-tailed Duck, and Surf Scoter. To look for landbirds in winter, pay a visit to Westcroft Gardens on the west side of the island. This is private property, but visitors are welcome to walk through this nursery, which hosts large evergreens and an understory of Rhododendrons, plus overgrown brushy areas that offer cover for semi-hardy wintering birds such as Hermit Thrush, Yellow-rumped Warbler, and White-throated Sparrow. The evergreens normally have wintering Red-breasted Nuthatches and Pine Siskins, with White-winged Crossbills in flight years.

GROSSE ILE

Pennsylvania Rd.

WYANDOTTE

Sibley Rd.

Bridge Rd.

Horse Mill Rd.

W. Jefferson Ave.

DETROIT

King Rd.

Westcroft Gardens (21803 W. River Rd.)

West River Rd.

Church Rd.

East River Rd.

West Rd.

RIVER

Ferry Rd.

Grosse Ile Pkwy.

Bellevue Rd.

Stony Island

Groh Rd.

Grosse Ile Airport

CANADA U.S.

CANADA U.S.

North

0 Kilometers 2

0 Mile 1

PROUD LAKE

Half day; summer

To reach Proud Lake from the Detroit Metropolitan Airport, go east on I-94 to I-275. Go north on I-275 to I-96, and go west on I-96 to the Wixom exit. Follow Wixom Road north for 6.2 miles to the headquarters entrance for Proud Lake State Recreation Area; turn right (east) down a corridor of evergreens to a parking lot at the end. Garden Road is 50 yards north of this entrance and goes west to a dead end at a pedestrian bridge.

The varied habitats at **Proud Lake** include marshes along the Huron River, old pine plantations, deciduous forest, and overgrown fields. In the extensive old pine plantations by the headquarters area there may be found a number of northern species that are hard to find elsewhere close to Detroit in the breeding season: Blue-headed Vireo, Red-breasted Nuthatch, Brown Creeper, Golden-crowned Kinglet (occasional), and Black-throated Green (occasional) and Pine Warblers. This is one of the few areas near Detroit where Pileated Woodpecker has occurred in recent years. Proud Lake is also a good place to find Black-billed Cuckoo. By taking Garden Road to the end, you will find marshes along the Huron River (canoe rentals available), where breeding birds include Sandhill Crane, Willow and Alder Flycatchers, and Sedge Wren.

BELLE ISLE

Half day; spring, fall, and winter

From downtown Detroit go east on Jefferson Avenue 2.4 miles to Grand Boulevard, bear right, and take the bridge over to **Belle Isle**. Traffic is one way (counterclockwise) around the island, with a few streets through the interior of the island.

This urban park near where Lake St. Clair drains into the Detroit River is a fine quick getaway for a birder visiting downtown Detroit. Its woods and open areas can harbor good numbers of migrant landbirds, and its lagoons and the surrounding Detroit River can be excellent for waterfowl in season. In fall, the first of the diving ducks, typically Ring-necked Ducks and Redheads, start to appear around 1 October at Blue Heron Lagoon at the east end of the island. It might not be until the end of the month that diving ducks start appearing in numbers on the river itself. Hooded Mergansers are particularly fond of the lagoons at the east end of the island in late October through early December. In fall, one or two Black-crowned Night-Herons roost on the wooded islands in these lagoons until the lagoons freeze over. The woods in the interior of the island can be excellent for migrant warblers after 1 May. Sometimes Red-headed Woodpeckers are found in these woods, even in winter. Birding around the perimeter of the island should present no unusual

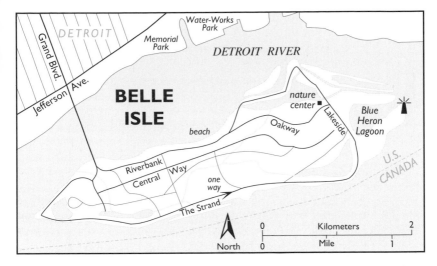

problems for birders, but birding the interior woodland may be risky for a lone female birder. Birding here in summer is not recommended because there are relatively few breeding birds and because crowds can be monumental late in the day and on weekends. There is, however, a large colony of Cliff Swallows under the bridge to the island.

CROSSWINDS MARSH

Half day; spring, summer, and fall

From Detroit Metropolitan Airport go west on I-94 to I-275. Go south on I-275 for 8.8 miles to the Will Carlton Road exit. Go west 3.3 miles to Haggerty Road. Go north 0.5 mile to the park entrance on the west side of the road; gates open at 8:00AM.

Crosswinds Marsh is only about a 20-minute drive from Metro Airport. Canoe rentals are available. At the present time bathroom facilities are rudimentary. There is an extensive system of boardwalks over the man-made marsh, which is home to the likes of Pied-billed Grebe, Hooded Merganser, Virginia Rail, and Marsh Wren. A pair of Bald Eagles attempted to breed there recently, and there is a good chance of seeing that species in the park. In late summer a few shorebirds, such as American Golden-Plover and both yellow-legs, appear on mudflats. The park's extensive marsh is complemented by a patchwork of fields and small woodlots that harbor a good diversity of migrant and breeding birds. There is a good population of Orchard Orioles here, a bird hard to find elsewhere in Michigan. Yellow-breasted Chats can be found in the brushy areas on the west side of the park.

PORT HURON STATE GAME AREA

Full day; late spring and summer

This area is approximately an hour-and-a-half from most parts of Metro Detroit. From Detroit go east (and north) on I-94 toward Port Huron. Where I-94 intersects I-69, go west on I-69 for 3.1 miles to the Wadhams Road exit. Turn right (north) on Wadhams, cross the Black River, and bear left onto Vincent Road. Go north on Vincent Road 3.5 miles to M-136. Go west on M-136 for 2.5 miles to a parking area on the south side of the road.

The above directions access the most productive area in this state game area. In the mixed deciduous and coniferous forest along the Black River you should find such southern warblers as Cerulean, Louisiana Waterthrush, and Hooded sharing the area with such northern species as Chestnut-sided, Black-throated Green, Blackburnian, and Mourning. An avian enigma about the **Port Huron State Game Area** is that for many years it has had sizable populations of both Blue-winged and Golden-winged Warblers, yet the Golden-winged population so far has not diminished. Acadian Flycatcher can be found along the Black River, whereas Alder and Willow can be found in brushier areas (try Shoefelt Road west of Vincent Road). Approximately 3.5 miles to the north of M-136, near the junction of Hewitt and Graham Roads, both Henslow's and Clay-colored Sparrows have traditionally bred, though suburban sprawl could soon doom them in that area. Both species were still being found there as of June 2000. In fallow fields in the general vicinity of the state game area look and/or listen for Northern Harrier, Northern Bobwhite, Upland Sandpiper, Grasshopper Sparrow, and Bobolink. Upland Sandpiper is regular in the fields at Wadhams and Smiths Creek Roads.

POINT EDWARD, ONTARIO, AND THE ST. CLAIR RIVER

Half day (fall); full day (winter)

The start of this tour is approximately an hour-and-a-half from most of the Detroit area. From Detroit take I-94 east to Port Huron. Cross over the Blue Water Bridge (toll) into Sarnia, Ontario. After clearing customs, take the first exit, which is marked Front Street/Point Edward. Bear left and turn left on Front Street. Go 0.7 mile to Michigan Street. Turn left on Michigan and go 0.4 mile to St. Clair. Go right one block to Victoria. Go left three blocks to Fort Street and take that to the parking lot at the end.

This tour is actually two different trips that start at the same location, a parking lot overlooking Lake Huron at **Point Edward, Ontario.** In the fall this is a birding destination by itself. In winter, however, this is just the first stop of many to look for winter waterfowl and gulls. Fall at Point Edward

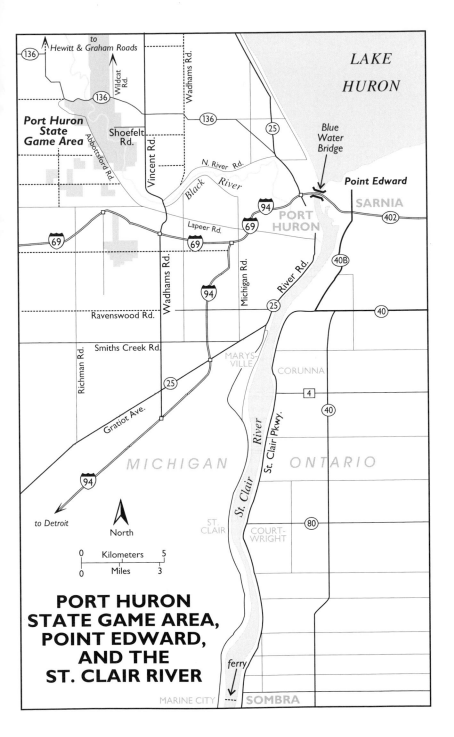

**PORT HURON
STATE GAME AREA,
POINT EDWARD,
AND THE
ST. CLAIR RIVER**

brings Michigan and Ontario birders scope to scope. Michigan birders come to this Canadian outpost for birds that are hard to get elsewhere in the state and which are essentially coastal or pelagic in habits—King Eider, Red Phalarope, jaegers, Black-legged Kittiwake, and Sabine's Gull. Mind you, none of these birds is common there, but there is a chance for them. The rule of engagement here is that the watery boundary-line between Michigan and Ontario runs from the middle of the Blue Water Bridge to the mid-point between a green buoy (in Michigan) and a red buoy (in Ontario).

A rule of thumb for all birders in the fall is that if you would feel comfortable loitering outside your car, you probably picked the wrong day to go to Point Edward! Cold and windy days seem to bring the best birds. Jaegers are the premier attraction at Point Edward, with all three species having been recorded in the fall. Long-tailed Jaeger borders on the accidental, with only three records. Parasitic Jaegers are the most regularly reported, with sightings from 27 August to 27 December. Black-legged Kittiwakes (almost always first-winter birds) are annual at Point Edward, appearing between mid-October and late December. Point Edward is excellent for all three species of scoters and for Long-tailed Duck. You also have a reasonable chance for seeing Red-throated Loon and Red-necked Grebe

As for winter birding, the main focus is on the **St. Clair River**. Point Edward is merely the starting line, with the finishing line being the town of Sombra, Ontario. Much like birding in the Niagara Falls area, the U.S. side of the river is heavily developed and difficult to access, whereas the Ontario side provides excellent access to the river. For winter birding on this route, the colder and the more ice the better, since the ice forces birds off Lake Huron to the north and off Lake St. Clair to the south—and onto the river. From Point Edward find your way back to Front Street and start driving south. Stop to look over Sarnia Bay if it is open, as there are often gulls—including Glaucous and Iceland—sitting on the ice. If there are Snowy Owls around, check the park around Sarnia Bay as well as the Sarnia Airport. Continue south along the St. Clair River, checking the pockets of open water for diving ducks, primarily Canvasback, Redhead, Greater Scaup, Common Goldeneye, and Common Merganser, with smaller numbers of other species. Look on the floating ice for unusual gulls (an Ivory Gull was here in mid-December 1995) and Bald Eagles. Harlequin Ducks are fairly regular, whereas Tufted Duck, King Eider, and Barrow's Goldeneye are rarely found here. If the ice is not a problem, take the Sombra ferry back to the U.S. Otherwise, you will have to backtrack to Sarnia and go back over the Blue Water Bridge.

PASSERINE MIGRANT SITES
Half day; spring

Spring migrants do not tend to linger long, so the more eyes looking for them the better. The following are three locations scattered around

Metro Detroit where in May you are likely to have plenty of company and thus plenty of help in trying to find as many migrants as possible. The same locations are also likely to have early spring migrants and fall migrants as well.

Nichols Arboretum, Ann Arbor: From Detroit Metro Airport, go west on I-94 to Ann Arbor. Go north on US-23 to the Geddes Road exit. Go west, crossing the Huron River onto Geddes Road. Look for the entrance to the Arboretum on your right (parking is a challenge here). These are hallowed grounds, where generations of birders and ornithologists studying or working at the University of Michigan have strained their necks looking for warblers in spring migration. The "Arb" turns up good birds on a regular basis, and species such as Kentucky and Worm-eating Warblers are found here more often than anywhere else in the state. The site is particularly known for Connecticut Warbler, which are best looked for between 18 May and 1 June.

Metrobeach Metropark: From Detroit take I-94 east to Metropolitan Parkway; take that road east to the end, which is at the park (entrance fee). This is more than just a spring migrant trap, as it has an extensive marsh with breeding Least Bitterns, and it can be excellent for waterfowl, being on the shores of Lake St. Clair. Over the years it has produced some stellar rarities, such as Magnificent Frigatebird, "Great White" Heron, and Heermann's Gull. Behind the Nature Center is a loop trail through a cottonwood grove that can be excellent for migrants.

Fairlane, at the University of Michigan–Dearborn: From Detroit Metro Airport go east to the Southfield Expressway (MI-39). Go north 4.5 miles to the Ford Road exit. Go west one mile to the Evergreen Road exit, then south, and after two stoplights turn west into the campus of the University of Michigan–Dearborn. The pedestrian entrance to the environmental study area is at the west end of the entrance road.

Henry Ford's estate, Fairlane, is preserved on the University of Michigan–Dearborn campus, and as befits a man who dabbled in birding himself, a large wooded area along the Rouge River has been preserved. These woods produce a fine variety of migrants, with a special emphasis on more-southern species that seem to turn up regularly here but are hard to find in general in southern Michigan. Julie Craves is the force behind the Rouge River Bird Observatory based here (*www.umd.umich.edu/dept/rouge-river*). See her article, "The Environmental Study Area at The University of Michigan–Dearborn," *Winging It*, September 1993.

ACKNOWLEDGMENTS

I would like to thank Mike Kielb for his help regarding the Nichols Arboretum in Ann Arbor, Jeff Schultz for his input on Lake Erie Metropark, and the late Dennis Rupert for the years of insight on birding in and around Sarnia, Ontario.

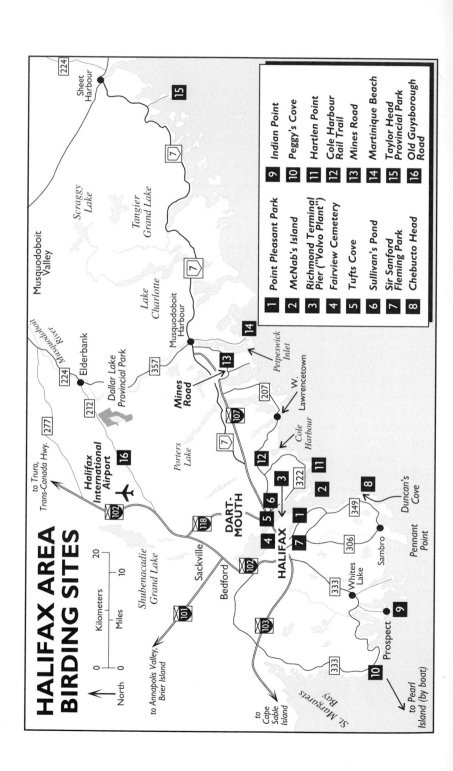

HALIFAX AREA BIRDING SITES

North

Kilometers
0   10   20
Miles
0   10

Legend:

1. Point Pleasant Park
2. McNab's Island
3. Richmond Terminal Pier ("Volvo Plant")
4. Fairview Cemetery
5. Tufts Cove
6. Sullivan's Pond
7. Sir Sanford Fleming Park
8. Chebucto Head
9. Indian Point
10. Peggy's Cove
11. Hartlen Point
12. Cole Harbour Rail Trail
13. Mines Road
14. Martinique Beach
15. Taylor Head Provincial Park
16. Old Guysborough Road

Sheet Harbour
Scraggy Lake
Tangier Grand Lake
Musquodoboit Valley
Lake Charlotte
Musquodoboit Harbour
Musquodoboit River
Elderbank
Dollar Lake Provincial Park
Perpeswick Inlet
W. Lawrencetown
Cole Harbour
Mines Road
Porters Lake
Halifax International Airport
to Truro, Trans-Canada Hwy.
Shubenacadie Grand Lake
Sackville
Bedford
DART-MOUTH
HALIFAX
Duncan's Cove
Sambro
Pennant Point
Whites Lake
Prospect
St. Margarets Bay
to Cape Sable Island
to Annapolis Valley, Brier Island
to Pearl Island (by boat)

224 · 7 · 357 · 224 · 212 · 277 · 102 · 207 · 107 · 7 · 118 · 322 · 349 · 306 · 333 · 101 · 103 · 333

HALIFAX, NOVA SCOTIA

Blake Maybank

Boreal forest, saltmarshes, deciduous uplands, seabird colonies, vagrants from all compass-points, year-round avian adventure—Nova Scotia is one of Canada's best year-round birding destinations. It is halfway between the North Pole and the equator, and it lies at the eastern edge of the continent. And Halifax is its center, offering an attractive mix of culture, nature, history, and urban sophistication. It's a favorite destination for people the world over, and yet retains an uncrowded, intimate demeanor.

Just before the turn of the millennium, the City of Halifax was administratively combined with Halifax County, as well as Bedford and Dartmouth, the other cities that also share Halifax Harbour. The new entity, the Halifax Regional Municipality (hereafter "HRM"), is enormous, requiring a three-hour drive end-to-end, although home to but 450,000 people. Against such a broad landscape this chapter cannot be comprehensive, and so features only selected sites within an hour's drive (usually) from either downtown Halifax or the Halifax International Airport.

ESSENTIAL INFORMATION

Getting Around: HRM is geographically large, but the greater part of its population is clustered around Halifax Harbour. Its effective public transportation, therefore, is restricted to the urban core of Halifax, Bedford, and Dartmouth. Buses are reliable and affordable, but they will not reach all sites described herein (bus routes are illustrated in the phone book's Blue Pages). Passenger ferries operate between Halifax on the harbor's west side and Dartmouth and Woodside on the east side. Taxis are safe but expensive, so most visiting birders will find rental cars the best option. In the specific birding sites described farther on, travel times assume a rental car. Add 50 percent to travel times if driving at rush hour in urban areas, and 100 percent if riding public transit.

Climate: Halifax's climate is volatile, strongly influenced by the sea, which makes for exciting birding. Atlantic waters are relatively cold, thereby

151

cooling spring and summer temperatures, moderating those of winter, and prolonging autumn. January temperatures at Halifax Harbour range from -8° to 0°C (17° to 32°F), while July temperatures at the harbour range from 13° to 21°C (55° to 70°F). Precipitation can occur anytime; 15 percent occurs as snow during the winter months. Fog is frequent, especially mid-spring through early summer, but usually retreats to the outer coast during the day. Fog or cloud obscures the sun for half the daylight hours annually. Nova Scotia is the stormiest region of Canada, with the most intense frontal systems occurring usually in autumn and winter. One or more hurricanes (or remnants thereof) touch provincial waters annually, though landfall is rare.

Safety: HRM is a safe, friendly city. However, it is a port, so don't leave all your protective instincts at home. Lock your vehicle, and don't leave valuables in plain sight, especially when parking in more-isolated areas.

Natural Hazards: This is Canada—bring your DEET. Black Flies bite from May–July, mosquitoes from June–October, neither in appalling numbers, and they are worse inland and earlier in the season, except in saltmarshes. Breezy coasts are often bug-free. There are no disease-bearing ticks, poisonous snakes, or cantankerous wildlife. (Dog Ticks do occur south of HRM, from Lunenburg County to the Yarmouth area.) Black Bears are present but are rarely noted. During hunting season (October–January, Sundays excluded) stick to coastal areas, roads, established hiking trails, or public parks.

Other Resources: Books include *Atlas of Breeding Birds of the Maritime Provinces* by Tony Erskine (1992, Nimbus Publishing) and *Birds of Nova Scotia* by Robie W. Tufts (1986, Nimbus Publishing). These are also viewable on the web; see web sites below. *Birder's Guide to Nova Scotia* by Blake Maybank is scheduled to be published by Nimbus in late 2002.

Some important phone numbers are the Nova Scotia Bird Society Bird Information Line, (902) 852-2428; the Halifax Visitor Information Bureau, (902) 490-5946; Weather, Environment Canada, (902) 426-9090; the Nova Scotia Tourism Information and Reservations, (800) 565-0000; and Metro Ferry Information, (902) 461-9939. Helpful web sites are numerous:

Birds of Nova Scotia on-line, *www.museum.gov.ns.ca/mnh/nature/nsbirds/bons.htm*
Halifax Field Naturalists, *www.chebucto.ns.ca/Recreation/FieldNaturalists/field nat.html*
Halifax Municipality Visitor Info, *www.halifaxinfo.com*
Metro Transit System, *www.region.halifax.ns.ca*
Museum of Natural History, *www.museum. gov.ns.ca/mnh/*
Museum of Natural History Birds, *www.museum.gov.ns.ca/mnh/nature/ns birds/*
Nova Scotia Bird Society, *www.chebucto.ns.ca/Recreation/ NS_BirdSoc/*
Nova Scotia Checklist, *www3.ns.sympatico.ca/ns/maybank/NS-Checklist.htm*
Nova Scotia's Provincial Parks, *www.parks.gov.ns.ca/index.htm*
Nova Scotia Tourism, *www.exploreNS.com/*
Weather (Environment Canada), *www.ns.ec.gc.ca/weather/ns_fortxt.html*.

THE BIRDING YEAR

The seasons and accompanying avian movements are blurred; there is no quiet time to the birding year. Nearly 400 species have occurred in HRM. Treat the following as a generalization (listed species are reasonably common unless otherwise noted).

Resident Birds: The following resident birds excite many visitors' interest: Great Cormorant (easiest in winter), American Black Duck, Common Eider, Bald Eagle, Spruce Grouse (elusive), Black Guillemot, Black-backed Woodpecker (secretive), Boreal Chickadee, Gray Jay, and White-winged Crossbill (irregular).

Spring Migration, late February to early June: In spring, birders focus on the coast. Winter birds begin departing in March, gannets and scoters move north along the coast in April, and "southern" herons, such as Great and Snowy Egrets and Little Blue Herons, are regular overshoots. Vagrant passerine overshoots, including Blue Grosbeak, Indigo Bunting, and Orchard Oriole, tend to be found at feeders. In spring most migrants arrive during May and breed locally—fewer are passing through on their way farther north. Shorebirds are particularly scarce, unlike in autumn.

Breeding Season, late May through mid-July: In breeding season the focus shifts away from the coasts and into the interior forests. Twenty-two breeding warbler species highlight a diverse list. Popular migrant breeders include Osprey, Piping Plover (Martinique Beach), American Woodcock, Willet, Atlantic Puffin (Pearl Island), Northern Saw-whet Owl, Yellow-bellied Flycatcher, Alder Flycatcher, Cape May and Mourning Warblers, Nelson's Sharp-tailed Sparrow, "Ipswich" Savannah Sparrow (migrates through Martinique Beach en route to Sable Island, but a few oversummer), and Rusty Blackbird (uncommon).

Autumn Migration, late June through early December: This is the most exciting time of the Nova Scotia birding year. There are many shorebirds, including American Golden-Plover, Hudsonian Godwit, and White-rumped, Baird's, and Buff-breasted Sandpipers. American Pipits, Lapland Longspurs, and Snow Buntings pass through later in the season. Birders focus on coastal migrant traps (islands and peninsula tips). "Rarity season" peaks from early September through late October. While almost anything is possible, "routine" annual rarities include Western Kingbird, Philadelphia Vireo, Warbling Vireo, Blue-gray Gnatcatcher, Brown Thrasher, Prairie Warbler, Eastern Towhee, Clay-colored Sparrow, Lark Sparrow, Grasshopper Sparrow, Blue Grosbeak, Indigo Bunting, and Dickcissel. The full list of HRM's vagrant species is too long to mention, but some stellar sightings include Little Egret, Zone-tailed Hawk, European Golden-Plover, Little Stint, Broad-billed Sandpiper, Ross's Gull, Fork-tailed Flycatcher, Eurasian Jackdaw, Townsend's Solitaire, Bell's Vireo, Virginia's Warbler, Black-throated Gray Warbler, Brewer's Sparrow, Lark Bunting, Golden-crowned Sparrow, and Chaffinch.

Winter, December through March: The annual provincial winter species count averages 190. Many "winter" birds begin arriving in early October, such as grebes (Red-necked and Horned), Rough-legged Hawk, winter gulls (Black-headed, Iceland, Glaucous), Purple Sandpiper, and Bohemian Waxwing (irregular). Northern Shrikes arrive in late October. Easterly gales in winter will blow Thick-billed Murres and Dovekies to the near-shore, where they will linger for days. Scarce but regular winter birds include Eurasian Wigeon, Tufted Duck, Barrow's Goldeneye, Mew (Common) Gull, and Lesser Black-backed Gull. Some rare passerines are routinely attracted to feeders and the "warm" oases of urban gardens, including Red-bellied Woodpecker, Orange-crowned and Pine Warblers, Yellow-breasted Chat, Eastern Towhee, Dickcissel, and Baltimore Oriole. Northern Cardinals and House Finches are scarce residents, but are gradually increasing in numbers.

URBAN DESTINATIONS

Travel times are from downtown Halifax by car. When the word "bus" appears after travel times, it means that regular bus service is available. To orient to many sites, you'll need a Metro street map (a reasonable one is located in the phone book's Blue Pages). The Nova Scotia tourism department provides free provincial highway maps.

Point **Pleasant Park** (10 minutes, 30 on foot, bus) is located on the south end of peninsular Halifax, and access is free. Forest birding is best in the breeding season, whereas the ocean is most rewarding between October and April. The main gate is opposite the south end of Young Avenue, and a huge billboard map of the park is at the parking lot. The park is covered in mature conifers, primarily Red Spruce, and the previous clearing of the understory has left the forest unproductive for passerines, although planned cutting due to an exotic-insect infestation may improve this situation. The park is heavily used by walkers, less so on side trails. The best birding for now is along the shoreline, where loons, grebes, and alcids are regular in winter. An excellent sewage outfall is visible from the path along the southwest shore of the park, where hundreds of Iceland Gulls congregate throughout the winter, and Glaucous Gull is regular.

McNab's **Island** lies at the mouth of Halifax Harbour. It is public land—undeveloped—with many trails, and may become a provincial park. The island is large, and well wooded with conifers, offering good forest birding within sight of downtown Halifax and Dartmouth. Access is via boat—twice-daily water-taxis leave from downtown Halifax at Cable Wharf and Murphy's On The Water, or you can arrange transport to fit your schedule from McNab's Island Outfitters at Eastern Passage, (800) 326-4563. The island is worth a visit any time of year, but access is more difficult in winter. An island guidebook is available at local bookstores.

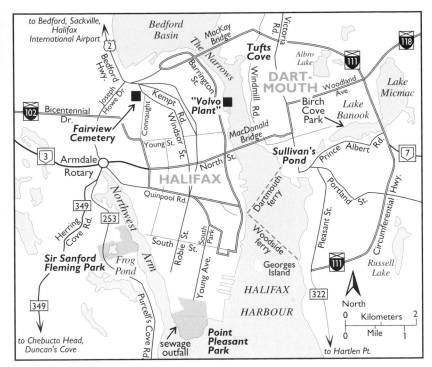

to Bedford, Sackville,
Halifax
International Airport

Bedford
Basin

Tufts
Cove

Albro
Lake

118

The Narrows

MacKay Bridge

Victoria Rd.

Bedford Hwy.

2

111

DART-
MOUTH

Woodland
Ave.

Lake
Micmac

Joseph Howe Dr.

Kempt Rd.

**"Volvo
Plant"**

Windmill Rd.

Birch
Cove
Park

Lake
Banook

102

Bicentennial
Dr.

Connaught

Windsor St.

MacDonald
Bridge

**Fairview
Cemetery**

Young St.

North St.

**Sullivan's
Pond**

Prince Albert Rd.

7

3

Armdale
Rotary

Quinpool Rd.

HALIFAX

Dartmouth ferry

Portland St.

Circumferential Hwy.

349

Northwest

253

South St.

Robie St.

South Park

Woodside ferry

Pleasant St.

111

Russell
Lake

Herring Cove Rd.

**Sir Sanford
Fleming Park**

Frog
Pond

Arm

Young Ave.

Georges
Island

349

Purcell's Cove Rd.

sewage
outfall

HALIFAX

HARBOUR

322

**Point
Pleasant
Park**

North

0   Kilometers   2

0   Mile   1

to Chebucto Head,
Duncan's Cove

to Hartlen Pt.

A fine sewage outfall is at **Richmond Terminal Pier** (10 minutes, bus), a site also known as **"The Volvo Plant"** (now gone). Follow the road downhill from the junction of Richmond Street and Barrington Street, turn left past the railway tracks, then right at the first buildings onto the wharf—the sewage outfall is close to shore, just over the wharf edge. From October through March this is a great place for Black-headed and Iceland Gulls, and occasionally for Lesser Black-backed, as well.

Fairview Cemetery (at Windsor Street and Kempt Road, entrance off Windsor, 15 minutes, bus), in addition to holding many victims of the *Titanic*, shelters autumn vagrants (e.g., Northern Mockingbird, Pine Warbler, once a Chaffinch). The best area is the wooded hillside along Windsor Street.

U rban Dartmouth offers several good sites for birding between November and March. **Tufts Cove**, viewable from Nootka Avenue off Windmill Road, is good for ducks, and Eurasian Wigeon is regular. Black-headed Gulls are common; they also feed at the sewage outfall off the power plant (scope needed), or roost on the playing fields adjacent to Nootka. **Sullivan's Pond**, bordered by Hawthorne Street, Crichton Avenue, and Prince Albert Road, is good for ducks and gulls, and Tufted Ducks have recently overwintered here. The brushy public area along the stream connecting the pond with upstream Lake Banook is good for passerines in late autumn. Nearby Birch Cove Park, off Crichton Avenue, is an autumn vagrant trap, as are surrounding streets. The tall conifers on Brookdale Court are frequented by Pine Warblers through the winter.

SUBURBAN DESTINATIONS
WEST OF HALIFAX HARBOUR

Sir Sanford Fleming Park (20 minutes, bus) is off Purcell's Cove Road. Birders also refer to it as "The Dingle" and "Frog Pond"; both sites are part of the park. There are trails for easy access. The forest is coniferous, and the pond has attracted vagrant herons. The park also borders the Northwest Arm of Halifax Harbour, where loons and grebes are regular in winter, and alcids (including Dovekie) have been spotted.

Chebucto Head (30 minutes) lies south of Portuguese Cove on Route 349 (take Herring Cove Road from the Armdale Rotary). Take the turn for Duncan's Cove and drive to the lighthouse—access is allowed. This is a sea-watch site, best in strong east or southeast winds in autumn and winter, but always worth a look for tubenoses, gulls, and alcids. A scope is essential. Nearby Duncan's Cove is a fine migrant trap—park on the road in the village (ask permission), as break-ins plague cars in the "designated" parking area uphill.

Few visitors to the province escape a visit to Peggy's Cove (60 minutes). Although it is an attractive area, some birders visit in June and July to take a half-day boat tour that visits nearby Pearl Island, the site of a small Atlantic Puffin colony (Peggy's Cove Water Tours, (902) 823-2349). En route to Peggy's Cove, check out the village of Prospect, at the end of Prospect Road off Route 333. Hike the trail at the end of Indian Point Road, and explore the stunning coastline and coastal barrens. Highlights include Fox Sparrow in summer, Whimbrel in autumn, and Harlequin Duck in winter.

SUBURBAN DESTINATIONS
EAST OF HALIFAX HARBOUR

Hartlen Point is 35 minutes from downtown Halifax. Follow Route 322 from downtown Dartmouth south to Eastern Passage, turn onto Shore Road, and follow it to the Hartlen Point Golf Course. Buses go as far as Shore Road and Caldwell—a two-kilometer walk remains.

Hartlen Point, guarding the northern entrance to Halifax Harbour, is a year-round destination and is generally considered the best mainland migrant trap in Nova Scotia. (Cape Sable Island in southern Nova Scotia, although

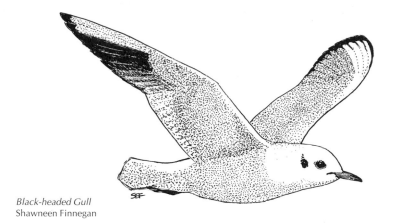

Black-headed Gull
Shawneen Finnegan

accessible via a causeway, is still considered an island.) Hartlen Point extends well out into the Atlantic, with a diversity of productive habitat that ties down migrant birds. Hartlen Point Golf Course also aids this process, its fairways a disincentive for quick dispersal. Habitats include mudflats, cobble beaches, alder thickets, a spruce bog, small hardwood groves, and the golf course. All of Hartlen Point belongs to the Department of Defence. Access by birders is tolerated, and even welcomed, as our presence discourages illegal hunting. Always yield the right-of-way to golfers.

Compared to downtown Halifax, Hartlen Point will be cooler, windier, and often foggier, the latter especially in spring through autumn during south or southwest winds. Resident birds are few in number; Boreal Chickadee is the most sought-after and encountered on every trip. But Hartlen is really a place for migrants, not for breeders.

In March-April, during spring waterfowl migration, the ocean is the focus. Scoters, Long-tailed Ducks, Common Eiders, and Red-breasted Mergansers can be abundant, and Double-crested Cormorants and Northern Gannets fly past. Inland is relatively quiet.

From late April through May, typical of Nova Scotia in general, there are few major movements of spring landbird migrants. In particular, northbound shorebirds are almost completely absent. The Main Beach and Back Cove are still worth checking, as migrants and vagrants do appear. With such birds as European Golden-Plover on the books, Hartlen Point should not be ignored in spring.

Local birders seldom bother with Hartlen from June to mid-July, but visiting birders might like to seek out Alder Flycatcher, Boreal Chickadee, Tennessee and Nashville Warblers, and Nelson's Sharp-tailed Sparrow, all of which are fairly common. Spruce Grouse, by contrast, are rare, and White-winged Crossbills are erratic.

Birding picks up in mid-summer. Shorebirds are a prime autumn attraction along the beach, Back Cove, and the fairways. The beach is best; check gravel bars as the tide exposes them, and closely examine accumulations of storm-blown seaweed. Shorebird numbers peak in August–September, and although flocks rarely exceed several hundred birds, a fine diversity occurs, and extraordinary rarities have appeared, including Little Stint and Broad-billed Sandpiper.

Large plovers favor the fairways, particularly when rain keeps the golfers at bay. During most years a few Buff-breasted Sandpipers pass through as well, usually in September. Back Cove holds fewer shorebirds, but it always bears checking, since the province's first Spotted Redshank was found here, and lesser lights have included Ruff.

With landbirds, anything is possible. Unusual species can occur at any time, but they are more likely following sustained winds with a westerly component. They can occur anywhere, but Back Cove is the favored locale. Seek out chickadee flocks. Expect the unexpected. A partial list of vagrants includes Boreal Owl, White-eyed and Yellow-throated Vireos, Mountain Bluebird, Northern Wheatear, Townsend's, Cerulean, Kentucky, and Connecticut Warblers, Western Tanager, Brewer's Sparrow, and Lark Bunting.

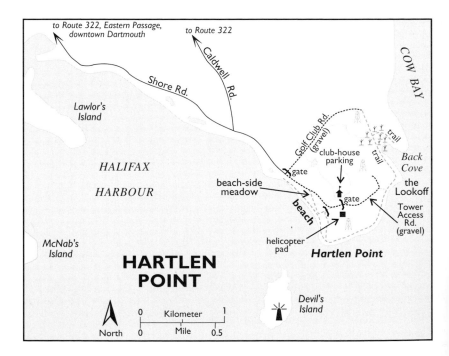

After mid-November Hartlen quiets somewhat. Small flocks of sparrows are found along the shoreline, and a few American Pipits try to over-winter. Gulls cruise up and down the tide line, with Iceland Gulls common and Black-headed Gulls regular. Rough-legged Hawks and Purple Sandpipers are intermittently present. In winter, the sea is the attraction, where loons, grebes, sea ducks, and alcids can be seen feeding or flying into and out of Halifax Harbour.

Hartlen Point begins when you arrive at the golf course. Golf Club Road is a gated gravel road to the east of Shore Road that cuts across two fairways to the northernmost tower, near the head of Back Cove, and continues to join with Back Cove Trail. This 1.5-kilometer road can be hiked at any time (yield to golfers!). The habitat is scrubby spruce, wet tamarack bog, deciduous patches, and fairways. Don't drive the road if the gate is open, lest you risk being locked in.

The beach extends from opposite the Old Club House Road to The Point. Devil's Island is visible to the south. A wet meadow lies between the road and the beach, with sedges, cattails, and a narrow stream mid-way. North-end beach access across the meadow is via two short, rough gravel roads.

The golf course occupies most of Hartlen Point. During golfing season (May–October) birders may use the club-house parking lot; park near the entrance gate. (The club's sewage settling-pond is just west of the lot and should be quickly checked for ducks.) When the course is closed, the lot is gated, so park on the road edge.

Where Shore Road turns sharply away from the Beach, a rough, gated gravel road leads to the beach. The left fork leads to the Point. The Lookoff Trail extends for 1 kilometer along the shore from the Point to the **Lookoff**. Along the way there is a gradual increase in the near-shore elevation, from near sea level to 10 meters.

Shortly past the parking lot, Shore Road ends at a locked gate. This is the **Tower Access Road**, which goes to the Lookoff, and then northwest to the middle communications tower. The Back Cove Trail runs from the Lookoff to the southern mouth of Back Cove and then continues just inland of the Back Cove shoreline around to the northern mouth of the Cove. For most of the inner portion of the Cove the trail is screened from the water and the saltmarsh by deciduous shrubs and trees. Look carefully for three different rough paths that provide access to the shoreline of inner Back Cove. Back Cove Trail is joined at its apex by the Golf Club Road. Along the eastern side of Back Cove, a short trail leads to a golf-cart path linking the two holes that run along the middle of the peninsula. There is a portable toilet here for golfers, and birders have been allowed to use it.

Back Cove is the hot-spot of Hartlen Point, especially during fall migration. A semicircular rocky reef, covered only at high tide, protects the cove from waves. The head of Back Cove is a marsh, bisected by a stream, with extensive mudflats where the stream flows into the cove. The stream-bed is treacherously muddy, and no attempt should be made to cross it; to reach both sides of the marsh, you'll have to use paths off the Back Cove Trail. The inner part of the marsh is less saline and supports a spreading cattail patch. Back Cove is also blessed by an abundance of birch, alder, aspen, and willow that host many passerines.

The future **Cole Harbour Provincial Park** (25 minutes, bus) is accessible off Bissett Road, opposite the Nova Scotia Rehabilitation Centre (slated for closure). These 300 acres provide the best landbird diversity close to Halifax. A parking lot and a trailhead are adjacent to the large barn opposite the Rehab Centre. Just a few minutes farther south on Bissett Road is the start of the **Cole Harbour Rail Trail**, a 7-kilometer hike (one-way) across the back of Cole Harbour to West Lawrencetown. Forests are productive at either end, but the best feature is the mudflats during southbound shorebird migration. Note that the tide in the estuary lags two to three hours behind Halifax Harbour.

The best pure boreal habitat close to Halifax Harbour is along **Mines Road** (50 minutes). Take Highway 107 to its end, turn right on Route 7, and right again on West Petpeswick Road. One kilometer before the road ends, turn right on the 5-kilometer-long gravel-surface Mines Road, best in breeding season but often good in autumn migration. The road is sometimes rough (but navigable) and is rarely traveled. Spruce Grouse, Black-backed Woodpecker, Gray Jay, and Boreal Chickadee are resident, and all the finches can occur. Yellow-bellied and Alder Flycatchers breed, as do Tennessee and Blackburnian Warblers (among the 20 species of warblers here). At the western end of the road, turn right to return to Highway 107.

Martinique Beach (60 minutes), at the end of East Petpeswick Road leading from the town of Musquodoboit Harbour, is a wildlife sanctuary popular with waterfowl in spring and autumn. It's a reliable spot for migrant "Ipswich" Savannah Sparrows breeding on offshore Sable Island, and Piping Plovers are here as well. It's good in all seasons and isn't crowded, even in summer.

A full day is needed to visit **Taylor Head Provincial Park**, off Route 7 east of Halifax (two hours). The park road is ungated only from late May to the second weekend in October, but it is wonderful for coniferous-forest breeding birds, migrant seabirds, and autumn shorebirds. At other times the park is rewarding but requires a 5-kilometer walk one way, through mature spruce forest.

NEAR HALIFAX INTERNATIONAL AIRPORT

If you are somewhat pressed for time, you can bird the edge of the boreal forest to the north of the airport parking lot. If you have a few hours (or more), rent a car, exit the airport, and turn left (before Highway 102) at the small sign for **Old Guysborough Road** (Route 212). After some odd turns the road eventually passes south of the airport and heads northeast toward Elderbank, some 25 kilometers distant. En route, it passes through field and forest, and skirts some small lakes. Traffic is light, although slightly heavier near the airport (which is noisy), and you can stop wherever you please. American Woodcocks and Northern Saw-whet Owls breed, as do many warblers and sparrows. Hay fields have Bobolinks, and the marsh just before Elderbank has American Bitterns. **Dollar Lake Provincial Park** is a worthwhile stop en route, with picnic sites, washrooms, and trails. The park is closed mid-October to mid-May (although you can still walk in).

FARTHER AFIELD

Brier Island is a four-to-five-hour drive southwest from Halifax, and is not only a superb year-round birding destination, but also the embarkation point for whale- and seabird-watching tours from June–October (Mariner Cruises, (800) 239-2189). Expect Greater, Sooty, and Manx Shearwaters, Wilson's Storm-Petrel, jaegers, South Polar Skua (Great Skua from late September onward), Razorbill, and Atlantic Puffin.

Cape Sable Island lies three hours south of Halifax and is an exceptional year-round site, with shorebird and passerine migrations a specialty, and, recently, is the site of Canada's only breeding American Oystercatchers. There is no finer accessible vagrant trap in Nova Scotia.

Cape Breton Island is a three-hour drive north from Halifax. Two or more days are needed just to start sampling its delights, including the Bird Islands Seabird Sanctuary (Great Cormorants, Black-legged Kittiwakes, Razorbills, Atlantic Puffins) and the world-famous Cabot Trail, which passes through Cape Breton Highlands National Park (breeding Northern Hawk Owls, rare, and Bicknell's Thrushes).

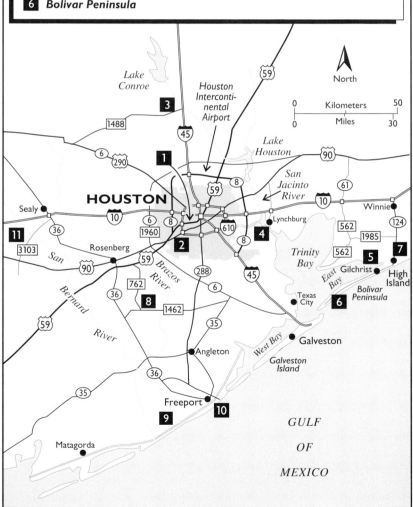

HOUSTON AREA BIRDING SITES

1 *Houston Arboretum/ Memorial Park*

2 *Russ Pittman Park and Discovery Nature Center*

3 *Jones State Forest*

4 *San Jacinto Battleground and State Park*

5 *Anahuac NWR*

6 *Bolivar Peninsula*

7 *High Island*

8 *Brazos Bend State Park*

9 *San Bernard NWR*

10 *Quintana*

11 *Attwater Prairie-Chicken NWR*

Lake Conroe

3

1488

Houston Intercontinental Airport

45

6   290

1

HOUSTON

Lake Houston

90

San Jacinto River

8

59

8

610

10

61

Winnie

Sealy

10

6   8

1960

2

Lynchburg

4

562

124

562

5

7

11

3103

36

San

Rosenberg

59

Bernard

Brazos River

288

6

45

Trinity Bay

East Bay

Gilchrist

High Island

90

762

36

8

1462

35

6

Texas City

Bolivar Peninsula

6

River

59

Angleton

West Bay

Galveston

Galveston Island

35

36

Freeport

10

9

Matagorda

GULF

OF

MEXICO

North

0   Kilometers   50

0   Miles   30

HOUSTON, TEXAS

David Sarkozi

L*ocation, location, location* rings as true for the birder as for a realtor. Situated 50 miles from the Gulf of Mexico along one of the great migration routes, the Houston area has recorded over 450 species of birds. Less than one hour's drive from downtown Houston you can find hardwood forest, pine forest, cypress swamps, vast marshes and prairies, sheltered bays, estuaries, extensive mudflats, and the open Gulf of Mexico. The city itself has some fine large parks, neighborhoods with old Live Oaks, and large greenways tracing the routes of the old bayous.

ESSENTIAL INFORMATION

Getting Around: Houston has a good public bus system, and the birding destinations in the city are reachable by bus. Taxis are plentiful in Houston; they are not typically hailed off the street but are called by telephone. Reliability is not great, with taxis arriving late or not at all; I do not recommend them for the visiting birder. Car rentals are widely available, and there are many rental locations scattered about town well away from the airports. An added plus is that many of the rental agencies will pick you up and drop you off. This is not a universal service but is available and worth asking about.

Houston has some of the worst traffic in the United States. Everything in Texas is bigger, and that includes rush hour, which is more like rush three-hours. Morning traffic is heaviest from about 7:00 to 8:30AM, and afternoon traffic is worse, from about 4:00 to 6:00PM. Houston's five-lane highways operate at capacity during these hours, and any "disturbance" such as construction (a perpetual state at least on I-45) or a traffic accident can turn them into parking lots. Add at least thirty minutes to your travel time during these hours if you're traveling inside Inner Loop 610.

Climate: Houston has three pleasant seasons, weather-wise, and one that even the locals can barely endure. Spring (March to May) and fall (September to December) on the Upper Texas Coast (UTC) have some of the best weather for birding that you could wish for. By May one can expect daily temperatures in the 90s Fahrenheit, and in July and August 100° is not uncommon. Houston is famous for its double 90s: 90 degrees with 90 percent humidity. When birding during the warm months, be sure to have plenty to drink and wear clothes that are loose-fitting and light-colored. It is a good idea to wear long sleeves and a hat that provides plenty of shade for your head. If you are accustomed to more northerly latitudes, you might not realize just how easy it is to get a nasty, even dangerous, sunburn in the South. Sunscreen is a must for anyone out birding between late spring and early fall.

Winters on the Upper Texas Coast are usually mild. In many years freezing temperatures are not recorded. From November through February expect temperatures in the 30° to 40° range at night and daytime temperates up to 60°. Winter days can be blustery, however. Many a birder has found out the hard way just how chilly one can feel when a wet wind blows in across the wet marshes and prairies. Plan to dress in layers.

Safety: Outside of Houston proper you and your car are reasonably safe. Inside the city you should take all the standard precautions. Don't leave valuables in sight in your car; lock them in the trunk if possible. Don't bird in deserted urban locations by yourself, especially early and late in the day. This precaution holds for men as well as for women.

Natural Hazards: Houston and the Upper Texas Coast are Bug Central. Most birding locations are loaded with horrendous numbers of mosquitoes. Insect repellent is a must most of the time. If flies are a problem, you may have to reapply your repellent often. Long sleeves are a good idea, in terms of protection both from insects and from the sun. Grassy fields can have ticks and their microscopic mite cousin the chigger, especially if there are cattle present. A few chigger bites can make you pretty miserable, producing large and very itchy welts that persist for days or even weeks. If you should find yourself burdened by these nuisances, try one of the 10-percent hydrocortisone creams on the market. They will stop the itching, and if applied regularly for a couple of days will reduce the welts. Tucking pants into your socks and spraying liberally with insect repellent or sulfur powder will help guard against ticks and chiggers. Fortunately, Lyme disease is rare in Texas.

Other Resources: Texas Parks and Wildlife and the Texas Department of Transportation have teamed up to create the Great Texas Coastal Birding Trail. This driving trail stretches from the Louisiana border to Brownsville in thrsee sections. The Upper Texas Coast section has nearly two hundred sites listed. Copies of the site guide and trail map can be obtained by calling, toll-free, (888) TXBIRDS. The Houston Audubon Society web site has excellent maps of Houston area birding sites, including the sanctuaries at High Island as well as Bolivar Peninsula (*www.houstonaudubon.org*). For a thorough treatment of the Upper Texas Coast also consult the ABA/Lane birdfinding guide *A Birder's Guide to the Texas Coast* by Harold Holt (1993); it also has detailed maps for some of the sites mentioned in this chapter.

THE BIRDING YEAR

The spring birding season begins when Neotropical migrants start returning to the Upper Texas Coast in late March. Early warblers include Northern Parula, Yellow-throated, Swainson's, and Kentucky. Local birders mass at area migrant traps during April. Checking the weather forecasts and your accumulated sick-time becomes a ritual. A cold front and/or rain that extend out into the Gulf of Mexico may produce a fall-out of migrants, at which time hundreds or even thousands of vireos, thrushes, warblers, tanagers, buntings, orioles, and other Neotropical migrants make emergency landings after a difficult crossing of the Gulf.

For many birders, the end of April is the end of spring migration. The birder who doesn't venture out during the first half of May, however, is missing a lot of good birding. Frontal passages can produce plenty of migrants both along the coast and well inland. Shorebirding can be excellent almost to June; mudflats on the coast and rice fields east and west of Houston host large concentrations.

Summer can be hot, muggy, and buggy, but before the middle of July the shorebirds are returning. Look for Magnificent Frigatebirds along the coast and post-breeding Wood Storks inland. By August the trickle of shorebirds turns into a steady stream. The end of summer birding is marked by the mass staging of Purple Martins. In late July and August martins roost in huge flocks of up to 100,000 birds. Exact roost sites change from year to year, so contacting local birders is a good way to find out current roost locations.

By Labor Day fall migrants are returning to the migrant traps. First come the flycatchers (including a better number and selection of *Empidonax* than in spring), then the warblers and the orioles. Fall is the best time for finding some of the rarer migrants, such as Swallow-tailed Kite and Black-throated Blue Warbler. Migration lasts into November and ends with the skeins of Snow and Greater White-fronted Geese arriving on the prairies.

Winter is the time of waterfowl, when the Central Flyway dumps millions of ducks and geese onto the coastal prairie. Hawks and sparrows become abundant, and driving back-county roads looking for them is a popular birding excursion at this time of year. Early winter is also the time for the annual Christmas Bird Counts. There are about 20 counts in the Houston area every year, virtually one on every day of the count season. Texans are known for their friendliness, and it is possible to join every count in the area. Several of the counts (e.g., Mad Island Marsh, Freeport, and Bolivar Peninsula) annually finish in the top ten in the U.S.

THE HOUSTON ARBORETUM
AND NATURE CENTER

Several hours; year round

Located in Houston's Memorial Park at 4501 Woodway, (713) 681-8433, the **Houston Arbotetum** is 15 minutes from downtown, 30 minutes from Intercontinental Airport, 30 minutes from Hobby Airport, and is a worthwhile several-hour visit. It consists of 155 acres of forest, pond, and prairie habitats. The dense vegetation screens the five miles of foot trails and makes it possible to forget that you are next to one of Houston's major highways. In summer some of the trails may be closed because of mosquitoes; bring insect repellent. The Arboretum and Memorial Park are a remnant patch of mixed southeastern pine/hardwood forest. Birds typical of the Pineywoods of east Texas can be found here in the spring and summer. Acadian Flycatcher, White-eyed, Yellow-throated, and Red-eyed Vireos, Wood Thrush, Pine, Swainson's, Kentucky, and Hooded Warblers, and Summer Tanager are fairly easy to find. The pond habitats harbor such birds as Yellow-crowned Night-Heron and White Ibis.

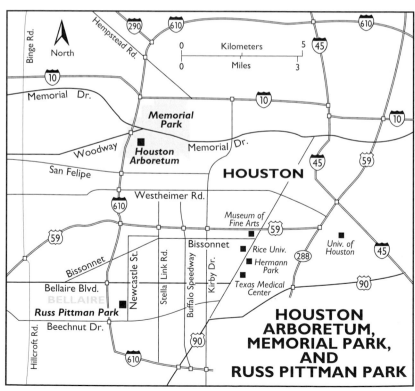

HOUSTON
ARBORETUM,
MEMORIAL PARK,
AND
RUSS PITTMAN PARK

A demonstration prairie was created when pine beetles killed the trees on the site. (There was once a natural Gulf Coast prairie on this site until pine trees moved in.) In this open area expect Eastern Kingbirds in spring and summer and sparrows in winter. In spring, the woods can be a great place for migrant songbirds. There are days when close to 20 warbler species can be found. In fall, the woods are often used as a roost for southbound migrant Mississippi Kites and Broad-winged Hawks.

Russ Pittman Park and **Discovery Nature Center** (7112 Newcastle Street in Bellaire, (713) 667-6550) are 15 minutes from downtown, 30 minutes from Intercontinental Airport, and 30 minutes from Hobby Airport. This small park has developed a reputation as a good spot to see migrants during the spring and fall. Many people have lunch with the birds and spend an hour or two birding the park. Ten or more species of warblers are regularly found on a visit during migration. Eastern Screech-Owls are resident in the park, and staff can often direct you to a spot from which to view a roosting owl. The park also has a growing reputation as a site for winter hummingbirds. It is well stocked with hummingbird feeders, which are kept filled all winter. Special attention also has been given to growing plants attractive to humming-birds. As many as five species may be present at one time, including Buff-bellied, Ruby-throated, Black-chinned, Broad-tailed, and Rufous. Rarer still, Allen's and Anna's have made appearances.

W.G. JONES STATE FOREST

Several hours; year round

W. G. Jones State Forest can be reached from Houston by traveling north on I-45 for 30 miles to FM-1488. Go west (left) on FM-1488 about two miles to the headquarters on the right side of the road. The main part of the park is on the south (left) side of the road. This is one of the easiest places in Texas to see Red-cockaded Woodpecker, and Brown-headed Nuthatch is resident in the park. In winter they may be joined by Red-breasted and White-breasted Nuthatches. Wood Thrush, Pine Warbler, Louisiana Waterthrush, Hooded Warbler, Yellow-breasted Chat, and Summer Tanager are common nesters. Eight species of woodpeckers are possible. There are several small lakes in the park, and Anhinga and Wood Duck are usually present year round.

The best way to see the Red-cockaded Woodpeckers is to visit on a weekday and pick up a map of the colonies at the headquarters. If you can't visit on a weekday, follow these directions. From I-45 go west on FM-1488 about one mile to the second road on the left (this is the first *paved* road on the left). Just after you turn onto this road turn left again onto the first dirt road. Just before you get to a T-intersection, park and walk to the T. Turn left and go about 200 yards to the nest trees (they are marked with rings of green paint) on the west side of the road. The best times to see the

Red-cockaded Woodpeckers are at dawn and dusk. The birds are out foraging during the day, but they return to the colony to roost. Even if you can't visit at dawn or dusk, with some effort you can usually find the woodpeckers foraging in the general area of a colony.

SAN JACINTO BATTLEGROUND AND STATE PARK

Several hours; year round

From Houston take I-10 east approximately 25 miles to the San Jacinto River. Once over the bridge take Lynchburg Road to the free ferry across the ship channel to the park entrance. The south end of the park is the best birding area. From July to October there are usually Wood Storks present, with the greatest numbers occurring in late summer (August). The park's location on Burnet Bay makes it a good migration stop in the spring. In winter, the park and Lynchburg Road are very good locations for Hooded Merganser and Osprey.

ANAHUAC NATIONAL WILDLIFE REFUGE

Half day; year round

Go east on I-10 from Houston for about 45 miles to the TX-61 exit. Head south to the intersection of TX-61 and TX-65. Continue straight though the intersection, where the road will change numbers to FM-562. Go another eight miles to FM-1985 and turn left. Continue about three miles to the main entrance of **Anahuac National Wildlife Refuge**. It takes at least a half-day to bird the whole refuge, but many birders make a quick pass around the best parts on their way to or from High Island.

Anahuac Refuge has two birdable tracts open to the public. The Old Anahuac Unit is the main tract and consists of most of the original purchase of the refuge. At 6,000 acres there is a lot to bird here. The hedgerows along the entrance road can be good for migrants during the spring. Those consisting of willow and hackberry host wintering Palm Warblers.

The **Shoveler Pond loop road** is the most popular part of the refuge. About a quarter-mile in on this loop there is a small stand of willows on your right. These trees often are full of migrants during the spring and fall. The small pond that they surround often has a small alligator or two. Continue to the Shoveler Pond impoundment, which the road circles. Water levels in the impoundment vary greatly. This is a good spot for herons. During the spring and summer you should be able to find several Least Bitterns; one of the best strategies for seeing one is to watch from the

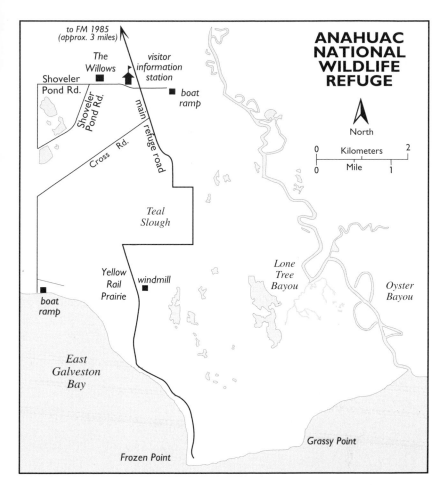

to FM 1985
(approx. 3 miles)

The
Willows

Shoveler
Pond Rd.

Shoveler
Pond Rd.

Cross Rd.

main refuge road

visitor
information
station

boat
ramp

**ANAHUAC
NATIONAL
WILDLIFE
REFUGE**

North

0 ___ Kilometers ___ 2

0 ___ Mile ___ 1

Teal
Slough

Yellow
Rail
Prairie

windmill

Lone
Tree
Bayou

Oyster
Bayou

boat
ramp

East
Galveston
Bay

Grassy Point

Frozen Point

observation platform on the east side of the loop. Purple Gallinule is reliable here in spring and summer. During migration, Virginia Rail and Sora can be numerous. King Rails are expected here, as well. In winter there can be large numbers of ducks visible from the observation platform. In spring and fall Fulvous Whistling-Ducks are usually present. Look here also for White and White-faced Ibises and Roseate Spoonbill. Glossy Ibis is scarce, but expected, in spring and summer. The tall patches of cattail and cane are full of Marsh Wrens in spring and summer. Their gurgling song is ubiquitous. A few Sedge Wrens occur in winter and spring.

Return to the main refuge road and turn south, then turn right onto the next road, Cross Road. The prairie fields on both sides of this road host nesting Dickcissels. At the end of the road turn left and continue down to East Galveston Bay. As you get closer to the bay, watch the canal on your left for Clapper Rails. There is a small earthen observation platform here.

From this platform scan the bay for grebes, pelicans, and ducks. In July and August, Wood Storks use the marshes behind the bay, and usually you can see a few from here. From the boat ramp there is a gravel road going to an old outbuilding. Along this road is an easy place to find a Seaside Sparrow, resident year round. Sedge Wren is common here in the winter and is quite vocal during April before departing.

Return to the main refuge road, turn right (south), and continue down to the bay. The road will zigzag a bit here. On the drive down you should be able to find a couple pairs of White-tailed Kites year round. The marshes on both sides of the road host wintering geese, including huge numbers of Snow Geese. Greater White-fronted, Ross's, and Canada Geese should also be present.

About one half mile before the bay you will see a windmill on the left side of the road and the entrance to the "Yellow Rail Prairie" on the right. Yellow Rails are present here from November through mid-April, but they can be very difficult to see. There are organized "rail walks" in the spring (late March through mid-April) that have a good success rate of seeing the birds. Check with the refuge office, (409) 267-3337, for the current schedule.

Seven miles east of the main refuge entrance on FM-1985 is the entrance to the **East Bay Bayou Tract**. This area features a wooded trail along the East Bay Bayou that can be good in spring migration, as well as several working rice fields. At least one rice field is flooded each spring for shorebirds and is good for Whimbrel, Hudsonian Godwit, and Buff-breasted Sandpiper. North of the refuge and FM-1985 there are numerous additional rice fields, which when flooded in spring are frequented by great numbers of shorebirds. In addition, there are several grazed short-grass fields along FM-1985 between FM-562 and TX-124 that host migrant American Golden-Plovers and Upland Sandpipers in spring.

THE BOLIVAR PENINSULA AND HIGH ISLAND

Half to full day; year round

To reach the **Bolivar Flats Shorebird Sanctuary** from Galveston take the free ferry across the channel to Port Bolivar and follow TX-87 about three miles to Loop 108. Turn right on Rettilon Road to the beach. Turn right on the beach, following the well-packed tracks to avoid getting stuck. Go about 3/4 mile to the sanctuary entrance at the telephone poles in the sand.

Bolivar Flats is one of the best shorebird spots in Texas. Created by the 100-year-old jetties that protect the entrance to Galveston Bay, it is a great expanse of accessible mudflats. The multitudes of herons, shorebirds, gulls,

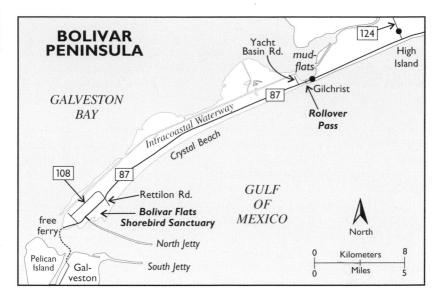

BOLIVAR PENINSULA

GALVESTON BAY

Yacht Basin Rd.

mud-flats

124

High Island

Intracoastal Waterway

87

Gilchrist

Rollover Pass

Crystal Beach

108

87

GULF OF MEXICO

Rettilon Rd.

Bolivar Flats Shorebird Sanctuary

free ferry

North Jetty

North

Pelican Island

Gal-veston

South Jetty

0   Kilometers   8

0   Miles   5

and terns include permanent and winter residents as well as migrants. Year round you can usually find Brown Pelicans, Reddish Egrets, and Roseate Spoonbills. In late summer and early fall look for Magnificent Frigatebirds. In the winter and early spring look for rare-but-regular Pomarine and Parasitic Jaegers. Except in the breeding season you can usually count on Black-bellied, Snowy, Wilson's, Semipalmated, and Piping Plovers. During migration, many species of shorebirds may blanket the flats. Willet, Ruddy Turnstone, Red Knot, Sanderling, Semipalmated, Western, and Least Sandpipers, and Dunlin are usually common. Good numbers of yellowlegs, Long-billed Curlews, Marbled Godwits, Stilt Sandpipers, and dowitchers can be expected some of the time. In winter and spring, great flocks of American Avocets are present. Look also for grebes and ducks in the calmer waters near the jetty. Surf Scoters are usually present in spring. At least ten species of gulls have been observed on the flats, including rarities such as California, Thayer's, Lesser Black-backed, Glaucous, Great Black-backed, and the state's first Kelp Gull. Nine species of terns have been observed, including Gull-billed, Sandwich, Least, and, rarely, Sooty..

Don't forget to check the *Spartina* grass behind the point. Here, Clapper Rail and Seaside Sparrow are residents, and in the winter and early spring they are joined by Sedge Wren and Nelson's Sharp-tailed and Le Conte's Sparrows. In the open areas, Horned Larks are present year round. Other birds to watch for in winter are Northern Harrier (common), Merlin, Peregrine Falcon (often seen on the flats), and Short-eared Owl (scarce).

About 14 miles east from the entrance to Bolivar Flats is Rollover Pass and Yacht Basin Road. **Rollover Pass** is an artificial cut in the Bolivar Peninsula. The south side offers good views of the Gulf of Mexico. This can be a good spot for jaegers, particularly when shrimpers are working close to shore and there are large gull flocks following the boats. In summer, scan here for Magnificent Frigatebirds. In the winter search for Northern Gannets and scoters. The bay side of the Pass has extensive mudflats. This is a good spot for Reddish Egret (year round) and Marbled Godwit (September through April). Large numbers of gulls and terns congregate here. All of the small plovers and sandpipers are present in season.

Yacht Basin Road is on the north side of the road about a quarter-mile west of the pass. This short road passes through some saline flats and *Spartina* grass. The flats are great in the spring for Whimbrels and Long-billed Curlews. Seaside Sparrows are present and will respond well to pishing. The ditches have large numbers of crabs, and Clapper Rails are easy to see. The end of the road offers a good view of several dredge-spoil islands, which support American Oystercatchers. Least and Black Terns are often found cruising the Intracoastal Waterway during the late summer.

High Island Bird Sanctuary is composed of four facilities maintained by the Houston Audubon Society at High Island; excellent maps are available at the society's web site, *www.houstonaudubon.org*. A small fee of $5 per day is good for all four sanctuaries; season passes are available. There is also a small sanctuary owned by the Texas Ornithological Society.

High Island is a legend in the birding world, famous for spring fall-outs of warblers and other migrant passerines. During spring migration (late March through the first week of May) when north winds or rain make the flight across the Gulf of Mexico difficult, great numbers of Neotropical migrants stop to rest at this "island of trees" on the coastal plain. High Island is built on top of a salt dome and is the only ground for many miles that is high enough and dry enough to support large numbers of trees. When the wind comes from the south, very few birds stop at High Island but continue onward and disperse north of I-10. On these days when you are seeing only a few migrants, remind yourself how many birds were able to safely complete the hazardous crossing of the Gulf of Mexico that day!

High Island is also excellent for fall migrants. At times you can have the sanctuaries to yourself and have lots of birds (especially when winds from the south bottle up migrants). Late September is the best time, but birding will be good between Labor Day and early November. Some of the hard-to-find migrants on the Upper Texas Coast are more common in the fall, such as a variety of *Empidonax* flycatchers and Black-throated Blue and Prairie Warblers.

Louis Smith Woods, also known as **Boy Scout Woods**, is located on 5th Street one block east of the Post Office and TX-124. Please park *only* in the parking lot and respect the residents of High Island by not blocking driveways. This sanctuary has good boardwalks and access for handicapped birders. **Smith Oaks**, the largest of the four sanctuaries, is on Old Mexico

Road on the north edge of town. During the spring migration please follow the signs to the parking lot on the south side of the sanctuary. This sanctuary has been expanded recently, and many improvements are being made. Boardwalks are being built, but most of the sanctuary does not have good access for the handicapped.

On spring weekends there are often hundreds of birders in town. If you don't like crowds, try visiting during the week. It's never very busy during the fall, and completely empty in winter. Spring is mosquito season, so bring your repellent, especially for use in Smith Oaks. In summer, birding is slow and the biting flies can be bad.

BRAZOS BEND STATE PARK

Half day; year round

To get to **Brazos Bend State Park** from Houston head south on TX-288 for 30 miles to the Rosharon exit. Turn right on FM-1462 and go about 10 miles to FM-762 and turn right. Go about one mile to the park entrance on the right. An alternate route is to take US-59 west from Houston to about one mile west of the Brazos River and FM-2759, where you drive south about one mile to FM-762, and then south on FM-762 about 12 miles to the park entrance on the left.

If your time is limited, head straight for the lake trails. Elm Lake and Forty-Acre Lake are very good for waterbirds. Reddish Egret is the only heron that I have not seen in the park, and it is not unusual to see all the rest in a single day (including the two bitterns). Anhingas are common year-round residents. Forty-Acre, Elm, and Pilant Lakes are the best places in the Houston area to see Black-bellied Whistling-Ducks (resident). Wood Duck, Mottled Duck, and Blue-winged Teal also nest in the park. Pilant Lake is also a reliable place to find Cinnamon Teal during the winter. Seeing ten species of ducks here is not unusual on a winter's day. Bald Eagles are regular winter visitors. Mississippi Kites and Red-shouldered Hawks nest in the park. On the farm roads west of the park Crested Caracaras are fairly common. Eastern Bluebirds, Prothonotary Warblers, Painted and Indigo Buntings, and Orchard Orioles are some of the common nesting passerines. The trail between the lakes is very good for Prothonotary Warblers from late March through August.

Hale Lake is good for seeing Northern Parula, and Pileated Woodpeckers, common in most of the park, seem even more so here. Last is the Creekfield Trail, which was one of the first handicap-access nature trails in the state. Paved trails and boardwalks go around and over Creekfield Lake and past the George Observatory. Birds here are much the same as at Elm and Forty-Acre Lakes, but the vegetation is denser so the visibility not as good.

Brazos Bend is one of the best places to see an alligator up close. It's not unusual to see them sunning on the shore 15 feet off the trail. They often don't move for hours (even days), but when they do, their speed is astonishing.

SAN BERNARD NATIONAL WILDLIFE REFUGE

Half day; year round

From Houston take TX-288 south to Lake Jackson. Go west on FM-2004 about 5 miles to TX-36 and FM-2611. Continue straight through the intersection onto FM-2611. Approximately one mile after the San Bernard River turn left on FM-2918. Go about one mile and turn right on the gravel CR-306 and continue another mile or so to the refuge entrance. The refuge is open daily from sunrise to sunset. Only about 20 percent of the refuge is accessible by car. Lots of water and trees means that mosquitoes can be bad here, even in winter. In summer, flies are a problem. Don't even roll your windows down before putting on the repellent!

Thousands of geese and ducks and many Sandhill Cranes make the refuge their winter home. The refuge is also a very good place to find Crested Caracara. The loop around Moccasin Pond is good for herons and waterfowl. During August and September expect to find Wood Storks. There are willows along the southern side of the loop where Barred Owls can be found roosting. During migration there should be some migrants here.

Along the slough across from the entrance to Moccasin Pond is the parking area for the foot trails into the woods. These trails can be very good for migrants in both spring and fall, and for Painted Bunting. About a half-mile past the entrance to the Moccasin Pond Loop is the Scissortail Trail Birding Loop. This trail passes through some dense brush and small woods and can be very good in migration. The road ends at a boat ramp at Cedar Creek. There are several oil-field roads off of the refuge road. Not all are passable or open to the public. Be careful and obey the signs.

QUINTANA

Half day; spring, fall, and winter

To reach **Quintana** take TX-288 south from Houston to Freeport. Continue on TX-288 to TX-36 and turn left (east). Go to the T-intersection and turn right. Cross the swing bridge (free) and turn left at the first stop sign. Continue about two miles to the small village of Quintana. The Quintana Neotropical Bird Sanctuary is located on this road directly across the street from the blue City Hall building. The Xeriscape Park is located two blocks north of this park.

The village of Quintana and its two parks have become hot-spots for neotropical migrants. These small woodlots can pack in a lot of birds in the spring and fall, and they seem to get more than their share of rarities, such as Black-whiskered and Yellow-green Vireos. The small size of the parks makes it an almost sure thing that a rarity will be detected if one is present.

In winter, check the Quintana Jetty, which has a paved walkway out to the end. From the end of the jetty, Northern Gannets and hard-to-find sea ducks such as scoters may be found. Check the Saltcedars along the entrance road to the jetty; Barn Owls often roost in them. To reach the jetty parking area continue on the main road past the City Hall building to the T-intersection and turn right. Just before the gated entrance to Quintana County Park turn left and follow the road to the base of the jetty.

ATTWATER PRAIRIE-CHICKEN NATIONAL WILDIFE REFUGE

Half to full day; spring, fall, and winter

To reach **Attwater Prairie-Chicken National Wildlife Refuge** head west from Houston on I-10 for 50 miles to Sealy, then go south on TX-36 about 2 miles to FM-3103. Turn right (west) on FM-3103 and continue about eight miles to the refuge entrance, which is just west of the San Bernard River, on the right. The refuge is open daily from dawn to dusk. Most of it is closed to the public to protect the few remaining prairie-chickens on the refuge, but the open sections can still be very productive. It is one of the best places to find resident White-tailed Hawk and Crested Caracara. During winter, Bald Eagles are often seen and Ferruginous Hawks are possible, as are Swainson's Hawks in spring and summer.

Sparrows abound; 19 species are listed on the refuge checklist. This is also a good spot for Sprague's Pipit in winter and early spring. Walking the mowed trails in the prairie areas at this season will usually produce some great looks at Le Conte's and Grasshopper Sparrows; watch also for the distinctive stair-step flight of Sprague's Pipit. The hedgerows along the fences harbor large numbers of White-throated and White-crowned Sparrows and the occasional Harris's.

Large numbers of waterfowl winter on the refuge. Teal Slough and Pintail Slough are often covered with grebes, geese, ducks, moorhens, and coots. Least Grebe appears to be regular here in the winter and spring. Watch the ditches along the roads for King Rails. Check along the river for the few woodland birds found on the refuge. Ash-throated Flycatchers and Fox Sparrows are regular in these woods in winter.

In spring, be sure to check shortgrass fields and stubble fields bordering the refuge for "grasspipers": American Golden-Plovers and Upland and Buff-breasted Sandpipers.

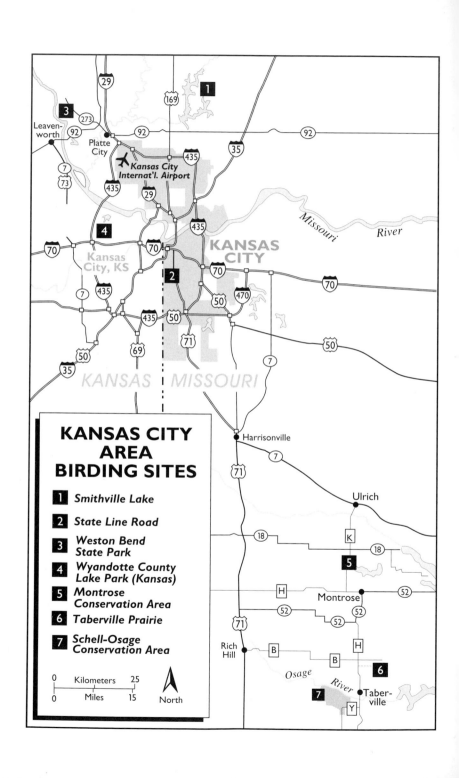

KANSAS CITY AREA BIRDING SITES

1 *Smithville Lake*

2 *State Line Road*

3 *Weston Bend State Park*

4 *Wyandotte County Lake Park (Kansas)*

5 *Montrose Conservation Area*

6 *Taberville Prairie*

7 *Schell-Osage Conservation Area*

0   Kilometers   25
0   Miles   15

North

KANSAS CITY, MISSOURI

Chris Hobbs

If St. Louis is the "Gateway to the West," then Kansas City is surely its ornithological crossroads. Bordered by tallgrass prairie to the west and south, glaciated plains to the north, and upland deciduous forest to the east, this friendly Midwestern city offers avian diversity which often comes as a pleasant surprise to visiting birders. Whether it's Great-tailed Grackle and Rusty Blackbird, Eastern and Spotted Towhees, or Black-capped and Carolina Chickadees, the Kansas City area offers subtle yet distinctive blends of birds and boundaries.

The Missouri River acts as a natural corridor for many migrant waterfowl, shorebirds, and passerines. Historically, it was an avenue for exploration of the West, beginning with Lewis and Clark In the early 1800s. During the spring of 1834, Thomas Nuttall and John Townsend traveled the "Mighty Mo" through Kansas City, where they collected and described science's first Harris's Sparrow. Many other species that primarily winter in, or migrate through, the interior of the country are regularly observed in the Kansas City area.

ESSENTIAL INFORMATION

Getting Around: Travelers typically fly into Kansas City International Airport, located 15 minutes north of downtown. A car is a necessity, and airline customers will find all major car-rental companies represented at the airport and at a few satellite offices in the suburbs. Cross-country travelers driving toward other destinations often pass through Kansas City, on either I-70 or I-35. All visitors to Kansas City will enjoy minimal traffic congestion, an uncomplicated highway system, and driving times from one side of the city to the other of 30 to 45 minutes.

Climate: Average daytime high temperatures are 87°F in summer, 60°F in fall, 35°F in winter, and 68°F in spring. The peak period of bird migration and diversity in spring occurs from mid-April through mid-May, when temperatures and precipitation are variable. Spring and early summer storms can be intense, as Kansas City is geographically on the fringe of "Tornado Alley." Once summer is underway, occasional thunderstorms interrupt the moderate heat present through mid-September. From that point through October, temperatures and precipitation are once again on a roller-coaster of proportions equal to the influx of fall migrants. Winters go through cycles of below-zero cold snaps and heavy snows, to mild, dry conditions. No matter how unpredictable the weather may be at any given season, there will almost always be an array of interesting avian species present in the area.

Safety: Most of the locations described are safe places to bird. However, as with any large community, an opportunistic criminal element exists, so take precautions to conceal any valuables that you might leave in an unattended vehicle. While tuning in the birds, don't tune out what's happening around you, and you'll have a safe, satisfying birding experience.

Natural Hazards: Few people encounter poisonous snakes while birding in the Kansas City area, but insect and similar pests such as mosquitoes and ticks are evident during the wet seasons of spring and early summer. Chiggers are present in areas of tall grass during the summer. No truly dangerous wild animals are found in Kansas City, though you may be lucky enough to spot a fleeting Bobcat.

Other Resources: The Burroughs Audubon Society of Kansas City publishes a brochure of local natural-history areas with directions to a variety of birding locales. The brochure is free and available by contacting their office, (816) 795-8177. Kansas City birds are frequently represented on the Missouri State Bird Report, (573) 445-9115. Both Missouri and Kansas have computer listserves, MOBIRD-L and KSBIRD-L, respectively, that can be accessed on the Internet or through the ABA web site (*www.americanbirding.org*).

Other considerations: If it happens that *you* are the hungry carnivore in Kansas City, don't forget Kansas City's heritage as a major cattle stockyard and beef-packing town. This "cow town" is famous for its beef. For steaks, try The Golden Ox or Hereford House. For barbecue, it's hard to beat Gates and Sons, Arthur Bryant's, or Smokehouse.

THE BIRDS

Birders in Kansas City have many local and regional destination choices, depending on their species of interest and available time. During the fall, area reservoirs attract large concentrations of Franklin's Gulls and a variety of waterfowl. At local prairies, turf farms, and marshes, such sought-after species as Buff-breasted Sandpiper, Sprague's Pipit, Le Conte's Sparrow, and Nelson's Sharp-tailed Sparrows are regular fall migrants but have narrow "windows" of occurrence. Clusters of planted Scots (Scotch) Pine and other conifers in area parks and cemeteries offer oases for wintering owls and finches. Also during the winter, Spotted Towhees and Harris's Sparrows can be found in brushy fence-rows, while open pastures and farmland yield Lapland and Smith's Longspurs; Smith's Longspur prefers "Three-Awn" and other short grasses of less than six inches height. Snow Buntings are occasionally found during early winter on the rip-rap of lakes. In the spring exposed mudflats attract migrant shorebirds, including Hudsonian Godwit and White-rumped, Baird's, and Stilt Sandpipers. Grassy fields and prairie offer habitat for the secretive and elusive Yellow Rail, which migrates through the area in April and again in late September/early October. Kansas City is on the western edge of the range for most migrant flycatchers and eastern wood-warblers, which peak in diversity and abundance during the second week of May. Of interest, both the Missouri and the Kansas Big Day records exceed 200 species, and both included valuable time spent in the Kansas City area.

SMITHVILLE LAKE

Half day; fall and early winter

Smithville Lake, a 7,200-acre Army Corps of Engineers reservoir about 20 miles north of downtown Kansas City, is situated amidst upland pastures and wooded draws. It is the largest reservoir near Kansas City, and it attracts a variety of migrant waterbirds. Red-throated and Pacific Loons, Red-necked and Western Grebes, Pomarine and Parasitic Jaegers, and rare gulls have visited Smithville on multiple occasions. Exploring the outlying areas should yield a variety of raptors, sparrows, and other landbirds.

From Kansas City, go north on US-169 to Smithville, then turn east on KS-92 and proceed 2.0 miles to County Road DD. Go north on DD for one mile to the **Jerry L. Litton Visitor Center** for a map of the area. Behind the Visitor Center are several feeders and a good vantage from which to scope the lake.

Leaving the Visitor Center, turn right (north) on DD to the next right, a paved road that crosses the dam. The small parking lot at the north end of the dam offers a good view of the lake and an opportunity to listen for fly-by Lapland or Smith's Longspurs, and rarely, a Snow Bunting. American Pipits occasionally linger late into the season and can be observed working the rip-rap along the dam. Watch for rare (but regular) Pacific Loons, and perhaps a Red-throated Loon, among the sometimes numerous Common Loons.

From the parking lot, continue driving 0.25 mile northwest, turning north on County Road F. A brief stop in **Little Platte Park** takes you past the golf-course entrance and park fee-collection booth ($5.00 daily, if open, for entire lake complex). If one looks east toward the lake, a hilltop picnic shelter is visible in the distance. From the shelter, the panoramic view of the lake affords a good vantage for scanning the water for ducks and gulls. In October, watch for a stray Sabine's Gull among the congregation of up to 20,000 Franklin's Gulls.

Returning to the Little Platte Park entrance, continue north 2.0 miles on County Road F, then turn right onto County Road W. After crossing an arm of the lake, W bends to the south. Watch for 192nd Street on the left, and take this gravel road through overgrazed upland pasture to see or hear Northern Harrier, Eastern and Western Meadowlarks, and during migration, waterfowl on the small ponds. Turn around when you come to the T-inter-section and return to W, then go left toward the small settlement of Paradise. At Paradise, jog a block west onto Collins Road, the street in front of Clyde's General Store, and continue south about 1.5 miles to **Camp Branch** and **Bauman Park**. The first entrance is the campground and shooting range, which is worth a quick tour. Northern Shrike has been found in this area, and the loop roads may yield sparrows and additional views of the lake and shoreline. *(Note: roads close to the lakeshore are sometimes closed during the winter months.)*

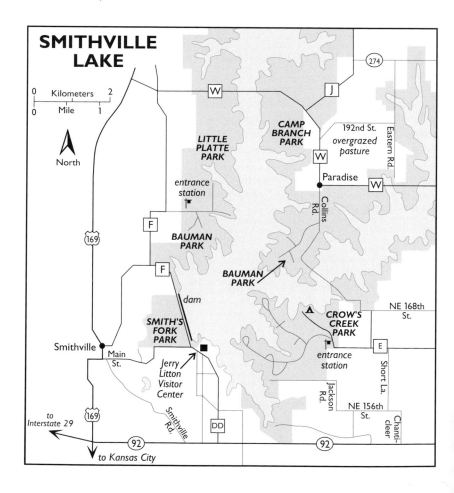

Return to Collins Road; the next entrance into Camp Branch includes a mini-beach that sometimes hosts late shorebirds and loafing gulls. Down the beach toward the main body of water, a short, rocky peninsula into the lake can at times attract an interesting variety of gulls, terns, and lingering shorebirds. Returning again to Collins Road, turn right, cross the narrow arm of the lake, and follow it to the stop sign at County Road E. Turn right and proceed to the entrance to **Crow's Creek Park**, turning left past the entrance booth. Beyond the booth, the next right turn leads to more campgrounds, but first stop briefly to check the small RV sewage ponds on the left for diving ducks. The campground is situated on a high, grassy peninsula that offers several viewing perspectives. Watch for Western and Clark's (rare) Grebes in the narrow inlet to the south, and check the main lake to the west for loons, scoters, and more diving ducks. Upon exiting Crow's Creek Park, turn south on any gravel road to zig-zag back to KS-92, whereupon driving west will lead to US-169.

STATE LINE ROAD IN MID-TOWN

Morning; spring and fall

In the suburbs along busy **State Line Road** between 64th Street and 63rd Street, an oasis exists for migrant passerines. Park at the First Lutheran Church on the corner of 64th and State Line in Mission Hills, Kansas, and walk along the creek and woods that border the parking lot and street. The area along the creek bordering the adjacent block to the east (in Missouri) is also good. Eleven species of flycatchers and over thirty species of warblers have been recorded in this residential area, including rarities such as Black-throated Blue and Prairie. Kansas's only record of Brown-headed Nuthatch was an individual that wintered in this compact migrant-magnet.

WESTON BEND STATE PARK

Half day; spring, summer, early fall

Twenty miles northwest of downtown Kansas City, along the Missouri River in Platte County, is 1,133-acre **Weston Bend State Park**. The park's riparian woodlands consist of an assortment of willows, cottonwoods, oaks, maples, and sycamores, and their proximity to the river attracts a wide array of migrants and breeding songbirds.

From downtown Kansas City, go north on I-29 past the airport to Exit 20, just north of Platte City. Go west to KS-273, then follow it northwest to KS-45. Turn south on KS-45 and watch for the park entrance (no fee) on the right. Upon entering the park, take the first left into the parking lot, which is the trailhead for a three-mile, paved, walking/biking loop.

In late April through most of May, this paved loop is one of the premier warbler hot-spots in the Kansas City area. Allow three or four hours to walk the complete loop, starting in a counter-clockwise direction. The first two miles pass through a variety of woodland habitats that should produce breeding Yellow-throated and Red-eyed Vireos, Wood Thrush, Kentucky Warbler, Louisiana Waterthrush, Rose-breasted Grosbeak, Summer and Scarlet (uncommon) Tanagers, as well as a host of migrants. Cerulean and Worm-eating Warblers are rare breeders in the park, and may be heard or seen during the first two miles. Connecticut Warbler has been detected several times during the latter half of May. During spring migration, over 30 species of warblers pass through the park. The last mile of the loop is through scrubby, upland, second-growth vegetation dominated by the songs of Bell's and White-eyed Vireos, Blue-winged Warbler, Yellow-breasted Chat, Eastern Towhee, and Field Sparrow. Spotted Towhees winter in the Kansas City area, and are often present until the first week of May.

After completing the loop, drive west through the park past the tobacco barn and park office to the Scenic Overlook parking lot. A short trail leads to the viewing platform overlooking the Missouri River and Fort Leavenworth,

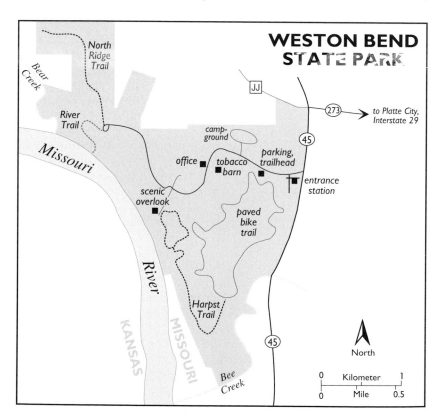

Kansas. At the edge of the clearing just south of the platform is a small sign marking an unpaved hiking trail. The trail follows the ridge through stands of maple and eventually drops down to connect with the three-mile, paved loop trail.

Departing the Overlook parking lot, drive west to the last lower parking lot near the Missouri River. Walk through the gate and cross the railroad tracks where a dirt trail leads to the river. In the open willow groves and cottonwoods, breeders and/or migrants include Black-billed Cuckoo, Alder and Willow Flycatchers (migrants), American Redstart, and Orchard and Baltimore Orioles. Scanning the Missouri River during the latter half of May or in mid-September may yield migrant Caspian Terns.

WYANDOTTE COUNTY
LAKE PARK, KANSAS
Half day; year round

Wyandotte County Lake Park in Kansas City, Kansas, can be easily accessed from the junction of I-435 and I-70. Head north on I-435 for 3 miles to Leavenworth Road. Go east on Leavenworth for 2.5 miles to 91st Street; turn left and proceed to the park entrance. A paved road meanders through the gently-rolling hills of oak-hickory woodlands and encircles the deep-water reservoir. With the Missouri River only one mile to the north, Wyandotte County Lake attracts a variety of expected, and unexpected, migrant and wintering geese, ducks, and gulls. A Harlequin Duck spent several days near the dam one winter. The scattered groups of pine and juniper trees have been productive during winter for Yellow-rumped Warbler. Several vantage points are available for viewing the lake and its many coves.

Uncommon in our region during the breeding season, Broad-winged Hawks and Scarlet Tanagers regularly nest in the park. Common nesting birds include Wild Turkey, Whip-poor-will, Kentucky Warbler, and Summer Tanager. During migration, the park attracts a diverse array of flycatchers, vireos, and warblers. Open areas with scattered walnut trees are best in spring; scrubby areas are preferred in fall.

MONTROSE CONSERVATION AREA, TABERVILLE PRAIRIE, AND SCHELL-OSAGE CONSERVATION AREA

Full day; year round

An hour-and-a-half south of Kansas City is the first of a cluster of refuges with distinctive personalities—each offering a variety of habitats and birds. To reach **Montrose Conservation Area** (hereafter CA) from southeastern Kansas City, drive south on US-71 to the KS-7 exit east toward Clinton. Proceed 20 miles to the Urich exit, turn left at the stop sign, then go a block to County Road K south. Go south on K about 8 miles and turn east on KS-18. In less than two miles, turn south on County Road RA and proceed 3.0 miles to the north end of Montrose CA.

The lake's water levels fluctuate, with lower water offering the best opportunity for a variety of birds. During migration, several species of shorebirds will use any exposed mudflats. Black-crowned and sometimes Yellow-crowned Night-Herons roost on the vegetated island. Red-shouldered Hawks are often seen or heard along the wooded hillside to the south. Warblers and sparrows can be found around the campground or across the road. Follow the paved road around the corner, past the campground, to the bridge separating the wildlife area from Montrose Lake to the east. This power-plant reservoir has a warm-water discharge that keeps it mostly free of ice during the winter. Concentrations of Double-crested Cormorants, geese, ducks, and gulls can be found during much of the year. Continue south 3.0 miles to the stop sign in the town of Montrose, then turn left on Highway 52 east. If food or gas is required, stop at Casey's convenience store.

From Casey's, go 1.0 mile east on Hwy. 52 and turn south on SW1101, the first gravel road. Proceed 1.0 mile to the junction of SW906, an eastbound gravel road. Check the (private) cattail-bordered pond on the southeast corner for ducks, Soras, and Marsh Wrens during migration. The adjacent fields (also private property) have Upland Sandpipers, Dickcissels, Grasshopper and Lark Sparrows, and sometimes Sedge Wrens during the breeding season. In late fall and early spring, watch for Smith's Longspurs, and for a variety of raptors year round. From the junction, continue south on the gravel road 2.0 miles to the T-junction. The field on the northwest corner has been reliable in fall for Sprague's Pipits, Smith's Longspurs, and an assortment of grassland sparrows. The farm pond regularly attracts ducks, gulls, terns, and sparrows, including several fall records of Nelson's Sharp-tailed Sparrow around the small willows. Turn west at the T-junction and go 1.0 mile to Highway 52 west, scanning for Greater Prairie-Chicken in winter and for Prairie Falcon in fall and winter.

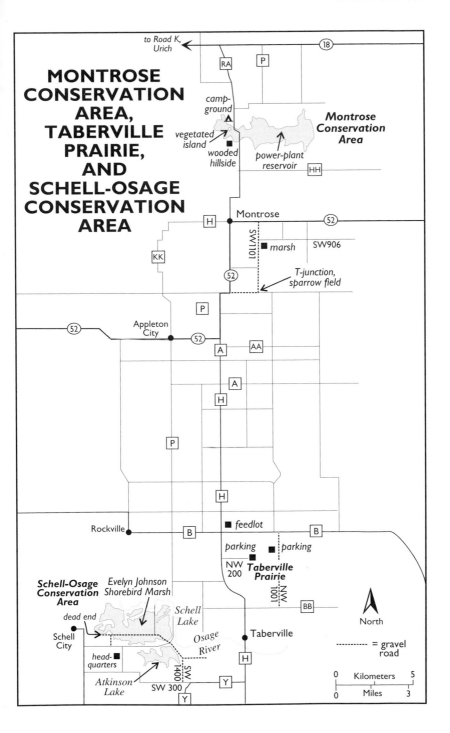

MONTROSE
CONSERVATION
AREA,
TABERVILLE
PRAIRIE,
AND
SCHELL-OSAGE
CONSERVATION
AREA

to Road K, Urich

18

RA

P

camp-ground

Montrose Conservation Area

vegetated island

wooded hillside

power-plant reservoir

HH

H

Montrose

52

SW1101

marsh

SW906

T-junction, sparrow field

52

KK

P

52

Appleton City

52

A

AA

A

H

P

H

feedlot

Rockville

B

B

parking

parking

NW 200

Taberville Prairie

Schell-Osage Conservation Area

Evelyn Johnson Shorebird Marsh

Schell Lake

NW 1001

BB

North

dead end

Schell City

head-quarters

Osage River

Taberville

---------- = gravel road

Atkinson Lake

SW 300

SW 1400

H

Y

Y

0   Kilometers   5

0   Miles   3

Smith's Longspurs
Shawneen Finnegan

Highway 52 soon turns south, then west again in 2.0 miles. Take County Road A south about two miles, then County Road H for 6.0 miles to County Road B. From the junction of B and H, proceed south on H for 1.0 mile, watching carefully for an inconspicuous, eastbound gravel lane marked NW200. Turn onto this narrow lane and drive 0.75 mile to the parking lot at the dead end, which is one of the entry points for Taberville Prairie.

Taberville Prairie is a 1,360-acre reserve that offers something interesting at every season. Northern Harrier, Scissor-tailed Flycatcher, Henslow's Sparrow, and Grasshopper Sparrow are breeders. During fall and spring migrations, Le Conte's Sparrows join the ranks of common grassland sparrows. Raptors are attracted to the prairie year round, but during winter and migration watch for Merlin, Prairie Falcon, and Short-eared Owl. Though declining in Missouri, Greater Prairie-Chickens are permanent residents; they will often flush. From the parking lot, walk to the north and east in a broad loop back to the parking lot. Returning to County Road H, go north 1.0 mile to County Road B and turn east. Sometimes during migration and winter the feedlot on the northeast corner of the junction attracts a variety of blackbirds, including Brewer's and Yellow-headed. Drive east 2.0 miles to NW1001, the first gravel road south, just past a farmhouse on the right. Drive south 1.2 miles to a small parking area on the west side of the road that is worth a brief hike along the edge of the prairie. From early to late spring, Greater Prairie-Chickens are often observed displaying in the mornings on the east side of the fence (in surprisingly sparse agricultural habitat). Continue south 2.0 miles to a T-intersection, which is County Road BB. Turn west on BB and go 1.5 miles back to County Road H.

To continue to **Schell-Osage Conservation Area**, go south on H about three miles through the small town of Taberville and across the Osage River to County Road Y. Turn west onto Y and go 2.5 miles, exiting onto SW300, a gravel road that continues west as Y bends to the south. (This gravel entrance to Schell-Osage CA comes with little warning.) Turn right on SW1400 and proceed through the Ozark-like oak woodlands, eventually descending to the shore of Atkinson Lake. On the northeast side of the road, the dead trees in the standing water are home to breeding Red-headed Woodpeckers and Prothonotary Warblers; Pileated Woodpeckers can also be seen year round, working the trees. Continuing around the lake, take the first right turn and follow this main dike road northwest among small bodies of water and marsh. The south side of Schell Lake has deep water that attracts diving ducks and gulls, whereas the willow-lined marshes between the river and dike road host herons, rails, shorebirds, and nesting Willow Flycatchers. Resident Pileated Woodpeckers and nesting Yellow-throated Warblers can be found at most access points near the Osage River. Water levels fluctuate with seasonal rains, and Schell-Osage can be productive for herons and shorebirds under favorable conditions. Roseate Spoonbill and several Ruffs are among the vagrants discovered here. Along the main dike road, check the Evelyn Johnson Shorebird Marsh for shorebirds during migration.

At the west end of the reservoir, you have the option of turning south or continuing straight west on a dead-end road. The dead-end has some interesting habitat worth a visit year round. Yellow-crowned Night-Heron, Red-shouldered Hawk, Pileated Woodpecker, and Prothonotary Warbler are regular during the breeding season, and migrant landbirds may be present during spring and fall. Taking the left turn leads south 0.5 mile to a junction with another main east-west road through the refuge. Turn east and go to the second gravel road, toward the headquarters. The south end of the headquarters complex is bordered by a strip of mature pine trees. Behind the pines are dense clusters of Red Cedar that have been reliable in winter for accipiters, roosting Long-eared Owls, and Hermit Thrushes. Schell-Osage is within the contact zone for Black-capped and Carolina Chickadees, and intergrades are routinely observed and heard throughout the area.

Continuing east on the main road leads back to County Road Y. To return to Kansas City, take Y east to H, and follow H north past Taberville Prairie to B. Turn west onto B and continue straight to Highway 71 at Rich Hill. From Rich Hill, go north on Highway 71.

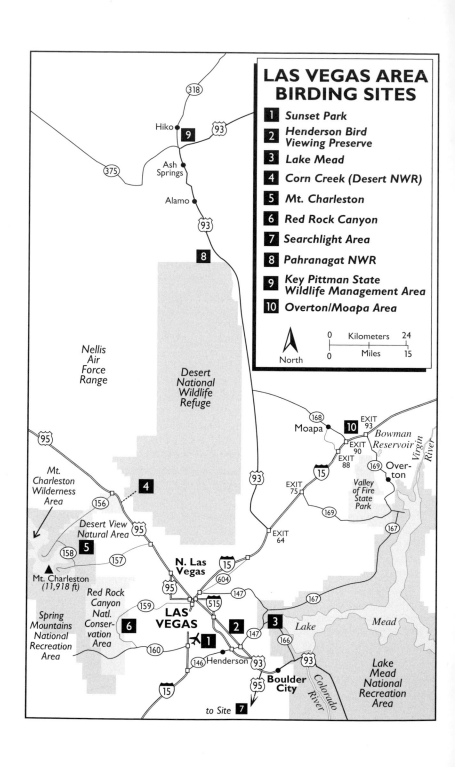

LAS VEGAS AREA BIRDING SITES

1 Sunset Park
2 Henderson Bird Viewing Preserve
3 Lake Mead
4 Corn Creek (Desert NWR)
5 Mt. Charleston
6 Red Rock Canyon
7 Searchlight Area
8 Pahranagat NWR
9 Key Pittman State Wildlife Management Area
10 Overton/Moapa Area

Kilometers 0 — 24
Miles 0 — 15

North

318

Hiko **9** 93

375

Ash Springs

Alamo

93

8

Nellis Air Force Range

Desert National Wildlife Refuge

168
Moapa **10** EXIT 93
Bowman Reservoir
EXIT 90
EXIT 88
169 Over-ton
Virgin River

95

Mt. Charleston Wilderness Area

156

Desert View Natural Area

95

158 **5**

157

93

EXIT 75

Valley of Fire State Park

169

4

EXIT 64

167

Mt. Charleston (11,918 ft)

N. Las Vegas

15

604

Red Rock Canyon Natl. Conservation Area

95

159

147

Spring Mountains National Recreation Area

6

LAS VEGAS

515

2

3 Lake

Mead

167

160

146 Henderson

1

147

93

166

15

95

Boulder City

93

Colorado River

Lake Mead National Recreation Area

to Site **7**

LAS VEGAS, NEVADA

James and Marian Cressman

L as Vegas brings to mind large resort hotels, an almost limitless supply of entertainment, and a town that never sleeps. The city is located in Clark County, Nevada's southernmost; found within the county's borders are three of the fastest-growing cities in the United States. Although "neon" is what most birders will think of when the words "Las Vegas" are spoken, the area surrounding the city supports some of the best desert birding on the continent. Although urban sprawl has wiped out some of the close-in birding locations, well over 300 species have been found in the vicinity of Las Vegas. Sunset Park, Henderson Bird Viewing Preserve, Lake Mead National Recreation Area, Desert National Wildlife Refuge (Corn Creek), Mount Charleston, Red Rock Canyon Recreation Area, the Searchlight area, and Pahranagat National Wildlife Refuge offer excellent and diverse birding potential.

Many of the visitors who are attending conventions try to bird around their scheduled meetings and seminars. In three cases the birding routes outlined here can be divided easily into separate, shorter trips.

ESSENTIAL INFORMATION

Getting Around: Most visitors arrive at McCarran International Airport, about four miles from "the Strip." Airport limousine service can be arranged at the airport. All major car-rental companies have outlets at the airport. Many of the large hotels have a car-rental agency on their premises. Unfortunately, none of the birding areas is reasonably accessible by public transportation.

Climate: The weather in spring and fall can be very pleasant. Winter mornings can be cool or cold, but most afternoons warm up nicely. Summer temperatures are normally over 100°F daily. During late July and August temperatures of 110°F are not uncommon. Early-morning trips are necessary in late spring and summer, since most birding activity will cease by 10:00AM unless one is in the mountains. Birders should wear hats, use sunscreen, and

189

drink lots of liquids. Temperatures on Mount Charleston can be 30 degrees cooler than on the desert floor, so a light sweater or a jacket might be necessary in spring and fall, especially early or late in the day.

Safety: Crime conditions are not appreciably different from those in any other large city. The birding areas described here are safe, and even a lone female birder should not have any problems. Do not leave any valuables on the seat of your car; thievery has been a problem at several locations.

Natural Hazards: Such hazards are not generally a problem except at the Henderson Bird Viewing Preserve, where gnats and mosquitoes can be common. Chiggers are not present. Rattlesnakes are seen occasionally in southern Nevada. While walking in the desert, be mindful also of scorpions and encounters with spiny plants.

Other Resources: A Rare Bird Alert covers southern Nevada, (702) 390-8463. The state chat group, Nevada Birds, can be subscribed to at *listserve@list.audubon.org*. Bird lists can be researched at *http://list.audubon.org/archives/nvbirds.html*. A number of local ABA members, listed in the ABA Membership Directory, are willing to provide current information.

Other Considerations: Do not bird on private property without securing permission. Generally, permission will be readily granted. Never enter a mining claim, generally fenced and marked. The federal government now charges $5 per day to visit Lake Mead and Red Rock Canyon Recreation Areas. Bring your Golden Age or Annual Passport. The state parks charge a $5 daily fee; county parks are free.

SUNSET PARK AND THE LAKE MEAD LOOP
Several hours to full day; year round

Sunset Park is located immediately southeast of McCarran International Airport. To reach the park, go east on Tropicana Avenue from "the Strip" to Eastern Avenue. Turn right (south) and follow it to Sunset Road, cross Sunset Road, and turn left (east) into Sunset Park at the second entrance. Park near the pond. Resident species include Gambel's Quail, Greater Roadrunner, Verdin, Black-tailed Gnatcatcher, Crissal Thrasher, Phainopepla, and Abert's Towhee. During spring and early summer look for Western Kingbird, Bell's Vireo, Cactus Wren, and Lucy's Warbler. Hike through the Rabbitbush/mesquite areas. Sunset Park can be excellent for migrant passerines in spring. In winter the pond supports a variety of waterfowl. Note that much of the park is heavily used by joggers and individuals exercising their dogs. Try to get there early!

To reach the **Henderson Bird Viewing Preserve** (in actuality, the City of Henderson sewage-treatment ponds), exit onto Sunset Road from Sunset Park, turn right (east), and drive approximately seven miles. Shortly after crossing Boulder Highway, make a left turn onto Moser Drive. Moser Drive

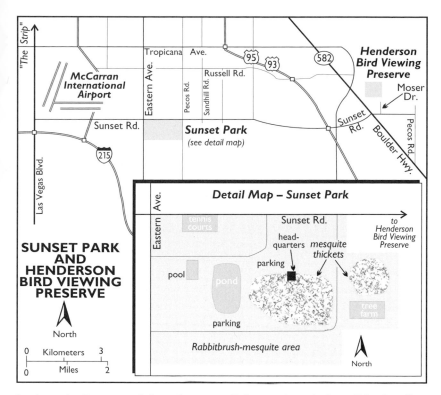

leads to the Preserve; follow the signs. If driving directly from "the Strip" to the Preserve, drive east on Tropicana or Flamingo Avenue to Boulder Highway, turn right (southeast), and go to Sunset Road. Immediately after the *Welcome to Henderson* sign, turn left (east) onto Sunset Road and then left onto Moser Drive.

The preserve is open 6:00AM to 3:00PM every day except Thanksgiving, Christmas, and New Year's Day. There is no fee, but you must sign a release-of-liability waiver. The preserve has 13 ponds (a scope is helpful) and requires more than an hour to walk at a rapid pace. One of the paths is paved to accommodate wheelchairs, benches overlook several ponds, and restroom facilities are provided. This is an excellent place for waterbirds and a number of desert passerines. About 250 species have been observed here. Resident species include Gambel's Quail, Virginia Rail, Sora, Greater Roadrunner, Verdin, Crissal Thrasher, and Abert's Towhee. Common Moorhens breed. At least 12 species of ducks are normally present in winter. A Peregrine Falcon visits from time to time. Shorebird numbers and variety can be excellent when sufficient appropriate habitat exists. Most species migrate through in late April and May and again in late July, August, and September, and include Snowy and Semipalmated Plovers, Black-necked Stilt, American Avocet, both yellowlegs, Western, Least, and Baird's (fall) Sandpipers, and

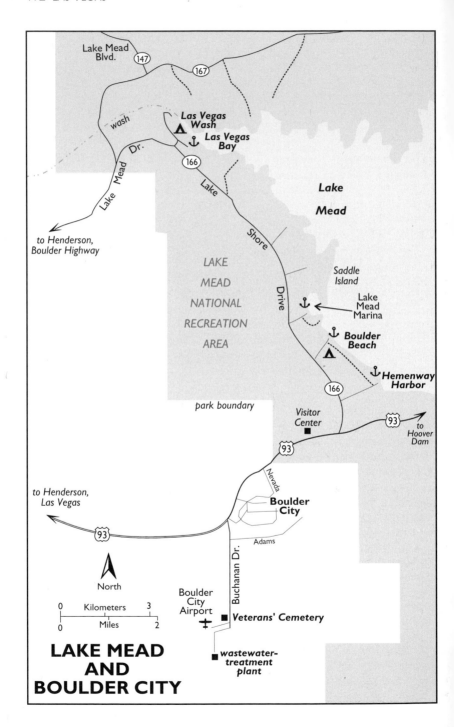

**LAKE MEAD
AND
BOULDER CITY**

Long-billed Dowitcher. Scarce migrants in fall include Solitary Sandpiper, Pectoral Sandpiper, Short-billed Dowitcher, and Stilt Sandpiper. Many rarities have been found here, including Black-bellied Whistling-Duck, Red-necked Stint, Ruff, Least Tern, and Black Skimmer. Passerine migrants and a few vagrants have been seen in the brushy areas surrounding the ponds, and the recent planting of native trees and shrubs should prove even more enticing to migrants in future years.

To get to **Lake Mead** from the preserve, return to the intersection at Sunset Road and Boulder Highway. Turn left (southeast) onto Boulder Highway and drive to NV-146 (also called Lake Mead Drive). Turn left onto Highway 146. Drive 9 miles to the Las Vegas Wash (Las Vegas Bay) area of Lake Mead. Check both the marina and the narrow bay behind the campground. Look for loons, Western and Clark's Grebes, waterfowl, and gulls (Ring-billed and California are most numerous, a few Bonaparte's and Herrings are found in migration and winter, and rarities such as Laughing, Franklin's, Mew, Thayer's, Yellow-footed, and Sabine's have been seen). The beach area should be checked for shorebirds. Rock Wrens are on the cliffs.

From here go southeast on NV-166 to the Lake Mead Marina. Check the shore and drive out on the dike at the south end of the marina to search the lake area for waterbirds. This is another good spot for rarities. Continue south on NV-166 to Boulder Beach. Walk through the campground. Costa's Hummingbirds are resident here and especially at feeders in the adjoining mobile-home community. This area is also good for Inca Dove and Greater Roadrunner. Also check the trees in the campground for migrants during spring and fall. Take the dirt road paralleling the beach south to Hemenway Harbor. Check for shorebirds and waterbirds. In winter watch for loons (four species have been seen here over the years) and gulls.

From Hemenway Harbor return to NV-166, turn left, and continue south until you reach US-93. Turn right to Boulder City. Drive south on Buchanan Drive approximately two miles. Turn right toward Boulder City Municipal Airport. Search the right (north) bank for Burrowing Owls. They have nested here for many years. Go back to Buchanan, turn right, drive past the Veterans' Cemetery (good in fall and winter for sparrow flocks) and take the first road to the Boulder City Wastewater-Treatment Plant. Remain outside the fence. Below the ponds is a discharge channel. Search the channel for Virginia Rails and Soras, and for hummingbirds and warblers in spring and fall. Check the power poles for Golden Eagles and other raptors. Return to US-93, turn left and drive north through Henderson back to Las Vegas.

Corn Creek
(Desert National Wildlife Refuge)
and Mount Charleston

Half to full day; spring, summer, fall

Take US-95 northwest approximately 20 miles from downtown Las Vegas, turn right at the **Desert National Wildlife Refuge** sign onto a good dirt road, and drive four miles to the headquarters area. On the way in, check the saltbush and Greasewood in spring for Brewer's,, Black-throated (also summer), and Sage Sparrows. During early spring look for Sage Thrashers. About two to three miles from US-95, walk out through the saltbush north of the road (the area to the south is private property) for these species as well as for Le Conte's Thrasher. Unfortunately, the latter species appears to be declining here. Take lots of water and be prepared for a long search.

The headquarters area **(Corn Creek)** is a classic desert oasis. Over 300 species of birds have been observed here. Cover the three ponds and the orchard, scout the pasture, and walk around the equipment yard and the hiking trail. The whole area is excellent for transient species in the spring and fall. Large numbers of flycatchers, vireos, warblers, tanagers, grosbeaks, and buntings may be seen. Some days only a few birds are present. In spring look for nesting Lesser Nighthawk, White-throated Swift, Lucy's Warbler, Scott's and Bullock's Orioles, and Lesser Goldfinch. Year-round residents include Greater Roadrunner, Verdin, and Crissal Thrasher. Corn Creek has many

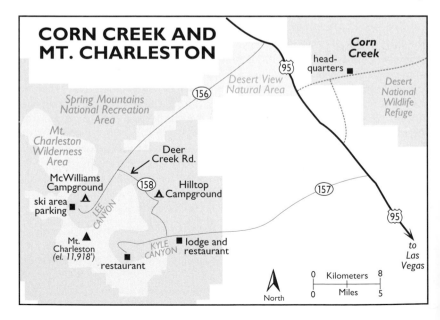

records of vagrants, mostly eastern passerines, as well as a few visitors from Arizona and points south. The best times for rarities are in May and from September to early November.

Return to US-95 and turn right, continuing north 3.5 miles to NV-156, which leads west to **Lee Canyon**. This road ascends to about 8,600 feet in the Spring Mountains **(Mount Charleston)**. Along the lower section of the road watch in spring and summer for Ladder-backed Woodpecker, Pinyon Jay, Verdin, and Scott's Oriole; higher up, search for Northern Goshawk (rare), Broad-tailed Hummingbird, Clark's Nutcracker, Pygmy Nuthatch, Mountain Bluebird, Grace's Warbler, Cassin's Finch, and Red Crossbill. Park in the Lee Canyon ski-area parking lot and, if time permits, hike part of the trail.

Go back 6 miles to **Deer Creek Road** (NV-158), where you turn right. On the right along this road watch for Townsend's Solitaire, Virginia's and Grace's Warblers, and Green-tailed Towhee. Walk through the Hilltop Campground and look for Red-naped Sapsucker, Mountain Chickadee, Red-breasted, White-breasted, and Pygmy Nuthatches, and Brown Creeper. Farther along Deer Creek Road is the Deer Creek Canyon Picnic Area, where Flammulated Owl and Cordilleran Flycatcher have been found on several occasions in late spring and early summer. Flammulated Owls are, in fact, fairly widespread in the Spring Mountains and are relatively easy to hear in May and June, if you spend the night. Northern Saw-whet Owls may be heard along the Deer Creek Road between the picnic area and Kyle Canyon. At NV-157 you have reached **Kyle Canyon**. Turn right and drive to the end of the road at a lodge/restaurant. Along the way check Kyle Canyon campground and the adjoining ranger residence area for hummingbirds at the feeders, Pygmy Nuthatch, Grace's Warbler, and Black-headed Grosbeak and the oak-covered slopes for Band-tailed Pigeon and Virginia's Warbler. At the restaurant check the hummingbird feeders for Broad-tailed Hummingbird. Nearby hiking trails to Charleston Peak provide access to mixed fir forest; breeders include Red-breasted Nuthatch and Ruby-crowned Kinglet, and Flammulated Owl and Red Crossbill are possible. Higher up there are Clark's Nutcrackers. Below Deer Creek Road on NV-157 is another restaurant with hummingbird feeders, where there are many Broad-taileds, sometimes a few Calliopes and Anna's, and, beginning in early July, southbound Rufous.

RED ROCK CANYON RECREATION AREA

Half day; year round, best in spring

From downtown Las Vegas go west on Charleston Boulevard, NV-159, approximately 15 miles to the entrance to **Red Rock Canyon** (fee). There is a 13-mile, one-way loop through this scenic area, with several

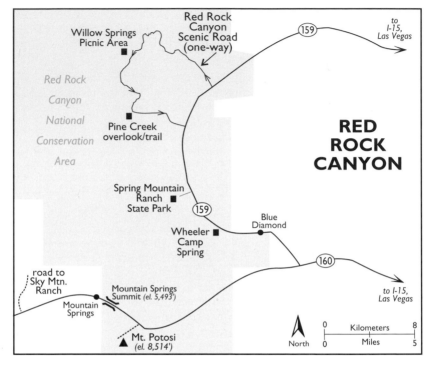

overlooks, stops with interpretive signs, and good photo opportunities. Drive slowly, watching for birds and bicyclists. The first good birding stop is Willow Springs Picnic Area. Park and walk the trails. In spring, watch for Gray Vireo and Black-chinned and Black-throated Sparrows. In late summer, Chukars come to the spring to drink. Year-round residents include Western Scrub-Jay (interior race), Rock and Canyon Wrens, and Spotted Towhee.

Continue around the loop road to Pine Creek Overlook and Trail. In winter, Sharp-shinned and Cooper's Hawks, Ladder-backed Woodpecker, Say's Phoebe, Western Scrub-Jay, and Juniper Titmouse are present. Western and Mountain Bluebirds and Townsend's Solitaire are possible. In spring, watch for Anna's Hummingbird and Cactus Wren.

As you leave the loop road, turn right and drive 2.5 miles to **Spring Mountain Ranch State Park** (fee). Year-round residents include Greater Roadrunner, Ladder-backed Woodpecker, Western Scrub-Jay, Juniper Titmouse, Mountain Chickadee, and Verdin. In spring and summer watch for Black-chinned Hummingbird, Say's Phoebe, Western Kingbird, Lucy's and Yellow Warblers, and Summer (in the oak grove) and Western Tanagers.

When you leave the ranch, turn right to drive 1.7 miles to Wheeler Camp Spring. This is a good spot in spring and fall, as hummingbirds, flycatchers, warblers, tanagers, and orioles migrate through the area. Cooper's Hawk,

Black-chinned Hummingbird, and Lucy's Warbler nest here. When you leave, turn right drive a half-mile to **Blue Diamond**. Drive into town and walk around the park and swimming-pool area. Observe the *No Trespassing* signs. Inca Doves have resided in the area for several years.

As you leave Blue Diamond, turn left to head back toward Las Vegas on Charleston Boulevard, or turn right and drive 2.5 miles to NV-160. Turn right on NV-160, drive 10.8 miles to the Mount Potosi road (unsigned) where there is a BSA Camp sign, and turn left. Search along both sides of this dirt road during the spring and early summer for Cassin's Kingbird, Gray Vireo, Black-chinned Sparrow, and Scott's Oriole. Much of the property here is private (and being rapidly developed), so stay on the dirt road. Leaving the Mt. Potosi road, turn left (west) on NV-160 and proceed five miles, then turn right onto the road to Sky Mountain Ranch. Gray Vireos and Virginia's Warblers have been found along this road. Also look for Steller's and Pinyon Jays.

SEARCHLIGHT AREA

Half day; spring and early summer

The **Searchlight** area, located about an hour southeast of the city, supports an extensive Joshua Tree forest that is home to several local and sought-after species found nowhere else in the state. From the junction of US-93 and US-95 east of Las Vegas and Henderson, take US-95 south for 56 miles to Searchlight. In Searchlight take US-164 west for 8.3 miles, turn right on a dirt road—the YKL Ranch Road—and drive for approximately four miles, searching the area for Gilded Flicker, Cactus Wren, Bendire's Thrasher (April-July), and Scott's Oriole. If your vehicle has four-wheel drive, continue farther up the road another 5 miles, past the power-line, until the road ends at a perennial spring. Hike among the junipers in this beautiful, rugged area, looking for Gray Vireo and Black-chinned Sparrow (both are common). This is the only reliable area in the state for Rufous-crowned Sparrow.

Return to Searchlight and follow signs east to Cottonwood Cove on the Colorado River. In winter, look for loons and ducks. In pockets of desert scrub there are resident Greater Roadrunners and Black-tailed Gnatcatchers. The residential area near the cove is worth checking for passerines during migration and winter.

Drive north from Searchlight on US-95 for 4.4 miles to Grampa's Road on the right (east). Cross the cattle-guard, then at the fork keep left, drive east, under the electric power-lines where the road forks again, keep right, and drive out to a mining claim. Stay outside the claim, but walk the dirt roads in this area, looking for Gilded Flicker, Ladder-backed Woodpecker, Cactus Wren, Black-tailed Gnatcatcher, Black-throated Sparrow, and Scott's Oriole. Just about anywhere with a good growth of Joshua Trees is worth checking.

Pahranagat National Wildlife Refuge and Vicinity

Full day; year round

From the junction of US-93 and I-15 northeast of Las Vegas, take US-93 north for 62.5 miles to the entrance to the lower lake at **Pahranagat National Wildlife Refuge**. At dusk in winter, check the marsh habitat that surrounds the lake for Short-eared Owl. The entrance to the refuge headquarters is 3.6 miles farther north, and the entrance to the upper lake is another one mile north. In late fall and winter (November to the end of February) look for Tundra Swan, large numbers of some 12 to 14 species of ducks, and impressive raptor concentrations, including Bald and Golden Eagles, Red-tailed, Ferruginous, and Rough-legged Hawks, and Prairie Falcon. In spring and fall watch for a variety of migrants, from herons to warblers, as well as Greater White-fronted Geese and Sandhill Cranes. Rarities in this area have included Common Black-Hawk, Zone-tailed Hawk, Red-headed Woodpecker, and a number of "coastal" species of waterbirds on the larger lakes. The hamlet of **Alamo**, five miles north of Pahranagat NWR, has a motel, gas station, and restaurant. A spring or summer drive along the frontage road (Richardsonville Road) on the west side of US-93 about a mile north of Alamo can be productive. Check the large cottonwoods and the farm fields for Yellow-billed Cuckoo, Vermilion and Brown-crested Flycatchers, Summer Tanager, Blue Grosbeak, and Lazuli (and possibly Indigo) Bunting. **Ash Springs,** north of Alamo, with a gas station, mini-mall, and snack bar, is a good rest stop. There are several nice stands of trees and a spring nearby.

Twenty miles farther north, near Hiko, on NV-318, is **Key Pittman State Wildlife Management Area**. This is an excellent area for studying Nevada's rare riparian breeders, including Yellow-billed Cuckoo and Willow Flycatcher *(extimus* subspecies). There are several lakes and farm fields managed by the Nevada Division of Wildlife. These lakes have swans, ducks, and eagles in winter. In spring and fall there may be good numbers of shorebirds. White-faced Ibises are often present. A scope is necessary. As you drive through the area in fall and winter, be sure to check the irrigation equipment in the hay fields for Ferruginous Hawks.

After visiting the Key Pittman complex, you might also stop at Crystal Springs, which is across the road on NV-375. During the spring and fall a few flycatchers, vireos, warblers, and other migrants are usually present. Great Horned Owls have nested here. Look for the historical marker and enter the spring area at that point.

OVERTON/MOAPA AREA

Half day; year round

Take I-15 northeast from Las Vegas to Exit 93 and turn right onto NV-169. Drive 3.7 miles and turn left onto an unsigned dirt road that leads to **Bowman Reservoir**. In winter, look for loons and waterfowl; in spring, check for Osprey and shorebirds. During the summer months the reservoir may be overrun with jet-skiers, but the surrounding vegetation can be good for lowland riparian breeders such as Summer Tanager and Blue Grosbeak.

Return to NV-169, turn left, and drive 9.8 miles to the **Overton Wildlife Management Area**. This area is normally open Monday–Friday; in winter, do not enter on a hunting day. (Check with an on-duty ranger.) Many ducks are resident, as are Wild Turkey, Ring-necked Pheasant, and Gambel's Quail; in spring look for herons and shorebirds. As you drive along NV-169, check the irrigated fields during spring and fall for flocks of White-faced Ibises, gulls, and other migrants. This is a good site for Least Bittern during the summer months, and Yellow-billed Cuckoo is here at that season as well.

Two additional areas nearby have only recently begun to receive birder coverage, and adventuresome readers might profit from some exploration on their own. The first area, going north from **Moapa**, is the Muddy River drainage, which is good for nesting Yellow-billed Cuckoos and Vermilion Flycatchers, migrant shorebirds and passerines, and wintering Sandhill Cranes and Ferruginous Hawks. A new Christmas Bird Count here might some day host the most species in the state. Much of the land here is private, but there is sufficient public access to allow for productive birding. Leave I-15 via Exit 88. Go left under I-15, follow the black-topped road to a dairy farm, and search the pastures for egrets, raptors, and a variety of field birds. Do not leave the black-topped road without permission. Follow the road as it loops right to join NV-168 through Moapa. Warm Springs Road is a loop off NV-168 from which one can scan palm groves, riparian vegetation, and desert habitats from the car. Resident species include Gambel's Quail, Greater Roadrunner, Ladder-backed Woodpecker, and Phainopepla; additional summer breeders include Yellow-billed Cuckoo, Vermilion and Brown-crested Flycatchers, Blue Grosbeak, and Hooded and Bullock's Orioles. There is good rarity potential here, too.

The second area is farther east, along the **Virgin River** east to Mesquite and the Arizona state line. Here, there are nesting Yellow-billed Cuckoos, *extimus* Willow Flycatchers, and possibly Clapper Rails. Be aware, however, that access may be a problem, and that the area is being developed rapidly.

ACKNOWLEDGMENTS

Helpful comments on a draft were provided by Paul Lehman, Bruce Lund, and Mike San Miguel.

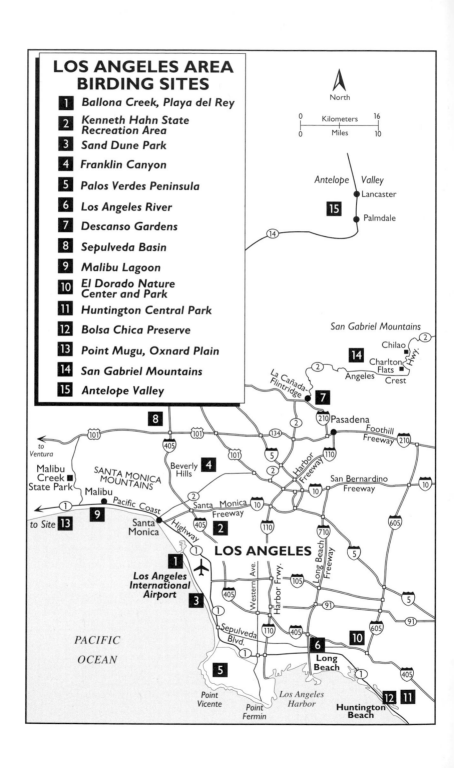

LOS ANGELES AREA BIRDING SITES

1. **Ballona Creek, Playa del Rey**
2. **Kenneth Hahn State Recreation Area**
3. **Sand Dune Park**
4. **Franklin Canyon**
5. **Palos Verdes Peninsula**
6. **Los Angeles River**
7. **Descanso Gardens**
8. **Sepulveda Basin**
9. **Malibu Lagoon**
10. **El Dorado Nature Center and Park**
11. **Huntington Central Park**
12. **Bolsa Chica Preserve**
13. **Point Mugu, Oxnard Plain**
14. **San Gabriel Mountains**
15. **Antelope Valley**

North

Kilometers 0 — 16
Miles 0 — 10

Antelope Valley
Lancaster
Palmdale

San Gabriel Mountains
Chilao
Charlton Flats
Angeles Crest

La Cañada-Flintridge
Pasadena
Foothill Freeway

to Ventura

Malibu Creek State Park
Malibu
Pacific Coast Highway
Santa Monica Mountains
Beverly Hills
Santa Monica Freeway
San Bernardino Freeway

to Site 13

Santa Monica

LOS ANGELES

Los Angeles International Airport

Sepulveda Blvd.
Western Ave.
Harbor Frwy.
Long Beach Freeway

Long Beach

PACIFIC OCEAN

Point Vicente
Point Fermin
Los Angeles Harbor
Huntington Beach

LOS ANGELES, CALIFORNIA

Jean D. Brandt and Kimball L. Garrett

Los Angeles is a City, a County, a Basin, a Greater Metropolitan area, and a state of mind, encompassing numerous cities, large unincorporated areas, vast blocks of suburbia, farms, ranches, parks, wilderness, and even an island or two. It is also a birder's paradise, with 478 species having been recorded in the county (including five "officially" established exotics). From anywhere in the urban area (roughly the Los Angeles Basin), one is within an hour or two of the mountains, the ocean, the desert, riparian habitats, chaparral, pine forests, wetlands, rivers, lakes and streams, and narrow canyons. It is the only place where, as someone once joked, "One can get frostbite in the morning and sunstroke in the afternoon on the same Christmas Bird Count."

No city in North America has been more vilified than Los Angeles, sometimes with good reason. Natural disasters are given worldwide press—earthquakes, fires, floods—as are the very real physical dangers incumbent in any urban area. For the birder, the most frustrating of all problems, however, is *gridlock*. Just *getting around* is difficult, and public transportation for birding itineraries is virtually non-existent. You must have a car, or a friend with a car, or borrow a car, or rent a car, or hire a taxi. The ABA Directory lists local birders willing to assist visiting birders.

ESSENTIAL INFORMATION

Getting Around: First Rule: *Get maps!* Your local auto club, book-store, or travel shop will have good local maps. They are essential. Second Rule: *Check on traffic conditions before heading out.* All of these trips will take longer than you expect. Radio station KFWB (AM 980) has traffic reports every five minutes and KNX (AM 1070) every six minutes.

Climate: Weather is rarely a problem in Southern California. Daytime temperatures in the Los Angeles Basin are rarely below the mid-50s Fahrenheit in winter, while 90° is a normal high in summer, although hot spells can bring a few days over 100°. Climate differences between habitats should be considered. It can be 50°F and drizzling along the coast, 70°F and smoggy in the basin, 90°F and clear in the valleys, 100°F and windy in the Antelope Valley, and 40°F and cloudy in the mountains—all on the same day! Between November and April, rain may come down in bucketfuls (when it comes at all), but it rarely continues for more than a day or two. Substantial snow may fall in the local mountains.

Natural Hazards: Insects should not be a problem, but ticks carrying Lyme disease have recently been reported in some chaparral areas. Poison Oak can be abundant in canyons and oak woodlands. Rattlesnakes are found throughout the area (but are rarely encountered), so watch for them.

Safety: While it is always safer (and more companionable) to bird with others, one must sometimes go into unfamiliar territory alone. Accidents can happen; if possible, carry a cell phone (911 works wherever you are). Please exercise utmost caution, whether in local parks or out in the "wild," particularly early in the morning or late in the afternoon. Los Angeles has its share of "bad guys" and you don't want to become an "incident."

Other resources: The Audubon House has a great book store and library, and has free advice from knowledgeable birders (Spotted Doves are resident at Audubon House); it is located in Plummer Park at 7377 Santa Monica Boulevard, West Hollywood, CA 90046, (323) 876-0202; weekly bird tape (323) 874-1318, *www.laaudubon.org*. Sightings are also reported on the Southern California Bird Box at (818) 952-5502; at the prompt you'll need to know that there have been five species of loons recorded in California.

The Natural History Museum Ralph Schreiber Hall of Birds is a renowned research collection, located in Exposition Park; contact Kimball Garrett, Ornithology Department, 900 Exposition Boulevard, Los Angeles, CA 90007, (213) 763-3368 (Ornithology Department); for general information, call (213) 763-DINO. (Allen's Hummingbirds and Yellow-chevroned Parakeets may be found year round in the park). The Los Angeles Zoo has a fine collection of species in flight cages and exhibit areas throughout the zoo; 533 Zoo Drive, Los Angeles, CA 90027, (323) 666-4650; good birding, including many chaparral species, is available on the zoo grounds.

Books include *A Birder's Guide to Southern California* by Brad Schram (ABA/Lane) is a very comprehensive 1999 update of the original Lane guide. *Where Birders Go In Southern California* by Hank Childs (1993, Los Angeles Audubon Society) has excellent directions to over 76 locations in Los Angeles County, along with notes as to what birds can be expected and site fees, if any. *Birds of Southern California, Status and Distribution* by Kimball Garrett and Jon Dunn (1981, Los Angeles Audubon Society; out-of-print) has valuable information on species seen in southern California, along with excellent bar-graphs. *California Birds, Their Status and Distribution* by Arnold Small (1994, Ibis Publishing) contains information on all of the species ever seen in California, and has excellent photos by the author and his son, Brian Small.

THE BIRDING YEAR

Any time of year will offer the traveling birder an excellent assortment of species. Some of our most-requested species are entirely or largely resident: Spotted Dove, Nuttall's Woodpecker, Oak Titmouse, California Gnatcatcher, Wrentit, California Thrasher, California Towhee. The earliest landbird migrants arrive by mid- or late January (some swallows, migratory Allen's Hummingbirds, etc.). Additional birds are in by the first half of March, including Swainson's Hawks, Pacific-slope Flycatchers, Warbling Vireos, orioles, etc. Migration peaks for most passerines in the latter half of April and the first ten days of May. A suite of late species (mid-May to early June) includes Willow Flycatcher, Western Wood-Pewee, and Swainson's Thrush.

Landbird diversity is lower in summer (June and July), but that is an ideal time to visit riparian habitats and the higher elevations. Allen's Hummingbirds (other than local resident birds) are southbound by late June; Orange-crowned Warblers disperse up-slope as early as late May. Passerine fall migrants are found from July through October, though different species have different date spans and peaks. Most common wintering passerines arrive after mid-September and remain through March or early April (a few species may remain later, e.g., Cedar Waxwings stay through May).

Winter bird diversity can be exciting in the region, with a variety of overwintering flycatchers, vireos, warblers, tanagers, orioles, and other birds often staked out by local birders in well-planted parks and residential neighborhoods on the coastal slope.

Seabird-watching: loons, Brant, and scoters (as well as Gray Whales) are best seen mid-March to mid-May from any of our coastal points, e.g., Point Dume, Long Point, Newport Pier. Black-vented Shearwaters are seen, frequently from shore, from October to March (with a few present all year); Pink-footed and Sooty Shearwaters are best from May to October. Storm-petrels (mostly Black, very rarely Least and Ashy) are sometimes seen from shore in summer and early fall. Terns are most abundant and diverse from May to September.

Shorebirds: Spring migration peaks for most species in April and early May. Fall migration of adult birds starts July–August (even late June for some species), and the juveniles are seen August–September.

SHORT TRIPS FROM THE AIRPORT

Several hours to half day; year round

Ballona Creek/Playa del Rey. Wandering Tattler, Black Turnstone, and Surfbird can be found along the jetties from September through April. Black Oystercatcher is resident on the detached breakwater. Watch for loons, grebes, Brown Pelicans, sea ducks, gulls, and terns. "Belding's" Savannah Sparrows are resident in the wetlands upstream, to the south of the Ballona

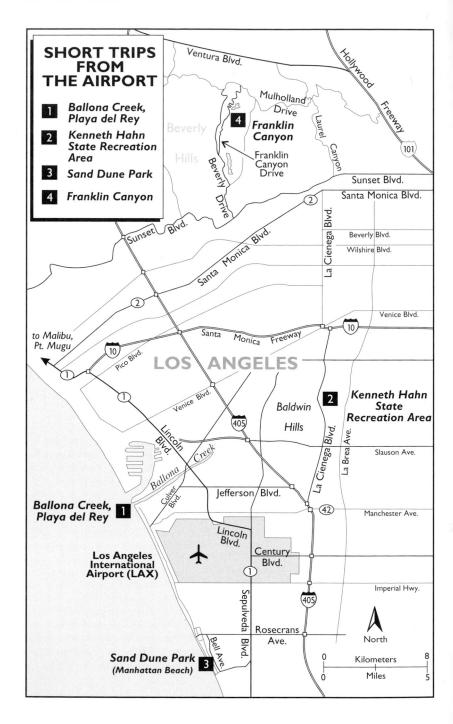

SHORT TRIPS FROM THE AIRPORT

1 *Ballona Creek, Playa del Rey*

2 *Kenneth Hahn State Recreation Area*

3 *Sand Dune Park*

4 *Franklin Canyon*

Ventura Blvd.

Hollywood Freeway

Mulholland Drive

Franklin Canyon

4

Beverly Hills

Franklin Canyon Drive

Laurel Canyon

101

Sunset Blvd.

Santa Monica Blvd.

Beverly Drive

Sunset Blvd.

2

La Cienega Blvd.

Beverly Blvd.

Wilshire Blvd.

Santa Monica Blvd.

2

Venice Blvd.

10

to Malibu, Pt. Mugu

10

1

Pico Blvd.

Santa Monica Freeway

10

LOS ANGELES

1

Venice Blvd.

405

Baldwin Hills

2 **Kenneth Hahn State Recreation Area**

La Cienega Blvd.

La Brea Ave.

Slauson Ave.

Lincoln Blvd.

Ballona Creek

Culver Blvd.

Jefferson Blvd.

42

Manchester Ave.

Ballona Creek, Playa del Rey 1

Lincoln Blvd.

Century Blvd.

Los Angeles International Airport (LAX)

1

Sepulveda Blvd.

405

Imperial Hwy.

North

Bell Ave.

Rosecrans Ave.

Sand Dune Park 3
(Manhattan Beach)

0   Kilometers   8

0   Miles   5

Creek channel. From Los Angeles International Airport (hereafter LAX), drive north on Sepulveda Boulevard to Lincoln Boulevard (at a Y-intersection). Take Lincoln Boulevard to Jefferson Boulevard. Turn left on Jefferson, which meets Culver Boulevard at another Y-intersection. Continue west on Culver for 1.0 mile to Pacific Avenue. Turn right. Pacific Avenue ends at the bridge over Ballona Creek. Walk across the bridge and bird west to the end of the jetty. Take your scope to view the breakwater. Return over the bridge and walk upstream along the Ballona Creek channel to view the wetlands. Diving ducks, gulls, and an occasional Ross's Goose winter on the small lagoon along Pacific Avenue.

Kenneth Hahn State Recreation Area (Baldwin Hills). This site is good for migrant and wintering landbirds, hummingbirds, breeding Bullock's and Hooded Orioles, and resident Spotted Doves. The Baldwin Hills include the largest remaining natural open space in the Los Angeles Basin, but many chaparral species (e.g., Oak Titmouse, Wrentit) are absent. Hahn Park is extensively landscaped, with some natural coastal-scrub areas. From LAX take Century Boulevard east to I-405 (San Diego Freeway); enter northbound I-405 and exit immediately at La Cienega Boulevard. Go north on La Cienega about 3 miles to the Hahn Park entrance. There is a parking fee on weekends.

Sand Dune Park (Manhattan Beach). This small, groomed park in a residential area is good for migrants, vagrants, Spotted Doves, and local resident birds (including Allen's Hummingbirds), and is easy to bird. From LAX, drive south on Sepulveda Boulevard to Rosecrans Avenue. Turn right (west) on Rosecrans and go just over 1 mile to Bell Avenue. Turn left (south) on Bell and go three blocks. Turn right into the park. Bird the trails on the hillside to the west.

North of the airport—but not truly "close" to the airport, given traffic conditions—**Franklin Canyon** in Beverly Hills can produce Black Phoebe, Oak Titmouse, Wrentit, California Thrasher, and other chaparral and oak woodland birds, all resident here. From LAX, drive north on I-405 to Sunset Boulevard. Turn right (east) and go to Beverly Drive. Turn left (north) onto Beverly Drive to Franklin Canyon Drive. Take Franklin Canyon Drive over the hill to the upper reservoir; there is a nice nature center here.

PALOS VERDES PENINSULA

Half day; year round

This tour includes a precise location for finding California Gnatcatcher and Cactus Wren. From LAX, drive east on Century Boulevard to I-405. Go south on I-405 to Western Avenue (about 8 miles). Turn right (south) on Western and drive through the hills to 25th Street. Turn right (west) on 25th, which turns into Palos Verdes Drive South. Continue on Palos Verdes Drive South about 2.5 miles to Forrestal Drive. Turn right on Forrestal and park at the end of the road. Walk uphill into the gravel quarries and listen for the birds in the sage scrub and cactus. (Note that some scrub species, notably Wrentit, are absent from the Palos Verdes Peninsula.)

For seabird and whale-watching from coastal bluffs, visit **Long Point**. Scan offshore (a spotting scope is recommended) for Black-vented Shearwater in fall and winter, three species of cormorants, "Black" Brant, scoters, shorebirds, gulls, and terns during migration, and, if you are lucky, even a few Parasitic and Pomarine (scarce) Jaegers in spring and fall. From Forrestal Drive (above), continue west on Palos Verdes Drive South to the entrance to Point Vicente Lighthouse (not accessible for birding). Make a 180-degree turn, and drive back east for about a half-mile to the parking lot on your right, overlooking the ocean and the rocky shore below. If time permits, the same species could also be looked for at **Royal Palms State Beach, White Point,** and **Point Fermin**. All three spots are located east of the southern terminus of Western Avenue, along the coast. Nearby **Averill Park** and **Peck Park** are good for Allen's Hummingbirds and migrants. Both parks are just east of Western Avenue; Averill is just south of 9th Street, and Peck is north of Summerland Avenue.

Harbor Regional Park offers a chance for Least Bittern (difficult to see; check the reeds near the south end of the lake) and resident Tricolored Blackbird, and is good for wintering birds and migrants. *Use extra caution when birding here (many people illegally make the park their home).* From LAX, drive south on I-405 to the I-110 Freeway. Exit on Pacific Coast Highway (Highway 1). After 0.5 mile turn right (west) to Vermont Avenue and turn left into the park. Check the lake from the west or the south; check the edge of the willows on the north side of the park for migrants, vagrants, and wintering birds. (Note: the golf course east of the lake is off limits.)

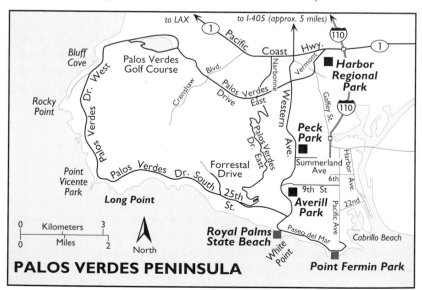

PALOS VERDES PENINSULA

LOS ANGELES RIVER
Half day; summer and fall

From June through November, or before the first winter rains scour the algae and other growth from the concrete-lined river bottom, the lower reaches of the **Los Angeles River** offer the best opportunity in the Los Angeles Basin for a good number and variety of shorebirds. Peregrine Falcons frequently hunt along this portion of the river, and, if you are looking for Nutmeg Mannikin and Orange Bishop, these species are common in the ditch on the east side of the bike path. It is better to bird the river in the morning, when the sun is at your back. Access the bike path on the east bank of the river by taking I-710 (Long Beach Freeway) to Del Amo Boulevard; go east over the river to Orange Avenue, then south no more than 100 yards from the intersection, and park. Walk west on the dirt path for 200 yards to the river. Another option is an additional three miles south on I-710 to Willow Street east over the river to Golden Avenue; go north a very short block and then west (left) onto 26th Way toward the river to De Forest, where you will park near a gate to the bike path east of the riverbank. These two sites will provide access to the best four birding miles of the river.

DESCANSO GARDENS
Half day; year round

Descanso Gardens, located in La Cañada-Flintridge, is good for Wood and Ring-necked Ducks on the pond in winter, migrants in spring and fall, and resident chaparral and oak-woodland birds in the well-maintained gardens. It's a lovely spot for birders and non-birders alike, located at 1413 Descanso Drive, La Cañada-Flintridge; open daily from 9:00AM to 4:30PM, entrance fee. The San Fernando Valley Audubon Society has a free birdwalk the second and fourth Sundays of every month at 8:00AM. From LAX, drive north to I-10 (Santa Monica Freeway). Go east to I-110 (Harbor Freeway) and north on I-110 to I-5 through downtown Los Angeles (you might want to pick a longer but better route if traveling during rush hour). The exit to I-5 is on the left. Go northwest on I-5 to Highway 2 (Glendale Freeway) and right (northeast) on Highway 2 to Verdugo Road. Turn right (east) onto Verdugo and go to Descanso Drive. Turn right and follow signs into the gardens.

SEPULVEDA BASIN AND WILDLIFE AREA
Half day; year round

Sepulveda Basin and Wildlife Area is good year round, but best from fall to spring. Located just west of the junction of the notorious I-405 and Burbank Boulevard in the San Fernando Valley, this large park has a wildlife area east of Woodley Avenue and north and south of Burbank Boulevard on the east side, and Lake Balboa (east of Balboa Avenue) on the west side. Look for American White Pelicans, American Bitterns, geese (mainly Canada, but often present are White-fronted, Snow, and Ross's), and ducks. Breeding birds include Yellow-breasted Chat, Spotted Towhee (south of Burbank Boulevard), and Blue Grosbeak (along the river between the model-airplane field and Lake Balboa). Tricolored Blackbirds are frequently found at Lake Balboa, and Lawrence's Goldfinches are occasional at any time (check the wildlife area).

MALIBU LAGOON AND MALIBU CREEK STATE PARK
Half day; year round

Malibu **Lagoon** is good for shorebirds in migration, ducks, gulls, and terns in winter, and unexpected rarities any time of year. King Eider, Piping Plover, Pileated Woodpecker, and Yellow Wagtail are one-time sightings here. Check the flowering Cape Honeysuckle east of the bridge on the ocean side of the highway for Allen's Hummingbirds (year round). Scope offshore for Black-vented Shearwaters (fall, winter). The total distance from LAX is approximately 25 miles. From LAX, drive north on I-405 to I-10. Go west on I-10 to the end and continue northwest on Pacific Coast Highway (Highway 1) to Malibu. The state park maintains a fee parking lot south of Pacific Coast Highway at Cross Creek Road, or you may look for parking along the south side of Pacific Coast Highway west of Cross Creek Road. Do not leave valuables visible in your car.

To reach **Malibu Creek State Park** continue a short distance farther west on the Pacific Coast Highway to Malibu Canyon Road and turn right. Continue up the canyon 5.0 miles, passing through the tunnel. Just past Piuma Road is the left-hand entrance to the Tapia Park portion of Malibu Creek State Park; 1.3 miles farther up the highway is the main entrance to the park (entrance fee). Both sections of the park have oak woodland, chaparral, and riparian habitats, and there are extensive open areas in the main part of the park (where several hiking trails traverse all habitats.) Watch for White-tailed Kite, Red-shouldered Hawk, Acorn and Nuttall's Woodpeckers, Oak Titmouse, Canyon Wren (gorge in main park), Western Bluebird, Wrentit,, California Thrasher, Rufous-crowned Sparrow, Lawrence's Goldfinch (erratic, scarcest in winter), and a good selection of migrants.

EL DORADO NATURE CENTER AND PARK
Half day; fall, winter, spring

El **Dorado Nature Center and Park**, located in Long Beach at 7550 E. Spring Street, is best during migration and winter. Take I-405 south approximately 24 miles to Studebaker and exit north to Spring Street. Turn right to the park entrance; closed Mondays, parking fee required. (Be sure to walk the trails at the Nature Center; a Blue Mockingbird wintered here in 1999–2000). The park is good for migrant and wintering Townsend's Warblers and a few Black-throated Gray Warblers as well as resident Allen's Hummingbird. Tricolored Blackbirds are often around the lakes in Areas II and III. The park is open from 7:00AM to dusk; the Nature Center opens at 8:00AM. This park and the two Huntington Beach sites can be done together in a long half-day.

HUNTINGTON BEACH

Half day; year round

Huntington Central Park and Bolsa Chica Preserve are located in Huntington Beach (Orange County). To reach the park, drive south on I-405 to Golden West Street; take Golden West south past Warner Street. Huntington Central Park is a few blocks farther south between Slater and Talbert. Good birding, especially for migrants and vagrants, can be found throughout the park both east and west of Golden West Street. Common Ground-Dove and Allen's Hummingbird are resident. To reach **Bolsa Chica Preserve** from Huntington Central Park, continue south on Golden West to the Pacific Coast Highway. Turn right (north) to the Bolsa Chica Preserve (about 2.5 miles). Nesting terns (including Elegant) and skimmers are numerous, and the preserve is also good for ducks and shorebirds during migration and winter and for herons year round.

POINT MUGU, OXNARD PLAIN, AND SANTA CRUZ ISLAND

Full day plus; year round

Point Mugu and the Oxnard Plain are reached fom LAX via Highway 1 past the Malibu Lagoon (see Malibu Lagoon section on previous page); continue west along the coast about 23 miles to just past Point Mugu Rock for a few hundred yards to where it becomes legal to cross the highway; make a U-turn back to the point. Do not try to cross over the double-yellow line at the Point; it is dangerous and the California Highway Patrol will issue you an expensive citation if you are caught. From Point Mugu scope the ocean for Black-vented (September through March) and Sooty and Pink-footed Shearwaters (scarce, but most common April through October), Black Storm-Petrel (scarce, summer), sea ducks, jaegers, gulls, and terns. On the way to Point Mugu, stop at Leo Carrillo State Park (15 miles) in the fall and winter to search for rocky shorebirds. Big Sycamore Canyon Campground, in Point Mugu State Park can be good for migrant passerines in spring and fall, including a few vagrant species, especially if there is water in the creek bed.

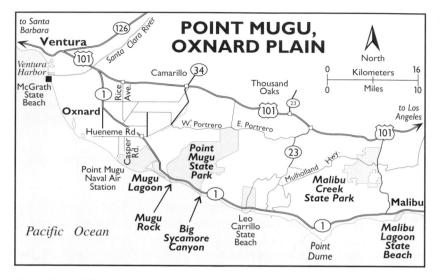

From Point Mugu, continue north—checking the lagoons on your left for herons, ducks, and shorebirds—for approximately 2.5 miles and take the Hueneme Road exit. Go west on Hueneme Road, checking the sod fields for shorebirds and rare longspurs (fall and winter). Turn left on Casper Road for more sod fields. Pacific Golden-Plover is regular in small numbers in the fall. *Bird these fields only from the public paved roads.*

Santa Cruz Island is a must for anyone wanting to see the endemic Island Scrub-Jay. Boats leave from Ventura Harbor, 90 minutes northwest of LAX via Highway 101. Contact Island Packers in Ventura, 1867 Spinnaker Drive, Ventura, CA 93001, (805) 642-7688, for recorded information, and (805) 642-1393 to make reservations. Island Packers runs year-round trips to and around this and other Channel Islands, where you should see a number of pelagic species (including Xantus's Murrelet, February–June). Island Scrub-Jays are easily found on trips that land at Prisoners' Harbor; to find them at Scorpion Anchorage (where most trips land) may require an easy hike of a mile each way. Allen's Hummingbirds are island residents.

SAN GABRIEL MOUNTAINS
Full day; year round

The **San Gabriel Mountains** along the Angeles Crest Highway offer the most accessible montane birding from LAX or Burbank Airport. Take the Angeles Crest Highway exit off the Foothill (#210) Freeway in La Cañada-Flintridge. Good mixed-coniferous forest areas are found around Charlton Flat and Chilao, beginning around 25 miles up the highway. Mountain Quail (try Chilao Visitor Center), White-headed Woodpecker, Red-breasted

Sapsucker, Pygmy Nuthatch, Brown Creeper, Red Crossbill (winter), etc., are all possible. At Buckhorn Campground and beyond, some additional high-mountain species are encountered, such as breeding Dusky Flycatcher, Green-tailed Towhee, "Thick-billed" Fox Sparrow, and resident Clark's Nutcracker and Williamson's Sapsucker (the latter usually requires hiking well above the highway; it's more widespread in fall and winter). Higher portions of the highway are closed in winter. A National Forest "Adventure Pass" (daily or annual fee) is required for parking. Passes may be obtained at any Forest Service ranger station or at many local sporting-goods stores.

ANTELOPE VALLEY
Half to full day; year round

The **Antelope Valley**, two hours north of LAX via I-405/I-5/Highway 14, includes sites from Quail Lake (along Highway 138) in the west to Saddleback Butte in the east, and Big Rock Creek in the south to Rosamond in the north. This is a huge area, and most of your birding will be short walks or done from the car. Quail Lake is best for wintering ducks. In late fall and winter, look for raptors (including Ferruginous Hawk and Prairie Falcon), and Mountain Plovers and Mountain Bluebirds in agricultural land north of Avenue A and 110th Street West. Le Conte's Thrashers nest widely but in small numbers in Joshua Tree/creosote scrub along small washes; one location is north of the Antelope Valley Country Club at Avenue O and Division in Palmdale. Scott's Orioles nest in the Joshua Trees west of Longview Road and Pallett Creek Road in the southeast valley; Ladder-backed Woodpeckers and Verdins are also resident in these habitats.

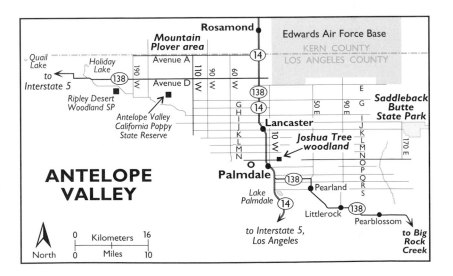

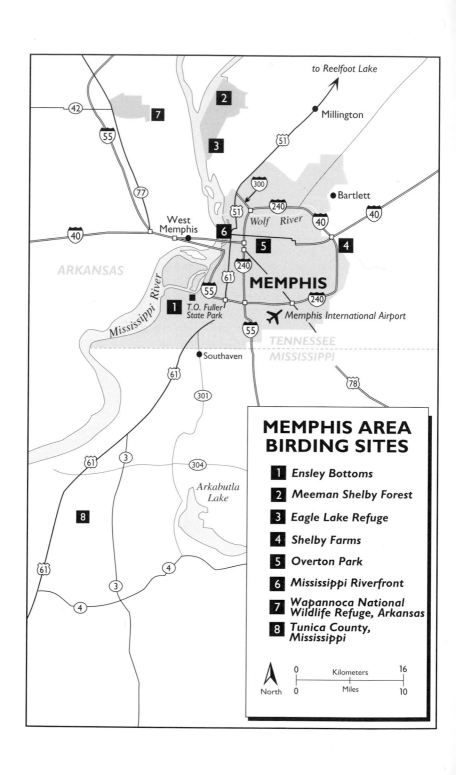

to Reelfoot Lake

42

55

77

7

2

3

Millington

51

300

240

Bartlett

40

40

West
Memphis

51

Wolf River

40

6

5

4

40

ARKANSAS

240

61

Mississippi River

55

MEMPHIS

1

T.O. Fuller
State Park

240

Memphis International Airport

55

TENNESSEE

Southaven

MISSISSIPPI

61

78

301

61

3

304

Arkabutla
Lake

8

61

3

4

4

3

4

MEMPHIS AREA BIRDING SITES

1 Ensley Bottoms

2 Meeman Shelby Forest

3 Eagle Lake Refuge

4 Shelby Farms

5 Overton Park

6 Mississippi Riverfront

7 Wapannoca National
Wildlife Refuge, Arkansas

8 Tunica County,
Mississippi

0   Kilometers   16

North 0   Miles   10

MEMPHIS, TENNESSEE

Jeff R. Wilson

Memphis, Tennessee, brings to mind images of Elvis Presley, barbecue, Beale Street (the home of the blues), cotton, and the mighty Mississippi River. You can get all that, plus fine birding, here in the Heart of the South and smack-dab in the middle of what is arguably the greatest flyway in North America. During the "Memphis in May Festival," the world's largest Bar-B-Q cooking contest is held on the banks of the Mississippi, Beale Street is playing the blues, and spring migration is in full swing. There is something here for the birder at all seasons. There is also an extra bonus for those working on their state lists: with Memphis being in the very southwest corner of Tennessee, it is just a short jump into prime habitat in adjoining Mississippi and Arkansas.

In the early days, the Mississippi River brought adventurers, explorers, and ornithologists to stay on its high bluff. Today, you can go north on the river and see a colony of Bank Swallows at the very location which John James Audubon wrote about on a journey that he took to New Orleans. It is written that the historic Mississippi Delta starts in the lobby of the famous Peabody Hotel in downtown Memphis. Here, every morning a group of Mallards is ceremoniously marched from their roost on the roof, down the elevator, and across the plush red carpet to reside in the beautiful lobby fountain. Within thirty miles of this historic hotel, prime birding habitats abound: upland and bottomland hardwoods, swamps, sloughs, agricultural fields, the largest concentration of catfish ponds in the South, city parks, state parks, national wildlife refuges, sand-bars, lakes, and, perhaps best of all, a birder-friendly sewage-treatment plant that attracts shorebirds by the thousands. A world-class zoo plus museums and a botanical garden are available for your non-birding pleasure.

ESSENTIAL INFORMATION

Getting Around: The Memphis International Airport is a major hub for Northwest Airlines and is served by most other major carriers as well. It is located at the crossroads of Interstate 40 and Interstate 55. Amtrak serves the city with the famous "City of New Orleans." Although freeway travel is generally not too bad, it can get bogged down from 7:00–8:00AM and from 5:00–6:00PM; alternate routes to all locations can be found with a good map.

Climate: While in the mid-South, you can expect moderate weather with average daily high temperatures of 60°F in winter, 77°F in spring, 91°F in summer, and 78°F in fall. The extremes can be just that, with the highest temperature recorded being 108°F and the low a bone-chilling -13°F. Average annual precipitation is 55 inches, with March and December having the most rainfall and August and October showing the least. Humidity can be high, with an average through the year at 3:00PM of 51 percent. The average wind speed is clocked at 7 knots.

Safety: Although Ensley Bottoms is an isolated area, it is relatively secure in that the Tennessee Valley Authority (TVA) has a continuous security patrol, and the treatment lagoons are in constant operation. The employees at the lagoons are on the alert for suspicious individuals, so keep your binoculars held high. The *No Trespassing* signs at the Earth Complex also help keep the traffic down to just birders and employees. Many of the resident women birders in the area bird there alone, but I do not recommend this practice. Usually, some birder in Memphis would be happy to bird with you. Even though Overton Park is located in the center of town, and thus receives much use, some caution should be taken on the more-remote trails. Normal precautions should be taken at all state parks and national wildlife refuges, although those mentioned here are safe. None of the areas listed below has a reputation for crime, but as anywhere on this good earth, being cautious and alert always pays off.

THE BIRDING YEAR

Each season passes one to another in stages that peel away like the layers of an onion, with only subtle separations at each end. The spring season changes in fits and spurts, with most migrants quickly continuing north, in a hurry to breed. The highest species diversity occurs during the second week in May, when the late/early migrants overlap the early/late birds. This is a magical time, and a good birding day can produce 130–140 species. Summer can be slow, but it can also be the most revealing and educational of all seasons. Sitting-and-watching produces many unexpected records during those long hot days. Fall in the South starts much earlier than most people believe; the hints come early when the first returning shorebirds show up in late June, and Dickcissels and Painted Buntings start to thin out in late July and August. In autumn, the changes in avian composition are brought about mostly by changes in the weather, as northern breeding species filter through largely during pre-set date spans, but the largest numbers are associated with the passage of fronts. Winter presents us with fewer species, but that lack is made up for in sheer numbers (particularly waterfowl). One hundred species in a day is an achievable winter goal in the area.

BIRDING SITES

Now for the meat and potatoes: Birding along the Mighty Mississippi River can produce just about any species, and during migration it produces *many* species. Some particularly good areas for the visiting birder are Ensley Bottoms and environs, Meeman Shelby Forest, Eagle Lake Refuge, Shelby Farms, Overton Park, and the Mississippi River Front. Still within a 30-mile radius of Memphis are the Wapannoca National Wildlife Refuge and nearby rice fields (in Arkansas) and Tunica County and Arkabutla Lake (in Mississippi).

For those birders with extra time, magical and historical **Reelfoot Lake** (25,000 acres in size, of which 15,000 are water) is located 100 miles to the north. This cypress-filled lake was formed in the early 1800s by what was likely the largest earthquake ever recorded in the U.S. in historic times, one that was felt far and wide, even ringing church bells in Charleston and Boston. To fill this great depression, the Mississippi River ran backward for three days. The lake and the surrounding area hold great treasures for birders, but they would take a whole chapter unto themselves to cover adequately.

ENSLEY BOTTOMS

Half or full day; year round

Of the birding sites within the city, **Ensley Bottoms** supports the greatest species diversity. Over 300 species have been recorded within a five-mile circle centered on TVA's Allen Steam Plant. Ensley is located in the extreme southwest corner of Tennessee but still inside the Memphis city limits. It is nestled in a large sweeping curve of the Mississippi River, and many birds take a short-cut and fly over the area. All the necessary habitats are present to produce a great variety of species in any season. The Maxson Water-Treatment Lagoons serve up the best in shorebirds. The area is called "The Earth Complex," after the tree-and-leaf recycling, sod production, and agricultural endeavors.

You should check in at the plant headquarters for information just in case the rules have changed. The signs read *No Unauthorized Vehicles* allowed, but birders are welcome. Over the years birders have had a great working relationship with the management and its employees. The main rules include *not* parking on any levees or roads, and immediately giving the right-of-way to any trucks or other equipment. These lagoons are easily birded as long as the levees are not wet, but even then they can be walked. Because of the "gumbo" clay, sometimes even a light rain can get you into trouble. Many of the roads are gravel; but always play it safe in case of a sudden rainstorm, and leave your car on firm ground. The good news is that the winds will dry these slick spots relatively quickly.

Of the 43 species of shorebirds that have been seen in Tennessee, 40 have been seen at The Earth Complex; additionally, Purple Sandpiper has occurred on the nearby river. There are shorebirds present during all months of the year. Spring migration gets into full swing in late March and continues until the last White-rumped Sandpipers leave in early June. Almost immediately, fall migration begins during the last week of June and continues well into October and November. The best month for a large variety of shorebirds is August, when up to 20 species can be seen on a good day, with a few more possible on a great day. The numbers build to some 3,000–6,000 birds (sometimes more) in September and October. Killdeer and Black-necked Stilts are regular breeders, and there is one nesting record of Spotted Sandpiper. Ensley is the Ruff headquarters of the South, with 13 records (including one bird that stayed for 60 days during the fall of 1994); females appear in the spring, usually around the first two weeks in May, and males in the fall from August into November. Other notable visitors include such vagrants as Long-billed Curlew, Sharp-tailed Sandpiper, and Red-necked Stint, plus occasional Piping Plovers, Hudsonian Godwits, and Whimbrels. Wilson's Phalaropes appear in the spring and fall, with Red-necked and Red Phalaropes and Red Knots found rarely in the fall.

An active Bald Eagle nest is located at Ensley Bottoms, and the first successful nesting of Western Kingbird for the state was recorded here in

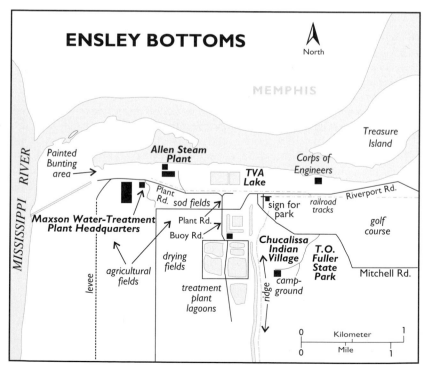

1999. Spotted Towhees have been spotted here four times, there are many records for Scissor-tailed Flycatcher and Western Meadowlark, and even a Vermilion Flycatcher has graced a birder's eyes at this magical spot. The agricultural fields and fallow areas provide habitat for breeding Horned Larks and wintering flocks of sparrows and Lapland Longspurs. During spring migration, impressive lists of flycatchers can be recorded along the edges of willow groves, with Eastern Wood-Pewee as well as Acadian, Yellow-bellied, Alder, Willow, Least, and Olive-sided Flycatchers, and Eastern Phoebe usually present around the middle of May. Multiple Philadelphia Vireos can be seen in the willows during migration and are easily compared to the Warbling Vireos that breed here. This area and nearby Presidents Island are the only reliable places in Tennessee to see nesting Painted Buntings. Willow Fly-catchers and Blue Grosbeak also breed here. The songs of Dickcissels will ring from every stalk and tree in the late spring and summer; those of Bobolinks may be heard from the extensive plots of vetch during spring migration.

At the TVA Lake you might see or at least hear Least Bittern (sometime breeder) or American Bittern (migrant). In winter, ducks trade in and out of the lake, including Greater Scaup mixed in with the Lessers. Long-tailed Ducks make periodic visits. The large roosting flocks of blackbirds harbor occasional Yellow-headeds. With the Mississippi River curving just to the north and west, many unusual migrants have appeared in this area: Neotropic Cormorant, Black-bellied Whistling-Duck, Garganey (two records), all three ibises, Western Tanager, and Lazuli Bunting (two records), to name a few.

From Ensley it is a three-minute drive to bird the woodlands found at the tail-end of the last Chickasaw Bluff, just a half-mile to the east at **Chucalissa Indian Village** and **T. O. Fuller State Park**, (901) 543-7581 or -7582. The woods here are 100 feet above those of the bottomland and offer great habitat for resident and migrant birds. There is an excellent and newly-renovated campground in the park, and the Indian museum at Chucalissa is highly recommended.

Directions: Coming from either north or south take Exit 9 (Mallory) off I-55, go east on Mallory one block, and then right (south) on Riverport. After 2 miles this road runs on top of a levee bordering some great wetland habitat that often produces many herons, including the occasional Tricolored, as well as ibis, Wood Stork, and Wild Turkey. Proceed to Plant Road; you will pass the signs for T.O. Fuller State Park and Chucalissa Indian Village (remember those for later). Making a right on Plant Road will take you past the TVA Lake (on a short dead-end spur road to the right) and Allen Steam Plant and straight into the parking lot of T. E. Maxson Water-Treatment Plant. Here you can check for information on existing conditions or restrictions. Reverse your course, and when you get back to Riverport continue straight and proceed south on Buoy Road past the drying and maintenance buildings to the lagoons.

Swainson's Warbler
Shawneen Finnegan

MEEMAN SHELBY FOREST AND EAGLE LAKE REFUGE

Half or full day; year round

Meeman Shelby Forest is a large (13,467-acre) wooded state park just north of Memphis; it straddles the Third Chickasaw Bluff, drops off into the rich flood-prone alluvial plain of the river, and supports an impressive list of resident and migrant species. A May morning spent from the top of the ridge down the 100-foot drop-off to the bottomland woods can reward the birder with 20-plus species of warblers, including breeding Cerulean and Swainson's. The most consistent area for finding these two species is on the road past the hunter check-in station. This road can be walked as it drops off the bluff and down to the floodplain. Ceruleans can be found all along the upper and especially the middle part before the road levels out. They also can be found along many of the trails that follow the bluff top. (Sometimes you can be looking straight out into the tops of the trees.) The Swainson's occupy at least three territories after the road levels out and on an old road that runs off to the right at the bottom of the bluff. Directions to the hunter check-in station are given below. The park's lakes, woods, and fields can easily occupy a birder for an entire day.

Eagle Lake Refuge is adjacent to and just south of Meaman Shelby Forest. It sits wholly in the floodplain at the base of the 100-foot Third Chickasaw Bluff and is strategically situated next to the Mississippi River. The refuge's 1,500 acres comprising woodlands, fields, and ponded areas are conveniently

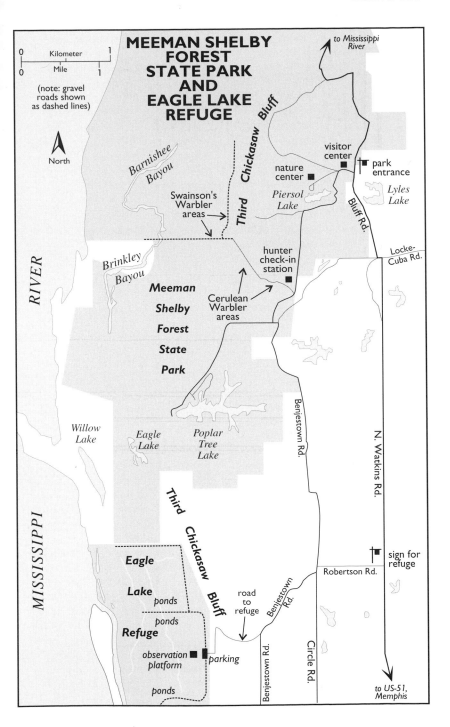

MEEMAN SHELBY
FOREST
STATE PARK
AND
EAGLE LAKE
REFUGE

Kilometer

Mile

(note: gravel
roads shown
as dashed lines)

North

to Mississippi
River

Barnishee
Bayou

Third Chickasaw Bluff

Swainson's
Warbler
areas

Piersol
Lake

nature
center

visitor
center

park
entrance

Lyles
Lake

Bluff Rd.

Locke-
Cuba Rd.

RIVER

Brinkley
Bayou

hunter
check-in
station

Meeman
Shelby
Forest
State
Park

Cerulean
Warbler
areas

Benjestown Rd.

N. Watkins Rd.

Willow
Lake

Eagle
Lake

Poplar
Tree
Lake

Third Chickasaw Bluff

MISSISSIPPI

Eagle
Lake
ponds

Robertson Rd.

sign for
refuge

ponds

Refuge

road
to
refuge

Benjestown Rd.

observation
platform

parking

Benjestown Rd.

Circle Rd.

ponds

to US-51,
Memphis

located for a quick morning or afternoon birding trip. It is a newly developed area, operated as a multi-purpose waterfowl/shorebird refuge by the Tennessee Wildlife Resource Agency in cooperation with Ducks Unlimited. The finest observation platform in the South was recently dedicated here; the ramped, multi-level platform is 36 feet high and is handicap-accessible. Spring floods recharge the ponded areas, but in dry years the managers have the facilities to pump water into the ponds. With appropriate water/soil management it is potentially the best combined waterfowl/shorebird viewing site in Tennessee. At this time the Tennessee Ornithological Society and Ducks Unlimited are helping to design and facilitate new management plans. The paved road down the bluff is a favorite place for Yellow-bellied Flycatcher in both spring and fall migration. American White Pelican, many species of waterfowl, and Bald Eagle are regular visitors, whereas Wood Stork, Tricolored Heron, Purple Gallinule, and Hudsonian Godwit may sometimes provide a wake-me-up.

To reach Meeman Shelby Forest, from Interstate Spur 300, which connects the north leg of I-240 to Highway 51 (Danny Thomas Boulevard), go north on Danny Thomas Boulevard for 2.75 miles to North Watkins. Make a left and proceed north to where this road meets Locke-Cuba Road at a T-intersection. Turn left and proceed 0.75 mile and turn right on Bluff Road. The entrance to the headquarters is 0.75 mile on your left. Information and trail maps can be obtained at the new headquarters building. To find the check-in station go west from the headquarters building and take the left fork, marked Piersol Lake; go approximately 2 miles to the sign for the station, turn right, and park in the lot, because the road is closed beyond this point. Some areas of the park are closed during hunting season and will be posted; to check this call (901) 876-5215 or -5216.

The Eagle Lake Refuge is located just south of Meeman Shelby off of Benjestown Road; signage can be followed from North Watkins. From the check-in station go south 0.75 mile and go left 0.2 mile to Benjestown Road. At Benjestown turn right and go 3.75 miles to a sign for the refuge.

MEMPHIS CITY PARKS

Half day; year round

Shelby Farms (4,500 acres) is the largest urban park in the world situated entirely within a city's limits. The park is a mix of agricultural, pastoral, and woodland settings combined with walking and bike paths, most of which are open to the public. Tree-canopied footpaths along the Wolf River, lakes, fish ponds, rolling hills, and agricultural and fallow fields hold many surprising species at all seasons. Tennessee's first White-winged Dove and second Black-bellied Whistling-Duck were found here, and these are only a few of the many good birds found there over the years. Smith's Longspurs are occasionally found here in November and December, if *Aristida* grass is present.

Directions: On the east leg of I-240 take Exit 13 for Walnut Grove and proceed east 0.75 mile; after crossing the Wolf River, you will find yourself in the middle of the Shelby Farms Complex.

Overton Park is a 315-acre park with a large stand of old-growth hardwoods located in the heart of Memphis. The Memphis Zoo and Brooks Art Museum adjoin Overton Park. The park is a convenient and excellent place for woodland migrants during spring and fall and is a fine location to see and hear Fish Crows, which nest here. Caution is warranted while walking on some of the more-remote trails.

MISSISSIPPI RIVERFRONT

Half day; year round

There are many places along the **Mississippi Riverfront** in Memphis from which to scan the river: the River Walk (which runs along the top of the bluff), Tom Lee Park (home of the World Championship Barbecue Contest), and Jefferson Davis Park all can be reached from Riverside Drive. Almost anything can fly by: jaegers, Little, Glaucous, and Sabine's Gulls have all been recorded from these riverfront sites.

But by far the best birding can be had on Mud Island in the residential section located just north of the Memphis Bridge. You can

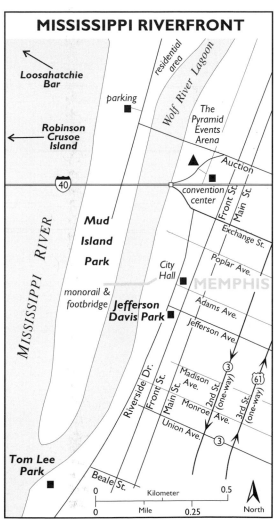

MISSISSIPPI RIVERFRONT

Loosahatchie Bar

residential area

Wolf River Lagoon

parking

Robinson Crusoe Island

The Pyramid Events Arena

40

Auction

convention center

Front St.

Main St.

Exchange St.

MISSISSIPPI RIVER

Mud Island Park

Poplar Ave.

City Hall

MEMPHIS

monorail & footbridge

Jefferson Davis Park

Adams Ave.

Jefferson Ave.

Riverside Dr.

Front St.

Main St.

Madison Ave.

2nd St. (one-way)

3rd St. (one-way)

3

61

Monroe Ave.

Union Ave.

3

Tom Lee Park

Beale St.

0   Kilometer   0.5

0   Mile   0.25

North

reach this island by driving north on Front Street past the Pyramid Events Arena and then taking a left onto Auction. Check the cottonwoods for nesting Baltimore Orioles and for raptors (winter). From here you have a close view of the river, the Loosahatchie Bar, and Robinson Crusoe Island. All of the area across the river from here is actually in Tennessee, as the mighty Mississippi River over the years has shown little respect for the state boundaries laid out by humans. The sand-bar has provided many exciting birds over the years, such as Wood Stork, Long-billed Curlew, and Purple Sandpiper. Peregrine Falcons are sometimes seen perched on or hunting from the Memphis Bridge.

WAPANNOCA NATIONAL WILDLIFE REFUGE AND RICE FIELDS, ARKANSAS

Half or full day; all seasons

Wapannoca National Wildlife Refuge is just 22 miles from the Memphis Bridge and contains fine bottomland hardwood forest and a large cypress-lined lake. Many successful Arkansas Big Days in early May have begun here, where by late morning you might record 120-plus species, including 25-plus warblers. It is truly a jewel situated in the broad agricultural desert in the delta country of northeastern Arkansas.

During the autumn of 1999, birders began to explore the birding (i.e., rail) potential of the rice-harvesting operations that take place only a few miles from Memphis and just west of I-55 and Wapannoca NWR. In late September–October 2000, fantastic results were had, with large numbers of Soras and Virginia Rails found, and as many as five Yellow and 11 Black Rails seen. The method used to see these birds is to find a rice field being harvested and then stand at the end of the field where the combines are turning around. Many of the rails will be seen as they flush. To see a Black Rail you should look down the fresh tire tracks and hope to see one run down or across these tracks as they scurry from small patch to small patch of remaining stubble. Similar results have been achieved since the 1980s by those observing late-fall rice-harvesting operations in southwestern Louisiana and east Texas.

Directions: For Wapannoca NWR, take I-55 or I-40 across the river into Arkansas. Go west approximately 8 miles and take I-55 north for 14 miles and exit at Highway 42 (Exit 21). Go east 1.5 miles, pass under a railroad bridge, and proceed to the entrance, which is immediately on your right. To find the rice fields for autumn railing, drive the roads in any direction off I-40 and I-55 west of Memphis in Arkansas.

TUNICA COUNTY, MISSISSIPPI

Half or full day; November through March

Great winter birding starts about 25 miles south of the Peabody Hotel Lobby in the "delta" region of **Tunica County, Mississippi**. Here, flat land stretches for miles and is filled with cotton, soybeans, and catfish ponds, all of which provide excellent birding opportunities. The recent introduction of rice farming in the area is responsible for the burgeoning flocks of ducks and Lapland Longspurs. Mixed-species flocks, including four species of geese and numbering 20,000–30,000 individuals, are found regularly. Huge flocks of Lapland Longspurs (2,000–5,000) feed in the rolled rice fields. Double-crested Cormorants, grebes, and waterfowl collect in numbers around the catfish ponds. Among the regular Bonaparte's, Ring-billed, and Herring Gulls there have been Franklin's, Laughing, and Glaucous. An amazing collection of Red-tailed Hawks can be found here, with dark-morph, rufous-morph, Harlan's (light and dark), Krider's, and Fuertes' recorded. A winter ride through the area can produce over 100 Red-taileds and 60 Northern Harriers, plus Sharp-shinned, Cooper's, Red-shouldered, and Merlin. If you follow the harriers to their evening roost-sites, you might well encounter Short-eared Owls. Recently small numbers of Sandhill Cranes have been found wintering in this area. The birding is best within the triangle formed by Highway 61, Highway 3, and Highway 4. (This area is located just to the east of the third-largest gambling center in the United States.) The overall area looks like any other largely denuded delta countryside, but persevere, for birds abound.

Just east of Tunica County and up in the hills you will find **Arkabutla Lake,** a large Corp of Engineers impoundment with surrounding pinewoods. In the winter you might find good numbers of loons, waterfowl, eagles, and gulls, and large flocks of American White Pelicans.

Directions: From I-55 take Exit 7 south onto Highway 61. Eight miles to the south you will enter Mississippi. Proceed 11 miles farther to the junction with Highway 3, which angles off to the left. You are now on the east leg of the "magic triangle," formed by Highways 61, 3, and 4. From here you can take Arkabutla Lake Road up onto the bluff and directly to the lake.

MIAMI AREA BIRDING SITES

1. Virginia Key
2. Bill Baggs Cape Florida State Recreation Area
3. Crandon Park
4. A.D. "Doug" Barnes County Park
5. Kenwood Elementary School
6. Baptist Hospital
7. Kendall Indian Hammocks Park
8. Pinecrest
9. Fairchild Tropical Gardens
10. Matheson Hammock County Park
11. Cutler Ridge
12. Miami Springs, Airport
13. Everglades National Park
14. John U. Lloyd State Recreation Area
15. Hugh Taylor Birch State Recreation Area
16. Spanish River Park
17. Wakodahatchee Wetlands
18. Florida Keys

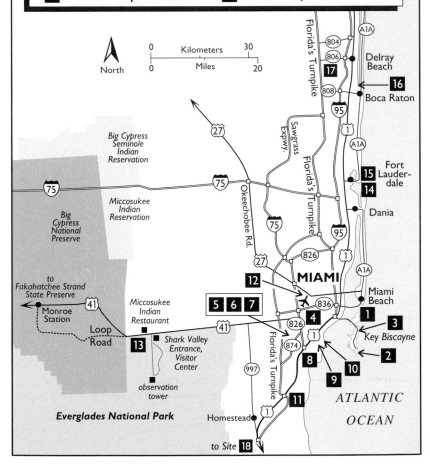

MIAMI, FLORIDA

Larry Manfredi and Mickey Wheeler

South Florida hosts a variety of birds—regional specialties, Caribbean strays, and exotics—that are difficult or impossible to find in other areas of the United States. Many of these birds can be found easily in Greater Miami, which offers excellent birding for the traveler who has a few hours to several days to spare. Specialties vary from season to season, but almost any time of year can yield birds unique to this area, one of the few true subtropical regions in the country.

ESSENTIAL INFORMATION

Getting Around: The City of Miami is located in east-central Miami-Dade County. Most of the birding areas discussed in this chapter are scattered over Miami-Dade, Broward, southern Palm Beach, and northern Monroe Counties. Because public transportation is limited, a car is essential. Car-rental agencies have offices at the Miami International Airport and at downtown locations. Miami-Dade County is laid out on a grid, with streets running east/west and avenues north/south. Rush-hour traffic on the Palmetto (SR-826) and Dolphin (SR-836) Expressways, on I-95, and on major east-west arteries such as Bird Road (SW 40 Street) and Kendall Drive (SW 88 Street) can be horrendous from 6:30 to 9:30AM and from 4:00 to 6:30PM.

Climate: South Florida has two seasons, a wet season from May through mid-October, and a dry season from mid-October to May. During the pleasant winter months there is little rain, and temperatures are usually in the 60s to 70s Fahrenheit, although the temperature can occasionally drop into the 40s. Water concentrates into ponds that can attract spectacular concentrations of wading birds and waterfowl. The summer months are extremely humid and hot, with temperatures typically in the 90s and frequent heavy, tropical rains. Wading birds are dispersed throughout the Everglades and are more difficult to see then.

Safety: As in many large urban/suburban areas, crime can be a problem anywhere, including parks. Always lock your car when you leave it. Never leave valuables exposed. Place these items in the trunk before you arrive at your destination. In less-affluent areas don't wander too far off the beaten track. Always note where you are, and pay attention to your surroundings.

Natural Hazards: Mosquitoes can be terrible in tropical hammocks, marshes, and other rural areas during the rainy season (primarily summer and fall). They are less of a problem during the drier winter and early spring and in developed areas. Cases of mosquito-borne viral encephalitis, including West Nile Virus, have been reported in Florida; precautions are advised. South Florida has a subtropical climate, so the sun can be intense, even in winter. Be sure to use sunscreen, wear a hat, and carry plenty of water.

Other Resources: The Tropical Audubon Society, 5530 Sunset Drive, Miami, FL 33134, (305) 666-5111, fax (305) 667-9343, maintains an electronic bulletin board for bird sightings, which is updated regularly. The TAS Miami Bird Board may be accessed through the TAS home page (*http://tropical.fl.audubon.org/*). The Doc Thomas House, the headquarters of Tropical Audubon Society, is located on Sunset Drive (SW 72 Street) on a beautiful piece of property that has many large trees and extensive native plantings. This mini-park can be a good place for migrant and wintering birds and for both countable and non-countable exotics. Call for information and to find out what hours the property is open.

Useful books include *Florida Bird Species: An Annotated List* by William B. Robertson, Jr., and Glen E. Woolfenden (1992, Florida Ornithological Society); *The Birdlife of Florida* by Henry M. Stevenson and Bruce H. Anderson (1994, University Press of Florida); *A Birder's Guide to Florida* by Bill Pranty (1996, ABA/Lane guide); and *A Birder's Guide to the Bahamas* by Anthony W. White (1998, ABA/Lane guide; includes photos of many of the Caribbean specialties that occasionally show up in South Florida).

THE BIRDS

South Florida is of interest to birders for both its native and its introduced bird species. Swallow-tailed Kite (March–July), Snail Kite, Short-tailed Hawk, Purple Gallinule, White-crowned Pigeon, Monk and White-winged Parakeets, Mangrove Cuckoo, Smooth-billed Ani, Burrowing Owl, Gray Kingbird (April–August), and Red-whiskered Bulbul can all be found within a two-hour drive of Miami. In addition, there is always the possibility of finding Caribbean strays at any time of year. Recent vagrants have included Key West Quail-Dove, Cuban Pewee, La Sagra's Flycatcher, Thick-billed Vireo, Bahama Mockingbird, Bananaquit, and Western Spindalis (formerly Stripe-headed Tanager). Finally, the Miami area can be an excellent place to view migrating raptors and passerines, especially at migrant traps such as Bill Baggs Cape Florida State Recreation Area, A. D. Barnes Park, and Hugh Taylor Birch State Recreation Area (Fort Lauderdale). Many readers will note that there are no specific Smooth-billed Ani sites discussed in this chapter. The reason is that there has been a substantial reduction in the Florida ani population, and the few remaining sites tend to be ephemeral in nature.

VIRGINIA KEY, KEY BISCAYNE, AND CRANDON PARK

Half to full day; year round

Located between the mainland and Key Biscayne, **Virginia Key** may from time to time host—among the more-common shorebirds, gulls, and terns—a Piping or a Wilson's Plover or a Lesser Black-backed Gull. It's worth a stop. Brushy vegetation here can yield winter sparrows. From the airport, go south on Le Jeune Road (NW 42nd Avenue) 1.3 miles to the SR-836 Expressway. Take SR-836 east to I-95 (about four miles) and then head south on I-95 for 2.4 miles to Exit 11. Exit and follow the signs for Key Biscayne. After paying the $1.00 toll, cross the Rickenbacker Causeway to Virginia Key. Check Hobe Beach on the right for shorebirds, gulls, and terns. Low tides and early morning are best. There is a small mudflat at the southern end of Virginia Key, 3.5 miles from the toll booth. To reach it cross the Bear Cut Bridge onto Key Biscayne. Turn right into the marina and right again toward Bear Cut. Park, walk back toward the bridge, and look over the mudflats.

The 400-acre **Bill Baggs Cape Florida State Recreation Area** ($4.00/vehicle, (305) 361-5811, hours 8:00AM to sunset) is located at the southern tip of Key Biscayne, 7.2 miles from the Rickenbacker Causeway toll booth. Before Hurricane *Andrew* hit in August 1992, the dominant vegetation was Australian Pine (Casuarina) and Brazilian Pepper, with very little native vegetation. Most of the Australian Pines were knocked down by *Andrew's* strong winds. The fallen trees were mulched to provide a good soil surface for the planting of native vegetation. As the new vegetation matures, the park will become better and better for birding. From the park entrance booth, go 1.3 miles to the last parking area, on the right side of the lighthouse. Park and follow the paved road toward the water, continuing past the sign that reads *Bicycles and foot traffic only.* This path is productive for migrants in both spring and fall, and is a possible locale for Caribbean strays. Check the dead trees in the fenced area to the right of the lighthouse for White-crowned Pigeon (year round) and Gray Kingbird (spring and summer). With some luck, Mangrove Cuckoo may be found in spring and fall. In fall, any place in the park can be good for raptors, including Merlins and Peregrine Falcons. Some of the rarities that have shown up at various seasons include Key West Quail-Dove, Thick-billed Vireo, Northern Wheatear, Bahama Mockingbird, and Western Spindalis.

As you exit Bill Baggs Cape Florida State Recreation Area, return 2.2 miles to **Crandon Park**, (305) 261-5421, on the right side of the road. After paying the entrance fee ($4.00/vehicle), park and head to the beach, which can be good for shorebirds, except on weekends, when there are just too many beach-goers. Walk along the beach to the north end of the parking area. A dirt road parallels the beach and goes through some coastal growth. This area is good for migrants, raptors in fall, and possible Caribbean strays. Check also for White-crowned Pigeon (year round) and Mangrove Cuckoo (spring and fall).

SUBURBAN MIAMI–DADE COUNTY
Half or full day; year round

Depending on the time available, this route through various county parks and suburban neighborhoods can yield some of South Florida's specialties, migrants, and exotics, including Red-whiskered Bulbul, Spot-breasted Oriole, and many kinds of parrots.

A. D. "Doug" Barnes County Park is an avian oasis in the midst of urban Miami-Dade County. The park contains a native pine and hardwood hammock, some cattail-lined ponds, and a picnic area with scattered pines, figs, oaks, and other hardwood trees. These areas provide food and shelter for a variety of resident, breeding, migrant, and exotic species. From the airport go south on Le Jeune Road (NW 42nd Avenue) approximately 1.3 miles to SR-836. Drive west 3.4 miles to SR-826. Go south on 826 another 3.4 miles and exit at Bird Road/SW 40th Street. Turn left (east) and go 0.5 mile to SW 72nd Avenue, then left (north) 0.2 mile to the park entrance on the right. Make a left at the T-intersection inside the park and follow the road for 0.2 mile to the Leisure Access Center and a maintenance yard, where parking is available. Enter the native hammock through the small gate next to the building with a bird mural. Follow the paved path to a small pond with a waterfall. Be sure to check the trees and the ground along the way for migrants. At the pond, bear left and follow either paved or dirt paths toward the back of the property. More than 20 species of warblers, including Swainson's (early spring) and Connecticut (second week of May), occur here annually. Chuck-will's-widow and Black-whiskered Vireo can also be found in spring and fall. This section of the park contains an elevated boardwalk that gives a view of the surrounding brush (watch your step if it's wet; the boardwalk can be covered with slippery algae and moss). Check this area for White-crowned Pigeons (year round); they like the fruit of the Strangler Fig trees here. Drive back to the T-intersection, proceed straight ahead (south), and park in the picnic area. Check the ponds for Least Bittern and Sora, and the trees (especially those in fruit) for migrants, White-crowned Pigeon, Monk, White-winged, and Yellow-chevroned Parakeets, Gray Kingbird (spring and summer), and Spot-breasted Oriole (especially in fall). Swallow-tailed Kites may nest in the park and are often seen soaring overhead from late February through July. A very small wooded area farther south is also worth a look.

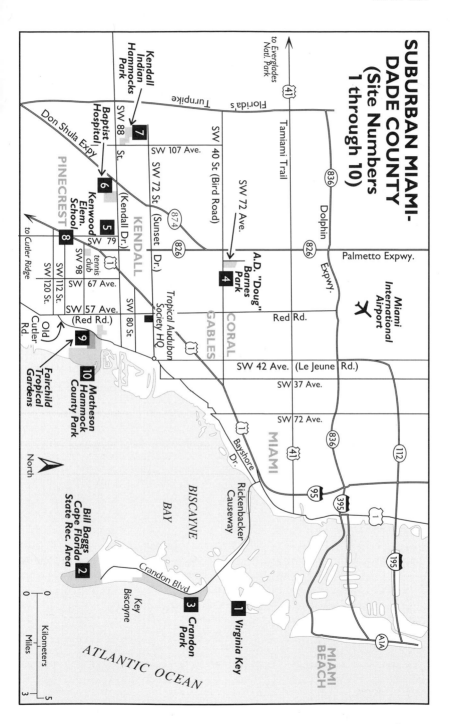

SUBURBAN MIAMI-
DADE COUNTY
(Site Numbers
1 through 10)

Kenwood Elementary School: After you exit A. D. Barnes Park, return to Bird Road. Drive 0.5 mile west to the Palmetto Expressway (SR-826), and take it south about 3 miles to Kendall Drive (SW 88th Street). Exit onto Kendall Drive West, immediately get into the left lane, and proceed 0.3 mile to SW 79th Avenue. Turn left (south) and go 0.2 mile to an opening in a fence (gate) on the right, just past a four-lane driveway. Park along 79th Avenue and enter into the small area with native plantings. Pay attention to signs indicating hours when parking is allowed along the street. Avoid times when children are entering and leaving school. Look here for Red-whiskered Bulbuls and Spot-breasted Orioles. These birds prefer flowering trees and bushes and any fruit that might be in season. Check here also for migrants (especially warblers), as well as Ruby-throated Hummingbirds and occasionally Rufous Hummingbirds (fall, winter).

Baptist Hospital: Return to Kendall Drive and drive west 1.0 mile. Turn left into the Baptist Hospital property, and park along the road between the two lakes. This area is good for Monk Parakeets, which nest in the Melaleuca trees bordering the large lake. In winter, the smaller lake east of the roadway may have a flock of Ring-necked Ducks. White-winged and Yellow-chevroned Parakeets, Fish Crow, Red-whiskered Bulbul, and, sometimes, Hill Myna may also be seen here. If you don't have luck with the parakeets and bulbuls, check the neighborhood across the street on the north side of Kendall Drive. The neighborhood is also good for Spot-breasted Oriole.

Kendall Indian Hammocks Park: Continue west on Kendall Drive 3.0 miles, turn right on SW 107th Avenue, and drive 0.4 mile to Kendall Indian Hammocks Park. Turn left into the 105-acre park, go 0.6 mile, and park on the left. The trails across from the parking area traverse a large oak hammock that can harbor large numbers of migrants in spring and fall. The area around the parking lot and ball fields can also have Gray Kingbirds in spring and summer. Check for Chuck-will's-widow in the wooded areas and for Spot-breasted Orioles in any flowering trees.

The village of **Pinecrest** is an affluent area with large lots planted in a variety of exotic tropical flowering and fruiting trees that attract many countable and non-countable exotics. Monk, Mitred, White-winged, and Yellow-chevroned Parakeets, Hill Myna, Red-whiskered Bulbul, and Spot-breasted Oriole are seen regularly. The most productive area to bird is from US-1 east to Red Road (SW 57th Avenue) and from Kendall Drive (SW 88 Street) south to SW 120 Street. The Royal Palm Tennis Club (on SW 98th Street just east of SW 72 Avenue) and the surrounding neighborhood are good for Red-whiskered Bulbuls and Spot-breasted Orioles, particularly in the early morning and late afternoon.

Matheson Hammock County Park and Fairchild Tropical Gardens are adjoining properties in Coral Gables. Both contain native and exotic vegetation that attracts a fine selection of spring and fall migrants and a variety of *Psittacids*. Monk, White-winged, and Yellow-chevroned Parakeets, Eastern Screech-Owls, Great Horned Owls, Pileated Woodpeckers, and Hill Mynas are resident here. Gray Kingbirds and Black-whiskered Vireos are present in spring and summer. White-crowned Pigeons may be seen at any time, and Mangrove Cuckoos are sometimes found, especially in the spring and fall. Short-tailed Hawks frequently soar over the area from August through February, and Swallow-tailed Kites, from late February through July. Rarities such as La Sagra's and Sulphur-bellied Flycatchers, Bahama Mockingbird, and Black-throated Gray Warbler have been seen in the Matheson Hammock picnic area, and Bananaquit has been recorded at Fairchild.

To reach these properties from US-1, drive east 2.5 miles on Killian Drive (SW 112 Street) to Red Road (SW 57th Avenue). Turn right and travel south on Red Road 0.35 mile to the first stoplight, then left onto Old Cutler Road. Follow Old Cutler northeast for 1.1 miles to the **Fairchild Tropical Gardens**, 10901 Old Cutler Road, Coral Gables, FL (305) 667-1651. (*Note: it is projected that by the fall of 2002 the main entrance to Fairchild Tropical Gardens will be relocated 0.3 mile farther northeast along Old Cutler Road, or 1.4 miles from Red Road.*) There is an $8 admission fee, which includes a guided tram tour; children under 13 are free. A cafe serves light lunches on weekends. The Gardens are open every day of the year except Christmas.

To continue to **Matheson Hammock County Park**, 9610 Old Cutler Road, Coral Gables, FL 33156, (305) 665-5475, turn right from the Fairchild Gardens parking lot onto Old Cutler and drive to a stoplight at the main entrance to Matheson Hammock County Park. Turn right onto the main park-access road. Park in the first parking lot on the left. The picnic area on the right is good for migrants, wintering vireos and warblers, and the occasional West Indian stray. White-crowned Pigeons, White-winged Parakeets, and Hill Mynas are not uncommon. Walk through the picnic area to its southwest corner and cross Old Cutler Road. Here a trail traverses a West Indian hammock and leads to a large field and plant nursery. The hammock may have migrants, as well as White-crowned Pigeons and Black-whiskered Vireos (spring and summer). Large Royal Palms in the open area at the edge of the hammock provide nesting cavities for White-fronted Parrots, Red-masked Parakeets, Pileated Woodpeckers, and Hill Mynas. Eastern Screech-Owls and Great Horned Owls are resident in the nursery area.

Farther into the park along the entrance road is a beach and marina. Access to these areas requires a $4.00/car entrance fee. Prairie Warblers nest in the Red Mangrove Hammock. Herons and shorebirds may be seen along the beaches, especially at low tide.

Cutler Ridge: Cave Swallows of the West Indian race nest under or near the Florida's Turnpike Extension overpass at SW 216 Street (Hainlin Mill Drive) in Cutler Ridge, located between Kendall/Coral Gables and Homestead. The greatest number of birds are usually present under the canal bridge on SW 216 Street just east of the Turnpike, or under the Turnpike itself immediately to the north. Although the swallows are most easily observed from April through September, sightings have been made during every month of the year, particularly during the early morning and late afternoon. To reach this colony, travel south via US-1 or the Turnpike to SW 216th Street. Turn left (east) onto 216th Street, drive under the Turnpike overpass, make an immediate left onto the northbound frontage road, and park on the grass along the right side of the road. You should be able to observe the Cave Swallows from here. If you choose to leave you car, be sure to lock it. Break-ins have occurred.

BIRDING NEAR THE AIRPORT

Several hours to half-day; year round

For those with limited time, there are several destinations very close to, or at, the airport. Find an agreeable cab-driver to help with these outings. Burrowing Owls can be found at several locations in the grassy areas at the southern part of Miami International Airport. The best spot is along the fence near NE 57th Avenue (Red Road). This area can be reached from a parking lot along Perimeter Road. *Psittacids*, including Monk, Mitred, and

Yellow-chevroned Parakeets, as well as several species of parrot, can be found just north of the airport in Miami Springs. From the Palmetto Expressway (SR-826), exit onto NW 36th Street and go east to the light at Curtiss Parkway (2.0 miles). Turn left (north) and follow the road for a mile as it curves right through the Miami Springs Golf Course. Park on Navarre Drive at the Fair Haven Nursing Home. Bird the block around the nursing home, and then walk the parkway median back to the golf course. Check the oaks, figs, and other trees in the median for *Psittacids*, Spot-breasted Orioles, and wintering or migrant landbirds. Gray Kingbird may be found in spring and summer.

EVERGLADES NATIONAL PARK AND BIG CYPRESS NATIONAL PRESERVE

Full-day; year round

Accessible areas of Everglades National Park and Big Cypress National Preserve can be visited easily in a day trip from Miami. South Florida specialties such as Snail Kite, Purple Gallinule, and Limpkin are possible. From the airport go south on Le Jeune Road approximately 1.3 miles to SR-836. Follow 836 west 7.5 miles to Florida's Turnpike south. Take the first exit onto SW 8th Street westbound. Continue west on SW 8th Street (US-41) for 24 miles, and pass the Shark Valley entrance of Everglades National Park. Just beyond the park entrance, on the right, is the Miccosukee Indian Restaurant. Check the snags along the canal behind the restaurant and the extensive marsh to the north for Snail Kites. Anhingas and Limpkins may also be seen here. If you don't see the kites here, continue west to the microwave towers at the bend in the road, park on the right, and scan the marsh.

Return to the Shark Valley entrance to Everglades National Park (fee $8/vehicle, hours 8:00AM to sunset). A two-hour tram ride ($10.50 adults, $9.50 seniors, $6 children 12 and under, (305) 221-8455) makes a 15-mile loop through prime Everglades habitat, with a tall observation tower at the mid-point. You can also rent bicycles or hike the paved loop at your own pace. Some of the birds that you might see in Shark Valley include Anhinga, Snail Kite (check the east side of the loop, just south of the parking area), Swallow-tailed Kite, King Rail, Sora, Purple Gallinule (in the canal on the west side of the loop), and Limpkin. There are sometimes spectacular concentrations of wading birds here during the winter.

After leaving Shark Valley, continue west on US-41 for 3.8 miles. At this point US-41 bends to the northwest, and Loop Road (SR-94) branches to the left. This primitive road, paved for the first eight miles, goes approximately 27 miles and makes a loop back to US-41 at Monroe Station. The road travels through cypress, hammocks, pinewoods, and saw-grass prairies. After the paved portion ends, travel can be rough, and portions of the road may be impassable during wet years. Those who wish to drive it should first check at the education center at the east end of Loop Road (indicated by a sign) for current road conditions. Some of the birds that are seen here include Wild Turkey, Barred Owl, Pileated Woodpecker, Carolina Wren, Eastern Blue-bird, Prothonotary Warbler (spring and summer), and various migrants.

From Monroe Station go west 24.4 miles to the Cypress Bend section of Fakahatchee Strand State Preserve (on the right side of the road). Park in the small parking area and walk to the north about 100 yards to the 2,000-foot-long boardwalk, which meanders through a virgin cypress forest. Look for Limpkin, Swallow-tailed Kite (spring, summer), Barred Owl, Yellow-bellied Sapsucker (winter), Pileated Woodpecker, Carolina Wren, Tufted Titmouse, Northern Parula, and lots of migrants in spring and fall. For information: Fakahatchee Strand State Preserve, PO Box 548, Copeland, FL 33926, (941) 695-4593.

EXTRA EFFORT

Three coastal parks north of Miami, in Broward and southern Palm Beach Counties, are noteworthy for an abundance and variety of migrants and for the relatively frequent occurrence of West Indian strays, particularly during April and May.

John U. Lloyd State Recreation Area (251 acres; entrance fee $4.00/car; opens at 8:00AM) is the southernmost of these. To reach this park from Miami, take I-95 north to Sheridan Street. Exit here and go east to US-1. Turn north on US-1 to Dania Beach Boulevard. Turn right (east) and follow signs to the park, which is 2.2 miles from US-1. Park at the north end of a parking lot located about 1 mile beyond the fee station. From here, the Barrier Island Nature Trail traverses a small mixed hammock which is good for migrants and sometimes a West Indian stray such as La Sagra's Flycatcher, Bahama Mockingbird, Western Spindalis, or Bananaquit. A jetty located at the northernmost end of the park is a good place from which to observe Northern Gannets and Magnificent Frigatebirds in winter.

Hugh Taylor Birch State Recreation Area (180 acres; $3.25/car; opens at 8:00AM) may be the best park in Broward County for migrants and West Indian strays. From I-95, exit east onto Sunrise Boulevard. Drive east across the Intracoastal Waterway to the park entrance on the left (about four miles from I-95). Follow signs to the Beach Parking Lot. From this lot the paved road goes about one mile through a West Indian hardwood hammock. Flowering and fruiting Gumbo Limbo and Strangler Fig trees attract migrants and West Indian strays, particularly in April and May. Key West Quail-Dove, La Sagra's Flycatcher, Thick-billed Vireo, Bahama Mockingbird, Western Spindalis, and Bananaquit have occurred here. Spot-breasted Orioles may be present, particularly from late August through early October. Check the roadside undergrowth for Swainson's Warbler in spring and fall and for Connecticut Warbler during the second week of May.

Spanish River Park is a city park in Boca Raton in southern Palm Beach County. The fee for parking inside the park is $8.00 during the week and $10.00 on weekends. Limited free parking may be available along Spanish River Boulevard west of SR-A1A. To reach the park, take I-95 north, exit onto Glades Road and go east to US-1. Turn left (north) and proceed to Spanish River Boulevard. Turn right (east), cross the Intracoastal Waterway, and park on the right. Walk south through the Australian Pines into the park. Although Spanish River has less native vegetation than does Hugh Taylor Birch, it still attracts a variety of migrants and a few West Indian strays, including Thick-billed Vireo, Bahama Mockingbird, Western Spindalis, and Bananaquit. The first U.S. record of Cuban Pewee was of a bird that spent a good part of March and April 1994 here. Swainson's Warbler can be seen in spring and fall and Connecticut Warblers occur primarily during the second week of May.

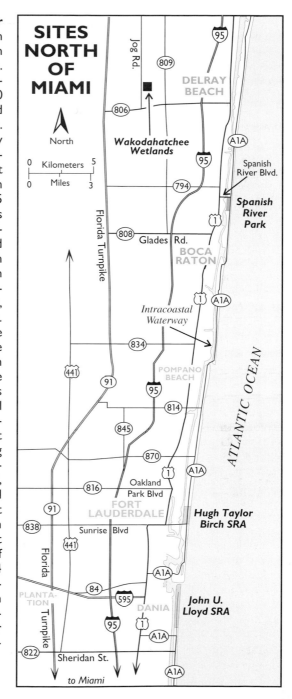

SITES NORTH OF MIAMI

North

0 Kilometers 5

0 Miles 3

Jog Rd.

809

DELRAY BEACH

806

Wakodahatchee Wetlands

A1A

95

Spanish River Blvd.

794

Spanish River Park

1

Florida Turnpike

808

Glades Rd.

BOCA RATON

1

A1A

Intracoastal Waterway

834

441

91

POMPANO BEACH

95

814

845

870

1

A1A

816

Oakland Park Blvd

91

FORT LAUDERDALE

Hugh Taylor Birch SRA

838

Sunrise Blvd

441

Florida Turnpike

84

A1A

PLANTA-TION

595

DANIA

1

John U. Lloyd SRA

95

A1A

822

Sheridan St.

to Miami

A1A

ATLANTIC OCEAN

In inland Broward and southern Palm Beach Counties two freshwater marshes created as wetland-mitigation projects have attracted an interesting array of mostly native species. An unnamed mitigation project on the north side of Sheridan Street, just east of the Southeast Regional Library near Pembroke Pines in Broward County, achieved prominence among birders for hosting two male Masked Ducks in May and June of 2001. This small marsh has a boardwalk. Pied-billed Grebes, Least Bitterns, Mottled Ducks, Purple Gallinules, and exotic Purple Swamp-hens breed here. All are easily observable, particularly during the nesting season. To reach this area, take either the Palmetto Expressway (SR-826) or Florida's Turnpike Extension north to I-75. Follow I-75 north and exit on Sheridan Street west. Proceed west for 1.3 miles and turn right into the Southeast Regional Library parking lot. The marsh lies immediately to the east of the parking lot.

The **Wakodahatchee Wetlands** is a water-treatment facility in southern Palm Beach County. Great effort and expense have been expended to manage this area for wildlife. Furthermore, an extensive boardwalk has been built into the marsh to facilitate wildlife observation and photography. Least Bitterns are common residents. They are most easily observed in the spring when they are nesting and actively feeding young. Other resident species include Pied-billed Grebe, a variety of herons, Mottled Duck, Limpkin, Purple Gallinule, and Common Moorhen. Winter visitors include American Bittern, Peregrine Falcon, Virginia Rail, and Sora. Black-necked Stilts and Least Terns are conspicuous in spring and summer. To reach Wakodahatchee, take Florida's Turnpike north and exit at Delray Beach. After paying the toll, proceed straight (south) 0.1 mile to a T-intersection at Atlantic Avenue. Turn left (east) onto Atlantic and drive 1.6 miles to Jog Road. Turn left (north) onto Jog Road and go 1.7 miles to the entrance on the right. Park in the small lot and proceed to the boardwalk. Use sunscreen; there is little shade.

The southern entrance to **Everglades National Park** ($10/vehicle) is located southwest of Florida City, about one hour from Miami. The park road travels through pinelands, sawgrass prairies, and mangrove swamps to its terminus at Flamingo. The park, covered in greater detail in Pranty's ABA guide, is our premier natural area and offers good birding, particularly in winter. Stops at Anhinga Trail, Paurotis Pond, Nine-mile Pond, and West Lake can yield a variety of herons, ibises, spoonbills, and waterfowl. Hammocks, including Royal Palm and Mahogany Hammock, can produce wintering passerines and, perhaps, a Barred Owl. Eco Pond, a sewage-treatment area at Flamingo, usually has a few rails and a large concentration of waders. Shrubby areas surrounding the pond can be excellent for wintering passerines. Short-tailed Hawks can be seen soaring anywhere in the park in fall and winter, but they are most often observed at Anhinga Trail (in the morning, when the Turkey Vultures rise) or in the Flamingo area. White-crowned Pigeons come to roost at dusk at Paurotis Pond.

The best spot to find Greater Flamingoes—often present in small numbers during the fall and winter (rarely into spring)—is at high tide at the end of the

1.8-mile Snake Bight Trail. The trail travels through mangrove forest (look for Mangrove Cuckoo in spring and summer, and occasionally in winter) and ends at a boardwalk with a panoramic view of the bay. Be aware that mosquitoes can be horrendous, particularly in summer. Large numbers of herons (including Reddish Egret), spoonbills, shorebirds (including Wilson's Plover and Marbled Godwit), gulls (check for Lesser Black-backed), and terns (including Gull-billed) may be present at the end of the trail, and Swallow-tailed Kites are common (March through July). Greater Flamingo may also be seen by taking a boat trip into Florida Bay from the marina at Flamingo. Trip itineraries can vary, so birders are advised to check with a park naturalist. For further information, contact Everglades National Park, 40001 SR-9336, Homestead, FL 33034, (305) 242-7700.

The **Florida Keys** are also an exciting place to bird. Spring and summer specialties include Magnificent Frigatebird, Reddish Egret, Roseate Tern, White-crowned Pigeon, Antillean Nighthawk, Gray Kingbird, and Black-whiskered Vireo. At the Dry Tortugas, 68 miles west of Key West, add Masked and Brown Boobies, Sooty Tern, and Brown Noddy. Pelagic trips yield Audubon's Shearwater and Bridled Tern. "Cuban" Yellow Warblers breed in the mangroves near the Card Sound Bridge toll booth, between the mainland and upper Key Largo. Short-tailed Hawks are found in winter. Sometimes there are also interesting West Indian strays to spice the mix. The middle and lower keys offer a fine fall raptor migration. The 128-mile US-1 travels the Keys, which have been developed to a great extent. Fortunately, the state is working to purchase the few remaining undeveloped hammocks, and mangrove forests are now protected from development. One such site open to the public and closest to Miami is the state botanical site on upper Key Largo. To reach this site from US-1 turn left onto SR-905 soon after arriving on Key Largo. After a very short distance on SR-905, park in front of the large pink arch on the right. A walk along the trails here in spring and summer should produce White-crowned Pigeon, Gray Kingbird, and Black-whiskered and White-eyed Vireos. Mangrove Cuckoos are present in the hardwoods on upper Key Largo, although they are not easy to see. Note: be sure to stay on designated trails, and do not walk in any posted areas.

ACKNOWLEDGMENTS

Assistance on the Broward and Palm Beach Counties sites was given by Wally George. Jill Rosenfield provided helpful comments on Miami-Dade. Jeff Weber provided editorial assistance.

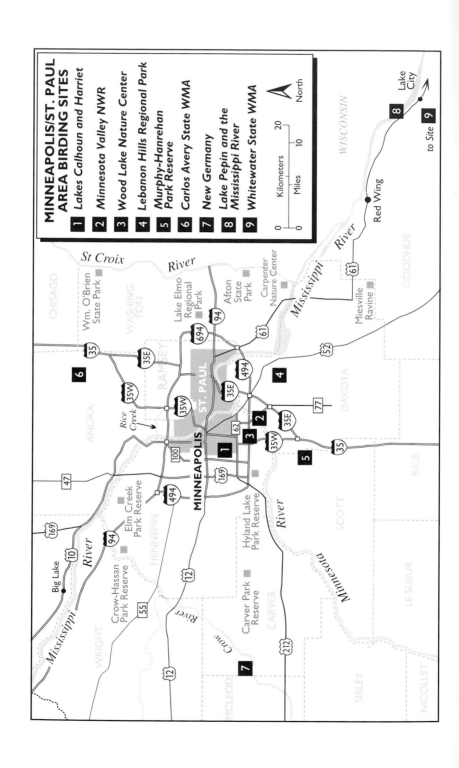

MINNEAPOLIS/ST. PAUL AREA BIRDING SITES

1 Lakes Calhoun and Harriet
2 Minnesota Valley NWR
3 Wood Lake Nature Center
4 Lebanon Hills Regional Park
5 Murphy-Hanrehan Park Reserve
6 Carlos Avery State WMA
7 New Germany
8 Lake Pepin and the Mississippi River
9 Whitewater State WMA

North

Kilometers   0   10   20
Miles   0   10

to Site **9**

MINNEAPOLIS/ ST. PAUL, MINNESOTA

Paul Budde and Mark Ochs

The Twin Cities area of Minneapolis/St. Paul is inhabited by almost three million people. It is the entertainment and cultural center of the upper Midwest and is noted for its fine theater, museums, and shopping. Yet amidst all these people and activities there are plenty of birding opportunities, including an excellent location just down the street from the Mall of America, the nation's largest shopping and entertainment complex. Three major rivers, numerous large lakes, and extensive parkland provide shelter for migrants and sufficient—though diminishing—habitat for breeding species. Spring and fall migration can be excellent, and winter usually brings surprises.

ESSENTIAL INFORMATION

Getting Around: While some of the locations described here are accessible by bus, for most birding you must have a car. Driving is relatively easy for a major metropolitan area. One point of confusion for visitors is that Interstate 35, which stretches from Texas to Duluth, splits into two segments through the Twin Cities. I-35E passes through St. Paul, and I-35W goes through Minneapolis. The worst traffic generally is limited to rush hour (7:00 to 9:00AM, 4:00 to 6:00PM) and the summer commutes to and from points northward at the beginning and end of each weekend. Because of the harsh winters and short summers, Minnesota keeps the road-repair industry fully employed when the snows are gone. Such construction projects can be an annoyance.

Climate: In the Twin Cities, spring and fall are typically short interludes between the long, cold winter and a warm, humid summer. Even the deepest city lakes freeze by mid-December. They thaw around mid-April. In the middle of winter the weather can be quite cold, with temperatures some days staying below 0°. If you venture farther north, the weather can be even 20 to 30 degrees colder than in the Twin Cities. None of this frigidness stops Minnesotans from going outdoors. One simply has to dress warmly and take proper precautions with one's vehicle.

Natural Hazards: Mosquitoes are present from the end of May into September. Deer and Horse Flies can be annoying in deciduous forests in the summer, though Black Flies are a problem only farther north in the state. Both Wood and Deer Ticks inhabit tall, dry grass. Some of the Deer Ticks carry Lyme disease, so take precautions. Though there is some Poison Oak present, Poison-Ivy is far more common. Watch for it at the margins of woods and fields.

Safety: While the Twin Cities have a lower crime rate than most large metropolitan areas, one should still be vigilant when visiting the area. All valuables should be locked in the trunk of your vehicle or, better yet, carried with you.

Other Resources: There are three Rare Bird Alerts available by telephone; currently all are revised weekly on Thursday. The statewide report is (763) 780-8890 or, from outside the metro area, (800) 657-3700. The number for Duluth and Northeast Minnesota is (218) 525-5952. A report is available for Northwest Minnesota at (800) 433-1888. Any unusual birds that you find can be reported by using these same telephone numbers, except for Northwest Minnesota, for which you should call (800) 542-3992.

More timely information on unusual birds in the area is available through two Internet mailing lists (listserves). The first is sponsored by the Minnesota Ornithologists' Union (MOU). Information about subscribing to this list can be found at the MOU's web site, *www.cbs.umn.edu/~mou/*. Check here for messages posted on the listserve over the most recent two-week period and for a wealth of additional information regarding birding in the state. The second list, known locally as MnBird, also focuses on birding in Minnesota. Information about subscribing to it and recent messages are available at *www.linux.winona.msus.edu/mnbird/*.

Another good resource for finding birds in Minnesota, including the Twin Cities, is Kim Eckert's *A Birder's Guide to Minnesota* (an updated fourth edition is currently in the works). In addition to describing where to bird in each of the state's 87 counties, it provides interesting reading about where rarities have appeared in the past. Robert Janssen's *Birds in Minnesota* (1987, University of Minnesota Press) contains information about the status and distribution of each species recorded in the state. The University of Minnesota runs a raptor-rehabilitation clinic on its St. Paul campus (*www.raptor.cvm.umn.edu/*).

THE BIRDING YEAR

Minneapolis and St. Paul are located at the confluence of the Mississippi and Minnesota Rivers. These river valleys and the nearby St. Croix River serve to funnel migrants through the region. Waterfowl follow the thawing ice and pass through in March and April. The bulk of the spring passerine migration runs from the last week of April through the end of May. Many flycatchers and vireos return after the first week of May; the largest variety of warblers can be found near mid-month. Breeding birds include those at the northern periphery of their range, such as Acadian Flycatcher, Blue-winged, Cerulean, and Hooded Warblers, and Louisiana Waterthrush, and others at the southern end of theirs, such as Common Loon and Golden-winged Warbler. Most fall migrants pass through from mid-August through mid-October. Shorebird migration starts even earlier—at the beginning of July—and can run through October. However, the Twin Cities have little habitat for shorebirds; they are more easily found in western Minnesota. Fall warbler movements are at their best between 20 August and 20 September. Sparrows come through in strong numbers during the last week of September and through October. Late fall is generally good for vagrants, and among these are gulls. Thirteen gull species were found in the Twin Cities during the 1990s. Prime winter birding locations include feeders at many regional parks and nature centers. In a good year, winter can be exciting, with one or more northern specialties making an incursion southward into the area. The Twin Cities are a gateway to these sought-after northern species, often found just a few hours away.

MINNEAPOLIS

Half day; spring and fall

Minneapolis has a good number of birding locales within its boundaries. The Mississippi River and Minnehaha Creek as well as six good-sized lakes lie within the city. Each of these sites is bordered by city parkland, and all can be productive during migration.

Some of the best birding areas in the city are located in its southwest corner. Waterfowl and gull-watching can be excellent at the right times of the year on **Lakes Harriet and Calhoun**, which lie west of I-35W between Lake Street (30th Street) and 50th Street The area between these lakes consists of a parkway, the T. S. Roberts Bird Sanctuary, and Lakewood Cemetery. Though this area is too small to provide much birding outside of migration, each of these areas can be enjoyable in the spring or fall. And while they are generally not as productive as the areas along the Minnesota River described below, some species of interest are regularly found here.

Both Lakes Harriet and Calhoun are fairly deep, are about three miles in circumference, and are bordered completely by city greenways with cycling and walking paths. During migration, Tundra Swans rest briefly on these lakes, though you are more likely to see or hear flocks flying over the city both during the day and at night. Horned and Pied-billed Grebes are common in both spring and fall, and a few Red-necked, Eared, and Western Grebes can be found every few years. Red-breasted Mergansers stage on the lakes in large numbers in the spring. Many other species of waterfowl are present annually (particularly in April and November), as are a few Common Loons.

One of the lakes' biggest attractions for birders is the thousands of gulls that roost in the fall. Numbers of Ring-billed Gulls begin increasing in August. Herring Gull numbers start rising in September. Franklin's Gulls appear for a short time in late September or early October. The first Thayer's Gulls show up at the beginning of October; they become more numerous through November until the lakes freeze. A few Glaucous Gulls usually arrive by late November. Iceland Gulls are not annual, and Black Dog Lake (part of the Minnesota Valley National Wildlife Refuge) is probably a better spot to look for them, given that by the time when they show up, the city lakes are often frozen. One or more Lesser Black-backed Gulls often roost on these lakes each fall. Bonaparte's Gulls pass through quickly, with more seen in spring than in fall. Birders should always be on the lookout for something more unusual. Little, California, Glaucous-winged, and Great Black-backed Gulls and Black-legged Kittiwake were all seen at one or the other of these lakes during the 1990s. Moreover, it is while surveying the gulls that birders occasionally discover a rarity such as Pacific Loon, Harlequin Duck, a scoter, or Long-tailed Duck. The best time to gull-watch on both lakes is in the half-hours before and after sunset. On most days you will want to set up your scope midway down the western shore so that the sun is at your back. Watch for where the gull flocks are forming, however, as wind conditions and competing sailboats and kayaks cause them to move around. On both lakes the flock tends to form in the middle of the lake. On Calhoun, however, the majority of Herring Gulls often initially form a loose flock closer to the western shore. Conveniently, many of the more-interesting larger gulls usually congregate with the Herrings. It is probably for this reason that birders tend to favor Calhoun, though Harriet should not be overlooked.

At the north end of Lake Harriet lies the **T. S. Roberts Bird Sanctuary.** "Roberts," as it is locally called, is named after Dr. Thomas Sadler Roberts, the dean of Minnesota ornithologists. It is a thin strip of woodlands and marsh, sandwiched between the lake and Lakewood Cemetery. The paths through the sanctuary might appear to be confusing, but the park is small, so you cannot get lost. Though only a quarter-mile in length, the area can be surprisingly good during migration for vireos, thrushes, warblers, and sparrows, both in spring (late April through first week of June) and fall (mid-August through early October). At other times of the year there is very little to be seen here.

Other wooded areas in Minneapolis that hold passerines during migration include the extensive parklands along the Mississippi, beginning at Fort Snelling State Park and proceeding upstream; the east and north shores of Cedar Lake, which is a half-mile northwest of Lake Calhoun; and Theodore Wirth Park (especially the area around the Eloise Butler Wildflower Garden) in the west-central part of the city.

MINNESOTA VALLEY NATIONAL WILDLIFE REFUGE

Half or full day; year round

This vast refuge, located along the Minnesota River in the southern metropolitan region, has some of the area's best overall birding locations. It extends from the confluence of the Minnesota and Mississippi Rivers to the southwest, well beyond the perimeter of the metro area. Five sites popular with local birders (and close to the airport) are described here.

Refuge Visitor Center: From the airport, go south on Highway 5 to I-494 westbound. Immediately exit onto 34th Avenue South and head south to 80th Street, then east 0.4 mile to the visitor center. A loop trail is just east of the building. It is fairly steep in places, but there are benches along the way and an observation platform at the bottom. It is approximately a 30-minute round-trip walk along the deciduous hillside. This is a good area for spring and fall migrant passerines, and the occasional rarity, such as White-eyed Vireo, Rock Wren, and Worm-eating Warbler, has turned up. Additionally, Prothonotary Warblers nest in the river bottom below the center. Another good birding trail leads southeast of the center into the Kelly Tract. Check with refuge staff to learn if this trail is currently open to the public.

Bass Ponds: Backtrack to 34th Avenue South and turn left. This route quickly becomes Old Shakopee Road. After 1.0 mile Old Shakopee makes a hard left at the Mall of America. Follow this turn and again turn left at the 86th Street traffic light. Within 100 yards veer left onto the narrow road at the Bass Ponds Environmental Study Area sign. Proceed to the parking lot. Walk past the gate and down the long hill to the loop trails around the series of ponds. (Over 2.5 million Largemouth Bass were raised in these ponds over a thirty-year period.) This area is excellent for spring and fall passerine migrants. Both Virginia Rail and Sora are present. The Hogback Trail provides an alternative hiking route (about 1.5 miles long) to the next site, Old Cedar Bridge. From the bottom of the hill, continue straight between the two ponds and then turn right.

Old Cedar Bridge: Return to Old Shakopee Road and go south/left. Continue across MN-77 (Cedar Avenue) to the traffic light at Old Cedar Avenue. Turn left and drive to the parking lot at the bottom of the hill. Trails go northeast toward the Bass Ponds and southwest into the wooded river-bottom. The best birding to the southwest is found as far as the second boardwalk. A side-trip to an observation platform out in the marsh commences a few hundred yards from the parking lot. This area is excellent in migration for passerines, as well as for Virginia Rail and Sora, which are best viewed from the old bridge at the bottom of the road. Additionally, Marsh Wren, Yellow-headed Blackbird, and, occasionally, Least Bittern can be found here.

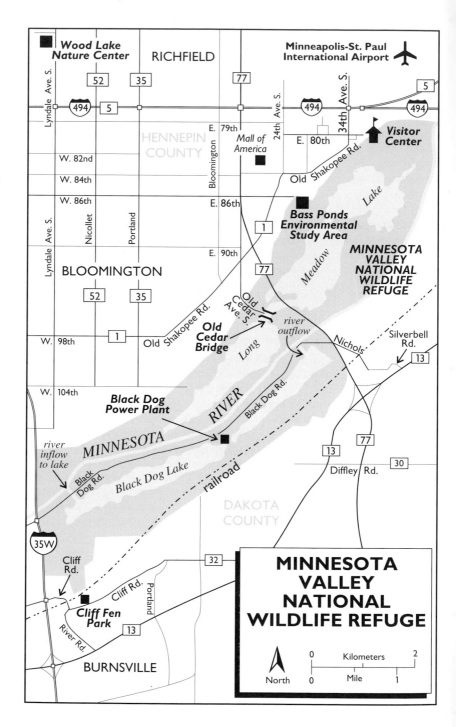

Wood Lake Nature Center
RICHFIELD
Minneapolis-St. Paul International Airport

Lyndale Ave. S.

52   35   77   5

494   5

HENNEPIN COUNTY

E. 79th
Mall of America
E. 80th

24th Ave. S.
34th Ave. S.

Old Shakopee Rd.

Visitor Center

W. 82nd
W. 84th

Lake

W. 86th
Bloomington

E. 86th

1

Bass Ponds Environmental Study Area

Lyndale Ave. S.
Nicollet
Portland

E. 90th

77

MINNESOTA VALLEY NATIONAL WILDLIFE REFUGE

Meadow

BLOOMINGTON

52   35

Old Shakopee Rd.
Old Cedar Ave. S.

river outflow

Old Cedar Bridge

Long

Nichols

Silverbell Rd.

13

W. 98th

1   Old Shakopee Rd.

W. 104th

Black Dog Power Plant

MINNESOTA   RIVER

Black Dog Rd.

river inflow to lake

Black Dog Rd.

MINNESOTA

Black Dog Lake

railroad

13   77

30

Diffley Rd.

DAKOTA COUNTY

35W

Cliff Rd.

32

Cliff Fen Park

Cliff Rd.

Portland

River Rd.

13

BURNSVILLE

MINNESOTA VALLEY NATIONAL WILDLIFE REFUGE

North

0   Kilometers   2

0   Mile   1

Black Dog Power Plant: This area consists of a coal-fired power plant, together with long cooling-ponds east and west of the plant. Because of warm-water discharges, at least parts of these ponds remain open year round. To reach this area, backtrack to MN-77 and head south across the Minnesota River. At the first intersection turn onto northbound Highway 13. Proceed 0.7 mile to the traffic light at Silverbell Road. Turn left and follow it 0.6 mile to a T-intersection. Turn right on Nichols Road and head down toward the river. Watch the wetlands on your right for waterfowl. Continue under the new Cedar Bridge to the first outflow of Black Dog Lake into the Minnesota River.

The area between the east outflow and west inflow, 3.2 miles ahead, is good for waterfowl, Bald Eagles, Rough-legged Hawks, gulls, and Northern Shrikes during the late fall and early winter (November–early January). Iceland, Lesser Black-backed, and Great Black-backed Gulls and Black-legged Kittiwake have been recorded more than once, and Thayer's Gull and Glaucous Gull are present every year. The first state-record Glaucous-winged Gull was also seen here for an extended period of time. Peregrine Falcons nest on the west side of the tallest chimney at the power plant. There is a trail and an observation platform midway down the length of the west pond. Watch for the parking area on your left about 0.5 mile past the power plant.

Cliff Fen Park: Continue west past the west inflow (check for gulls) to I-35W. Proceed south on I-35W 1.0 mile to Cliff Road. After exiting, turn left on Cliff Road and continue under the freeway for 1.0 mile to Cliff Fen Park on the north side of the road. Park and walk northeast around the soccer field to the railroad tracks. Follow the tracks to the right (east) a few hundred yards to a track-side sign with a *15* on it. This area is characterized by wet grass interspersed with willow clumps and is good in summer for Black-billed Cuckoo, Willow Flycatcher, Sedge Wren, and an occasional Bell's Vireo. Additionally, American Woodcocks can be seen and heard performing their courtship ritual at dusk and dawn from late March to early June.

WOOD LAKE NATURE CENTER

One to three hours; spring, summer, and fall

Wood Lake is a 150-acre area located in Richfield, a suburb just south of Minneapolis. It is south of the Crosstown Expressway (MN-62) and east of I-35W. The reserve consists mostly of marshes bordered by tall cottonwoods and other deciduous trees to the north, east, and west, and by some brushy fields to the south. The entrance is along Lake Shore Drive, a short road that runs south from 66th Street and west from Lyndale Avenue. The best time to visit is during spring migration, when on the right day just about any vireo, thrush, or warbler can be found. Also watch for sparrows in the weedy patches.

During summer Wood Lake is the best-known location in the Twin Cities to look for Least Bittern. A few seem to be present every year; they are most easily found toward dusk. Walk the paths around the ponds and watch for birds at the margins of the cattails. Be sure to check both ends of the boardwalk that bisects the marsh from east to west, and the area around the bridge visible to the south from the western end of this boardwalk. Other interesting birds in summer include Virginia Rail, Sora, Warbling Vireo, Marsh Wren, and in some years Yellow-headed Blackbird. Great Egret, Green Heron, and Black-crowned Night-Heron are also regular during the summer.

LEBANON HILLS REGIONAL PARK

Half day; spring, summer, and fall

Lebanon Hills is a large (2,000-plus acres) regional park located 20 minutes south of the airport in Eagan and Apple Valley. It consists mostly of rolling deciduous woods with small lakes and ponds, and a network of trails for walking, biking, and/or horseback-riding. Birding is best during spring and fall migrations; however, a number of interesting species can be found during the breeding season as well. Although there are numerous access points, only two will be discussed, because much of the habitat is similar.

Schulze Lake is probably the best overall birding area in the park. It is located 3.5 miles east of I-35E on the south side of Cliff Road (County 32). Drive in at the large sign and gatehouse. A winding road leads to the main parking lot. If you visit at any other time of year and find the main gate closed, drive a few hundred yards east on Cliff Road and enter to the south (right) via a short dirt road that ends at McDonough Lake. Here you will find a paved walking path that leads around the lake to the main Schulze Lake parking lot. The trailhead from Schulze Lake begins at the cluster of pines beyond the parking lot and left (east) of the swim beach. This trail winds around the lake and back to the entrance road. Trails are well-marked with signs but still can be confusing to a first-time visitor. Use the lake as a reference point.

Spring (the last three weeks in May) and fall (mid-August to the end of September) migrations are good for flycatchers, vireos, warblers, and tanagers. The best areas are the mature oak trees on the south and west sides of the lake. Eastern Towhees breed here and can be found around the parking lot. The west side of the entrance road has Field Sparrows and Indigo Buntings in the clearings, and nesting Blue-winged Warblers can be found in the same area—usually in the trees beyond the open area. Mourning Warblers can occasionally be found during breeding season—typically on the west side of the lake. Cooper's, Red-shouldered (rare), and Broad-winged Hawks, Yellow-throated Vireos, and Scarlet Tanagers also can be found in the park.

For another entrance into the park, go west on Cliff Road 2.8 miles to Johnny Cake Ridge Road. Turn south 0.5 mile to the trailhead on the

west/right side of the road. Walk west and up the hill through the planted
pines. You will encounter open areas to the south and rolling deciduous
woods farther west. The birds to be found here are similar to those around
Schulze Lake, except that there are fewer warblers.

MURPHY-HANREHAN PARK PRESERVE

Half day; spring, summer, and fall

Murphy-Hanrehan lies in western Dakota and eastern Scott Counties.
It, like Lebanon Hills, consists of 2,000-plus acres of rolling deciduous
woods and small lakes and ponds. In light traffic it is a 30-minute drive from
the airport. The park is home to nesting Red-shouldered Hawk, Acadian
Flycatcher, Wood Thrush, Blue-winged, Cerulean, and Hooded Warblers,
and Scarlet Tanager. Occasionally, Alder Flycatcher and Chestnut-sided and
Mourning Warblers can be found during the summer months. Spring and fall
migrations can be excellent; however, the large size of the park tends to
disperse the birds.

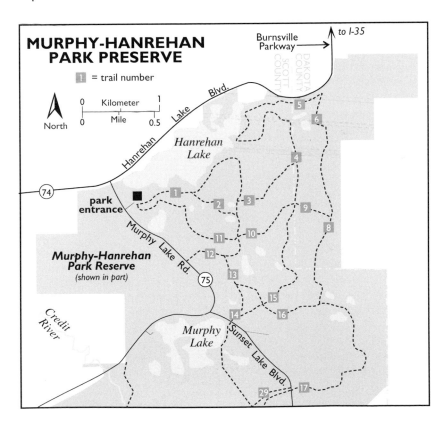

Head south on I-35W from Minneapolis to Dakota County 42 (Crystal Lake Road). Go west 2 miles to Burnsville Parkway, then turn south (left). This road curves to the right and becomes Hanrehan Lake Boulevard as it crosses into Scott County. After 2.4 miles you will pass Hanrehan Lake on your left. Turn left onto Murphy Lake Road, and park in the lot on your left. Pick up a park map from the display or mailbox at the trailhead. An entrance fee (currently $5.00) is required to park along any of the roads or walk the trails. Park personnel regularly patrol and ticket unregistered vehicles.

Continue up Murphy Lake Road to the left for 1.0 mile, then left on Sunset Lake Boulevard for 0.2 mile. There is a trailhead (#14) on your left. Park on the side of the road and head up the trail. Mourning Warblers are irregularly found along this part of the trail in summer. At the first split, #13 is to the left and #15 to the right, and #16 is to your right once you reach #15. Hooded Warblers are most frequently found between trail markers #15 and #16. Scarlet Tanagers are common in the triangle formed by markers #13, #14, and #15. Wood Thrushes and Blue-winged and Cerulean Warblers are found regularly throughout the park. Acadian Flycatchers, which are at the northern edge of their breeding range, are more difficult to find. (Because several of these southern species occur in Minnesota in very low numbers, the use of tapes is strongly discouraged.) Alder Flycatchers are also rare; they tend to be found bordering marshy areas at the northern edge of the park. Barred Owls are commonly heard at night from the trailhead itself. The terrain is hilly, and the mosquitoes and flies can be pretty thick in summer; however, the variety of species in and around the park makes it a worthwhile visit.

CARLOS AVERY STATE WILDLIFE MANAGEMENT AREA
Half to full day; year round

Carlos Avery State WMA is 23,000 acres of productive wetlands, grasslands, and deciduous woods located 30 miles north of the Twin Cities. To reach this excellent refuge, take I-35E or I-35W north to Forest Lake. Exit onto County 2 and turn left. Upon entering Anoka County the road changes to County 18. Continue for 4.0 miles from the county line, then turn right onto Zodiac Street and drive 1.0 mile to the refuge headquarters. Check the conifers bordering the driveway for birds, including crossbills in winter. Be sure to pick up a map at the headquarters, as this area, with its poorly marked roads, can be confusing.

From the headquarters, begin driving due east through open and wooded areas. Eventually, the road curves to the north and passes several large pools, which can be good for herons or shorebirds if water levels are right. Watch and listen for Sandhill Cranes in open areas; they breed here regularly. Less

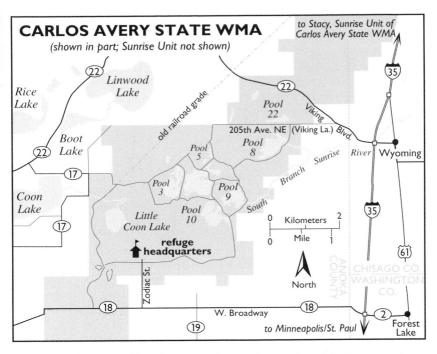

CARLOS AVERY STATE WMA
(shown in part; Sunrise Unit not shown)

to Stacy, Sunrise Unit of
Carlos Avery State WMA

Rice Lake

Linwood Lake

Pool 22

old railroad grade

Viking

205th Ave. NE (Viking La.) Blvd.

Boot Lake

Pool 5

Pool 8

Sunrise River Wyoming

Branch

Coon Lake

Pool 3

Pool 9

South

Little Coon Lake

Pool 10

refuge headquarters

Zodiac St.

Kilometers

Mile

North

ANOKA COUNTY

CHISAGO CO.

WASHINGTON CO.

W. Broadway

to Minneapolis/St. Paul

Forest Lake

frequently, Common Moorhens—at the northern edge of their range—have been found in some of the pools.

The wooded tracts of the refuge can be excellent for passerines during migration and summer. Check especially the western edge of the refuge and along the road running due north from County 17 toward the eastern side of Boot Lake. This road passes by a small cemetery and then through a spruce-tamarack bog where warblers expected farther north in summer can sometimes be found. Birds in these areas include both cuckoos, Alder Flycatcher, Golden-winged, Blue-winged, Chestnut-sided, and Pine Warblers, and Northern Waterthrush. In winter, watch for hawks, owls, Northern Shrikes, and Common Ravens. The spruce-tamarack bog east of Boot Lake, as well as the headquarters area, are also good places to look for crossbills, although these birds are absent more often than present.

NEW GERMANY

Half day; late summer and fall

Away from Carlos Avery State WMA, shorebirds can be difficult to find near the Twin Cities. Although there are sod farms and other fields that have potential from year to year, these are scattered throughout the area, and whether they have water and shorebirds is highly dependent on recent weather conditions. One of the more reliable nearby spots is the Crane Creek drainage between New Germany and Lester Prairie in western Carver County.

To visit this spot, head west on Highway 7 from Minneapolis. About 13 miles past I-494 you will see the **Carver Park Reserve** to the south. This excellent site, a large regional park with hiking and biking trails, is well worth checking if you have time, either on the way to or from New Germany. The park consists of deciduous woods, prairies, and small ponds. The feeders at its Lowry Nature Center can be productive.

To reach **New Germany**, continue west on SR-7 from the turn-off to Carver Park another 12.5 miles to the junction with County 33. The town of New Germany is about a mile to your left. Instead, continue on SR-7 for another 2.3 miles. Just across the McLeod County line the Crane Creek drainage meets SR-7. Pull far off the shoulder of this heavily traveled two-lane road and look for shorebirds to the south. *Please note that all of this area is private property and that all birding should be done from the road.* After you are satisfied with your viewing, return east to Yancy Avenue, the first gravel road heading south (right). Go south 1.5 miles, where the road turns left. Before making this turn, you will see a pond to your right that is worth checking for herons and shorebirds. Continue as the road turns first left and then right. At this point it is now Yale Avenue. At the next paved road, County 30, turn right and scan the two ponds on the north side of the road for shorebirds. Traffic, though infrequent, moves quickly on this road, and there is very little shoulder. If you are uncomfortable, pull ahead to Yancy Avenue, a quiet gravel

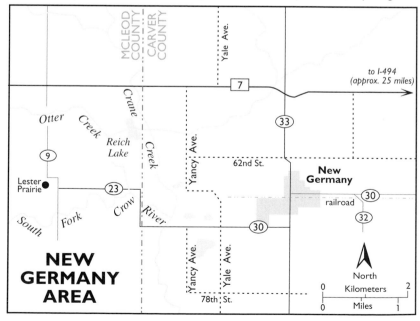

road on the left where you can leave your car to return on foot to bird these ponds. Be careful to watch the grassy edges in late July and August for possible Buff-breasted Sandpipers. Continue south on Yancy Avenue and study the large pond, which begins about 150 yards ahead on your left. Be alert for Black-billed Cuckoos and Red-headed Woodpeckers in the area. Large flocks of American White Pelicans often can be seen soaring overhead. During late September and October, watch the weedy edges for migrant sparrows. Continue down Yancy, turning left on 78th Street and again left at Yale. This eventually brings you to the opposite side of the large pond that you first studied from Yancy Avenue. Unfortunately, during spring migration the water levels are too high, and it is rare that good shorebird habitat exists.

LAKE PEPIN AND THE MISSSISSIPPI RIVER

Full day; spring or fall

The **Mississippi River** below Minneapolis/St. Paul is a migration corridor for many birds. One can easily fill a whole day by stopping at the sites described below. Any of the places along this route could be interesting at the right times of year. Plan your day based on the month of your visit and the amount of time you have.

Start in Red Wing, which is about 40 miles southeast of St. Paul along the Mississippi, and head south. In the late fall through early spring a stop at Colville Park along the river can produce waterfowl, eagles, and gulls. There is a nuclear power-plant just upstream whose warm-water discharge keeps the river open. Watch for a sign for the park just southeast of Red Wing, before you reach the Training School.

Hok-Si-La is a park on the shores of **Lake Pepin**, just north of Lake City. It offers good birding during spring migration. The pine grove can be good for owls during late fall and winter. Prothonotary Warblers nest in the wooded backwaters. There are also several places from which you can scan Lake Pepin, on which a few scoters can sometimes be found among the approximately 10,000 Common Mergansers during the late fall. Also watch for loons and gulls. Head farther south on Route 61 to Lake City. In the center of town is a marina and a point of land that offer good vantage points from which to scan the lake.

Just beyond the southeast end of Lake Pepin is an excellent area to look for Bald Eagles from late fall through early spring. Early December is probably the best time, when one can often find as many as several hundred eagles. Although there is an observation platform built in the town of Wabasha, more of the eagles are actually farther north near Reads Landing.

Continuing south along Route 61 past Wabasha to Kellogg, take County 84 to the east. This road meanders between Route 61 and the river through some sandy Nature Conservancy grasslands that during breeding season have both cuckoos and Lark and Clay-colored Sparrows. County 84 rejoins 61 in Weaver. If you continue south on 61, watch for staging Tundra Swans in November and December. Thousands of these birds rest here and across the river in Alma, Wisconsin, in preparation for the last leg of their trip to the Atlantic Seaboard.

A side-trip good at any time of the year is to go southwest along SR-74 from Weaver into the **Whitewater State Wildlife Management Area**. In winter watch for Golden Eagles and Red-shouldered Hawks, both of which regularly winter here, and check the junipers for Townsend's Solitaires (rare) and the feeders at the headquarters. During the breeding season watch for herons, and for many of the passerines that barely make it north into Minnesota, such as Willow Flycatcher, Bell's Vireo, and Louisiana Water-thrush. If you visit during deer-hunting season (the first half of November), wear orange, because this area is very popular with hunters!

OTHER NOTEWORTHY SITES

Some of the better regional parks omitted earlier for lack of space are **Lake Elmo** in Washington County and **Elm Creek**, **Hyland Lake**, and **Crow-Hassan** in Hennepin County. In Elm Creek, for example, one can find both species of cuckoos, Acadian Flycatcher, Sedge Wren, Wood Thrush, Blue-winged Warbler, and Clay-colored Sparrow. The sparrows can be found at the dog-run field at the intersection of Elm Creek Road and County 202. The biking trail just north of here takes you through areas where the other birds can be found.

Afton and **William O'Brien State Parks** and **Carpenter Nature Center** attract migrants moving along the St. Croix River. **Rice Creek** in Ramsey County is another good place to look for migrant warblers. Walk the trails along the creek between Highways 47 and 65 in Fridley, about 7 miles due north of downtown Minneapolis. **Miesville Ravine**, located in the extreme southeast corner of Dakota County, is good for both spring and fall migrants, and is a reliable area for breeding Whip-poor-wills. The latter can be found along the Goodhue County line where 280th Street becomes Orlando Avenue.

There are often one or more Snowy or Northern Saw-whet Owls around the Twin Cities in the winter. During late July and August there are usually some Buff-breasted Sandpipers to be found on local sod farms. For all of these species your best bet is to check the local birding reports.

EXTRA EFFORT

As good as birding can be in the Minneapolis/St. Paul area, some would argue that the best birding in the state is in **Duluth**, 150 miles from the Twin Cities. **Hawk Ridge** is a spectacular hawkwatching site from September through November. Winter finches and Bohemian Waxwings can be found at local feeders and in Mountain Ash trees during many winters. A few Snowy Owls usually inhabit the frozen bay near the harbor, and in some winters a Gyrfalcon may also be present. Red-throated and Pacific Loons and all three scoters are found in most fall seasons and briefly during spring. Passerine migration can be excellent. In summer, this is the gateway to the Minnesota boreal forests with nesting owls, flycatchers, and warblers. And once you are this far, particularly if it is during fall, why stop here? The farther up the North Shore of Lake Superior that one travels, the more likely one is to encounter the species and vagrants that concentrate along the Lake Superior shoreline.

Aitkin County has year-round populations of Sharp-tailed Grouse, Great Gray Owl, and Black-billed Magpie. In winter, watch for Northern Hawk Owl, Snowy Owl, Bohemian Waxwing, and all the winter finches. During the summer Yellow Rails and Le Conte's and Nelson's Sharp-tailed Sparrows can with patience be found—or at least heard—at the **McGregor Marsh** (along SR-65 a mile or two south of SR-210). Many of the boreal specialties that are more common farther north are here at the southern edge of their breeding ranges: Alder and Yellow-bellied Flycatchers, Gray Jay, Boreal Chickadee, and Golden-winged and Connecticut Warblers. A good place to look for Great Gray Owl is along Pietz's Road, which runs north of County Road 18, beginning two miles west of County Road 5. Walk the snowmobile trail south of road 18 to find the warblers and flycatchers. (In summer, bring lots of mosquito repellent!)

Mille Lacs Lake, in central Minnesota, is over 200 square miles in area. It is best known to Minnesotans as a Walleye fishing-ground, but birders head there in the fall looking for waterfowl of the type which one might better expect to find on Lake Superior. Four loon species, three scoters, Barrow's Goldeneye, Red Phalarope, and Pomarine and Parasitic Jaegers have been found on Mille Lacs Lake. Common Loons and Bonaparte's Gulls are present in large numbers in October. Look for Little Gull among them. From the Twin Cities, take I-94 northwest to Rogers, then north on Highway 101 across the Mississippi River. When 101 meets US-10, continue north on US-169 to Mille Lacs. Here you can decide to circumnavigate the lake either clockwise or counter-clockwise. Do not ignore the passerines in the trees; such vagrants as Magnificent Hummingbird, Painted Redstart, and Western Tanager have been found along the lakeshore in fall.

For these areas you should check the MOU web site or the RBA for news of recent sightings; Eckert's book has detailed directions to the best locations.

ACKNOWLEDGMENTS

We gratefully acknowledge the review offered by Parker Backstrom, Steve Carlson, Drew Smith, and Tom Tustison, who critically read and contributed to this account.

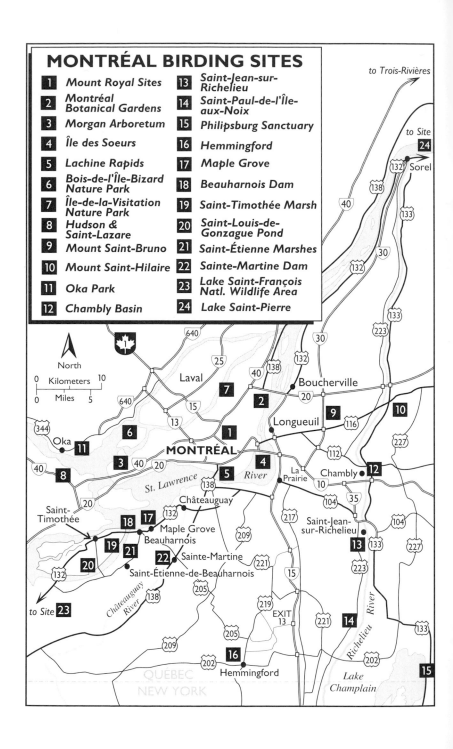

MONTRÉAL BIRDING SITES

1	Mount Royal Sites	**13**	Saint-Jean-sur-Richelieu
2	Montréal Botanical Gardens	**14**	Saint-Paul-de-l'Île-aux-Noix
3	Morgan Arboretum	**15**	Philipsburg Sanctuary
4	Île des Soeurs	**16**	Hemmingford
5	Lachine Rapids	**17**	Maple Grove
6	Bois-de-l'Île-Bizard Nature Park	**18**	Beauharnois Dam
7	Île-de-la-Visitation Nature Park	**19**	Saint-Timothée Marsh
8	Hudson & Saint-Lazare	**20**	Saint-Louis-de-Gonzague Pond
9	Mount Saint-Bruno	**21**	Saint-Étienne Marshes
10	Mount Saint-Hilaire	**22**	Sainte-Martine Dam
11	Oka Park	**23**	Lake Saint-François Natl. Wildlife Area
12	Chambly Basin	**24**	Lake Saint-Pierre

North

Kilometers 0 — 10

Miles 0 — 5

to Trois-Rivières

to Site **24**

Sorel

to Site **23**

Laval

Boucherville

Oka **11**

Longueuil

MONTRÉAL

La Prairie

Chambly

Saint-Timothée

Châteauguay

Maple Grove

Beauharnois

Sainte-Martine

Saint-Étienne-de-Beauharnois

Saint-Jean-sur-Richelieu

Châteauguay River

Hemmingford

EXIT 13

Lake Champlain

QUEBEC
NEW YORK

St. Lawrence River

Richelieu River

MONTRÉAL, QUÉBEC

Pierre Bannon and Richard Yank

Whether you are coming to Montréal for a business trip or for a vacation, you will be fascinated by this scenic and enjoyable city, its European style, its great restaurants, and its many festivals and special events. The Montréal area lies within the St. Lawrence River lowlands. The relatively flat topography of this area is punctuated by a series of hills known as the Monteregian Hills. Mount Royal, which dominates the city of Montréal, is one of these hills. It offers excellent birding opportunities very close to the downtown area for birders with only a couple of hours at their disposal. The Botanical Gardens, Nuns' Island, the Lachine Rapids, and a network of five Nature Parks, all easily accessible by public transport, also contribute to making the city of Montréal a very good birding destination.

The topography of the surrounding lowlands is such that the St. Lawrence River has expanded in some places into vast bodies of water, known as Lakes Saint-François, Saint-Louis, and Saint-Pierre. During spring flooding, most of the "Greater" Snow Goose population and 75 percent of all the Canada Geese migrating through southern Québec stage for a few weeks in the floodplain of Lake Saint-Pierre. In fall, almost 165,000 scaup of both species use Lakes Saint-François and Saint-Louis during migration.

With a checklist of 303 regularly occurring species, plus an additional 70 casual visitors, the Montréal area has the richest avifauna in Québec. Moreover, winter birding has gained in popularity in recent years, with local birders tallying lists of between 100 and 120 species for the three winter months.

ESSENTIAL INFORMATION

Getting around: Dorval Airport, on the island of Montréal, about 20 minutes from the downtown area by car, handles all domestic and international flights except for some international charters. Canada's main national airline (Air Canada) and a number of U.S. and overseas carriers offer regularly scheduled flights to Montréal. Via Rail Canada provides transcontinental rail service within Canada. Via Rail's Montréal terminus will leave you at the downtown central station at 935 de la Gauchetière Street West. Consult Via Rail Canada at their web site, *www.viarail.ca/*, or telephone (514) 989-2626. The city of Montréal is built on an island. Although the city has an excellent subway system (The Metro), there are still plenty of cars on the roads, and rush hours can be a nightmare. For trips on the island, it can be difficult to travel by car on weekdays, so public transportation should be considered. For help and directions to access any of the Montréal Island sites by public transport, call the Société de Transport de la Communauté Urbaine de Montréal (STCUM) at (514) AUTOBUS (288-6287) or consult their web site at *www.stcum.qc.ca/*. For trips off the island, it is much better to have a car, but it is essential to leave early, especially on weekdays, to avoid traffic jams on highways and bridges. Montréal's Central Bus Station is at 505 de Maisonneuve Street East (corner of Berri). The Voyageur bus company has a web site at *www.voyageur.com/infoe.htm*. For access to sites outside the island of Montréal, call (514) 842-2281 for bus schedules and fares.

Montréal is second in size only to Paris among the French-speaking cities of the world. So, although knowledge of French is not essential, it is a precious advantage, especially when traveling outside Montréal itself.

Climate: From late spring to early fall, temperatures are usually pleasant, with average daytime highs near 80°F in mid-summer and 70°F the rest of the time. Be prepared for mosquitoes in June and July. From late fall to early spring, birders need warm clothing, including hats, gloves, and boots. Daytime temperatures average 20°F in January and February but can be as low as 0°F or less early in the morning. A thick blanket of snow usually covers the ground from December through March, at times limiting access to woods and fields unless you are equipped with snowshoes or skis.

Safety: Montréal is recognized internationally as a very safe city. However, visitors should not leave binoculars, telescopes, or cameras in view within their cars when using public parking areas.

Other Resources: We suggest the site guide *Birdfinding in the Montréal Area* by Pierre Bannon (1991, Province of Québec Society for the Protection of Birds and Centre de conservation de la faune ailée de Montréal). Rare Bird Alert telephone numbers are (514) 989-5076 (English) and (450) 687-6740 (French). The French hotline is updated daily. Two excellent web sites are *Rare Birds of Québec*, maintained by Louise Simard at *www.total.net/~simardl/oiseauxraresqc.index/rares.htm*, with information concerning recent sightings across the province (French), and *Birds of Québec* by Denis Lepage, with numerous links: *www.oiseauxqc.org/quebangl.html* (bilingual).

Other destinations: One outing that might interest birders is the Montréal Biodome, where one can find live birds, mammals, and plants associated with four ecosystems: the Tropical Forest, the Laurentian Forest, the St. Lawrence Marine Ecosystem, and the Polar World. It is located at 4777 Pierre-de-Coubertin, near the Montréal Botanical Gardens. Another interesting destination is the Redpath Museum, at 859 Sherbrooke Street West, which houses a large natural-history collection, including some 1,500 bird specimens. It is located at 859 Sherbrooke Street West.

THE BIRDING YEAR

Spring and fall are the best birding seasons in Montréal. Spring migration begins at the end of March and finishes in early June. Raptors and waterfowl pass through in March and April, whereas passerines and shorebirds arrive mostly in May. During the last two weeks in May, approximately 200 species can be found in the Montréal area, and it is possible to see 140 on a Big Day. About 190 species nest in the area, mostly in June. In mid-July, birding slows down in the Montréal area, and a visiting birder might be interested to head north to the Laurentian Hills in search of eastern warblers and boreal species. Mont Tremblant Park, near Saint-Jovite, is a good birding destination at this season; it can produce Spruce Grouse, Black-backed Woodpecker, Gray Jay, and Boreal Chickadee.

Migrant landbirds start to return to the Montréal area in mid-July, and in most years some can be found into December. Although they are never seen in huge numbers, a good variety of shorebirds visit the area, especially in August and early September. Gull migration is at its peak in November and early December. After the leaves have fallen in late October, passerines become scarce and local woodlands become quiet. Although Montréal has a rather frigid winter climate, this is nonetheless an extremely interesting season for the birder. It is the time to watch for northern species such as Iceland and Glaucous Gulls, Snowy Owl, Northern Shrike, American Tree Sparrow, Lapland Longspur, Snow Bunting, White-winged Crossbill, and Common Redpoll. Other, less-common, northern visitors include Gyrfalcon, Northern Hawk Owl, Great Gray Owl, Boreal Owl, Three-toed Woodpecker, Black-backed Woodpecker, Gray Jay, Boreal Chickadee, Bohemian Waxwing, Pine Grosbeak, and Hoary Redpoll.

MOUNT ROYAL

Half day; mainly spring, summer, fall

Mount Royal overlooks the city of Montréal from an altitude of 700 feet and is easily accessible from the downtown area within a few minutes. There are three excellent birding sites on the mountain: Mount Royal Park, Mount Royal Cemetery, and Westmount Summit Park. **Mount Royal Park** was created in 1874 and today represents one of the largest remaining green spaces on the island of Montréal. This park was designed by architect Frederick Law Olmsted, who also designed New York's Central Park. Birding is best in spring and fall, but the park also provides ready access to a good variety of nesting species, as well as wintering birds. In spring, local birders are attracted by waves of northbound warblers and migrating hawks. In winter, finches come to feeders provided by the city, while American Robins prefer to feast on mountain-ash berries. Rarities have included Townsend's Solitaire, Varied Thrush, and Hooded Warbler. By car, Mount Royal parking lots can be reached from the east via Camillien Houde Parkway at the corner of Mont-Royal and Park Avenues, or from the west from Côte-des-Neiges Road. Note that coins will be required for the meters. For travel by bus, take Bus 11 from the Mont-Royal Metro station.

Adjacent to the park is **Mount Royal Cemetery**, also a popular destination for local birders in spring and fall. Eastern Screech-Owls are present year round, while summer residents include Red-shouldered Hawk, Pileated Woodpecker, and Eastern Bluebird. To the west of Mount Royal Park is **Summit Park**, a tiny wooded area owned and maintained by the City of Westmount. In May birders from across the province flock to this heavily-used urban oasis to witness impressive concentrations of passerines that regularly pause here during migration. No fewer than 33 species of warblers have been sighted over the years. By car, from Côte-des-Neiges Road, take Belvedere Road up the mountain (across from Remembrance Road). Turn right onto Summit Road and drive to Summit Circle, which goes

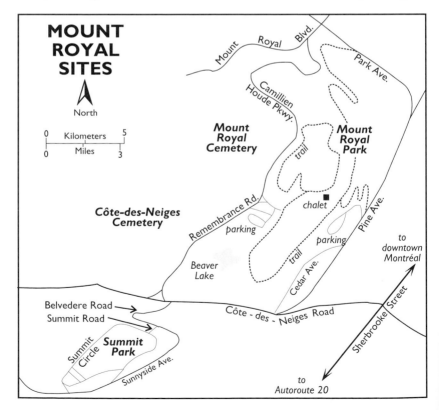

all the way around the park. By public transport, from Guy-Concordia Metro station take Bus 66, 165, or 166 to Côte-des-Neiges and Belvedere.

MONTRÉAL BOTANICAL GARDENS AND MORGAN ARBORETUM

Half day, year round

Although most visitors are attracted to this 180-acre site by exquisite floral displays, birdwatchers have also found the **Montréal Botanical Gardens** of great interest. Spring and fall offer a nice variety of migrant passerines, while feeders attract winter birds, and therefore raptors, in good numbers. Bohemian Waxwings are also found regularly in winter. By car from downtown Montréal, take Autoroute 40 east and Pie IX south to the corner of Sherbrooke Street, or, alternatively, Notre Dame Street east and Pie IX north. By public transport, take the Metro to Pie IX station. Those wishing to visit indoor aviaries can visit the nearby Biodome, open year round.

The **Morgan Arboretum** is a sanctuary of 600 acres forming part of Macdonald College in Sainte-Anne-de-Bellevue at the western tip of the island of Montréal. It has the largest remaining woodlands on the island, including a tremendous variety of trees and shrubs, both native and exotic. It offers good birding at all seasons along a network of well-marked walking trails. Nesting species include Pileated Woodpecker, Ovenbird, and Scarlet Tanager. During autumn, the south boundary of the Arboretum, near Autoroute 40, offers one of the best sites in southern Québec from which to observe raptor migration. By car, take Autoroute 40 west to Exit 41 toward Chemin Sainte-Marie. At the first intersection turn left to the entrance. A modest parking fee is collected. The nearby Ecomuseum, open throughout the year, offers a collection of native fauna.

ÎLE DES SOEURS AND LACHINE RAPIDS

Half day, year round

Despite a rapid loss of habitat to urbanization in recent years, the western tip of **Île des Soeurs** (Nuns' Island) still attracts a variety of birds. Pied-billed Grebes nest on the pond, Northern Waterthrushes and Rusty Blackbirds visit the moist woods in spring, owls and woodpeckers appear frequently in winter, and Gray Partridge (difficult to find) and an occasional Short-eared Owl inhabit the fields. Offshore, Red-throated Loons and Red-necked Grebes are spotted each year in migration. An impressive 283 species have been reported over the years, including 34 species of warblers. By car, take Décarie Boulevard (Highway 15) or the Bonaventure Autoroute. Take the Île des Soeurs exit just before the Champlain Bridge. Park at the end

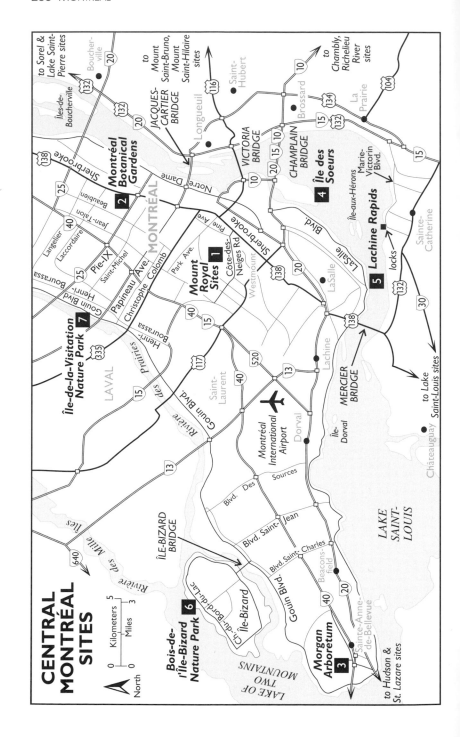

CENTRAL MONTRÉAL SITES

North

Kilometers 0 5
Miles 0 3

1 Mount Royal Sites
2 Montréal Botanical Gardens
3 Morgan Arboretum
4 Île des Soeurs
5 Lachine Rapids
6 Bois-de-l'Île-Bizard Nature Park
7 Île-de-la-Visitation Nature Park

to Sorel & Lake Saint-Pierre sites
Boucherville
Îles-de-Boucherville
to Mount Saint-Bruno, Mount Saint-Hilaire sites
to Chambly, Richelieu River sites
Saint-Hubert
Longueuil
Brossard
La Prairie
Sainte-Catherine
JACQUES-CARTIER BRIDGE
VICTORIA BRIDGE
CHAMPLAIN BRIDGE
Marie-Victorin Blvd.
Île-aux-Hérons
locks
Montréal Botanical Gardens
Sherbrooke
Beaubien
Jean-Talon
Langelier
Lacordaire
Pie-IX
Saint-Michel
Papineau Ave.
Christophe Colomb
Henri-Bourassa
Gouin Blvd
Henri-Bourassa
LAVAL
Rivière des Prairies
Île-de-la-Visitation Nature Park
Notre Dame
Park Ave.
Pine Ave.
Sherbrooke
Côte-des-Neiges Rd
Westmount
LaSalle
LaSalle Blvd
Lachine Rapids
Saint-Laurent
Gouin Blvd.
Montréal International Airport
Dorval
Île-Dorval
Lachine
MERCIER BRIDGE
to Lake Saint-Louis sites
Châteauguay
Rivière des Mille Îles
ÎLE-BIZARD BRIDGE
Ch.-du-Bord-du-Lac
Île-Bizard
Bois-de-l'Île-Bizard Nature Park
Blvd. Des Sources
Blvd. Saint-Jean
Blvd. Saint-Charles
Beaconsfield
Gouin Blvd.
Sainte-Anne-de-Bellevue
Morgan Arboretum
LAKE OF TWO MOUNTAINS
LAKE SAINT-LOUIS
to Hudson & St. Lazare sites

of Île des Soeurs Boulevard or at the Elgar Shopping Centre. By public transport, from the LaSalle Metro Station, take Bus 12 to the end of Île des Soeurs Boulevard.

The **Lachine Rapids**, one of the finest natural features along the St. Lawrence River, are located just west of Île des Soeurs and can be birded from the LaSalle waterfront. Herons, ducks, gulls, and terns abound at the bottom of the rapids. Caspian Tern can be spotted in summer, and Eurasian Wigeon and Arctic Tern have appeared in late May and early June. Wintering ducks are present in large numbers and include primarily American Black Duck, Mallard, Common Goldeneye, and Common Merganser. By car, this site is located along LaSalle Boulevard. There is a municipal parking lot at the corner of 6th Avenue. Also check the bottom of the rapids at the corner of Fayolle Street to the north. By public transport, take Bus 110 from the Angrignon Metro station to the corner of Central and Bishop Power Streets. Walk to LaSalle Boulevard. The Lachine Rapids can also be birded from the south shore at **Côte-Sainte-Catherine**. The St. Lawrence Seaway locks at Sainte-Catherine provide a splendid view of the waterfowl and gulls that congregate below the rapids. Even in mid-winter a variety of ducks and gulls (including Iceland and Glaucous) frequent the fast-moving waters, sometimes attracting a Snowy Owl or a Bald Eagle. Double-crested Cormorants are plentiful from spring to fall. Nests of Great Blue Heron, Great Egret, and Black-crowned Night-Heron are visible among the taller trees on Heron Island, situated mid-river across from the locks. By car, head south across the Champlain Bridge, take the first exit after the bridge toward New York (State Route 15 south or Highway 132 west); take Exit 46 (LaPrairie/Salaberry) and turn right onto Marie-Victorin Boulevard. Drive 5.2 kilometers and turn right at the Sainte-Catherine Locks. Or alternatively take the Mercier Bridge. At the south end of the bridge, take the left exit (LaPrairie, 132 East), drive 6.5 kilometers, turn left onto Rue Centrale, and go to Marie-Victorin Boulevard. The locks are a little farther on. By public transportation, Les Autobus Ménard, (800) 363-4543, provide service from the Voyageur bus terminal in downtown Montréal (at the Berri/UQAM Metro station).

NATURE PARKS OF MONTRÉAL

Morning or half day; mainly spring, summer, fall

The Montréal urban community is endowed with five beautiful Nature Parks. From west to east these are Cap-Saint-Jacques, Bois-de-l'Île-Bizard, Bois-de-Liesse, Île-de-la-Visitation, and Pointe-des-Prairies. All are accessed from Gouin Boulevard, which runs parallel to Rivière des Prairies along the north shore of Montréal island. The following web site provides further details: *www.cum.qc.ca/cum-an/parc/coorpara.htm*. Each of these parks can be visited in a couple of hours or in a half day. Only two are described here.

Bois-de-l'Île-Bizard Nature Park, occupying 440 acres on Île Bizard, is by far the largest and most interesting of these parks. The varied habitats include swamps, abandoned fields, mature Silver Maple/Beech forest, and stands of White-Cedar. A rich variety of birds is found here: Great Horned Owl and Red-shouldered Hawk regularly nest in the forest, and Least Bittern (rare), Virginia Rail, and Sora inhabit the marshy areas. The 10-kilometer system of trails and boardwalks is heavily used by cyclists during the summer. By car, take Highway 40 to Boulevard Saint-Jean north; continue to Gouin Boulevard and turn left (west). Follow signs to the Île Bizard Bridge. Once across the bridge, watch for signs directing you to the north side of the island and the park entrance along Chemin du Bord du Lac. There is a parking fee.

The smallest of the regional parks, **Île-de-la-Visitation Nature Park**, is located along Rivière des Prairies and is especially interesting to birders for its winter concentrations of gulls. In late afternoon, thousands of Great Black-backed and Herring Gulls, accompanied by Iceland and Glaucous Gulls, congregate above the dam to spend the night. An occasional Lesser Black-backed Gull has been seen. By car, take Highway 40 to the Christophe Colomb/Papineau Avenue exit; turn north on Papineau Avenue. Turn right onto Henri-Bourassa Boulevard, left onto Rue de Lille, right onto Gouin Boulevard, and left into the parking area. By public transport, from the Henri-Bourrassa Metro station, take Bus 69 to Rue d'Iberville, and walk north for one block.

HUDSON AND SAINT-LAZARE

Half to full day; year round

These two sites are about 45 minutes west of downtown Montréal. With its 120 nesting species, **Hudson** is one of the most attractive summer birding sites near Montréal. Among the several points of interest, Aird's Pond is highly recommended. It is located 8 kilometers west of Hudson village on Main Road. The pond is found at the back of the parking lot at Finnegan's Market, on the south side of the road. This private property is available to birders, so be respectful. Check the pond and then take the path along its western edge to the railroad track. Walk along the track to the right. Check the marshy area on both sides of the track and the fields farther to the west, where Green Heron and Sedge Wren have nested in recent years.

Nearby **Saint-Lazare** has large stands of Eastern White Pine and spruce hosting nesting Blue-headed Vireo, Golden-crowned Kinglet, Hermit Thrush, Cape May Warbler, and Dark-eyed Junco. The pinery along Chemin Poirier is recommended for wintering Three-toed and Black-backed Woodpeckers, as well as White-winged Crossbills, which are seen almost every year. By car from Montréal, take Highway 40 west, then Exit 22 to Chemin Côte Saint-Charles. Drive north to Main Road and turn left for Finnegan's Market. To reach Chemin Poirier from Finnegan's Market, backtrack to Chemin Côte

Saint-Charles and drive south past Highway 40. Turn right on Chemin Sainte-Angélique and then left on Chemin Poirier. Parking is forbidden along the pinery, so birding should be done from the road, near the car. Otherwise, parking will be found to the east at the Base de Plein Air Les Cèdres, at the north end of Chemin Saint-Dominique. There is an admission fee. Near the Centre is a large, partly flooded sand pit visited by waterfowl and shorebirds in late summer.

THE MONTEREGIAN HILLS

Half to full day; mainly spring, summer, fall

The topography around Montréal is highlighted from west to east by a string of ten hills jutting out of the surrounding lowlands. Mount Royal is one of these, the others being the Oka Hills, Mount Saint-Bruno, Mount

Saint-Hilaire, Mount Rougemont, Mount Saint-Grégoire, Mount Yamaska, Mount Shefford, Mount Brome, and Mount Mégantic. Although Mount Mégantic is well to the east, outside the Montréal area, birders with a day to spare may be interested in making the long trip to this mountain for its nesting Bicknell's Thrushes (June–July).

Mount Saint-Bruno, Mount Saint-Hilaire, and Oka Park in Oka will be described here. **Mount Saint-Bruno,** only 30 minutes east of Montréal, is recognized as one of the most beautiful and ornithologically productive sites in the area. Among the more unusual resident species are Turkey Vulture, Red-shouldered Hawk, Barred Owl, and Pine Warbler. By car from Montréal, take the Jacques-Cartier Bridge, Taschereau Boulevard, and Highway 116 to Autoroute 30, or, as an alternative, the Champlain Bridge and Highway 10 to Autoroute 30. Exit via Chemin des 25 and follow signs to the park.

Mount Saint-Hilaire has been designated a United Nations Biosphere Reserve; much of the area is owned and managed by McGill University. A nature center and interpretative program are offered to the public. Nesting Peregrine Falcons and Common Ravens are of special interest. By car, it is reached in 45 minutes from downtown Montréal. Take the Jacques-Cartier Bridge and Taschereau Boulevard to Highway 116 to the town of Mont St. Hilaire. From west of downtown, take the Champlain Bridge and Highway 10 east to Exit 29. Follow Highway 133 north to the town of Mont St. Hilaire. Once there, follow signs to the nature conservation center: from Highway 116, take Rue Fortier, then Chemin Ozias Leduc to Chemin de la Montagne. Turn left at Chemin des Moulins and then left to the Gault Estate.

Oka Park is located northwest of Montréal along Lake of Two Mountains, just east of the village of Oka. Bordered by sandy beaches, marshes, and the lake to the south, and by the Oka Hills to the north, this 4,400-acre park offers a wide diversity of habitat that has attracted a total of 210 bird species. The White Pine forest within the park is home to nesting Pine Warblers, while stands of Sugar Maple harbor the locally rare Yellow-throated Vireo. By car from Montréal allow 45 minutes. Take Autoroute 13 north, then Autoroute 640 west to the end, and turn right on Highway 344 toward the west. Signs will direct you to the park (fee). In summer, the park can also be reached by car ferry from Hudson, which is located just across the Ottawa River from Oka.

RICHELIEU RIVER
Half to full day, spring or fall

The Richelieu River, flowing north from Lake Champlain to the St. Lawrence River at Sorel, is a major flyway for ducks and geese. The following sites can be visited singly in half-day trips or combined to make a full day afield. Our first site is the **Chambly Basin**, located just 45 minutes east of Montréal.

This is an excellent site for grebes, waterfowl, and gulls. Horned and Red-necked Grebes are easy to find during migration, especially during spring but also during fall. Small gulls are usually abundant in November and early December. Most will be Bonaparte's, but check for Black-headed, Little, and Ross's (two records) and Black-legged Kittiwakes, which have appeared in the past few years. Ospreys are common in spring. An Ancient Murrelet caused great excitement here in October 1998. By car, take Highway 10 east from the Champlain Bridge to Exit 22. Drive north on Fréchette Boulevard, then turn right on Bourgogne Street at the basin. Park at Fort Chambly (historic site) and walk behind the old fort to scan the basin.

Saint-Jean-sur-Richelieu lies farther south along the Richelieu River. This site is interesting mostly in late fall when migrating waterfowl stop near the bridge that crosses the river here. Barrow's Goldeneye is seen annually, and a Greater White-fronted Goose or a Harlequin Duck will occasionally show up. Flocks of Bonaparte's and other gulls also congregate at this site. By car, take Highway 10 east from the Champlain Bridge to Exit 22 toward Saint-Jean-sur-Richelieu. Drive south on Highway 35 and then take the exit to Boulevard du Séminaire-Sud. At the traffic lights, go straight to the river and turn right on Champlain Boulevard. Soon you will see a parking area along the river on the left. Scan the river from there. Another parking area is found one kilometer north of the bridge.

Except after a very dry winter, the fields on the west side of the Richelieu River between Saint-Jean-sur-Richelieu and Saint-Paul-de-l'Île-aux-Noix are flooded each spring. Check all flooded fields from the many side streets between Highway 223 and the river. In early spring, search for waterfowl. Later in the season (May), check for shorebirds and egrets. Ruff and Marbled Godwit have appeared almost annually in recent years; vagrant American Avocet and Curlew Sandpiper have occurred. By car, same as for Saint-Jean-sur-Richelieu, but at the exit turn right on Boulevard du Séminaire-Sud. This road will lead you to Highway 223.

From Saint-Paul-de-l'Île-aux-Noix, two excellent sites are accessible within a 30-minute drive: the Philipsburg Sanctuary to the southeast and Hemmingford to the southwest. To reach the **Philipsburg Sanctuary**, continue south on Highway 223, turn left on Highway 202, and right on Highway 133. About one kilometer past the flashing amber light in Philipsburg, look for the Motel Frontière on the left. You will find a small parking lot just south of the motel. This bird sanctuary is the pride and joy of the Province of Québec Society for the Protection of Birds (PQSPB). It covers about 1,200 acres on both sides of Highway 133, between the village of Philipsburg and the U.S. border. Situated on the shore of Missisquoi Bay where the foothills of the Green Mountains meet the plain of the St. Lawrence Valley, the sanctuary offers a sampling of most ecosystems found in the region. Most bird species occurring in southern Québec and northern New England have been seen here. Among species generally uncommon in Québec but regularly breeding here are Yellow-throated Vireo, Northern Rough-winged Swallow, Eastern Towhee, and Field Sparrow. The Beaver pond supports Least Bittern, Wood Duck, Virginia Rail, and Sora. Golden-winged Warblers have nested, and Cerulean Warblers have regularly been observed in stands of mature maple near the border. A dirt road to the east of the highway, near the Canadian Customs House, gives quick access to the habitat occupied by the Ceruleans. Recently, Tufted Titmice have been found nesting in the area. In late fall, stop at the Philipsburg wharf and scan the bay for loons, jaegers, and rare gulls. Directly from Montréal, this site can be reached in about 60 minutes. Take the Champlain Bridge from Montréal, Autoroute 10 east to Highway 35 south, and then Highway 133 south. In Philipsburg, proceed as described above.

To reach the **Hemmingford area** from Saint-Paul-de-l'Île-aux-Noix, keep south on Highway 223, then turn right on Highway 202, and follow directions to Hemmingford. This rural area located near the U.S. border is favored by birders looking for Wild Turkey. Nesting raptors and Clay-colored Sparrows are also sought-after specialties. Wild Turkeys can be found almost anywhere along the secondary roads between Highways 15 and 219. Fisher Road is particularly good in this respect. To reach it, take Highway 219 north out of Hemmingford and turn right after 7 kilometers at Fisher Road. Directly from Montréal, Hemmingford can be reached in 45 minutes. Take the Champlain Bridge and Autoroute 15 south. Exit at Murray Road (Exit 13).

LAKE SAINT-LOUIS

Half to full day; spring, summer, fall

The area south of Lake Saint-Louis is situated immediately southwest of Montréal and can be reached in about 45 minutes from the downtown area. The following six sites can be visited one at a time or as part of a full-day loop. The first stop is at **Maple Grove**, the most reliable site in southern Québec at which to find Caspian Tern. August is the best month. The Île de la Paix Wildlife Sanctuary, located offshore, hosts nesting herons, ducks, and Black Terns. A few shorebirds are usually present each fall. From Montréal, take the Jacques-Cartier, Champlain, or Mercier Bridge to Highway 132 west. In Léry, turn right on Chemin de la Gare, left on Chemin du Lac, and then right on McDonald Street. Drive to the end and park near the playground on the right. Walk along the fence toward the shoreline. Look offshore for Caspian Terns.

To reach the **Beauharnois Dam**, backtrack to Highway 132 by turning west along Rue Saint-Laurent upon leaving the previous site, and continue west past the municipality of Beauharnois. The area surrounding the Beauharnois hydroelectric station is one of the best anywhere in Québec for observing gulls and terns. From September to January concentrations have reached 10,000 birds, with all the common species (Ring-billed, Herring, and Great Black-backed) and an astounding number of vagrants (including such rarities as Laughing, Franklin's, Little, Black-headed, Mew, California, Lesser Black-backed, Sabine's, and Ivory) having been encountered. There are also large rafts of scaup and mergansers in November.

The **Saint-Timothée Marsh**, located 10 minutes from the Beauharnois Dam, features a small heronry, nesting Least Bitterns, Common Moorhens, and numerous ducks. In late summer this is an excellent site for Great Egrets, especially when they come in to roost in the evening. Recently, Bald Eagles have also been regular in late summer. Willow Flycatchers nest in the willow thickets bordering the marsh. From the Beauharnois Dam, drive through the tunnel under the seaway, at the first gas station turn left onto Chemin Sainte-Marie. Drive 5 kilometers on Chemin Sainte-Marie and then on Rang Saint-Joseph to a small parking area on the left. Walk across the bridge to the marsh.

LAKE SAINT-LOUIS
BIRDING SITES

North

Kilometers 0 — 5
Miles 0 — 3

LAKE SAINT - LOUIS

Île de la Paix Wildlife Sanctuary

Châteauguay

Léry {132}

{132}

Châteauguay River

Beauharnois Dam

Maple Grove

Mercier

Melocheville

Beauharnois

{132}

{236}

{205}

{138}

Saint-Timothée

Chemin Sainte-Marie

Saint-Joseph

Canal

Rang Ste.-Anne

Sainte-Martine Dam

Sainte-Martine

Boul Pie XII

Saint-Timothée Marsh

Beauharnois

Saint-Étienne Marshes

Rang St-Georges

{205}

Saint-Louis-de-Gonzague Pond

Rang Saint-Joseph

Rivière Nord

Saint-Louis

Saint-Étienne

Rang St-Laurent

{236}

Rang Chemin

St.-Louis-de-Gonzague

Rang du Trente

Rang du Vingt

Rang du Dix

{138}

{203}

Châteauguay River

The **Saint-Louis-de-Gonzague Pond** attracts thousands of "Greater" Snow Geese in late fall (mid-October to mid-November). Greater White-fronted and Ross's Geese and Eurasian Wigeon also turn up occasionally. A vagrant Pink-footed Goose caused great excitement here in 1996 and 1997. This site is only 10 minutes from the Saint-Timothée marsh. From the latter, continue southwest along Rang Saint-Joseph and turn left onto Boulevard Pie XII. Park just before the bridge and walk along the gravel road which goes west along the Beauharnois canal. Scan the pond for waterfowl.

Numerous marshes are maintained by Ducks Unlimited on the south side of the Beauharnois canal. These marshes, collectively known as the **Saint-Étienne Marshes**, are interesting from early April until November for herons, waterfowl, rails, and shorebirds. Least Bitterns nest among the reeds. During the fall, huge concentrations of blackbirds roost in the vegetation. From the Saint-Louis-de-Gonzague Pond, take the bridge across the canal, turn left on Chemin Saint-Louis and then left on Rang Sainte-Anne to the end of the road. To get to the ponds, you must walk behind some farm buildings on the left side of the road.

The **Sainte-Martine Dam**, located along the Châteauguay River, is excellent for shorebirds from mid-July to late October. About 25 species have been reported, including Baird's and Stilt Sandpipers, Long-billed Dowitcher, and Wilson's Phalarope, all of which occur annually. Osprey, Merlin, and Peregrine Falcon are also fairly regular during this period. A good variety of southern herons have also turned up below the dam. This site is less than 20 minutes from the Saint-Étienne Marshes. From the marshes, backtrack to Highway 236 east toward Beauharnois. In Beauharnois, turn right onto Highway 205 and then right onto Highway 138 until you reach Sainte-Martine. Look for Restaurant Grégoire on the right; park behind the restaurant and walk to the shore. From Montréal, take the Mercier Bridge and Highway 138.

LAKE SAINT-FRANÇOIS
Full day; spring, summer, fall

Although it is rather distant and isolated, **Dundee**, southwest of Lake Saint-François, is regularly visited by Montréal birders. The Lake Saint-François National Wildlife Area, a territory of 12 square kilometers covered mostly by marshlands, is one of the most remarkable birding sites in southern Québec. Herons, ducks, and rails are the main groups of birds to be found. Specialties include Great Egret, Yellow Rail, Willow Flycatcher, and Sedge Wren. Among the many points of interest, we recommend the Great Egret Trail that takes you on a 3.7-kilometer dike surrounding a pond managed by Ducks Unlimited. This site is accessible from Highway 132, 0.8 kilometer before reaching Point Fraser Road. At the end of Point Fraser Road is an interpretive center and observation tower, an area well worth exploring. The extreme southwest section of the refuge deserves a visit, but requires crossing into the U.S. To reach this area, follow Highway 132 to the border. Once across, make a right turn in the village of Fort Covington and take Point Hopkins Road, which follows the Salmon River. This road winds through a vast marsh where Yellow Rails can be heard at night during May and June, but they are very difficult to see. From the south shore of Montréal, take Highway 132 west to Dundee. This site can also be reached from eastern Ontario by crossing the St. Lawrence River at Cornwall and taking U.S. Highway 37 East.

LAKE SAINT-PIERRE

Full day, mainly spring

Approximately 90 minutes east of Montréal is Lake Saint-Pierre, a wide section of the St. Lawrence dotted with low-lying islands and rimmed by extensive freshwater marshes that attract a terrific number and variety of waterbirds. Two sites are described, one on the north shore and the other on the south. **Baie-du-Febvre,** located on the south shore of Lake Saint-Pierre, is a major spring staging-area for "Greater" Snow Geese. In recent years, April counts have exceeded 200,000 birds. A few Greater White-fronted and Ross's Geese have also been found each year among the flocks of Snows. Check for Snowy and Short-eared Owls in early spring. Rough-legged Hawks are numerous in April, and Redheads, Ruddy Ducks, and Black Terns nest in summer. Following the departure of the geese in May, the still-flooded fields continue to attract shorebirds, including such rarities as American Avocet, Black-tailed Godwit, and Curlew Sandpiper. Hunting is permitted in the refuge during the fall. Take Autoroutes 10 or 20 east to access Autoroute 30 east to Sorel. Once at Sorel, continue east on Highway 132 to Baie-du-Febvre. Visit the excellent interpretive center in the village to obtain current birding information.

Saint-Barthélemy is situated on the north side of Lake Saint-Pierre. Similar to the previous site, flooded fields in spring represent the main attraction. Large concentrations of waterfowl including Snow Geese and a variety of ducks are present throughout April. Shorebirds stop over in May. In late summer check the Route du Fleuve along Lake Saint-Pierre for Great Egrets. In winter, Snowy Owls are easily found every year along the secondary roads north of Autoroute 40. From Montréal, take Autoroute 40 east to Exit 155 at Saint-Barthélemy and make your way to the side road that runs parallel to Autoroute 40 on the south side. A loop taking one from Baie-du-Febvre to Saint-Barthélemy would necessitate a very long day or preferably two days. From Baie-du-Febvre, drive east on Highway 132 and cross the river at Trois-Rivières. Then drive west on Highway 138 toward Saint-Barthélemy.

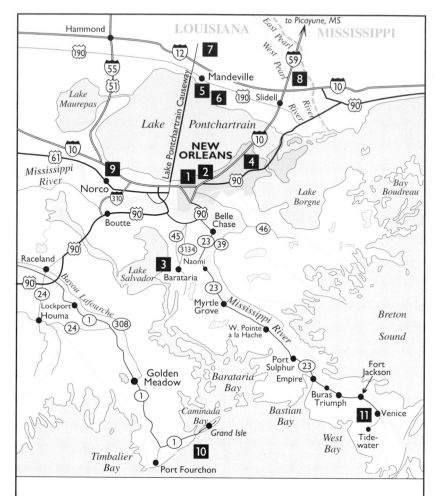

NEW ORLEANS AREA BIRDING SITES

1 City Park

2 Lake Pontchartrain shoreline

3 Barataria Preserve

4 Bayou Sauvage National Wildlife Refuge

5 Mandeville

6 Fontainbleau State Park

7 Abita Springs

8 Honey Island Swamp

9 Bonnet Carre Spillway

10 Grand Isle, Fourchon Beach

11 Venice area

North

0   Kilometers   50

0   Miles   30

NEW ORLEANS, LOUISIANA

Dan Purrington

Sometimes called America's most interesting city—it is one of the most popular tourist destinations in the U.S., the birthplace of jazz, and home to some of North America's best food. New Orleans really *is* "The Big Easy," the "City that Care Forgot." Residents here think first about where they're going to eat next and where the good music is, and only later consider what is on the desk at work. The *Vieux Carre*, or French Quarter, is the main attraction, but food and music are to be had everywhere. Although a Creole rather than a Cajun town, New Orleans is the gateway to Acadian Louisiana, and much Cajun food and music can be found in the city. Big annual events are the Sugar Bowl at New Year's, Mardi Gras in February or March, and the Jazz and Heritage Festival in late April and early May. If a convention or a family visit brings you here, leave plenty of time for carousing, and, of course, birding.

New Orleans also conjures up images of lush flowers and stately homes. But birders will probably think of John James Audubon and the woods and marshes in which he hunted and painted, the trackless Baldcypress/Water Tupelo and bottomland swamps, and the excitement of spring migration on the coast.

Although not an avian wasteland, New Orleans, like most urban areas, presents a challenge to the birder with limited free time. Urban sprawl, accompanied by draining and filling of marsh and swamp, has pushed undisturbed habitat well away from the center of the city. City Park, the Lake Pontchartrain shoreline, Bayou Sauvage National Wildlife Refuge, and the Barataria Preserve unit of Jean Lafitte National Park do offer excellent and diverse birding possibilities, but only the first two are reasonably accessible by public transport. Still, more than 400 species have been found in the vicinity of New Orleans in southeast Louisiana, the majority in the metropolitan area. This richness reflects the diversity of habitats accessible in a one-day trip from the city: fresh, brackish, and saline marsh, coastal "cheniers," Gulf beach, open water, Baldcypress/Water Tupelo and bottomland hardwood swamps, pine woodland, and a variety of brushy, disturbed habitats.

Spring and fall migrations offer the opportunity to watch hordes of trans-Gulf migrants arriving from the Yucatán in spring or staging for the southbound flight in fall. New Orleans' sweltering summers will test the stamina of the visiting birder, but the weather is actually no worse than in many other major Eastern cities (e.g., Atlanta or Washington, D. C.), and early-morning trips to nearby swamp or pinewood habitat can be rewarding. The coastal marsh and Gulf beach can be interesting in summer, the only hiatus in shorebird migration being (nominally) the period 10 June–10 July. Gulf breezes will provide some relief as well.

The visiting birder who has two days free for birding might consider the 250-mile trip to Cameron Parish in southwest Louisiana, where the best birding in the state (except perhaps in mid-summer) is usually to be found.

ESSENTIAL INFORMATION

Getting Around: The best birding possibilities are at least 30 miles away from the city center, requiring an automobile. New Orleans' modest public transportation system is ill-suited to the needs of the birder without wheels. Most visitors arrive at the New Orleans International Airport, about 15 miles west of downtown, which can be reached by taxi or limousine. There are accommodations near the airport, but most visitors, in town for a convention or to indulge a bit, will stay in the central business district in or near the French Quarter. Other hotel districts are in Metairie, which is between the airport and New Orleans, and on the eastern edge of the city. Public transportation in the outlying areas is primitive to nonexistent, so if one wants to bird on foot, a stay in the city is recommended. The St. Charles streetcar will get the visitor to Audubon Park and to the Audubon Zoo, which offer birding possibilities, and City Park and the lakefront can be reached, with some difficulty, by bus. Taxis, of course, are available.

Safety: New Orleans' crime is almost as famous as its food, but conditions are not appreciably different from those in other large cities. Your hotel can help steer you away from high-crime areas. Most of the birding areas described here are safe, the primary exception being the best birding areas of City Park, which are secluded and not appropriate for a solitary female birder.

Natural Hazards: Insects will generally not be a problem in the city (bring repellent, nonetheless), but mosquitoes, gnats, and Deer Flies can easily ruin a birding trip to outlying areas (especially marshes or swamps). In the pine flats, chiggers may be a problem, and Poison-Ivy is widespread and often the dominant understory plant in near-coastal areas. Finally, watch where you stand; it may be a Fire Ant mound!

Other considerations: With some notable exceptions (Barataria Preserve, Bayou Sauvage, Pearl River Wildlife Management Area, Fontainbleau State Park, City Park), much of the birding in the New Orleans area is done on private land. This restriction may only mean walking a few feet off the road or birding a residential neighborhood on Grand Isle. Sometimes it is possible to identify the landowner and ask permission; more often it is not. If you choose to go onto private property, however briefly and innocently, remember that it is private and that your presence there is at the discretion of the owner.

Other Resources: Information on the birds of the New Orleans vicinity and Louisiana in general can be found in the Orleans Audubon Society's *Guide to Birding Southeast Louisiana*, available on the OAS web site, *www. jjaudubon.net/guide.htm* (includes maps); on the OAS Hotline, (504) 834-2473; in George Lowery's *Louisiana Birds;*, from the listserve *LABIRD's* web site, *www.museum.lsu.edu/~Remsen/LABIRDintro.html*; and from the following web sites: *www.homeport.tcs.tulane.edu/~danny.labirds.html* and *www.losbird.org*. For a weekend trip to the southwest parishes, one should obtain a copy of Bruce Crider's *Birding Guide to Southwest Louisiana* from the Southwest Louisiana Convention and Visitors Bureau, (800) 456-7952, or write for a free copy of the brochure, "Birds of Louisiana," by the Office of Tourism, 1051 N. Third Street, Baton Rouge, LA 70802, (800) 395-1939, *www.louisiana travel.com*.

THE BIRDING YEAR

Migration, depending on the weather, can be exciting and intensely rewarding, especially in the spring. New Orleans can be good, particularly if rain comes at the right time (overnight in fall; late afternoon and early evening in spring). The best spot is along the outer coast at Grand Isle, or near it at Venice, close to the mouth of the Mississippi River. In spring it is possible to see 130 or more species in a 20-mile stretch of the coast from Fourchon Road (LA-3090) to the east end of Grand Isle. Many of the birds that breed in the central and northern United States migrate through the northern Gulf Coast to or from Mexico and Central America, though birds riding strong tailwinds in spring will fly inland without landing on the coast, and thus the coastal woods (*cheniers*) may be empty.

Pine flats north of Lake Pontchartrain harbor the usual southern pine-woods specialties: Red-cockaded Woodpecker, Brown-headed Nuthatch, Pine Warbler, and Bachman's Sparrow, though the woodpecker is extremely local and the sparrow is hard to find when it is not singing. The creek and river bottoms are best in breeding season (late April–early July), when the woods are filled with the songs of Prothonotary, Swainson's, Kentucky, and Hooded Warblers. A Swallow-tailed Kite might be soaring overhead.

The short, intense spring migration occurs between about 5 March–15 May, with the peak being 15 April–5 May. The more leisurely fall migration begins in mid-to-late July and ends about mid-November. There is consider-able movement outside these dates, however, with shorebird migration tapering off in early June and picking up again in early July.

City Park
and Lake Pontchartrain Shore
Half day; fall, winter, spring

City Park—three square miles of mostly Live Oak trees, many festooned with Spanish Moss—offers a variety of migrants in spring or fall, though there is little undergrowth and a lot of human activity on weekends. The New Orleans Museum of Art is located here, and birders can combine birding near the museum with a look at its interesting collections. To reach City Park from the central business district, drive north up Canal Street approximately 3 miles to City Park Boulevard, where Canal takes a jog at the cemeteries. You can also reach City Park Boulevard by taking I-10 west to Metairie Road, and exiting to the right, or by taking Esplanade Avenue. The Canal Boulevard bus will take you to City Park Boulevard or to Harrison Avenue; the walk to the park is about one-half mile. To reach the best birding area in the park, turn left off City Park Boulevard at the southwest corner of the park onto Marconi Drive, and drive north about 2 miles to Harrison Avenue. Turn right, and after about 0.3 mile, pull off into the parking area on the north side of Harrison. Go left (north) into an extensive patch of woods bordered on the left by a lagoon. This area, known as Couterie Forest, is set aside for birding and other nature activities. The woods, dominated by hardwoods but with extensive understory, can be excellent in migration and sometimes interesting in winter. There is a well-maintained trail, and a circuit can be made, turning always to the right, that ends back on Harrison Avenue. These areas are remote and are not recommended for solo birders.

The shore of **Lake Pontchartrain**, north of City Park, offers a variety of gulls and waterfowl. Most of the gulls are Laughing, Ring-billed, and Herring, but Lesser Black-backed, Great Black-backed, and Glaucous Gulls have been seen. In winter you might find Common Loon, Horned Grebe, Bonaparte's Gull, and Royal and Forster's Terns. To get to Lake Pontchartrain from City Park, take Marconi Drive about 2.5 miles north to the shore of Lake Pontchartrain, or take the Canal Boulevard bus. You can also bird around Lake Vista, a residential development from City Park to the lakefront and east from Marconi Drive. It consists of oaks with little understory, but can be excellent in migration.

Lakeshore Drive from the marina/yacht-club area at the west all the way east to "Seabrook" Bridge (about four miles) can be interesting in winter. Occasionally, scoters or unusual gulls are seen, and the Seabrook Bridge area itself has a breakwater and a boat launch. The nearby East Campus of the University of New Orleans is also worth checking. The New Orleans Marina and Southern Yacht Club can be reached from Robert E. Lee Boulevard at the west end of Lakeshore Drive. A drive out to the breakwater opposite the yacht club might be of interest. There are seafood restaurants here and at Bucktown, just across the 17th Street Canal; try Bruning's or Sid-Mar's.

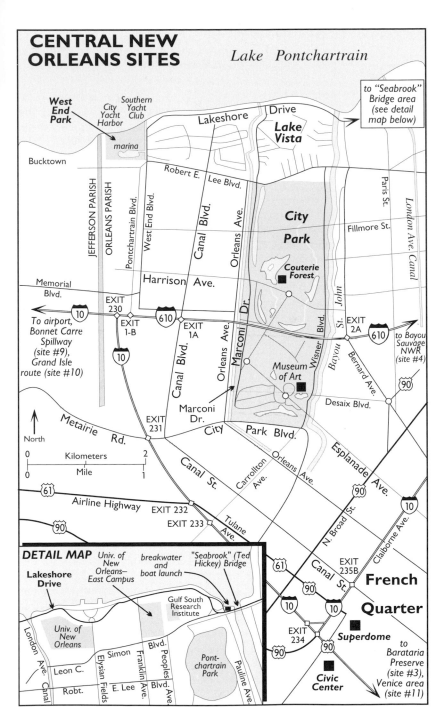

CENTRAL NEW ORLEANS SITES

Lake   Pontchartrain

BARATARIA PRESERVE UNIT
Half day; year round

Some of the most interesting birding near the city can be found in the **Barataria Preserve Unit** of Jean Laffite National Park and Preserve, a little over six miles from the Mississippi River bridge on the west bank of the river. The rangers and naturalists there are very helpful and can explain where the best trails are and what birds you might see. In particular, the Bayou Coquille trail leads into the marsh where a great many waders may be seen at any season, including all the regular herons, both *Plegadis* ibises, and White Ibis. Other recommended trails are the Ring Levee, Visitor Center Loop, Palmetto Trail, and Plantation Trail, which offer mature hardwood and Baldcypress/Water Tupelo swamp habitat, with typical southern breeding birds, including Red-shouldered Hawk, Barred Owl, Northern Parula, and Prothonotary, Hooded, and Yellow-throated Warblers. Canoes can be rented for a more intimate look at the marsh and the swamp. You will see Nutria, alligators, and an excellent variety of birds. To reach the park from downtown, cross the Mississippi River bridge (Crescent City Connection) onto the Westbank Expressway, which is US-90. Drive west until you reach Barataria Boulevard, LA-45. Exit, drive south for about 5 miles, and follow the signs to the park. For information call (504) 589-2330 or check *www.gov/jela/jelaweb.htm*.

BAYOU SAUVAGE NATIONAL WILDLIFE REFUGE
Half day; fall, winter, spring

Bayou Sauvage is a new urban national wildlife refuge at the eastern edge of the city, consisting mostly of Live Oak woods on the natural ridge along Bayou Sauvage and several thousand acres of marsh. It can be interesting at any season, but especially from early fall through May. In summer, heat, insects, and spider webs may deter all but the hardiest. The refuge can be reached from downtown by taking I-10 to the east and exiting at Paris Road. Go south to Chef Menteur Highway (US-90) and turn east for three to four miles, passing a water tower on the left. Look on the left for the refuge parking lot and signs indicating the *Ridge Trail*. If you reach Power's Junction, the intersection of US-90 and US-11, you have gone too far (but see below). There is a parking lot, but as yet no interpretive center. You can walk a boardwalk trail on the Bayou Sauvage ridge about one-half mile to view some of the marsh and the swamp. Alternatively, walk north along the levee (Maxent Levee) as far as you want, watching the willows for passerines and the lagoons to the east for ducks (in winter) and other waterbirds.

Continue east on US-90 to Power's Junction, turn left onto US-11, and almost immediately park at a spot on the left where there are concrete barricades. This spot provides access to another part of the ridge, which can be walked back to the west for at least several hundred yards. This area is remote and secluded, and normal caution should be used. Carry insect repellent and wear boots.

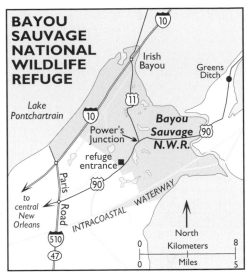

Continue northeast on US-11 through the refuge, noting ponds on the left that may have ducks, shorebirds, gulls, and terns, depending on the season. Eventually, you reach I-10 again (at Irish Bayou) where you can return to the city, being careful not to go east across the five-mile bridge on I-10 or the US-11 bridge to Slidell (unless you're headed to Honey Island Swamp).

URBAN "LAGNIAPPE" (a little extra)

The **Audubon Louisiana Nature Center**, in Joe Brown Park in New Orleans East, consists of 68 wooded acres with marked trails and an interpretive center. The center maintains hummingbird feeders in winter that often attract western hummingbirds. The fenced center provides a safe alternative to City Park for general birding, though it is difficult to reach by public transportation. Birding is best from fall through spring. Contact information: (504) 246-5672, *www. auduboninstitute.org*; the fee is currently $4.75.

Audubon Park is recommended mainly because of its accessibility (via the St. Charles street car); it is most interesting in spring. The best place to see Eurasian Collared-Doves in the city is in the Audubon Park/Zoo area, especially in the zoo itself and behind it near the river, where one may also find Bronzed Cowbirds. Monk Parakeets are regular, as well.

Visitors to the city during the fall and winter (mostly October to March) might want to try to take advantage of the opportunity to observe some wintering (mostly western) **hummingbirds** at area feeders. Ten species have been recorded in the New Orleans area, and four—Buff-bellied, Ruby-throated, Black-chinned, and Rufous—are either relatively numerous or at least somewhat regular in winter. To see such birds typically will involve contacting individual hummingbird enthusiasts. The best way to do this is through LABIRD (*www.museum.lsu.edu/~Remsen/LABirdintro.html*) or the LSU hummingbird site, HUMNET, at *www.museum.lsu.edu/~Remsen/HUMNETintro. html*.

Or take a swamp tour by boat either from the foot of Canal Street, in the Pearl River basin, or west toward Raceland and Houma (inquire at your hotel). Take Airline Highway (US-61) toward Norco to bird in the Sarpy Swamp and Good Hope Oil Field, or to Pass Manchac for some swamp-edge birding and fried catfish at Middendorf's.

MANDEVILLE LAKEFRONT
AND ST. TAMMANY PARISH

Half to full day; year round

The **Mandeville harbor** and the pine flats of **St. Tammany** and surrounding parishes provide two different habitats for birders. The typical southern pinewoods species are present, including Red-cockaded Woodpecker, Brown-headed Nuthatch, Pine Warbler, and Bachman's Sparrow, but the creek bottoms and clear-cut areas enhance bird diversity; about 150 species are counted on the northshore Christmas Bird Count. Along the Mandeville harbor in winter there will be Common Loons, Horned Grebes, Bufflehead, perhaps Common Goldeneye, and certainly Lesser Scaup. You might see an Osprey or a Bald Eagle, or an interesting gull. In migration or in winter the oaks and pines along the lakefront can be worthwhile.

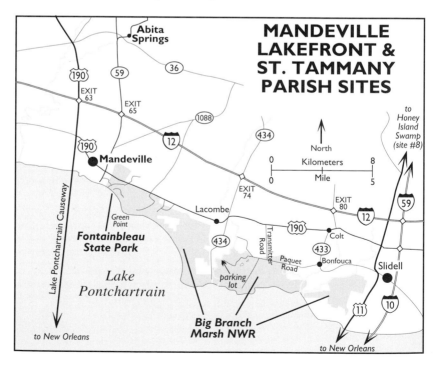

To reach Mandeville from downtown New Orleans, take I-10 toward the west to Causeway Boulevard, and thence north to the 24-mile Causeway Bridge over Lake Pontchartrain (current toll is $3.00, southbound only). After reaching the north shore, follow the curve to the right toward Mandeville; when US-190 joins from the left, follow it into Mandeville. Take one of several streets south to the lakefront (including LA-59) and drive the lakefront from one end to the other, about one mile.

Leaving Mandeville, birders can drive three miles east on US-190 to **Fontainbleau State Park** (fee), which offers pines, oaks, lakeshore, and, to the east, marsh. Look for Red-headed and Pileated Woodpeckers and an excellent diversity of other landbirds. Alternatively, continue east toward Lacombe (passing La Provence, one of the area's best restaurants) and beyond, watching for signs to newly created **Big Branch National Wildlife Refuge**. About 2.3 miles beyond LA-434, turn right on Transmitter Road, then right at a T-junction, and go about one mile to a road to the left, where there is a refuge parking lot. This large area of marsh and pinewoods on the north shore of the lake is excellent for pinewoods species, and it harbors at least a few Red-cockaded Woodpeckers.

Another alternative from Mandeville is to take LA-59 north and drive directly to **Abita Springs**. Anywhere in this vicinity can be interesting, either in winter or in the breeding season. During the latter, all of the bottomland species will be present (e.g., Barred Owl, Acadian Flycatcher, Wood Thrush, Northern Parula, and Prothonotary, Kentucky, and Hooded Warblers), as well as the pinewoods specialties. Most of the habitat consists of pinewoods, clear-cut successional pine tracts, broomsedge fields, and brush. In the cut-over pine flats, typical breeding birds will include Prairie Warbler, Yellow-breasted Chat, and Blue Grosbeak. In summer in the right kind of brushy areas, you may find Painted and Indigo Buntings. In winter you may flush a Le Conte's or a Henslow's Sparrow from the broomsedge. Henslow's prefers some pine canopy and at least a small amount of brushy understory, whereas Le Conte's seems to thrive in more-open broomsedge fields. Bachman's Sparrows are found in habitat similar to that of Henslow's, but finding them when they are not singing is problematic, and forestry practices are eliminating their habitat. Remaining good examples of the proper habitat can be found along LA-36 east of Abita Springs toward and beyond LA-434 (about nine miles). Other typical species include Eastern Bluebird and Pine Warbler year round, and Broad-winged Hawk, Chuck-will's-widow (crepuscular), and Eastern Wood-Pewee in spring and summer. A caveat is that continuous lumber harvest means that the best spots for a given species change as timber is cut or as clear-cuts re-grow.

HONEY ISLAND SWAMP

Half to full day; year round

One of the best introductions to bottomland hardwood swamp habitat can be had in the **Pearl River Wildlife Management Area**, in the **Honey Island Swamp**. To reach Honey Island Swamp, take I-10 east from the city, past Slidell, and when I-10 bears right to the Mississippi coast, continue straight onto I-59. After crossing the West Pearl River, watch for a right turn into Honey Island Swamp and the Pearl River Wildlife Management Area, especially good in the breeding season. A Louisiana hunting or fishing license (a three-day non-resident license) can be obtained at a Wal-Mart, or you may want to obtain a Louisiana Wildife Stamp, which is required for those without a Louisiana hunting license. Contact the Louisiana Department of Wildlife and Fisheries at (888) 765-2602 or *www.wlf.state.la.us.*

When you arrive at the Wildlife Management Area, the narrow asphalt road travels generally eastward and dead-ends at Indian Bayou. There are also two gravel roads that leave the pavement to the south, and one to the north; all are recommended. There is no through traffic, so you can park anywhere along the road and listen for typical bottomland species (Barred Owl, Acadian and Great Crested Flycatchers, Red-eyed and Yellow-throated Vireos, Wood Thrush, Northern Parula, Prothonotary, Kentucky, and Hooded Warblers, Summer Tanager). Swainson's Warbler breeds here, especially along the only gravel road that goes to the left, as does American Redstart. Although many

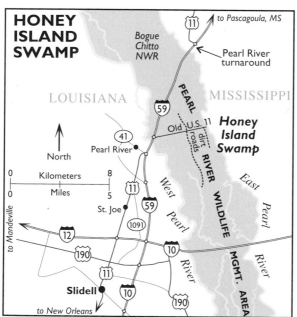

Swallow-tailed Kites breed in the Pearl River Basin, the canopy is so dense that seeing one is a matter of luck. Arrive early to avoid the heat of the day and to enjoy the bird song, or strike out into the swamp, which is usually mostly dry, in hopes of seeing the elusive Swainson's Warbler.

Continue east on I-59 to the Pearl River Turnaround (4.0 miles), where there is a gravel pit and brushy habitat that is good for Yellow-breasted Chat and Painted Bunting. Here and elsewhere along I-59 watch for Swallow-tailed Kite or the more-common Mississippi Kite. If you drive under the I-59 bridge, you can return to New Orleans via I-59, or, if you feel adventuresome, take the small dirt road that parallels the interstate. This dusty road passes through pine flats, bottomland, and Baldcypress/Water Tupelo swamp, offering many birding possibilities in the nesting season. American Redstarts are especially common breeders. There is no exit, however, and you must return to the East Pearl River bridge to get back on I-59.

BONNET CARRE SPILLWAY

Half day; year round

Here you can explore a network of dirt roads offering brushy habitat, shorebirding in season, and, in winter, a good place to look for raptors. Sprague's Pipits and Le Conte's Sparrows are frequently found during winter in the short grass near the spillway structure at River Road. Typical breeding species of the bottomland forest are present in summer. There is probably no other area its size in southeast Louisiana with such a variety of habitats.

To reach the **Bonnet Carre Spillway**, take I-10 west beyond the airport to I-310. Exit right onto US-61 (Airline Highway) toward Norco. Just past Norco, you reach the spillway, which is a large open area of fields and woods through which some flow from the Mississippi River is occasionally diverted. Here you can drive the east (south) levee to the lake, parking anywhere that interests you, or perhaps driving into the spillway itself. You can also, conditions permitting, immediately drop down into the spillway and drive left toward the river.

The spillway is good for raptors, has good brushy habitat for sparrows, and some ponds that might harbor ducks. This area is best to visit in fall and winter, but it has enough deep woods toward the lake to be interesting during the breeding season.

FOURCHON BEACH AND GRAND ISLE

Full day; year round

The **Fourchon/Grand Isle** area offers some of the best birding possibilities in southeast Louisiana. The drive itself, about 100 miles one-way, has great potential. Leave New Orleans by I-10 to the west, turn south on I-310 west of the airport, and pick up US-90 near Boutte. The elevated I-310 passes through pristine cypress swamp in which you will see Wood Ducks, White Ibises, herons, and perhaps a Bald Eagle. West on US-90 you will see ponds, Baldcypress/Water Tupelo swamp, and lots of willows.

You may see Anhinga, White-faced or Glossy Ibises, White Ibis, and Mississippi Kite (after mid-April). You certainly should see Red-shouldered Hawks. Eventually, US-90 turns south toward a crossing of Bayou Lafourche, leading to Houma. Just before the highway crosses Bayou Lafourche, exit to the right and turn south on LA-308 along the east side of the bayou (you can also drive the west side, LA-1; a bit slower). The next 25 miles or so will pass sugar-cane fields, oyster boats, and shrimpers, and eventually lead to Golden Meadow, where you will cross the bayou at a bridge with a high superstructure, just beyond a Burger King on the left, to LA-1. Take LA-1 south for about a mile and make the right turn toward Grand Isle when it splits. When you reach the four-lane LA-1 bypass after about 0.5 mile, turn left toward Grand Isle. (Note that speed limits are rigorously enforced here.)

Below Golden Meadow, you will travel through mostly saline coastal marsh, full of herons and Clapper Rails. At Leeville (on both sides of a drawbridge), look for Brown Pelicans and, on the radio towers, Peregrine Falcons (winter).

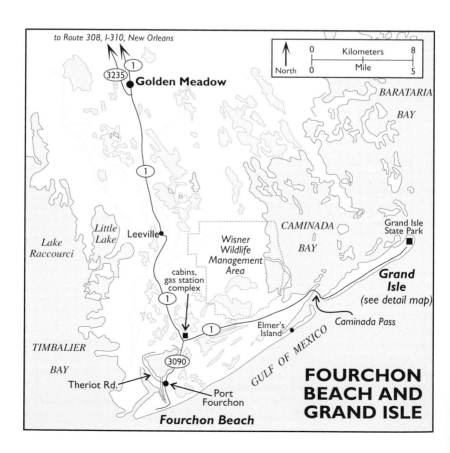

About six miles south of Leeville, you will notice a collection of fishing camps (cabins), a gas-station complex (decent restaurant), and an oil installation, which are at the intersection of LA-1 and LA-3090 (A. O. Rapellet Road), known locally as **Fourchon Road**. Turn right and explore the length of Fourchon all the way to the Gulf (4.0 miles). Three roads go to the right, offering various possibilities for exploring the edge of the impoundment (threatened) that LA-3090 skirts. The first road turns just past the Port Fourchon headquarters at the north end of the lagoon and goes back to its west side, a good spot to scan the lagoon and to bird the low trees in migration. Under fall-out conditions almost anything might be found here: flycatchers, warblers, buntings, Dickcissels, Bobolinks (late spring). The main lagoon harbors ducks, shorebirds (if the water level is right), gulls, and terns. At the lower end of the lagoon, Theriot Road provides another opportunity to scan the lagoon and shorebird habitat. Along the final road (Estay Road, closest to the Gulf), Yellow-headed Blackbirds often can be found in flocks of Red-winged and other blackbirds. Across from this road is a boat launch with restrooms. Mottled Ducks are seen frequently, as are Brown and American White Pelicans; Roseate Spoonbills may be spotted.

Continuing on Fourchon Road toward the Gulf, you will cross a small bridge and drive to the beach through more salt marsh with Black Mangrove (**Fourchon Beach**). Depending on your vehicle and the state of the beach, you may be able to drive about 2 miles west to the mouth of Belle Pass. Beware of soft sand, however. Often a four-wheel-drive vehicle is required, and rescue is very expensive. Along the beach there may be interesting gulls (e.g., Lesser and Great Black-backed). Typical birds of the beach are Semipalmated, Piping, and, rarely, Snowy Plovers, with Wilson's being conspicous in the breeding season and Red Knots during migration. It is conceivable that you might see a Kelp Gull here, or a Kelp x Herring hybrid. Often Merlins or Peregrines are seen, and in winter, especially February to April, Northern Gannets can be seen diving offshore. Just north of the mouth of the pass is an active heronry (summer), which has Reddish Egrets and Roseate Spoonbills among at least seven species.

Return to Highway 1 and continue east to Caminada Pass and the bridge onto Grand Isle. It might be worthwhile to explore the west end of the island, where there is a beach, a jetty where Purple Sandpiper has been seen, and brushy habitat. Drive east to the center of the island, marked by the Sureway Supermarket. You can begin to bird the woods there or travel east to **Grand Isle State Park** ($2.00 admission). The latter offers beach views and a long spit on which gulls and terns rest in winter, large areas of Wax Myrtle that can harbor migrants, and salt marsh with Clapper Rail. There is primitive camping, and you can walk the beach about a mile to the east to the spit where gulls, terns, and Brown Pelicans congregate. The entire east end of the island is dominated by shortgrass fields, which may have large numbers of shorebirds in migration if there have been recent rains. In spring, American Golden-Plover, Upland Sandpiper, Baird's Sandpiper, and Buff-breasted Sandpiper might be seen in these fields. Access to these fields by private auto is generally allowed by Exxon, but please remember that this is private property.

Return to the main road (LA-1) and head west, carefully examining the large fields north of the road for shorebirds. Turn right at the water tower. Drive 0.25 mile to a junction and turn right into a collection of Mulberry trees and feeders that can offer spectacular birding in April, harboring dozens of tanagers, grosbeaks, buntings, Dickcissels, orioles, and even warblers. Brush and woods about 200 yards to the northeast can be interesting at any time other than mid-summer.

Back on the main road, return west to a series of streets that trend right (north) into extensive, mostly Live Oak, woods. Although the area is residential, there are two large woods: behind the Sureway Supermarket and about two blocks to the west on Naccari Lane. (The latter woods are now owned by The Nature Conservancy.) Coming from the east, the first street of interest is Ceme-

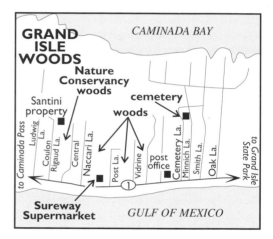

tery Lane, just before the Grand Isle Post Office. Park at the historic cemetery and bird the surrounding Live Oaks. This—and the next three or four streets to the west—offer the best landbirding on the island. During inclement weather or northerly winds in spring, huge numbers of migrants may drop into the trees in a spectacular fall-out. At other times, there may be no migrants at all. All of these woods, from the cemetery west, can be birded in one long walk. Remember that some of this is private land; respect the privacy of the landowners. At the end of Coulon Rigaud Lane, you can park and bird the oaks, Mulberry trees, ridges, and brush. A Western Kingbird or a Scissor-tailed Flycatcher might be seen here, or a flock of Groove-billed Anis in winter. The owner (Bobby Santini) of the property on the right at the end of the lane usually will have feeders out, attracting large numbers of seed-eaters, including buntings and grosbeaks, but also Bronzed and possibly Shiny Cowbirds, which now breed nearby. Eurasian Collared-Doves and White-winged Doves (winter) may be present.

A typical trip to Grand Isle will begin at 6:00AM in New Orleans, reach Fourchon Road at 8:30AM, the island by about noon, and end at 5:00 or 6:00PM on the island. On a good day, one might see 130 or more species on such a trip. There are a few B&Bs and many motels on the island.

VENICE

Full day; fall, winter spring

While no place in Louisiana exceeds the **Venice** area in the numbers of winter vagrants, it is a remarkably difficult area to bird, and is correspondingly difficult to describe. Much of the birding is done in small patches of willows or brush, and often it is hard to distinguish the habitat from a dump. On the other hand, Venice is *the* place to find vagrant *Myiarchus* flycatchers in winter, and perhaps not even south Florida can beat a typical Venice CBC list of 14 to 15 species of wintering warblers. It is one of the best places to see several regional specialties, such as White-faced and Glossy Ibises together (lower road, toward Tidewater), or Groove-billed Ani in winter. It offers extensive woodlands that are not far from the open Gulf, so migration can be spectacular, given the right weather conditions.

To reach the area, cross the Mississippi River bridge and take General DeGaulle Drive south to either Behrman Highway or Woodland Drive, thence right (west) to Belle Chase Highway, LA-23. Once on this road, one can continue all the way to Venice, some 65 miles. En route you will drive through Port Sulphur, bypass Empire, and cross the Empire Canal (good view of the subsiding marsh and the river) on a high-rise bridge. Birding possibilities along the way include Myrtle Grove (where White-tailed Kites are sometimes seen in winter), Lake Hermitage Road below Myrtle Grove, or near Pointe-a-la-Hache.

About two miles farther down LA-23 is **Fort Jackson**, worth examining for both birding and historical reasons; across from it is a very large area of scrub, brush, and small trees (public land) that often has Brown-crested and Ash-throated Flycatchers in winter. Immediately below Fort Jackson is a large patch of mature woods (parish-owned) whose edges may be interesting in migration and that usually has flocks of wintering warblers in season. From here it is about eight miles to Venice; along the road there are small patches of woods that can be full of birds in spring or may hold vagrants in late fall and winter. About one mile below the fort, you might see a Groove-billed Ani in the roseau cane (*Phragmites*, tall stands of grass) in winter as you drive by.

At Venice, the road jogs to the right, past willow-lined and Water-Hyacinth-choked bayous, to Tidewater. One can see a bittern of either species (depending on season), three ibis species, waterfowl, Common Moorhens, Ospreys (in winter), or a vagrant Vermilion Flycatcher. The extensive willows along the road to Bud's Boat Rental and Venice Marina often harbor western vagrants or wintering warblers, and the area is perhaps the best place in the U.S. to see both species of *Plegadis* ibises together.

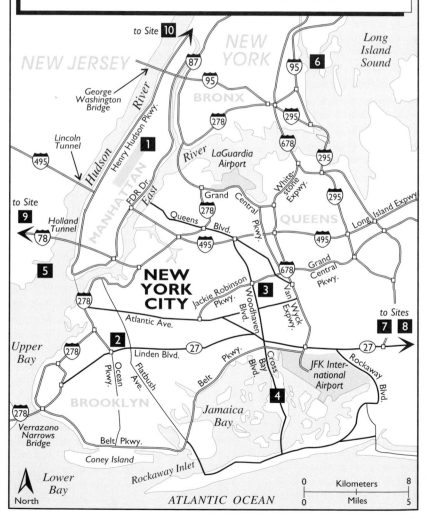

NEW YORK CITY AREA BIRDING SITES

1 *Central Park*

2 *Prospect Park*

3 *Forest Park*

4 *Jamaica Bay Wildlife Refuge*

5 *Liberty State Park*

6 *Pelham Bay Park*

7 *Jones Beach and Vicinity*

8 *Montauk Point*

9 *Great Swamp NWR*

10 *Bear Mountain, Doodletown Road*

to Site **10**

Long Island Sound

NEW YORK

87

95

95

6

NEW JERSEY

George Washington Bridge

Hudson River

Henry Hudson Pkwy.

BRONX

278

River

LaGuardia Airport

678

295

295

Lincoln Tunnel

495

MANHATTAN

FDR Dr.

1

East

Grand

Queens

278

Central Pkwy.

White-stone Expwy.

295

to Site **9**

Holland Tunnel

78

Blvd.

495

Long Island Expwy.

NEW YORK CITY

Jackie Robinson Pkwy.

Woodhaven Blvd.

3

Van Wyck Expwy.

678

Grand Central Pkwy.

5

278

Atlantic Ave.

to Sites **7** **8**

2

278

Linden Blvd.

27

Pkwy.

Cross Bay Blvd.

JFK International Airport

27

Rockaway Blvd.

Upper Bay

Ocean Pkwy.

Flatbush Ave.

Belt

4

BROOKLYN

278

Verrazano Narrows Bridge

Belt Pkwy.

Coney Island

Jamaica Bay

North

Lower Bay

Rockaway Inlet

ATLANTIC OCEAN

| 0 | Kilometers | 8 |
| 0 | Miles | 5 |

NEW YORK, NEW YORK

Peter Joost

It's easy to think of New York City as being long on concrete, short on natural attractions. But, like most stereotypes, on examination this one proves false. New York has much to recommend it to nature lovers and, in particular, to birders. The metropolitan area's bird list stands at well over 400 species, with more than 175 breeding birds.

There are reasons for this diversity. Geographically, New York City stands at the intersection of three life zones and, as a result, its birdlife includes breeding species with southern as well as those with northern affinities. Situated along the Atlantic Flyway, the region's coastline is a highway for many migrants, especially in the fall. Other species use natural landmarks surrounding the city, such as the Hudson River and Kittatinny Ridge. The region's climate and topography also contribute to its seductiveness to birds. Altitudes ranging from sea level to more than 1,800 feet (in northern New Jersey) provide considerable variability. In the course of a year, temperatures may range from 100°Fahrenheit in summer to sub-zero in winter, with considerable local divergences.

Finally, there is the diversity of habitats. These include a marine environment, the Hudson estuary, ponds, lakes, rivers, freshwater and saltwater marshes, many forest types, and a few grasslands, as well as numerous sanctuaries and parks. Even urban skyscrapers attract birdlife: Peregrine Falcons nest in uptown, midtown, and downtown Manhattan and on several bridges. Together these varied habitats attract a plethora of birds to satisfy any drop-in visitor, as well as the dedicated locals who have systematically charted the region's birdlife.

ESSENTIAL INFORMATION

Getting Around: Visitors come to New York via almost every mode of travel: air, bus, train, car, even boat. And transport from transit centers is abundant and generally reasonably priced, once you've arrived. Buses, subways, and trains serve all of New York City's five boroughs 24 hours a day (with reduced service during late hours). Bus and subway maps appear in the telephone yellow pages of each borough. For free maps, send a request with a self-addressed stamped envelope to MAPS, Box NYBT, NYC Transit Authority, 370 Jay Street, Brooklyn, NY 11201. In addition, maps are posted at each bus stop, subway station, and subway car, and sometimes at token booths. For more information, call (212) 330-1234 or check the MTA New York City Transit web site, *www.mta.nyc.ny.us/index.html*. Taxis in Manhattan are numerous. For travel to outer boroughs, a car service can make a trip much easier; use the Yellow Pages and do some comparison shopping. When traveling by car service or taxi, make sure that you have directions. Also, arrange to be picked up at a specific time (car service only). There are many car-rental services in the region. When picking up a car on the weekend, be sure to allow time; lines may be long. Remember that traffic can be dispiritingly slow during rush hours and near the shore during beach season.

Climate: Although New York does not have a climate of extremes, it can exhibit a wide range of conditions in a short period of time. Proximity to the Atlantic Ocean has a slightly moderating effect on temperatures, but summers can be hot and muggy and winters are cold and, less regularly, snowy.

Natural Hazards: Poison-Ivy is widespread. Mosquitoes and biting flies may be numerous in spring and summer at some coastal marshes. Ticks are present during any of the warmer months and include Deer Ticks, some of which carry Lyme disease.

Safety: New York's reputation as a high-crime area is in need of revision. Nevertheless, it is wise to be observant, as in any urban setting, particularly when an area is likely to be relatively deserted. Even in so apparently rustic a venue as Pelham Bay, be vigilant. It is best to bird with one or more companions in the less-traveled sections of most city parks.

Other Resources: Several local birding and natural-history groups offer guided weekend walks. During spring migration, early-morning walks are offered in Central Park on weekdays, as well. For information about New York City Audubon Society trips and programs, call (212) 691-7483, or check their web site, *www.nycaudubon. org*. The Linnaean Society of New York offers a year-round schedule of weekend trips, usually of a local nature, and two evening programs a month (held in the American Museum of Natural History). For information, write to The Secretary, The Linnaean Society of New York, 15 West 77th Street, New York, NY 10024, call (212) 252-2668, or view the web site, *www.linnaeansociety.org*. Another local organization that offers trips is the Brooklyn Bird Club; check *www.brooklynbirdclub.org*.

The National Audubon Society and the Linnaean Society of New York jointly sponsor a Rare Bird Alert that covers the metropolitan area and which is usually updated each Friday; call (212) 979-3070. New Jersey Audubon maintains a statewide alert, (908) 766-2661. The Connecticut number, also statewide, is (203) 254-3665. Daily postings on New York area birdlife as well as reports of local RBAs can be found on e-birds at *http://users.nac.net/ bencl*. This resource is also a good place to make inquiries of local birders.

There are several good books that cover the area: *The New York City Audubon Society Guide to Finding Birds in the Metropolitan Area* by Marcia T. Fowle and Paul Kerlinger (2001, Cornell University Press), *Where to Find Birds in New York State* by Susan Roney Drennan (1981, Syracuse University Press), *A Guide to Birdfinding in New Jersey* by William J. Boyle, Jr. (1994, Rutgers University Press, being updated), and *New York's 50 Best Places to Go Birding In and Around the Big Apple* by John Thaxton (1998, City & Company).

Other destinations: The American Museum of Natural History at 79th–81st Streets and Central Park West is a great spot on rainy days or even after an exciting morning in Central Park's Ramble. The Central Park Zoo (on the East Side at 64th Street) has an interesting rainforest exhibit, and the Bronx Zoo (now called the Wildlife Conservation Society) has attractive exhibits featuring exotic birds.

THE BIRDING YEAR

B irding is excellent year round in the New York City region. Christmas Bird Counts attest to the surprising number of lingerers in early winter: the Brooklyn count regularly exceeds 125 species; Central Park alone can exceed 50. Jones Beach and other coastal spots are productive all winter for waterfowl, Snowy Owls (irregular), and interesting gulls.

The spring migration begins in March and April, but the pace grows frenetic during the month of May. Greatest numbers occur typically in the second or third week of the month, lasting for a week. This is the time to be in Central Park, Prospect Park in Brooklyn, or other city parks. The North and South Gardens at Jamaica Bay Wildlife Refuge also provide excellent warbler viewing. Some highlights can include Golden-winged (rare but regular in our immediate area), Blue-winged, Chestnut-sided, Ovenbird, Northern Waterthrush, Hooded, and American Redstart. A second group arrives in mid-May: Tennessee (small numbers), Magnolia, Cape May, Blackburnian, Bay-breasted, Blackpoll, Wilson's, Canada, and Yellow-breasted Chat (small numbers). The very last of the warblers to show up is Mourning, typically during the last week of May or even into early June.

In June, as migration winds down, Doodletown Road/Bear Mountain north of the city and New Jersey's Great Swamp are good places to observe birds on territory. Many shorebirds linger into early June, and, by the end of the month, the first of the Arctic breeders, Least Sandpipers and Short-billed Dowitchers, are beginning their southward return. Shorebirding can be rewarding from late June to mid-October, with the heaviest concentrations between mid-July and early September. Landbirding picks up again in August. September is the fall equivalent of May for sheer numbers, especially toward the middle of the month. Cold fronts push waves of landbirds south, and Jones Beach is one of several good places to be when northwest winds cause many migrants to drift to the coast. Hawk migration is well underway in September, and early October is the best time for accipiter migration. Waterfowl and sparrows show up in increasing numbers in October. Late fall is a good time to check migrant traps for western rarities. Many winter residents—including loons, gannets, and scoters and other sea ducks— arrive in November. Buteo hawks, especially Red-tailed and Red-shouldered, migrate in greatest numbers during November.

CENTRAL PARK

Half day; spring, fall, winter

No birder visiting New York in the spring should miss the avian spectacle at **Central Park**. Migration viewed from the vantage of "the Ramble" is truly one of the City's unique experiences. And there are few better places to find birds, concentrated as they are in this 862-acre oasis. Fall is excellent also, and even winter can be worthwhile. There are 200 species, including 32 nesters, that have been regularly or occasionally seen in the park since the 1970s, with 67 more rarities reported during this period.

The park—accessible by bus, subway, or cab—is located between Fifth Avenue and Central Park West, and extends from 59th to 110th streets. The Ramble (72nd to 79th streets), a forested section with extensive underbrush and many winding paths, borders the Lake and features a pond and a meandering stream. It can be reached easily from either Fifth Avenue or Central Park West. Virtually every northeastern passerine has at some time been found in the Ramble, on occasion in surprising numbers. Particular places to check are Cherry Hill (south of the Ramble across Bow Bridge), especially in the early morning, when warblers and other migrants land in the tall trees here before dispersing; Strawberry Fields, west of the southern corner of the Lake, near Central Park West between 72nd and 73rd streets; the Point, a peninsula extending into the Lake; the lowland area around the large willow at the base of the Point; Azalea Pond; and Pin Oak Swamp in the Ramble's center. The open area and edges south of Belvedere Castle are also worth exploring. Another excellent area, recently restored and very productive, is between the Loch at 104th Street and the Harlem Meer in the park's northeastern corner. Follow the path that encircles a swampy stream running north into the Meer. The brushy areas on both sides can be productive, as well. This area of the park is well patrolled but can sometimes be rather deserted. Local birders advise going with a partner.

Central Park has birds in winter, too. Hawks and owls (sometimes including Barn (rare), Long-eared, and Northern Saw-whet) are usually present, and in recent years Red-headed Woodpeckers have been resident in the area just north of Belvedere Castle. Also check the Central Park Reservoir for ducks, gulls, and other species. A hawkwatch from August into

December is held at Belvedere Castle. In the 1995 season, nine Golden Eagles were tallied.

For information contact The Central Park Conservancy at (212) 315-0385. The Conservancy has a bird checklist, which is available at various locations in the park, including Belvedere Castle near the Ramble, the Dairy (just west of the zoo), and Dana Discovery Center at the north end of the park. The Central Park web site includes maps: www.centralparknyc.org.

Two other New York City parks are worth noting. Brooklyn's 530-acre **Prospect Park** is, like Central Park, a marvelous place to be during migration periods. The best areas are, moving south from the north end of the park, the Vale of Cashmere, the Midwood, the Lullwater, and the Peninsula (which extends into Prospect Lake), as well as Lookout Hill, slightly to the west of the Lake. Best birding times are from mid-April to early June and mid-August to mid-October, but any month can be worthwhile. Prospect Park is in the process of being lovingly restored with native plantings by the Prospect Park Alliance. Safety here is improving, but it is wise to be cautious in secluded areas, and perhaps to go with a companion. The Brooklyn Bird Club, New York City Audubon Society, and Prospect Park Alliance all conduct tours. Since the fall of 2001, the National Audubon Society and the Alliance have operated an environmental-education center,

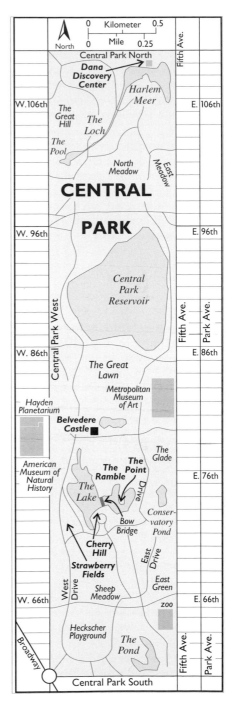

located in the Boathouse. The Park is easily reached by public transportation; consult NYC transit, (718) 330-1234 or *www.mta.nyc.us*. The web site for the park, *www.prospectpark.org*, contains a map and directions.

Forest Park is another celebrated birding area, located on the Harbor Hills moraine in the borough of Queens. Although much of the 538-acre park is given over to other activities, the eastern section is a mature woodland that can be excellent in migration, spring and fall, but is less productive at other times. The most famous spot in the park is the Water-Hole, in the North Woods, a kettle pond that at times presents an extraordinary spectacle of bathing birds. The birding area of the park is isolated, and birders should exercise appropriate care; do not bird alone here. Reach Forest Park by subway (E or F train, Kew Gardens/Union Turnpike stop) and a short walk west on 80th Road, or by car—the Long Island Expressway (I-495) to Woodhaven Boulevard, left on Myrtle Avenue, and left on Park Lane South, with access to the park.

JAMAICA BAY WILDLIFE REFUGE

Full or half day; year round

J amaica Bay Wildlife Refuge is one of North America's premier birding hot-spots. More than 325 species have been recorded at this 9,000-acre refuge, as well as an interesting variety of insects (especially butterflies), reptiles, and amphibians. Check the log-book at the refuge headquarters to see what is around and where. You can also pick up a bird checklist and a map of the refuge, which is part of the Gateway National Recreation Area.

To reach the refuge by subway, take the A train to the Broad Channel station in Queens, walk west several blocks on Noel Road to Cross Bay Boulevard, then right (north) to the refuge headquarters (about three-quarters of a mile). An alternate route is to take the E, F, or R subway line to the Jackson Heights/Roosevelt Avenue stop and catch the Q53 express bus to the Rockaways. Ask to be let off at the JBWR Visitor Center. For bus information, call (718) 335-1000. By car from mid-Manhattan, take the Midtown Tunnel to the Long Island Expressway (I-495) and exit south onto Woodhaven Boulevard. Proceed to Cross Bay Boulevard and continue through Howard Beach to the refuge parking lot, slightly more than one mile from the North Channel Bridge on the west (right) side of the road. From downtown Manhattan, take the Brooklyn-Battery Tunnel or Brooklyn Bridge to the Brooklyn-Queens Expressway (I-278) toward the Verrazano Bridge. Be vigilant when the road divides, and do not go over the bridge—stay right on the Belt Parkway. Proceed to Cross Bay Boulevard (Exit 17S) and follow directions as above.

Birders with several hours between flights at John F. Kennedy International Airport can make it to the Jamaica Bay Wildlife Refuge if they plan in advance.

The refuge is only 15 to 20 minutes from the airport, and a taxi ride is not too expensive. It is important to give the driver specific directions, because taxi drivers at the airport are rather notorious for getting "lost" or for taking a round-about route. From Kennedy, take the Belt Parkway heading west (toward the Verrazano Bridge). Go approximately three exits to Cross Bay Boulevard South, then follow the directions above. Taxis do not run regularly past the refuge, so your best bet is to arrange for a car service to pick you up at an appointed time. There is a public phone at the refuge headquarters, and the staff has telephone books. Make sure that the car service knows how to get to the refuge; it is not a well-known spot among the transit community.

Two areas in the refuge are the focus for birding. The **West Pond**, on the west side of Cross Bay Boulevard, is encircled by a gravel path leading from the refuge headquarters. This freshwater impoundment, partly surrounded by saltmarshes, can be filled with waterfowl, particularly during migration. In spring the water level is lowered to create a skirt of mudflat, attractive to resting ducks and terns as well as to feeding shorebirds. During both spring and fall, shorebirding can be good, especially at high tide. (This is the site of the celebrated Broad-billed Sandpiper which occurred in

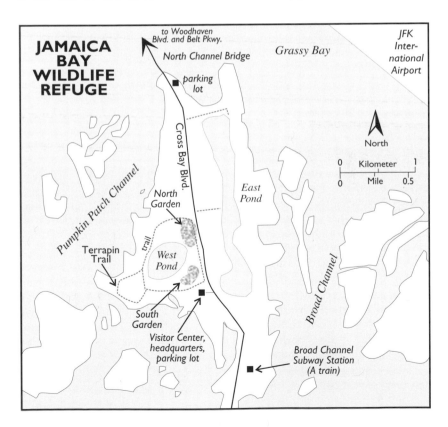

September 1998.) The path also branches and meanders through an area of mixed brush and woodland, the North and South Gardens, attractive to a variety of landbirds during both spring and fall migrations.

The **East Pond**, also managed seasonally for shorebirds and waterfowl, is even more famous for its rarities—such as Red-necked and Little Stints, Sharp-tailed and Curlew Sandpipers—found there over the years, as well as for the aggregations of shorebirds that gather in late summer and early fall, especially when management practices lower the pond's water levels and when high tide shrinks the available mudflats in the bay. Hudsonian Godwit and Western, White-rumped, and Stilt Sandpipers are regular at that time. Rare but regular species include American Avocet, Marbled Godwit, Baird's Sandpiper, and Wilson's Phalarope. The refuge is a fine place to wrestle with the fine points of peep identification, since the birds often can be seen at very close range. Indeed, virtually any East Coast shorebird may be seen here, with the exception of those with very southern distributions, or, like Piping Plover or Purple Sandpiper, confined to a specific habitat. To fully explore this area when water levels are lowered, be prepared to walk along the muddy edge of the pond. Bring rubber boots or old sneakers. Keep close to the phragmites edge to minimize disturbance to the feeding and roosting ducks, shorebirds, and gulls.

Jamaica Bay has attractions all year, but it is especially exciting from mid-July to mid-October, when the shorebirds are present in large concentrations. Landbirds and other waterbirds are here, too. Check the West Pond and marshes for Tricolored Heron, Yellow-crowned Night-Heron, and Boat-tailed Grackle. A fall walk through the North and South Gardens will often produce a variety of warblers and other passerines, as well as an occasional American Woodcock. Woodcocks (along with some 70 or so other species) breed at the refuge; in early spring they can be seen displaying at dusk in the open area just south of the visitor center.

In winter impressive numbers of waterfowl, including large numbers of Brant and Snow Geese, use the refuge, and it can be a good place to find Barn, Snowy (irregular), Short-eared, and Northern Saw-whet Owls. (Barn Owls inhabit the nest boxes dotted around the refuge; for Snowy and Short-eared scan the marshes and the open field circled by Terrapin Trail. Your best bet for fall and winter Saw-whets is the juniper trees in the North Garden.) During spring, the marshes attract Glossy Ibis, herons, rails (Clapper Rails are resident), and migrant shorebirds.

Along the outer beach to the south, the Breezy Point section of Gateway National Recreation Area (including Jacob Riis Park and Fort Tilden) has nesting Piping Plovers, terns and skimmers, wintering Purple Sandpipers, "white-winged" gulls, "Ipswich" Savannah Sparrows, and Snow Buntings, as well as migrant passerines during spring and, especially, fall.

In all seasons except winter Jamaica Bay can be buggy, with ticks, biting flies, and mosquitoes; bring repellent. Be aware of Poison-Ivy along the trails.

For information contact the Gateway NRA–Jamaica Bay Wildlife Refuge, Floyd Bennett Field, Brooklyn, NY 11234, (718) 318-4340 or *www.nps.gov/gate.*

LIBERTY STATE PARK, NEW JERSEY

Half day; year round, but especially winter, spring, fall

For a different mix of birds from those of Central Park, **Liberty State Park**—a 1,212-acre site just across the Hudson at the foot of Manhattan—is an excellent choice. Although much of the park is used for other activities—there is the Liberty Science Center, a restored railroad terminal (built in 1889), a marina, playgrounds, the Interpretive Center and Liberty Park Natural Area, and a ferry service for Liberty and Ellis Islands—it provides a good vantage point for scanning the birds in Upper New York Bay, and has other interesting habitat as well, including one of the last remaining saltmarsh habitats along the Hudson River.

From Manhattan take the Holland Tunnel to the New Jersey Turnpike. Take the first exit, 14B, and follow signs to the park. There are various modes of public transportation from New York City. Take a PATH train to Journal Square in New Jersey and catch a bus to Liberty State Park at Platform A3. Tell the driver where you want to go (Interpretive Center or parking lots),

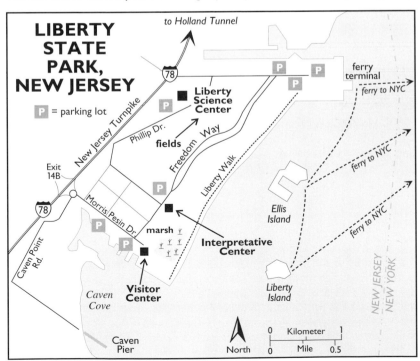

and also get a schedule of the bus, as the runs are infrequent in winter. An alternative route is to take the PATH train to Exchange Place in Jersey City. Walk a short distance to the Hudson-Bergen Light Rail station for shuttle buses to the Park. There is also a water-taxi service from lower Manhattan to Liberty Landing Marina (at the north end of the park).

During late fall, winter, and early spring, scan the cove from the first and second parking lots along Morris Pesin Drive for grebes, Great and Double-crested Cormorants, ducks, and gulls. Red-necked Grebe and "white-winged" gulls are occasionally found. Many duck species can be seen offshore, including all three scoters, Long-tailed Duck, and Red-breasted Merganser. A host of puddle ducks, including an occasional Eurasian Wigeon, can be found in the saltmarsh across the road. In winter check the marsh for Short-eared Owl and Northern Harrier; in spring listen for Marsh Wren. Look for sandpipers around the jetty. The area near Flag Plaza, east of the visitor center, offers numerous vantages for scanning. At the west end of the marsh, Freedom Way heads north toward the Interpretive Center, which is devoted to nature study. The Japanese Black Pines (succumbing to a fungus blight and gradually being replaced by other species) on both sides of the road are attractive to migrants and winter finches, as well as to owls—especially Barn, Northern Saw-whet, and, rarely, Long-eared. The trail leading from behind the center can also be productive. Continue along Freedom Way to the northern part of the park, and check the fields in late fall (especially) and winter for Horned Larks, Snow Buntings, and Lapland Longspurs (scarce). Two nearby areas, Caven Pier and Caven Cove, are also worth a look. Both can be reached by a left turn at the traffic circle just before the turnpike entrance. You can walk part way out the pier to look for shorebirds and gulls. Snowy Owls are occasionally found at these spots as well. Snow Buntings can be found on the pier in winter.

For information contact Liberty State Park, Morris Pesin Drive, Jersey City, NJ 07305, (201) 915-3401, or visit the web site (which includes a map and other information) at *www.libertystatepark.com.*

PELHAM BAY PARK

Half day; winter

This 2,000-acre Bronx county park is an excellent place for wintering waterbirds and owls. Up to five species of owls have been seen in a single outing, and during most winters one can expect to find at least two or three species. There are several productive areas. Check the waters off Hunter and Twin Islands for loons, grebes, and waterfowl, especially Brant, American Black Duck, American Wigeon, Canvasback, both scaup species, Common Goldeneye, Bufflehead, and Red-breasted Merganser. Great Cormorants join

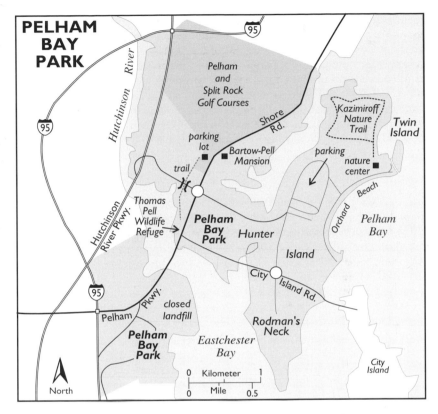

PELHAM
BAY
PARK

Hutchinson River

Pelham
and
Split Rock
Golf Courses

Shore Rd.

Kazimiroff
Nature
Trail

Twin
Island

parking
lot

Bartow-Pell
Mansion

parking

nature
center

Beach

trail

Thomas
Pell
Wildlife
Refuge

Pelham
Bay
Park

Hunter

Pelham
Bay

Hutchinson River Pkwy.

Island

Orchard

City Island Rd.

closed
landfill

Pelham

Pkwy.

Rodman's
Neck

Pelham
Bay
Park

Eastchester
Bay

City
Island

North

0   Kilometer   1

0   Mile   0.5

over- wintering Double-cresteds on the rocks offshore. Twin Island is a good place from which to scan for Harbor Seals.

On Hunter Island take the Kazimiroff Nature Trail, reached at the northeast end of Orchard Beach. Check the upper (pine) and lower (spruce) evergreen groves for owls, especially Barn, Great Horned, and Long-eared. Also check nearby tangles for Northern Saw-whets. After following Shore Road to the Split Rock Golf Course and Bartow Mansion, search both areas for owls and accipiters, particularly the young pines along Shore Road, as well as the set of pines facing the mansion's front. A path leads from the golf course parking lot under a rail trestle toward the Thomas Pell Wildlife Refuge, a tract of saltmarsh and oak-hickory woodlands worth investigating. Rodman's Neck, in the southern part of the park, can be good for Northern Harriers and Short-eared Owls. The traffic circle at Rodman's Neck is Pelham's most reliable area for Barn Owls. And, finally, don't neglect to scan the closed landfill on the west shore of Eastchester Bay for Red-tailed and Rough-legged Hawks and Northern Harriers.

Pelham Bay Park is the end stop for the Lexington Avenue #6 subway. The walk from there north and east to Hunters Island is approximately two miles. By car take the Hutchinson River Parkway and exit at the City Island/Orchard Beach exit. Continue east into the park, past the traffic circle to the parking area on Hunter Island. From the west take Pelham Parkway, which enters the park. Continue north to the traffic circle. Turn east and continue to Hunter Island. For information on Pelham Bay, including directions, call (718) 430-1890, or check the web site at *www.newyorkled.com/pelhambay.htm*. Groups that lead tours to Pelham Bay include New York City Audubon Society, (212) 691-7483, the Bronx Urban Park Rangers, (718) 430-1832, and Pelham Bay Nature Center, (718) 885-3467.

JONES BEACH AND VICINITY

Full or half day; year round, especially late spring, fall, and winter

The 2,500-acre **Jones Beach State Park** occupies eight miles of the 17-mile barrier beach east of Jones Inlet in Long Island's Nassau County. The remainder of the beach, stretching to Fire Island Inlet, includes several other parks and is mostly public land (although access is limited during summer). You can reach Jones Beach via the Meadowbrook or Wantagh Parkways. For information contact Jones Beach State Park, (516) 785-1600, and Theodore Roosevelt Nature Center, (516) 679-7254.

The entire area, including Point Lookout on the west side of Jones Inlet, offers excellent birding in all seasons. One caveat: the park is a major destination for New York City beachgoers, and summer traffic, even into early fall, can be very heavy. In fall, when winds blow out of the northwest, the birding can be spectacular. At such times, migrant passerines pile up along the coast, and lawns, trees, and bushes can be literally filled with birds feeding

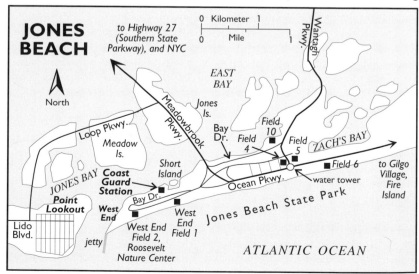

or simply taking a breather. Virtually any migrating East Coast landbird can be seen here, especially in September, including such regular rarities as Dickcissel and Clay-colored and Lark Sparrows. And for sheer numbers, one cannot fail to be impressed by the massive September flights of swallows (mostly Tree), by Northern Flickers nervously darting up at every turn, or Eastern Kingbirds atop nearly every tree or bush. Fall is also the best season for migrating hawks, especially Osprey, Sharp-shinned and Cooper's Hawks, American Kestrel, Merlin, and Peregrine Falcon. The July–October period is excellent for shorebirds, including such hard-to-find species as Baird's and Buff-breasted Sandpipers (mostly in September); check any rain pools in the dunes between Parking Fields 1 and 2.

During the winter, Jones Beach can be an excellent spot to find owls, including Snowy, Short-eared, and Northern Saw-whet. Hawks, which can be numerous in migration, are present in winter as well—including Northern Harrier and an occasional Rough-legged Hawk. Offshore, an array of winter ducks and other waterbirds can be seen: loons, grebes, gannets, eiders, and scoters. An occasional "white-winged" gull is present (check Point Lookout and Field 6), as well as a small number of Little and Black-headed Gulls among the ubiquitous Bonaparte's working the outgoing tides at the inlets. In early 1994 and 1995 a Ross's Gull was present across the inlet off Point Lookout. Black-bellied Plovers, Purple Sandpipers, Sanderlings, Dunlins, a few American Oystercatchers, and Red Knots winter locally. During flight years, Jones Beach is a good place for winter finches, including crossbills, redpolls, and siskins. Flocks of Horned Larks and Snow Buntings (and occasional Lapland Longspurs) can be found in the dunes or the parking lots.

Summer is worth a visit, as well. Piping Plovers breed in roped-off areas toward the jetty. Gulls and terns (Common, Least, and a few Roseate) nest nearby, as do Black Skimmers, numerous herons, and Glossy Ibis. Chuck-will's-widow is a scarce summer resident near Oak Beach, and Virginia and Clapper Rails breed in the marshes. Gull-billed Terns are regularly seen hawking for insects over wet areas in the dunes. Shorebird migration begins to build in July.

Some of the best places to check, moving west to east, are as follows. The area around the jetty at **Point Lookout**, a residential community on the western side of Jones Beach Inlet, is worth scanning, especially in fall and winter. This can be a good place to check the Bonaparte's Gull flock, and Harlequin Ducks are often present. To reach this area, take the Loop Parkway off the Meadowbrook Parkway. Go left onto Lido Boulevard, follow it to the end, and look for a parking spot. The town beach, to the right along the inlet, affords good vantages for viewing.

Back across the inlet, take Bay Drive off Ocean Parkway (which runs most of the length of the barrier beach). Turn right into the **Coast Guard Station** and park in the lot fronting the boat basin. The small island just offshore is Short Island, attractive to cormorants, shorebirds, and gulls. The pines in front of the station is a magnet to migrating passerines, and the adjacent shrubby field is also worth investigating; take the path which leads in from the driveway. Drive to **West End** Field 2, park, and walk across the dune field toward the jetty. The area of heath and dune between the parking lot and the jetty is worth walking to find Snowy and Short-eared Owls, Horned Larks, Snow Buntings, and winter sparrows (including "Ipswich"). Purple Sandpipers often frequent the jetty itself, and Harlequin Ducks are regularly found on its edges.

The **Theodore Roosevelt Nature Center** is located at West End Field 1; there is a bird log here, as well as displays on the ecology of the barrier beach. Farther east the north edges of Fields 4 and 5 and the trees near the maintenance building at Field 10 can be productive for migrants and for owls in winter, although many of the Japanese Black Pines are dying. After parking at Field 6, walk west to scan from the boardwalk for gulls on the ocean. (There are restrooms and a restaurant here.) Search for landbirds in the fields, bushes, and trees along its margins and around the large covered pavilion (restaurant) area, which is especially good for late warblers and occasional rarities. The huge tower at the circle is a favored Peregrine Falcon roost (one winter it even hosted a Gyrfalcon). A tunnel leads to Zach's Bay, also worth a look for Great Cormorant, Brant, shorebirds, and passerines.

Gilgo Village, farther east, is another magnet for migrants. Search the paths around the cottages; be respectful of homeowners' privacy. Farther east still, check Fire Island Inlet in summer for Roseate Tern, and in winter and early spring for Bonaparte's Gull concentrations, possibly containing a Little or a Black-headed Gull.

EXTRA EFFORT

Birders with extra time in late fall and winter may want to consider a one- or two-day trip to the **Montauk Point** area, at the eastern tip of Long Island. It is the best place near the metropolitan region to look for eiders and alcids. Razorbills and Black-legged Kittiwakes are present most years, and on rare occasions Dovekie can be found. Regular species include Red-throated and Common Loons, Horned Grebe, Northern Gannet, all three scoters, Red-breasted Merganser, Purple Sandpiper, and Bonaparte's Gull. In recent years Common Eiders have been numerous, and there are often one or two King Eiders present as well. "White-winged" and Lesser Black-backed Gulls are rare but regular. For the best waterbirding, scan the waters off Montauk Point State Park near the lighthouse, as well as the entrance to Montauk Harbor (Lake Montauk). Because of the distance (some 100 miles from the city), it is often advisable to spend one or two nights, and you will need a car. During the summer, there are whale-watching trips—good also for viewing seabirds—available from the marina at the end of West Lake Drive. To get to Montauk, follow the Long Island Expressway (I-495) east to Exit 70, then Route 111 to the Sunrise Highway (Route 27), which, after many miles, finally ends at the point. For more information, call Montauk Point State Park, (631) 668-2461.

Also on eastern Long Island, check Hook Pond in the town of East Hampton, an excellent location for wintering waterfowl, including Tundra Swan (rare), Common Merganser, and an occasional Eurasian Wigeon. Farther west, try Moriches and Shinnecock Inlets, both good for nesting American Oystercatchers, migrant shorebirds, and a variety of wintering waterfowl, as well as occasional rare gulls and alcids, and Dune Road between them along the barrier beach. Dune Road, excellent for waterfowl and shorebirds, and Snowy Owls in some winters, is reached off the Montauk Highway (27A) at Hampton Bays, or from the towns of Quogue or Westhampton Beach (in all these areas, follow signs to the beach). Roseate Terns summer (mid-May to late August) on islets east of the Ponquoge Bridge (Route 32); check from the parking lot at the base of the fishing pier, and from the end of Road 1.

Less than an hour's drive from Manhattan (and even closer to Newark Airport) is the **Great Swamp National Wildlife Refuge**, a surprisingly wild oasis in the midst of New Jersey's suburbia. Much of the habitat is wetland, but there are also ponds, streams, old fields, pastures, and upland forests. Birding is good year round, and it is even worth a visit during the doldrums of June and July. Birds of interest here include Least Bittern (summer), American Woodcock, Barred Owl, Pileated Woodpecker, Eastern Bluebird, and Bobolink. Great Blue Heron nests are visible from a pull-out on Pleasant Plains Road. To reach Great Swamp, near Chatham, follow I-78 West to Route 24, toward Morristown and Summit. Take the Morris Avenue exit in Summit to River Road. Follow River Road through Chatham (where a left turn is required) for a total of about four miles to Fairmount Avenue. Turn right, then take the second left onto Meyersville Road, and then, after two-and-a-half miles, right onto New Vernon/Long Hill Road. In two miles you will reach the refuge observation center. For information, contact Great Swamp NWR, RD 1, Box 152, Basking Ridge, NJ 07920, or call (973) 425-1222.

A favorite of New York birders in spring and early summer is **Bear Mountain** and nearby **Doodletown Road**, on the western side of the Hudson River, an hour's drive north of New York City. It offers perhaps the best place in the region for Black Vulture and nesting Golden-winged (rare), Cerulean, and Hooded Warblers. Take the New York State Thruway to the Palisades Interstate Parkway north to the Perkins Drive exit. Follow the road to a traffic circle and take the first right turn to Route 9W. On Route 9W, park a short distance south, near Iona Island Road, and take the steep trail (formerly Doodletown Road) on the opposite side of the road. Iona Island is worth investigating for waterbirds. For information, call (914) 889-4100.

ACKNOWLEDGMENTS

Helpful comments were provided by Richard Cech, Robert V. DeCandido, Gina Provenzano, Don Riepe, and Marie Winn.

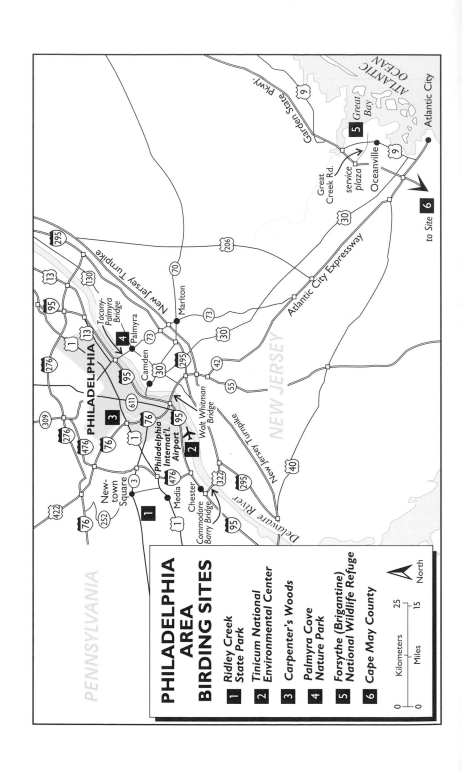

PHILADELPHIA AREA BIRDING SITES

1. Ridley Creek State Park
2. Tinicum National Environmental Center
3. Carpenter's Woods
4. Palmyra Cove Nature Park
5. Forsythe (Brigantine) National Wildlife Refuge
6. Cape May County

Kilometers 0 — 25
Miles 0 — 15

North

PENNSYLVANIA

NEW JERSEY

ATLANTIC OCEAN

Atlantic City

Great Bay

Oceanville

service plaza

Great Creek Rd.

Garden State Pkwy.

Delaware River

to Site 6

Atlantic City Expressway

New Jersey Turnpike

Philadelphia International Airport

Walt Whitman Bridge

Commodore Barry Bridge

Tacony-Palmyra Bridge

Palmyra

Camden

Marlton

Media

Chester

Newtown Square

PHILADELPHIA

PHILADELPHIA, PENNSYLVANIA

John J. Harding

The Delaware Valley region consists of eastern Pennsylvania, central and southern New Jersey, and northern and central Delaware. With Philadelphia at its hub, this tri-state area has a long history steeped in birding tradition, beginning with such luminaries as John James Audubon and Alexander Wilson. Well over 400 species have been recorded in the region. Although the Philadelphia area has its share of vagrants and rarities, the region is perhaps most famous for the large number and variety of spring and fall migrants, including myriad waterfowl, raptors, shorebirds, and passerines. The wealth of habitats is reflected in the diversity of birdlife. The Atlantic Ocean, saltwater and freshwater marshes, barrier beaches, pine barrens, meadows and successional fields, deciduous woodlands, and Canadian-zone forests are all within a two-hour reach of downtown Philadelphia.

ESSENTIAL INFORMATION

Getting Around: Many visitors to Philadelphia arrive at Philadelphia International Airport or at the Amtrak Railroad Station at 30th and Market Streets. Car-rental facilities are located at both sites, and driving is the recommended mode of travel to the various hot-spots. Most birding locations in the Delaware Valley region are less than a two-hour drive from the city, with many half-day trips only 30 minutes away. This allows the visiting birder to stay overnight in Philadelphia, which is renowned for its accommodations and historic sites. Rush-hour traffic in the region can be a problem.

Climate: Daytime high temperatures in the summer average 80–92° Fahrenheit, while the winter norms range between 25° and 45°. Spring (mid-April through May) is probably the best time to be afield and is often absolutely glorious, with temperatures in the 60s and 70s. Autumn weather can be beautiful as well, particularly from mid-September to late October, and the late October foliage can be stunning. The sea-breezes along the coast can make for more-pleasant summer birding (beware of crowds), but they may generate bracing wind-chill factors during the winter.

Natural Hazards: Serious hazards are rare, but nuisances such as Poison-Ivy, biting flies, ticks, and mosquitoes can be present from April through October, depending on the locale and recent weather. Repellent is a good idea, especially near coastal marshes. There have been many reports of Deer Ticks transmitting Lyme disease, so be careful.

Safety: Personal safety of birders has not been a problem in the tri-state area. Although safe to date, some of the more isolated trails at Tinicum, Carpenter's Woods, Palmyra, and behind the Philadelphia Airport could be problematic—so bird with a companion. It is advisable to hide valuables left in your locked car.

Other Resources: The Delaware Valley Ornithological Club (DVOC), formed in 1890, is one of the oldest and most active birding organizations in the U.S. To learn more, visit *www.acnatsci.org/dvoc/*. The DVOC's meetings are held twice monthly at the Academy of Natural Sciences in downtown Philadelphia at 19th and the Parkway, (215) 299-1000. The Academy, founded in 1812, is renowned for its Department of Ornithology and for its VIREO (Visual Resources for Ornithology) collection of photographs of over 5,000 species of birds. The Philadelphia Birdline at (215) 567-BIRD has weekly bird reports (updated Friday). Other Rare Bird Alerts of the Delaware Valley region are New Jersey (908) 766-2661, Cape May (609) 861-0466, and Delaware (302) 658-2747.

Books include *A Guide to Bird Finding in New Jersey* by William, J. Boyle, Jr. (1994, Rutgers University Press), *Birding the Delaware Valley Region* by Harding and Harding (1980, Temple University Press), *A Guide to the Birds of Lancaster County, Pennsylvania* by H. B. Morrin, ed. (1984, Lancaster County Bird Club), *Birds of Delaware County, Pennsylvania* by Nick Pulcinella (1999, Birding Club of Delaware County), and *The Birds of Cape May* by David Sibley (1997, Cape May Bird Observatory). An article by Colin Campbell and Ellen Short in the May 1994 *Winging It* describes nearby Delaware shorebirding. The web site *www. delawarevalleybirding.com* contains helpful regional birding information.

THE BIRDING YEAR

The greatest concentrations and number of species are seen during the spring and fall migrations. For waterfowl, these peaks occur from March through mid-April and again from October through early December, with many birds wintering over. Birds of prey abound in the autumn, September through November, along both the Appalachian ridges and the coast (most notably at Cape May), particularly following passage of a cold front. Most spring shorebirds come through the area during May; their fall migration is more drawn out, starting in early July and ending mostly by early November. Over 30 species of shorebirds have been recorded on a regular basis, with the Delaware refuges and Brigantine (Forsythe) National Wildlife Refuge being the best sites. The peak movement of spring landbirds also occurs in May. Their autumn migration extends over a longer period as well, usually from mid-August through mid-November.

Ridley Creek State Park

Half day; spring, summer, and fall

Ridley Creek State Park is a 2,600-acre tract of deciduous woodlands and brushy successional meadows located only twenty miles west of Philadelphia. It attracts great numbers of both migrant and nesting landbirds. In particular, a 1.5-mile stretch of creek along Sycamore Mills Road (closed to auto traffic) in the extreme southeastern portion of the park is ideal for observing the representative birds of the area. Birding early in the morning on a weekday maximizes privacy (cyclers, fishermen, and hikers favor the weekends). A several-hour walk during the spring or fall migrations may yield up to 25 species of warblers, five species of vireos, and several flycatchers and thrushes, plus various species of woodpeckers, swallows, wrens, sparrows, and orioles. The first three weeks in May and again from late August through September are the best times. Many typical eastern landbirds nest at Ridley Creek State Park. More than a few regular breeding species found here are uncommon elsewhere in the Delaware Valley region.

To reach the park, travel from the City Line Avenue exit off the Schuylkill Expressway (I-76) for 3.5 miles along US-1 South (City Avenue) to the intersection with Route 3 (West Chester Pike). Turn right (west) onto Route 3 and drive 5.8 miles to Route 252 in Newtown Square. At the next light (0.1 mile farther), turn left onto Bishop Hollow Road (which becomes Ridley Creek Road) and travel 3.3 miles to Chapel Hill Road. Make a right onto Chapel Hill Road across the narrow Sycamore Mills Bridge. Barren Road is to the left (to Tyler Arboretum), and the birding tour is immediately to the right. For information: Ridley Creek State Park, Sycamore Mills Road, Route 36, Media, PA 19063, (610) 892-3900.

From the parking lots by the bridge at the junction of Ridley Creek Road and Chapel Hill Road, the first upstream mile of Ridley Creek hugs Sycamore Mills Road, shaded by a canopy of towering hardwoods. This is the place to be during migration, even on slow days. Eventually, Ridley Creek veers away from Sycamore Mills Road. Moist thickets dotted with islands of second-growth hardwoods line the right side of Sycamore Mills Road for the next half-mile, and then open to a clearing. Scan the sycamores along the gravel road leading to the youth hostel on the right.

An equally good birding route is along Forge Road, which leads off to the left up the substantial hill from Sycamore Mills Road, approximately one-quarter mile from the parking lot. During May, the feeders at the colonial house near the junction host Ruby-throated Hummingbirds, various woodpeckers, and lingering White-throated Sparrows. Deciduous woodlands crowd the gradual incline for the next half-mile or so and then open to a series of brushy successional fields and second-growth woodlands surrounding Picnic Area #17 to the right. As Forge Road mercifully levels off, continue several hundred

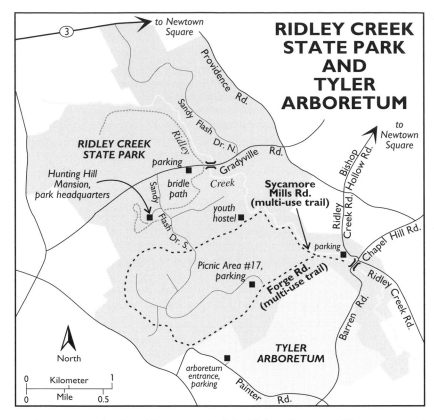

yards to a gutted colonial house on the left. Yellow-breasted Chat has nested near here the last few years, along with Blue-winged, Chestnut-sided, and Prairie Warblers. Picnic Area #17 also serves as a back-up parking lot, from which you would walk downhill on Forge Road toward Ridley Creek.

Over 20 warbler species are commonly seen during migration; a dozen are regular breeders, including Blue-winged, Northern Parula, Chestnut-sided, Prairie, Black-and-white, American Redstart, Ovenbird, Louisiana Waterthrush, Kentucky, and Yellow-breasted Chat; Pine and Hooded Warblers are less frequently observed in summer.

All six species of eastern vireos may be seen during migration; White-eyed, Yellow-throated, and Red-eyed remain to nest. Warbling Vireo favors several creekside locations. Check below the youth hostel, along the bridle path, and especially above Rose Tree Bridge, just outside the park. Six species of thrushes are seen here during migration; Wood Thrush and Veery remain to breed. Many other eastern landbirds are to be expected during migration, and some remain to nest in the general area: Broad-winged Hawk, Pileated Woodpecker, Acadian Flycatcher, Scarlet Tanager, Rose-breasted Grosbeak, and Orchard and Baltimore Orioles are among the favorites.

Some birders with less time prefer to hike the bridle path that meanders along Ridley Creek under Gradyville Road Bridge. To reach it, regain your car at the parking lot at the Sycamore Mills Bridge, turn left onto Ridley Creek Road, and proceed 0.4 mile to Providence Road. Turn left, and after 0.4 mile make another left at the stop sign onto Gradyville Road. Wind along 0.4 mile to the next stop sign, bear left, and after 0.4 mile park off the road to the right, immediately past a gate blocking the bridle path.

The bridle path is a one-hour, half-mile condensed version of the previous walks. Most of the migrant and breeding landbirds of Ridley Creek State Park can be found here, as well. As you bear right along the bridle path to the bridge, scan the huge oaks and sycamores. Heading upstream along the bridle path in the opposite direction, one eventually comes to "Hunting Hill," a densely wooded hilltop off to the left. This is a reliable spot to hear and hopefully see nesting Kentucky and Hooded Warblers.

Tyler (Painter) Arboretum, adjacent to Ridley Creek Park, covers an additional 700 acres. From the Sycamore Mills Bridge, drive 1.2 miles along Barren Road to Painter Road, and turn right. Proceed another mile to the Arboretum's parking lot on your right. An entrance fee is charged. A detailed map of the various trails and plantings can be obtained at the visitor center (open daily) next to Lachford Hall. For information: Tyler Arboretum, 515 Painter Road, Media, PA 19063, (610) 566-5431.

Visiting Tyler in the spring or summer after birding Ridley Creek may add Pine Warbler (at the Pinetum), along with Brown Thrasher (declining), Indigo Bunting, and Field Sparrow in the tree-studded meadows and along woodland edges. Eastern Bluebirds use the scattered nesting boxes.

JOHN HEINZ NATIONAL WILDIFE REFUGE (TINICUM) AND THE PHILADELPHIA AIRPORT

Half day; year round

Tinicum was established as a National Environmental Center in 1972 to preserve the last remaining freshwater/brackish tidal marsh along the Delaware River. Tinicum was renamed **John Heinz National Wildlife Refuge** following the death of the conservation-minded senator in 1990. This unique preserve, totaling 1,200 acres, is surrounded by industrial complexes and housing and is only two miles from Philadelphia International Airport.

Tinicum's main attraction is a freshwater impoundment whose depth is controlled by rainfall and adjustable flow-gates to tidal Darby Creek. With water levels usually high, the impoundment is often a shallow lake dotted with islands of vegetation. The gravel dike that separates the impoundment from Darby Creek serves as the main vantage point for birding the refuge. Beginning at the visitor center and snaking around the western boundary of the preserve for 1.5 miles, the dike leads to an observation blind overlooking the tidal mudflats of Darby Creek; look for shorebirds here. The dike is flanked by narrow strips of scattered trees, with cattails and rushes edging the banks. Meadows, dotted with thickets of second-growth woodland, serve as the marsh's eastern boundary. A service road meanders through this section and leads into deciduous woodland separating the southern part of the marsh from nearby Bartram Avenue. Recently, a swath was clear-cut between the service road and the impoundment.

To reach Tinicum from the airport, follow Route 291 East for one-half mile and turn left at the first traffic light onto Island Avenue. Drive 0.4 mile (by-passing the entrance to I-95 South) and turn left onto Bartram Avenue. Proceed 0.3 mile, turning right at the light onto 84th Avenue. Drive 0.7 mile to the second light at Lindbergh Boulevard, turn left, and proceed 0.2 mile farther to Tinicum's entrance on your right. Park in the lot by the visitor center. The dike road around the preserve begins here but must be walked since it is closed to auto traffic. Another entrance to the refuge, closer to Darby Creek's mudflats, is found off Route 420. For information: John Heinz National Wildlife Refuge at Tinicum Visitor Center, 86th Street and Lindbergh Blvd., Philadelphia, PA 19153, (215) 365-3118.

Beginning in mid-March, wintering ducks are joined by good numbers of migrant waterfowl. Most species are more plentiful during the fall (October–December), and many individuals winter over if the water doesn't freeze. Snowy Egrets and Little Blue and Tricolored Herons are occasionally seen, particularly from late summer through early fall. Secretive Least and

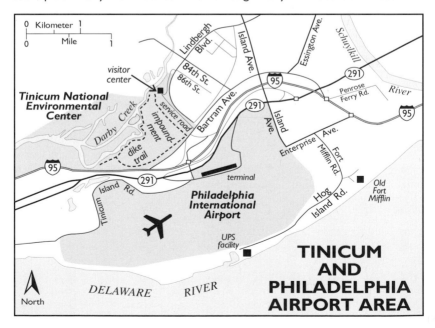

American Bitterns were formerly more regular. Virginia Rail and Sora are uncommon migrants.

Early May heralds the spring shorebird migration, although nesting American Woodcocks will have arrived already in March. Late summer and early fall (late July through mid-October) promise more species and greater concentrations. Pectoral Sandpiper, Dunlin, and Short-billed Dowitcher are to be expected during this period. Additional species are occasionally seen on the tidal flats.

May signals the major landbird movement. Many of the species seen at Ridley Creek are encountered here, too, but usually in lower numbers. Many of the migrants can be found working their way through the brush and trees along the dike. Willow Flycatchers nest along the dike and the service road. Both Fish and American Crows frequent the refuge at all seasons. Brown Thrasher and Yellow-breasted Chat occasionally breed in the brushy areas adjoining the east side of the impoundment. Warbling Vireo and sometimes Orchard Oriole nest in taller shade trees lining the dike.

Many sparrows may be found from October through April. The trail through the meadows and briers along the eastern border of the marsh is a favorite for American Tree, Field, and White-crowned Sparrows during the colder months. Swamp Sparrows occur year round.

Nearby, the **Delaware River** and **Philadelphia Airport** can be rewarding for a variety of waterbirds as well as open-country birds. Great Cormorant is regular during the colder months. Laughing Gull is a common warm-weather visitor, with Forster's and occasionally Caspian Terns seen along the river from August through October. If the tide is low, exposed mudflats and sand-bars may host some herons and shorebirds. During spring and summer, check the ponds near the junction of Fort Mifflin and Hog Island Roads for marsh birds. Willow Flycatcher and Blue Grosbeak nest in the scattered groves of trees along the river. Wintering Northern Harriers quarter the extensive airport fields along Hog Island Road, while Rough-legged Hawk and Short-eared Owl (both rare) are bonuses. Check the cropped airport fields for Horned Lark, Snow Bunting (irregular), and Lapland Longspur (rare).

From the airport follow Route 291 east for one-half mile and turn right at the traffic light onto Island Avenue. Continue past the airport and bend left onto Enterprise Avenue, then right onto Fort Mifflin Road, which soon becomes Hog Island Road. This road parallels the back side of the airport for a couple miles to its end overlooking the river and the tidal flats, next to the large United Parcel Service (UPS) facility. Bring a scope!

WISSAHICKON VALLEY
AND CARPENTER'S WOODS

Half day; spring and fall

The **Wissahickon Valley**, a section of Philadelphia's Fairmount Park, extends approximately seven miles from the mouth of Wissahickon Creek by the Schuylkill River northwest to the city limits near Chestnut Hill College. The valley's main attraction is Wissahickon Creek, which courses through a large wooded ravine. The principal habitat is mixed deciduous hardwoods with scattered conifers. Carpenter's Woods, a famous birding hot-spot of only several acres, branches off the Wissahickon Valley proper. Large numbers of landbirds funnel through here during their spring and fall migrations.

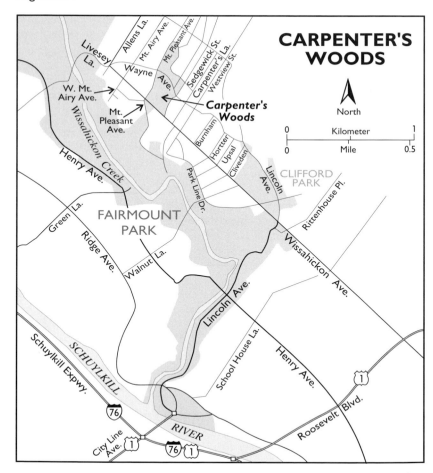

To reach Carpenter's Woods, travel to the junction of US-1 and I-76 and take the exit off I-76 for Kelly and Lincoln Drives. Go 1.5 miles along Lincoln Drive to the first light. Bear right onto Rittenhouse Place, following signs for Wissahickon Avenue, and turn left at the light onto Wissahickon Avenue (northwest). Drive 1.1 miles on Wissahickon Avenue (past four traffic lights) to Carpenter's Lane. Proceed one block farther and make a right onto Sedgewick Street. Park on the left before the intersection with Wayne Avenue.

The best times to visit **Carpenter's Woods** are the first three weeks in May and again from late August through September. The migrant and resident birdlife of Wissahickon Creek is very similar to that of Ridley Creek. Warblers are the main reason to visit, especially in May. Carpenter's Woods is particularly good for migrant Tennessee, Black-throated Blue, Blackburnian, and Bay-breasted Warblers. Unfortunately, Louisiana Waterthrushes are becoming scarcer as breeders along Wissahickon Creek, and nesting Kentucky Warblers have virtually disappeared. Cerulean Warblers once favored the tall trees adjoining the creek between the covered bridge (near Thomas Mill Road) and Bells Mill Road.

If you have more time, explore West Mount Airy Avenue and Livesey Lane, within walking distance of Carpenter's Woods.

PALMYRA COVE NATURE PARK, NEW JERSEY
Half day; fall

Palmyra, New Jersey, a 300-acre oasis, is a premier fall birding site bordering the Delaware River across from Philadelphia. During autumn migration, certain passerines occur here more predictably than elsewhere in the region, save possibly at Cape May, the latter a two-hour drive. A good trail system accesses the Delaware River, brushy fields, deciduous woods, and freshwater marsh.

From I-76, take US-1 North (Roosevelt Boulevard) and drive 7 miles to the signs for Route 13 and the Tacony-Palmyra Bridge. Turn right onto Robbins Street and proceed approximately two miles and then across the bridge. After the tolls make a left at the first light onto Souder Avenue (0.2 mile). Turn left at the T-intersection with Temple Street, make a sharp right after the guard rail (yield sign), and follow the sign for Palmyra Cove Nature Park under the bridge to a gravel parking lot. Among the many regularly occurring passerines seen between late August and mid-October are such uncommon species as Yellow-bellied and Least Flycatchers, Philadelphia Vireo, and Cape May and Wilson's Warblers. This is one of the best locations in the Delaware Valley region to search for Connecticut Warbler during

September and for Lincoln's Sparrow during October. Vagrants have included Clay-colored, Lark, and Le Conte's Sparrows.

EDWIN FORSYTHE (BRIGANTINE) NATIONAL WILDLIFE REFUGE, NEW JERSEY

Full day; year-round

Brigantine National Wildlife Refuge was combined in 1984 with Barnegat National Wildlife Refuge and renamed Edwin Forsythe National Wildlife Refuge. Brigantine is a birding jewel only 20 minutes from the casinos of Atlantic City, and less than two hours from Philadelphia. An eight-mile, one-way auto loop allows access to the refuge's varied habitats. Extensive tidal saltmarshes and bays, nearly 1,400 acres of freshwater and brackish impoundments, brushy fields, and woodlands have attracted almost 300 species. The impoundments are magnets for most of the refuge's species and vary from shallow lakes to marshes to extensive mudflats, depending on the season, precipitation, and management practices.

From Philadelphia proceed east across the Delware River on the Walt Whitman Bridge. Follow the signs for Atlantic City/Route 42 South. Pick up the Atlantic City Expressway and drive 35 miles to the northbound Garden State Parkway. Proceed north on the parkway for 4 miles to the service plaza in the median. Go to the north end of the plaza and take the signed ramp downhill to Jimmie Leeds Road (avoid re-entering the parkway northbound). Turn right at the light and proceed east for a third of a mile, there angling off to the left onto Great Creek Road. Take this road 3 miles to the light at Route 9 in Oceanville. Continue straight another mile to the fee station, refuge parking lot, restrooms, and information booth (which has refuge brochures, a map, and a sightings log). An entrance fee, Duck Stamp, or Golden Eagle Passport is required. Birding is very good year round, especially during spring and fall migrations. A scope is a necessity for viewing many of the birds. Insect repellent is essential on many days from June through September. For information: Edwin Forsythe NWR, Great Creek Road, P.O. Box 72, Oceanville, NJ 08231, (609) 652-1665.

Wintering and migrant waterfowl occur in great numbers at Brigantine, including Tundra and Mute (resident) Swans and thousands of Snow Geese (including a few blue-morph birds and sometimes a rare Ross's Goose). Brant and Long-tailed Duck are more wedded to the adjacent saltwater bays.

April marks the wading-bird invasion, when good numbers of herons (including Little Blue and Tricolored), egrets, and Glossy Ibis arrive. Least and American Bitterns are both secretive and declining in numbers, with the latter occasionally found in winter. Clapper Rails dart out regularly from the saltmarsh vegetation.

May heralds the spring shorebird migration, although their autumn movement (July through early November) brings larger numbers and variety. The edges of the West Pool and the eastern flats of the East Pool are particularly good if water levels are appropriate. By far the greatest concentrations of shorebirds will be present on the two pools around high tide. In addition to the common East Coast species, White-rumped Sandpiper is a regular migrant (particularly at and north of the West Pool), and Western, Pectoral, and Stilt Sandpipers and Long-billed Dowitchers can be found during fall migration. Whimbrel is a regular migrant, frequenting the saltmarshes, whereas American Oystercatcher and Willet are common breeders in the Brigantine area. American Golden-Plover, Hudsonian and Marbled Godwits, and Wilson's and Red-necked Phalaropes occur in small numbers every fall. American Avocet, Baird's and Buff-breasted Sandpipers, and Ruff are annual.

Gull-billed (check the north side of the West Pool), Common, and Forster's Terns and Black Skimmer are numerous during the breeding season, whereas Caspian, Royal (more common along the outer coast), and Least Terns are most likely during late summer.

Migrant and nesting landbirds are somewhat underrepresented at Brigantine. However, check the Purple Martin colonies near the parking lot, and listen for Whip-poor-will and Chuck-will's-widow in spring and early summer along Leeds Point and Scott's Landing Roads, to the north. Saltmarsh Sharp-tailed and Seaside Sparrows nest in their preferred habitats. Nelson's Sharp-tailed Sparrow occurs as a migrant in October and November and again briefly in May. Rough-legged Hawk and Short-eared Owl are uncommon winter residents, and a few Bald and Golden (scarce) Eagles are seen then. The best place for winter eagles is at the end of Motts Creek Road, located off Route 9 three miles north of the refuge. Look for resident Peregrine Falcons at the hacking boxes located on the dike between the East and the West Pools and at tour stop 11; or you may see them instilling panic in the waterfowl or shorebirds which you are trying to observe.

Over the years, Brigantine Refuge has hosted quite an array of rarities, including Reddish Egret, Black-bellied Whistling-Duck, Garganey, Gyrfalcon, Spotted Redshank, Black-tailed and Bar-tailed Godwits, Red-necked Stint, Fork-tailed Flycatcher, and Northern Wheatear.

CAPE MAY COUNTY, NEW JERSEY

Full day; year round

Cape May is one of the premier birdwatching sites in the eastern United States. Its strategic coastal location at the tip of a peninsula, as well as a collage of habitats, provide excellent year-round birding, with the autumn migration being particularly renowned. A passing cold front followed by northwesterly winds is often ideal for fall raptors and passerines. "Cape May" refers to a collection of birding locations within Cape May County, where just over 400 species have been recorded, 140 of which have nested since 1980. Cape May also hosts many vagrant species over a year's time, with the best season for oddities being late October through November.

Several birdfinding guides (e.g., Harding and Harding 1980, Boyle 1994, Sibley 1997) and Cape May Bird Observatory (CMBO) brochures/maps describe the county in detail. Call the CMBO Hotline at (609) 861-0466, updated weekly on Thursday. When arriving in Cape May County, stop at one or both of the CMBO centers; the first, the Center for Research and Education, is near the Delaware Bayshore on Route 47 a mile south of Route 657 in Goshen; the other, the Northwood Center, is in Cape May Point just a few blocks from Cape May Point State Park and the landmark lighthouse. Check the sightings logs and obtain a free birding site map, bird and butterfly checklists, and program schedule. Both centers have great bookstores, too. For information: CMBO, 701 East Lake Drive, P.O. Box 3, Cape May Point, NJ 08212, (609) 884-2736 (Northwood Center); or 600 Route 47 North, Cape May Court House, NJ 08210, (609) 861-0700 (Center for Research and Education). Both centers are open from 10:00AM to 5:00PM daily.

The Cape May Point State Park fall hawkwatch averages 55,000 birds of prey annually. Merlins and Peregrine Falcons exceed several hundred individuals each in late September and early October. Many of the seventeen or so raptor species have preferred windows-of-passage; early October provides the greatest variety. Also check Bunker and Lighthouse Ponds for

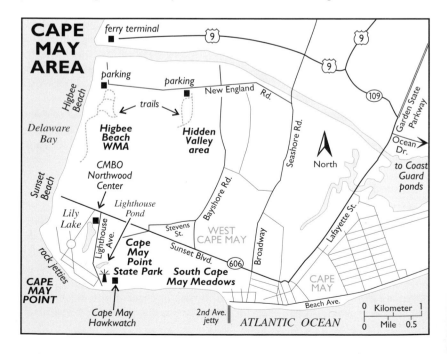

waterfowl, terns, and nesting Least Bittern, and scan offshore from the park pavilion or beach. Nearby **Lily Lake** can be good for waterfowl, as can the **Coast Guard Ponds** along Ocean Drive between Cape May and Wildwood Crest. The extensive marshes at the nearby Two-Mile Landing are good for Seaside and Saltmarsh Sharp-tailed Sparrows from May to December, and for Nelson's Sharp-taileds during migration, as well as for herons, Brant, American Oystercatchers, and other shorebirds.

Higbee Beach Wildlife Management Area is famous for migrant passerines, especially in fall (mid-August–early November). Walk the trails radiating from the parking lot southward through brushy fields and along woodland edges. Early morning is best, and also is recommended to ensure a parking spot during a prime spring or fall weekend. Just after dawn, on mornings with north, northwest, or west winds, one may see thousands of warblers passing through. A particularly good place to see these birds, though only in flight, is from atop the dike along the rim of the dredge-spoil impoundment a short walk north of the parking lot. Although uncommon, Yellow-bellied Flycatcher, Philadelphia Vireo, Orange-crowned (October), Connecticut, and Mourning (September) Warblers, and Lincoln's Sparrow (October) are practically synonymous with Higbee Beach and adjacent **Hidden Valley** (also part of Higbee Beach WMA) back to the east (see map). Most warblers and flycatchers peak during late August and September, whereas kinglets, bluebirds, late warblers, sparrows, and numbers of American Woodcock predominate in October and early November. There is a long list of rarities from these two sites.

Nearby **South Cape May Meadows,** along Sunset Boulevard, is Nature Conservancy property famous for small numbers of Piping Plovers and Least Terns nesting on the upper beach. Late-summer and early-fall shorebirding can be good if water levels are low. Check the marsh vegetation for nesting Least Bitterns and rails. Almost anything can turn up here and has, including North America's first Whiskered Tern.

Between late fall and early spring, the rock jetties and the "Concrete Ship" around Cape May Point should be checked for loons, both cormorants, Northern Gannet, scoters, and Purple Sandpiper, and from spring through fall for large numbers of terns. The Avalon Seawatch at the end of 7th Street in **Avalon** is excellent in fall for watching the southward passage of thousands of coastal seabirds.

Stone Harbor Point and **Nummy's Island**, located along the Atlantic coast approximately ten miles north of Cape May, are excellent for herons (including Yellow-crowned Night-Heron), Clapper Rail, shorebirds (including resident American Oystercatchers and occasional Marbled Godwits), gulls, terns, and marsh sparrows.

Along the Delaware Bayshore, **Reed's Beach** and several nearby roads that lead to the Bay are famous for hordes of May shorebirds (and gulls) that feed on Horseshoe Crab eggs. **Jake's Landing** to the north is excellent for nesting marshbirds and Pine and Yellow-throated Warblers (in the pines), as well as wintering raptors (including Short-eared Owl). Nearby **Belleplain State Forest**, particularly in the vicinity of the Sunset Road bridge, is excellent for "southern" breeding passerines including Acadian Flycatcher, Yellow-throated, Prothonotary, Worm-eating, and Hooded Warblers, Louisiana Waterthrush, and Summer Tanager. Whip-poor-wills are numerous; Chuck-will's-widows are scattered elsewhere in the county. Do *not* leave the roads here, as Deer Ticks abound, many of which carry Lyme disease.

OTHER SITES

Florence, New Jersey (off Route 130, south of Trenton), is situated on the Delaware River across from the huge Tullytown/Penn Manor landfill north of Philadelphia. Florence is a gull-watcher's paradise during the winter months, except on Sundays when the dump is closed and the gulls have scattered. Among the upwards of 60,000 birds present, as many as 75 Lesser Black-backed Gulls and small numbers of both Iceland and Glaucous Gulls can be tallied in a day. From one to four Thayer's have been reported annually. From the two public parks in Florence you can scan the large rafts of gulls roosting on the river. The best vantage point is usually from the small park with the boat-launching ramp (Carey Park); the other park is slightly more wooded and is found farther to the south. Great (and Double-crested) Cormorants, Common Mergansers, and Bald Eagles also may be seen.

Peace Valley Nature Center (near Doylestown off Route 313) and **Nockamixon State Park** (near Quakertown off Routes 412/313) in Bucks County, north of Philadelphia, support deciduous woodlands, brushy fields, and large freshwater lakes. The areas are good for migrant and wintering waterfowl and gulls, Wild Turkey, and a variety of migrant and nesting passerines.

Hawk Mountain Sanctuary, Berks County, Pennsylvania (near Kempton off Routes 61/895) is famous for autumn hawkwatching , the scenery, and its conservation heritage. Northern Goshawk, Red-shouldered and Broad-winged Hawks, and Golden Eagles favor these Appalachian ridges. Hawk Mountain is also good for winter finches and several breeders typical of the Canadian-zone forests of the Poconos (e.g., Winter Wren, Hermit Thrush, and Black-throated Green and Canada Warblers). Closer to Philadelphia, hawkwatches at Militia Hill in Fort Washington State Park (off Route 309) and at Rose Tree Park (near Media) lack Hawk Mountain's scenery and raptor numbers, but they are more easily accessible for those with limited time.

Lancaster County, Pennsylvania, contains fertile farmlands pitching gently westward to the Susquehanna River. The river is fed by numerous tributaries, each guarded by remnant corridors of woodlands hosting nesting species uncommon elsewhere. During the colder months, check freshly manured fields of the Amish farms west of New Holland (take South Groffdale Road off Route 23). Horned Lark, Snow Bunting, and Lapland Longspur (uncommon) may be found in winter. Search for Rough-legged Hawks, also in winter.

The town of Washington Boro (Routes 999/441 near Millersville) provides views of a chain of wooded islands and their interconnecting mudflats—the **Conejohela Flats**—in the Susquehanna River. The mudflats attract numerous herons and shorebirds, and some gulls and terns, between July and October. Migrant and wintering waterfowl, especially Tundra Swans, also use the area. A scope is essential; birds are distant.

Farther south along the Susquehanna River, check **Muddy Run Park** and the adjacent Susquehannock State Park (off Route 372) for waterfowl and locally nesting Osprey and Bald Eagle. Look for Worm-eating, Kentucky, and Hooded Warblers plus Louisiana Waterthrush nesting in the steep, densely vegetated "river hills" along the river. Cerulean and Yellow-throated Warblers prefer large sycamores. Prothonotary Warbler is occasionally found singing from the wooded swamps.

Just across the Maryland state line along US-1, **Conowingo Dam**, on the Susquehanna, is known for its wintering Bald Eagles and especially the large concentration of winter gulls ("white-winged" species, Lesser Black-backed, and the occasional rarity). Cross the dam on US-1 to the south (west) side and make your first left, then left again, downhill to the parking lot below the dam.

The Delaware Refuges, including Bombay Hook National Wildlife Refuge, Port Mahon Road, Little Creek and Ted Harvey Wildlife Management Areas, and Prime Hook National Wildlife Refuge (Broadkill Beach), among others, form a string of birding pearls along Route 9 and the Delaware Bay near Dover. Birdlife is similar to that of Brigantine, with superb fall shore-birding (July–October). In addition to the Brigantine species, Curlew Sandpiper and Ruff are annual, and American Avocet and Black-necked Stilt are locally common in Delaware. During the past decade, such rarities as Little Egret, Northern Lapwing, Black-tailed Godwit, Sharp-tailed Sandpiper, Red-necked and Little Stints, and Whiskered and White-winged Terns have been seen. Greater White-fronted and Ross's Geese occur annually, the latter in very small numbers.

Pelagic Trips out toward the deep-water canyons of the Atlantic Ocean are offered usually in late May, August, and September, with an additional one or two winter trips. Brielle, Barnegat Light, and Cape May, New Jersey, and Lewes, Delaware, are departure points, with most trips lasting 12–16 hours. Each season has its unique assortment of seabirds and marine life. For information call the Philadelphia Birdline or visit the DVOC's web site.

ACKNOWLEDGMENTS

Special thanks to Ted Floyd (Pennsylvania), Stephen Lawrence (Carpenter's Woods), Paul Lehman (New Jersey), and Nick Pulcinella (Pennsylvania) for their input.

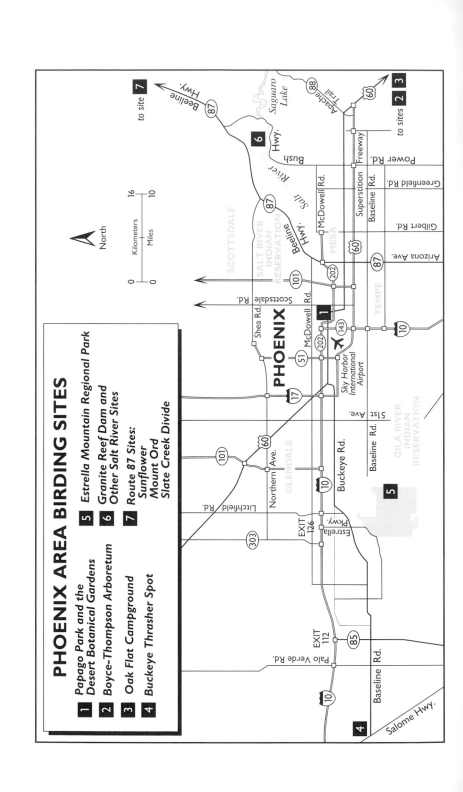

PHOENIX AREA BIRDING SITES

1 Papago Park and the
Desert Botanical Gardens

2 Boyce-Thompson Arboretum

3 Oak Flat Campground

4 Buckeye Thrasher Spot

5 Estrella Mountain Regional Park

6 Granite Reef Dam and
Other Salt River Sites

7 Route 87 Sites:
Sunflower
Mount Ord
Slate Creek Divide

PHOENIX, ARIZONA

Richard Ditch

When birders think of Arizona, they immediately envision the world-famous hot-spots in the southeastern corner of the state, places such as the Santa Rita, Huachuca, and Chiricahua Mountains, Patagonia, and the San Pedro River. By contrast, Phoenix is a large city located in the middle of a desert: it is hot, dry, and rapidly expanding. The cooler, wetter canyons of southeastern Arizona are not to be found here. Still, there are many birding opportunities around Phoenix for the traveling birder, and if your itinerary does not allow you to wander to other parts of the state, you can nevertheless leave with a satisfying Southwestern birding experience.

Tucson is only about 100 miles to the south, easily reached via I-10. From Tucson, all of the southeastern Arizona hot-spots are reachable. These sites are thoroughly described in birdfinding guides to southeastern Arizona.

ESSENTIAL INFORMATION

Getting Around: Public transportation is very limited in the metro area, so don't expect to get to the recommended birding spots by bus or train. Taxis are available, but you should probably plan on a rental car to reach most birding locations. All the major rental companies operate out of Sky Harbor Airport.

Rush hour can extend from 6:30 until 9:00AM and again from 3:00 until 6:30PM. Inbound morning traffic backs up on both I-10 and the Superstition Freeway (US-60) where they meet southeast of Sky Harbor Airport, as well as on I-10 from the West Valley and on I-17 from the north. Avoid US-60 eastbound from I-10 in the late afternoon and early evening.

Climate: "Hot" is the operative word for Phoenix in summer. Temperatures in the high 90s and 100s Fahrenheit are the norm, with 110–115° for the hotter periods. Nighttime temperatures typically drop into the 80s in the city, and upper 70s outside of town. Winter is much more pleasant. Expect highs in the 60s or low 70s, with night-time temperatures in the 40s. Skies are mostly clear blue and cloudless. The sun's direct rays are strongly felt on clear days year round. Indeed, the biggest danger to visitors may be the intense sun and the summer temperatures. Use plenty of sunscreen (and wear a long-sleeved shirt and long pants). Sunglasses are essential year round, and a hat with a brim will make birding much more comfortable. Carry water with you at all times, and drink it: the "dry heat" will dehydrate you much sooner than expected. Rain is a rare event around Phoenix, with brief but heavy rains possible during the July and August monsoon; gentle rain is possible in winter.

Natural Hazards: Rattlesnakes are present throughout the metro area, especially in rocky hillside parks and in sandy washes. They are seldom seen and usually do not want a close encounter any more than you do. But if you are one of the few who meets up with a snake around Phoenix, show it due respect and count yourself fortunate to see a secretive native desert animal. Biting insects are virtually non-existent, so don't worry about insect repellent. But be alert for swarms of angry bees; Africanized bees make the local news each summer. If you think that you've stirred up a nest of them, the recommended action is to run as fast as possible directly away to the nearest closed shelter, such as your car. Dust storms are an uncommon but nasty possibility along open stretches of I-10; these storms can limit visibility to zero and have caused large traffic pile-ups that close I-10 for hours at a time. Avoid driving into such a storm.

Other Resources: The Maricopa Audubon Society meets at the Phoenix Zoo on the first Tuesday of the month, September through May. Call their recorded information line at (480) 829-8209 for details on upcoming meetings and field trips. The society also maintains a web site at *www.maricopaaudubon.org*. Recommended books include *Birds of Phoenix and Maricopa County Arizona* by Janet Witzeman, Salome Demaree, and Eleanor Radke (1997, Maricopa Audubon Society), *A Birder's Guide to Southeastern Arizona* by Richard Cachor Taylor (1999, ABA/Lane Birdfinding Guide Series), and *Finding Birds in Southeast Arizona* by William A. Davis and Stephen M. Russell (1999, Tucson Audubon Society).

THE BIRDS

The Phoenix region is home to many species of birds. The key to finding the more interesting ones is to identify and visit the proper habitats, including open desert, riparian, open water, and montane scrub and forest. The trips outlined below sample all of these major habitats.

Breeding-season specialties include Black-bellied Whistling-Duck, Common Black-Hawk, Zone-tailed Hawk, Black-chinned Hummingbird, Gray Vireo, Olive Warbler, and Rufous-crowned, Black-chinned, and Black-throated Sparrows. Winter brings large flocks of sparrows to grasslands and agricultural fields; these are mostly White-crowned, but also include Savannah, Brewer's, Sage, Vesper, and Lark; Lark Buntings may be present in large numbers or may be almost entirely absent. Other winter birds in the Phoenix

Le Conte's Thrasher
Dan Lane

area include more ducks than might be expected in a desert, numerous hawks, including Ferruginous, and occasional Mountain Plovers. A regional specialty is the variety of thrashers: Curve-billed, Bendire's, Le Conte's, and Crissal can be found year round, and Sage Thrashers occur in winter and early spring.

PAPAGO PARK
AND THE DESERT BOTANICAL GARDENS

Half day; year round

If you've never been birding in Arizona, or if you have only a very limited amount of time, then a visit to **Papago Park** and the **Desert Botanical Gardens** provides a chance to see many of the common desert birds while also providing an introduction to desert plants. The Gardens are located off Galvin Parkway, between Mill and McDowell Streets, next to the Phoenix Zoo. Hours are 8:00AM to 8:00PM, October through April; 7:00AM to 8:00PM, May through September (closed Christmas Day); (480) 941-1217. There is an admission charge of $7.50 per adult, with discounts for seniors and children. This is one of the few places to which taxi service from Sky Harbor Airport would be reasonable; it's a mere 15 minutes away. A non-birding companion should enjoy the plants. Paved and dirt walks let the visitor stroll about. Resident birds include Harris's Hawk, Gambel's Quail, Inca Dove, Anna's Hummingbird, Gila and Ladder-backed Woodpeckers, Gilded Flicker (if you don't see one around the parking lot, walk the Desert Peoples' Trail), Verdin, Cactus Wren, Black-tailed Gnatcatcher, Curve-billed Thrasher, Abert's Towhee, and occasionally Loggerhead Shrike. Black-chinned Hummingbird and Hooded Oriole are possible March through August; White-winged Dove is common from April through August. Lesser Nighthawks are active at dusk from April through September, and Elf Owls nest in Saguaro cavities around the parking lot. Phainopeplas are found October through May, while Costa's Hummingbirds are most often seen November through May. Look in the large trees near the Archer House for migrant warblers and winter vagrants.

The Phoenix Zoo property also can be good for migrant and wintering passerines, and should be checked for Bendire's Thrasher and Bronzed Cowbird.

BOYCE-THOMPSON ARBORETUM AND OAK FLAT CAMPGROUND

Half to full day; year round

The **Boyce-Thompson Arboretum** is located about 50 miles east of the I-10/US-60 junction along Highway 60, 3 miles west of Superior. Allow 60 minutes for the drive. Hours are 8:00AM to 5:00PM daily except Christmas; there is a $6.00 admission fee. The Arboretum is a migrant trap in spring and fall, an escape from the brutal heat of metro Phoenix in summer, and a place to see some interesting wintering birds. With lush woods along a stream that has some water most of the year, it offers opportunities for seeing both desert and non-desert birds. Watch for Harris's Hawks on utility poles along US-60 around Apache Junction and near the turn-off to Queen Valley. Get a trail map at the entrance, make your first stop at the demonstration garden and picnic area, and then follow the main trail along the creek. Loop up the hill and visit man-made Ayers Lake, and return to the entrance past the cactus garden.

Expected birds year round include Pied-billed Grebe, White-winged Dove (near the houses by the entrance in winter), Inca Dove, Anna's Hummingbird, Gila Woodpecker, Gilded Flicker (around Saguaro Cacti), Common Raven, Black Phoebe, Verdin, Cactus, Rock, Canyon, and Bewick's Wrens, Curve-billed Thrasher, Phainopepla, Northern Cardinal, Canyon and Abert's Towhees, Rufous-crowned Sparrow, and Lesser Goldfinch. In winter, expect Ring-necked Duck, Sora, "Red-shafted" Northern Flicker, Red-naped Sapsucker, Say's Phoebe, White-breasted Nuthatch, Hermit Thrush, "Audubon's" Yellow-rumped Warbler, Green-tailed and Spotted Towhees, and "Oregon," "Pink-sided," and "Gray-headed" forms of Dark-eyed Junco.

Migrants can include almost anything; expect most of the western *Empidonax* flycatchers, Plumbeous and Cassin's Vireos, and Orange-crowned, Black-throated Gray, and Townsend's Warblers. In summer there are Black-chinned Hummingbirds, Bell's Vireos, Lucy's Warblers, and Yellow-breasted Chats, and Hooded Oriole. Uncommon to rare birds include Zone-tailed Hawk (March to September), Williamson's Sapsucker (winter), Rufous-backed Robin (almost annual in winter, possible wherever shrubs or trees have fruit), White-throated Sparrow (winter), and "Slate-colored" Fox Sparrow (winter). A fair number of eastern vagrants have occurred over the years, mostly in fall and winter.

A good way to spend some more time birding in this area is to continue east on US-60 to **Oak Flat Campground**, about 4 miles east of Superior. Look for a turn on the south side of the road just after it levels out from the scenic drive up the canyon and through the tunnel. The change in elevation from the arboretum brings different species. Acorn Woodpecker, Juniper Titmouse, Western Bluebird, Crissal Thrasher, and Canyon Towhee can be found year round. In some winters there are Lewis's Woodpeckers, Western Scrub-Jays, and "Slate-colored" Fox Sparrows. Look for Scott's Oriole from May through September. Gray Vireos are sometimes found nesting on the hillside past the campground.

BUCKEYE THRASHER SPOT AND ESTRELLA MOUNTAIN REGIONAL PARK
Half day; best in winter and early spring

The desert west of **Buckeye** is good for finding Crissal, Bendire's, and Le Conte's Thrashers, Black-tailed Gnatcatcher, and wintering Sage, Black-throated, and Brewer's Sparrows. If possible, visit early in the morning when the thrashers are more likely to perch in the scattered trees and larger bushes. The Le Conte's are most likely to be heard singing from late January through March.

Take I-10 west from Phoenix to Exit 112 for Highway 85. Go south about 3.8 miles to Baseline Road. Go west (right) on Baseline for 8.5 miles until it reaches a T-intersection with Salome Highway. Park near this intersection. Look for Le Conte's Thrashers anywhere in this area; the west and northeast sides are usually best. Crissal Thrashers favor the washes where vegetation is denser. Scoping is the best approach. As an added bonus, Sage Thrasher is a migrant in the area from late January through March.

Estrella Mountain Regional Park makes a convenient stop on the return trip to metro Phoenix. Take Exit 126 from I-10 and follow the Estrella Parkway south about 5 miles. Turn left after crossing the bridge, then right to enter the park, where there is a modest fee. The mesquites around the picnic area should be checked for wintering Gray Flycatchers. Gilded Flickers are resident. Look throughout the area for common species such as Gambel's Quail, Greater Roadrunner, Ladder-backed Woodpecker, and Curve-billed Thrasher. Also check the riparian habitat along the river as time permits.

GRANITE REEF DAM AND SALT RIVER ACCESS
Half day; spring and fall

For spring and fall migrants, try the area east of Phoenix along the **Salt River**. Take US-60 east from I-10 about 16 miles to the Power Road exit (#188). Go north about 8 miles until the road curves east along the Salt River. Here, Power Road becomes the Bush Highway, which connects with Highway 87 a few miles farther east. Check the **Granite Reef Dam Recreation Area** picnic area and use the fishermen's trails to the cottonwood area (to the left of the parking area, toward the dam). The next picnic area, also on the left, is Phon D. Sutton. Still farther, again on the left, is Coon Bluff. Granite

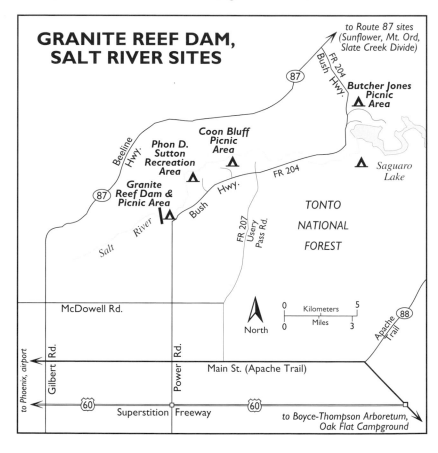

Reef and the area beyond Coon Bluff are the two best spots to view the desert-nesting Bald Eagles that often visit this part of the Salt River. Ospreys are also seen in this area. Another spot to check is the Butcher Jones Picnic Area (fee area) on the north side of Saguaro Lake, farther east along the Bush Highway. All of these spots are extremely popular with picnickers and fishermen, so plan to visit as early in the day as possible, or go during the middle of the week. Avoid the area entirely on popular holiday weekends when crowds of river-rafters invade the area.

Nesting birds found along this stretch of the Salt River include Gila and Ladder-backed Woodpeckers, Black Phoebe, Vermilion Flycatcher, Bewick's Wren, Black-tailed Gnatcatcher, Phainopepla, Lucy's and Yellow Warblers, and Hooded and Bullock's Orioles. Also look for Harris's Hawk, Ash-throated Flycatcher, Loggerhead Shrike, Canyon Wren, and Black-headed Grosbeak. Wintering birds may include Red-naped Sapsucker, Gray Fly-catcher, and both Blue-gray and Black-tailed Gnatcatchers.

ROUTE 87

Full day; spring and summer

There are a number of good birding spots located along the **Beeline Highway (Route 87)**, which runs northeast toward Payson. Reach the Beeline Highway from the I-10/US-60 junction by following US-60 east to the Country Club Drive Exit (#179) in Mesa. Follow this north; it soon becomes Route 87. Or from the Granite Reef birding spots discussed above, continue east on the Bush Highway until it joins Route 87. Traffic along this route is heavy, especially on summer weekends, but a recently completed highway project has improved matters.

Sunflower is a tiny community along Highway 87, about 50 miles from the I-10/US-60 junction. Allow an hour to reach this area on busy weekends in the summer. Common Black-Hawk has nested right along Sycamore Creek here in May and June since 1992. The road realignment has isolated a section of the old highway from the heavy traffic flow and saved the nest. Look for a left turn near mile marker 218. After crossing the southbound lanes of the new highway you will be on a now-quiet section of the old road, with the creek bed on your right. At 0.8 mile from the turn-off look for the nest in the line of trees between the road and the creek on the right. Look for a pull-out nearby that does not block access to any private property; unfortunately, the ranches along this section of old highway seem ready for imminent subdivision for new houses. Do not approach the nest or otherwise stress the nesting birds. The old road rejoins the new road in several miles. There are many pull-outs and good birding all along this section, so stop anywhere that seems birdy. Look for nesting Cassin's Kingbird, Summer Tanager, Blue Grosbeak, Spotted Towhee, and Lesser Goldfinch.

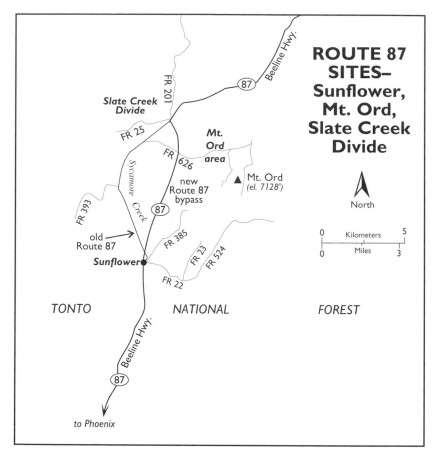

ROUTE 87 SITES– Sunflower, Mt. Ord, Slate Creek Divide

North

Kilometers 0 — 5

Miles 0 — 3

Beeline Hwy.

FR 201

87

Slate Creek Divide

FR 25

Mt. Ord area

FR 626

Sycamore Creek

new Route 87 bypass

Mt. Ord (el. 7128')

87

FR 393

old Route 87

Sunflower

FR 385

FR 23

FR 524

FR 22

TONTO   NATIONAL   FOREST

Beeline Hwy.

87

to Phoenix

Continue on the old road 0.8 mile past mile marker 223, where another unmarked road leads off to the left. This road becomes graded dirt in a short distance, and in 1.3 miles leads to the junction of Forest Roads 25 and 201. This area is known to local birders as **Slate Creek Divide**. Take the road to the right (FR-201) up the steep grade (high-clearance vehicle recommended) and look for a cattle-pen off to the left (0.6 mile). The slope to the left of FR-201 and below the cattle-pen is a good place to find Gray Vireo. Also look for nesting Rufous-crowned and Black-chinned Sparrows here. Crissal Thrasher is also in this area, but harder to find. For the adventuresome birder with the proper vehicle, traveling another six or so miles may produce nesting Spotted Owl, Whip-poor-will, Mountain Chickadee, and Red-faced Warbler. *Note that road work continues along the graded dirt road at the time this is being written, so there could be more changes soon in this area.*

Return to old Route 87 (about 1.9 miles from the cattle-pen) and turn left. In 1.2 miles this connects to the new Route 87. Directly across the divided highway is the start of FR-626, 6.1 miles of rough and winding dirt road that leads to microwave and fire towers at the top of Mount Ord. As you head up FR-626, scan the skies for Zone-tailed Hawk, which could occur anywhere along the route up or down. This rough road may require up to 30–45 minutes of driving to reach the top (longer with birding stops along the way). A high-clearance vehicle is recommended, but not strictly necessary if you drive with care.

Mount Ord is located on the Maricopa County line at an elevation of 7,000 feet. At lower elevations (before reaching the trees) look for Gray Vireo, Rufous-crowned Sparrow, Black-chinned Sparrow, and Scott's Oriole. At 2.9 miles another dirt road branches off FR-626 on the right. Park opposite this road and walk the road through the pine woods looking for Bushtit, Pygmy Nuthatch, Western Bluebird, Virginia's, Black-throated Gray, and Grace's Warblers, Painted Redstart, Olive Warbler, Hepatic Tanager, and other high-elevation birds. A water-trough for cattle and wildlife is on the hillside of this unmarked road not far from the start.

Return to your car and drive another 3.2 miles up FR-626 to a gate and park. Do not drive past the gate even if it is open. Walk up toward the top; when the road splits, choose either direction, since both roads join at the top under the tower. Look for the high-elevation birds you may have missed earlier, plus Band-tailed Pigeon and Acorn Woodpecker. On your return to your car, walk down whichever road you didn't climb earlier.

On the drive back down to Route 87 there is another road that splits off from FR-626 at 1.9 miles from the locked gate; stay left for FR-626 and the way back to the main road.

ACKNOWLEDGMENTS

I would not have been able to prepare this material without the assistance of the many expert birders of the Phoenix area. I thank Janet Witzeman, who has done a more thorough job for the area in *Birds of Phoenix and Maricopa County, Arizona*. The extensive bar-charts in Janet's guide should be consulted for precise data on species occurrence in the area. I especially wish to thank Steve Ganley for answering all my questions and providing other input to this chapter.

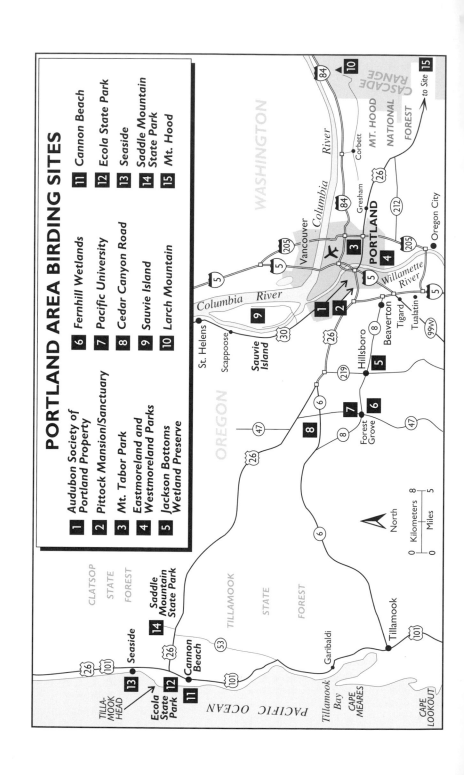

PORTLAND AREA BIRDING SITES

1 Audubon Society of Portland Property
2 Pittock Mansion/Sanctuary
3 Mt. Tabor Park
4 Eastmoreland and Westmoreland Parks
5 Jackson Bottoms Wetland Preserve
6 Fernhill Wetlands
7 Pacific University
8 Cedar Canyon Road
9 Sauvie Island
10 Larch Mountain
11 Cannon Beach
12 Ecola State Park
13 Seaside
14 Saddle Mountain State Park
15 Mt. Hood

PORTLAND, OREGON

Jeff Gilligan and Owen Schmidt

The Willamette and Columbia Rivers converge at Portland, Oregon, at the north end of the Willamette Valley and at the west end of the Columbia River Gorge. With the Pacific Ocean about an hour-and-a-half to the west and the Cascade Mountains and the high desert two hours or so to the east, Portland offers a wide variety of habitats not requiring an overnight stay away from the city.

ESSENTIAL INFORMATION

Getting Around: Portland has a well-developed bus and light-rail system, but birders will need a car for nearly all recommended locations. Portland traffic can be as bad as it gets during peak hours on all major routes in all directions. Try to avoid travel Into the city from 7:00–9:00AM and out of the city from 4:00–7:00PM. Listen to traffic reports on local radio stations.

Climate: The temperate climate here is a product of low elevation and the moderating influence of the Pacific Ocean, which is only about 75 miles to the west. This climate supports both spruce trees and the hardiest species of palms. Native forests are dominated by evergreens such as Douglas-fir and Western Redcedar, and in riparian areas by willows, Oregon Ash, and Black Cottonwood. Snow is rare, but rain is frequent from November through April, and neither May nor June is typically anything approaching arid. A dry season usually starts soon after 4 July and continues into late September or October. Summer days can occasionally reach into the 90s Fahrenheit, whereas summer nights are usually cool and the humidity low. Mid-winter temperatures are typically in the 40s for highs and high 30s for lows.

Natural Hazards: Mosquitoes can be a problem on Sauvie Island in spring and early summer, as well as at higher elevations in the Cascades in early summer. Ticks are a problem only on the eastern slope of the Cascade Mountains in spring.

Safety: None of the areas mentioned is considered dangerous, but we recommend against leaving valuables in a vehicle when it is not occupied.

Other Resources: The Rare Bird Alert is maintained by the Audubon Society of Portland at (503) 292-0661. Oregon Field Ornithologists maintains a web site with a current checklist of Oregon birds and useful links at *www. oregonbirds.org*. There are two birding guides for Oregon: *The Birder's Guide to Oregon* by Joseph E. Evanich, Jr. (1990, Portland Audubon Society), and *Wild in the City* by Michael C. Houck and M. J. Cody, editors (2000, Oregon Historical Society). Another useful title is *Birds of Oregon: Status and Distribution* by Jeff Gilligan et al. (1994, Cinclus Publications). The Audubon Society of Portland maintains a well-stocked bookstore and nature shop at Audubon House, 5151 N.W. Cornell Road, (503) 292-9453. Staff at the bookstore, which is open seven days a week, can provide helpful advice or refer the traveling birder to members of the active local birding community. Local birders typically gather at Audubon House at 7:30PM the first Tuesday of each month. Visiting birders with or without slides or video are always welcome.

THE BIRDS

Species commonly found in or very near Portland that are of particular interest to birders visiting the Pacific Northwest include Blue Grouse, Mountain Quail, Band-tailed Pigeon (summer = S), Western Screech-Owl, Northern Pygmy-Owl, Vaux's Swift (S), Anna's Hummingbird, Rufous Hummingbird (S), Red-breasted Sapsucker, Olive-sided Flycatcher (S), Western Wood-Pewee (S), Hammond's Flycatcher (S), Pacific-slope Flycatcher (S), Cassin's Vireo (S), Hutton's Vireo, Violet-green Swallow (S), Steller's Jay, Western Scrub-Jay, Chestnut-backed Chickadee, Bushtit, American Dipper, Western Bluebird, Townsend's Solitaire, Varied Thrush, Black-throated Gray, Hermit, and MacGillivray's Warblers (all S), Townsend's Warbler (winter), Western Tanager (S), Black-headed Grosbeak (S), Lazuli Bunting (S), Spotted Towhee, Golden-crowned Sparrow (winter), Western Meadowlark, Brewer's Blackbird, Bullock's Oriole (S), and Evening Grosbeak (mainly in spring). The nearby montane and marine habitats add substantially to this list.

AUDUBON SOCIETY OF PORTLAND PROPERTY

Several hours; year round, best in spring

The **Audubon Society of Portland** has a small forested reserve near downtown Portland adjacent to the large Forest Park. The feeders at Audubon House are great for close-up views of Band-tailed Pigeon, Steller's Jay, Black-capped and Chestnut-backed Chickadees, Varied Thrush (winter), Black-headed Grosbeak, Spotted Towhee, and Evening Grosbeak. Owls seen here include Western Screech-, Northern Pygmy-, Barred, and Northern Saw-whet. To reach **Audubon House**, drive west on Lovejoy Avenue from downtown Portland. At 27th Lovejoy becomes Cornell Road and starts up

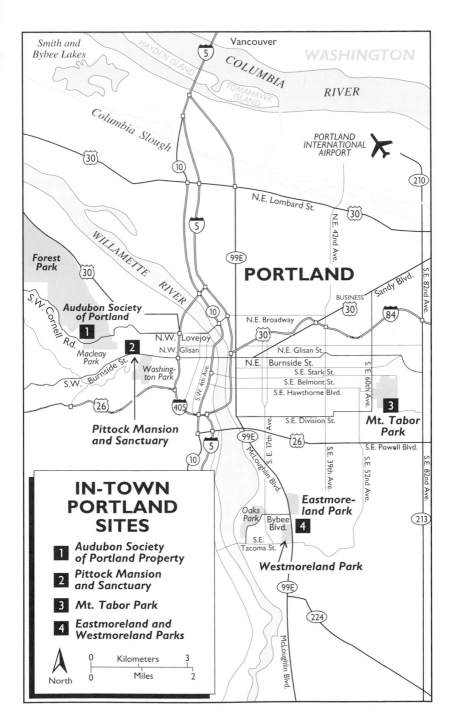

Smith and
Bybee Lakes

WASHINGTON

COLUMBIA

RIVER

HAYDEN ISLAND

TOMAHAWK
ISLAND

Vancouver

5

Columbia Slough

30

10

5

WILLAMETTE RIVER

PORTLAND
INTERNATIONAL
AIRPORT

210

N.E. Lombard St.

N.E. 42nd Ave.

30

99E

PORTLAND

BUSINESS
30

Sandy Blvd.

S.E. 82nd Ave.

84

Forest
Park

30

Audubon Society
of Portland

1

N.E. Broadway

N.E. Glisan St.

N.E. 60th Ave.

S.W. Cornell Rd.

N.W. Lovejoy

N.W. Glisan

30

N.E. Burnside St.

2

Macleay
Park

S.W. Burnside St.

Washing-
ton Park

S.W. 4th Ave.

S.E. Stark St.

S.E. Belmont St.

S.E. Hawthorne Blvd.

3

26

405

**Pittock Mansion
and Sanctuary**

S.E. Division St.

**Mt. Tabor
Park**

5

99E

26

S.E. 39th Ave.

S.E. 52nd Ave.

S.E. Powell Blvd.

S.E. 82nd Ave.

10

McLoughlin Blvd.

S.E. 17th Ave.

213

**IN-TOWN
PORTLAND
SITES**

Oaks
Park

Bybee
Blvd.

4

**Eastmore-
land Park**

S.E.
Tacoma St.

Westmoreland Park

1 Audubon Society
of Portland Property

2 Pittock Mansion
and Sanctuary

3 Mt. Tabor Park

4 Eastmoreland and
Westmoreland Parks

99E

224

McLoughlin Blvd.

North

0   Kilometers   3

0   Miles   2

into the west hills. At one point, a sharp right is required as one goes uphill. Next pass through two tunnels in the West Hills of Portland and watch for signs on the right.

PITTOCK MANSION
AND PITTOCK SANCTUARY
Several hours; spring

Pittock Mansion and its grounds are located not far from Portland Audubon. A visit during spring migration often is productive for migrants. As elsewhere in Portland, the hardy Anna's Hummingbird can be found here in small numbers all year. To reach Pittock Mansion, drive west on West Burnside up into the West Hills and watch for signs to Pittock Mansion. Turn right and again follow the signs through the labyrinth of streets to the mansion. Park and walk the grounds of the mansion for sometimes superb panoramic views of the city and surrounding snow-capped peaks. Pick up a trail map at the trailhead parking lot.

MT. TABOR PARK
Several hours; spring

Mt. Tabor Park is an island of large second-growth trees surrounded by the city. This small, extinct volcano is sometimes very productive on spring mornings between about 20 April and 10 May. Mt. Tabor Park sits between Stark and Division Streets in southeast Portland. The best access is on the west side, off S.E. 60th Avenue. Turn east from 60th onto S.E. Salmon Street and drive a few short blocks to park along the street near the park. The northeast access is from S.E. 69th Avenue. Follow the switchbacks uphill from the border of the park about 0.4 mile to a parking lot. This access is nearer the peak, which is another half-mile on foot. It may be safer to park anonymously in the neighborhood and walk into the park; do not leave valuables in your car.

EASTMORELAND
AND WESTMORELAND PARKS
Several hours; winter

Both Eastmoreland Park and Westmoreland Park in southeast Portland host a variety of wintering waterfowl and gulls for close inspection, often including Eurasian Wigeon and Mew, California, Thayer's, and Glaucous-winged Gulls. Westmoreland is accessible from Highway 99E (McLoughlin Boulevard). Eastmoreland is accessible from S.E. Bybee.

FERNHILL WETLANDS, JACKSON BOTTOMS, PACIFIC UNIVERSITY CAMPUS, CEDAR CANYON ROAD
Half day; year round

These areas are located in western Washington County near Oregon's so-called Silicon Forest. **Jackson Bottoms Wetland Preserve** is a restored wetland habitat near Hillsboro along the Tualatin River. The first of two access spots is 0.3 mile south of downtown Hillsboro on Highway 219, where there is a small parking lot with a covered viewing area. A second parking lot is 0.8 mile farther south and provides access to walking trails into the Reserve as well as a soon-to-be-built nature center. This area is marked with signs for a Water Quality Laboratory and Wetlands Hiking Area. Both areas are wheelchair-accessible. Birds include various species of waterfowl in winter, and in summer may include Wood Duck and Cinnamon and Blue-winged Teal. Depending on water levels, shorebird habitat may be accessible along the trails. Wintering sparrows include "Sooty" Fox, Lincoln's, Swamp (rare), Golden-crowned, White-crowned, and White-throated (rare).

The **Fernhill Wetlands** are a short distance west of Hillsboro just southeast of Forest Grove. The area is wheelchair-accessible. The wetlands are a combination of sewage-treatment ponds that have been converted to a wildlife area, and marshes created as a wetland-mitigation bank. Fernhill Lake is adjacent to the parking area. Its open water provides

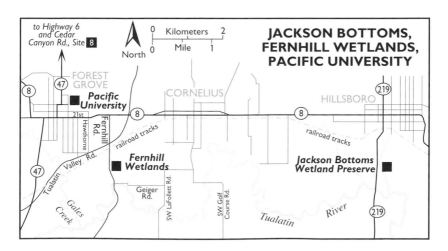

habitat for grebes, geese, ducks, and occasional loons. Cattail Marsh is over the berm. American Bittern, Virginia Rail, Sora, American Coot, Marsh Wren, and Yellow-headed Blackbirds are regular. Take Highway 8 west toward Forest Grove, turn left on Highway 47-Bypass, after about a half-mile turn left on Fernhill Road, and then after 0.2 mile south, cross the railroad tracks and turn left into a parking lot at the old sewage-treatment plant. A grid of more than two miles of berms with trails makes most parts of Fernhill Wetlands accessible.

Eagle's Perch Pond is next; it can be viewed from your car at the intersection of Fernhill Road and Geiger Road. A Bald Eagle nest has been viewable from the wetlands for several years. Scan the trees along the Tualatin River. The eagles often perch on the snags in the marshes behind Fernhill Lake. Shorebird habitat is present when water levels are low.

Oregon White Oaks on the campus of **Pacific University** in nearby Forest Grove support resident Acorn Woodpeckers and "Slender-billed" White-breasted Nuthatches (*Sitta carolinensis aculeata*). Take Highway 8 (Pacific Avenue in Forest Grove) west to College Way in the center of Forest Grove, turn north on College Way, and the campus is immediately on the right. Park along College Way or just to the west in the residential section around 21st Avenue or University Avenue.

Cedar Canyon Road** provides excellent access to marsh birds in early spring when displaying American Bitterns are visible from the road. To reach this area go west on Highway 6 to about 5.8 miles west of the intersection with Highway 26, turn right on Cedar Canyon Road, and keep right at the first turn. The best viewing is at 1.2 miles, around the bridge where N.W. Killin Road "Ts" to the left.

SAUVIE ISLAND
Half day; year round

Sauvie Island** is a large alluvial island at the confluence of the Willamette and Columbia Rivers. Although the refuge on the island maintained by the state of Oregon is largely off-limits to birders from early October into mid-April, the island is worth visiting at any season.

A vehicle parked at any of the Oregon Fish and Wildlife Department parking areas must have a day or annual parking permit, which can be purchased at the store on Sauvie Island near the island end of the entrance bridge off Highway 30. Sauvie Island is also the last stop for Tri-Met bus-line #17. Maps to the island are available at the Wildlife Management Area Headquarters on Sauvie Island Road a short distance past its intersection with Reeder Road.

In spring and fall hundreds of Sandhill Cranes use the island as a stopover; smaller numbers winter locally as well. Raptor-watching is often good; several dozen Bald Eagles winter on the island. Geese and ducks are numerous in migration and winter. Tundra Swans are also common winterers. Although Canada Geese are most common, Snow Geese also winter on the island, but Greater White-fronted Geese are mostly transients.

Beyond the headquarters on Sauvie Island Road, look for a small parking area for Virginia Lake. A trail leads to the grassy, seasonally-wet lake, but the woods around it are more interesting. Red-eyed Vireos nesting here are near the western edge of their range. Red-breasted Sapsucker, Pileated Woodpecker, Willow Flycatcher, and Bullock's Oriole are regular.

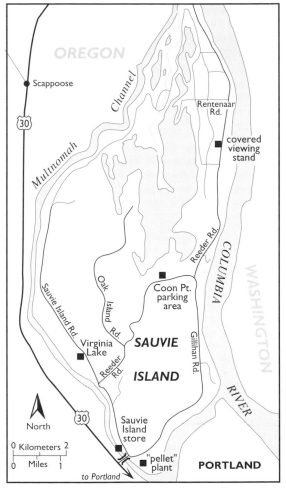

Return to the intersection of Sauvie Island Road and Reeder Road and turn left onto Reeder Road. Oak Island Road leads to Oak Island (now permanently connected to Sauvie Island). When open to the public, its oak forest is good for landbirds, including Bullock's Oriole. Return to Reeder Road and turn left to the Coon Point parking area. An overlook from the dike provides viewing possibilities for waterfowl and Bald Eagles. Shorebirds are possible when water levels are down.

Continue on Reeder Road past the intersection with Gillihan Road until you reach another parking area with a covered viewing stand.

Depending on water levels, waterfowl and raptors can be common here. Farther on Reeder Road, turn left at the gravel Rentenaar Road. This road can be excellent for wintering sparrows as well as for viewing opportunities for waterfowl and raptors. Eurasian Wigeon and "Eurasian" Green-winged Teal (very rare) are possible in winter here, as elsewhere on the island. Birders are welcome to walk Rentenaar Road year round, but be sure to stay on the road during the closed season (early October to mid-April).

R eturn to the intersection of Reeder Road and Gillihan Road and head south. Where Gillihan reaches its southmost point, there is a gravel road and a manufacturing facility where pellets are made for domestic fowl (locally known as the "pellet plant"). This area often attracts large numbers of gulls and some waterfowl between late fall and early spring. If you visit at such times, the gull activity should be apparent. You might also consider starting your Sauvie Island day at this location, which is very close to the entrance bridge, because the gulls come and go during the day. Multiple visits are suggested. The flock in winter usually has Ring-billed, California, Herring, Thayer's, Glaucous-winged, and hybrids of that species and the more coastal Western Gulls. Western and Glaucous Gulls often can be seen. In several recent winters one or more Slaty-backed Gulls have also joined the flock. Mew Gulls are often seen in fields away from the above-named ruffians.

LARCH MOUNTAIN

Half day; late spring to early fall

L ocated in the Cascade Mountains about an hour east of Portland, 4,055-foot **Larch Mountain** offers the nearest access to some of the species typical of the Cascades. Hermit Warblers nest at higher elevation, whereas Black-throated Grays predominate lower down. Other summer species include Blue and Ruffed Grouse (resident), Northern Pygmy- and Northern Saw-whet Owls (resident), Red-breasted Sapsucker, Olive-sided, Hammond's, and Pacific-slope Flycatchers, Gray Jay (at the picnic area on top), Chestnut-backed Chickadee, Townsend's Solitaire, Hermit Thrush, Varied Thrush, MacGillivray's Warbler, Western Tanager, Black-headed Grosbeak, Lazuli Bunting, and Evening Grosbeak. Try taping out Mountain Quail in spring in brushy areas. (That method is your best hope of seeing the species in the Coast Range as well, unless you have many hours to spend driving logging roads.) On a clear day, the view from the top of Larch Mountain to Mt. St. Helens and Mt. Hood is spectacular.

To reach Larch Mountain, take I-84 east from downtown Portland for approximately 57 miles. Take Exit 22, turn right on Corbett Hill Road, drive up this winding road to near the top, and take a left on East Crown Point Highway. The unmarked town of Corbett is at this intersection. Follow

Crown Point Highway 1.9 miles to a fork, take the right fork, and proceed about 14 miles to the top of Larch Mountain. Taking a left at the fork would yield a scenic tour of the Columbia River Gorge down to Multnomah Falls, Oregon's most-visited attraction and an excellent location for American Dipper.

On the way to Larch Mountain, you might want to check out a spot around the Sandy River Delta between I-84 and the Columbia River, as well as the Sandy River itself. Take the exit at the Sandy River, about 17 miles from downtown Portland. Park on either side of the freeway. This spot is being reclaimed as a natural area. The birding area is on the north side of the interstate, where a trail leads into the riparian forest. Summering species include Willow Flycatcher, Warbling Vireo, Red-eyed Vireo, Yellow Warbler, Lazuli Bunting, Bullock's Oriole, and other riparian species.

CANNON BEACH, SEASIDE, ECOLA STATE PARK

Full day; year round

Located approximately 75 miles west of Portland, **Cannon Beach** and nearby sites are the locations closest to Portland for seabirds. In Cannon Beach the great sea-stack called Haystack Rock (one of at least three along the Oregon coast by that name) hosts a variety of nesting seabirds. Most sought-after are the Tufted Puffins that nest in burrows on the grassy slopes from early April into late July. Look for them perched outside the burrows or flying to and from the ocean. Pelagic Cormorants and Pigeon Guillemots nest on the ledges of the sheer cliffs, whereas Brandt's Cormorants and Common Murres use the more-gentle slopes higher up. Western Gulls (of the lighter-mantled northern subspecies) are ubiquitous. The lower rocky areas support a pair or two of Black Oystercatchers, and, from fall into spring, may also have Black Turnstones, Surfbirds, and Rock Sandpipers (rare). Wandering Tattlers use these rocky habitats during both migrations.

The water around the rock and its associated smaller rocks often host Harlequin Ducks, which may be present year round. Check low-lying rocks for roosting birds. At times all three scoter species can be seen. Bald Eagles and Peregrine Falcons frequent the area when nesting seabirds are present.

Nearby **Ecola State Park** on Tillamook Head provides similar habitat for many of the same seabird species. The remnant old-growth coastal forest within the park is good habitat for nesting Northern Pygmy-Owl, Pileated Woodpecker, Olive-sided and Pacific-slope Flycatchers, Chestnut-backed Chickadee, Swainson's and Varied Thrushes, Hutton's Vireo, and Orange-crowned, Townsend's (except summer), Hermit, and Wilson's Warblers. Check areas of thick Salal bushes for Wrentits, which reach their northern range limit not far north of here on the south bank of the Columbia River. The Indian Beach area is especially good for Black Oystercatchers and other rock-loving shorebirds.

The town of **Seaside** is just north of Tillamook Head. It is the most honky-tonk of any Oregon coastal town, but if you are in the area, it may be worth taking a quick look on the south edge of town at **"The Cove,"** as it is known to the locals. Loons, Western Grebes, scoters, and rock-loving shorebirds are all possible. The small estuary of the Necanicum River can be accessed from a stairway across the street from the high school. Various shorebirds, gulls, and Caspian Terns are among the expected species.

East of Seaside and just north of Highway 26 is **Saddle Mountain State Park**. The park itself and the area around the road leading to it support many of the species mentioned for Ecola State Park. Add the possibilities of Blue Grouse (often heard calling from the evergreens in spring) and Gray Jays (which often are present at the picnic area).

To reach these coastal sites, take any of the several exits off Highway 101 marked for **Cannon Beach**. Haystack Rock is obvious from downtown Cannon Beach. The northernmost exit from Highway 101 leads directly to **Ecola State Park**. To get to The Cove in **Seaside**, turn west off Highway 101 onto Avenue U, take the first left onto Edgewood, which soon turns into Ocean Vista. To bird the Necanicum River estuary on the north side of Seaside, return to Highway 101, head north, and turn left onto 24th Avenue just before the Necanicum River bridge. After crossing the river,

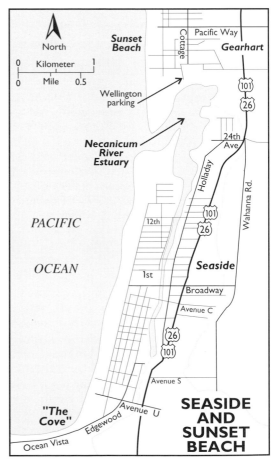

SEASIDE AND SUNSET BEACH

turn left again onto Holladay. The Necanicum River estuary overlook is about a half-mile ahead on the right, across from the high school.

For another access to the Necanicum River estuary, return to Highway 101 north to Gearhart and turn west onto Pacific Way. Turn left onto Cottage, continue to the T-intersection, turn right, and then immediately left onto Wellington. Park and walk the short distance to the estuary.

To check for sandpipers and gulls (and sometimes seabirds) on **Sunset Beach**, return to Cottage, cross Pacific Way, and continue for approximately a quarter-mile to where you can turn left and drive onto Sunset Beach. This beach extends 10 miles north from here and is, in fact, considered a public road in Oregon. Beware the loose sand and the many hazards of driving a car along an ocean beach.

On your return to Portland, you will reach the access to Saddle Mountain State Park off Highway 26 about 9 miles east of its junction with Highway 101.

MT. HOOD

Full day; spring, summer, fall

Oregon's highest peak is about 1.5 hours east of Portland off Highway 26. A trip to **Timberline Lodge** and the forests below it adds possibilities that are not afforded at Larch Mountain. Follow the signs left off Highway 26 at the crest of the Cascades up to Timberline Lodge. Gray Jay, Clark's Nutcracker, Mountain Chickadee, and Mountain Bluebird are regular around the lodge. Gray-crowned Rosy-Finches nest above timberline and are sometimes seen at or near the lodge. The boreal-like forests below have both Three-toed and Black-backed Woodpeckers, as well as Williamson's Sapsucker (usually on the mountain's eastern flanks). Calliope Hummingbird and Cassin's Finch are also possible farther down the east side of the mountain, and other species await the birder on the Cascades' east side, such as Red-naped Sapsucker, Pygmy Nuthatch, and Green-tailed Towhee.

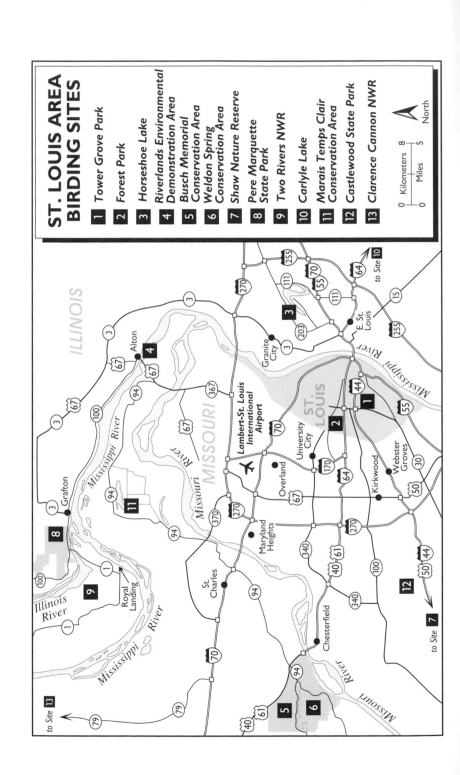

ST. LOUIS, MISSOURI

Bill Rowe and Randy Korotev

Situated halfway between Canada and the Gulf of Mexico, St. Louis has variably hot summers, variably cold winters, and long, mostly pleasant but unpredictable spring and fall seasons. The birdlife exemplifies a similar overlap between south and north, with (as random examples) a few nesting Mississippi Kites in summer and a few vacationing Glaucous and Thayer's Gulls in winter.

By local tradition, the St. Louis area extends fifty miles in all directions from the city limits. The Mississippi, Illinois, and Missouri Rivers converge here, serving as conduits for migrating waterfowl and other birds. The countryside varies from flat, open agricultural land to Ozark-border hills and streams, with a few large lakes, scattered remnants of marsh, and many tracts of forest, including riparian cottonwood/sycamore and upland oak/hickory. Native prairie is unfortunately missing except for prairie-restoration areas in parks and refuges. The City of St. Louis lies at the core of the region, surrounded on the Missouri side by the broad suburban band of St. Louis County (a separate political entity), which in turn is surrounded by peripheral counties that are now the hot-spots for population growth. Across the Mississippi River lies a large swath of Illinois, also developing apace. Good, diverse birding can be found on both sides in all seasons; about 370 species have been recorded here.

ESSENTIAL INFORMATION

Getting Around: Only the City of St. Louis has public transportation that would be useful to the visiting birder, and even then only to get to the two large city parks (see below). For the rest of the area a car is essential. On the other hand, the distance from the center to the best birding sites is not too great; a 30-to-60-minute drive will get you to most of them.

Safety: Birding any of the listed sites during daylight should not present safety problems. Some local birders prefer to have company when they visit Tower Grove Park, Forest Park, and the Horseshoe Lake area, but the likelihood of trouble is very low.

Natural Hazards: Mosquitoes, chiggers, and ticks are plentiful in warm weather. Poison-Ivy, the one hazardous plant, is common and must be recognized and avoided. Copperheads and Timber Rattlesnakes occur in some wooded areas but are retiring and are virtually never encountered.

Climate: To estimate clothing needs in any season, check the forecast for the coming week. Only the summer months are predictable (warm to hot). In any other season, the temperatures and precipitation are too varied to give any rules, except that winter averages fairly cold.

Other Considerations: All sites described are public. If you bird around private property, follow the ABA *Code of Birding Ethics*. The average landowner in rural Missouri or Illinois will not understand what you are doing.

Other Resources: The best resource is *Birds of the St. Louis Area: Where and When to Find Them* (1998, Webster Groves Nature Study Society; similar in format to ABA/Lane birdfinding guides). The most useful web sites are *www.wgnss.org*, Webster Groves Nature Study Society, and *www.stlouisaudubon.org*, St. Louis Audubon Society. Locally, the Tyson Nature Line at (314) 935-8432 reports the comings and goings of area birds without focusing exclusively on rarities. The Missouri Rare Bird Alert at (573) 445-9115 covers the entire state and often mentions St. Louis. In addition, the Audubon Society of Missouri web site *www.mobirds.org* contains a complete annotated checklist of Missouri birds. Authoritative but expensive are *Birds of Missouri* by Mark Robbins and David Easterla (1992, University of Missouri Press), and *The Birds of Illinois*, by H. David Bohlen (1989, Indiana University Press).

THE BIRDING YEAR

St. Louis's birding timetable is representative of the central Midwest. The first spring migrants are the waterfowl, beginning in late winter and peaking in March. Shorebirds start arriving in March (American Golden-Plover, Pectoral Sandpiper) and peak in late April and May, although luck with these birds varies with habitat conditions. Spring hawk migration is modest; the latest to arrive (mid-May) is the scarce but regular Mississippi Kite, nesting in well-wooded St. Louis County suburbs. Gull variety may still be good in early March but diminishes with warm weather, just as the terns begin to pass through. Passerine species that winter in the southern U.S. tend to return in March and April—kinglets, Brown Creepers, Hermit Thrushes, Yellow-rumped Warblers, and sparrows—along with some migrant breeding species such as Northern Parula and Yellow-throated Warbler. The main movement of Neotropical passerine migrants is concentrated between late April and mid-May, when the trees resound with Tennessee Warbler song, and the birder has a chance of seeing 35 other warblers, along with cuckoos, flycatchers, vireos, thrushes, tanagers, grosbeaks, and orioles. Late May brings the last waves of warblers, including Mourning and an occasional Connecticut, and the late flycatchers, such as Alder and Yellow-bellied.

Summer-resident passerines generally continue singing through the end of July, at least off and on, and many remain findable by sight or call-notes well into September. Wetlands, especially in Illinois, always have herons, whose numbers gradually increase into early fall. The southbound migration of adult shorebirds begins in early July; juveniles arrive in August, along with cormorants, Ospreys, terns, and migrant passerines.

Fall migration is more protracted and less concentrated but generally mirrors that of the spring, with peaks for warblers in September, sparrows in October, and waterfowl (along with loons and grebes) in November. More hawks come through, with the Broad-wing movement focused in late September and other species averaging later. American White Pelicans, which formerly were found only in fall, may now occur at any time and are seen in the thousands.

Much publicized in winter are the Bald Eagles that patrol the Illinois and Mississippi Rivers from November to March; over 100 in a day are possible if the weather has been cold. Icy conditions also increase the chances of seeing the rarer gulls, for which Riverlands and Carlyle Lake are the best bets. A fine winter day's birding can be had at most of the sites below; local Christmas Bird Counts typically tally between 55 and 85 species.

For information on finding the area's one unique species, the permanent resident and introduced Eurasian Tree Sparrow, see the side-bar.

EURASIAN TREE SPARROW

Released in 1870 at St. Louis, the Eurasian Tree Sparrow gained a foothold in North America that it has never lost. Currently, it is most common on the north and east sides of the St. Louis area, scarce or absent to the south and west, and spotty in the center. Of the major sites described in this book, three are good for the "ETS": Horseshoe Lake, Riverlands, and the Two Rivers National Wildlife Refuge. It cannot be expected at the others. The birds may be around residential areas, along with House Sparrows, or (especially in winter) in single-species flocks in hedgerows, brush, and dense weeds.

Within the city of St. Louis, the ETS is reliable in residential neighborhoods that lie just south of the west end of Forest Park, that is, just south of I-64/US-40 and east of McCausland Avenue, although the birds may move around from year to year. Within a 15-minute drive of the airport, they are found in Sunset Park (north St. Louis County) and in the vicinity of St. Stanislaus Park (northwest St. Louis County), both on local maps.

For precise, up-to-date directions to ETS locations, check the Webster Groves Nature Study Society web site, *www.wgnss.org*, and the St. Louis Audubon web site, *www.stlouisaudubon.org*.

TOWER GROVE
AND FOREST PARKS, MISSOURI
Half day; mainly spring and fall

Tower **Grove Park** and the **Kennedy Forest** of Forest Park, both in the city of St. Louis, are the two best migrant traps in the area. In April and May, and again from mid-August through October, both parks offer excellent opportunities to find migrant passerines. On a good day in early May, more than 20 species of warblers can be found in a few hours. The parks are also good for migrant hawks and resident owls (Eastern Screech-, Great Horned, and sometimes Barred).

Tower Grove Park is easier to bird, and preferable if you have only an hour. From either I-64 or I-44, proceed south on Kingshighway Boulevard. The northwest corner of the park (Kingshighway and Magnolia Avenue) is about one-half mile south of I-44. Turn left onto Magnolia and park on the right side of the street between one and two short blocks east of Kingshighway. Walk south across the park grounds a few hundred feet to the heart of the best birding area, the Gaddy Bird Garden. At the center of the Bird Garden thicket, the fountain (a bubbling rock) is a remarkable bird magnet. After birding the thicket, meander eastward as far as the horse stables. Another productive area is the "cypress tree circle," about halfway between the center of the park and the east entrance on Grand Avenue. At this writing, there are plans to build a bird-friendly pond near this site. Although birding is best in the morning, it can be fruitful any time of the day and can be combined with a trip to the Missouri Botanical Garden, immediately to the

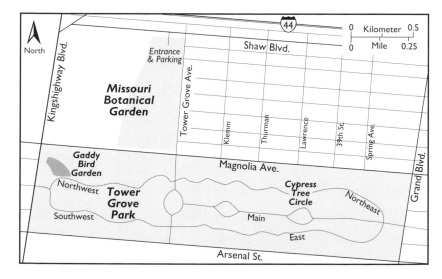

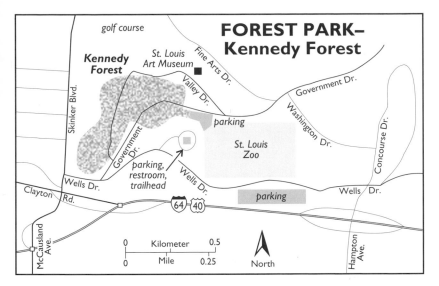

FOREST PARK–
Kennedy Forest

golf course

Kennedy
Forest

St. Louis
Art Museum

Fine Arts Dr.

Valley Dr.

Skinker Blvd.

Government Dr.

Washington Dr.

Concourse Dr.

parking

St. Louis
Zoo

Government Dr.

parking,
restroom,
trailhead

Wells Dr.

Wells Dr.

Clayton Rd.

Wells Dr.

parking

Wells Dr.

64 40

McCausland Ave.

0   Kilometer   0.5

0   Mile   0.25

North

Hampton Ave.

north of the park. Information about the park, with maps, can be found at *www.stlouis.missouri. org/parks/tower-grove/maps.html*.

The **John F. Kennedy Forest** lies in the southwest corner of Forest Park, immediately west of the St. Louis Zoo and south of the St. Louis Art Museum. From I-64, take the McCausland exit (eastbound) or the Clayton Road exit (westbound). From the intersection of Clayton (E-W) and Skinker/McCausland (N-S) at the southwest corner of the park (large Amoco sign), proceed north a very short distance on Skinker Boulevard and turn right into the park on Wells Drive. At the fork, go right (Wells Drive) to the official trailhead, or left (Government Drive) and park at one of the two well-marked points where the pedestrian trail crosses the road. On weekends, it's best to arrive before 10:00AM; after that, traffic can present a problem.

Kennedy Forest, unlike Tower Grove Park, is wild and unkempt. As a consequence, it's more of a challenge to bird, but 150 species of birds have been seen there. The best procedure is to follow the two-mile maintained trail, which crosses Government Drive and Valley Drive each twice, and detour occasionally on side trails. South of Government Drive, a portion of the trail is wheelchair-accessible (start at the trailhead). Be sure to check the old oaks that border the portion of the woods with dense understory, the savanna on the west edge of the woods, and the bird fountain, just south of the trailhead at the edge of the woods. Birding along Valley Drive can also be productive. Work is imminent, however, to remove the portion of Valley Drive that goes through the forest and to build some ponds in its place. A timetable for the spring passerine migration and a map of the Kennedy Forest are available at *www.levee.wustl.edu/~rlk/wgnss/nn99kf/*.

HORSESHOE LAKE, ILLINOIS

Half day; year round

Just across the Mississippi River from downtown St. Louis, **Horseshoe Lake** (not to be confused with the National Wildlife Refuge of the same name in southern Illinois) offers handy birding opportunities at all seasons. It is a reliable area for Little Blue Heron, Snowy Egret, Cattle Egret, and Black-crowned Night-Heron, for gulls and terns in season, for shorebirds when lake levels are low, and for raptors and passerines at all times. Eurasian Tree Sparrows are common.

Both the west and east sides, accessed separately, are worth checking. For the west side, cross the bridge just south of the Arch downtown, following signs for I-70/I-55. After about three miles, just beyond the exit for I-64, comes another exit for IL-203. Take that exit and stay left for 203 North, leading you past a truck stop on your right and an auto raceway on your left. At the second stoplight, turn right onto Big Bend Road. The portion of Horseshoe Lake that is now on your left, and the crop fields on your right, are private property, but you can often see birds by judiciously stopping and scanning as you drive along. In about two miles, just beyond railroad tracks, veer right to stay on Big Bend Road (the only junction with a paved road). You are now on public land, although care must be taken during hunting season (signs usually posted). Following Big Bend Road to its end (about 1.5 miles, including a sharp left and a sharp right) will take you through an interesting mix of habitats—fields, brush, woodlots—ending at a wooded area near the lake.

Now return to the Big Bend Road junction, turn right on Layton Road, and follow it to the end, where there is public parking along the lakeshore (part of the State Park). Here you can scope the lake in spring and fall for loons, grebes, waterfowl, gulls, terns, and raptors, including Osprey. Though sometimes nearly devoid of birds, the lake can be very productive and has yielded a long list of rarities, such as Pacific Loon, Western Grebe, and Little Gull. In the nesting season, common lakeside birds include Warbling Vireo and Baltimore Oriole. Except in very cold weather, you will usually share the lakeshore with people fishing. Access to this area may change in the future with the construction of a new bridge across the Mississippi.

To access the east side, return to IL-203, turn left, and proceed to the turn for I-55/I-70 north and east. Take the interstate only as far as the first exit, at IL-111; turn left (north) and go 3 miles to the Horseshoe Lake State Park entrance on the left. As you enter, keep an eye out for Eurasian Tree Sparrows. From the entrance drive you can go right, around the lakeshore, or left, across a causeway to Walker's Island. Pull off on the shoulder of the causeway (as do the fishermen) to scan the lake and its shoreline in all directions for herons, waterfowl, gulls, terns, etc.; in August the water may be drawn down, leaving temporary shorebird habitat. On the island, you may drive a loop road through the campground, or walk a path along the lake margin at the far end of the loop, starting from the grassy parking area.

To expand this trip into a full day, continue north on IL-111, west on I-270 into Missouri, and north on MO-367 to Riverlands as described below (30-minute drive); or backtrack on I-55/I-70 to I-64 (east) to Carlyle Lake (45 minutes).

RIVERLANDS ENVIRONMENTAL DEMONSTRATION AREA, MISSOURI/ILLINOIS

Half day (or full day if combined with other nearby sites); year round

Riverlands—created by the U.S. Army Corps of Engineers—is one of the region's main birding attractions. Visit in summer for wading birds and open-country passerines such as Sedge Wren and Dickcissel, in winter for waterfowl, raptors (especially Bald Eagles), and gulls (18 species recorded), and in spring and fall for shorebirds and terns. From December through February you may see Trumpeter Swans that make their winter home here; they do not yet count as wild birds because they originate from breeding programs in Minnesota and Wisconsin. Occasional Tundra Swans join them. The impressive rarity list includes single records of Neotropic Cormorant, Harlequin Duck, Smew, and Ross's and Glaucous-winged Gulls. In bad weather you can see a lot by simply cruising in your car and pausing on the shoulders. Most of the restored prairie is closed to public entry, so please watch from roadsides, parking areas, and marked trails. Chances are good that you will run across other birders.

From I-270 on the north side of St. Louis County, take MO-367 north toward Alton. Cross the Missouri River, pass the junction of MO-94, and continue 2.5 miles almost to the Mississippi River bridge, where there is a final right-turn opportunity at a gas station. Take this right and proceed past the gas station to the Wise Road junction, where you will see a Riverlands sign. Go straight ahead on Riverlands Way, checking both sides of its two-mile length. Stop at the visitor center on the left, where you can obtain a map and a bird list, and birdwatch from an observation room if the weather is poor. In winter, the feeders here may attract Horned Larks, Lapland Longspurs, and sparrows, as well as Eurasian Tree Sparrows. Eagles adopt prominent perches on the trees across the bay; on the water look for flocks of ducks (if open) or gulls (if frozen). An observation deck here is handicap-accessible.

As you continue east on Riverlands Way, the restored prairie to the south (right) will have grassland nesting birds in warm weather and Northern Harriers, Red-tailed Hawks, American Kestrels, and possibly Rough-legged Hawks and Short-eared Owls at other seasons. "Heron Pond," a little over halfway along on the right, often has the best shorebird and wading bird habitat; it may also have numbers of ducks and geese (Ross's Goose has become somewhat regular here in the colder months). To the left, a broad view of the river channel and dam allows you to scope for waterfowl, gulls, and terns. The road eventually dog-legs to the left and takes you down to a parking lot below the spillway, where you may see eagles and gulls, or spot the occasional Peregrine Falcon.

Returning to the Wise Road intersection, go left a short distance and pause at the Teal Pond parking area to check the pond for waterbirds and scan the prairie to the south for raptors. Continuing down Wise Road, you will have more chances to see sparrows (Le Conte's is regular but difficult to observe, November-March), as well as raptors, Ring-necked Pheasants, and blackbirds.

Starting again from the gas station, take the road opposite the station, perpendicular to Riverlands Way and parallel to US-67; it takes you right along the bay, with a handy parking lot not far down, at the beginning of Ellis Island. Continue around the corner, along the riverbank under the bridge (watch for nesting Cliff Swallows), and turn right at the sign for Lincoln-Shields Recreation Area. Here you may scan another large bay; this can be one of the congregating points for winter duck and gull flocks or for migrant pelicans.

A Riverlands trip is not complete without checking the Illinois side. Return to the highway and cross the bridge to Alton; stay in the right lane and turn right onto IL-143. In about two miles, turn right again at a stoplight to take the access road back to the dam and its large new visitor center. Here, right beside the lock, you can watch waterfowl and gulls up and down the river. The spillway is now hidden from view, but you may get close scope

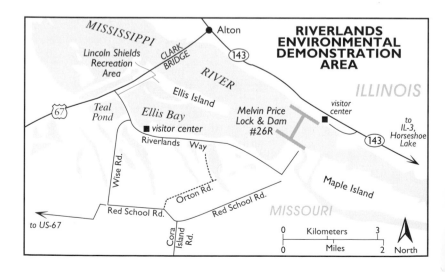

views of gulls perched on the retaining walls, or on ice in the river. Among the abundant Ring-billed and Herring Gulls, this spot offers a good chance of finding a "regular" rare gull (Thayer's, Lesser Black-backed, Glaucous) or one of the "better" ones (Iceland, Great Black-backed, Black-legged Kittiwake).

To continue with a visit to Horseshoe Lake, keep going east on IL-143 to IL-3 south, then take I-270 east and IL-111 south; or turn around and go back past the bridge and through Alton to head for the Two Rivers Refuge as described under that section.

BUSCH MEMORIAL
AND WELDON SPRING
CONSERVATION AREAS, MISSOURI
Half to full day; year round

Few major metropolitan regions have such a large area of public land (over 14,000 acres) available within 45 minutes of downtown as that afforded by the **Busch** and adjacent **Weldon Spring Conservation Areas** (Missouri Department of Conservation). If you have one day to spend in the St. Louis area and want to see the greatest variety of bird species, this is the place to go. The area can be birded well by car or on foot. Many Ozark-border species, particularly edge species such as Blue-winged Warbler and Yellow-breasted Chat and streamside species such as Northern Parula and Louisiana Waterthrush, are common here In spring and early summer. The Busch area contains several lakes that attract ducks, Osprey, and terns. The area is excellent for sparrows in fall, winter, and spring. Any of the region's raptors may be encountered.

Proceed west from downtown on I-64/US-40. After crossing the Missouri River, take the MO-94 exit and head south (left). At 0.9 mile you will see the parking lot for a tract of the **Weldon Spring Conservation Area** (hereafter "CA") on the left, just before the access road for a federal clean-up site. A hike up the gravel road from the parking lot and into the adjacent fields in spring or early summer can produce Bell's Vireo, Blue Grosbeak, Dickcissel, and possibly Henslow's Sparrow. Back on MO-94, go 0.3 mile and turn right onto County Highway D. The main entrance to **Busch Conservation Area** is 2.0 miles ahead on the right. Enter and turn right at the T, and head to the visitor center to obtain maps of both Busch and Weldon CAs and a bird list for Busch. Areas especially worth visiting within Busch are the Fallen Oak Nature Trail and Hampton Memorial Lake (both near the headquarters); the Busch Hiking Trail, excellent for flycatchers, vireos, warblers, and tanagers; the Lakes 24, 34, and 35 loop; and Lake 33 (the largest lake) and the nearby wetland area (two pools, sometimes shorebirds) and Dardenne Creek Trail.

Returning to MO-94, turn right and go another 1.3 miles to reach a parking lot and trailhead for the Lewis and Clark Trails, on your left. These offer

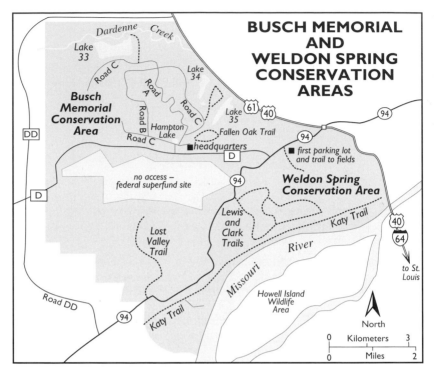

five-mile and eight-mile options for extended hikes through a fine wooded tract of the Weldon Spring CA.

Another 2.8 miles west brings you to a signed left turn for Katy Trail State Park, a linear corridor that runs along the base of the bluff. When not crowded with hikers and bikers, this trail can provide a great birding hike, especially on a calm winter morning, when Eastern Bluebirds and Yellow-rumped Warblers can be common, along with other woodland species.

To reach a reliable place to find breeding Cerulean Warblers, return to MO-94, turn left, proceed 0.8 mile to the bottom of the hill, and turn right into the parking lot for the Lost Valley Hiking/Biking Trail (Weldon Spring CA). The first part of the trail parallels a sycamore-lined creek, home to Cerulean and Yellow-throated Warblers, Northern Parula, and Louisiana Waterthrush. These two CAs are multi-use areas, where fishermen, dog-trainers, picnickers, and hunters far outnumber the birders; nearly all the sites mentioned here, however, are no-hunting zones. See more information at *www.conservation.state.mo.us/areas/stlouis/buschca*.

SHAW NATURE RESERVE, MISSOURI

Half to full day; year round

Most of the birds characteristic of the Ozarks can be found at the **Shaw Nature Reserve** of the Missouri Botanical Garden. Its 2,500 acres contain diverse habitats, including managed collections, prairie and savanna restorations, glades, upland forest, ponds with a boardwalk, and the Meramec River floodplain. With 13 miles of hiking trails, the reserve is highly accessible by foot, but not by car. At least 14 species of warblers have nested here, including Blue-winged, Pine, Prairie, Cerulean, Prothonotary, and Worm-eating. Other specialties include Red-shouldered Hawk, Acadian Flycatcher, Sedge Wren, and Henslow's Sparrow (some years; in restored prairie). The best birding strategy is to drive to one of the parking lots near the pond, hike to the Meramec River on one set of roads and trails, and return on another. There are many options. Brush Creek Trail is a good starting point. Water and restrooms are available at the Trail House.

The reserve is about 45 minutes southwest of downtown St. Louis via I-44. Exit at Gray Summit (Exit 253), turn left across the interstate, then right, and the entrance is on your left immediately. A small entrance fee is required, and a map available at the Visitor Center is necessary. The grounds are open to hiking year round from 7:00AM to sunset, but the Visitor Center is not open until 8:00AM (weekdays) or 9:00AM (weekends). More information is available at *www.mobot.org/MOBOT/arboretum*.

PERE MARQUETTE STATE PARK AND TWO RIVERS NATIONAL WILDLIFE REFUGE, ILLINOIS

Half to full day; year round

These two fine areas, only a few miles apart, complement each other well. The state park is a large (8,000 acres) tract of upland forest, good for breeding and migrant passerines, whereas the refuge provides a mix of open water, edge, bottomland forest, and crop fields, attracting waterfowl in large numbers (with a winter-resident flock of Snow Geese), shorebirds when the habitat is right, raptors (especially eagles), and its own assortment of smaller birds, such as winter sparrow flocks and year-round Red-headed Woodpeckers.

From central St. Louis, it takes about an hour-and-a-quarter to reach these sites. Follow the directions to Riverlands (above), and stop there first if you wish. Proceed across the bridge to Alton and turn left, then left again when you reach the intersection by the casino, to follow the scenic Great River Road (IL-100) along the Mississippi River. If it happens to be autumn, watch out for the traffic as you admire the view and the foliage like everyone else on the road. Other distractions will be Bald Eagles soaring over, October–March, and Turkey Vultures, March–October.

In about 15 miles you will enter the town of Grafton at the confluence of the Mississippi and Illinois Rivers. By the time you reach the far side of town, you will be following the Illinois River. Drive on about six miles, passing the Brussels Ferry on your left, to the **Pere Marquette State Park** visitor center on your right. Here you can obtain a park map and plan a hike; one of the best overlooks is McAdams Peak, from which you can scan the countryside and look for migrating hawks. Back at the park entrance, you can cross the highway to check the river itself and the lower end of Stump Lake. Two miles farther on IL-100, a left onto Dabbs Road will take you to upper Stump Lake for herons, waterfowl, shorebirds, and riparian passerines.

To reach the largest unit of the **Two Rivers NWR**, take the Brussels Ferry (free) across the Illinois River. On the other side, either go straight on the paved highway (Route 1) or make an immediate right for the "scenic route," a gravel road along the river where you can search for eagles and Eurasian Tree Sparrows. This road loops back to join the highway, where you continue to your right. All land now on your right is refuge property,

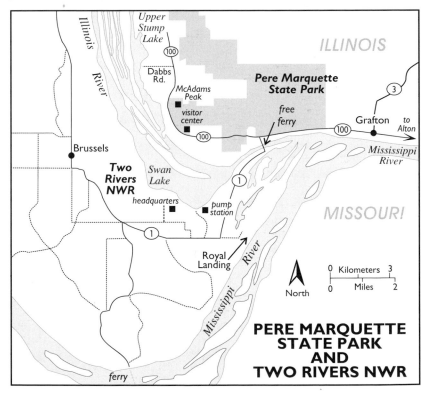

with Illinois state land to your left. Within two miles, you will see signs on the left for Pohlman Slough and Royal Landing, both worth checking.

About a half-mile past the Royal Landing turn, turn right onto an inconspicuous gravel access road that leads into the refuge and down to a small parking area by a pump station, from which you walk out to an observation point on "Swan Lake." This is a large backwater of the Illinois River that may have flocks of waterfowl and pelicans scattered across it and Bald Eagles around its margin. In winter, a resident flock of Snow Geese averaging 10,000 birds may be resting on the lake; with care and luck you might pick out a Ross's Goose. You can also walk the gated service road for landbirds and views of the lake. Spring and fall may bring flocks of shorebirds to the wetland cells that you pass on the way in and out.

Back at the highway, go 1.2 miles farther to a right turn marked with a refuge sign. More signage will lead you through several turns to the modern headquarters building, open weekdays and sometimes on weekends. From the deck here, you can scan fields, a large pond below you, and the wooded lake margin. The shrubbery and prairie grass in this area can yield a good variety of sparrows (e.g., American Tree, Field, Savannah, Song, Swamp, White-crowned) in fall, winter, and spring, and Blue Grosbeaks in summer. Be aware that this spot is the only part of the refuge open to the public during duck-hunting season, normally 15 October to 15 December. From the point where you made the final right turn into headquarters, you can walk or drive the gravel road on down the hill and into the large bottomland woods, to view Swan Lake from another excellent vantage point for pelicans, ducks, eagles, other raptors, shorebirds, and woodland birds.

CARLYLE LAKE, ILLINOIS

Full day; year round

It is possible to get to **Carlyle Lake** and back in half a day, but it takes a full-day trip to do this area justice. The largest lake in the region, Carlyle was formed by damming the Kaskaskia River. The lake supports sailing, fishing, and hunting in addition to excellent birding. Because of the lake's size, a scope is an absolute necessity. Fall is the premier season, with migrant Common Loons, Horned Grebes, Double-crested Cormorants, geese, ducks, and Franklin's and Bonaparte's Gulls, as well as shorebirds if the habitat is right in peripheral areas. Rarities are always possible, notably Sabine's Gull in late September and early October; Carlyle offers one of the best opportunities in the Midwest for this species. Lesser Black-backed Gulls have occurred as early as September. Fall also brings the possibility of rare loons (Red-throated, Pacific), grebes (Red-necked, Eared, Western, Clark's), waterfowl, gulls, and the chance of a jaeger. Wintry conditions assemble gull flocks that may include Thayer's, Glaucous, Great Black-backed, Black-legged Kittiwake, and others. In addition to the lake itself, birders should spend time

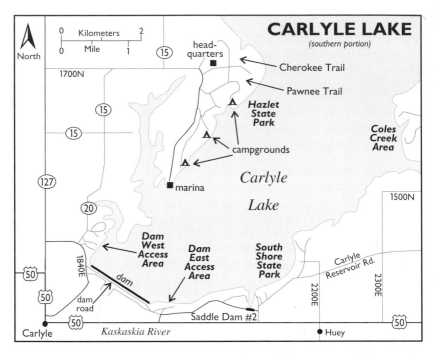

in the woods and brush of the state parks and drive around the nearby countryside for raptors and landbirds

Go east across the I-70/55/64 bridge downtown and continue until I-64 diverges ("Louisville") in about a mile. Follow I-64 to Exit 19 and go north on US-50 for just half-a-mile; turn right to stay on US-50 and continue (with a couple of right-angle turns) through the town of Lebanon. It is now 24 more miles on US-50, through open farmland, to the T-junction with IL-127 on the outskirts of the town of Carlyle. Go left, then immediately right at McDonald's, and proceed into the Dam West Recreation Area, veering to the right along the lake shore, where a small sand beach is often a resting place for gulls whenever no humans are around. Scan the Ring-billeds here for anything unusual. Go to the visitor center opposite the beach for a map of the area (as essential as your scope) and a bird list. You are close to the end of the dam here, and you may walk out on it, but a better view can be had by driving to the bottom of the hill and turning left onto a paved road that leads to the center of the dam. From the parking lot, take the stairs up onto the dam and scan the entire lower lake for just about anything. When Sabine's Gulls or jaegers are present, they can sometimes be seen from this point; scarce ducks can include Greater Scaup, Long-tailed Duck, and scoters.

For other good morning stops, return to IL-127 and proceed south to the center of town, then east (left) on US-50 a couple of miles to a sign for *Dam East Recreation Area*. Turn left here, then left again to reach the east end of the dam, a water's-edge view of the lake, and a wooded trail. Then backtrack, follow the road across the Saddle Dam #2 (a raised causeway), and try the next boat-launch area (on the left). A little farther along, you reach a T-junction; turn left and go on to visit some of the lakeside picnic and campground areas of South Shore State Park; recommended are Hickory Hollow and Deer Run. From these points you get broad vistas of the lake, with the sun behind you in the morning. Farther north and east, the Coles Creek area has recently hosted small numbers of Eurasian Collared-Doves.

In the afternoon, you are better off back on the west side. One good route is to turn right off IL-127 at McDonald's again, then make a left (north) for Hazlet State Park. Enroute, detour right at Jim Hawn Access, checking for landbirds in the trees and shrubbery as you drive in; from the parking lot, walk out toward the lake, where ducks, shorebirds, and gulls may be resting.

Continuing north, swing right on road 1700 N and enter Hazlet State Park, where you may make any number of interesting stops. For landbirding, especially during migration, try the woodland and brush of the Cherokee and Pawnee Trails (get park map or check Corps of Engineers map). The boat-ramp area, the lakeside campgrounds, the Peppenhorst boat-launch area, and (southmost) the pavilion overlook just outside the gated marina all provide views of inlets or of the lake proper. Not far from the headquarters building, groves of pine and juniper may harbor Long-eared and Northern Saw-whet Owls during the colder months. Note that the pheasants in Hazlet are released for hunting, and be careful if it's pheasant season.

Various other areas on both sides of the lake may be productive. Check your Corps of Engineers map and explore on your own. A complete checklist of Carlyle Lake birds and frequent updates on what's around can be found at *k12.il.us/websites/dkassebaum/report.htm*.

A FEW ADDITIONAL GOOD SITES

Marais Temps Clair Conservation Area (St. Charles County, Missouri): Managed wetland, open country, woodland edge. Waterfowl, raptors; sometimes bitterns, rails, shorebirds; Willow Flycatchers in summer. 45-minute drive from downtown. **Castlewood State Park** (St. Louis County, Missouri): Riparian and woodland habitats with walking trails. Fish Crows (spring and summer), Cerulean, Yellow-throated, and Prothonotary Warblers. 25-minute drive. **Clarence Cannon National Wildlife Refuge** (Pike County, Missouri): Mississippi River bottomland refuge with managed wetlands, riparian forest. Waterfowl, raptors, rails, passerines; Bald Eagles nest. 1.5-hour drive. En route is Lock and Dam #25 at Winfield for ducks, eagles, gulls, and Eurasian Tree Sparrows.

ACKNOWLEDGMENTS

We thank Charlene and Jim Malone for their helpful comments and suggestions.

SALT LAKE CITY AREA BIRDING SITES

1 City Creek Canyon/ Memory Grove

2 Tanner Park/ Hansen Hollow

3 City Cemetery

4 Jordan River Parkway

5 South Shore of Great Salt Lake

6 Bountiful Landfill

7 Farmington Bay WMA

8 Antelope Island

9 Willard Bay

10 Bear River Migratory Bird Refuge

11 Millcreek Canyon

12 Parley's Canyon

13 Big Cottonwood Canyon

14 Provo Canyon/ Mount Timpanogos

15 East Canyon Sage Grouse Lek

16 Skull and Rush Valleys

17 Ophir Canyon

18 Uinta Mountains

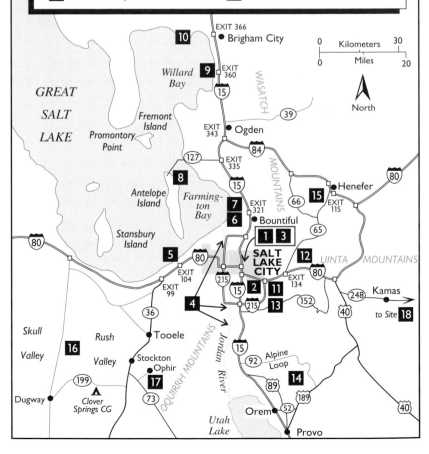

SALT LAKE CITY, UTAH

Ella Sorensen, Georgene Bond, and Robert Bond

Salt Lake City sits in a high basin surrounded by mountains. It is a land of great contrasts. The descent from the surrounding peaks, which tower over 11,000 feet, traverses such habitats as alpine lakes and tundra, spruce-fir forests, open meadows, aspen groves, hillsides covered with scrub oak, pinyon-juniper woodlands, fast-flowing mountain streams, and sagebrush flats. It ends at roughly an elevation of 4,200 feet on the shores of Great Salt Lake, one of the world's largest saltwater lakes, and its adjacent 400,000-acre complex of fresh, brackish, and saline wetlands.

Salt Lake City lies on the eastern rim of the Great Basin. The West Desert, as the Utah portion is called, covers roughly a third of the state. Much of the Great Basin is covered with sagebrush and pinyon-juniper woodlands. Far from being devoid of birdlife, as these habitats may seem to the traveler speeding along a highway, they support such breeding species as Ferruginous Hawk, Chukar, Greater Sage-Grouse, Burrowing Owl, Pinyon Jay, Juniper Titmouse, Sage Thrasher, and Black-throated and Sage Sparrows.

Several nearby mountain ranges offer great birding opportunities. The Wasatch and Uinta ranges of the Rocky Mountains extend into northern and central Utah. The Uinta Mountains, the tallest U.S. range with an east-west axis, contain peaks that are over 13,000 feet in elevation and are dotted with hundreds of glacially-formed lakes. The Stansbury and Oquirrh Mountains are fault blocks that rise in elevation from the desert floor of the Great Basin. Regularly seen in this idyllic montane setting are Blue and Ruffed Grouse, Williamson's and Red-naped Sapsuckers, Three-toed Woodpecker, Dusky, Hammond's, and Cordilleran Flycatchers, Gray Jay, American Dipper, Black Rosy-Finch, Cassin's Finch, and Pine Grosbeak.

To the west and north of Salt Lake City lies the Great Salt Lake itself, perhaps the best-known feature of Utah's landscape. Its wetlands are legendary and have long been considered one of the birding hot-spots of North America. Most of the interior western species of grebes, ducks, shorebirds, and other water-associated species are easily observed here.

Essential Information

Getting Around: Many travelers arrive at the Salt Lake International Airport, located approximately eight miles west of downtown Salt Lake City. Major hotels/motels are located at the International Center just west of the airport, as well as downtown and south along I-15. Traffic congestion may be extreme during morning and evening commutes, and if possible, travel at those times should be avoided. Light-rail and bus services are available in the city, but they will be of little help to the birder.

Climate: Utah is blessed with four very distinct seasons, each of which provides a unique birding experience. Temperatures in mid-summer average in the 90s Farhenheit, but the dry climate makes these temperatures more tolerable than one might imagine. Mid-winter daytime temperatures average in the mid-30s, with snow present off and on for about four months. Annual precipitation in Salt Lake City averages around 14 inches, with March and April being the wettest months. Higher elevations receive considerably more precipitation, mostly in the form of snow.

Other Considerations: Utah is dry, summers are hot, and many of the birding locations described here are at fairly high elevations, so plan accordingly. Elevations described in this guide reach nearly 12,000 feet. Sunscreen or protective clothing is a must. Higher elevations may be surprisingly cool even in mid-summer. Mosquitoes may be numerous in the mountains or in wetter areas. Rattlesnakes are common, though rarely encountered, in the foothills and mountains. Lyme disease and Rocky Mountain Spotted Fever are extremely rare, but other tick-borne diseases such as Colorado Tick Fever are more common. Most, but not all, of the birding areas are on public property, but please observe all posted regulations and signs.

Safety: Most areas in Salt Lake City are considered relatively safe, although appropriate precautions should be taken, as is the case in all cities. Some of the mountain roads are narrow, winding, and rough. Conventional vehicles should be adequate, but please drive with care in such areas.

Birding Resources: The statewide rare bird alert is (801) 538-4730. *Birding Utah* by D. E. McIvor (1998, Falcon Press) is the only statewide birding guide for Utah. An excellent Internet site is *www.utahbirds.org*; it provides a great deal of pertinent information regarding Utah birds.

City Sites

Several hours to half day; year round

Four good areas for finding birds within Salt Lake City proper are described. **City Creek Canyon and Memory Grove** are within walking distance of downtown Salt Lake City. A small, rock-strewn mountain creek lined with cottonwoods and maples runs through patches of conifers in the upper area,

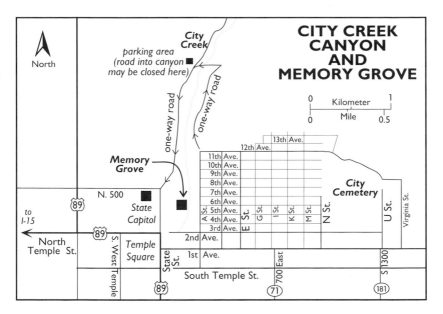

while submontane shrub dominates the lower portion of the canyon. More than 100 bird species have been recorded here, with 50 occurring regularly. Memory Grove is a good area in which to look for California Quail (introduced). In winter, Bohemian Waxwings often can be found in this section of the canyon—if it is a good year for this erratic species. Watch also for Winter Wrens. As you continue up the canyon in spring or summer, watch for Golden Eagle, Broad-tailed Hummingbird, Western Scrub-Jay (resident), American Dipper (resident), Townsend's Solitaire (resident), Virginia's Warbler, Black-headed Grosbeak, and Lazuli Bunting. In the coniferous areas look for resident Steller's Jay, Mountain Chickadee, Brown Creeper, and Golden-crowned Kinglet. Blue and Ruffed Grouse have been observed in the upper portions. Common Poorwills call in late spring and early summer at night from dry hillsides high in the canyon. Western Screech-, Great Horned, Northern Pygmy-, Long-eared, and Northern Saw-whet Owls are reported fairly regularly.

Memory Grove is reached from the center of the city by going about a half-block east of State Street on North Temple, turning north onto Canyon Road (120 East), and following this road into Memory Grove. The upper portion of City Creek Canyon can be reached by following the canyon road that begins at 11th Avenue and B Street. Go 0.7 mile and turn right into the canyon. Automobiles are usually not allowed in the canyon itself, but there is parking at the mouth, and the hike, along a paved road, is not overly strenuous.

Tanner Park/Hansen Hollow: Hansen Hollow is a small natural area preserved amid the hustle-and-bustle of freeways and houses. A cottonwood-and-brush-lined creek traverses the gully; on the slopes, scrub oak predominates. Within this small area, Black-chinned Hummingbird, Black-headed Grosbeak, and Bullock's Oriole are commonly found in spring and summer. California Quail, Black-billed Magpie, and American Dipper are year-round residents. During migration, most regularly occurring passerines migrating through Utah can be found here. In winter, birds are often few in number, as is the case in much of northern Utah. Northern Shrike is occasional, and many of Utah's records of Harris's Sparrow have come from here.

To get to Tanner Park/Hansen Hollow, take I-80 east to the 2300 East exit. Almost immediately after exiting, take the first left and continue east for 0.4 mile, watching for Tanner Park, a small park on the left. Leave your car in the upper parking lot. To enter the gulch, walk to the back (northeast corner) of the park and follow the road into the gulch. Note: The birding experience may be somewhat compromised by the fact that Hansen Hollow is a prime area for east-side Salt Lake City residents to run their dogs.

City Cemetery: Many species in Utah carry out altitudinal migrations: they breed in the mountains and drop to lower elevations in winter. City Cemetery can be a good place to look for these and other species in winter. Look for Steller's Jay (in some winters they remain in the mountains), Black-billed Magpie, Brown Creeper, Golden-crowned Kinglet, Townsend's Solitaire, Bohemian and Cedar Waxwings, and Red Crossbill. Western Screech-Owls are regularly observed in the cemetery trees and are present year round. A good variety of species passes through in migration. City Cemetery can be reached by going east from Main Street on South Temple to E Street. Turn left (north), continue to 11th Avenue, and turn right (east). City Cemetery is between N and U Streets. If the gate is open, you may enter by car; otherwise, enter on foot. The cemetery can also be entered from 4th Avenue between N and U Streets. This entire 4th Avenue area is also worth checking in winter for Bohemian Waxwings, if it is a good year for the species locally.

The Jordan River Parkway: The Jordan River runs south to north through the center of the Salt Lake Valley, connecting Utah Lake in the south with the Great Salt Lake. A trail in the Jordan River Parkway follows much of the Salt Lake County portion of the river and provides access to interesting birding, especially in migration. The trail courses through wetlands, deciduous wooded areas, open meadows, and, in the south, along sagebrush hills. (Map is on page 365.)

Three recommended access points include the Utah State Raceway in the north part of the valley, 4800 South in the mid-valley, and 12300 South in the south valley area. The first is reached from the corner of Redwood Road and North Temple. Travel north on Redwood Road for 2.3 miles. Turn left on 1700 North and go west to Rose Park Lane (0.4 mile). Turn right and follow Rose Park Lane to where it dead-ends (0.4 mile) at the Jordan Park State Park

ORV area. Walk across the fields toward the mountains, then follow the trees and stream south for a mile or so. In winter Northern Shrike as well as various raptors may be found in this area.

The 4800 South trailhead may be reached by traveling west 1.0 mile from 4800 South and State Street. Just past 500 West turn left into the parking area on the south side of the road. Walking a mile or so south can be productive in spring and fall. Nesting species include Yellow-breasted Chat, Black-headed Grosbeak, Yellow-headed Blackbird, and Bullock's Oriole. Barn and Great Horned Owls may occasionally be seen or heard during the evening.

The south valley parkway trailhead is reached via Exit 294 (12300 South) from I-15. Travel 1.6 miles west on 12300 South, and turn left onto a small dirt road into the parking area. The paved trail may be walked for one to two miles south through shrub, Russian-olive trees, open fields, wetlands, and sagebrush. This area should be very productive during spring and fall migrations because the mountains converge here, funneling the birds through a fairly narrow corridor.

GREAT SALT LAKE

Half to full day; year round

Some of the most accessible birdfinding opportunities are along the south and east sides of the **Great Salt Lake**, particularly where the Bear, Jordan, and Weber Rivers enter the lake. Six Great Salt Lake sites are described here: South Shore of the Great Salt Lake, Bountiful Landfill, Farmington Bay Wildlife Management Area, Antelope Island and Causeway, Willard Bay, and Bear River Migratory Bird Refuge.

South Shore of the Great Salt Lake: Approximately 11 miles west of the Salt Lake International Airport, westbound I-80 approaches the Great Salt Lake. Exit 104 leads to the Saltair Resort. Check the numerous ponds along the access roads. At the resort, turn left and drive the gravel road to the sailboat marina, again checking roadside ponds and the shoreline. This general area can be good in winter for ducks, gulls, and Bald Eagle. In spring any number of shorebird species as well as California Gull and Caspian Tern can be found. Although not necessarily a worthy birding destination in and of itself, this area is along the way as you travel to any of the west-desert locations described in this guide, and it can be an interesting stop.

Bountiful Landfill: The best hot-spot for gulls in winter in the Salt Lake City area is the Bountiful Landfill, located approximately ten miles north of the downtown area. From I-15, take the 400 North exit in Bountiful (Exit 321). At the stop sign turn left (west) onto 400 North. At 0.9 mile, turn right (north) on 1100 West and go 0.8 mile, turning left (west) onto 1600 North. In another 0.3 mile you reach the gate to the landfill. At the entrance station,

GREAT SALT LAKE SITES

Bear River Migratory Bird Refuge

Bear River Bay

Willard Bay

Willard Bay State Park

GREAT SALT LAKE

campground
causeway
Buffalo Point
Visitor Center
Antelope Island
Garr Ranch House

Farmington Bay

Farmington Bay WMA
Bountiful Landfill

Saltair Resort
South Shore

to Rush and Skull Valleys

EXIT 366
Forest St.
Brigham City

EXIT 360
Willard

dike

North

0 Kilometers 8
0 Miles 5

89
15
39 EXIT 348 Ogden
126
EXIT 343
84
127 EXIT 335 89
Syracuse
EXIT 333 109
15
Farmington
Glover La. EXIT 327
106
EXIT 322
400 North EXIT 321
Bountiful
EXIT 316
215 89
Salt Lake City International Airport
80 SALT LAKE CITY
EXIT 104
EXIT 102 201
2100 South
West
Redwood Rd.
State St.
215 80
15
EXIT 99 36 111

ask permission to watch birds, and then use care to park in areas that do not interfere with landfill traffic. In mid-winter, search through the thousands of Ring-billed, California, and Herring Gulls for less-common species including Thayer's, Glaucous, and, rarely, Glaucous-winged and Lesser Black-backed. Numerous raptors frequent this area in winter, including Bald Eagle, Rough-legged Hawk, and Prairie and Peregrine Falcons. When you tire of the "dump" atmosphere, you can continue birding a few miles to the north at Farmington Bay Waterfowl Management Area.

Farmington Bay Waterfowl Management Area: This state-owned refuge located at the mouth of the Jordan River has long been a popular birding spot, partly because of its proximity to the Salt Lake City population center. Breeding birds found in the area include Eared, Western, and Clark's Grebes, American White Pelican, Snowy Egret, White-faced Ibis, Black-necked Stilt, American Avocet, Willet, Franklin's Gull, Caspian and Forster's Terns, and Yellow-headed Blackbird. The mudflats host large numbers of migrant shorebirds, including Snowy Plovers. Most western waterfowl species can be found in migration. In winter, Thayer's and Glaucous Gulls appear sporadically among the regular larids, until the bay freezes over in mid-winter. Also in winter, numerous Bald Eagles fish and roost in the area, whereas Rough-legged Hawks and Short-eared Owls hunt along the dikes.

To reach Farmington Bay, take I-15 north to the Centerville exit (Exit 322). Head east and turn immediately left onto the frontage road that parallels the Interstate. At 3.1 miles turn left (west) on Glover Lane, crossing over I-15. In another 1.4 miles turn left into Farmington Bay. The gate is open from 8:00AM until 5:00PM year-round. Some interior roads are closed during the nesting season. Ponds at the west end of Glover Lane can be excellent for shorebirds.

Antelope Island and Causeway: Roughly 16 miles long and 7 miles wide, Antelope Island is the largest island in the Great Salt Lake. Sagebrush, greasewood, and grasses are the predominant vegetation. Common summer birds include Say's Phoebe, Rock Wren, Sage Thrasher, Loggerhead Shrike, and Brewer's, Vesper, and Lark Sparrows. The island is probably Utah's most accessible location to see Chukars year round. The seven-mile causeway provides access to the middle portion of the Great Salt Lake, where some birds considered rare or accidental in the state have made appearances. These include Greater Scaup, all three scoters, Long-tailed Duck, Harlequin Duck, and Barrow's Goldeneye. An incredible sight from the causeway is the staging of hundreds of thousands of Red-necked and Wilson's Phalaropes during migration in late summer. Eared Grebes also congregate in large numbers. In spring, it seems that almost any shorebird may show up along the causeway, but species and numbers vary from year to year. In winter, Lapland Longspur and Snow Bunting (both rare) have shown a special affinity for the edges of the causeway, where they occasionally mix with Horned Larks.

To reach the causeway and island, travel north from Salt Lake City on I-15. Take Exit 335 (Syracuse), turn left at the stoplight, and head west. In 6.9 miles you reach the entrance station (fee). At 2.2 and 6.3 miles the causeway crosses waterways that allow water to flow from the south to the north side of the road. These areas are particularly good for waterbirds. The island proper is reached after seven miles. Take the right fork and check the sagebrush and grasslands for Sage Thrashers and sparrows. After a mile, turn left to the Visitor Center. Chukars may be seen among the rocks near here. Just beyond the turn-off to the center, search both sides of the road for Burrowing Owls. The feeders at the center should be checked in winter.

In another 1.3 miles a turn-off to the right goes to the **Bridger Bay Campground**. Park at the far end of the campground loop by the Shoreline Trailhead. A walk along the first one-half mile of the trail will almost certainly produce Chukars. They are usually heard before they are seen, clucking and chattering amongst the rocks on the hillside to the left. This is also an excellent area for Rock Wrens. Another good spot for Chukars is **Buffalo Point**. Return to the main road, turn right, and at the next road junction at the yield sign, turn right again, and go to the end of the paved road. Walk to the trailhead past the gift center, and pay close attention for Chukars on the rocky hillsides on the north side of the trail. The hike to the top of the knoll is recommended simply to enjoy the spectacular 360-degree view of the Great Salt Lake and the mountains beyond. After the hike, one can—if so inclined—enjoy a buffalo-burger from the concession stand at the parking lot. Antelope Island is home to one of the largest free-roaming Bison herds in the United States.

When leaving the area, travel northeast back toward the causeway. Before the causeway, a road turns back and follows the east side of the island south for 11 miles to the Garr Ranch House. There are trees and a large grassy area near the old ranch, and a spring and a related riparian area attract numerous passerine migrants in spring and fall. A resident pair of Great Horned Owls resides in the barn in winter and in the trees at other seasons. About one mile north of the ranch a hacking tower can be seen at a distance on the edge of the Great Salt Lake. A pair of Peregrine Falcons can usually be seen here during the nesting season. Returning north, one can stop and listen for Grasshopper Sparrows on the west side of the road toward the hillside.

Back on the mainland, park near the entrance station and walk the shoreline south for a mile or so. Snowy Plovers nest on the playas or open mudflats.

Willard Bay is a freshwater impoundment adjacent to the Great Salt Lake created by a large dike. This is a popular summer recreation area and should be avoided during June, July, and August. In mid-winter the water may be frozen. The best time to visit is during migration. Grebes, pelicans, swans, ducks, shorebirds, gulls, and terns can be seen from various vantage points here. The campground (fee area) is a mixture of thick brush, cottonwoods, a small pond and marsh, and a creek. If visited during migration, the area can be excellent for western migrant passerines. In winter, Bald Eagles congregate in the large trees. To reach Willard Bay drive north from Salt Lake City about 50 miles on I-15. Take Exit 360 and head west into Willard Bay. The dike is straight ahead, and the campground is to the left.

Bear River Migratory Bird Refuge: Most birders have undoubtedly heard of Bear River Migratory Bird Refuge. Created by Congress in 1929, it is a major migration stopover point for waterbirds. Sometimes, however, the 14-mile route between I-15 and the refuge is more interesting than the refuge itself. A multitude of factors affect birding in this area, and the good spots sometimes change daily. Some of the species that breed or forage in summer on the refuge or along the route to the refuge are Eared, Western, and Clark's Grebes, American White Pelican (which flies in to feed from its nesting site on Gunnison Island in the Great Salt Lake), American Bittern, White-faced Ibis, Cinnamon Teal, Virginia Rail, Sora, Snowy Plover, Black-necked Stilt, American Avocet, Willet, Franklin's and California Gulls, Caspian, Forster's, and Black Terns, Marsh Wren, and Yellow-headed Blackbird. In migration, huge numbers of ducks visit the area. Western and Least Sandpipers can also be abundant; Semipalmated and Baird's occur in smaller numbers. Flocks totaling thousands of Long-billed Dowitchers often have a few Short-billed Dowitchers or Stilt Sandpipers mixed in. The Great Salt Lake is also a major stop-over point for migrant Marbled Godwits. November is traditionally a month when over 20,000 Tundra Swans use the refuge. Winter and early spring may be excellent for gulls, including "white-winged" species. In mid-winter the water is often frozen, but raptors can still be seen, and Lapland Longspurs and Snow Buntings are occasionally found along the road to the refuge.

To reach Bear River refuge, drive north on I-15 approximately 55 miles to Brigham City and Exit 366, which will put you on Forest Street. Turn left (west) and drive to the refuge, which is about 15 miles ahead. Once at the refuge you can also take the 12-mile auto-tour route. The refuge is open from sunrise to sunset.

WASATCH MOUNTAINS

Half to full day; summer (spring for grouse trip)

The Wasatch Range extends from northern to central Utah and rises abruptly from the valley floor. Most of Utah's human population inhabits the base of this range. Creeks and glaciers have carved canyons, of which many are easily accessible on paved roads. Knowing the habitat requirements of desired species can help the observer find these birds in other mountain ranges in the state, as well.

Millcreek Canyon: This is a steep-walled, stream-carved canyon reaching the eastern edge of Salt Lake City. Travel east on I-80 to I-215, which curves south. Take the 3900 South exit (Exit 4). Turn left (east) and proceed to the signal at Wasatch Boulevard. Turn left (north) and go one block to the signal at 3800 South. Turn right and proceed east up the canyon. At 3.1 miles, the road to a picnic area crosses the creek, and American Dipper can usually be seen here, as well as anywhere from here on up the stream. In just another 0.2 mile, just past the Millcreek Inn, turn into the parking and picnic area on the right. The Desolation Trailhead is located here. Birding along this trail is facilitated by the fact that no stream parallels the trail, so bird song is more easily heard.

In the summer daylight hours an impressive list can be tabulated along this trail, including such species as Northern Goshawk, Cooper's Hawk, Golden Eagle, Blue Grouse, White-throated Swift, Black-chinned and Broad-tailed

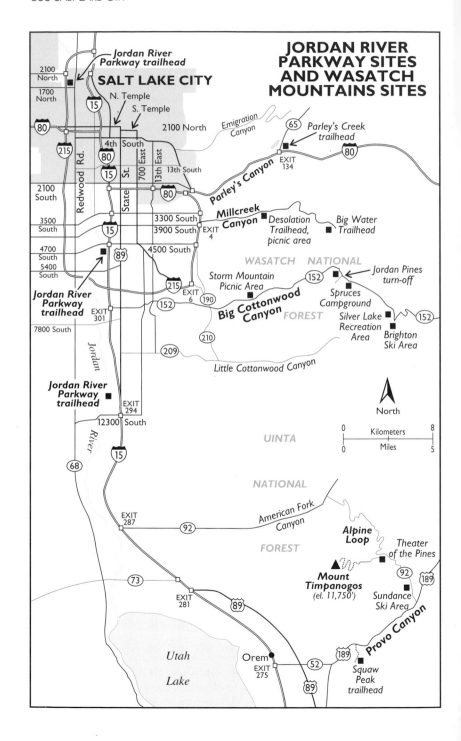

Jordan River Parkway trailhead

SALT LAKE CITY

JORDAN RIVER PARKWAY SITES AND WASATCH MOUNTAINS SITES

2100 North

1700 North

N. Temple

S. Temple

2100 North

Emigration Canyon

Parley's Creek trailhead

EXIT 134

4th South

13th South

Parley's Canyon

2100 South

3300 South

Millcreek Canyon

Desolation Trailhead, picnic area

Big Water Trailhead

3500 South

3900 South

EXIT 4

4700 South

4500 South

WASATCH NATIONAL

5400 South

Jordan River Parkway trailhead

EXIT 301

Storm Mountain Picnic Area

Jordan Pines turn-off

Spruces Campground

7800 South

Big Cottonwood Canyon

FOREST

Silver Lake Recreation Area

Brighton Ski Area

Little Cottonwood Canyon

North

Jordan River Parkway trailhead

EXIT 294

12300 South

Kilometers   8

Miles   5

UINTA

NATIONAL

EXIT 287

American Fork Canyon

Alpine Loop

Theater of the Pines

FOREST

Mount Timpanogos (el. 11,750')

Sundance Ski Area

Provo Canyon

EXIT 281

Utah

Lake

Orem

EXIT 275

Squaw Peak trailhead

Hummingbirds, Dusky Flycatcher, Clark's Nutcracker, Steller's Jay, Townsend's Solitaire, Swainson's and Hermit Thrushes, Orange-crowned and MacGillivray's Warblers, Western Tanager, Green-tailed Towhee, and Black-headed Grosbeak. After dark, Flammulated, Northern Pygmy-, and Northern Saw-whet Owls, as well as Common Poorwills, are all regularly heard along the first three-quarters of a mile of the trail. At 1.3 miles farther up the canyon, a road to the right leads to the Terraces Picnic Area. Flammulated and Northern Saw-whet Owls have been found in this area, as well.

For a wonderful hike as well as great montane birding, travel up the canyon to nearly the end of the road and park in the parking area on the right at the Big Water Trailhead, open only in summer and fall. The two-and-a-half mile hike to Dog Lake is pleasant and might produce Blue and Ruffed Grouse, Three-toed Woodpecker, Olive-sided Flycatcher, and Pine Grosbeak. Be forewarned that mountain bikers are allowed on this trail on even-numbered days, so odd-numbered days are preferred by hikers and birders.

Parley's Canyon: A few miles east of Salt Lake City is Parley's Canyon. Drive east on I-80 out of Salt Lake to Exit 134 for East Canyon. At the stop sign, turn left onto Highway 65 and go 0.4 mile. Immediately after crossing the creek, park on the right side of the road. Walk around the gate—open to hikers—and follow the old road/trail for two to three miles up the canyon. The open sage-covered hills to the left of the creek provide prime habitat for Broad-tailed Hummingbirds and Green-tailed Towhees. Along the riparian habitat to the right are multiple Beaver dams and an excellent area for a multitude of birds in spring and summer. This is one of the few areas near Salt Lake where Gray Catbirds can sometimes be seen. Calliope Hummingbirds have nested in this area.

When you have returned to your car, you may wish to take the drive up the canyon on Highway 65 (closed in winter and early spring) into the aspen and fir forests, which can be productive for montane birds. Flammulated Owls may be heard at night.

Big Cottonwood Canyon: This major ski area is open all year, although birds are sparse in winter. In summer the canyon is a cool relief from the hot temperatures in the valleys below. Birds can be found anywhere in the canyon. Several prime areas are described here. To reach Cottonwood Canyon, travel on I-215, driving either east from I-15 or south from I-80, and take Exit 6 for 6200 South. Follow the signs to Big Cottonwood Canyon and the Solitude and Brighton ski areas. Turn left (east) at the signal at 7200 South at the mouth of the canyon. At 2.8 miles is the Storm Mountain Picnic Area. It is often heavily used by picnickers, especially on late spring and summer weekends, but by wandering the trails toward the back of the picnic area you can usually find Black-chinned Hummingbird, Virginia's Warbler, Black-headed Grosbeak, and Lazuli Bunting. Proceed another 6 miles and park beside the road at the Jordan Pines turn-off on the right. For birding purposes, it is best to walk, not drive, this road. Black-chinned, Broad-tailed, and Calliope Hummingbirds all nest, and Rufous Hummingbirds are seen after mid-July.

Red-naped Sapsucker, Olive-sided, Hammond's, Dusky, and Cordilleran Fly-catchers, Mountain Chickadee, Townsend's Solitaire, MacGillivray's Warbler, Western Tanager, Lincoln's Sparrow, and Cassin's Finch all breed here.

Another 0.8 mile up the main road, the Spruces Campground (fee area) offers a similar palette. In another 4.4 miles, a parking lot and visitor center are found at the Silver Lake Recreation Area. Trails around the lake and beyond, as well as the roads in the area, may produce Three-toed Wood-pecker, Williamson's Sapsucker, Red Crossbill, and Pine Grosbeak. Similar birds can be found on the Lake Mary, Martha, and Catherine Trails above the Brighton Ski Lodge at the end of the road.

Provo Canyon/Mount Timpanogos: Black Swift is one species of interest that has been found regularly in Provo Canyon in summer. Take I-15 south to Exit 275 (8th North, Orem) and go east. Watch for signs to Provo Canyon. At 3.8 miles bear left over the overpass onto US-189 and go 1.9 miles, turning right at the sign indicating Squaw Peak Trail. After about 1.4 miles, turn left onto a dirt road (which may be somewhat hard to see). Park at the beginning of this road and hike onto the knoll on the left. Looking east toward the backdrop of towering peaks, it is frequently possible to see the swifts riding the thermals. They often pass close by overhead. A good time of the day to look is around 8:30AM. In the evening the swifts are often seen flying over the knoll or moving east up the canyon; they may also be seen at Bridal Veil Falls along UT-189. There are also many White-throated Swifts in this area. If you continue farther up the Squaw Peak Trail, this general area is said to have many Blue and Ruffed Grouse.

The **Alpine Loop**, open only in summer, is a beautiful but time-consuming return route to Salt Lake City. A winding, narrow, paved road goes through submontane shrub, coniferous forest, and aspen groves. It traverses the back side of Mt. Timpanogos, one of the highest peaks in the Wasatch Range at 11,957 feet, eventually returning to I-15. One particularly attractive hike is along the first couple of miles of the trail to the top of Mt. Timpanogos. To reach the Alpine Loop, turn left from U. S. 189 onto State Highway 92 and proceed about five miles, past the Sundance ski resort and Aspen Grove, to the Theater of the Pines on the left. The trail to Mt. Timpanogos begins at the parking lot. The first mile-and-a-half of the trail is paved and winds up through a broad valley, with a willow-lined stream and cascading waterfalls. Some species regularly seen in summer are White-throated Swift, Broad-tailed and Calliope Hummingbirds, Red-naped Sapsucker, Olive-sided, Ham-mond's, Dusky, and Cordilleran Flycatchers, MacGillivray's Warbler, and Green-tailed Towhee. Both Hammond's and Cordilleran Flycatchers fre-quent the trees in the open amphitheater near the parking lot.

East Canyon Greater Sage-Grouse Lek: Within about an hour's drive of Salt Lake City is an accessible Greater Sage-Grouse lek. Drive north on I-15 to Farmington and exit onto Highway 89 North. Follow the highway to I-84, then take I-84 eastbound for approximately 25 miles to Henefer. Take Exit 115, the second Henefer exit. Turn right at the stop sign, go through

Henefer, and turn left onto Highway 65 toward East Canyon Recreation Area. At 6.5 miles the road crests by a sign indicating Morgan County. A parking area by a historical marker is located on the right side of the highway. The lek is beside the road, primarily on the right side, although some birds seem to prefer to display on the left or even in the middle of the highway. Activity begins at the end of March and lasts until the beginning of May, with peak activity in mid-April. One should arrive near dawn, which during April is 6:15 to 6:30AM . The birds usually disperse around 8:00AM. Although these birds seem more to be acclimated to people than most, care should be taken to minimize disturbance.

After observing these incredible birds, to add diversity to the trip continue traveling south on Highway 65 to East Canyon Reservoir. Bear right at the junction onto Highway 66. Several observation points are located along the reservoir. In spring, one can find Common Loon, Western and Clark's Grebes, Common and Red-breasted Mergansers, and a variety of other ducks. One may then return to I-84 at Morgan. Utah birders have found the Spring Chicken Inn in Morgan an ideal place for a late breakfast to conclude the trip.

GREAT BASIN AND WEST DESERT

Half to full day; year round (best in winter)

Utah's west desert, part of the Great Basin, is one of the best winter raptor areas on the continent. Bald Eagles are usually associated with water, but many years ago biologists were amazed to find large concentrations of this species in Utah's west desert far from water. Rough-legged Hawks (winter), Golden Eagles, and Prairie Falcons occur regularly. Merlins are occasionally seen in winter. In summer, Swainson's and Ferruginous Hawks may be sighted. Raptor populations in Utah tend to be somewhat cyclical. In some years individuals seem to be on every pole, and in other years they are much less numerous. Following the west desert tour described below will almost always produce a Northern Shrike in winter; Loggerhead Shrikes occur year round. The west-desert tour makes a large loop through Rush and Skull Valleys, with side trips to Vernon, and into the Oquirrh and Stansbury Mountains.

Skull and Rush Valleys: Take I-80 west from Salt Lake City to Exit 99 (Tooele/Grantsville) and onto UT-36 South. Watch the fields, poles, and sky for raptors. Shrikes are often seen perched on utility wires, bushes, or trees. Continue through Tooele (about 11 miles from I-80). Just before leaving the small town of Stockton, turn right onto a dirt road that winds down to Rush Lake. The lake varies in size from year to year; in some years it is dry. The best time to visit the lake is during spring and in fall before the lake freezes in November or December. During the summer, there is usually too much competition from windsurfers. Check the brushy areas on the way to the lake for Sage Thrasher and Brewer's and Vesper Sparrows.

Back on UT-36, there are several pull-offs that can be used to scan Rush Lake from a distance. A side-trip to Ophir can be made (see below); otherwise, continue on UT-36 South. This road goes through Rush Valley and is an excellent area for raptors in winter and other sagebrush-associated species in any season. Pinyon Jays are sometimes found just past Vernon where the pinyon-juniper vegetation comes close to the road.

If time is short, turn right at Highway 199 and go 1.4 miles to Clover. Pinyon Jays can often be found in or near the town. The route then climbs through pinyon-juniper habitat to Johnson Pass and descends into Skull Valley. As you climb, watch the stream for American Dipper.

At 8 miles out along 199, Clover Springs, a BLM campground, is situated by a beautiful spring and stream surrounded by cottonwoods set in pinyon-juniper surroundings. Gray Flycatcher (summer), Western Scrub-Jay, Pinyon Jay, Juniper Titmouse, and Virginia's and Black-throated Gray Warblers (both summer) can be found in this area. For several years a pair of Northern Pygmy-Owls was resident here.

Just before reaching Dugway, an Army base with restricted access, swing to the right and continue north through Skull Valley, watching for many of the same Great Basin species. Several small ranches along the way may be worth checking, especially in migration. Vagrants are occasionally found here in spring and fall. Horseshoe Springs is good for Virginia Rail and Sora. It is approximately 37 miles from Dugway to the I-80 interchange at Timpie.

Ophir Canyon: This is a steep-sided canyon carved by a perennial stream found on the west side of the Oquirrh Range. Ophir, once a small picturesque mining town, has recently been partially reinhabited but still retains much of its rustic flavor. The road, usually open all year, may be closed after snowstorms and can sometimes be quite slick. From pinyon-juniper habitat at its beginning, the road climbs into coniferous forest and aspen groves. In the winter it is an excellent area in which to find hundreds of roosting Bald Eagles. The eagles can be seen flying up and down the canyon at dawn or dusk.

Turn left (east) off UT-36 onto UT-73. Watch for Sage Thrashers, Loggerhead and Northern (winter) Shrikes, and Brewer's, Vesper, and Lark Sparrows. At 5.6 miles from UT-36, turn left and follow the road into the canyon to the town of Ophir. The pinyon-juniper areas may produce Juniper Titmice and Black-throated Gray Warblers during the summer. In winter, Ophir usually has Steller's Jays, Mountain Chickadees, and Townsend's Solitaires. Recently, in winter, Western Screech-Owl s and Northern Pygmy-Owls have been located within a half-mile above Ophir. Great Horned, Long-eared, and Northern Saw-whet Owls also are resident in the canyon. American Dippers are common along the stream. The road is paved to Ophir but turns to dirt thereafter. In the winter, park in the small pull-off just beyond Ophir and walk along the snow-packed road. At times this is a popular snowmobiling area.

UINTA MOUNTAINS
Half to full day; summer

The **Uinta Mountains**, 130 by 45 miles in extent, are the highest range in Utah, with 13,528-foot King's Peak being Utah's highest point. The word "uinta" is from the Ute Indian language and means "pine land," undoubtedly referring to the extensive coniferous forests found there. Magnificent mountain scenery and great birding opportunities abound. The three areas described, good samples of this region, are easily accessible, and concentrate mainly on three species: Three-toed Woodpecker, Gray Jay, and Black Rosy-Finch. These three species are often easier to find in the Uinta Mountains than elsewhere in Utah. The sites are accessible only in summer: because of snow, the road may not be passable in some years until late June.

Trial Lake: To reach this area, travel east from Salt Lake City on I-80 to Highway 40 south to Highway 248, and east to Kamas. From Kamas take UT-150 east toward Mirror Lake. After about 23 miles watch for the sign pointing to Trial Lake. Turn left and park near the lake. It has been said that Three-toed Woodpecker is the most numerous woodpecker in this area. Try the trails around the campground and around the various lakes in the area. This species has also been seen by parking in safe areas along Route 150 just below the turn-off to Trial Lake and exploring the spruce-fire forest between the road and the stream. Gray Jays, Pine Grosbeaks, Cassin's Finches, and Red Crossbills can also be found in this general area.

Bald Mountain: Return from Trial Lake to UT-150, turn left (east) and continue up the canyon. Watch for the Bald Mountain Picnic Area sign near the summit (3.8 miles) and turn left into the parking lot at the Bald Mountain Trailhead. The talus slopes of this near-12,000-foot peak are ideal breeding habitat for Black Rosy-Finches and American Pipits. The easiest approach is to walk to the restrooms near the Bald Mountain Trailhead and climb the small rise to the right. Walk along the base of the talus slope that forms the side-face of Bald Mountain. Scan the rocks, especially those near snow banks. If this short hike is not successful, the fairly strenuous two-mile hike to the top of Bald Mountain may be in order. The latter hike is often required later in the summer when the snow has melted off the lower slopes. The top of Bald Mountain gives a spectacular view of some fifty glacially-formed lakes. (Rosy-Finches have been observed less frequently at the main parking lot and along the adjacent highway, particularly early in the season.) Other species seen in this area in summer include Three-toed Woodpecker, Mountain Bluebird, Townsend's Solitaire, and Cassin's Finch.

Mirror Lake: From Bald Mountain Pass the road drops into the basin that holds Mirror Lake, one of the most popular lakes in the area. Watch for the sign to the lake (2.4 miles), turn right, and proceed to the parking lot. The campground and surrounding spruce-fir forest is a good area in which to find Three-toed Woodpeckers, Gray Jays, Pine Grosbeaks, and Cassin's Finches.

SAN DIEGO AREA BIRDING SITES

1. **Cabrillo National Monument**
2. **Fort Rosecrans National Cemetery**
3. **Point Loma Nazarene College**
4. **La Jolla**
5. **San Diego River Flood-Control Channel**
6. **J Street Marina, Chula Vista**
7. **Marine Biology Study Area**
8. **Tijuana Slough National Wildlife Refuge**
9. **Mission Dam**
10. **Lake Hodges**
11. **San Diego Zoo**
12. **Cuyamaca Rancho State Park**
13. **Anza-Borrego State Park**
14. **Salton Sea**
15. **Wild Animal Park**

to Riverside

15

15

Escondido

10 San Dieguito River Park

Rancho Bernardo

North

Kilometers 0 — 12
Miles 0 — 8

15

52

9

visitor center

San Diego River

Mission Gorge Rd

to Sites 12 13 14

521

4

805

5

15

El Cajon

Mission Bay

163

Friars Rd.

La Mesa

5

8

8

5

94

3

San Diego Bay

11

SAN DIEGO

Sweetwater Reservoir

2

Otay Lakes

1

Point Loma

South San Diego Bay

75

5

805

Chula Vista

6

Imperial Beach

7

8

117

U.S.
MEXICO

Border Field State Park

Tijuana

BAJA CALIFORNIA NORTE

SAN DIEGO, CALIFORNIA

Richard E. Webster

San Diego's idyllic climate and diverse habitats contribute to excellent year-round birding. San Diego further provides the easiest access to the Salton Sea and Colorado Desert, only peripherally treated here. Catering to tourists is a major part of San Diego's economy, and there is no lack of non-birding indoor and outdoor activities to round out a visit.

ESSENTIAL INFORMATION

Getting Around: San Diego is part of car-culture California; a car is the only efficient way to get around. Buses do reach many areas but are time-consuming; taxis are expensive and not omni-present. Traffic, although relatively benign by big-city standards, is getting worse, and is "big-city bad" on the major freeways during traditional rush hours. Still, an excellent freeway system provides quick access to many areas at times other than rush hour.

Climate: The city's climate is mild, with no extremes in the coastal zone. Minor warnings: it may seem pleasant in the asphalt jungle of the city, but the traditional afternoon wind comes off of a cold ocean, so take a wrap with you to the coast. Rain is minimal (under 10 inches per year, mostly November through March), but San Diego is still affected by most Pacific fronts, so watch the weather maps to plan landbirding for calm periods. The coastal influence extends only about 15 miles inland, producing warm summer days and chilly winter nights in the inland valleys and farther east; and the mountains and deserts can present life-threatening extremes to the unprepared.

Safety: San Diego is safe for a big city, but it *is* a big city, so basic caution is required. This region, and areas along the immediate border in particular, receives a substantial flow of illegal aliens and the accompanying prevalence of border-patrol agents. This situation can be uncomfortable for some, but general birder experience is that illegal aliens wish to be left alone and do not add to the risk of crime.

Natural Hazards: Poison Oak is locally abundant in canyons; insects are very seldom a problem (no chiggers, few mosquitoes or ticks, and Lyme disease is rare).

Other Resources: The San Diego Rare Bird Alert, (619) 688-2473, is updated daily if there are fresh sightings, and is reproduced on the BIRDWEST listserve. The 1998 ABA/Lane book, *A Birder's Guide to Southern California* by Brad Schram, provides additional detail on San Diego and nearby mountains, deserts, and the Salton Sea. *Where Birders Go in Southern California* by Henry E. Childs, Jr. (1993, Los Angeles Audubon Society) is less detailed but still useful. The status and distribution of San Diego's avifauna are expertly covered in *The Birds of San Diego County* by Philip Unitt (1984, San Diego Society of Natural History, Memoir 13). For general travel information contact the San Diego Visitor Information Center, 2688 East Mission Bay Drive, San Diego, CA 92109, (619) 276-8200 or *www.sandiego.org*.

THE BIRDING YEAR

San Diego provides excellent birding all year. Summer has less overall diversity because most waterbirds are present in numbers only in migration (which starts in early July for shorebirds) and winter, but summer is still good because many target species of visiting birders are permanent residents or summer breeders. Spring and fall migrations are excellent for diversity, although there are seldom "fall-outs." Peak periods for migrant western landbirds are 15 April to 20 May and 15 September to 20 October. Although San Diego's CBC has slipped from national contention, the winter birding is still in that league. San Diego's strengths are (1) outstanding waterbirding, including inshore waters, rocky and sandy shorelines, bays, salt marshes and estuaries, and large mudflats; (2) a full complement of chaparral and coastal sage-scrub species; (3) good locations at which to search for passerine migrants; and (4) quick access to oak woodlands and a modest variety of species typical of montane coniferous forests.

Pelagic birding out of San Diego is fairly good, but it is not nearly so good as that out of Monterey or Bodega Bay, and there are vastly fewer organized trips (recently, just one early September trip organized by the Western Field Ornithologists). San Diego has a large sportfishing fleet with excellent boats, and half-day and full-day fishing trips can be joined at any number of outlets (e.g., along Scott Street on Point Loma and in Quivira Basin in Mission Bay). You will see pelagic species on such a trip, but you will be hostage to the fishing conditions (half-day trips usually fish close to shore with a limited selection of species, but a few tubenoses, jaegers, and alcids are to be expected; full-day trips go well offshore, but if you are particular about your ABA-Area list, you should know that some of these trips travel into Mexican waters). Whale-watching trips (for Gray Whales, January to March; check with the standard sportfishing companies) are to inshore waters but are good for Black-vented Shearwater, Parasitic Jaeger, and Rhinoceros Auklet.

POINT LOMA

One to four hours; best in spring and fall

Point Loma offers great views of San Diego along with a moderate list of chaparral birds, viewing points for rocky shores and inshore waters, and great potential for migrant landbirds. Migration is best April–May and September–October. Summer is slow, and winter adds only a few species to the residents (e.g., Townsend's Warbler in conifers, Golden-crowned Sparrow in chaparral). Mornings are best for landbirds, while the late afternoon offers better scenery (the morning marine layer may have cleared; also, the light is behind you then). The visitor will be interested in the wide variety of flycatchers, vireos, thrushes, warblers, and sparrows typical of western North America; the locals also search for rarities, an extraordinary variety of which have been found over the years (mostly eastern species, but an occasional Mexican or Siberian species, as well).

There are three main areas to bird, all reached from Catalina Boulevard. **Cabrillo National Monument** (fee: $3; free with Golden Eagle Pass) includes a visitor center and has the best views. Check the ornamental vegetation around the visitor center, parking lot, and en route to the Old Lighthouse (the "Myoporum Grove") for migrants. The adjoining coastal sage-scrub, more of which is to be found down the Bayside Trail, supports resident California Quail, Western Scrub-Jay, Bushtit, Bewick's Wren, Wren-tit, California Thrasher, and California and Spotted Towhees. Flowering Bottlebrush (introduced) and natives (e.g., Black Sage) are good for humming-birds in spring, including Anna's, Rufous, and Allen's, and a few Calliopes and Costa's. Orange-crowned Warbler is a common breeder and migrant. A road to the west just before the Monument's entrance kiosk leads steeply down to the coast, where there are three small parking lots that offer the chance to check the rocks and the ocean (scope recommended). La Jolla (see below) is much better, but, if your time is limited, you have a chance here for loons and scoters, Brown Pelican, all three cormorants, Wandering Tattler, Black Turnstone, many gulls and terns, and the occasional pelagic species.

Fort Rosecrans National Cemetery (free) is located along both sides of Catalina Boulevard. It can be worthwhile to check every tree in the place, but walking a loop through the central part of both sides will cover the best areas. This spot is best in migration (and not worth the time otherwise). Birds are thinly and rather uniformly distributed; watch for small flocks of warblers and sparrows. A few days are truly awful, with almost no birds, but on most days there is at least a sprinkling of migrants.

Point Loma Nazarene College is reached by taking Dupont Street west from Catalina and parking near the barrier. For the best birding, walk both north and south along paths between the residential fence-line and the college buildings. Otherwise, "follow your nose" to the northern and southern ends of the college and other good clumps of trees. The college is

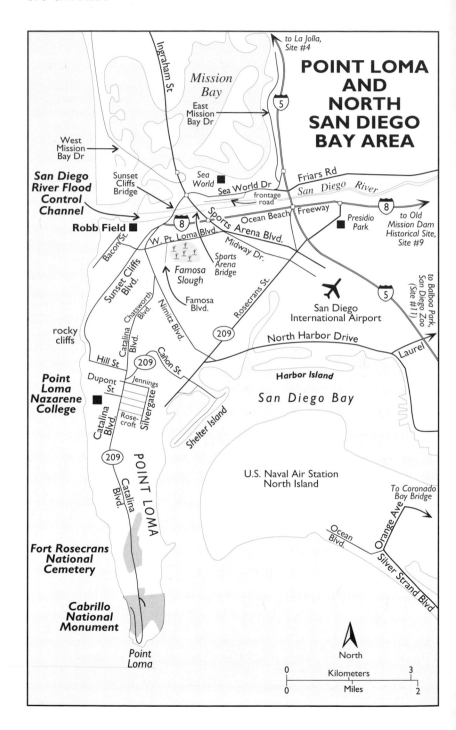

**POINT LOMA
AND
NORTH
SAN DIEGO
BAY AREA**

to La Jolla,
Site #4

Mission
Bay

Ingraham St

East
Mission
Bay Dr

West
Mission
Bay Dr

Friars Rd

Sea
World

Sea World Dr

San Diego River

**San Diego
River Flood
Control
Channel**

Sunset
Cliffs
Bridge

frontage
road

Presidio
Park

to Old
Mission Dam
Historical Site,
Site #9

Ocean Beach Freeway

Robb Field

W. Pt. Loma Blvd.

Sports Arena Blvd.

Bacon St.

Midway Dr.

Sports
Arena
Bridge

**Famosa
Slough**

San Diego
International Airport

Famosa
Blvd.

Rosecrans St.

Sunset Cliffs Blvd.

North Harbor Drive

to Balboa Park,
San Diego Zoo
(Site #1)

**rocky
cliffs**

Chatsworth Blvd.

Nimitz Blvd.

Laurel

Hill St

Cañon St

Harbor Island

**Point
Loma
Nazarene
College**

Catalina Blvd.

Dupont
St

Jennings

Silvergate

San Diego Bay

Rose-
croft

Shelter Island

Catalina Blvd.

P O I N T   L O M A

**U.S. Naval Air Station
North Island**

To Coronado
Bay Bridge

**Fort Rosecrans
National
Cemetery**

Catalina Blvd.

Ocean
Blvd.

Orange Ave

Silver Strand Blvd.

**Cabrillo
National
Monument**

Point
Loma

North

0   Kilometers   3

0   Miles   2

especially good in spring migration and birdy in fall and winter; summer offers little. Similar birding is found in residential areas near the college, by covering Dupont Street, Silvergate Avenue, and Rosecroft Lane to the east of Catalina.

There is some strategic planning to be done. The Monument and Cemetery are on a government reservation that, on weekends and holidays, is open only from 9:00AM to 5:00PM. On weekdays, the gate opens earlier, and well-behaved birders are tolerated at the Monument and Cemetery after 7:00AM. *Note: during the summer the Monument may remain open until sunset (call for hours)*. If the government reservation is not open, the college and the adjacent residential area are the places to start birding until it *does* open.

LA JOLLA
Two hours; year round

La Jolla offers some of the best ocean birding in Southern California (scope recommended). It is also a lovely and expensive piece of real estate. What that means is that unless you go early in the morning, be prepared to lose your temper negotiating the narrow streets in search of the true rarity, a parking space. That said, although early morning offers good light and good seabird activity, an early start is not necessary here and could be better spent elsewhere. Viewing late in the day is more difficult as the sun sets over the ocean. The best opportunity for tubenoses and other pelagic species is during and immediately following winter storms with strong west winds. Birders generally head for Point La Jolla (along Coast Boulevard at the north end of Browning Scripps Park, reached from I-5 by way of Ardath Road and Prospect Street), but there is no magic spot, and walking north and south along the coast from there will usually be necessary to find the flocks of rock-loving shorebirds (Surfbird, Black and Ruddy Turnstones, Wandering Tattler, Whimbrel; August through April is best). Numbers of migrant and wintering loons (three species) and Surf Scoter are regular, three species of cormorant are resident, and a good variety of gulls and terns pass by. Scanning offshore is productive for jaegers (mostly Parasitic with a few Pomarine; check behind fishing boats), and, thanks in part to a nearby submarine canyon, there is an appreciable chance for tubenoses and a few alcids. The most likely shearwater is one of the most wanted: Black-vented (largest numbers September–March). La Jolla is interesting all year, although avian variety is reduced in summer.

BAYS AND ESTUARIES
One hour to half day; year round

All of the following spots are good and are moderately similar; pick the ones that are convenient or fit your time constraints. A telescope is strongly recommended. Get the tide information and plan accordingly. Any tide above 7.0 feet is significantly high (think rails), and above 6.0 feet will work some of the time; any negative tide is significantly low. Tides in the upper parts of the bays will lag one to two hours behind the typical outer-beach tide that is published in the newspaper.

The San Diego River Flood-Control Channel is just north of the airport and near Sea World. There is a variety of vantage points, including some bike paths. For the outer area west of the Sunset Cliffs Bridge, better for roosting gulls and terns and some shorebirds such as Snowy Plover, try the south side by taking Bacon Street into Robb Field and parking at the edge of the levee. For tidal mud and marsh, try the north side upstream from the Sports Arena bridge, looking for the small frontage road (once on it, give bicycles and pedestrians the right of way); this area has the largest number of herons, ducks, and shorebirds. In between the two bridges is some deeper water with grebes, "Black" Brant, and diving ducks in winter. Nearby **Famosa Slough** is also worth a check. Take West Point Loma Boulevard east from Nimitz Boulevard, turn right on Famosa Boulevard, and find a parking spot.

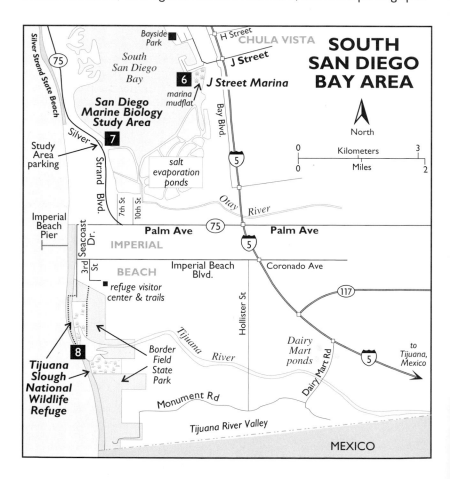

Although San Diego Bay is large, an easy spot from which to bird is the **J Street Marina** in Chula Vista, reached easily from I-5 (take the J Street exit, head west, take the left to the south edge of the marina). Look at the large, tidal mudflat to the south of the marina. Perhaps the best area is the **San Diego County Marine Biology Study Area** on the west side, reached by going north from Imperial Beach on the divided Silver Strand Boulevard (Highway 75). On your right within the first mile after leaving Imperial Beach are several large impoundments, part of the vast salt-works at the south end of the Bay, with several pull-offs. Then comes the paved Study Area parking lot, where the impoundments end and the Bay begins. You can walk along the edge (be careful—the bike path looks convenient but is dangerous for walkers) and out onto a couple of the levees. The tidal flats just to the north of the Study Area parking lot are good for large numbers of shorebirds at low tide. San Diego Bay has large numbers of diving ducks and a small flock of "Black" Brant in winter. The impoundments are usually at a water level good for ducks and phalaropes, but are sometimes lowered and then become good for herons and shorebirds. In summer, there is a large tern colony (mostly Elegant and Forster's, but also Caspian and Black Skimmer, with small numbers of Least, Royal, and Gull-billed) on dikes in the inner salt-works.

The **Tijuana Slough National Wildlife Refuge** is just to the south. In Imperial Beach take Seacoast Drive (formerly First Street) south to the end. On the east side is a healthy saltmarsh with resident "Light-footed" Clapper Rails (seen most easily at high tide) and "Belding's" Savannah Sparrows. Watch also for small numbers of the migratory "Large-billed" Savannah Sparrows, mostly September to February. Park at the end and walk south down the beach for about 20 minutes (more difficult on a very high tide) to the river mouth, where the sandy flats are good for Snowy Plover and the tidal flats are good for shorebirds, gulls, and terns. The east side of the marsh may be reached by trails from the Visitor Center (from Imperial Boulevard go south on 3rd Street and then east on Caspian Way), and from a parking lot at the south end of 5th Street.

MISSION DAM

One hour to half day; year round

This is the best spot in the San Diego area for a mix of breeding/resident landbirds, and it can be productive for migrants as well. The area is most fun in spring and early summer, when all the breeders are present and singing, but it is productive in any month. Morning is always best for landbirding, but this is particularly true in the summer, when it becomes hot after mid-morning. Allow a half-hour drive from the airport, but as little as an hour can be enough to find a nice variety of birds in the riparian area. Several hours are needed for greater coverage of the varied habitats. The riparian area is easily birded around **Lake Kumeyaay** and downstream to the historic Old

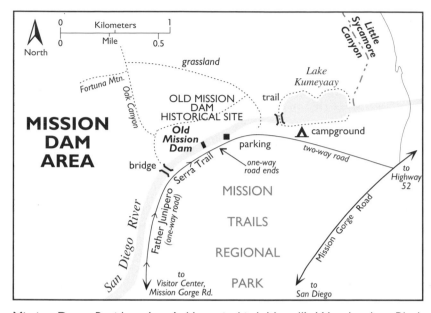

Mission Dam. Resident Anna's Hummingbird, Nuttall's Woodpecker, Black Phoebe, and Hutton's Vireo (uncommon) are joined in spring and summer by Pacific-slope Flycatcher, Bell's Vireo (endangered; no tapes allowed), Yellow Warbler, Yellow-breasted Chat, and Black-headed and Blue Grosbeaks. The gorge along the one-way (upstream) road that is downstream from the dam has several pairs of Canyon Wrens. Just below the dam a bridge across the "river" (this is the San Diego River) leads to a network of trails. The trail up Oak Canyon initially goes through coastal sage-scrub; look for Costa's Hummingbird in spring and summer and resident California Gnatcatcher (tough; easier at Lake Hodges) and Rufous-crowned Sparrow. Farther up this little canyon is chaparral with California Quail, California Thrasher, and a variety of sparrows: a few "Bell's" Sage, occasional Black-chinned, and moderate numbers of wintering Fox (a variety of subspecies—check them carefully), White-crowned, and Golden-crowned. The grasslands support White-tailed Kite and Grasshopper Sparrow.

LAKE HODGES

Two to four hours; year round

Located a half-hour northeast of San Diego along increasingly congested I-15, **Lake Hodges** is the recommended spot for California Gnatcatcher and other species of coastal sage-scrub. Early to mid-morning is strongly recommended. In addition, the lake is good for Clark's Grebes (with Westerns) and a variety of other waterbirds, and it seems to be reliable for

Cassin's Kingbird on a year-round basis. Exit I-15 south of the lake at the West Bernardo Drive/Pomerado Road exit and turn west and then right in approximately 0.5 mile at the stoplight and park. From the Jocelyn Senior Center, a network of small trails fans out through the coastal sage-scrub toward the lake. There are several pairs of gnatcatchers (*endangered; don't use a tape and please stay on the trails*); they can be quiet and sneaky, but with a little patience are usually found. The coastal subspecies of Cactus Wren occurs in low numbers (check the Prickly Pear cactus on the hills), and this is a good site in spring and early summer for Costa's Hummingbird. Some residents are White-tailed Kite, Greater Roadrunner (a few), White-throated Swift, California Thrasher, California and Spotted Towhees, and Rufous-crowned and "Bell's" Sage Sparrows. Another spot for California Gnatcatcher is San Elijo Lagoon, a half-hour north of San Diego on I-5; see Schram's *A Birder's Guide to Southern California* for details.

SAN DIEGO ZOO AND WILD ANIMAL PARK

Two hours to full day; year round

The San Diego Zoological Society's **San Diego Zoo** (Balboa Park, San Diego) and **Wild Animal Park** (near Escondido, just north of Lake Hodges) are among the world's few great zoos, and include many fabulous birds. And there are some native birds, especially in winter, such as Orange-crowned and Townsend's Warblers in flowering eucalyptus at the Zoo, and raptors at the Wild Animal Park (Golden Eagle and the rare winter Zone-tailed Hawk).

CUYAMACA RANCHO STATE PARK

Half to full day; year round

By the standards of the West, San Diego's mountains are small and support only a modest variety of montane species. The birder with more time will wish to head north for the San Jacinto, San Bernardino, or San Gabriel Mountains, Mt. Pinos, and/or the Sierra Nevada. However, absent bad traffic, you can cover the 50 miles from the airport to the mountains in an hour and add some very different scenery and birds to your San Diego visit. There is no one magic spot, but the standard trip is to head for **Paso Picacho Campground** in **Cuyamaca Rancho State Park**. The woodland here is a mixture of oaks and conifers with a resulting mix of birds, including Mountain Quail (difficult to find), Band-tailed Pigeon, Acorn, Nuttall's, and White-headed (scarce) Woodpeckers, Hutton's Vireo, Steller's Jay, Mountain Chickadee, Oak Titmouse, White-breasted and Pygmy Nuthatches, Western Bluebird, and Purple Finch. Summer adds much, including Ash-throated Flycatcher, Violet-green Swallow, Black-headed Grosbeak, Lazuli Bunting (streams and meadows), and Bullock's Oriole. Winter can bring additional rewards, including Lewis's Woodpecker, Williamson's Sapsucker, Golden-crowned Kinglet, Townsend's Solitaire, and various finches, but numbers are small and/or the species are erratic. With some time, energy, and no winter snow, walk the fire road to **Cuyamaca Peak**. This walk offers lovely views as well as some of San Diego's scarce breeders, such as "Audubon's" Yellow-rumped Warbler and Fox Sparrow (*stephensi*, a huge-billed, gray-backed type; other subspecies occur here in winter). There are many other pleasant trails to explore (Azalea Glen, Milk Ranch Road, and Middle Peak). Although erratic, Lawrence's Goldfinches are present in many months of the year—the Green Valley area has proven to be especially good—but this species is difficult to nail down.

Cuyamaca Lake is easily checked (best in wet years; good for ducks outside of summer), and a loop back to Interstate 8 through the Laguna

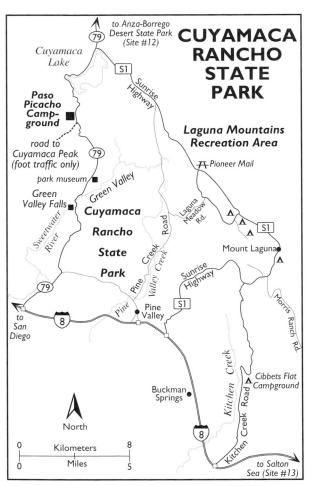

Mountains provides great views out over Anza-Borrego State Park and more chances to stop and explore chaparral and pine-oak woodland. One more spot to consider in this region is **Kitchen Creek**, an exit off I-8 7.6 miles east of the S-1 (Sunrise Highway) exit. The montane chaparral found three to six miles north of I-8 is one of the relatively few spots where Gray Vireo breeds near San Diego (early April to early July). This habitat, of which there is a great deal here and en route to Cuyamaca Mountain, is good for skulky Mountain Quail and Black-chinned

Sparrow (breeding season). A gate across the road just past Cibbets Flat Campground may or may not be open. If it is not open, walk the first half-mile beyond. See Schram's guide for more details.

THE DESERT AND THE SALTON SEA
Full day or overnight; year round

Anza-**Borrego State Park** is the closest desert to San Diego; it supports most of the standard desert species. The wildflowers are, one year in seven, "world class" in February and March; try the local flower hotline at (760) 767-4684 or, more generally for Southern California including Anza-Borrego, the Wildflower Hotline at (818) 768-3533. This region is most productive (pleasant) in winter and spring. A long day trip is reasonable, including a loop involving I-8, S-2, and the Laguna Mountains; Agua Caliente County Park and Yaqui Well/Tamarisk Grove Campground are particularly recommended. Enticements include White-winged Dove, Long-eared Owl, Costa's Hummingbird, Black-tailed Gnatcatcher, Le Conte's Thrasher, Phainopepla, Black-throated Sparrow, and Scott's Oriole. In winter there are Brewer's and Sage Sparrows. See Schram's Southern California guide for details.

The **Salton Sea** provides incredible waterbirding and offers additional desert landbirds. The only regular place in the U.S. for Yellow-footed Gull (mostly summer and fall, a very few in winter), the Salton Sea's other attractions include the opportunity to see hundreds, often thousands, of birds such as Eared Grebes, American White Pelicans, White-faced Ibises, Ross's Geese, Black-necked Stilts, American Avocets, and Long-billed Curlews. Flocks of wintering Mountain Plovers roam the agricultural areas in search of the "right" field. Desert bonuses include Burrowing Owl, Lesser Nighthawk, and Abert's Towhee. Winter is most pleasant, spring and fall migration the most diverse, and summer the most interesting for rarities from the Gulf of California. The summer half of the year brings six months of 100°-plus temperatures. Only two-and-one-half hours from San Diego, it can be visited in one day, but for people new to the region, an overnight visit is strongly recommended to reduce frustration levels and the need for an extremely early start. See Schram's Southern California guide for more details.

BIRDING FOR NON-BIRDING AND SEMI-BIRDING SPOUSES

Particularly recommended are the Zoo and/or Wild Animal Park; Pt. Loma, especially on a beautifully clear afternoon for the views; La Jolla; whale-watching boat trips (winter); and the Cuyamaca Peak/Laguna Mountains region for a walk in the pines and great views. For a quickie divorce, try the Salton Sea in July without air-conditioning.

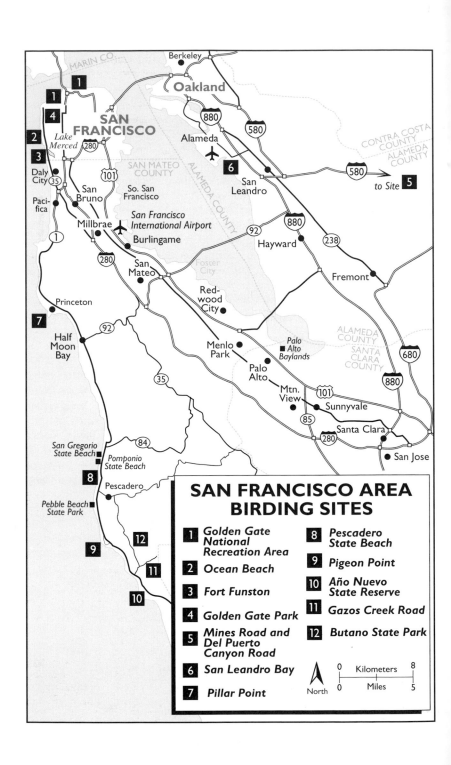

SAN FRANCISCO AREA BIRDING SITES

1 Golden Gate National Recreation Area

2 Ocean Beach

3 Fort Funston

4 Golden Gate Park

5 Mines Road and Del Puerto Canyon Road

6 San Leandro Bay

7 Pillar Point

8 Pescadero State Beach

9 Pigeon Point

10 Año Nuevo State Reserve

11 Gazos Creek Road

12 Butano State Park

North

| 0 | Kilometers | 8 |
| 0 | Miles | 5 |

SAN FRANCISCO, CALIFORNIA

Alan Hopkins

San Francisco is known for its hills, cable cars, Victorian houses, restaurants, and the fog-shrouded Golden Gate Bridge. It is not surprising that San Francisco is among North America's favorite tourist destinations. The Bay Area's geography and climate—impacted greatly by the Pacific Ocean and San Francisco Bay itself—interact to create a fine variety of habitats and a great diversity of birds. Bay Area birders can find over 300 species annually. The visiting birder will find birding San Francisco a rewarding experience.

ESSENTIAL INFORMATION

Getting Around: Most San Francisco birding sites can be accessed via public transit. The focal point of public transit in San Francisco is along Market Street. Buses and electric streetcars run along the surface streets, whereas trolleys and Bay Area Rapid Transit (BART) trains are located mostly below ground. For more information contact the San Francisco Municipal Transit (MUNI) at (415) 673-6864, Bay Area Rapid Transit (BART) at (415) 992-2278, and ferry information at (800) 229-2784. Trips to Mines Road, the San Mateo Coast, and most other Bay Area sites require a car. Expect *very* congested rush-hour traffic on the major freeways.

Climate: With a summer dry season and a winter wet season, the climate is technically "Mediterranean." The Pacific Ocean's cold California Current, however, can create cool, damp conditions along the coast throughout the year. During the summer months, "low clouds and fog extending inland during the night and morning, clearing to the coast, and breezy in the afternoon" is a Bay Area weatherman's mantra. Summer temperatures along the immediate coast may reach only into the mid-60s Fahrenheit, while in the hills around Mt. Hamilton in the East Bay it can be over 90°. During the winter months, fog is more common in inland valleys than it is along the coast. At that season temperatures can again vary greatly. Bay Area birders typically dress in layers and bring sunscreen and a hat.

Safety: The birding sites discussed here are all quite safe; however, a few precautions are worth considering. Crime is very rare at these sites, but don't leave valuables in plain view, pay attention to your surroundings, and stay on established paths. Some places in extreme eastern Golden Gate Park, not mentioned here, have a large population of homeless people.

Natural Hazards: Poison Oak is common everywhere in the Bay Area. Rattlesnakes and ticks may be encountered along Mines Road and Del Puerto Canyon Road. Even on a calm day the interaction of ocean waves, tides, rip currents, and undertow make the tidal zone a dangerous place to walk.

Other Resources: Useful contacts include the Golden Gate Audubon Society, (510) 843-2222, www.goldengateaudubon.org; Golden Gate National Recreation Area, (415) 566-0560; Golden Gate National Park Association, (415) 776-0693; Golden Gate Raptor Observatory, (415) 331-0730; Northern California Bird Box, Rare Bird Alert voice-mail, (415) 681-7422; Joe Morlan's California Birding Pages, www.fog.ccsf.cc.ca.us/~jmorlan; San Francisco Bay Area Nature-Related Events Calendar, www. best/~folkbird/calendar/. Detailed maps of the region may be obtained from AAA and Rand McNally (595 Market Street, San Francisco). The Golden Gate National Parks Association has trail maps of San Francisco's Pacific Shore and the Marin Headlands. Books include *Birding Northern California* by J. Kemper (1999, Falcon Press), *San Francisco Peninsula Birdwatching* by C. Richer et al. (1996, Sequoia Audubon Society), *Birding at the Bottom of the Bay* by B. Wyatt, A. Stoye, and C. Harris, editors (1990, Santa Clara Valley Audubon Society), and *Birds of Northern California: An Annotated Field List* by G. McCaskie, P. DeBenedicitis, R. Erickson, and J. Morlan (1979, Golden Gate Audubon Society).

Other Destinations: Alcatraz, (415) 705-1045; California Academy of Sciences, (415) 750-7145; The Exploratorium, (415) 561-0360; and San Francisco Zoological Gardens, (415) 753-7061.

THE BIRDING YEAR

Most San Francisco parks have been planted with pine, cypress, and eucalyptus. Common birds are Anna's and Allen's (February–August) Hummingbirds, Western Scrub-Jay, Chestnut-backed Chickadee, Bushtit, Brown Creeper, Pygmy Nuthatch, California Towhee, and White-crowned Sparrow. During the non-breeding season, Winter Wrens, Ruby-crowned and Golden-crowned Kinglets, Townsend's Warblers, and Golden-crowned and "Sooty" Fox Sparrows are numerous. Spring migration peaks between mid-April and late May; fall migration runs from mid-August to mid-October. The number of migrants and rarities found within the city's limits keeps birders active. Recent exceptional sightings have included Manx Shearwater, Bar-tailed Godwit, Gila Woodpecker, Dusky-capped Flycatcher, Yellow-green Vireo, and Northern Wheatear.

The Pacific coastline is frequented by many wintering loons, grebes, and scoters. Wintering shorebirds include Snowy Plover, Wandering Tattler,

Marbled Godwit, Black Turnstone, and Surfbird. In summer, the offshore rocks provide nesting sites for Brandt's Cormorant, Black Oystercatcher, and Pigeon Guillemot. San Francisco Bay is the winter home of thousands of loons, grebes, ducks, shorebirds, and gulls.

GOLDEN GATE NATIONAL RECREATION AREA

Half or full day; year round

The **Golden Gate National Recreation Area** (GGNRA) consists of a patchwork of parks stretching from Marin County south to San Mateo County. In San Francisco, the GGNRA encompasses parks along the City's northern and western waterfronts. If you have limited time, or are using public transit, the highlights of this tour are the Seal Rocks and the Cliff House, Lands End, and Crissy Field.

At Ninth Street and Market, take Hayes Street two blocks west and turn right onto Van Ness Avenue. Follow Van Ness two miles past North Point Street to Aquatic Park. **Aquatic Park** has wintering loons, grebes, and scoters along the semicircular Municipal Pier. Wintering and migrant land-birds can be found in the trees bordering Fort Mason across from the small art-deco building.

Return to Van Ness and turn west onto Bay Street toward the Golden Gate Bridge. Follow Bay Street four blocks (0.3 mile) and turn right onto Laguna Street. After one block Laguna Street becomes Marina Boulevard. Stay on Marina for eight blocks (1.0 mile). Just beyond Baker Street head straight, leaving the main thoroughfare, onto Mason Street and into **The Presidio**. After entering the Presidio, watch for the Beach Access signs (0.1 mile) and turn right into the parking area for **Crissy Field**. In the mid-1990s Crissy Field was an abandoned airfield, but in November 1999 the National Park Service opened the channel that let the bay waters flood into the newly-created Crissy Field Wetland. Still a work-in-progress, the Crissy Field Wetland looks to become one of San Francisco's favored birding sites. A number of migrant shorebirds that can be difficult to find elsewhere in the City have been spotted here. Wintering waterbirds using the marsh include Western and Clark's Grebes and a variety of waterfowl. The birding is best from the marsh's south side along the path that parallels Mason Street. The Crissy Field Visitor Center is located across Mason Street, near the observation ramp.

Continue west about one mile along Mason Street. To visit the Gulf of the Farallones National Marine Sanctuary Visitor Center, take the first right; otherwise, take the second right onto Crissy Field Avenue. At the top of the hill, merge onto Lincoln Boulevard. At this point a brief detour can be taken by following the signs to historic Fort Point at the foot of the Golden Gate

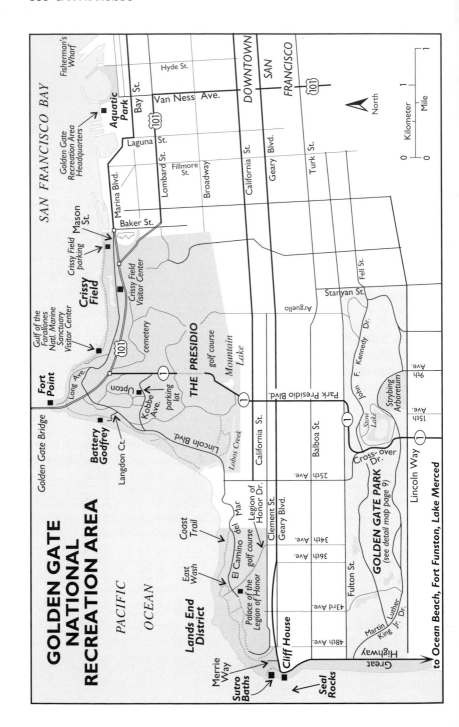

GOLDEN GATE NATIONAL RECREATION AREA

PACIFIC OCEAN

SAN FRANCISCO BAY

Fisherman's Wharf

Hyde St.

Bay St.

Van Ness Ave.

DOWNTOWN SAN FRANCISCO

Aquatic Park

Golden Gate Recreation Area Headquarters

Laguna St.

Fillmore St.

Lombard St.

Marina Blvd.

Broadway

California St.

Geary Blvd.

Turk St.

Baker St.

North

Kilometer

Mile

0

0

Crissy Field parking

Mason St.

Gulf of the Farallones Natl. Marine Sanctuary Visitor Center

Crissy Field Visitor Center

Crissy Field

Fell St.

Stanyan St.

Arguello

cemetery

THE PRESIDIO

Mountain Lake

golf course

Fort Point

Long Ave.

Upton

Kobbe Ave.

parking lot

John F. Kennedy Dr.

Park Presidio Blvd.

9th Ave.

15th Ave.

Golden Gate Bridge

Battery Godfrey

Langdon Ct.

Lincoln Blvd.

Lobos Creek

California St.

Balboa St.

Strybing Arboretum

Stow Lake

Cross-over Dr.

Lincoln Way

Coast Trail

Legion of Honor Dr.

El Camino del Mar

Clement St.

Geary Blvd.

25th Ave.

34th Ave.

36th Ave.

GOLDEN GATE PARK
(see detail map page 9)

East Wash

golf course

Palace of the Legion of Honor

Lands End District

Fulton St.

43rd Ave.

48th Ave.

Martin Luther King Jr. Dr.

Cliff House

Merrie Way

Sutro Baths

Seal Rocks

Great Highway

to Ocean Beach, Fort Funston, Lake Merced

Bridge. The waters flowing under the bridge provide excellent fishing opportunities for grebes and all three cormorants.

Return to Lincoln Boulevard, take it 0.6 mile, and then go right onto Langdon Court. Turn left and then right around the building to the overlook at Battery Godfrey. Below, watch for cormorants and shorebirds on the rocks, and loons, grebes, and scoters in the water. Standing on the battery can provide a great place from which to watch for migrating hawks in autumn. The highest peak on the Marin Headlands across the water is Battery 129. Also known as Hawk Hill, it is monitored by the Golden Gate Raptor Observatory and is the best place on the West Coast to watch fall raptor migration.

Return to Lincoln Boulevard and turn right. After 0.2 mile turn left onto Kobbe Avenue, continue another 0.3 mile, and park on the left in the lot at the intersection of Kobbe and Upton Avenues. In this area watch for resident California Quail; in spring and summer look for Olive-sided and Pacific-slope Flycatchers, Pygmy Nuthatch, and Hooded Oriole.

To continue, retrace your route back to Lincoln Boulevard and turn left. After you follow Lincoln Boulevard for one mile, it becomes El Camino del Mar. Following the Scenic Route signs, head west 0.5 mile to just beyond 32nd Avenue, where you enter the **Lands End** District of the GGNRA and the **Lincoln Park** Golf Course. The Lands End sign marks a trailhead for the Coast Trail. From this point it is possible to walk the spectacular and birdy trail to the Merrie Way parking area above the Sutro Baths.

Continuing the tour, the 0.3-mile stretch of trees that line El Camino del Mar to the top of the hill are worth checking during migration. Olive-sided Flycatchers and Pygmy Nuthatches nest in the conifers. At the top of the hill a golf-cart road leads down the hill to the northwest. Just before the third fairway, near a willow patch, a dirt path leads to an open area known as the East Wash, which can be outstanding during migration. Returning to the top of the hill, turn left onto Legion of Honor Drive and go past the museum of the Palace of the Legion of Honor and down the hill to the south for 0.4 mile. Continue straight past Clement Street on 34th Avenue and turn right onto Geary Boulevard. At 36th Avenue, Geary forks to the south; stay on the main thoroughfare, however, which becomes Point Lobos Avenue. Head down Point Lobos past 48th Avenue and turn right into the Merrie Way parking area above the **Cliff House, Seal Rocks,** and **Sutro Baths.**

Located where the rocky cliffs of Lands End wrap around to meet Ocean Beach, the Cliff House and Sutro Baths are the best places in San Francisco to look for wintering Wandering Tattler, Black Turnstone, Surfbird, and pelagic birds. At The Cliff House there are restaurants, public restrooms, and a GGNRA Visitor Center (open 10:00AM to 5:00PM). To check the rocks for shorebirds, watch for the narrow stairway between the two Cliff House buildings leading to the observation decks. In summer, Brandt's Cormorant and Black Oystercatcher nest on the rocks. The first turnstones arrive in July. Other birds that you may see during the non-breeding season include Brown Pelican, Marbled Godwit, Whimbrel, Willet, and Ruddy Turnstone. Offshore, watch for Red-throated and Pacific Loons, Western and Clark's Grebes, and Black and Surf Scoters. During some winters Marbled Murrelets are present, and occasionally an Ancient Murrelet is seen. In spring and summer Common Murres and Pigeon Guillemots are numerous. Spring, summer, and fall can bring thousands of Sooty Shearwaters close to shore. From August to October watch for Parasitic Jaegers chasing the Elegant Terns. Although the rocks are called Seal Rocks, the common mammals there are California Sea Lions, with Harbor Porpoise, Bottlenose Dolphins, Sea Otters, and Gray Whales occasionally seen offshore.   Once a glass-covered swimming palace, the Sutro Baths now are visited by wintering ducks and the common coastal gulls, including Heermann's (June–February), Mew (mid-October–April), California, and Glaucous-winged (October–May).

To the south of the Cliff House is five-mile-long **Ocean Beach**. The beach is habitat for Snowy Plovers (July–May), which prefer the upper beach between Lincoln Way and Pacheco Street To look for the plovers, take the Great Highway south from the Merrie Way parking lot to a parking lot just before Lincoln Way (1 mile). From this point either park and walk south along the beach or, to drive, turn left onto Lincoln Way and then immediately right onto the (lower) Great Highway. Proceed along the Great Highway 0.8 mile to Noriega Street, cross the upper Great Highway, and check for the plovers by walking the seawall. During late summer, Elegant Terns roost on this section of beach.

At the southern end of Ocean Beach, wintering rafts of Black, Surf, and White-winged Scoters are found off northern Fort Funston. To look for the scoters, continue south on the Great Highway for 3.9 miles to Sloat Street, then go 0.2 mile to the second parking lot. During the spring and summer, **Fort Funston's** cliffs to the south are home to a colony of Bank Swallows. A good place for landbird migrants at Fort Funston is the "Skyline Grove," found by following the trail that parallels the Great Highway and Skyline Boulevard to the south.   The grove is approximately one-half mile from the parking lot.

To return to Van Ness Avenue or Market Street, exit the southern Ocean Beach parking lot onto the Great Highway for 0.3 mile and turn left at the stop sign onto Skyline Drive. Follow Skyline for 0.7 mile and turn left onto Sloat Street and return to the Great Highway. Follow the Great Highway past the Cliff House and back onto Geary Boulevard, which eventually returns to Van Ness and then Market.

Lake Merced has a great diversity of birdlife and has produced a number of rarities over the years. Clark's Grebes nest on the lake. The best birding is from the end of Sunset Boulevard and around the South Impoundment along John Muir Drive. Bank Swallows forage over the lake in summer; look for Thayer's Gulls in winter.

GOLDEN GATE PARK

Half day; year round

Golden Gate Park, San Francisco's best-known park, has great birding. The Park's thirteen small lakes provide habitat for waterfowl, and there is enough botanical diversity to attract both resident and migrant landbirds. The eastern half of the Park is more developed and contains the California Academy of Sciences, Steinhart Aquarium, de Young Museum, Conservatory of Flowers, and Strybing Arboretum. To the west of Cross-over Drive (Highway 1) the park is more rustic. The most popular birding spots are Strybing Arboretum and Stow Lake in the eastern part of the park and the Chain of Lakes in the western section, but many other sites can be rewarding as well.

From Ninth and Market Streets, take Hayes Street four blocks west, turn left onto Gough Street, and then almost immediately right onto Fell Street. Fell is one-way for 19 blocks until it enters the park. Continue to the left for 0.5 mile (Fell has become Kezar Drive at this point) and turn right at the signal into the inconspicuous entrance at Martin Luther King, Jr., Drive (MLK Jr. Drive). Follow MLK Jr. Drive for 0.4 mile to the intersection with Ninth.

By public transit from Market Street, take Bus 5-Fulton to the Great Highway and Ocean Beach; or the N-Judah Streetcar to Ninth Avenue and Irving, then walk one block north on Ninth to the Park; or take Bus 71-Haight-Noriega, which starts at the Ferry Terminal, to 9th or 23rd Avenues.

The main gate for the **Strybing Arboretum and Botanical Gardens** is located at MLK Jr. Drive and Ninth Avenue; it opens at 8:00AM weekdays and 10:00AM on weekends and holidays. There is a store located near the main gate where maps, checklists, and field guides are available. The Arboretum is a consistent spot to find wintering Red-breasted Sapsucker, Varied Thrush, and White-throated Sparrow. The Arboretum's diverse plant communities frequently provide a winter food source for scarce over-wintering warblers, tanagers, and orioles. The most productive spots are the duck pond, the California and Succulent Gardens, and along the Muir Nature Trail.

Stow Lake is encircled by Stow Lake Drive. To reach Stow Lake take MLK Jr. Drive west and watch for the Stow Lake/Chinese Pavilion sign pointing to the one-way entrance. There is a snack bar with restrooms located along the lake's northern edge. Thayer's Gulls can sometimes be found in the flocks of wintering Glaucous-wingeds. Strawberry Hill in the center of the lake is a

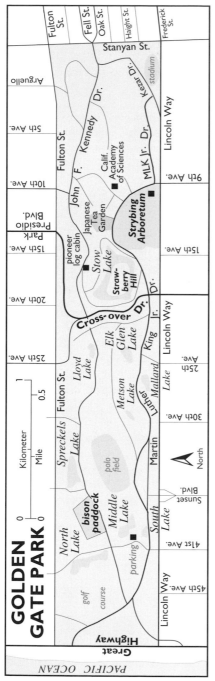

good place for migrant and wintering birds and resident Hutton's Vireos. Hooded Orioles occasionally nest in the palm trees near the Chinese Pavilion.

The best birding in Golden Gate Park west of Cross-over Drive is around its seven small "lakes." Follow MLK Jr. Drive 1.3 miles past the intersection with Cross-over Drive (Highway 1). At Elk Glen Lake (0.3 mile) the trees to the north can have Red-breasted Sapsuckers in winter, and the trees around the pump-house can be good during migration. Mallard Lake is 0.2 mile west of Elk Glen Lake. Here, look for dabbling ducks and Varied Thrush in winter and early spring. Continue west to the third stop sign near South Lake and turn right onto Chain of Lakes Drive (0.9 mile). Just beyond the equestrian stop sign, turn right into the parking lot for Middle Lake.

The **Chain of Lakes** are three small lakes that are the most frequently birded areas in the city; they have an impressive list of rare migrants. The lakes are encircled by paths, all of which are worth checking. Tall flowering eucalyptus trees at Middle Lake are full of warblers and Western Tanagers in autumn. The western edge of North Lake is also a good spot for migrants. Cooper's and Red-shouldered Hawks nest nearby. Public transit: 5-Fulton to 43rd Avenue.

To check some of the other spots in the western half of the park, turn right out of the parking lot, and then right (east) onto JFK Drive for 0.1 mile to the **Bison Paddock**. The Paddock can be a good place for sparrows, blackbirds, and, occasionally, wintering Cattle Egrets. Just 0.1 mile east of the Paddock is **Spreckels Lake**, which has wintering diving ducks and gulls. **Lloyd Lake** is 0.8 mile east of Spreckels Lake. Wintering Hooded Mergansers may be found, and occasionally Eurasian Wigeons are seen among the Americans. To return to the starting point, turn right onto Transverse Drive, which returns to MLK Jr. Drive, or continue along JFK Drive (closed weekends and holidays) to Kezar.

MINES ROAD/DEL PUERTO CANYON ROAD AND SAN LEANDRO BAY

Full day, year round

Birders make the trip east to **Mines Road** and **Del Puerto Canyon Road** to see many birds not found at other Bay Area sites. Narrow roads meander through the dry hills northeast of Mt. Hamilton and in the western Central Valley. Some of the birds found along the route are Greater Roadrunner, Costa's Hummingbird, Lewis's Woodpecker, Nuttall's Woodpecker, Western Kingbird, Yellow-billed Magpie, Canyon Wren, Wrentit, California Thrasher, Phainopepla, "Bell's" Sage Sparrow, and Lawrence's Goldfinch. On the return trip to San Francisco, a brief detour to San Leandro Bay for waterbirds can boost the day's list to over 100 species.

It is best to start this route as early in the morning as possible. Temperatures can reach above 90°F during the late spring and summer. In winter, nearby peaks can be dusted with snow. Birding along both roads consists of stopping at many of the pull-outs, but mid-day weekend traffic can make birding difficult. Be sure to have a full tank of gas, food, and fluids before you leave Livermore. The only public restrooms are located at Frank Raines County Park and Deer Creek Campground (fee) near the end of the tour, and at San Antonio Junction.

The tour passes through three counties: Alameda, Santa Clara, and Stanislaus. The roads are painted with large mile markers (mm), which are used here to highlight recommended stops (e.g., a stop for Sage Sparrow at "mm-20+.3" is 0.3 mile past mile-marker 20). Note that the numbering system changes at each county boundary. The numbers increase along Mines Road in Alameda County, and then decrease once the road enters Santa Clara County. Thus, there could be two mm-8 markers along the route.

From the Bay Area, take I-580 east. Upon reaching the east end of Livermore, take the Vasco Road exit south toward the Lawrence Livermore National Laboratory. South Vasco ends in about three miles at Tesla Road. Turn right on Tesla, continue 0.8 mile, and then go left onto Mines Road. After 3.3 miles watch for a left turn to continue on **Mines Road**. Yellow-billed Magpies are among the first birds to be encountered. As the road begins to climb into the hills, watch for Greater Roadrunner, California Thrasher, Phainopepla, and Lawrence's Goldfinch.

The road crosses several small ravines that are worth checking for migrants and Phainopeplas. The pull-out at mm-11 is a good place to scan for Wild Turkey (introduced) and roadrunner. At mm 20, the Arroyo Mocho crossing, Mines Road becomes San Antonio Valley Road as it enters Santa Clara County. Just after mm-25, the road passes the summit of a sage-covered hill. From the pull-out just beyond the summit look for California Thrasher and "Bell's" Sage Sparrow. As the road descends into the San Antonio Valley, check the small pond at mm-21+.7 for Wood Duck and the surrounding area for Lawrence's Goldfinches. The sage-covered out-croppings at mm-20+.3 may have Sage Sparrows. Lawrence's Goldfinch sometimes can be found near the fire station just before San Antonio Junction.

At the junction of San Antonio Valley Road and Del Puerto Canyon Road, take the former toward San Jose and Mt. Hamilton. Check the oaks along the road for Lewis's Woodpeckers. Continue to a small bridge and look for

wintering Say's Phoebes and Tricolored Blackbirds along the stream. Proceed to the second ("Bill Gehri") bridge; the willows here can be good for resident and migrant passerines.

Turn around and return to the junction with **Del Puerto Canyon Road** and take it east toward Patterson. The pond at mm 24+.7 is worth checking for Wood Duck, Nuttall's Woodpecker, and Lawrence's Goldfinch. After the road crosses into Stanislaus County, it begins to drop into the canyon. Watch the spring wildflowers along the roadside for hummingbirds; most will be Anna's, but migrant Rufous and Calliope are possible.

At mm-16 is the Deer Creek Campground. The area around the campground is an off-road-vehicle area, so birding may be difficult. On weekdays the area may be quieter and birding along the creek can be good. Phainopeplas have nested in the campground. The entrance fee is $2, undeveloped camping is $12, and full trailer hookup is $16. Frank Rains Regional Park is half a mile past Deer Creek Campground. It has water, restrooms, and tables, and is free (undeveloped camping is $12). Acorn Woodpecker, Oak Titmouse, and Western Bluebird are common.

Continue down Del Puerto Canyon Road to a large pull-out at mm-11+.6, where Costa's Hummingbirds and Canyon and Rock Wrens have nested. The wrens also can be found near mm-8+.5; the road is narrow at this point, and it is necessary to drive past the rock face and walk back. Rufous-crowned Sparrow may be seen here, as well.

As the road winds out of the canyon, look for Golden Eagles. Patches of Tree Tobacco line the road; watch here for hummingbirds feeding on its yellow flowers. Costa's Hummingbirds can be found between the large rock outcropping at mm-4+.2 and a small rock outcropping at mm-4+.5. The last miles of Del Puerto Canyon Road pass through grasslands; look for Burrowing Owl and Grasshopper Sparrow (spring and early summer), and, in the winter, for Mountain Bluebird. At I-5 (the Patterson exit) head north toward Sacramento. After 13 miles take I-580 toward Oakland and San Francisco.

San Leandro Bay Detour. Species possible here include Western and Clark's Grebes, Blue-winged and Cinnamon Teal, Eurasian Wigeon, Clapper Rail, Snowy Plover, Whimbrel, Long-billed Curlew, Marbled Godwit, Red Knot, and Elegant and Least Terns. From I-580 about 20 miles west of Livermore, exit from the left lanes onto I-238 for 2 miles, then take I-880 north. After 4 miles take the Hegenberger Road exit, turn left onto Edes Avenue, and then left on Hegenberger, which you follow for one mile before turning right onto Pardee Drive. Continue to Swan Way, turn left, and watch for the entrance gate to the Martin Luther King Jr. Regional Shoreline and Arrowhead Marsh on the right.

The half-mile road to **Arrowhead Marsh** is lined by small hills worth checking for Burrowing Owl. On the east side of the road is a newly-created

wetland. Many birds feeding far out on the San Leandro Bay mudflats at low tide come to this site at high tide. At the end of the road, just beyond the parking area, scope San Leandro Bay for grebes, Cinnamon Teal, scoters, and sometimes Barrow's Goldeneye (winter). Clapper Rails can be seen from the boardwalk that extends into the marsh.

Return to the entrance gate, turn right onto Swan Way, and then turn right again onto Doolittle Drive. After approximately 1-1/2 miles turn left onto the Harbor Bay Expressway. Take the expressway 2.2 miles and make a U-turn and park near the palm trees next to the pond. During breeding season watch for Least, Forster's, and Caspian Terns. There are sometimes Snowy Plovers among the shorebirds. Scanning the Bay beyond the pond can produce loons, grebes, Brown Pelicans, and scoters.

To return to San Francisco, backtrack to the signal at Doolittle Drive and turn left. Follow Doolittle over the bridge and turn right onto Fernside Boulevard. Follow Fernside one mile and turn right onto High Street. Follow High Street east to I-880.

THE SAN MATEO COAST

Full day; year round

B irdwatchers taking a drive along the **San Mateo County** coast will find miles of mostly undeveloped shoreline backed by open rolling hills. Some of the species to watch for are Pacific Loon, Sooty Shearwater, Pelagic Cormorant, White-tailed Kite, Rock Sandpiper (rare), Wandering Tattler, Pigeon Guillemot, Marbled Murrelet, Band-tailed Pigeon, Black Swift, Varied Thrush, and Tricolored Blackbird. The coastline is a patchwork of state parks, many of which may be worth checking. The most-productive areas for coastal birds are **Pillar Point and Harbor, Pescadero Marsh Natural Preserve, Pigeon Point**, and **Año Nuevo State Reserve**. For landbirds visit **Gazos Creek Road** and **Butano State Park**. There is a $5.00 day-use fee for the state parks and beaches. From San Francisco, take I-280 toward San Jose. In Daly City, as Highway 1 merges from the left, stay to the right to exit onto Highway 1 southbound, toward Pacifica and Half Moon Bay. Stay on Highway 1 for approximately 13 miles, and exit at the southern end of the Half Moon Bay Airport onto Capistrano Road.

A fter exiting onto Capistrano Road, turn right onto Prospect Way. At Broadway turn left and then immediately right onto Princeton. Follow Princeton until it ends at West Point Avenue and turn right. Follow West Point Avenue around the marsh and park in the West Shoreline Access Parking lot at **Pillar Point**. From the parking area, walk south along the path at the base of the cliff, along the edge of the harbor. The harbor is a good place to see wintering loons, grebes, and scoters. The jetty at the end of the path is frequented by Black Oystercatcher (resident), Wandering Tattler, and Black Turnstone. Check the Surfbirds carefully for the occasional Rock Sandpiper (November–March). After birding Pillar Point, backtrack to the town of Princeton. At the intersection of Prospect Way and Capistrano Road, turn right onto Capistrano, and follow it to Highway 1 at the traffic light. Turn right and head south 3.8 miles to the town of Half Moon Bay and the intersection with Highway 92. (After one leaves Half Moon Bay, services are limited.) From Highway 92 continue south on Route 1 for 10.8 miles to San Gregorio State Beach, which has a small lagoon worth checking for shorebirds and gulls.

O ne-and-one-half miles south of San Gregorio is the north parking lot of **Pescadero State Beach** and the North Pond of **Pescadero Marsh Natural Preserve**. North Pond can be good for waterfowl and shorebirds. From the parking lot, cross the highway to the trail around North Pond, where Bewick's Wrens and Wrentits are common. At the south end of North Pond the trail crosses a ridge where there is an observation platform, which gives an unobstructed view of the southern part of Pescadero Marsh.

To check Pescadero Lagoon, go south 0.7 mile from the North Pond parking lot. Just past the bridge watch for the right turn into the second Pescadero Beach parking lot (free). At the north end of the lot it is possible to view the lagoon and southern marsh; shorebirds are found along the rocky coast. To reach the lagoon, take the stairway from the parking lot, walk north back over the bridge, and then go back under the bridge to the trailhead. At 0.2 mile south of the intersection with Pescadero Road is another opportunity to check for rocky shorebirds. The southeast marsh can be checked by driving Pescadero Road east toward the town of Pescadero.

Two miles south of the intersection of Highway 1 and Pescadero Road is Pebble Beach State Park, where in some years a wintering Rock Sandpiper has been found. Harbor Seals are common on the inshore rocks.

At 3.3 miles south of Pebble Beach, Pigeon Point Road leads to the lighthouse at **Pigeon Point**. When conditions are right, scoping for seabirds from the dirt pull-out near the lighthouse can be spectacular. Marbled Murrelets are regular here but are frequently overlooked. Rhinoceros Auklets can be seen among the Common Murres, and all of the common West Coast shearwaters have been seen from here. In some fall seasons Black-vented Shearwaters are seen in good numbers, and a few Black-footed Albatrosses have been seen in spring. Coastal seabird migration surveys have been conducted here in spring. During their migration in late winter and early spring, Gray Whales can often be seen.

Follow Pigeon Point Road south back onto Highway 1. There is the option of looking for landbirds along Gazos Creek Road (see below) or to bird at Año Nuevo State Reserve. Gazos Creek Road winds to the north back to Pescadero Road, so it is more efficient to check Año Nuevo first.

Año **Nuevo State Reserve** was created to protect the Northern Elephant Seals that breed on the point's beaches; as a result, human access is restricted. During the seal's breeding season (December through March) there are guided tours that require reservations. It is a good idea to check your options for birding at the entrance gate or visitor center. The walk to the point is 1.5 miles, and walking over the dunes is strenuous but well worth it. Just after the trail begins, it splits. Take the Pond Loop Trail to the pond, which has gulls and possibly phalaropes during migration, as well as Bank Swallows in summer. From the trail, scope the cliffs at the north end of the beach for nesting Pelagic Cormorants and Pigeon Guillemots.

Follow the Pond Loop Trail past the pines and into an open area, looking for White-tailed Kites and, during their nesting season from late May through August, Black Swifts. At the staging area with painted seals, take the trail to the left, from which Marbled Murrelets can be seen close to shore. Sea Otters, seabirds, shorebirds, Black Swifts, and Wrentits may be seen by taking the spurs that lead to the cliff's edge from the main trail. After crossing the dunes, the trail ends at Bight Beach, where elephant seals haul out. When mounds of seaweed accumulate along the beach, the number and diversity of shorebirds here can be impressive. For information: Año Nuevo State Reserve, (415) 879-0227.

Gazos Creek Road, 4.3 miles north of Año Nuevo, follows Gazos Creek through a narrow valley. There are few places to park along the Creek, so birding is done by walking from the pull-outs that do exist. Some of the species to look for along the road are Band-tailed Pigeon, Red-breasted Sapsucker (winter), Pacific-slope Flycatcher, Varied Thrush (winter), MacGillivray's Warbler, and Black-headed Grosbeak. After 1.8 miles the road forks. The right fork follows the creek for 9 miles through redwoods to where it dead-ends. Just beyond the right fork there is a trail from which to bird. To continue, take the left fork onto Cloverdale Road, which leaves the valley and crosses rolling hills.

Butano State Park is located 1.2 miles along Cloverdale Road. Species frequenting the park are similar to those found along Gazos Creek. The park has picnic tables and camping ($16.00), plus a number of trails through the redwoods. Marbled Murrelets nest in the campground trees and may be seen and heard before dawn from late April through July. During the summer, reservations for camping may be necessary months in advance (Butano State Park, (415) 879-2040). The next seven miles along Cloverdale Road pass through ranchland. Watch for Western Bluebird, Western Meadowlark, and Tricolored Blackbird in winter, and for Grasshopper Sparrow in spring and summer. At the intersection with Pescadero Road turn left toward the town of Pescadero. During migration, the bridge that crosses Pescadero Creek along Stage Road is worth checking for migrants. From town it is two miles back to the coast and Highway 1.

OTHER SITES

It is impossible to do justice to the Bay Area's many birding sites in this brief summary. A few other excellent destinations include the following. Lake Merritt in Oakland is famous for wintering ducks, including Barrow's Goldeneye. The Palo Alto Baylands (and nearby Mountain View Shoreline) in Santa Clara County support large numbers of wintering and migrant waterbirds (herons, waterfowl, shorebirds, gulls, and terns), and can be good for Black Rail and Nelson's Sharp-tailed Sparrow during times of the highest winter tides. Point Reyes in Marin County is famous for seabirds, shorebirds, and passerine migrants and vagrants during the late spring and much of the fall. Nearby Bolinas Lagoon to the south and Bodega Bay (Sonoma County) to the north are also excellent. In the Central Valley, well to the east, federal and state wildlife refuges—such as Sacramento, Gray Lodge, and Los Banos—support White-faced Ibises, many thousands of wintering Tundra Swans, Greater White-fronted, Snow, and Ross's Geese, and Sandhill Cranes.

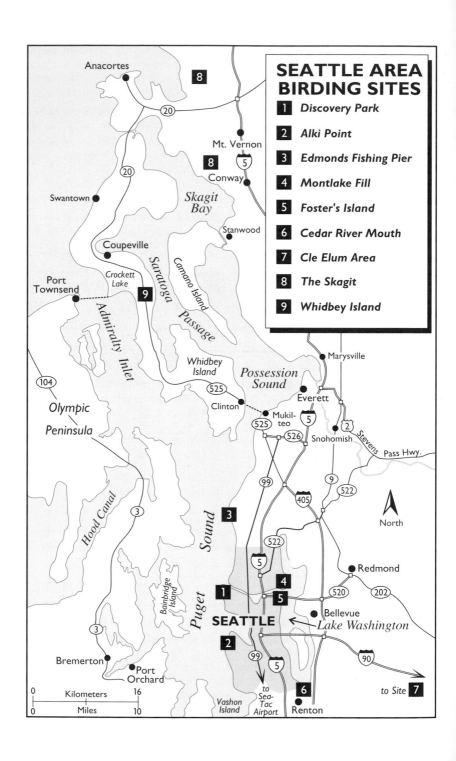

SEATTLE AREA BIRDING SITES

1 **Discovery Park**

2 **Alki Point**

3 **Edmonds Fishing Pier**

4 **Montlake Fill**

5 **Foster's Island**

6 **Cedar River Mouth**

7 **Cle Elum Area**

8 **The Skagit**

9 **Whidbey Island**

SEATTLE, WASHINGTON

Steven G. Mlodinow and Kevin Aanerud

In many folks' minds, Seattle = Rain. There is some truth to this rumor, though not in total precipitation. Many cities clearly exceed us there. The truth lies in persistence. Virtually every day has some clouds, and excepting mid-July to mid-September, the majority of days have some rain. But Seattle's rain does not arrive in gushing downpours but rather in mists and drizzles that can feel, at times, like the infamous Chinese Water Torture. What Seattle does have is a very temperate climate that rarely sees extremes of heat and cold, and the total number of birding days lost to weather is low. Furthermore, when the sun does shine, you can hardly top the glory of the shimmering Puget Sound sandwiched between the jagged, snowy Olympic and Cascade Mountains.

Birding opportunities around Seattle are as varied as the landscape. Within a 90-minute drive, there are superb shorebirding areas, great wintering raptor sites, enormous flocks of wintering waterfowl, and decent mountain birding. For those willing to put in a longer day, there are even more opportunities, including the excitement of the unpredictable (weather and birding) outer coast, the tremendous shorebirding of Vancouver, British Columbia, and the very different avifauna of the dry Eastside.

ESSENTIAL INFORMATION

Getting Around: Seattle is bereft of adequate public transportation for commuting as well as for birding. A rental car is therefore essential. A wide range of companies is located at SeaTac Airport, and some have of them have satellite offices elsewhere in King County and vicinity. Traffic is worsening, but it is not a horrid problem when compared to such burgs as Los Angeles and Chicago. Rush hours can be slow going, especially on Friday afternoons.

Climate: Seattle is generally cool and damp. Summer high temperatures average just over 70° Fahrenheit, while the lows average just over 50°. Winters are usually fairly benevolent, with low temperatures typically around 35° and highs about 45°. From October through April, fleece is the material of choice for your garments. It will keep you warm and shed enough rain for most days (and on the other days, you'll probably want to stay indoors anyway). Just remember, 40° and misting can be quite bone-chilling. Even May and June can be pretty cool and rainy, so be prepared. Reliably sunny and dry weather does not arrive until mid-July and typically disappears sometime in September.

Natural Hazards: One advantage of the weather is a general lack of bothersome insects. Mosquitoes are rarely a problem, chiggers are absent, and ticks are rare.

Safety: Seattle generally lives up to its reputation as a kinder, gentler city. Crime and safety issues are fewer than in many major cities, though the use of common sense is urged. Birding locations within Seattle have no notable crime issues; those outside Seattle are fairly rural and have little crime.

Other Resources: For information on birding Washington as well as the Seattle area, see *A Guide to Bird Finding in Washington* by T. R. Wahl and D. R. Paulson (1991, self-published), *Birding in Seattle and King County* by E.S. Hunn (1982, Seattle Audubon Society), *Birding in the San Juan Islands* by M.G. Lewis and F.A. Sharpe (1987, The Mountaineers), and *Birds of the Tri-Cities and Vicinity* by H. R. Ennor (1991, Lower Columbia Basin Audubon Society). And look for a new ABA guide in 2002, *A Birder's Guide to Washington*, by Hal Opperman and Andy Stepniewski (editors).

The Birds

One of the advantages of Seattle's climate is the high number of species present year round, despite the northerly latitude. A one-hundred species day is achievable in any month. Year-round residents in the Seattle area cover a broad spectrum, including Pelagic Cormorant, Bald Eagle, Peregrine Falcon, Pigeon Guillemot, Marbled Murrelet, Rhinoceros Auklet, Anna's Hummingbird, Red-breasted Sapsucker, Hutton's Vireo, Gray Jay, American Dipper, Varied Thrush, Townsend's Warbler, and Red Crossbill. Passerine migration is uninspiring when compared with much of North America, especially in spring, but shorebird migration is impressive, particularly in fall. Even more magnificent is the tremendous diversity and abundance of seabirds and waterfowl, not only during winter, but in summer as well.

Discovery Park

Half day; year round

Discovery Park is a popular birding site within Seattle that is well worth a visit. This 530-acre park has a wide variety of habitats, including open grassland, deciduous woods, and coniferous forest, as well as beaches, tidal flats, and excellent views of Puget Sound. Birding Discovery Park thoroughly

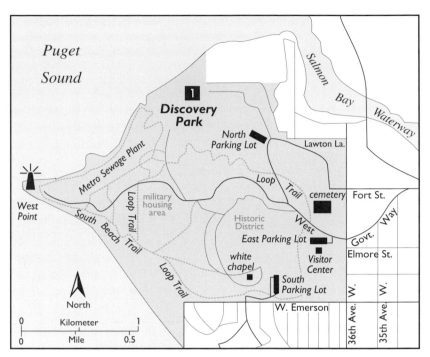

Puget
Sound

1

Discovery Park

North
Parking Lot

Lawton La.

cemetery | Fort St.

Loop Trail

West Point

Metro Sewage Plant

military
housing
area

Historic
District

West

East Parking Lot

Govt. Way

Elmore St.

South Beach Trail

Loop Trail

white chapel

Visitor
Center

South
Parking Lot

Loop Trail

W. Emerson

36th Ave. W.

35th Ave. W.

North

| 0 | Kilometer | 1 |
| 0 | Mile | 0.5 |

requires several miles of walking, though you can also enjoy an hour or two of non-strenuous birding here. The park is located just south of Shilshole Bay and northwest of the Magnolia Bluff neighborhood. From downtown, drive north on Western Avenue and watch for an easy merge onto Elliott Avenue. After veering to the right, the street (now 15th Avenue NW) will pass under the Magnolia Bridge. Take the Dravus Street exit and turn left onto the overpass. Turn right onto 20th Avenue West. Stay on the main arterial for 1.7 miles, during which stretch it becomes Gilman Avenue and eventually West Government Way, which directly enters the Park. Just inside the park is the visitor center, where you can purchase a bird checklist and a park map. Permits to park near the lighthouse can be obtained for those who are handicapped, over 62 years of age, or have children under five years old. For easiest access to the beaches below the bluff, it is best to drive to the South Parking Lot. To get there, before entering the main entrance, turn left on 36th Avenue West, which follows the eastern border of the Park. Turn right on W. Emerson Street and enter the park at the gate. The South Parking Lot is at the end of the road, a short distance inside the park.

The recommended walk will take you from the South Parking Lot to the beach and back, and is 2 to 3 miles round trip. If you intend on seabirding from the beach, a scope will be useful. Start by finding the steps near the northwest corner of the parking lot. Walk west toward the white buildings (which include the historic Post Chapel) and continue toward the open meadows and south bluff. There is a variety of trails and roads to choose from, and any will do as long as you are trending in the correct direction. From the bluff, follow the trail heading north through a brief wooded section. Just beyond a small clearing, look for the South Beach Trail, which descends through steeply sloped woods. This trail will soon meet with the main road, which leads to the Metro Sewage Plant. Walk the path paralleling this road until you reach the beach, and follow the beach to the West Point Lighthouse.

Birding begins at the parking lot, where a mixture of Scotch Broom, blackberry brambles, and an assortment of trees attracts numbers of migrants in fall (mid-August through mid-October). During October and November look for Varied and Hermit Thrushes, Purple Finch, Red Crossbill, Pine Siskin, and Evening Grosbeak. Anna's Hummingbirds are fairly easy to find here year round. The grounds around the Chapel are also excellent for migrant passerines. On a good fall day, the tall Lombardy Poplars can be full of warblers, predominantly Yellow-rumped, Orange-crowned, and Yellow, but frequently also Black-throated Gray, Townsend's, MacGillivray's, and Wilson's. The open meadows often have a Northern Shrike during winter, and in summer there are breeding Anna's and Rufous Hummingbirds and Willow Flycatchers. Unusual birds seen here have included Lewis's Woodpecker, Northern Mockingbird, and Black-throated Sparrow. The South Beach Trail usually has a flock or two of mixed-woodland species, including Hutton's Vireo, Chestnut-backed and Black-capped Chickadees, Bushtit, Bewick's Wren, Brown Creeper, and Golden-crowned and Ruby-crowned Kinglets.

The first section of beach that you encounter will have expansive mudflats even at mid-tide. From late July into October large numbers of gulls and terns gather to rest. The gulls are predominantly Glaucous-winged, Glaucous-winged x Western hybrids, Bonaparte's, Mew, and California, while the terns are mostly Common and Caspian. Rarities such as Little and Franklin's Gulls have been seen, as well as Elegant, Forster's, and Arctic Terns. Brant are numerous in spring. Shorebirding is not usually very impressive, although 24 species of shorebirds have been reported from Discovery Park. From July through September, Semipalmated Plover, Least and Western Sandpipers, Sanderling, and even Baird's Sandpiper are often present.

The **West Point Lighthouse**, which can be a very effective screen from the wind, is the best spot for observing alcids within Seattle. Rhinoceros Auklets can be seen year round, but they are most numerous from late summer through fall, and scarce in winter. Pigeon Guillemots are usually present. Marbled Murrelets are permanent residents that are most easily found during April and May when pairs linger near shore. Ancient Murrelets are brief visitors, usually from mid-October through November. A number of seabirds rarely seen in Puget Sound waters have been reported from West Point. To the north of the lighthouse, North Beach has a rock seawall and deeper water offshore where all three scoters and both goldeneyes can be found (November–March).

Retracing one's steps is the quickest way of returning to the South Parking Lot. The energetic birder can explore other areas of the park by hiking up the trail that begins at the end of the seawall. From the top of the bluff, trails lead in all directions. The main Loop Trail leads through the most heavily forested regions of the park. Barred (resident), Great Horned (winter), and Northern Saw-whet (fall and winter) Owls are often found here. By continuing on this trail for another mile you will reach the South Parking Lot.

If you are interested in seabirds but your time is too limited for the trek to the lighthouse, there are two alternatives accessible by car: **Alki Point** in West Seattle and the **Edmonds Fishing Pier**. Both locations are good for grebes (Western, Red-necked, and Horned), cormorants (Double-crested, Brandt's [winter only], and Pelagic), scoters (mostly Surf and White-winged), and alcids. To get to **Alki Point** from I-5, take the West Seattle Freeway and exit onto Harbor Avenue SW. The road will follow the curve of the

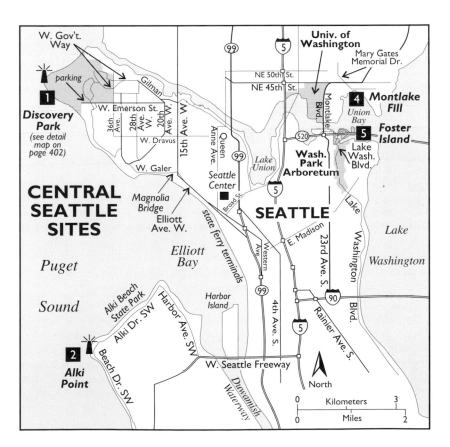

shoreline and become Alki Avenue SW. (A warm weekend will attract crowds, so the route may take longer than expected.) Continue past the sandy beaches and restaurants, and the road will lead you to the Alki Point Lighthouse. Just beyond, the street is named Beach Drive SW; a sidewalk promenade with railing indicates that you have arrived. Most of the species found at West Point occur here, and Harlequin Ducks are usually present October through March. Black Turnstones and Surfbirds are also regular visitors in winter.

The **Edmonds Fishing Pier** is a fine place for seabirding from August through May, with late fall being especially rewarding. Take I-5 north from Seattle about 15 miles to WA-104. Take WA-104 west 4 miles and watch for signs to the ferry, taking the exit ramp to the right marked *Kingston Ferry*. Follow this road downhill and turn left at the first streetlight onto Dayton Street. Cross the railroad tracks and, after the road veers left, park on the street or in the parking lot on your right. The fishing pier is accessible from the north end of the marina. Several fishing stations on the pier provide some protection from strong winds and stormy conditions, which can be opportune times to find rarities. In good years Ancient Murrelets (November–December) have been seen swimming directly under the pier. Close encounters with Common Murres, Pigeon Guillemots, and Rhinoceros Auklets are likely in late fall and early winter, and the rafts of Western Grebes are worth scanning for Clark's Grebe (October–April). From August through October, Parasitic Jaegers are fairly regular here. Rarities seen from Edmonds include Black-headed Gull, Little Gull, and Long-billed Murrelet.

LAKE WASHINGTON

Half day; fall, winter, spring

There are several quality birding areas along the shores of Lake Washington, including the **Montlake Fill**, **Foster Island**, and the **Cedar River Mouth**. The Montlake Fill, also known as the Union Bay Natural Area, is a bit of freshwater marsh and weedy grassland owned by the University of Washington. This patch was left in idle neglect (to the delight of birdwatchers) for 25 years but in recent years has experienced a more hands-on approach, which birders are watching with some anxiety.

At least 220 species of birds have been seen at the **Montlake Fill**, including many vagrants to western Washington. Two of the three existing ponds (not counting springtime rain puddles) provide decent habitat for shorebirds; 26 species have been recorded. Although shorebirding can be interesting in spring, the fall migration offers the greatest variety and opportunities for finding rarities. The first adult shorebirds arrive in July, and mid-August through September is the most active time of year, with October and November still interesting. Scanning Union Bay from the Fill during late fall and winter should reveal several species of waterfowl, usually including one or two Eurasian Wigeons. The willows, alders, and cottonwoods on the northeast edge of the Fill provide excellent habitat for passerine migrants in the fall and, to a lesser extent, in spring. Black Swifts are often seen flying over the Fill on the dreariest of days during summer. Northern Shrike, Lapland Longspur, and unusual sparrows are most often found during October to November. If one is hurrying along, the Montlake Fill can be birded in an hour-and-a-half, but if the weather has brought with it a rash of new migrants, it could be worth a half day.

To get to the Montlake Fill, take I-5 to the N.E. 45th Street exit. Continue east across the 45th Street Viaduct. Bear left at the light and turn right at the second light onto Mary Gates Memorial Drive. You can park on the street and walk through the Horticulture grounds to get onto the Fill. On Sundays and Saturday afternoons, campus parking is free, so you can park in the lots nearby, but it is best to avoid Husky football game days.

Foster Island is not far from Montlake Fill, and during migration it can be interesting, and a rarity or two are also found in winter. From Montlake Fill drive west on NE 45th Street. From either of the left two lanes you will merge onto Montlake Boulevard. Drive past Husky Stadium, across Montlake Bridge, and turn left at the third light onto Lake Washington Boulevard. Drive one-half mile, winding right and then left. After the first stop sign and before the road turns right again, turn left at the second stop sign into the Arboretum on Foster Island Road. The road ends in a short distance at a spot where you can park. Walk the trail that begins at the end of the road and cross the footbridge. Foster Island has woods comprised of a variety of trees, including many species of conifers, oaks, cottonwoods, alders, and madrona. Impressive numbers of passerines (late April to early June, mid-August to late October) take advantage of the food and cover available here. Rarities seen include Least Flycatcher, Blue-gray Gnatcatcher, Tennessee and Black-and-white Warblers, and American Redstart. The usual resident woodland species can be found here, including Hutton's Vireo. During winter, Townsend's Warblers are often present. Anna's Hummingbirds are easy to find in all but the most adverse weather conditions.

The **Cedar River Mouth** in Renton, at the south end of Lake Washington, is the Seattle area's best place for winter gulls. The easiest route is to drive south on I-5 from Seattle and exit for I-405 North. Take the second exit, following signs for Renton, and be prepared to make a quick right onto Rainier Avenue. Take Rainier for 1.2 miles and turn left onto Airport Way. The road curves to the left and becomes Logan Avenue North. At 6th Street turn left and enter Cedar River Park. Drive to the end of the park and scope from the small hill. Also look for gulls from the west side of the Renton Airport or from Gene Coulon Memorial Beach at the southeast corner of Lake Washington. A Glaucous Gull or two are usually present along with some Western Gulls and many Glaucous-winged, Herring, Thayer's, and Mew

Gulls. Be aware that many of the large gulls are hybrids, predominantly Glaucous-winged x Western, but also Glaucous-winged x Herring and other combinations. Late afternoon is best, as hundreds more gulls come to Lake Washington to roost after feeding at the Cedar Hills landfill.

CLE ELUM AREA
Full day; spring and summer

About 75 minutes east of Seattle, you can leave the wet fir forest behind and enter the dry pine woodlands, grassy meadows, and willow-lined riparian habitats of the "Eastside." The starting point for this venture is Cle Elum (pronounced CLAY EL-umm). From here you can quickly reach areas along the Teanaway River and around Swauk Pass.

To reach the **Teanaway River**, take the second Cle Elum exit off I-90 eastbound, turn left over the interstate, and then turn right onto WA-970. Drive nearly two miles and turn right onto WA-10. Within a mile this road crosses the Teanaway River. Park on either side of the bridge on the ample shoulder. Birding this fine riparian habitat is best accomplished by walking up and down the road or by scrambling up onto the railroad tracks (while using good sense and extra caution to avoid cars or trains). The area is excellent for breeding passerines such as Western Wood-Pewee, Willow Flycatcher, Warbling and Red-eyed Vireos, Veery, Gray Catbird, Yellow Warbler, and Black-headed Grosbeak. American Dippers are sometimes seen from the bridge. Drive another half-mile east on Highway 10 to look for Lazuli Bunting.

Drive 0.8 mile east of the Teanaway River bridge and turn left onto Taylor Road. This small dirt road reaches a T-intersection (Hart Road) within a short distance. Either left or right is worth birding. To the right in about 200 yards is a recent burn (1998), which is usually the most productive area. In spring, Blue Grouse may be heard, if not seen. Common Nighthawk, Calliope Hummingbird, Dusky Flycatcher, Mountain Chickadee, House Wren, Nashville Warbler, Cassin's Finch, and Evening Grosbeak are usually present. Going left will lead to more riparian worth exploring. Most of this area is private property with *No Trespassing* signs posted; bird only from the road.

To find higher elevation species and Golden Eagle, Williamson's Sapsucker, and Gray Jay, return to WA-970 and head east. After a few miles turn left onto Swauk Prairie Road, a dependable spot for Horned Lark, Western and Mountain Bluebirds, and Vesper Sparrow, especially around the small cemetery. At seven miles WA-970 meets US-97. Turn left and drive north toward **Swauk Pass**. To bird this area, turn onto any of the smaller Forest Service Roads and leave the busy traffic. A left onto the old Blewett Pass Road is especially good, or turn right at the turn-off to the tiny town of Liberty and drive Forest Service Roads 9712 or 9718. These dirt roads (usually in good shape even for passenger vehicles) head north to higher elevations, eventually rejoining US-97 at Swauk Pass for a quick return to I-90. You should encounter Calliope and Rufous Hummingbirds, Western Wood-Pewee, *Empidonax* flycatchers (Dusky, Hammond's, and Pacific-slope), Cassin's and Warbling Vireos, chickadees (Mountain, Black-capped, and Chestnut-backed), Swainson's Thrush, warblers (Nashville, Yellow, Townsend's, Yellow-rumped, MacGillivray's, and Wilson's), Cassin's Finch, and other species. On summer nights, this area is excellent for Spotted and Flammulated Owls and Common Poorwill.

THE SKAGIT

Half to full day; fall, winter, spring

The **"Skagit"** refers to the Skagit and Samish Deltas in western Skagit County, about a 60- to 90-minute drive north from Seattle. This area is best known for its wintering raptors and waterfowl, but it can also excel in wintering sparrows. The **Samish Flats** lie predominantly west of Chuckanut Drive and north of Allen West Road. The basic birding strategy is to drive the roads, pulling off onto the shoulder to scan fields for raptors and waterfowl. The big draw here is Gyrfalcon, with one to five present each winter, mostly from mid-November to mid-March. The most reliable area is between Sunset and Field Roads west of Thomas Road. Search by scanning low posts and dirt mounds. Also worth checking for Gyrfalcons are the fields and

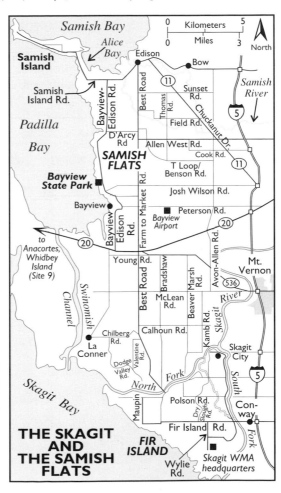

THE SKAGIT AND THE SAMISH FLATS

telephone poles along Bayview-Edison Road (north of D'Arcy Road) and Samish Island Road. While working these areas, you should also encounter Bald Eagle (common), Red-tailed (common), "Harlan's" (fairly common), and Rough-legged (common) Hawks, Northern Harrier (common), Peregrine Falcon(common), and Merlin (fairly common). A Prairie Falcon, rare in western Washington, is present in most winters. For Short-eared Owl, try Samish Island Road at dusk; during some winters, Snowy Owls can be found, too.

Non-raptors to be looked for on the Samish Flats include Eurasian Wigeon (up to 80; found throughout the flats, but especially along Samish Island Road from October to April, with January–March being best), Trumpeter and Tundra Swans (hundreds, can be anywhere, but most often in the northeastern part of the flats, November–March), "Eurasian" Green-winged Teal (scarce but annual, December–April), Northern Shrike (fairly common, October–March), and Snow Bunting (scarce, mostly November). Also, the fields in winter can have sizable flocks of gulls and roosting Black-bellied Plovers and Dunlin. Alice Bay, viewed mid-tide, can have fair-sized shorebird flocks and Brant (November–April), mostly "Black" Brant but also including a few "gray-bellied" types (a recently-recognized population from Melville Island that may be a distinct subspecies). To reach Alice Bay, take Samish Island Road 1.3 miles north and west from its intersection with Bayview-Edison Road and turn right onto a very steep and short boat ramp. Rarities seen on the Samish Flats in the past include Eurasian Kestrel, Iceland Gull, Tropical Kingbird, Clay-colored Sparrow, and Orchard Oriole.

To get to the **Samish Flats** from Seattle, take I-5 north past Mount Vernon to WA-20 and go west. In a few miles you will cross Best Road; the next traffic light is at Bayview-Edison Road. Turn right here and follow the road through the small town of Bayview. A brief stop at **Bayview State Park** can produce some common passerines and provides a view of Padilla Bay, where you can look for loons, waterfowl (including Brant), and gulls. About two miles later, the road drops into the Samish Delta lowlands (this spot will be obvious), where you should look for raptors and waterfowl.

Fir Island, as a birding area, lies mostly between Fir Island Road and the north fork of the Skagit River. As with the Samish Flats, the main birding strategy is to drive the roads, pulling off onto the shoulder to scan fields or *pish* at brush piles. The primary attractions are wintering swans and Snow Geese. Mixed Tundra/Trumpeter Swan flocks of up to 1,000 birds are not unusual (November–March). The best places to look are along Skagit City Road, between Fir Island and Polson Roads, and along Polson Road, although flocks can be anywhere in open fields. The Snow Geese, numbering 20,000 or more, are most often found along Fir Island Road west of Mann Road or along Maupin Road. Occasionally, other species are mixed in, including, very rarely, Ross's Goose. Fir Island is also a fair place for raptors. It is worth birding brush piles and looking at feeders in farmyards. Sparrow flocks here can be impressive (October–March), including numerous Song, White-crowned (both *pugetensis* and *gambelii*), Golden-crowned, "Sooty" Fox, and Lincoln's, plus Spotted Towhees and "Oregon" Dark-eyed Juncos. Uncommon to rare (but regular) are American Tree, Savannah, White-throated, and Harris's Sparrows, plus "Slate-colored" Dark-eyed Juncos.

To reach Fir Island, take I-5 north from Seattle to the Conway/McMurray Lake exit (#221). Turn left at the end of the exit ramp and go 0.25 mile to Fir Island Road. Turn right onto Fir Island Road and follow it through the tiny town of Conway and then over the south fork of the Skagit River. After crossing the bridge, continue straight along Fir Island Road, or turn right onto Skagit City Road to start your drive through the farmlands.

WHIDBEY ISLAND

Full day; year round

Whidbey Island is awesome in its beauty and fabulous in its birding, yet it is distinctly undercovered by birders. Despite this poor coverage, however, nine species of alcids and 40 species of shorebirds have been found here. One wonders what might fly by unnoticed.

What can a visiting birder expect on Whidbey? Birding on the Island is excellent year round, with June the slowest month. Shorebirding, one of Whidbey's main attractions, is best from early July to late September, though mid-April to mid-May can be good, depending on water levels. In addition to shorebirds, birders visit Whidbey year round to look for saltwater species such as loons, cormorants, and alcids (though not tubenoses, which are quite rare here). Common Murres, Pigeon Guillemots, Marbled Murrelets, and Rhinoceros Auklets can be found all year, but Ancient Murrelets are best sought during November and December. Loons, surprisingly, also can be found year round, as is best evidenced by three summer records of Yellow-billed Loon during the 1990s! Similarly, Pelagic Cormorant, Harlequin Duck, and White-winged and Surf Scoters are present all year, but there are several saltwater species, such as Red-necked Grebe, Brandt's Cormorant, Brant, Black Scoter, and Long-tailed Duck, that are rare during summer but fairly common otherwise. Heermann's Gulls are best found from June to October.

Whidbey Island is reached from Seattle by taking I-5 north to Exit 189, WA-526. Go west on WA-526 for 5.0 miles to the third traffic light and turn right. Go 0.4 mile to the second traffic light, and turn right again onto WA-525. In approximately 1.75 miles, this road ends at the Mukilteo Ferry landing. This 15-minute ferry ride will take you onto the southern end of Whidbey Island, about a 40-minute drive from Crockett Lake. With minimal traffic, reaching the ferry landing from Seattle takes about 40 minutes. The ferries run about every 30 minutes after 6:00AM, but the line can be long after mid-morning. For ferry information, call (206) 464-6400, or visit web site

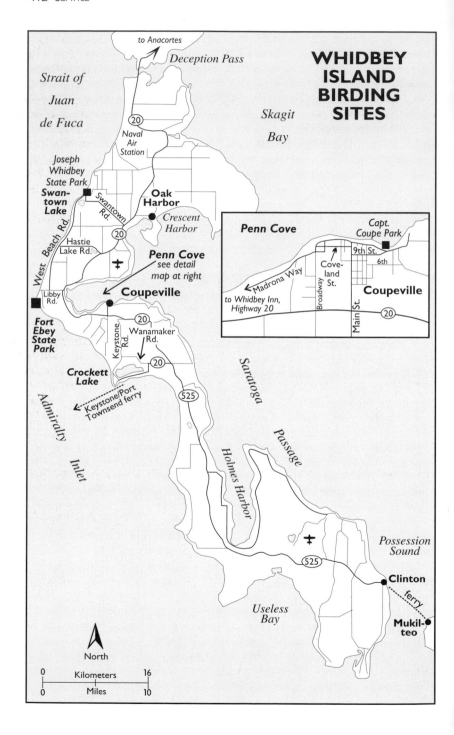

to Anacortes

Deception Pass

Strait of

Juan

de Fuca

Skagit

Bay

WHIDBEY ISLAND BIRDING SITES

20

Naval Air Station

Joseph Whidbey State Park

Swan-town Lake

Oak Harbor

Crescent Harbor

Swantown Rd.

20

Hastie Lake Rd.

Penn Cove
see detail map at right

Coupeville

Libby Rd.

Fort Ebey State Park

20

Wanamaker Rd.

Keystone Rd.

20

Crockett Lake

Keystone/Port Townsend ferry

Admiralty

Inlet

West Beach Rd.

525

Saratoga

Passage

Holmes Harbor

Penn Cove

Capt. Coupe Park

Madrona Way

Cove-land St.

9th St.

6th

Broadway

Main St.

Coupeville

20

to Whidbey Inn, Highway 20

Possession Sound

525

Clinton

ferry

Mukil-teo

Useless Bay

North

| 0 | Kilometers | 16 |
| 0 | Miles | 10 |

www.wsdot.wa.gov/ferries/. To reach Whidbey from the north end (and without a ferry crossing), take WA-20 west from I-5 through the Skagit area. Just before Anacortes, WA-20 turns south and onto Whidbey Island. Exiting the island via this northerly route is recommended on summer weekends.

Crockett Lake is approximately two square miles of shallow lake, mudflat, and *Salicornia* marsh. It is the premier birding spot on Whidbey Island. The level of the lake is manually controlled to some extent, with levels typically low in summer and early fall but fairly high during winter and early spring. Crockett Lake's biggest draw is shorebirds. From early July through mid-September, its shores are usually crawling with Western (thousands) and Least (hundreds) Sandpipers. Semipalmated Plovers, both yellowlegs, and both dowitchers are common as well, and during August so are Red-necked Phalaropes. In October these birds are replaced by Dunlins, along with a few lingering peeps. A number of other shorebirds that are typically considered uncommon to rare in western Washington are regular at Crockett, including Semipalmated Sandpiper (July–August), Baird's Sandpiper (August), Pectoral Sandpiper (September–October), Stilt Sandpiper (August–September), and Wilson's Phalarope (July–August). Indeed, Crockett Lake is the most reliable spot for Semipalmated Sandpiper in Washington, and during July and August, there is almost always at least one present.

Beyond fall shorebirding at Crockett, there are other attractions. Often, but not always, spring shorebirding here can be interesting, as well. If the water level is right, a look at any time from mid-April through May can be rewarding, though diversity during spring is considerably less than in autumn. Also, Crockett has a good variety of dabbling and diving ducks; during fall the muddy shores sometimes attract Lapland Longspur. Flocks of California and Heermann's Gulls and Caspian Terns often loaf on the mud (July–September). Rarities that have occurred at Crockett Lake include Little Blue Heron, Snowy Egret, Hudsonian Godwit, Buff-breasted and Sharp-tailed Sandpipers, Ruff, and White Wagtail.

After birding Crockett Lake, you might want to ride the nearby Keystone/Port Townsend Ferry. This run can be very birdy throughout the year, with maximum diversity from August into October. Particularly numerous are alcids and gulls. Jaegers are regular from mid-August to early October. The ferry landing is just across the street from Crockett Lake's west end.

To get to Crockett Lake, take WA-525 from the south or WA-20 from the north to Wanamaker Road. Go west on Wanamaker just over one mile to Keystone Road. Go south on Keystone Road and follow it as it bends to the west along the south side of Crockett Lake. Crockett Lake can be birded from anywhere along the road. It is also okay to walk out to the lakeshore, but be aware that the mud can be treacherous.

The west side of Whidbey Island from Hastie Lake Road to Swantown Road has been dubbed "**Swantown**" by birders. Several access points here allow good views of the Strait of Juan de Fuca, excellent spots for loons, grebes, cormorants, scoters, Harlequin Duck, Long-tailed Duck, Heermann's Gull, and alcids. The gravelly shore at the end of Hastie Lake Road is a good spot for Black Oystercatcher, except at high tide. Just south of Swantown Road and east of West Beach Road is **Swantown Lake**. This lake is a small version of Crockett Lake, although the water levels are not as consistently good for shorebirds. Nonetheless, it has had its share of uncommon shorebirds, including rarities such as Sharp-tailed Sandpiper and Ruff.

To get to the Swantown area, take Hastie Lake Road west from WA-20 until it dead ends at the shoreline; scan from here. Then go north along West Beach Road 2.6 miles; on your left there will be a pull-off overlooking the Strait of Juan de Fuca from a bluff, and Swantown Lake will be apparent to the right. Scan the Strait from here. Then continue north along West Beach Road, stopping to scan Swantown Lake. After passing the lake, there will be another pull-off to the left (0.8 mile from the first) from which to scan the Strait. The Swantown area can also be reached from the north by turning west onto Swantown Road from WA-20 in the town of Oak Harbor.

Penn Cove is another major attraction on Whidbey Island. This bay provides a sheltered, rich feeding area for many species. Numerous here are Common and Red-throated Loons (September–April), Red-necked and Western Grebes (September–April), White-winged and Surf Scoters (year round), Harlequin Duck (year round), Common and Barrow's Goldeneyes (November–April), Black Turnstone and Surfbird (mid-July to late April), and Pigeon Guillemot (year round). Marbled Murrelet and Rhinoceros Auklet are fairly common, as well (year round), and during most winters a few Black Scoters and a Rock Sandpiper or two are present (November–March). Unlike the case along Whidbey Island's western shore, Pelagic and Brandt's Cormorants, Heermann's Gull, and Ancient Murrelet are distinctly uncommon in Penn Cove. Penn Cove is a good spot to search for Clark's Grebe. This rare visitor to western Washington is almost annual here. Also, pay attention to the landbirds along the cove's edge. Look for California Quail (year round), Rufous Hummingbird (April–July), Olive-sided Flycatcher (May-August), Hutton's Vireo (year round), Chestnut-backed Chickadee (year round), Bushtit (year round), Bewick's Wren (year round), Spotted Towhee (year round), "Sooty" Fox Sparrow (October-April), Golden-crowned Sparrow (September-April), and Red Crossbill (year round). A number of rarities have been found at Penn Cove, the most exceptional of which was a Whiskered Auklet.

To bird Penn Cove, take WA-20 to Coupeville and turn north onto Main Street. Take Main Street to NE 9th Street and turn right. Go 0.35 mile to Captain Coupe Park and turn left into the park. Scan here for birds on the water. After looking here, return to Main Street, turn right, and then almost immediately left onto Coveland Street. Take Coveland about 0.2 mile and then veer left onto Madrona Way. From this point, scan the cove from pull-offs at 0.45 and 0.95 miles (these are the best pull-offs, but any sufficiently wide spot with a view can be worthwhile). The wooden structures below are for growing mussels. These platforms are favorite loafing sites for Harlequin Ducks, and rocky shorebirds often feed on the platforms, sometimes with Dunlins and Sanderlings. Around the platforms there are often large flocks of scoters. The pull-offs are also good places to *pish* and check for some of the above-mentioned passerines. Continuing along Madrona Way, at 2.45 miles, just past the Captain Whidbey Inn, turn into a smallish grassy parking area and scan the cove, paying attention to the shoreline for rocky shorebirds, as well. Next, continue on Madrona Way to where it meets WA-20. Here is a tidal lagoon that can be good for shorebirds, including turnstones and Surfbirds. Turn right onto WA-20 and go 0.6 mile to a private pier. Park at the base of the pier (without blocking access to it) and scan the shore. This is a favored spot for rocky shorebirds, except at high tide.

After you bird Penn Cove, a trip to **Fort Ebey State Park** can be worthwhile. The park's woodlands have all of the passerines mentioned above for Penn Cove, plus nesting Pacific-slope Flycatcher, Western Wood-Pewee, Varied Thrush, Townsend's Warbler, Black-throated Gray Warbler, and others. To reach the park, take Libbey Road west from WA-20 to Hill Valley Road and turn left. Go 0.6 mile and turn right into the park.

FARTHER AFIELD

If you have the time for a lengthier trip, a visit to the outer coast is often worthwhile. The best spots include Ocean Shores, Tokeland, and pelagic trips out of Westport. Ocean Shores has hosted such rarities as Eurasian Dotterel, Bristle-thighed Curlew, Bar-tailed Godwit, Curlew Sandpiper, Horned Puffin, wagtails (Yellow, White, and Black-backed), and McKay's Bunting. Tokeland has also produced significant rarities and is arguably the best spot south of Alaska for Bar-tailed Godwit (July–October). Westport pelagic trips usually provide a good selection of Pacific seabirds (including Black-footed Albatross and a few Fork-tailed Storm-Petrels, plus occasional Laysan Albatross, Flesh-footed Shearwater, and South Polar Skua) and have had their fair share of rarities, including Shy and Short-tailed Albatrosses, Mottled and Murphy's Petrels, Manx Shearwater, Red-legged Kittiwake, Parakeet Auklet, and Horned Puffin.

For information on Ocean Shores, see *A Birder's Guide to Coastal Washington* by Robert Morse (2001, R. W. Morse Co.). An article on Ocean Shores (also by Morse) appeared in the October 1996 *Birding* (28: 388-397). For Tokeland information, see Morse (2001) and *America's 100 Most Wanted Birds* by S.G. Mlodinow and M. O'Brien (1996, Falcon Press); for Westport information, contact Westport Seabirds at (360) 268-5222, *www.westport-seabirds.com*.

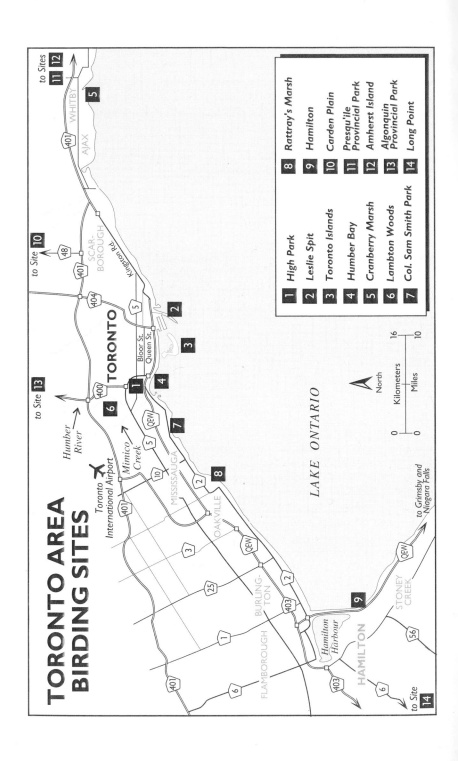

TORONTO AREA BIRDING SITES

to Sites [11] [12]

WHITBY

[5]

AJAX

401

SCAR-
BOROUGH

Kingston Rd.

to Site [10]

48

401

404

5

2

3

TORONTO

Bloor St.
Queen St.

1

4

to Site [13]

400

6

Humber
River

7

QEW

Mimico
Creek

5

Toronto
International Airport

407

10

MISSISSAUGA

OAKVILLE

3

2

8

25

QEW

BURLING-
TON

1

403

2

QEW

FLAMBOROUGH

401

6

403

HAMILTON

Hamilton
Harbour

9

56

STONEY
CREEK

QEW

to Grimsby and
Niagara Falls

to Site [14]

6

LAKE ONTARIO

North

Kilometers
0   16

Miles
0   10

[1]	High Park	[8]	Rattray's Marsh
[2]	Leslie Spit	[9]	Hamilton
[3]	Toronto Islands	[10]	Carden Plain
[4]	Humber Bay	[11]	Presqu'ile Provincial Park
[5]	Cranberry Marsh	[12]	Amherst Island
[6]	Lambton Woods	[13]	Algonquin Provincial Park
[7]	Col. Sam Smith Park	[14]	Long Point

TORONTO, ONTARIO

Hugh Currie

For seven years Canada has been named by the World Bank as the best country in the world in which to live. Toronto contributes to this ranking as a cosmopolitan and fascinating city with something for everyone. The streets are safe and the inhabitants friendly. The theater district is world-class. Prices are very reasonable for the U.S. tourist because of the favorable exchange rate.

Located on the north shore of Lake Ontario, Toronto is less than 100 miles from the Canadian Shield to the north. The current checklist shows 390 avian species in the Greater Toronto Area, of which 190 have bred locally.

ESSENTIAL INFORMATION

Getting Around: All major car rentals are available at the airport and throughout the city. Toronto Transit Commission information can be obtained by dialing (416) 393-4636, and transit-system maps are available at any subway station. Traffic is definitely a problem in the city and suburbs during rush hours, Monday to Friday. Otherwise, it is manageable.

There are several large parks offering excellent birding right in the city. The Toronto Islands and the Leslie Street Spit are each worth a half day or perhaps more. The former is a short ferry ride away from the downtown area, whereas the latter is about a half-mile from the nearest public transportation; thus, a taxi may be preferred. Most birding areas in Toronto can be managed by public transport, but the other areas mentioned in this chapter will require rental cars, with the possible exception of the Niagara Falls area.

Climate: Winter weather can be severe from December to March and even beyond. The Great Lakes, however, have an ameliorating affect on temperature. Very often snowfall is heaviest in the lee of the Great Lakes. At times, in winter, Toronto has no snow, while at the same time a town on the east side of Lake Huron, or just across the lake in upstate New York, may be buried under several feet. At most seasons, Toronto's climate is little different from that of, say, southern Minnesota or northern New England.

Safety: Toronto's murder rate is about one-tenth that of New York and most U.S. cities, and the rates of other crimes are also very low. Nonetheless, normal precautions are recommended as for any large urban area. Women usually travel in pairs or groups in the urban parks. Theft from cars is a possibility, and it is wise to keep valuables hidden.

Natural Hazards: Insects are never a problem in the city, but mosquitoes and Black Flies can be bad to the north in June and July. Ticks are possible along the Lake Erie shoreline, and these include Deer Ticks. Poison-Ivy is common in southern Ontario, so beware of this three-leaflet menace.

Other Resources: The best local publication is *A Birdfinding Guide to the Toronto Region* (1988) published by Clive E. Goodwin, but now unfortunately out-of-print and somewhat out-of-date. Another publication covering all of Ontario, including Toronto, is Clive Goodwin's *Birdfinding Guide to Ontario* (1995, University of Toronto Press); it is very thorough. The Toronto Rare Bird Alert number is (416) 350-3000, ext. 2293. It is updated every Friday at supper time and at about 9:30PM on Sunday evening (or Monday if it's a holiday weekend). It is also updated frequently for current news of extreme rarities in the Toronto area and elsewhere in Ontario. The Toronto RBA is currently headed by Harry Kerr at (416) 481-7948, Jerry Guild at (905) 823-1973, and Ron Scovell at (416) 745-9111, all of whom will be glad to help visiting birders. (You need to dial all 10 digits even if you are calling within the same area code.) Members of the RBA phone each other immediately when a rarity is found.

On the Internet, check the ONTBirds postings, courtesy of the Ontario Field Ornithologists, and the University of Toronto Zoology Department's Bird Sightings. ONTBirds is at *www-stat.wharton.upenn.edu/~siler/ontb.html*; the zoology department's web site is *www.zoo.utoronto.ca/fun.birds/html.*

Other Destinations: The Royal Ontario Museum at University and Bloor is a popular tourist destination and has displays of mounted birds. The best bookshop for natural-history titles is Open Air at Adelaide and Toronto Streets in the downtown area.

THE BIRDING YEAR

A ll things being equal, the best time of the year is mid-May, when migration is at its peak. An overnight rain usually means a fall-out in either spring or fall. Waterfowl migration, however, begins much earlier—in early March—and is best viewed at Humber Bay and Cranberry Marsh in the east or, best of all, at Long Point on Lake Erie. April brings sparrows and early migrants, which are best seen on the Toronto Islands. In May, the vireos and warblers arrive, with the most-southern species appearing first. Any and all patches of woods near the shoreline can be good, especially during a fall-out. Connecticut Warblers are best found on the east side of the Toronto Islands, south of the community on Ward's Island, during the last ten days of May.

By June, the birds are nesting, including the resident Peregrine Falcons at Victoria and King in the downtown area, and at Islington and Bloor at the west end of the city. July sees the beginning of the southward shorebird movement. The Toronto Conservation Authority has had many successes, but creating shorebird habitat on the Leslie Spit has not been one of them so far. Cranberry Marsh is perhaps the best area locally for shorebirds. Excellent shorebirding can be had at Presqu'ile Provincial Park, 1.5 hours east, until duck hunting begins in late September on alternate days.

Fall migration can be intense on a fall-out day on the Toronto Islands. Warblers begin moving in August and continue to early October. Northern Saw-whet Owls come through the region in the second half of October, and a few stay in suitable patches of woods at the Nature Sanctuary of Toronto Island, on Leslie Spit, or in the area of Lynde Shores Conservation area in Whitby to the east. The woods behind Humber College on Highway 27 can also be good. Generally speaking, precise owl locations are not given on the rare-bird hotline because of harassment by unethical birders and photographers. The last week of February is the optimal time for owls, when up to nine species can be seen in a day during a good winter.

Moving into winter, the number and variety of birds declines, but some interesting species appear for the first time. Bohemian Waxwings often turn up at Bolton or in the Claremont Conservation area to the east. Rarities such as Yellow-throated Warbler, Summer and Western Tanagers, and Harris's Sparrow may appear at a feeder. A Townsend's Solitaire or a Varied Thrush might be present in the Toronto region, often frequenting a feeder. Long-tailed Duck, Common Goldeneye, and Bufflehead are found along the waterfront. Snowy Owls are often seen at the Toronto Island Airport or on Leslie Spit, but they are currently trapped and removed from the larger Lester Pearson Airport for airplane-safety reasons. Harlequin Ducks often winter on the Toronto waterfront, either at Humber Bay or on the Leslie Spit. Northern Shrikes may turn up anywhere, but Leslie Spit is as good a place as any. Winter finches such as Pine Grosbeak, Common and Hoary Redpolls, and Pine Siskin may frequent feeders or natural food sources on the outskirts of the city. Snow Buntings and Lapland Longspurs are best looked for during February in manured fields on McGillivray Road just north of Rutherford Road or on Ashburn Road just northwest of the town of Brooklin.

Although technically beyond the scope of this chapter (but covered briefly in later pages), Algonquin Provincial Park (2.5 hours north) is a popular destination for boreal species. It offers sought-after species such as Spruce Grouse, Black-backed Woodpecker, Boreal Chickadee, Gray Jay, and possibly some northern finches. Mid-winter can offer driving difficulties, and deep snow may keep you confined to the roads rather than walking the trails. Northern owls can be found closer to the Toronto area during certain winters. The world-famous migration hot-spot Point Pelee is 3.5 hours away, being actually much closer to Detroit. To Canadians, this is banana-belt country, with several Carolinian species not found elsewhere in Ontario. Best time for a spring visit is mid-May; in fall, try late August through October. Slightly over an hour's drive from Toronto is Niagara Falls, which this book covers in a different chapter. Apart from the majestic falls themselves, the gulls can provide an excellent day's birding in late November or December: 19 species have been identified there, including such mega-rarities as Slaty-backed, Ross's, and Ivory.

HIGH PARK

Half day; fall through spring

High Park is an extensive wooded area with a large pond on the west side named Grenadier Pond. At the north end of Grenadier is a cattail marsh that formerly held Sora and Virginia Rails, but the newly arrived Coyotes are believed to have eliminated them. Orchard Orioles currently nest near the floral flag in the southwest part of the park. One can reach the park by subway, getting off at High Park Station and walking south. In spring, walk a little west, then south along the creek, checking for both waterthrushes. Continue along the creek's bank and up the hill to the restaurant. If the birding has been slow, try the woods farther south near Colborne Lodge; then go east, checking the ponds in the southeast corner, then north along Springbank Road. In fall, be sure to visit the High Park Hawkwatch, just north of the Grenadier restaurant parking lot, where hawks are tallied every day from September to November. The season totals usually exceed those of Hawk Mountain, Pennsylvania. Eastern Screech-Owls may be encountered anywhere in the park, even during the day.

LESLIE SPIT

Half to full day; early fall through late spring

Leslie Spit, also called Tommy Thompson Park, is open to the public only on weekends. If using public transport, take the Queen streetcar to Leslie Street, then walk south 0.5 mile to the beginning of the spit. The official list of Leslie Spit's birds is now exactly 300 species (as of June 2001) with the addition of Heermann's Gull in spring 2000.

In spring and fall, check the copse of woods about 200 yards southwest of the parking lot for passerines and owls. Walk south, looking for sparrows in the open areas. Continuing south for three miles, one may encounter a variety of ducks and likely a few raptors. In spring and early summer there is an enormous Ring-billed Gull colony along with Common and Caspian Terns, plus Double-crested Cormorants and Black-crowned Night-Herons. In recent years, Canvasbacks have bred in the ponds. From 24 May to about

10 October (Canadian Thanksgiving), a free bus, which can be flagged anywhere on its route, takes you out about two of the three miles, and will take you back. Otherwise, it is a very long, and in winter, a very cold walk, but one with excellent views of the lakeshore and downtown Toronto.

TORONTO ISLANDS
Half day; year round

These islands are very close to downtown Toronto but can be reached only by ferry from the foot of Bay Street. The round-trip fare is currently $5. In winter, the only ferry goes to Ward's Island on the east side, but during the warmer months there are also frequent ferries to Hanlan's Point in the west and Centre Island in the middle.

Toronto birders often start at **Hanlan's Point**, working their way along the fence bordering the airport. They then go west to the beach (except perhaps in summer, when it becomes a nudists' playground). Ducks and shorebirds can be found in season, and the airport is your best chance for Snowy Owl in winter. Next, walk south, checking the scrub to the right around to the lighthouse. It was here that two birders, on their first visit to the Toronto Islands, found Toronto's rarest bird, a Variegated Flycatcher, in October 1993. This species, normally found only in the tropics, attracted hundreds of birders from all over North America. Next, one comes to the new nature school, where one should check the feeder. Immediately north of the school is the nature sanctuary, which has extensive woods and ponds. The sanctuary offers an escape from the picnicking human throngs in summertime. If you find any owls, they will likely be here. Continuing east, check the pier on the south side of the island, where Cliff Swallows nest. There are several small islands accessible by bridge on the north side that should be checked if you have time. The area south of the village on **Ward's Island** can hold a variety of migrants, including Connecticut Warblers in late May.

HUMBER BAY
Half day; late fall to early spring, best in winter

Humber Bay is easily reached from downtown by taking a Queen Street streetcar going west. It is also fairly close to Lester Pearson Airport. Like Leslie Spit, the peninsulas were created a truckload at a time from the fill taken from construction sites. Humber Bay East is usually the more rewarding. Ducks of a dozen species or more can be seen at close range in winter in the enclosed harbors. Ross's Goose has been recorded here, as have Harlequin Ducks. Mimico Creek flows between the two peninsulas. A few shorebirds are possible in migration among the numerous resting gulls. Humber Bay West has a boardwalk leading to a gazebo where ducks and gulls

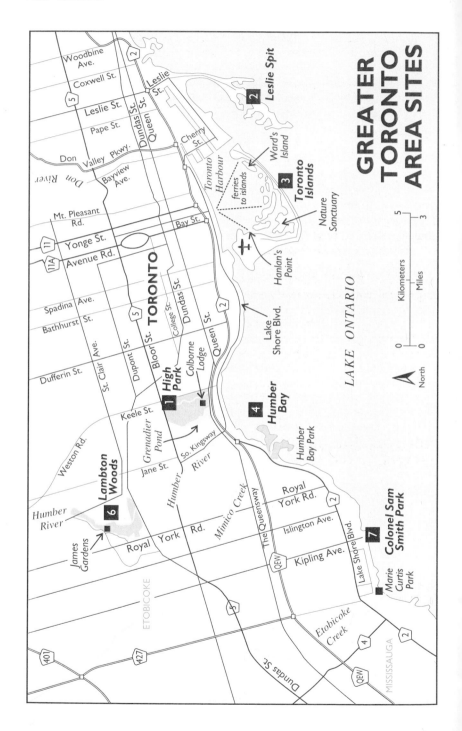

GREATER TORONTO AREA SITES

LAKE ONTARIO

North

Kilometers
Miles

2 Leslie Spit

3 Toronto Islands

Ward's Island

ferries to islands

Nature Sanctuary

Hanlan's Point

Toronto Harbour

Leslie St.

Cherry St.

Queen St.

Dundas St.

Woodbine Ave.

Coxwell St.

Leslie St.

Pape St.

Don Valley Pkwy.

Bayview Ave.

Don River

Mt. Pleasant Rd.

Yonge St.

Avenue Rd.

Bay St.

Spadina Ave.

Bathhurst St.

St. Clair Ave.

Dufferin St.

Dupont St.

Bloor St.

College St.

Dundas St.

Queen St.

Lake Shore Blvd.

TORONTO

1 High Park

Colborne Lodge

Keele St.

Grenadier Pond

Jane St.

So. Kingsway

Humber River

Weston Rd.

6 Lambton Woods

Humber River

James Gardens

Royal York Rd.

4 Humber Bay

Humber Bay Park

Mimico Creek

The Queensway

Royal York Rd.

Islington Ave.

Kipling Ave.

QEW

Lake Shore Blvd.

7 Colonel Sam Smith Park

Marie Curtis Park

ETOBICOKE

Etobicoke Creek

MISSISSAUGA

Dundas St.

401

427

QEW

can be studied at leisure. Continue to the end of Humber Bay West, where scoping of the ducks may reveal a Harlequin or perhaps a scoter.

CRANBERRY MARSH AND THE EAST
Half day; spring and fall

A favorite destination for Toronto birders is **Cranberry Marsh**, only a 30-minute drive east of town (not accessible by public transport). Exit Highway 401 at Harwood and go south to the second set of traffic lights, then left on Bayly Road to the Ajax/Whitby town line, then 0.5 kilometer farther east, where Hall's Road goes to the right. This turn-off can be easily missed. There are two viewing platforms from which the many geese, ducks, and shorebirds can be seen (best in the afternoon). At the south platform, there is a daily raptor watch from September to November. Many rarities have been recorded in this area, which includes a woods just to the northeast; the entire area is called the **Lynde Shores Conservation Area**. Another good stop a few kilometers farther east, especially in spring, is **Thickson's Woods** at the foot of Thickson Road. When you reach the lake, the woods are on your left on the east side. This oasis of vegetation has turned up many good finds in migration over the years, including such rarities as Townsend's and Black-throated Gray Warblers.

LAMBTON WOODS
A morning or half day; late fall to late spring

There are dozens of ravines and parks in the Toronto area that offer good birding opportunities, and one of these is **Lambton Woods**, located off Royal York Road on Eden Bridge Drive and north of Dundas Street on the Humber River. Park at James Gardens and begin walking south. Almost immediately, one comes to marshes that should be checked. Then walk up the hill to the top, where warblers are often found in spring. A Hermit Warbler turned up here in 1984.

Go back to the bottom of the hill and walk south. The woods that you are entering often have Red-bellied and Pileated Woodpeckers in winter, Olive-sided Flycatchers and many warblers in spring, and Eastern Screech-Owls at any season. Continue walking south, checking the feeder beside the trail in winter, and taking brief excursions to the right. When you reach the Dundas Bridge, do a U-turn and walk along the bank of the Humber River, checking the ducks. The river has birds all along its mostly wooded banks from Lake Ontario for several miles north, and you can extend the walk greatly to the north or, especially, to the south from Lambton Woods.

COLONEL SAM SMITH PARK
Half day; late fall to late spring

This is another fill site built one truckload at a time; it is located at the foot of Kipling Avenue in west Toronto. As you walk south from Lakeshore Road, check the tall spruces for warblers and other passerines. Upon reaching the base, there are several ponds and marshes that may hold a good bird or two. Next, continue out on the spit, checking the interior bay for shorebirds in season. Whimbrels often roost here in late May. Farther out, species such as American Pipit, Lapland Longspur, and Snow Bunting are possible at the appropriate seasons. Looking out on the lake, a variety of diving ducks may be seen, including scoters in winter. This site may be the closest lakeshore birding location to the airport. Marie Curtis Park slightly farther west is also very close.

RATTRAY'S MARSH
Half day; early fall to late spring

Located in Mississauga, west of Toronto (actually, Mississauga is now unified with Toronto politically), **Rattray's Marsh** offers a variety of habitats. It is located at the foot of Bexhill Road, which is near Southdown Road. It is perhaps best known for the flock of Red-necked Grebes that is present almost year round just offshore in Lake Ontario. There is a cattail-lined pond that may have extensive mudflats for shorebirds. Dabbling ducks are found on the pond, and, of course, diving ducks may be seen on the lake in season. Migrant passerines are found in the extensive woods.

HAMILTON
Half to full day; year round

Only 45 minutes west of Toronto (less from the airport), **Hamilton** has a favored location at the west end of Lake Ontario. From mid-September to mid-November, especially in stiff east or northeast winds, birders congregate at Van Wagner's Beach in front of Hutch's Fish and Chips Restaurant. Looking eastward with a telescope, one has perhaps the best opportunity in the region to see rare-but-regular seabirds such as Northern Gannet, Red and Red-necked Phalaropes, all three jaegers, Sabine's Gull, and Black-legged Kittiwake.

A short distance to the east along the Lake Ontario shoreline is **Stoney Creek** (follow the North Service Road), where huge numbers of diving ducks often congregate in late fall and winter to feed on Zebra Mussels. The ducks

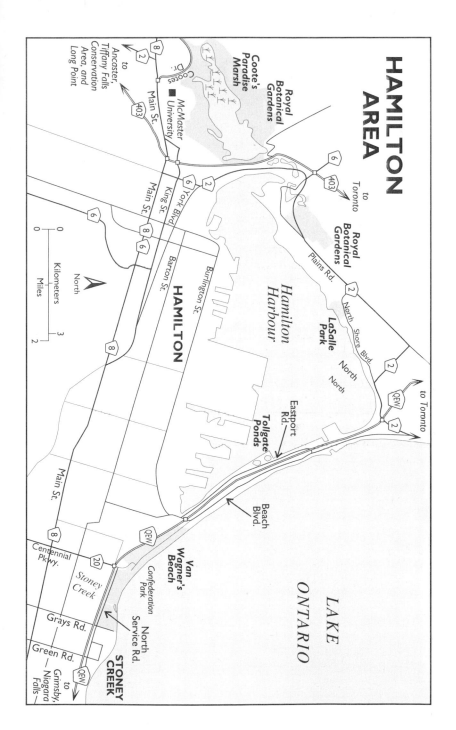

HAMILTON AREA

to Ancaster, Tiffany Falls Conservation Area, and Long Point

Royal Botanical Gardens

Coote's Paradise Marsh

Coote's Dr.

McMaster University

Main St.

403

Main St.

King St.

York Blvd.

Barton St.

Burlington St.

HAMILTON

6

8

6

2

6

403

to Toronto

Royal Botanical Gardens

Plains Rd.

North Shore Blvd.

2

LaSalle Park

North

North

2

QEW

2

to Toronto

Hamilton Harbour

Eastport Rd.

Tollgate Ponds

Beach Blvd.

QEW

20

8

Van Wagner's Beach

Confederation Park

North Service Rd.

Centennial Pkwy.

Stoney Creek

Grays Rd.

Green Rd.

Main St.

LAKE ONTARIO

STONEY CREEK

QEW

to Grimsby, Niagara Falls

North

0   Kilometers   3
0   Miles   2

can be viewed from the lake end of a number of roads between Grays Road and Green Road. Among the throngs of scaup, Long-tailed Ducks, Common Goldeneyes, and mergansers may be seen smaller numbers of scoters, perhaps a few King Eiders, and the odd rarity such as Tufted Duck, Common Eider, Harlequin Duck, or Barrow's Goldeneye.

Immediately to the north of McMaster University lies the **Coote's Paradise Marsh**, where the birding is always good, especially in fall. Exit Highway 403 at Main Street West (not Main Street East). Turn left (west) on Main Street West, and just after McMaster University turn right onto Coote's Drive. Proceed down the hill to the stoplight, then go right, do a U-turn, back to the stoplight and go left (east), parking just before a small bridge. Walk north, exploring the many trails. One pair of Prothonotary Warblers has nested here in recent years, and Nelson's Sharp-tailed Sparrows occur regularly in early October. Fast streams along the escarpment in Ancaster may hold nesting Louisiana Waterthrushes. The waterfalls at the Tiffany Falls Conservation Area are perhaps your best bet.

The **Royal Botanical Garden** off Plains Road has many trails and well-stocked feeders that make this a good destination in winter. **LaSalle Park**, on the north shore of Hamilton Harbour, often holds a rarity or two. Finally, the **Tollgate Ponds** and other ponds along Eastport Drive can be good for shorebirds. Try to visit Tollgate by driving south because the ponds are on the west side, and be careful to park well to the right.

Raptor aficionados will enjoy the **Grimsby Hawkwatch** in March and April. From Hamilton, go east on QEW to Christie Street (Exit 71), then south to the top of the hill. Go right on Regional Road 79 for 1.7 kilometers, then right into Beamer Point Conservation Area.

CARDEN PLAIN
Full day; late May and June

This magical area holds several species that can be difficult to find elsewhere in Ontario. An additional reward is the wildflowers and butterflies to be seen in June and July. Travel about 1.5 hours northeast to the town of Kirkfield. Leave Highway 48 here, go north to the lift lock, and check for Cliff Swallows. Continue another 2.4 kilometers to a curve and make a sharp right; then, after 0.2 kilometer, make a left so that you are going north again. Along this narrow road Upland Sandpipers, Common Snipe, and Eastern Bluebirds are easily seen. Loggerhead Shrike, now extremely rare in northeastern North America, can usually be found along this road. At 2.9 kilometers from the curve there is an extensive sedge marsh that in season always has Sedge Wren, American Bittern, and rails (including Yellow Rails in early May some years). Golden-winged Warblers nest in the poplar stands, Clay-colored, Grasshopper, and Vesper Sparrows are in the fields, and at night Whip-poor-wills and Common Nighthawks can be found. After another 9.5 kilometers there is a T-intersection; go left for 4.9 kilometers, then left again for 4.2 kilometers to Highway 503. Go left for 5.1 kilometers, then right to Canal Lake, where an Osprey nest can be seen on the telephone poles at very close range.

PRESQU'ILE PROVINCIAL PARK

Full day; year round, best in early fall and spring

A little over one hour's drive east along Highway 401, take Exit 509 for Brighton, then follow signs to **Presqu'ile Provincial Park**. There is a daily admission fee during the summer season. Just before you get to the park, a bridge crosses over an extensive marsh that may contain both bitterns, rails, moorhens, and other marsh birds. Once you have entered the Park, you will see signs announcing Beaches 1, 2, 3, and 4. Beaches should be checked for shorebirds, etc., with Beach 4 being the best.

At Beach 4, walk west to the lake from the parking lot, then, in August or September, take the trail left to Owen Point. At times over 1,000 shorebirds can be seen at close range, and as many as 19 species have been noted in a day. The most famous Presqu'ile shorebird was a Mongolian Plover in 1986. Equally surprising was the Sulphur-bellied Flycatcher at the Calf Pasture in

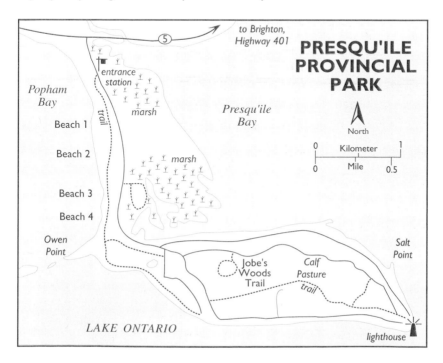

1986. Continuing south from Beach 4, then east, go right at the fork to visit Jobe's Woods, where Ruffed Grouse, American Woodcock, Pileated Woodpecker, and other woodland species may be seen. Continue east, then north through the Calf Pasture (good for sparrows) to a patch of woodland and an overlook of the bay for ducks. In March and April, the bay contains many thousands of waterfowl, with possibilities of rarities. Birders should note that in late fall duck-hunting occurs on alternate days.

Continue east to the lighthouse. The gift shop sells bird books, checklists, and other items of interest to the birder. A short loop walk here should turn up some migrant passerines; the lakeside should be checked for waterfowl.

AMHERST ISLAND

Full day; late winter best, good in spring and fall

Although the drive may be less than two hours to the ferry, the total journey will be longer before actual birding can begin. At certain times, however, the trip is well worth it, especially to those southerners who dream of seeing our northern owls. There is a large resident vole population that often attracts large numbers of hawks and owls to Amherst Island in winter. Peak owl season is typically during February and early March. Regular species include Long-eared, Short-eared, and Northern Saw-whet Owls. During invasion years Snowy, Northern Hawk, Great Gray, and Boreal Owls may be found. There is the added possibility of a Gyrfalcon or a rare duck such as

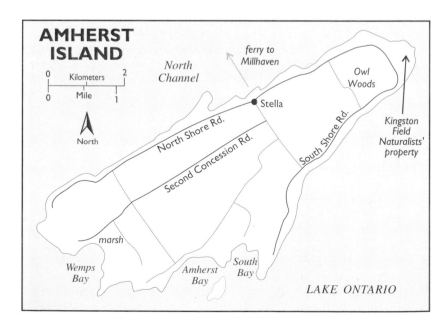

Barrow's Goldeneye. On a single weekend in mid-January 2001, over 500 birders visited the island, and all came away well pleased, having seen many owls and some of the specialties noted above. In 1979, a peak year, 10 owl species were present on the island, including 34 Great Gray Owls.

To get to **Amherst Island**, drive east on Highway 401 to Exit 593. Proceed south on County Road 4 to Millhaven on Lake Ontario. The ferry dock is 200 meters west on Highway 33. A round-trip on the ferry costs $3.50 Canadian; this fee includes your vehicle, and you may wish to take advantage of the restroom on the ferry. The first ferry leaves the mainland at 6:20AM, and then every hour on the half hour from 7:30AM. The ferry leaves the island every hour, on the hour, until 1:00AM. Once you reach the island, take the first left in the village of Stella and proceed east for 3.4 kilometers (2.1 miles). At this point, you either drive or walk 1 kilometer south, depending on the condition of the road. At the jog in the road walk northeast 250 meters to the beginning of the "Owl Woods." Dr. Alex Scott owns part of this property and welcomes visitors; however, it is best to inquire from local birders about access beforehand. Boreal and Northern Saw-whet Owls are usually found in the cedars at the beginning of the woods. In the Red Pine plantation behind, those two species also may be found, along with Long-eared Owls. In the open areas farther east, Short-eared Owls roost on the ground. Short-eareds begin flying as early as 3:30PM in winter and are best seen from the road farther to the east. Great Gray Owls, if present, are found in the woodlots farther west on the island.

Amherst Island is good at other seasons, too. The Kingston Field Naturalists Club owns the eastern tip of the island. In the ponds near the tip there are breeding Wilson's Phalaropes, and a good variety of ducks and shorebirds can be seen here during migration. The drive to **Wemps Bay** at the extreme west end can also be rewarding. There is a marsh, about a kilometer from Wemps Bay, on the south side of the road bisecting the island, that may hold Eurasian Wigeon and some of the more-common dabbling ducks.

ALGONQUIN PARK

Full day; spring and early summer, can be good in winter

This huge park, a 2.5-hour drive from Toronto, technically should not be included in this book because of the distance, but many Toronto birders go there on one-day trips. The park holds several species that cannot be found farther south, such as Spruce Grouse, Black-backed Woodpecker (possibly even Three-toed Woodpecker), Boreal Chickadee, and Gray Jay. Many other boreal-nesting species can be found here, such as Mourning Warbler and Lincoln's Sparrow. Beware, however, of Black Flies and mosquitoes during June, which can make life miserable if you don't have a good supply of DEET-based repellent.

There are two "best" locations to see the northern specialties. One is along the **Mizzy Lake Trail**. From the west entrance to the park, go 15.4 kilometers to Arowhon Road, then north 4.8 kilometers to an old railway bed. Turn right, drive 0.6 kilometer, and park at the locked gates; walk east past several ponds, watching for any of the "big four" species named, plus Olive-sided Flycatcher in June. The second location is **Spruce Bog Trail**, which is 42.5 kilometers from the West Gate. The first 100 meters are best for Spruce Grouse, but these birds often remain motionless and are difficult to find. Another half-kilometer east on Highway 60 brings you to the park interpretive center, where you can get a meal at the restaurant and perhaps some birdfinding assistance from the many expert naturalists on staff.

It would be possible to visit the Carden Plain and Algonquin Park on the same trip in one full day. The Ontario big day record of 200 species set in late May 2000 was begun at Carden, then visited Algonquin at dawn for singing boreal species, then Carden again, then the Lake Ontario region, Rondeau Provincial Park, Lake St. Clair, and, finally, Point Pelee after dark.

LONG POINT

Full day; best in spring, summer, and fall

Located on Lake Erie, this region boasts huge marsh areas, Carolinian woods, and the completely unpopulated and forested 20-mile point itself. At 100 miles from Toronto, it is at the limit of a two-hour drive, but this site can be well worth the effort. Long Point Bay formerly attracted most of the eastern population of Tundra Swans during March, as a stopover site on their way from Chesapeake Bay and the Atlantic Coast to Manitoba and thence to the Arctic. There are still thousands of Tundra Swans in March along with vast numbers of migrant waterfowl, but in recent years most Tundra Swans have been found inland or at Lake St. Clair.

The waterbirds can be seen from the causeway connecting the mainland to the beach, and by taking the dike trail on the west side of the causeway. The whole area to the west is called **Big Creek National Wildlife Area**. The trail is 1.0 kilometer past the bridge. Other vantage points are reached by turning right at the south end of the causeway along Hastings Drive, or by turning left at the end of the causeway and checking vantage points on the left, and from Lee Brown's, which is 3.9 kilometers west of Highway 59. To reach **Lee Brown's pond**, turn west at the last intersection before the causeway.

Forster's Terns are present during the breeding season, and Sandhill Cranes may be seen at any time, including winter. Be sure to visit the **Old Cut banding station**. The bird-banding program here is the oldest in North

America, and is active during April and May and from August to October. Check their sightings board for news of recent good birds. **Long Point Provincial Park** is located at the limit to where one can legally go east along the sand spit. (The whole length of the wooded point is privately owned.) The sedge areas in the park may hold Common Snipe and Sedge Wren during the breeding season.

To see Carolinian species in late spring and early summer, return to the intersection of Highways 59 and 24 and go west. Take the second left at 3.7 kilometers, then turn right (west) at the sand road at 1.4 kilometers. You are now approaching the **Wilson Tract**. The trails in these woods should lead you to Yellow-billed Cuckoo, Acadian Flycatcher, Cerulean and Hooded Warblers, and other southern species. There is a chance to hear Chuck-will's-widow among the din of Whip-poor-wills at night. Mosquitoes can be bad here. The more-open areas may contain Blue-winged Warblers, and the open fields often host Grasshopper Sparrows. Streams and ponds are good for Louisiana Waterthrushes, which are easiest to find when they are singing in May.

Returning again to Highways 59 and 24, go south 1.4 kilometers to the first dirt road and turn left (east). You will soon be in the **Backus Woods**, which holds many of the same species as the Wilson Tract, with two additions. Barred Owl is more likely to be heard at night here, and Prothonotary Warblers may be seen and heard in the wet areas by going north on the well-marked trail. Do not play tapes or disturb these warblers in any way, as they are now extremely rare anywhere in Ontario.

There are two sewage lagoons in this general area. The Port Rowan lagoon is off Regional Road 42, one kilometer east of Highway 59, on the north side. The Townsend Lagoons are reached by going 14.2 kilometers east of the town of Simcoe to Regional Road 69; continue north 1.4 kilometers and then take the first left after the railroad tracks. Currently, the lagoons can be visited on weekends only. Ducks and shorebirds, sometimes including rarities, may be seen at either of these lagoons. Just southeast of the town of Jarvis is another set of lagoons, but they aren't usually as good for birds.

Another place to visit in migration is **Turkey Point**, to the east of Long Point. The sand-bars often hold shorebirds and gulls (up to hundreds of Little Gulls can be seen here at times).

ACKNOWLEDGMENTS

I am indebted to Clive Goodwin and to the Ontario Field Ornithologists, whose site guides were invaluable in the preparation of this chapter.

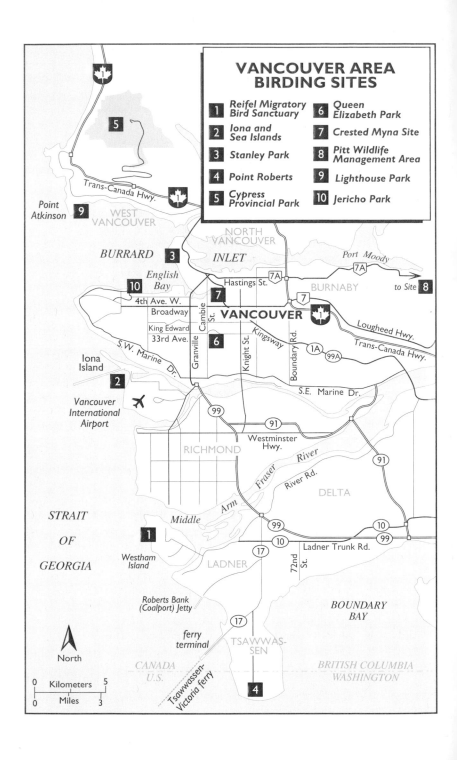

VANCOUVER AREA BIRDING SITES

1 Reifel Migratory Bird Sanctuary
2 Iona and Sea Islands
3 Stanley Park
4 Point Roberts
5 Cypress Provincial Park
6 Queen Elizabeth Park
7 Crested Myna Site
8 Pitt Wildlife Management Area
9 Lighthouse Park
10 Jericho Park

Point Atkinson

9

WEST VANCOUVER

Trans-Canada Hwy.

NORTH VANCOUVER

5

BURRARD   **3**   INLET

Port Moody

7A

to Site **8**

English Bay

Hastings St.   **7**

BURNABY

10

4th Ave. W.
Broadway

VANCOUVER   **1**

King Edward
33rd Ave.

Granville St.

Cambie St.

6

Knight St.

Kingsway

Boundary Rd.

Lougheed Hwy.

1A   99A

Trans-Canada Hwy.

Iona Island

2

S.W. Marine Dr.

S.E. Marine Dr.

Vancouver International Airport

99

91

RICHMOND

Westminster Hwy.

Fraser   River

River Rd.

91

DELTA

STRAIT OF GEORGIA

Middle   Arm

99

10

10

99

Ladner Trunk Rd.

1

Westham Island

LADNER

17

72nd St.

Roberts Bank (Coalport) Jetty

BOUNDARY BAY

ferry terminal

17

TSAWWASSEN

North

CANADA
U.S.

BRITISH COLUMBIA
WASHINGTON

Tsawwassen-Victoria ferry

4

0   Kilometers   5
0   Miles   3

VANCOUVER, BRITISH COLUMBIA

Wayne C. Weber

Vancouver, the largest city in western Canada, has a metropolitan population approaching two million—about half of all those living in British Columbia. Greater Vancouver extends from the lower slopes of the North Shore mountains across the Fraser River to the U.S. border. Despite rapid urban growth and congested traffic, Vancouver has a lot to offer the birder. Habitats in the Vancouver area range from the huge intertidal mudflats of Boundary Bay and large areas of farmland (protected from most kinds of development) to heavily forested mountain slopes. Vancouver owes much of its renown as a good birding area to its location at the mouth of the Fraser River. About 400 bird species have been recorded in the area—more than 80 percent of the total British Columbia list.

ESSENTIAL INFORMATION

Getting Around: Greater Vancouver has a good public-transit system, called TransLink (*http://www.translink.bc.ca*), consisting mainly of buses, but also including the Skytrain rapid-transit system. This system works well within Vancouver proper. Places such as Stanley Park, Jericho Park, Queen Elizabeth Park, and even Lighthouse Park in West Vancouver are easy to reach from downtown by bus. However, bus service to the suburbs is much poorer, and there is no public transit to many key birding areas, including Iona Island and the Reifel Bird Sanctuary. Rental cars are readily available at the airport and in downtown Vancouver.

Vancouver has worse traffic problems than most cities its size, in part because there is no freeway running through the city center. Try to avoid driving during weekday rush hours. The worst bottlenecks are the bridges from Vancouver to North Vancouver and those spanning the Fraser River, as well as the Massey Tunnel between Richmond and Delta. Most local radio stations feature rush-hour traffic reports.

433

Climate: In a nutshell—usually delightful in summer, but dismal in winter. Even in winter, snow is rare at sea level; summers are mild and sunny, but not hot. Mean daily high and low temperatures in January are 5°and 0°C (42° and 32°F), and 22° and 13°C (72°and 55°F) in July. Annual precipitation, most falling between October and April, averages 41 inches at the airport but more than 60 inches downtown. In winter, heavy downpours are rare, but overcast skies with long periods of light rain or drizzle are typical.

Natural Hazards: Biting insects are typically not a problem near the coast, but they may be a nuisance during late spring and summer in the mountains.

Other Considerations: Tides are a crucial factor when birding salt-water shorelines around Vancouver. The average tidal range is 10 feet, with extreme tides of up to 16 feet. Some areas are useless for birding at high tide, and others (e.g., Boundary Bay) are useless at low tide—the birds are near the water's edge, too far out to be identified. Check the daily papers or television weather reports; if you plan a long stay, buy a set of local tide tables from a marina or bookstore. Vancouver birders live and die by the tides.

Safety: Vancouver is probably one of the safest large cities in North America. A caution for persons hiking in the North Shore Mountains (Cypress or Mount Seymour Provincial Parks): stay on hiking trails and exercise caution. These mountains are rugged and deceptively dangerous, and several hikers and skiers are killed or seriously injured every year. Thefts from cars have been frequent at Iona Island and on the roads leading to Boundary Bay (64th, 72nd, and 104th Streets), so take necessary precautions.

Other Resources: The most comprehensive birding guide to the area is *The Birder's Guide to Vancouver and the Lower Mainland* by C. J. Aitchison (2001, Vancouver Natural History Society), a revised and expanded edition of a book first published in 1993. The Vancouver area also gets some coverage in *A Bird-finding Guide to Canada*, 2nd edition, by J. C. Finlay (2000, McClelland and Stewart). This book has somewhat spotty coverage of Canada, but it is very useful for the areas it does cover.

The Vancouver Natural History Society, founded in 1918, operates a web site at *http://www.naturalhistory.bc.ca/VNHS/index.htm*, which includes directions to, and a brief summary of, the birds to be found in each of the 31 sites covered in the *The Birder's Guide to Vancouver and the Lower Mainland*. The VNHS has field trips almost every weekend. The Society has a phone line at (604) 737-3074; when the message begins, punching the number 4 will take you to the Vancouver Rare Bird Alert—one of the best-maintained RBA tapes in North America. The tape is updated several times a week, and often once a day during peak migration times or when a mega-rarity is present. (Punching 2 will play a list of current field trips.) Transcripts of the tape are posted to BIRDWEST, TWEETERS (Washington State's e-mail group), and BCVAN-BIRDS (the Vancouver birding e-mail group). (Subscription information for these and other state/province chat groups is available on the ABA web site, *www.americanbirding.org*.)

THE BIRDING YEAR

In Vancouver's maritime climate, the seasons change slowly, with little change in temperature from November through March. Spring migration extends from late February through the first week of June. During most spring seasons, however, there are conspicuous waves of songbird migration. The conventional wisdom that "warbler waves don't happen along the West Coast" is not applicable to Vancouver, where strong storms in April and early May can produce excellent spring fall-outs.

The first Tree and Violet-green Swallows arrive in mid-to-late February. In March, concentrations of Brant and other waterfowl can be found. By late March, hordes of Varied Thrushes, kinglets, and other early songbirds are moving through. The peak migration period for most songbird species is 20 April to 10 May, although waves of flycatchers, vireos, and warblers can be seen as late as 5 June. The best places for songbird migrants are Queen Elizabeth Park, Point Grey (on and near the University of B.C. campus), and Jericho Park. Spring shorebird migration is also spectacular at places like Iona Island, Boundary Bay, and the Roberts Bank jetty. Movements peak between 20 April and 10 May, at which time one might see tens of thousands of Western Sandpipers and Dunlin, and smaller numbers of many other species.

Summer rarely produces large bird concentrations, but the weather is pleasant and most breeding passerines are in full song. Southbound shorebirds appear by 20 June, and large flocks are present through most of July. For many shorebird species, a July peak of adults is followed by a second, August–September peak, mainly juveniles. Late June and early July can be a good time to look for vagrants such as Red-necked and Little Stints.

Fall landbird migration, extending from early August to late November, is even more protracted than spring migration. Movements of most flycatchers, vireos, warblers, and some sparrows peak between 15 August and 15 September. A few species such as Yellow-rumped Warbler and White-crowned and Golden-crowned Sparrows peak later, in late September and October. Vancouver birders tend to focus on shorebirds in August through early October, with good reason. Many rare shorebirds occur annually (e.g., American and Pacific Golden-Plovers, Marbled and Bar-tailed Godwits, Sharp-tailed, Stilt, and Buff-breasted Sandpipers, and Ruff), and even greater rarities are possible.

Despite short days and frequent adverse weather conditions, winter can be exciting. The diversity and numbers of birds are impressive. Christmas Bird Counts for Ladner (covering most of the Fraser Delta) and Vancouver average 130 to 135 species. About 50,000 dabbling ducks and 40,000 Dunlins winter in the Fraser Delta area, and raptors winter in impressive numbers, too. Snowy Owls can be numerous in flight years, and a few are usually present even in non-flight years. One or two Gyrfalcons usually over-winter. Northern songbirds such as American Tree Sparrow, Snow Bunting, and Common Redpoll winter in small numbers in most years.

REIFEL MIGRATORY
BIRD SANCTUARY AND VICINITY

Half day; fall, winter, spring

The **George C. Reifel Migratory Bird Sanctuary**, open from 9:00AM to 5:00PM daily, is located on Westham Island. It is operated under lease by the non-profit B.C. Waterfowl Society, which charges a small admission fee (currently $4.00 for adults, $2.00 for children and seniors). The sanctuary is undoubtedly the most popular and best-known birding spot in Greater Vancouver, and it can be crowded on weekends. Its location at the mouth of the Fraser River, one of the largest and most productive estuaries on the Pacific Coast, accounts for its status as an outstanding location for migrant and wintering waterfowl, birds of prey, and shorebirds. Several miles of walking paths surround marshy or water-filled enclosures. There are several viewing blinds, plus a tall viewing tower at the northwest corner of the sanctuary, which overlooks the Fraser marshes and mudflats. At the entrance, a gift shop sells checklists for the sanctuary and the Vancouver area, as well as books and other birding paraphernalia. The gift shop staff can usually provide information about any unusual species that have been seen recently.

Next door is the Alaksen National Wildlife Area and the regional offices of the Canadian Wildlife Service. Permission to bird Alaksen on weekdays from 8:30AM to 4:30PM can be obtained at the CWS office. The remainder of Westham Island is accessible by a road network that offers good birding when the sanctuary and Alaksen NWA are closed. (The dikes surrounding the island, however, are privately owned and are off-limits to birders.)

One of the main attractions in winter (October to April) is a flock of up to 20,000 Snow Geese, which breed on Wrangel Island off Siberia and winter on the Fraser Delta and nearby Skagit Delta in Washington. In mid-winter (January and February), most of the geese usually move to the Skagit. Several hundred Trumpeter Swans winter here, as well. Depending on tides and other factors, the swans and geese may feed either in the intertidal marshes offshore (visible with a scope) or in farm fields on Westham Island, sometimes offering extremely close views. Up to 10,000 or more dabbling ducks consist mainly of Mallards, American Wigeons, Northern Pintails, and Green-winged Teal. Eurasian Wigeon is easy to find here, especially when ducks are feeding in the fields; it is usual to see up to 10 or 20 male Eurasians in a flock of several thousand American Wigeons. Diving ducks are present in much smaller numbers, mainly on the three freshwater sloughs (Robertson, Fuller, and Ewen Sloughs). In willows next to Fuller Slough, there is usually a winter roost of two to six Black-crowned Night-Herons. This is the only place in British Columbia where this species is seen reliably. The extensive brackish cattail marshes, visible from the outermost dike, are home year round to American Bitterns, Virginia Rails, and Marsh Wrens.

Reifel is renowned as a good place for birds of prey in winter, including Northern Harrier, Rough-legged Hawk, Merlin, Peregrine Falcon, and Barn, Great Horned, Long-eared, Short-eared, and Northern Saw-whet Owls. Northern Goshawk, Gyrfalcon, Snowy Owl, and Barred Owl are sometimes present. Bald Eagles nest on the island, and concentrations of up to 30 or 40 can be seen, especially in spring.

A guided bird walk around the sanctuary is offered at 10:00AM every Sunday, year round. If you want to see some of the more secretive owls, such as Barn, Long-eared, or Northern Saw-whet, you should join this walk, which often features a special effort to find them.

The wooded dikes, especially the east dike of the Central Field, are great in winter for sparrows (including "Sooty" Fox and Golden-crowned) and other passerines—in part because of the well-stocked feeders. Scarcer species such as Swamp, White-throated, and Harris's Sparrows are seen several times every year. Passerine migrants are often present in good numbers in the wooded areas in spring and fall.

Reifel is also noted for shorebirds. In spring and fall, large numbers, sometimes including rarities, may roost during high tide at some of the ponds, but they are usually out feeding on the mudflats at low tide. The best spots (depending on water levels in the various impoundments) are usually

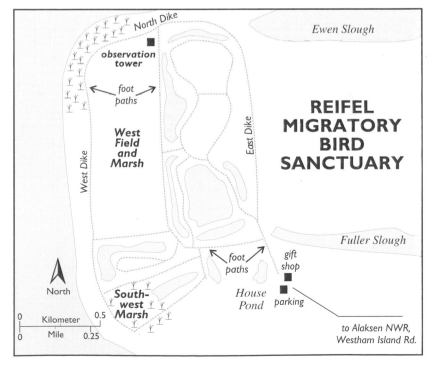

the "West Field," "Southwest Marsh," and "House Pond" (next to the refuge entrance and the gift shop). Less-common species include Semipalmated, Baird's (fall), Pectoral (fall), Sharp-tailed (rare but regular, late September and early October), and Stilt (rare, August and September) Sandpipers, and Ruff (rare, September). True rarities have included Black-necked Stilt, Spotted Redshank, Hudsonian Godwit, and Temminck's Stint.

Summer (June to early August) is the quiet season at Reifel. Although a good variety of breeding species is present, numbers are small, and relatively few waterfowl and raptors are present.

IONA
AND SEA ISLANDS
Half day; year round

Iona and Sea Islands are also part of the Fraser Delta. Iona Island is home to the Greater Vancouver sewage-treatment plant, as well as the Iona Island Regional Park. Sea Island, once mainly agricultural, is now 80 percent covered by the sprawling Vancouver International Airport. These islands are noted for waterfowl and birds of prey from October through April or May, and for shorebirds all year, but especially in spring and fall. Iona Island is probably the best place in western Canada to see unusual shorebirds.

To access **Iona Island** from the Vancouver Airport, drive east on Grant McConachie Way until you reach a traffic light at Templeton Drive. Turn left (north), go to Grauer Road, and turn left (west) again. Proceed westward on Grauer, which becomes Ferguson Road, until you reach the west end of Sea Island. The road then curves to the right (north) and approaches the Iona sewage plant, which is within a chain-link fence. During office hours (Monday–Friday, 9:00AM to 5:00PM) you may park in the visitor spaces next to the office. Preferably, keep on the road a short distance as it swings to the left, and park next to a gate that is left unlocked for birders to enter the sewage-ponds area. Check the sightings log there. Or, to bird the west end of Iona Island or the Iona South Jetty, continue on and park at the Iona Beach Park parking area (opens at 8:00AM), next to the restrooms.

Note: access routes to the Vancouver Airport are undergoing a major reconstruction, and the current access roads to Iona Island will change soon.

The sewage plant contains four settling-ponds. Ponds full of water (or treated sewage) usually have waterfowl; those with a mixture of exposed sludge and water serve as roosting areas for shorebirds—often thousands of them. Birding is best within two hours on either side of high tide. At low tide, there are usually only a few shorebirds present. During fall migration (late June through late October), all of the common mudflat species can be found, plus several others that are scarce in spring (e.g., Semipalmated and

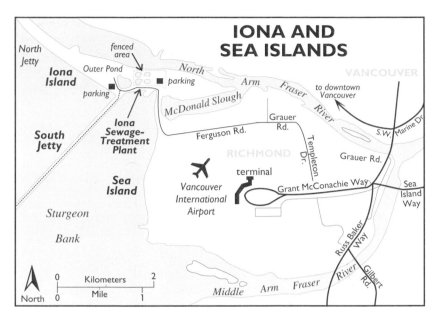

IONA AND SEA ISLANDS

North Jetty

Iona Island

Outer Pond

fenced area

parking

North parking

Arm *Fraser* *River*

to downtown Vancouver

VANCOUVER

McDonald Slough

Grauer Rd.

Ferguson Rd.

South Jetty

Iona Sewage-Treatment Plant

Templeton Dr.

Grauer Rd.

S.W. Marine Dr

RICHMOND

Sea Island

Vancouver International Airport

terminal

Grant McConachie Way

Sea Island Way

Sturgeon

Bank

Russ Baker Way

Gilbert Rd.

0 Kilometers 2

North 0 Mile 1

Middle *Arm* *Fraser* *River* Rd.

Pectoral Sandpipers). In addition, American Golden-Plover, Hudsonian Godwit, Sharp-tailed, Stilt, and Buff-breasted Sandpipers, and Ruff are usually seen from one to several times each fall. Greater rarities, such as Red-necked and Little Stints, Curlew Sandpiper, and even a Spoonbill Sandpiper, have been seen at Iona and/or Sea Island.

From September to May, the sewage ponds, "outer pond," and adjacent mudflats support dozens to many hundreds of dabbling and diving ducks, sometimes including Eurasian Wigeon. Look carefully for a rare Tufted Duck among the scaup on the outer pond. In summer (May to September) the ponds host Blue-winged and Cinnamon Teal, and the outer pond has nesting Yellow-headed Blackbirds—the only colony in the Vancouver area.

Two jetties extend out from the west end of Iona Island. The North Jetty borders the North Arm of the Fraser River. It is a stone-block jetty, and birders *should not* attempt to walk out on it—much of it is submerged at high tide! The sandy west end of Iona Island extends about 1.5 miles northwestward to the base of the North Jetty, and generally offers unexciting birding. However, the **South Jetty**, extending southwestward for 2.3 miles from just south of the Iona Beach Park restrooms, has a roadway (closed to private vehicles) on it, plus a huge pipe (atop which you can walk) that carries the treated sewage out into Georgia Strait. It takes about an hour to walk to the end. Birding along the jetty is usually mediocre at high tide, but it is much better at low or intermediate tides, when the flats are partly exposed and often teeming with waterfowl, shorebirds, and gulls.

From September to May, the intertidal areas north and south of the South Jetty feature loons, grebes, Snow Geese (spring and fall), all three scoters, and Bonaparte's, Mew, and Thayer's Gulls. Look especially for Thayer's along shorelines and in fields on **Sea Island**. Many of these species can be seen without walking out the jetty, but only at high tide. In late spring (May) there are often thousands of Bonaparte's Gulls on the flats. Parasitic Jaegers and Common Terns are frequent in May and September. Deepwater species such as Brandt's Cormorant, Pigeon Guillemot, Rhinoceros Auklet, and occasional rarities such as King Eider might be found from the tip of the South Jetty. However, these species are more likely to be seen, and without requiring a 4.6-mile walk, at Point Roberts.

Sea Island is very good for birds of prey. The fields along Grauer and Ferguson Roads are the winter home of many Northern Harriers, Red-tailed and Rough-legged Hawks, Barn Owls, and (in some years) Short-eared Owls. Bald Eagles, Merlins, and Peregrine Falcons are seen along shorelines. In fact, the latter two species attack shorebirds at the sewage ponds often enough to be a major nuisance to birders! Passerine migration is sometimes noteworthy on Iona and Sea Islands, although forest-dwelling species are usually scarce. Sparrows in particular are abundant at times. A good area for passerines is along the north dike of Sea Island, between McDonald Beach Park and the northwest corner of Sea Island. You can park either at the west end of this dike (unmarked parking area where Ferguson Road takes a sharp bend to the right, before starting onto the Sea/Iona causeway) or at McDonald Beach Park, and then walk as far as you like. A long list of passerine rarities has been found on Iona and Sea Islands.

STANLEY PARK

Half day; year round

Stanley Park, Vancouver's premier city park, is a peninsula jutting out into Burrard Inlet, close to downtown Vancouver. Most of its 1,000 acres are native conifer forest dominated by Douglas-fir, Western Redcedar, and Western Hemlock, although windstorms have destroyed or damaged many of the largest trees. The park is bisected by the Stanley Park Causeway, a high-speed traffic artery leading to the Lions Gate Bridge and to North and West Vancouver. East of the causeway, toward Brockton Point, and west of Lost Lagoon, there are grassy fields and ornamental gardens.

Stanley Park is easily reached from downtown Vancouver by car or via TransLink bus routes 23, 35, and 135, which travel along Hastings Street and end at the Lost Lagoon bus loop. There is bus service within the park in summer; contact TransLink for information. There are two main automobile entrances, at Beach Avenue and Georgia Street. (A good map of the park is a must.) Most park roads are one-way. Pay-parking is available at many locations. One of the park's most attractive features is a masonry seawall, topped by a broad asphalt path, which extends around the entire shoreline, but which is often very crowded with walkers, joggers, and cyclists. There is also an extensive trail network through the forested interior. Robberies and assaults are rare, but a lone female birder should avoid some of these trails.

Lost Lagoon, a small freshwater lake near the Georgia Street entrance, is choked with waterfowl and gulls in winter. A few Ring-necked Ducks and Redheads are often present. Tufted Duck is seen almost every year, with one sometimes staying for weeks. Hundreds of Common and Barrow's Goldeneyes roost on the lagoon at night, but feed along nearby shorelines in the daytime. Lost Lagoon is one of the best places anywhere to get close views of normally shy diving ducks down to distances of less than 10 feet. Ignore any Mute Swans, Black Swans, or Mandarin Ducks that you see; these are either wing-clipped birds or escapees.

The entire **Stanley Park seawall** is great for birding from September through May, but the best area is on the west (English Bay) side of the park, from the Beach Avenue entrance north to Siwash Rock. Regular winter species include Red-throated and Common Loons, Horned, Red-necked, and Western Grebes (the latter often in rafts of thousands), Pelagic Cormorant (Brandt's are regular on the Burnaby Shoal marker buoy off Brockton Point), Harlequin Duck, Long-tailed Duck, Surf Scoter, Common and Barrow's Goldeneyes, Bald Eagle, and Mew and Thayer's Gulls. Alcids (Common

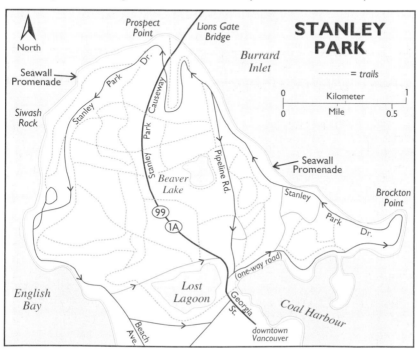

Murre, Pigeon Guillemot, and Marbled Murrelet) are present, usually well offshore, although Marbled Murrelets have become much scarcer in recent years as their old-growth forest habitat has been reduced by logging. A special feature is the seabird colony at **Prospect Point**, just west of the Lions Gate Bridge. A cliff about 200 feet high has a few dozen breeding pairs each of Pelagic Cormorant and Pigeon Guillemot. They can be viewed from above at the scenic Prospect Point lookout, or from the seawall below.

In the forested areas, birds present year round include Barred Owl, Pileated Woodpecker, Black-capped and Chestnut-backed Chickadees, Brown Creeper, Winter and Bewick's Wrens, Golden-crowned Kinglet, Hutton's Vireo (uncommon), Red Crossbill (sporadic), and Pine Siskin. A few additional species are found in winter, including Red-breasted Sapsucker, Varied Thrush, and "Sooty" Fox Sparrow. In spring and summer, additional breeding species include Rufous Hummingbird, Olive-sided, Hammond's, and Pacific-slope Flycatchers, Swainson's Thrush, Cassin's and Warbling Vireos, Orange-crowned, Black-throated Gray, Townsend's, MacGillivray's, and Wilson's Warblers, Western Tanager, Black-headed Grosbeak, and Purple Finch. In June and July, the **Beaver Lake** area has the greatest variety of birds, partly because the forest stands are particularly dense there. This is the best spot for Hammond's Flycatcher, Townsend's Warbler, and the occasional summering Varied Thrush. In the shrubbery near the lake, look for Willow Flycatcher. The lake itself has breeding Pied-billed Grebes and Wood Ducks.

Large numbers of passerine migrants can be seen on some days in April, May, late August, and September. The best areas, especially in spring, are not necessarily the forested areas, but the ornamental plantings west of Lost Lagoon and the Brockton Point area—especially where there are maples, which seem to provide many insects.

Stanley Park has produced many exciting birds over the years. Examples include Common Eider, Smew, Great Gray Owl, Black Phoebe, Philadelphia Vireo, Clark's Nutcracker, White-breasted Nuthatch, Black-and-white Warbler, Ovenbird, and Grasshopper Sparrow.

Ambleside Park, located in West Vancouver directly across First Narrows from the west side of Stanley Park, has a much smaller forested area, but offers similar habitats and a similar variety of species. It is easily reached by bus, and can be birded in two hours or less.

QUEEN ELIZABETH PARK

Several hours; spring

Queen Elizabeth Park is located atop Little Mountain, the highest hill in Vancouver. The park is an arboretum, and the spring flower displays are spectacular. There is a viewpoint offering a good view of downtown Vancouver and the North Shore Mountains, and the park is a favorite tourist destination. Although the vegetation is mostly manicured and non-native, there are some patches of native trees (especially Vine Maples) on the west, north, and south sides of Little Mountain, as well as some very large Western Redcedars and Douglas-firs. The main parking area (fee) is on the very top of Little Mountain and is most easily reached from the east via 33rd Avenue. There are a couple of smaller pay-parking areas as well, and there is free parking along most of the roads within and bordering the park.

The park has an unspectacular birdlife in summer and winter. However, in April and May, it becomes one of the best migrant-trap hot-spots in the Vancouver area. On most days in April and May there will be at least a few migrant passerines in the park. The best conditions occur when a storm crosses the Vancouver area after several days of fine weather, at which times the park can be hopping with songbirds. If the weather remains cool and damp, the concentrations can remain for several days before the migrants move on. Fair numbers of migrants are sometimes seen in fall.

Migrant birds occurring regularly and often in substantial numbers include Rufous Hummingbird, Olive-sided, Hammond's and Pacific-slope Flycatchers, Western Wood-Pewee, Cassin's Vireo, Swainson's, Hermit, and Varied Thrushes, Yellow-rumped ("Audubon's" and "Myrtle"), Black-throated Gray, Townsend's, and MacGillivray's Warblers, and Lincoln's and Golden-crowned Sparrows. Other, scarcer species that occur in ones or twos include Calliope Hummingbird, Red-naped Sapsucker, Dusky Flycatcher, Hutton's Vireo, and Nashville Warbler. The first three of these species were once considered vagrants in Vancouver, but they are now reported annually in spring here.

POINT ROBERTS, WASHINGTON

Half day; year round

Point Roberts is located south of the 49th parallel in Washington State, yet is accessible by land only from Canada, separated from the rest of Whatcom County by Boundary Bay. The name "Point Roberts" is applied to the U.S. portion of the peninsula, which covers an area of about 5 square miles. Point Roberts has been included for decades in the Vancouver bird checklist area, and there are at least 10 to 15 species found more easily there than anywhere else near Vancouver. The total list of bird species recorded is more than 240. Much of the Point is covered with a second-growth forest dominated by Douglas-fir, Grand Fir, Red Alder, and Broadleaf Maple. It is a good place for conifer-forest birds, but it is even more noted for marine birds, especially those that prefer deep water and strong currents. The best birding spot on the Point is **Lighthouse Marine Park** at the southwest corner.

From the intersection of Highway 17 and 56th Street (Point Roberts Road), drive south on 56th Street, through the business district of Tsawwassen, for 2.9 miles (4.7 kilometers) to the Canada/U.S. border crossing. This is a border crossing like any other (open 24 hours a day), so make sure that you have proof of identity, and be prepared for a vehicle inspection. Beyond the border crossing, 56th Street becomes Tyee Drive and continues southward. Lighthouse Marine Park can be reached in two ways. From the border crossing, drive south 1.1 miles (1.8 kilometers) to Gulf Road, turn right, and then left (south) onto Marine Drive to reach the park entrance. Alternately, continue south on Tyee Drive another 0.25 mile (0.4 kilometer) from Gulf Road to APA Road; continue on Tyee Drive, which immediately swings to the right, skirting the Point Roberts Marina, and eventually becomes Edwards Drive, paralleling the shoreline until it reaches Lighthouse Marine Park. The park has a $3.00 day-use fee for non-county residents. There are picnic tables (with wind shelters!) and restrooms, as well as a small campground.

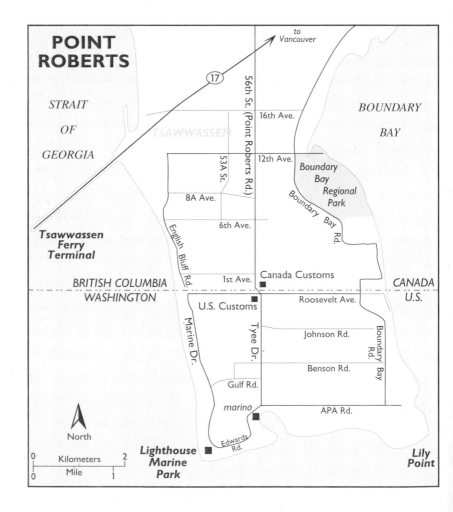

Here, the deep waters of Georgia Strait come close to shore, and strong currents often bring fish or other edibles to the surface, attracting many seabirds. Gulls (Bonaparte's, Mew, and Glaucous-winged) and cormorants (Double-crested, Pelagic, and, in fall and winter, Brandt's) usually form the nucleus of such flocks. Pacific Loons sometimes appear in the hundreds; Red-throated and Common are more frequent, but less numerous. In fall (late September-November) Heermann's Gulls and Ancient Murrelets are often seen. Lighthouse Marine Park is the best place near Vancouver to see alcids: Common Murres are often numerous from September through April or May, a few Pigeon Guillemots are seen all year, and Rhinoceros Auklets are scarce but regular from May through October or November. Marbled Murrelets were once seen regularly throughout the year, but they are now harder to find. Up to 30 Harlequin Ducks are seen all year near the Point and along the gravelly beach to the east. All three scoters can be seen from fall through spring, with Surf Scoters the most common. At low tide, Black Turnstone are often present on the beach (except in summer). During most of the year (except summer), a constant procession of marine birds flies by the point, often offering close views; they include grebes, "Black" Brant, Long-tailed Duck. In spring (May) and fall (September and October), Parasitic Jaegers are seen harassing flocks of Bonaparte's Gulls and Common Terns.

The other outstanding spot is **Lily Point**, at the southeast corner of Point Roberts. From the intersection of Tyee Drive and APA Road, drive east for 3.1 miles (5.0 kilometers) on APA Road until you reach a small cemetery surrounded by forest. Park your car next to the cemetery, then follow a broad path that leads east and then southeast. (Despite the No Trespassing signs, both local residents and birders have used the Lily Point area for many years without a problem.) About 0.5 mile along this (bulldozed) trail through the forest, next to an area of slumping gravel bluffs, a well-used but unsigned path leads down a hill to a large, flat beach area (Lily Point itself), where many of the same birds found at Lighthouse Marine Park can be seen. There are a couple of viewpoints between Lily Point and the cemetery, from which a large expanse of Boundary Bay can be scanned with a scope—but don't get too close to the edge of the bluffs!

The conifer forest near Lily Point and elsewhere on Point Roberts is good for Barred Owl, Pileated Woodpecker, Chestnut-backed Chickadee, Hutton's Vireo (all are year round); Pacific-slope Flycatcher, Swainson's Thrush, and Black-throated Gray Warbler (summer); and Red-breasted Sapsucker and Varied Thrush (mainly winter).

Other spots worth checking for marine birds include the west end of Gulf Road, the end of South Beach Drive (off APA Road), and the end of Simundson Drive, on the east side of the marina. There is public access to the beach here, but not at most other points on the shoreline. Expect to see many birds offshore, but do not expect to see fly-byes at close range the way you do at Lighthouse Marine Park.

The Tsawwassen Ferry Terminal, from where ferries depart to Vancouver Island, is at the end of a 3-kilometer jetty. There is a parking area (for dropping off and picking up passengers) in which parking is free for up to one hour; all other parking is pay parking. Many of the marine birds listed for Point Roberts can also be found here, although views of some of the species are not as good. A few species rare at Point Roberts are possible here. Black Oystercatchers nest on or near the jetty, and two to four birds can often be seen; a few Surfbirds sometimes accompany the Black Turnstones in winter; and Snow Buntings are often seen from November through March.

CYPRESS PROVINCIAL PARK

Several hours; spring, summer, fall

For mountain birding near Vancouver, **Cypress Provincial Park** is one of the best and most-accessible locations. Mount Seymour Provincial Park, in North Vancouver, offers very similar birding. Both parks feature large and very popular ski developments, with access roads that terminate at an altitude of about 3,000 feet. And each has a network of hiking trails that can be used from about May through early November.

The Cypress Provincial Park access road leaves Highway 1 at Exit 8, only a few miles north of downtown Vancouver. As you climb the mountain, stop at the Hi-View Lookout, about three-quarters of the way up the road. Here, there are spectacular views of Vancouver and English Bay (when it's not fogged in!), and the site is good for Band-tailed Pigeon and several breeding species not found higher up, such as Willow Flycatcher, Black-headed Grosbeak, and sometimes Black-throated Gray Warbler. The best area for summer birding in the park is the Yew Lake loop trail, which leads north from the uppermost parking area. This trail is about 2 kilometers long and hosts a representative sample of mid-mountain habitats (heavy forest, open bogs, and small ponds) and birds. Breeding species along the Yew Lake Trail and nearby include Blue Grouse, Northern Pygmy-Owl, Vaux's Swift, Black Swift (scarce and probably not breeding close by), Red-breasted Sapsucker, Olive-sided Flycatcher, Steller's and Gray Jays, Hermit and Varied Thrushes, Townsend's and MacGillivray's Warblers, and Red Crossbill (in some years). "Slate-colored" Fox Sparrows recently have colonized the area as a breeding species and can be found in brushy areas such as that near the parking lot. Another worthwhile hike for birds is from the lowest major parking lot—near the toboggan course—through heavy forest up to Hollyburn Lodge.

The upper parking lot of Cypress Provincial Park has potential as a hawkwatching spot in fall. In late September and October, more than 100 raptors have been noted passing on some days with northwest winds.

Winter birding in the park is sparse at best and is usually a lost cause because of the noise and hubbub created by the throngs of skiers from late

November to early April. However, if one arrives very early in the morning, one can usually find Gray Jays, Red-breasted Sapsuckers, and a few other species, sometimes including Red or (less often) White-winged Crossbills. Look for Northern Pygmy-Owls perched on roadside treetops.

MINOR BIRDING SITES

The south end of Cambie Street Bridge, Vancouver, was the only reliable location remaining as of July 2001 for the introduced **Crested Myna**. The best spot is in an industrial area around the intersection of Wylie Street and Second Avenue, or within two or three blocks of this site, which is just east of the south end of the bridge, immediately south of downtown. The mynas, which became established in Vancouver around 1897, once numbered in the thousands. They have declined sharply since the 1970s, largely the result of competition with European Starlings. They will likely be gone soon.

Jericho Park is located on West 4th Avenue in Vancouver. It combines some of the birding features of Stanley Park and those of Queen Elizabeth Park. There are two large freshwater ponds and a marsh, as well as saltwater shoreline on English Bay. Natural vegetation consists mainly of some dense stands of Red Alder, but most of the park has lawns and scattered trees. This park serves as a migrant trap in spring—less so than Queen Elizabeth Park, but more so than Stanley Park. Because of the variety of habitats, however, it is a much better year-round birding area than Queen Elizabeth Park.

Lighthouse Park, West Vancouver, is a scenic municipal park that includes 185 acres of virgin forest surrounding the Point Atkinson lighthouse. Breeding landbirds include Blue Grouse, Band-tailed Pigeon, Red-breasted Sapsucker, Pileated Woodpecker, Olive-sided and Hammond's Flycatchers, and Cassin's and Hutton's Vireos. Wintering waterbirds include Western Grebe, Barrow's Goldeneye, Harlequin Duck, Black Turnstone, Surfbird, Rock Sandpiper (rare), and Pigeon Guillemot. The Grebe Islets, two small, rocky islets off the west side of the park, have nesting Black Oystercatchers, and they are also the best area to look for other marine birds and shorebirds.

The area around the south end of **72nd Street** at **Boundary Bay** near Ladner is good for Peregrine Falcons, shorebirds (scope needed), and, at dusk, Barn and Short-eared Owls. It is also a good place to check for Snowy Owls during flight years.

The **Pitt Wildlife Management Area** is located at the south end of Pitt Lake, 24 miles (38 kilometers) east of Vancouver. Birding here is best in spring, summer, and early fall. Most of the area is wetland and marsh, but the wooded dikes are often good for migrant passerines. This is the best spot near Vancouver for American Bittern, Sandhill Crane (breeding), Eastern Kingbird, Gray Catbird, American Redstart (occasionally breeding), and Bullock's Oriole. Pitt WMA is large, and a half-day is needed to thoroughly bird the area.

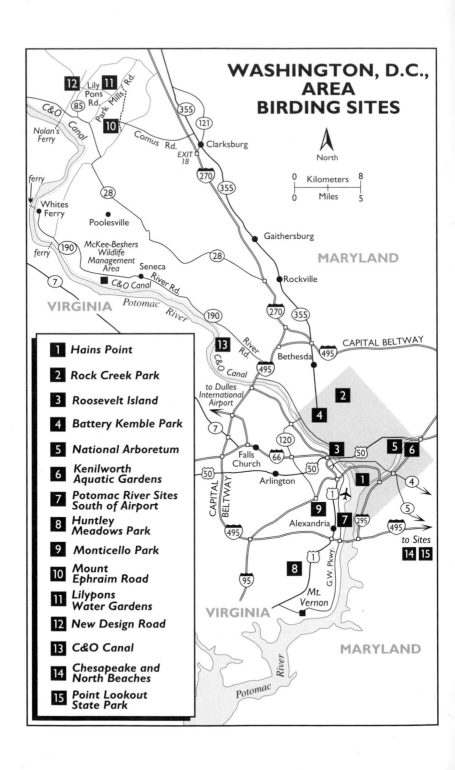

WASHINGTON, D.C., AREA BIRDING SITES

North

Kilometers 0 — 8
Miles 0 — 5

12 Lily Pons Rd. **11**
85 Park Mills Rd.
10
Comus Rd.
C&O Canal
Nolan's Ferry
355
121
355
Clarksburg
EXIT 18
270
355
ferry
Whites Ferry
28
Poolesville
190
McKee-Beshers Wildlife Management Area
Seneca
28
River Rd.
C&O Canal
Gaithersburg
Rockville
MARYLAND
7
VIRGINIA
Potomac River
190
270
355
CAPITAL BELTWAY
13
River Rd.
C&O Canal
495
Bethesda
495
to Dulles International Airport
7
120
2
4
Falls Church
66
3
50
50
5 **6**
50
Arlington
1
4
CAPITAL BELTWAY
9
7
295
5
495
Alexandria
495
8
1
G.W. Pkwy.
to Sites **14** **15**
95
Mt. Vernon
VIRGINIA
MARYLAND
Potomac River

1 Hains Point

2 Rock Creek Park

3 Roosevelt Island

4 Battery Kemble Park

5 National Arboretum

6 Kenilworth Aquatic Gardens

7 Potomac River Sites South of Airport

8 Huntley Meadows Park

9 Monticello Park

10 Mount Ephraim Road

11 Lilypons Water Gardens

12 New Design Road

13 C&O Canal

14 Chesapeake and North Beaches

15 Point Lookout State Park

WASHINGTON, D.C.

Ottavio Janni and Rob Hilton

Birding opportunities may not be the first thing to spring to one's mind when thinking of Washington, D.C., but in fact the city and its surroundings offer some excellent year-round destinations. The joys of spring migration were immortalized in Louis J. Halle's classic *Spring in Washington,* but fall is just as good, and winter has its rewards, too. For the visitor with little time to spare, the variety of passerine migrants that can be found within a 15-minute drive of downtown Washington makes the city a very attractive destination during migration seasons. And indeed the variety of warblers that can be seen at an urban migrant trap such as Rock Creek Park can easily hold its own against many other better-known East Coast hot-spots. In winter, gull aficionados will have to go no farther than such a quintessential Washington landmark as the Tidal Basin to study large flocks and to search for rarities. For those with more time, the city's surroundings offer a diverse mix of habitats that, depending on the time of year, can produce migrant shorebirds, wintering waterfowl, and breeding landbirds, including an excellent selection of typically southern passerines. Washington's proximity to the Chesapeake Bay provides yet another set of habitats and birding opportunities, and birders with a few days to spare may want to head over to the Delmarva Peninsula and the Atlantic coast.

ESSENTIAL INFORMATION

Getting Around: Although a few birding areas within the city limits can be reached by public transport, an automobile is a real convenience, and is essential for birding outside the city. Many visitors arrive at Reagan Washington National Airport, which is a short taxi or subway ride from downtown, where many hotels are located; some will fly to Dulles Airport, which is a fair clip outside of the city, or to Baltimore-Washington Airport. All airports have the usual car-rental outlets. City traffic is frequently congested, including areas other than downtown, and at times other than rush hour. Rush-hour traffic is among the worst in North America; summer weekend beach traffic, sports events, and arena concerts can cause additional slowdowns.

449

Special note: This chapter was completed in mid-2001. At press time it was not known what, if any, changes in access or birding quality may occur at any of these sites in the wake of the attacks on September 11, 2001, or because of construction projects on The Mall and near Jones Point and Hunting Creek.

Climate: Although spring and fall are generally pleasant, the summer months from June to August can be unbearably hot and humid. Winter weather is highly variable. Winter highs average in the low to mid-40s Fahrenheit. Summer highs can soar well above 90°, and afternoon and evening thunderstorms are frequent during summer. Winter-season snow totals average around 24 inches (60 cm); snowfalls in excess of 8 inches (20 cm) can disrupt area businesses and transportation.

Safety: Washington, D.C., has a reputation for violent crime, but the areas described here are generally safe. Common-sense precautions (as in any large city) should be used when birding in the city, particularly in northeast D.C. (Kenilworth Aquatic Gardens and the National Arboretum), and to a lesser extent in Rock Creek Park.

Other Resources: The best birdfinding guide for the region is Claudia Wilds's *Finding Birds in the National Capital Area* (1992, Smithsonian Institution Presss), which covers all of D.C., Maryland, and Delaware, as well as much of eastern Virginia. In addition, Virginia is well covered by the 1997 ABA guide, *A Birder's Guide to Virginia*. The Maryland Ornithological Society (*www.mdbirds.org*), the Audubon Naturalist Society (*www.audubonnaturalist.org*), and the Virginia Society for Ornithology (*www.ecoventures-travel.com/vso*) all have active field-trip programs. MOS can be reached by phone at (800) 823-0050; ANS at (301) 652-9188. Three birding listserves cover the area: MDOsprey, VA-Bird, and DE-Birds, and they are excellent sources of information on birds in the greater D.C. area. Information on subscribing to these and other state chat groups can be found on the ABA web site, *www.americanbirding.org*.

THE BIRDING YEAR

L ate February marks the beginning of spring as the first waterfowl begin to move north. Waterfowl numbers and variety peak in March, and spring is in full swing by early April. Bonaparte's Gulls, Caspian Terns, and swallows wing their way up the Potomac, while the first warblers (Northern Parula, Yellow-throated Warbler, Louisiana Waterthrush) begin establishing their territories. Landbird variety increases through April, and migrants peak during the first two weeks in May. Migrant traps can hold a spectacular variety of warblers (observers have recorded up to 31 species in one day in the immediate metropolitan area) and other passerines. In late May landbird migration is winding down (although some of the more uncommon species, such as Olive-sided Flycatcher and Mourning Warbler, occur then), but spring shorebird numbers are peaking. By June, migration is all but over, and while birding in the city is generally quiet, nearby Frederick County, Maryland, can offer a wide variety of breeding landbirds. July marks the beginning of adult shorebird migration on the Eastern Shore of Maryland's Chesapeake Bay and at Hunting Creek, and by mid-August, migration is in full swing again: shorebird numbers are high (and the first juveniles have arrived). Early cold fronts can produce a good variety of migrant landbirds. Passerine diversity peaks in September; a good day at Rock Creek can rival the best May days in terms of variety. Shorebirds are still present in excellent numbers; migrating raptors start to move after the first strong cold front. Neotropical migrants wind down in October, but sparrows and other short-distance migrants are peaking, as are raptors and many waterfowl. Landbird migration slows considerably after early November, but spectacular concentrations of waterfowl occur on the Eastern Shore, and hawkwatching can be rewarding. By December, winter is settling in. From now until March, waterfowl and gull-watching can be good along the river, particularly during a freeze (not every year), which concentrates waterfowl on patches of open water and brings in large numbers of gulls (often including "white-winged" species) to roost on the frozen Tidal Basin and Washington Channel. Landbirding in the city is slow but can be rewarding at the National Arboretum or Kenilworth Aquatic Gardens, while the fields of southern Frederick County provide habitat for sparrows and Lapland Longspur. The Eastern Shore is excellent for waterfowl and raptors.

DOWNTOWN D.C. – THE MALL AND NEARBY AREAS

Half day; fall through spring

The best birding in downtown D.C. can be found at East Potomac Park, known to birders as **Hains Point.** To reach this area from downtown, take 17th Street N.W. south from Constitution Avenue. Turn right (westbound) onto Independence Avenue, then make an immediate left turn to get onto eastbound Independence. Get immediately in the right-hand lane and fork right on Maine Avenue. After the traffic light, fork right again, then look for an intersection (with a brown East Potomac Park sign) that leads left under the highway bridge; do not miss this turn, or you will be in Virginia before you realize it. Ohio Drive loops one-way around the golf course on East Potomac Park. Birders can either walk or drive this three-mile loop. In winter, birds to watch for include a variety of diving ducks, and as many as six Merlins roost every evening in isolated trees on the golf course. Gulls provide the most excitement, however, particularly in the early morning and late afternoon. Lesser Black-backed Gull is almost always present from November to March among the abundant Ring-billed, Herring, and Great Black-backed Gulls. If Washington Channel freezes, numbers skyrocket, and Iceland and Glaucous Gulls are likely, while rarities such as Thayer's and

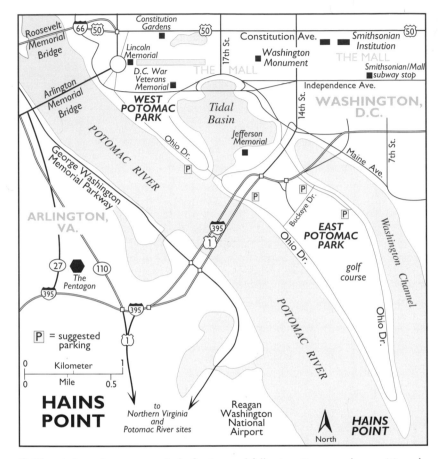

HAINS
POINT

California have been recorded. Spring and fall migrations can be exciting. In April, Bonaparte's Gulls, Caspian Terns, and swallows fly along the river; other landbird migrants concentrate in the small groves of trees (especially by the service road at the south end of the golf course) in April and May. Loons, grebes, and ducks peak in March and early April. In fall, landbird migrants are scarcer, but the large flocks of Laughing Gulls roosting on the golf course should be checked for the occasional Franklin's. Hains Point is particularly rewarding during or just after stormy weather; rain puddles on the golf course attract shorebirds in spring and fall (although over 20 species have been recorded, only a few will be present at any one time), and November Nor'easters sometimes produce coastal birds such as scoters. Hains Point is D.C.'s premier rarity site, with records of Pacific Loon, Tufted Duck, Little Gull, and Snowy Owl (twice), among others. The Tidal Basin nearby can be just as good for gulls as Washington Channel (especially when frozen), while Constitution Gardens just north of Independence Avenue is a nice little migrant trap, especially in spring. Check the grove of trees immediately around the D.C. War Veterans Memorial. Be warned that traffic on pleasant weekend afternoons from April to October is heavy; visiting at these times is not recommended. Major foot races are held several times a year, and all downtown roads can be closed for hours. (These events are usually announced in the Friday newspapers.) If the traffic loop is closed around Hains Point, the best parking is on Ohio Drive west of the Tidal Basin, or where Ohio intersects Buckeye, west of Washington Channel.

ROCK CREEK PARK, D.C.

Half day; spring and fall

The area near the nature center in **Rock Creek Park** is the premier landbird migrant hot-spot in the metropolitan area. To reach the best areas from downtown, take Connecticut Avenue north to Nebraska Avenue. Make a right, then turn right onto Military Road. After about 0.75 mile go right onto Glover Road into the park, fork left, pass the Nature Center, and park at picnic areas #17/18. On a good day the amount of activity in the first hour or two after dawn can be exhilarating, with birds flitting everywhere about the tops of the sunlit trees. Check the clearing at picnic areas 17/18, then walk south to the horse corral at picnic areas 25. In spring, trails into

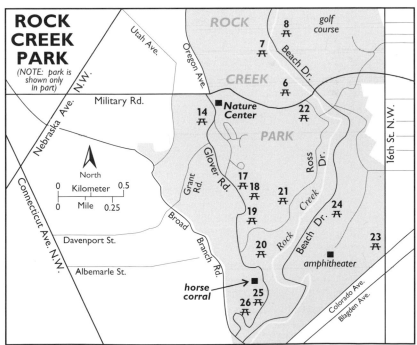

the forest (particularly the one that goes down to Rock Creek opposite the horse corral) can also be productive. The area immediately around the Nature Center is also very productive. Drive back north on Glover Road and park in the Nature Center lot. Check the edges of the parking lot, the small open area just behind the Nature Center, and in spring, the Life of the Forest loop trail, which starts behind the Nature Center (good for *Catharus* thrushes and Hooded Warbler). From there, continue to the Maintenance Yard (actually an open area adjacent to the Maintenance Yard). From the Nature-Center parking lot, walk about 100 yards to the horse stables, then take the wide path to your left downhill into the woods. After about 200 yards you will see an open area on your right. While not particularly appealing visually, this overgrown weedy field and forest edge is excellent for migrants, particularly in fall. It is especially good for such sought-after migrants as Red-headed Woodpecker, Olive-sided and Yellow-bellied Flycatchers, Orange-crowned and Mourning Warblers, and Lincoln's Sparrow (all rare but regular), while rarities have included Lark and Clay-colored Sparrows. Back in your car, return to the overgrown field at Picnic Area 14 (intersection of Glover and Military Roads) to look for migrants, especially in the fall.

All the eastern flycatchers, vireos, and warblers migrate through Rock Creek Park. During the first two weeks of May, finding 20 warbler species in the park is routine, and seeing 25 is quite possible. Later in May variety diminishes, but uncommon migrants such as Gray-cheeked Thrush and Mourning Warbler are regular. The fall migration is more drawn out, and peak days can come anytime between late August and early October, invariably after the passage of a cold front. While day-to-day species variety is lower in fall, the potential for uncommon species is better. The much sought-after Connecticut Warbler is regular in September, in weedy patches (particularly those containing Giant Ragweed) adjacent to woodland edges. Philadelphia Vireo averages about 10 individuals each fall, mostly in September. Although Neotropical migrants decline after mid-October, the remainder of the month can be excellent for sparrows, and later still in November, Picnic Areas 17/18 can be good places to listen for winter finches (e.g., Purple Finch, Pine Siskin, and Evening Grosbeak) flying overhead early in the morning.

THEODORE ROOSEVELT ISLAND TO CHAIN BRIDGE, D.C.

Half day; year round

For the birder with limited time, this short itinerary can prove rewarding in spite of the low-flying airplanes. It starts at **Roosevelt Island,** reachable by car only from the northbound lanes of the George Washington Memorial Parkway in Virginia, or on foot (30 minutes) from the tourist area of Georgetown by crossing the Key Bridge to 19th Street, and Arlington Ridge

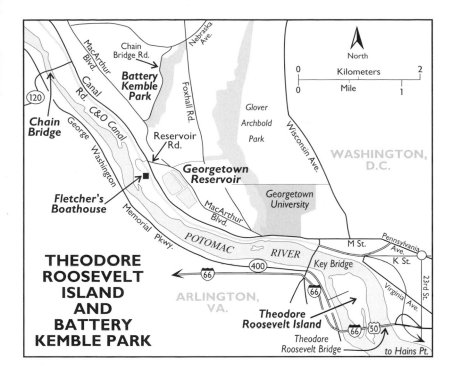

THEODORE ROOSEVELT ISLAND AND BATTERY KEMBLE PARK

Road to the footpath. The entire island, particularly the more-elevated areas near the Roosevelt Memorial, is excellent for landbird migrants in spring (activity is often good well into late morning, making it a perfect complement to Rock Creek), and the small marsh holds Black-crowned Night-Heron, Wood Duck, and an occasional surprise. After you bird the island, a return to D.C. for the additional sites in this section will require going north on the George Washington Parkway. There are two choices—one is to exit after about one mile to the left onto Spout Run Parkway and go about one-half mile to reach a U-turn exit road that will return you to the southbound parkway, from which you can reach Key Bridge back into D.C. Alternatively, continue north on the parkway another two miles (beyond Spout Run) to exit for Route 120/Chain Bridge into D.C. Either route will require getting onto Canal Road once you cross the river, and thence onto MacArthur Boulevard to reach **Georgetown Reservoir**. This small body of water is good for ducks in winter and migration (especially Canvasback and Ring-necked Duck), gulls, including Lesser Black-backed (the first Yellow-legged Gull recorded in the U.S. spent five winters here from 1990-1994), and raptors in fall (watch from the large lawn just east of the reservoir; Golden Eagle is regular in early November). Just past Georgetown Reservoir is a left turn onto Reservoir Road. At the bottom of the hill there is a tricky left-hand merge onto Canal Road, and an immediate exit down a steep driveway to Fletcher's Boathouse and the C&O Canal. (Note that Canal Road is one-way the wrong way on weekday mornings.) This is a very pleasant spot in spring, with breeding Yellow-throated Warblers and Orchard and Baltimore Orioles, as well as Caspian Terns and swallows over the river. Walking west along the towpath for about a mile takes you to Chain Bridge. The bridge offers a fine view of the marsh below, which can have waterfowl in migration and Yellow-crowned Night-Heron in summer. Go back to MacArthur Boulevard and make a left; after about 0.5 mile make a sharp right onto Chain Bridge Road; after 0.5 mile go right into the dirt parking lot for **Battery Kemble Park**, another outstanding site for landbird migrants; several sought-after species such as Olive-sided Flycatcher and Mourning Warbler are easier here than at Rock Creek. Concentrate on the isolated groves of trees on the hilltop. Veery breeds in the woods.

THE NATIONAL ARBORETUM
AND KENILWORTH AQUATIC GARDENS
Half day; year round

These two parks in Northeast D.C. combine beautiful flowers and great birding. From downtown D.C. take New York Avenue eastbound, then turn right onto Bladensburg Avenue N.E. After about 0.4 mile turn left onto R Street and into the **National Arboretum.** Some of the best winter landbirding in the city can be found here, with large flocks of Cedar Waxwings, good numbers of Eastern Bluebirds, Red-breasted Nuthatches in the pines, and the occasional lingering warbler. Great Horned and Barred Owls are resident. Spring migration is also rewarding; Fern Valley in particular is good for *Catharus* thrushes, whereas the large field with the Greek-style columns often has Bobolink in May. Fields can be swarming with sparrows in October. The Arboretum opens at 8:00AM and closes at 5:00PM. To reach **Kenilworth Aquatic Gardens**, get back onto eastbound New York Avenue (Route 50), and just after crossing the bridge over the Anacostia River take the first exit onto Kenilworth Avenue, and then the very next exit at the sign for Quarles Street. Follow the signs to Kenilworth Aquatic Gardens. The park opens at 7:00AM (though the gate is usually open earlier) and closes promptly at 4:00PM. The park has several acres of artificial water-lily ponds, and the Marsh Trail skirts the edge of a recently restored marsh, ending with views over a tidal pond and mudflats. A new boardwalk at the back left corner of the artificial ponds allows access through prime marsh habitat, and overlooks the same tidal flats. Birding is good year round. In winter, dabbling ducks and Hooded and Common Mergansers are often found, and landbirding can be interesting. In spring, Kenilworth is by far the best place in the city for herons, including American Bittern; the mudflats at the end of the Marsh Trail have a few shorebirds, and a wide variety of landbird migrants can be found. In early summer, several species that are otherwise difficult to find in the city breed here or nearby (e.g., Willow Flycatcher, Warbling and Yellow-throated Vireos, Marsh Wren, Prothonotary Warbler, Yellow-breasted Chat, Blue Grosbeak). Fall migration can also produce shorebirds. Rusty Blackbird occurs in April and October.

NATIONAL AIRPORT TO MOUNT VERNON

Half day; fall through spring

The best waterbirding in the metropolitan area is to be found along the **Potomac River.** The area just south of Reagan National Airport in particular provides good opportunities for watching shorebirds in fall, waterfowl in winter, and assorted migrants in spring. The recent proliferation of the exotic plant *Hydrilla* on this stretch of the Potomac (from July to November) has played a key role in attracting an outstanding variety of waterbirds. Head south from National Airport onto the George Washington Memorial Parkway. After about a mile, turn left into the parking lot for the **Washington Sailing Marina** and check the cove for waterfowl in winter and shorebirds in fall. Getting back onto the southbound G.W. Parkway, you will reach the city of Alexandria. There are several vantage points along its waterfront from which the Potomac can be scanned for waterbirds. The best two are **Founders Park**, reached by turning left onto Oronoco Street and following it until it ends, and **Jones Point**, farther south. To reach the latter, take the G.W. Parkway over the Capital Beltway, fork right before the first light for a jug-handle turn onto South Street, cross the parkway, drive under the Beltway at the sharp left, take the first right on Jones Bridge Road, and proceed to the end. Construction began in 2001 on a new bridge across the Potomac River, parallel to the existing Woodrow Wilson Memorial Bridge; access to Jones Point might become problematic.

As soon as you exit Alexandria on the G.W. Parkway, you will cross a small stone bridge over the mouth of **Hunting Creek**, the single best shorebird spot within an hour's drive of D.C. (Note that noise from the construction of the new bridge might have an effect on the birdlife here.) Park either at the Belle Haven Picnic Area lot about one mile to the south, or along South Street. From July to October an excellent variety of shorebirds can be seen on the tidal mudflats both east and especially west of the stone bridge. More-common species include Black-bellied and Semipalmated Plovers, Killdeer, both yellowlegs, Spotted Sandpiper, Semipalmated, Western, Least, Stilt, and Pectoral Sandpipers, Dunlin, and Short-billed Dowitcher. Rarities have included American Golden-Plover, Ruddy Turnstone, Sanderling, White-rumped and Baird's Sandpipers, Wilson's Phalarope, and Long-billed Dowitcher, but these do not occur every year. Good numbers of herons, gulls (Franklin's is rare but annual from August to October), and terns

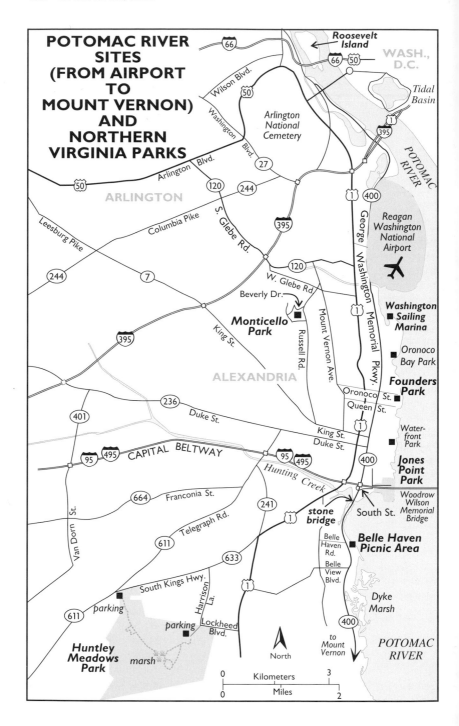

POTOMAC RIVER SITES (FROM AIRPORT TO MOUNT VERNON) AND NORTHERN VIRGINIA PARKS

also frequent the mudflats; later in fall excellent numbers of dabbling ducks can be seen here. Bald Eagle is common. The George Washington Parkway continues on to Mount Vernon. In fall and winter, large numbers of diving ducks can be seen from any of the parkway pull-offs that provide views of the river.

HUNTLEY MEADOWS
AND OTHER NORTHERN VIRGINIA PARKS
Half day; year round

A few miles south of the Capital Beltway (I-495) in Fairfax County, Virginia, lies **Huntley Meadows Park**, a jewel of an area containing a variety of habitats. It is most famous for its nesting King Rails. To reach the visitor center, take US-1, Richmond Highway, south from Exit 177 of the Capital Beltway (and south from the city of Alexandria). From downtown D.C., take US-1 over the Fourteenth Street Bridge and exit left for Route 1 and Crystal City. Proceed about 3.1 miles south of the Beltway to the traffic light at Lockheed Boulevard; this light is near the bottom of a long hill. Turn right and drive about 0.7 mile, until the road bends sharply to the right. Follow the signs and carefully turn left into the park, driving to the parking lot. Past the center, walk along the path through the forest to the boardwalk (go straight where the Cedar Trail goes left). The woods host typical eastern forest birds. Near the boardwalk listen and look for Prothonotary Warblers. Continuing on the boardwalk you will immediately come out to the marsh. Start looking for King Rails (usually resident except in cold winters), which can be seen and heard from any part of the boardwalk. Virginia Rails and Soras occur during migration, and Mississippi Kites have been seen over the marsh during May and June of recent years. Wood Ducks and Hooded Mergansers, among other ducks, as well as several heron species, can be seen. American and Least Bitterns nest occasionally. Continue to the observation tower, which you should climb in order to scan the marsh. In spring, displaying American Woodcocks can be seen at dusk from the other entrance to Huntley Meadows, which is reached by returning to the entrance gate at Lockheed Boulevard and going straight onto Harrison Lane (don't go right onto Lockheed). Drive up the hill to the traffic light and turn left onto South Kings Highway. Go about 1.5 miles, until you are approaching the traffic light at Telegraph Road at the bottom of the hill. Turn left just before this traffic light, park, and walk down the Hike-Bike Trail. In about a mile look for a wayside exhibit on woodcock; to the west (right) is an area where American Woodcocks display, and Barred Owls and old-field birds are often found. The park is good for migrant sparrows, especially Lincoln's Sparrows, in fall.

For the visiting birder with but a lunch-hour or two to spare, few places can be better in spring than **Monticello Park,** a narrow strip of left-alone woods in a valley between suburban houses. During the peak of spring migration, it is an excellent place to look for vireos, thrushes, warblers, and other migrants as they fly down to the stream to bathe. Pretty much every regular species of passerine migrant has been found here, and many birds can be seen at very close range. Late morning is best. In Arlington County, from the interchange of I-395 with South Glebe Road (Route 120) proceed south (left if you are driving from downtown D.C.). At the first traffic light completely away from the interchange (second light on South Glebe if you are coming from D.C.), take West Glebe Road across a small bridge into the City of Alexandria; South Glebe Road bears to the left at this light. Follow West Glebe Road about 0.9 mile to the second traffic light, Russell Road. Make a right, go about 0.3 mile, turn right onto Beverly Drive, and park carefully just before the wooded park on the left. Nearby parks such as Lubber Run and Long Branch Nature Center also act as migrant traps in spring and fall.

SOUTHERN MONTGOMERY AND FREDERICK COUNTIES, MARYLAND

Half to full day; year round

Perhaps the best year-round birding within an hour's drive of Washington can be found in southern Montgomery and Frederick Counties, Maryland. This itinerary starts from Exit 18 of I-270, the Clarksburg exit, about 18 miles north of the Washington Beltway. From here, drive 0.5 mile on Route 121 northeast to MD-355, and turn left. After about one mile on 355, turn left onto Comus Road, and proceed about 6 miles to a T-intersection. From there, turn right onto **Mount Ephraim Road** (dirt). This is one of the best roads in the Washington area for breeding songbirds, with Worm-eating, Kentucky, and Hooded Warblers among them. The road traverses private property (*stay strictly on the road*), and is excellent for spring migrants, particularly near the small open area 1.1 miles west of the Comus Road intersection. Mount Ephraim Road ends after 3.9 miles at Park Mills Road. Turn left and then right after 0.9 mile onto Lily Pons Road.

After about a half-mile the entrance to **Lilypons Water Gardens** will be on your right; you may park near the office building, but *pay attention to the operating hours posted at the entrance gate so that your car is not locked in.* This large area of artificial ponds is used for raising water lilies. In spring and fall, the drained ponds are attractive to herons and shorebirds and a variety of landbird migrants. In summer, breeding birds include Least Bittern and Willow Flycatcher; Loggerhead Shrike is barely hanging on. In fall and winter, the bushy hedgerows between ponds attract sparrows (including White-crowned and American Tree), and the ponds hold a modest selection of waterfowl. Lilypons has attracted rarities at all seasons and is always worth a look. *Remember, this area is a commercial business and private property—be considerate of the land and the employees, and do not enter any wet area!*

After leaving Lilypons, continue west on Lily Pons Road until the intersection with MD-85. Past this intersection, Lily Pons Road becomes Oland Road and ends after 0.7 mile at a T-intersection with **New Design Road**. Because of recent encounters between residents and birders, we urge you to park on the north (right, according to this itinerary) side of the road; *do not venture off the road under any circumstances*. The extensive fields in this area are worth birding anytime. In spring, they attract large flocks of Bobolinks, and Vesper, Grasshopper, and Savannah Sparrows breed, along with several pairs of Dickcissels in most years. Upland Sandpiper is regular in July/August. In late fall and winter, bare fields (especially if recently manured) attract large flocks of Horned Larks that usually contain small numbers of Lapland Longspurs and Snow Buntings. Pay attention to raptors as well: Rough-legged Hawk and Short-eared Owl show up occasionally.

Once you are on New Design Road, continue south for 3.3 miles until the road ends at Nolan's Ferry on the C&O Canal. The towpath west of here can be excellent for spring migrants, and it holds the usual Canal breeding birds, such as Acadian Flycatcher, Yellow-throated Vireo, Northern Parula, Yellow-throated and Prothonotary Warblers, and Louisiana Waterthrush. An alternative for spring migrants is Greenfield Road, reached by making a left turn off MD-85 one mile south of the intersection with Lily Pons Road. The stretch of road that parallels the Monocacy River is especially interesting.

The **C&O Canal** in Montgomery County is also worth birding for passerine migrants in either spring or fall. There are many access points (all left turns off River Road, Exit 39 on the Washington Beltway), and some of the best are described below, from east to west. Pennyfield Lock can be reached by taking Pennyfield Lock Road 8.4 miles from I-495. Violette's Lock (off Violette's Lock Road, 11 miles west of I-495) can be an excellent place to scan the Potomac, especially during stormy weather. Rarities have included American White Pelican, Pomarine Jaeger, Black-legged Kittiwake, and Arctic Tern; Long-tailed Duck and scoters are regular in spring and late fall. River Road meets a T-intersection 0.3 mile west of Violette's Lock Road. Continue left, and go 0.7 mile to Riley's Lock Road; turn left onto it and you will reach Seneca, which attracts many of the same species as Violette's Lock. About 4 miles west of Riley's Lock Road, a left turn at the sign for Hughes Road will take you to McKee-Beshers Wildlife Management Area (known to birders as Hughes Hollow). The impoundments, fields, and woods here hold a nice variety of breeding birds (Least Bittern and Willow Flycatcher among them), as well as migrant herons, waterfowl, and passerines. Hunting is allowed between September and May, currently not on Sundays. Back on River Road, head west and turn left after 0.3 mile on Sycamore Landing Road to the Canal. The towpath near here is one of the best places in the D.C. area for breeding Cerulean Warblers. This entire area is particularly recommended for birders who are also interested in butterflies and dragonflies.

If you haven't yet visited Lilypons (covered in the first part of this section) you could head there now from here. On Sycamore Landing Road, turn left (mile 0.0) at River Road, right onto West Willard at 0.2 mile, and right onto Fisher Avenue in Poolesville at 4.8 miles. Take the immediate left onto Elgin Road (Route 109), turn left onto MD-28 (Darnestown Road) at mile 7.3, right onto Park Mills Road at mile 13.0, and left onto Lily Pons Road at mile 16.3.

CALVERT AND SAINT MARY'S COUNTIES, MARYLAND
Full day; year round

For visitors with a little more time, the western shore of the Chesapeake Bay in Calvert and Saint Mary's Counties is an excellent bet. An area not too far from Washington is the **Chesapeake Beach/North Beach** area. From the Beltway, take Route 4 east/south about 14 miles, to the left exit for Route 260. Take Route 260 to the traffic light in Chesapeake Beach some 9 miles from Route 4. During winter, a wide variety of waterfowl can be seen here; waterfowl numbers build up during migration, and birding can be very interesting in March and April. Northern Gannets are often present, Eared Grebe is annual among the many Horned Grebes, Long-tailed Ducks and scoters (hard to find closer to Washington) are in excellent numbers, and a Little Gull very rarely shows up among the migrant Bonaparte's. Later in spring, and during the shorebird migration season (through October) the tidal pond in North Beach on the west side of Route 261, 1.5 miles north of Route 260, is worth checking. Herons, waterfowl, and an excellent variety of shorebirds can all be studied here at close range, and rarities are sometimes found. Lighting is best in the morning. From Chesapeake Beach, take Route 260 west to Route 2; turn left (south) on Route 2 and drive about 4.5 miles until you rejoin Route 4. Follow Route 4 for about 32 miles until it ends at Route 235 (this is about 55 miles from the Beltway directly via Route 4). Turn left (south/east) onto Route 235 and proceed to **Point Lookout State Park,** a distance of about 21.5 miles.

Point Lookout is an excellent place for waterbirds year round, and for passerine migrants and rarities in fall. Park by the restrooms at the end of the road. Check the bay and the Potomac River for Brown Pelican year round (especially in summer), waterfowl in winter, and Northern Gannet from November to April (but especially in March). The pilings just offshore can have Great Cormorant in winter (among the common Double-cresteds) and terns in summer, including, rarely, Sandwich. Just north of this parking lot, the marshy pond on the west side of the road is worth checking for herons, shorebirds, and marsh sparrows; it once hosted a Wood Stork. Forested areas are worth checking for landbird migrants, especially following the passage of autumn cold fronts. Brown-headed Nuthatch is resident in the pine woods, and Pine Warbler is a common breeder. Look for the nuthatch in the campground, especially along Periwinkle Point Trail, which is an abandoned railroad bed that one can enter behind the Visitor Center. To reach Periwinkle Point, take a right turn into extensive pine woods; the Point is a good place for Clapper and Virginia Rails, Marsh Wren, and Seaside and both Sharp-tailed Sparrows in their respective seasons.

In summer, a round-trip ferry cruise leaves Point Lookout at 10:00AM, Wednesday through Sunday, for Smith Island in the Chesapeake Bay. Wilson's Storm-Petrel is regularly seen from the ferry, and the island hosts breeding Yellow-crowned Night-Heron, Little Blue and Tricolored Herons, and Seaside Sparrow, among others. For information: *www.smithislandcruises.com*.

ADDITIONAL SITES

For birders with more time, there are plenty of outstanding birding sites within a three-hour drive of D.C. All the sites below are covered in Claudia Wilds's book, and some have been treated in more detail in recent birdfinding articles in ABA publications. The Delmarva Peninsula in particular offers many alternatives. **Bombay Hook National Wildlife Refuge** and **Little Creek Wildlife Management Area** in Delaware are two of North America's best shorebird hot-spots (see the May 1994 issue of *Winging It*, "Delaware Shorebirding"). **Blackwater National Wildlife Refuge** and nearby areas in **Dorchester County, Maryland**, have outstanding waterfowl and raptor concentrations in winter, as well as breeding Black Rails and southern passerines (see the article "Maryland's Everglades: Southern Dorchester County" in the April 1999 issue of *Birding*, 31:140-154). Also in Maryland, coastal **Worcester County** offers some of the best winter birding in the region; also it can have excellent passerine fall-outs in fall.

Farther south in Virginia, **Chincoteague National Wildlife Refuge** is excellent for waterfowl and shorebirds. The **Cape Charles** area can rival Cape May, New Jersey, as a fall migration hot-spot, and the **Chesapeake Bay Bridge and Tunnel** has Great Cormorant, Purple Sandpiper, and coastal waterfowl in winter, passerine migrants in fall, and rarities (such as the Black-tailed Gull that spent several winters there). See the article "Birding the Cape Charles Area" in the August 1995 issue of *Birding*, 27:270-281.

The **Appalachian Mountains** in western Maryland and Virginia hold many species that do not breed closer to Washington. **Garrett and Allegheny Counties** in Maryland and **Highland County** in Virginia are particularly recommended; consult Claudia Wilds's birdfinding guide.

ACKNOWLEDGMENTS

We wish to thank Lisa Shannon, who provided invaluable help with mileages; Patty Craig, who assisted with the St. Mary's County portion and provided helpful information about Point Lookout State Park; Kurt Gaskill, who provided information about Huntley Meadows Park; and Paul Pisano, who provided overall inspiration.

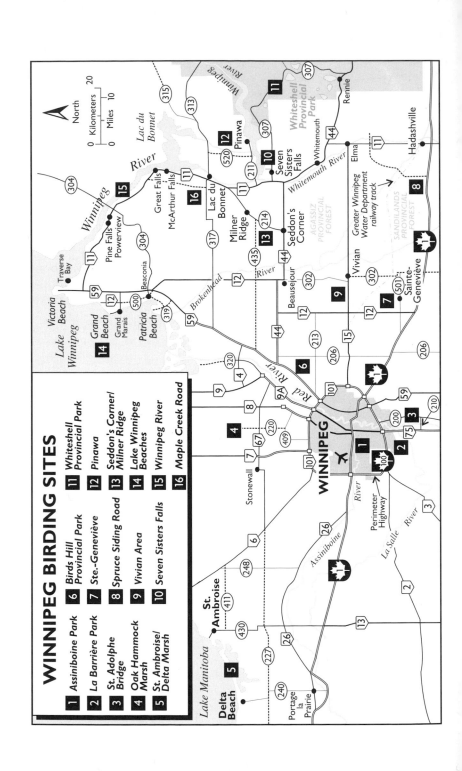

WINNIPEG BIRDING SITES

1 Assiniboine Park
2 La Barrière Park
3 St. Adolphe Bridge
4 Oak Hammock Marsh
5 St. Ambroise/ Delta Marsh
6 Birds Hill Provincial Park
7 Ste.-Geneviève
8 Spruce Siding Road
9 Vivian Area
10 Seven Sisters Falls
11 Whiteshell Provincial Park
12 Pinawa
13 Seddon's Corner/ Milner Ridge
14 Lake Winnipeg Beaches
15 Winnipeg River
16 Maple Creek Road

WINNIPEG, MANITOBA

Rudolf F. Koes and Peter Taylor

Located in the prairie/parkland ecotone, within an hour's drive of the boreal forest and two major freshwater lakes, Winnipeg offers something to birders year round. Although many provinces and states surpass Manitoba in total number of species recorded, few can rival the variety that can be seen in one day between mid-May and early September. Manitoba Big Day records include the Canadian all-time mark of 205 species as well as the North American record for June. This impressive birding was accomplished within easy driving distance of Winnipeg. In contrast, winter birding is extremely sparse, but it includes a number of sought-after boreal and subarctic species.

Although Winnipeg has never quite lived up to its early promise as a center of commerce and transportation, a "Chicago of the North," it is still a major business and cultural center with good airline connections across Canada and to several U.S. destinations. Perhaps most important for birders, Winnipeg Airport is the gateway to Churchill. Most birding tours visiting Churchill include in their itinerary at least a few days in southern Manitoba.

ESSENTIAL INFORMATION

Getting Around: Downtown Winnipeg is a 15-minute taxi ride from the airport. Car-rental outlets are available both at the airport and downtown. The airport is also served by a regular bus route. Public transportation in Winnipeg is efficient, and a $1.65 fare will get you anywhere in the city. Outside the city, however, renting a car is a must, unless you are fortunate enough to talk a local birder into a day out. In that event, insist at least on paying your host for the gas. Although there are no freeways, city streets are not often congested, even at rush hour. A trip from downtown to the outskirts typically takes 20 to 25 minutes, except during the occasional snow storm in winter. Beyond the city limits, provincial highways and other paved roads are good for all-weather travel, except in blowing snow or the most torrential thunderstorms. Unpaved roads with Provincial Road (PR) numbering are usually passable, but may be treacherous when wet or icy. All other roads should be traveled with caution, especially the many dirt roads that can gradually deteriorate or even end in the middle of nowhere.

Climate: From bitter cold in winter (-40°C/F) to blistering heat in summer (35°C or 100°F), the Manitoba climate is one of extremes, so be prepared. Local birders go out in winter (from mid-November to mid-March), even on the coldest days. Dress in layers, making sure to protect the head and feet. Most of us wear a parka, a toque (woolen cap), long underwear, mitts, and mukluks or snowmobile boots. In spring and fall, be prepared for a variety of conditions, and pack a hat, thick sweater, and gloves. In summer, a hat and sunscreen are advisable.

Other Considerations: Mosquitoes can be a nuisance from late May through September, as can Black Flies in the boreal forest. Wood Tick season is from late April through early summer. Carry DEET, tuck in long pants, and avoid long grass as much as possible. Black Bears are present in the boreal forest, but encounters are rare. Give them a wide berth, especially females with cubs. Poison-Ivy is common, even in some city parks. Stay on the trails if you are not familiar with this plant, or at least remember the old adage, "leaflets three, let it be."

Safety: Virtually all areas of the city are quite safe, and birding locations mentioned here, in particular, may be visited without worry about potential hazards. As in any large city, Winnipeg's core has its panhandlers and occasional drunks, but they rarely become overly pushy. Car break-ins do occur, particularly around the Manitoba Museum of Man and Nature, so lock valuables in the trunk. Although Manitobans are friendly people, do not trespass onto private property. When in doubt, stay away or ask permission.

Other Resources: Visitors who are staying for more than a day or two, or who would like to venture beyond the sites described here, should consider acquiring the following books: *Birder's Guide to Southeastern Manitoba* by N. J. Cleveland et al. (1988, Manitoba Naturalists Society); *Wings along the Winnipeg* (The Birds of the Pinawa-Lac du Bonnet Region, Manitoba) by P. Taylor (1985, Manitoba Naturalists Society); *A Bird-Finding Guide to Canada* edited by J. C. Finlay (2000, McClelland and Stewart); and *Field Checklists of the Birds of Manitoba* (2000) and of *the Birds of Southeastern Manitoba* (1995) by Manitoba Avian Research Committee.

For information on upcoming bird outings, contact the Manitoba Naturalists Society, 401-63 Albert Street, Winnipeg, MB R3B 1G4, (204) 943-9029 or *www.manitobanature.ca*. An alternative source is the Manitoba Museum of Man and Nature, 190 Rupert Avenue, Winnipeg, MB R3B 0N2, (204) 956-2830 or *www.manitobamuseum.mb.ca*. There is no Rare Bird Alert in Manitoba, but bird news circulates by phone and e-mail. For current information, check out the local birding chat group at *www.groups.yahoo.com/group/Manitobabirds*, or contact the Manitoba Naturalists Society (details above).

Maps and lodging information are available from Explore Manitoba Centre, 21 Forks Market Road, Winnipeg, MB R3C 2T7, (204) 945-3777. Free provincial maps and lodging guides are also available at many gas stations.

Other Destinations: For the non-birding companion, or on non-birding days, consider a visit to the following city attractions: Manitoba Museum of Man and Nature (address above), a superb museum and a must if time allows (check the new Hudson's Bay Company exhibit, and see how many birds you can spot in the Boreal Forest Gallery); Winnipeg Art Gallery, 300 Memorial Boulevard (houses world's largest Inuit art collection); The Forks, Forks Market Road (river-walk, shops, restaurants, market, tourist information, etc. at the confluence of the Red and Assiniboine Rivers); Winnipeg Zoo, in Assiniboine Park (see Assiniboine Park site map; don't miss the Tropical House); and Fort Whyte Centre, 1961 McCreary Road (captive and wild waterfowl, bison herd, and interpretive centre).

THE BIRDING YEAR

S pring birding starts in earnest with the arrival of waterfowl and raptors, beginning in March and usually peaking in the first half of April. For raptors, visit St. Adolphe at that time; for waterfowl, check Oak Hammock Marsh from early April through May or the Seven Sisters Dam in late April or early May. The latter period is also the best time for sparrows in Assiniboine Park or other city parks, or for locating various migrants at St. Ambroise and Delta. Deciding where to go becomes difficult in mid- and late May, when almost all areas offer a great variety. City parks, the boreal forest, and the "Beaches" may all be crawling with flycatchers, thrushes, and warblers.

June is prime time for breeding passerines in the boreal forest, or for trips to southwestern Manitoba or to Churchill, both beyond the scope of this guide. Shorebirds return between July and early September, tailing off until freeze-up around the end of October. Depending on water levels, Oak Hammock Marsh may provide excellent viewing. August and early September bring warblers to Assiniboine Park; waterfowl are at their best from mid-September into early November at Oak Hammock. Local birders check the "Beaches" and the Red and Winnipeg Rivers from October into early December for "sea ducks," Bald Eagles, and northern gulls. Winter is the best time to scour the boreal forest for grouse, owls, and the two "three-toed" woodpeckers, Gray Jays, Boreal Chickadees, as well as winter finches.

ASSINIBOINE PARK

Morning or half day; spring and fall, sometimes winter

N estled along the south bank of the Assiniboine River about six kilometers (four miles) west of downtown Winnipeg, **Assiniboine Park** is the premier birding location within city boundaries. Take a westbound #11 or #21 bus along Portage Avenue to Overdale Street and cross the footbridge south of Portage Avenue. Vehicles can be parked along Overdale. Access is also possible south of the river along Corydon Avenue, but directions are more complicated.

Invariably the most productive area is the wooded strip along the river, extending from the English Garden to beyond the park boundary to the east. A foot/bicycle path and various trails make for easy birding, although neck strain is a common complaint after a morning of warbler-watching! Beware of Poison-Ivy off the trails, and be alert for cyclists and rollerbladers along the main path.

Birding in the winter is generally slow, but Bohemian Waxwings and winter finches (Pine Grosbeak, crossbills, redpolls) are frequently present, especially in the upscale residential area immediately east of the park. Some early migrants may arrive in March, but the park is at its best from late April through May. First sparrows appear, then a rapid succession of thrushes, warblers, vireos, and flycatchers, with peak variety in mid-May. One may find five species of vireos, including Yellow-throated and Philadelphia, and 20+ warbler species. Elusive skulkers, such as Connecticut and Mourning, are possible beneath the underbrush, while "easier" species such as Cape May and Black-throated Green forage higher up. In the English Garden, visibility of both canopy- and ground-feeders is better than elsewhere in the park. This is also the prime spot for Harris's Sparrows, whose numbers usually peak during the second week of May. Yellow-bellied Flycatchers are often present in late May and the first few days of June.

Summer is a quiet time, although Yellow-throated Vireos remain to breed. By early August, southward migration of passerines is well underway. From

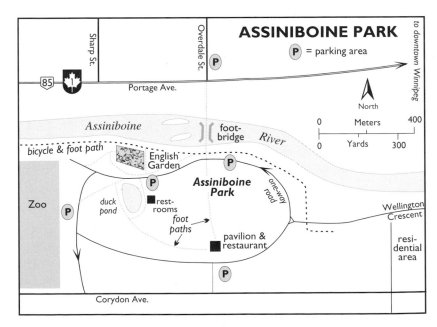

mid-August to mid-September Ruby-throated Hummingbirds, Rose-breasted Grosbeaks, and Baltimore Orioles enliven the English Garden, assorted passerines feast on Red-osier Dogwood berries along the river bank, and *Empidonax* flycatchers present identification challenges, while warblers *seep* and *zeet* everywhere. Check along the river for Great Blue Herons, Wood Ducks, and the occasional shorebird. From mid-September to mid-November the variety gradually diminishes to winter levels. Eastern Screech-Owls frequent this and other city parks year round; check with local birders for current information.

The park can become crowded on nice spring and summer days, so come early and avoid mid-day, especially on weekends. The nearby zoo (see map) is worth a visit, and the pavilion houses a collection of paintings (free admission), as well as a superb restaurant. Birders on a budget can try the coffee shop at Portage and Overdale.

Located along the Red River in the south of the city, **St. Vital Park** is smaller than Assiniboine Park, but at times it can be just as good, with the one advantage of better access to the riverbank to see grebes and ducks (April), swallows (May), and a host of warblers and sparrows (May, August/September). Farther south and on the west side of the Red River, King's Park is another alternative.

LA BARRIÈRE PARK

Morning or half day; spring and summer

South of the Perimeter Highway (Highway 100/101)—Winnipeg's ring road and unofficial boundary—lies **La Barrière Park**. Comprised of river-bottom forest, Bur Oak woodlands, and meadows, it offers fewer migrants than the large city parks, but it is home to several interesting summer residents. Broad-winged Hawk, Great Horned Owl, and Long-eared Owl nest sparingly in the woods, as do Great Crested Flycatcher, Yellow-throated Vireo, Scarlet Tanager, and Indigo Bunting. The trees around the parking lot are usually reliable for Orchard Oriole, while woodland edges and fields south of the parking lot often harbor Loggerhead Shrike, Eastern Bluebird, and Lark Sparrow. The park is most productive from late May to early July and to a lesser extent in late August and early September. There is no public transportation to the park, which is about 20 kilometers (13 miles) from downtown. Access is via southbound Route 80 (Waverley Street), or alternatively, via Route 42 (Pembina Highway) and the Perimeter Highway to Waverley Street. The bridge over the LaSalle River on Route 80 may be flooded in spring, but La Barrière Park can still be reached via PR-247 south of St. Norbert.

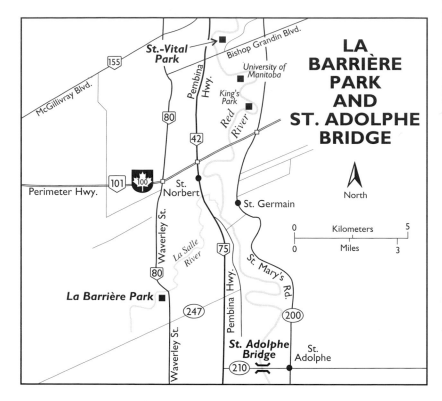

St.-Vital Park
155
McGillivray Blvd.
Bishop Grandin Blvd.
University of Manitoba
Pembina Hwy.
King's Park
80
Red River
42
Perimeter Hwy.
101
100
St. Norbert
Waverley St.
La Salle River
80
La Barrière Park
247
Waverley St.
Pembina Hwy.
75
St. Germain
St. Mary's Rd.
200
St. Adolphe Bridge
210
St. Adolphe

LA BARRIÈRE PARK AND ST. ADOLPHE BRIDGE

North

| 0 | Kilometers | 5 |
| 0 | Miles | 3 |

St. Adolphe Bridge

Half or full day; early spring

From early March to mid-April, birders congregate at the **St. Adolphe Bridge** to witness the annual spectacle of hawk migration. Accipiters, buteos, eagles, and falcons use the Red River Valley, a northern extension of the Mississippi Flyway, as their migration corridor in spring. Woodlands along the riverbank provide the necessary thermals for the migrating birds, particularly when snow still covers the surrounding agricultural land. Counts in the hundreds of birds are regular, and on exceptional days 1,000-plus hawks have been tallied. Red-tailed Hawks predominate, but double-digit numbers of Bald Eagles, Northern Harriers, Sharp-shinned and Cooper's Hawks, and Rough-legged Hawks are also possible. Northern Goshawks are cyclical; in some years dozens may be seen on a mid- or late March day, while more typically only a few are counted in a season. There is always the chance of seeing a Golden Eagle or a Peregrine Falcon, and possible rarities include Red-shouldered Hawk, Ferruginous Hawk, and Gyrfalcon. Although Bald Eagles, Northern Harriers, and Rough-legged Hawks start appearing in early

March, most migrants pass through in late March and early April. Sunny days with light winds are usually best.

In addition to diurnal raptors, many other birds follow the river on their northward journey. Skeins of honking Canada Geese, tight little groups of Common Mergansers, gulls, Northern Flickers, swarms of blackbirds, and retreating redpolls are just a few of the birds that will make most visits worthwhile.

The bridge is located on PR-210, which connects Highway 75 and PR-200, roughly 25 kilometers (16 miles) from downtown or 11 kilometers (7 miles) from the Perimeter Highway. Pull off the road onto the wide, gravel shoulder at the east side of the bridge over the Red River and scan the southern skyline. Traffic can be busy, so be careful when stepping onto the road.

OAK HAMMOCK MARSH

Half day; spring, summer, fall

In its heyday in the 1970s and 1980s **Oak Hammock Marsh Wildlife Management Area** was a magical place, full of birds—a surprise around every corner, it seemed. Natural succession, increased public use, marsh management policies, and cultivation of surrounding pastureland have all diminished its former glory, but it is still deservedly the most popular birding destination in the Winnipeg area. Nowhere else can one see a comparable variety of waders, waterfowl, raptors, shorebirds, and grassland species so close to the city.

About half-an-hour north of the Perimeter Highway (25 kilometers, 16 miles), the marsh can be reached via Highway 7 or Highway 8. At Highway 67 turn right (east) from #7 or turn left (west) from #8 until PR-220 is reached. Turn north and the Interpretive Centre at the edge of the marsh complex appears in the distance. Walking trails on the dikes provide ready access to the marsh; spotting scopes can be set up on the three observation mounds (north, central, and south) to scan the area.

In winter this is a desolate place. Roads are often blocked by snowdrifts, and few birds are present, although Sharp-tailed Grouse, Snowy Owls, and Snow Buntings are all possible along the west side, and a few ducks linger in some of the creeks that remain open. Canada Geese and attendant Bald Eagles return in late March, and by mid-April the marsh is a hive of activity. Snow Geese and ducks are abundant; Northern Harriers, Rough-legged Hawks, and Short-eared Owls patrol the grasslands; and flocks of Lapland Longspurs swirl over the bare fields. Shorebird numbers fluctuate from year to year, depending on water levels, but mid-May to early June is usually the best time. The marsh list ranges from regular visitors such as American Avocet and Wilson's Phalarope to strays such as Black-necked Stilt and Ruff. In early summer up to five grebe species are possible. Around the fringe of

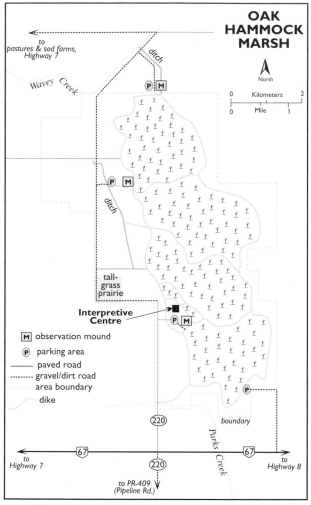

OAK HAMMOCK MARSH

North

| 0 | Kilometers | 2 |
| 0 | Mile | 1 |

to pastures & sod farms, Highway 7

Wavey Creek

ditch

ditch

tall-grass prairie

Interpretive Centre

M observation mound
P parking area
—— paved road
------- gravel/dirt road
...... area boundary
⌒⌒ dike

220

boundary

Parks Creek

67

to Highway 7

220

67

to Highway 8

to PR-409 (Pipeline Rd.)

the marsh, Yellow Rails turn up in wet years, and Sedge Wrens and Le Conte's Sparrows are common, and Nelson's Sharp-tailed Sparrow is very local.

Swainson's Hawk and Upland Sandpiper frequent the pastures and sod farms northwest of the marsh in summer. Both Black-bellied and American Golden-Plovers are frequently found here during migration, and Buff-breasted Sandpipers sometimes make a brief stop in August. Late summer is also the time to check for wandering egrets and Prairie Falcons. In September and October goose numbers peak, and a few Ross's Geese can usually be found amongst the thousands of Snows. Bald Eagle and Common Raven numbers start to build up, and in November dozens of each species feast on goose and duck carcasses. Snowy Owls also drift in from the north, and Rough-legged Hawks are once again prominent.

A few spots between the city and the marsh are worth checking. The vicinity of Pipeline Road (PR-409) and all along PR-220 to the marsh are often good for Swainson's Hawk, Gray Partridge, Western Kingbird, Loggerhead Shrike, and Orchard Oriole. Partridges are present year round, but they are most visible in winter; their numbers fluctuate from year to year.

ST. AMBROISE/DELTA MARSH COMPLEX

Full day; spring, summer, fall

The vast marshes that fringe the southern shore of Lake Manitoba have long attracted birders and other naturalists. The narrow forested sand ridge that separates the marsh from the lake supports exceptional breeding densities of several species, including Least Flycatcher and Yellow Warbler, and migrants funnel through here in untold numbers.

There are a number of accessible areas, but only the two best sites are described here. The first is **St. Ambroise Provincial Park**, which can be reached most directly via Highway 6 to PR-411 West and PR-430 North, which terminates at the lake. Park your vehicle near the former park entrance gate and walk in. Scan the lake and small offshore islands for American White Pelican, grebes, ducks, and terns. Clark's Grebe is possible among the many Western Grebes, but it is very rare, and hybrids do occur. Walk west on the gravel road for one to two kilo-

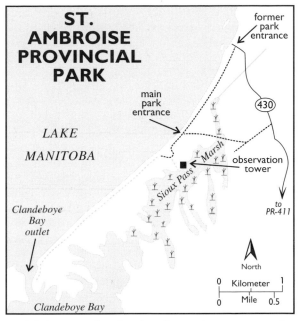

meters (one-half to one mile), keeping alert for thrushes and sparrows on the ground, warblers in the trees, and other migrants overhead, or in late spring and summer listen to the chorus of song that surrounds you.

Return to your vehicle, backtrack to the first gravel road on your right and proceed to the main park entrance. A park pass or fee is required, but one can walk in free; as at most Provincial Parks, the gate is staffed from late May to early fall. Follow the gravel road west (left) a short distance, then scan the lake, explore the trail west from the end of the road, and check the boardwalk leading south to an observation tower overlooking the marsh.

To reach **Delta** from St. Ambroise, return south on PR-430, turn west on PR-227 and north on PR-240. Make sure to check the dump on PR-227,

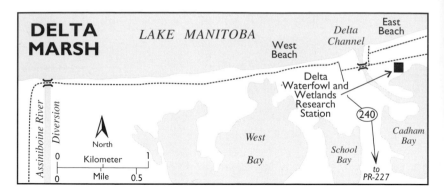

a few kilometers west of PR-430, as it usually hosts a few California Gulls amongst the hordes of Ring-billed and Herring Gulls in spring and early fall. At the terminus of PR-240, turn right, cross Delta Channel, and turn left. Just before the cottages, a beach-access point allows you to scan for waterfowl, shorebirds, gulls, and terns. At times exposed sand bars are full of plovers, turnstones, and terns. Again, check Western Grebes for Clark's. On a good day in migration, the trees are dripping with flycatchers, vireos, and warblers; be sure to walk along the paved road to the east.

Returning across the channel, drive slowly west from the end of PR-240, again looking for passerines. At times the sky above the woods is filled with streams of swallows and blackbirds, or Sharp-shinned and Broad-winged Hawks. After about 3 kilometers (2 miles), you will reach the Assiniboine River Diversion outlet, another good vantage point from which to scan the lake. If water levels permit, the concrete spillway can be crossed here; do so at your own risk. Drive south on the road along the dike at the west side of the Diversion to PR-227, checking the marshes and ponds on both sides of the dike. Obey all signs; do not enter posted areas. Upon reaching PR-227 turn left (east) and return to Winnipeg.

The whole area is justly renowned for its birdlife. There are two research stations and a banding station, and over the years such diverse rarities as Yellow-billed Loon, Tricolored Heron, Garganey, King Eider, Black-necked Stilt, Sabine's Gull, Worm-eating Warbler, and Golden-crowned Sparrow have been spotted here. See what *you* can find!

EXPLORING THE BOREAL FOREST

Half to full day; year round

The edge of the boreal forest crosses Manitoba diagonally from around Swan River in the west down to the southeast corner of the province. Aspen parkland forms a broad band of wooded grassland between the true boreal forest and the prairie, a distinction that is muddied by extensive agricultural clearing. Slightly elevated "islands" of forest, such as Riding Mountain, Spruce Woods, and Turtle Mountain, extend southward to the North Dakota border. Four major highways (1, 15, 44, and 59) radiate eastward from Winnipeg toward the boreal forest. All distances from Winnipeg start from the Perimeter Highway. **Birds Hill Provincial Park** is the closest extensively forested area to Winnipeg, barely 10 minutes from the city on Highway 59, but it is well worth the extra drive to reach the larger expanses of forest farther east. Most small towns have gas stations, but few keep birders' hours, so fill the tank before leaving Winnipeg.

Near the **Trans-Canada Highway, Sainte-Geneviève and Spruce Siding**: The Trans-Canada is not well-suited for birding, but it does give access to some productive areas. In recent years, Golden-winged Warblers have been found reliably in the **Sainte-Geneviève area** (27 kilometers east on Highway 1, north on Highway 12, and east on PR-501), especially in and around the old sand quarry near Monominto Road. This spot is also good for Great Crested Flycatcher, Scarlet Tanager, Eastern Towhee, and various warblers. It could justify a half-day outing in its own right, or be a stop on a full day.

Spruce Siding Road (north of Highway 1 about 71 kilometers from Winnipeg and 11 kilometers before Hadashville) is celebrated for April or May owling trips. It is no longer a numbered provincial road, but the surface is still good, albeit prone to local flooding in spring. In reasonably dry conditions, it is passable throughout (north, then east) to Highway 11. Great Gray Owls nest in the forest adjoining this road, but they are not always visible or audible in spring. Barred and Northern Saw-whet Owls respond to discreet use of taped calls. Try driving slowly, with frequent stops in spruce-tamarack bogs and near old fields or marshy clearings. The coniferous bogs are also excellent for listening for Connecticut Warblers, but the deep roadside ditches will likely curtail any forays into the woods. The large marsh just north of the Greater Winnipeg Water Department railway track and aqueduct is excellent for rails (including Yellow Rail in most years), American Bittern and rarely Least Bittern, and Sedge and Marsh Wrens.

Northeast to **Whiteshell Park**: Highways 15 and 44 offer an attractive birding loop, including possible side-trips to Pinawa or into Whiteshell Provincial Park. Eastern Bluebirds can be seen on roadside wires along Highway 15 near **Vivian**, and Brown Thrashers and Eastern Towhees alternately sing from exposed perches and skulk in the oak scrub. Note that some sites for Golden-winged Warblers along PR-302 north of Vivian, described in earlier guides, are no longer reliable; however, the birds can be found across the highway from the weather radar dome 0.6 kilometer west of Vivian. The forested stretch of Highway 15 between Sainte Rita and Elma (50 to 70 kilometers from Winnipeg) attracts good numbers of Northern

Hawk Owls and Great Gray Owls in invasion winters, and the odd individual in off-years.

Take Highway 11 north from Elma and turn west on Highway 44 toward **Whitemouth** (the eastbound route to Rennie would add too many miles for a single day). Highway 44 west through Whitemouth heads back toward Winnipeg via Beausejour, and has several side attractions. The network of farm roads (of varying quality) north of Whitemouth is well worth exploring for Sandhill Cranes from April to September, and can be excellent for Rough-legged Hawks and other raptors in early spring and late fall.

S even Sisters Falls is reached by taking Highway 11 north from the north junction of Highway 44, then traveling a mile east on PR-307. Just after the Whitemouth River bridge (check here for Hooded Merganser), a firm dirt road, *not maintained in winter*, leads north to a delightful picnic site at Whitemouth Falls. In spring and summer, American Redstarts swarm in the maple understory along the way, and American White Pelicans often provide entertainment near the falls. The best look-out spot at Seven Sisters Falls is the hydroelectric dam, which is accessible by a paved road running north from PR-307 at the east end of the village. **Natalie Lake**, the forebay of the dam, can be outstanding for waterbirds during migration, but numbers fluctuate from year to year and from day to day. Spring highlights include loons, grebes, Greater Scaup, White-winged Scoter (in some years), and mergansers, whereas all three scoter species are possible in October. Even in midsummer, it is worth scoping the rocks below the dam for Common and Hooded Mergansers and even Caspian Tern. A long list of rarities has accumulated here over the years. A telescope is essential, and visibility is best early or late in the day.

A s one continues eastward on PR-307 into **Whiteshell Provincial Park**, there is excellent songbird habitat in the cottage areas near Otter Falls and eastward to Nutimik Lake (remember that a vehicle permit is needed year round within the park). This stretch is especially good for Northern Parula, Black-throated Green Warbler, Mourning Warbler, and Scarlet Tanager from late May to early July. The road is narrow and busy on summer weekends, but the frequent cottage "block roads" provide plenty of opportunities to explore on foot.

Closer to Seven Sisters Falls, try walking some of the dirt roads, especially Homestead Road, that lead into Black Spruce forest. Forestry Road 28, which runs south of PR-307 just west of the park entrance, is also excellent. *Do not drive this road beyond the gravel stockpile about 1 kilometer south of PR-307, because it is very poorly maintained*; a leisurely walk beyond this point can be most rewarding in the breeding season. Philadelphia Vireo has nested in the aspens at the gravel depot, Alder Flycatchers abound, and Olive-sided

Flycatcher and Northern Parula can usually be found. In winter, this area can be good for Northern Goshawk and Black-backed Woodpecker.

Northern Hawk Owl
Louise Zemaitis

The **Pinawa** area (PR-211 east of Highway 11) is also excellent for songbird variety, especially the cemetery road that runs north of PR-211 just outside town. Park at the cemetery and walk the treacherous dirt road beyond; many an unwary driver has had to have his vehicle towed out of the mud or snow here! This road is especially productive at the peak of warbler migration; later in the summer, mosquitoes may dampen your enthusiasm. In winter, Pinawa feeders swarm with Pine and Evening Grosbeaks (in the morning), and Great Gray and Northern Hawk Owls are frequently seen along the western half of PR-211.

Provincial Road 520, running north off PR-211 west of Pinawa, travels through an interesting mixture of forest and marginal farmland, the latter good for Le Conte's Sparrow and (especially in winter and early spring) Sharp-tailed Grouse. Another good road to explore (with caution), especially for warblers, runs west off PR-520 opposite the Old Pinawa Provincial Recreation Park to some sand quarries in the forest. A little farther north, Tower Road and its branches are good for Sharp-tailed Grouse, as well. North another mile or so, pick up PR-313 into Lac du Bonnet, whence PR-317 and Highway 59 provide the most direct route back to Winnipeg.

If you take Highway 44 west toward Beausejour, the **Seddon's Corner** area has an attractive assortment of birds. North of Seddon's Corner, PR-435 runs west and downhill into a fine stretch of spruce-tamarack bog. Piecemeal logging has diminished this site, but it still attracts many boreal birds. Connecticut Warblers are fairly common and can be coaxed to the roadside by judicious tape-playing. It is more sporting to walk them up, but the going is very heavy even if you can get across the ditch. Other possibilities at appropriate seasons include Black-backed and Three-toed Woodpeckers, Yellow-bellied and Olive-sided Flycatchers, Blue-headed Vireo, Gray Jay, Winter Wren, Mourning Warbler (especially on the slope down from PR-214), and White-winged Crossbill. If you have only a few hours free to sample the boreal forest, this is the place to go. Even the occasional Spruce Grouse has been known to wander onto the road!

There are several good places for American Woodcock along PR-214, especially at the forest edge near Highway 11 (south of Lac du Bonnet). If you find yourself there at twilight (about one-half hour after sunset) in April or May, stop frequently until you hear one close by the road.

LAKE WINNIPEG BEACHES AND THE WINNIPEG RIVER
Full day; spring, summer, fall

Another loop, which is most productive in early spring or late fall, can be made by following Highway 59 to **Patricia, Grand, and Victoria Beaches** and, if time allows, returning along the Winnipeg River. Local birders scour the beaches and river late every fall for scoters, Long-tailed Ducks, and other northern waterbirds. Glaucous Gulls are possible in November, and hope springs eternal that an Ivory Gull will show up one day!

Patricia Beach is the least developed of the three major beaches, and also the closest to Winnipeg (PR-319 west of Highway 59). In early spring, snowdrifts on the wooded beach ridge melt much later than in the surrounding countryside, and access beyond the park entrance may be difficult even in May. The ridge extends north about a mile to the outlet from a large natural lagoon. The woods here offer a variety of passerines similar to those of St. Ambroise and Delta, but the birds occur in smaller numbers. The lagoon is good for Caspian and Forster's Terns, as well as for a few shorebirds, especially in September. Note that this secluded area is also used by nudists in summer; be discreet! Check the lake and lagoon for Western Grebes, and beware of pale immatures that can easily be mistaken for Clark's Grebes. In late fall, this area has numerous Bald Eagles. Snow Geese are common from mid-September until mid-October, and the odd Ross's Goose is possible. Check flocks of Bonaparte's Gulls for vagrant Little or Sabine's Gulls.

Returning along PR-319, turn left just past the railway track and follow the gravel road leading to PR-500 and the busier resorts of Grand Marais and **Grand Beach**. Needless to say, birding is best here before and after the holiday season. This area has a vestigial population of Piping Plovers, which should in no way be disturbed. From Grand Beach, Highway 59 takes you north to **Victoria Beach** (the numbering of Highways 12 and 59 is a bit confusing here). Beach access is off-limits to motor vehicles between mid-May and early September. The combination of the forested cottage area and the lakeshore offers excellent birding variety almost year round. Bird feeders in winter are often reliable places to spot Bohemian Waxwings, Pine Grosbeaks, and Pine Siskins. After viewing the beaches, if time permits take Highway 11 from Traverse Bay along the **Winnipeg River**, returning to Winnipeg via PR-304 from Pine Falls, PR-317 from Lac du Bonnet, or Highway 44 as described above. The most-productive spots are usually the rapids at Pine Falls (access along the wood stockpile at the paper-mill) and Seven Sisters Dam (see above), but it is worth checking the other dams at Powerview, Great Falls, and McArthur Falls.

Though enjoyable at any season, **Maple Creek Road** is best known for winter birding (December to March), especially for Great Gray Owls. A leisurely 24-kilometer (15-mile) drive along this narrow but well-maintained gravel road is easily incorporated into a trip along the Winnipeg River. The inconspicuous southern end of the road is on PR-317, about 90 kilometers (55 miles) northeast of Winnipeg and just 5 kilometers (3.2 miles) west of the junction with Highway 11 at Lac du Bonnet. The well-indicated northern end is on Highway 11, 4.5 kilometers (2.8 miles) northwest of Great Falls.

Heading north from PR-317, the first two miles run through open cropland, good only for Snow Buntings and rarely a Snowy Owl. Prospects improve as the road rises through marginal farmland to a low, rocky ridge and then descends through a more heavily wooded area with a few meadows. Park where the road jogs sharply east (8 kilometers, 5 miles), taking care not to impede other traffic, and walk west for a mile or so down the wide snowmobile trail (be prepared to jump aside for a few machines, whose drivers can be fast and inattentive). No two hikes here are the same, and nothing is guaranteed, but frequently-observed species include Three-toed and Black-backed Woodpeckers, Gray Jay, Boreal Chickadee, Pine Grosbeak, White-winged Crossbill, and both Common and Hoary Redpolls.

After a warm-up coffee, drive east for a mile and then north again. Great Gray Owls are possible anywhere in the strip of farmland for the next 5 miles, especially in early morning and late afternoon. Most conspicuous on calm days, they may be perched at the forest edge or even in farmyard trees. Black-billed Magpies are numerous, and other possibilities include Sharp-tailed Grouse, Northern Hawk Owl, Northern Shrike—and with luck, even a Northern Goshawk or Gyrfalcon. Forest fragments and transmission towers, especially near the second eastward jog in the road, are good for Northern Hawk Owl. The last few miles before Highway 11 are relatively unproductive, except for Snow Buntings.

ACKNOWLEDGMENTS

The maps in *Birder's Guide to Southeastern Manitoba* by N. J. Cleveland were a helpful resource for the preparation of several maps in this chapter.

OTHER GUIDES IN THE ABA SERIES

A Birder's Guide to the Bahamas
Anthony R. White

A Birder's Guide to Idaho
Dan Svingen and Kas Dumroese

A Birder's Guide to Virginia
David Johnston

A Birder's Guide to Colorado
Harold R. Holt

A Birder's Guide to Florida
Bill Pranty

A Birder's Guide to New Hampshire
Alan Delorey

Birdfinder: A Birder's Guide to Planning North American Trips
Jerry A. Cooper

A Birder's Guide to Southeastern Arizona
Richard Cachor Taylor

A Birder's Guide to Arkansas
Mel White

A Birder's Guide to Eastern Massachusetts
Bird Observer

A Birder's Guide to Churchill
Bonnie Chartier

A Birder's Guide to the Texas Coast
Harold R. Holt

A Birder's Guide to Wyoming
Oliver K. Scott

A Birder's Guide to the Rio Grande Valley of Texas
Mark W. Lockwood, William B. McKinney
James N. Paton, Barry R. Zimmer

A Birder's Guide to Southern California
Brad Schram

American Birding Association Sales

PO Box 6599, Colorado Springs, Colorado 80934
Phone: 800/634-7736 or 719/578-0607 Fax: 800/590-2473 or 719/578-9705
www.americanbirding.org

AMERICAN BIRDING ASSOCIATION

ABA is *the* organization of North American birders, and its mission is to bring all the excitement, challenge, and wonder of birds and birding to you. As an ABA member you will get the information you need to increase your birding skills so that you can make the most of your time in the field.

ABA supports the interests of birders of all ages and experiences, and promotes birding publications, projects, and partnerships. It focuses on bird identification and birdfinding skills and the development and dissemination of information on bird conservation. ABA also champions ethical birding practices.

Each year members receive six issues of ABA's award-winning magazine *Birding* and twelve issues of *Winging It*, a monthly newsletter. ABA conducts regular conferences and biennial conventions in the continent's best birding locations, publishes a yearly *Membership Directory and Yellow Pages*, compiles an annual *Directory of Volunteer Opportunities for Birders*, and offers discount prices for many bird books, optical gear, and other birding equipment through ABA Sales. The organization's *ABA/Lane Birdfinding Guide Series* sets the standard for accuracy and excellence in its field.

ABA is engaged in bird conservation through such institutions and activities as Partners in Flight and the American Bird Conservancy's Policy Council. ABA also actively promotes the economic and environmental values of birding.

ABA encourages birding among young people by sponsoring birding camp scholorships and "ABA/Leica Young Birder of the Year" competition, and by publishing *A Bird's-Eye View*, a bimonthly newsletter by and for its younger members.

ABA also publishes *North American Birds*, a quarterly which reviews all imprortant bird sightings and significant population trends for the US, Canada, Mexico, Central America, and the West Indies.

In short, ABA works to ensure that birds and birding have the healthy future that they deserve. In the words of the late Roger Tory Peterson, the American Birding Association is "the best value in the birding community." The American Birding Association gives active birders what they want. Consider joining today. You will find a membership form on the other side of this page.

American Birding Association Membership Services
PO Box 6599
Colorado Springs, CO 80934
telephone 800/850-2473 or 719/578-1614 - fax 719/578-1480
e-mail: member@aba.org
web site: www.americanbirding.org

AMERICAN BIRDING ASSOCIATION
Membership Application

All memberships include six issues of *Birding* magazine, monthly issues of *Winging It*, ABA's newsletter, and full rights of participation in all ABA activities.

Membership Classes and Dues:

❑ Individual - US	$40.00 / yr	❑ Student - Canada**	$30.00 / yr
❑ Individual - Canada*	$50.00 / yr	❑ Family - US	$47.00 / yr
❑ Individual - Int'l	$50.00 / yr	❑ Family - Canada*	$58.00 / yr
❑ Student - US**	$20.00 / yr	❑ Family - Int'l	$58.00 / yr
❑ Hooded Merganser - US $140.00 / yr		❑ Hooded Merganser - Int'l	$150.00 / yr

*Canadian dues include GST, which is paid to the Canadian government.
All membership dues include $30 for *Birding* magazine and $10 for *Winging It* newsletter.
** **Students** - Write your date of birth, name and location of school, and expected date of graduation on the bottom of this form. This information is **required** to receive Student rates.

Application Type
❑ New Membership   ❑ Renewal   ❑ Gift

Please call 800/850-2473 or 719/578-9703 for information about how you may subscribe to ABA's other publication, *North American Birds*.

Member Information
Name _____

Address _____

_____

Phone _____ E-mail _____

Payment Information
❑ Check or Money Order enclosed (US funds only)
❑ Charge to VISA / MasterCard / Discover (circle one)

Account Number _____

Expiration Date _____

Signature _____

Send this completed form with payment to:
> **ABA Membership**
> **PO Box 6599**
> **Colorado Springs, CO 80934**

Or log on to ABA's web site to join: *www.americanbirding.org/memform.htm*

MET11/01

PRINCIPLES OF BIRDING ETHICS

Everyone who enjoys birds and birding must always respect wild-life, its environment, and the rights of others. In any conflict of interest between birds and birders, the welfare of the birds and their environment comes first.

CODE OF BIRDING ETHICS

. Promote the welfare of birds and their environment.

(a) Support the protection of important bird habitat.

(b) To avoid stressing birds or exposing them to danger, exercise restraint and caution during observation, photography, sound recording, or filming.

Limit the use of recordings and other methods of attracting birds, and never use such methods in heavily birded areas or for attracting any species that is Threatened, Endangered, or of Special Concern, or is rare in your local area.

Keep well back from nests and nesting colonies, roosts, display areas, and important feeding sites. In such sensitive areas, if there is a need for extended observation, photography, filming, or recording, try to use a blind or hide, and take advantage of natural cover.

Use artificial light sparingly for filming or photography, especially for close-ups.

(c) Before advertising the presence of a rare bird, evaluate the potential for disturbance to the bird, its surroundings, and other people in the area, and proceed only if access can be controlled, disturbance can be minimized, and permission has been obtained from private land-owners. The sites of rare nesting birds should be divulged only to the proper conservation authorities.

(d) Stay on roads, trails, and paths where they exist; otherwise keep habitat disturbance to a minimum.

. Respect the law and the rights of others.

(a) Do not enter private property without the owner's explicit permission.

(b) Follow all laws, rules, and regulations governing use of roads and public areas, both at home and abroad.

(c) Practice common courtesy in contacts with other people. Your exemplary behavior will generate goodwill with birders and non-birders alike.

. Ensure that feeders, nest structures, and other artificial bird environments are safe.

3(a) Keep dispensers, water, and food clean and free of decay or disease. It is important to feed birds continually during harsh weather.

3(b) Maintain and clean nest structures regularly.

3(c) If you are attracting birds to an area, ensure the birds are not exposed to predation from cats and other domestic animals, or dangers posed by artificial hazards.

4. Group birding, whether organized or impromptu, requires special care.

Each individual in the group, in addition to the obligations spelled out in Items #1 and #2, has responsibilities as a Group Member.

4(a) Respect the interests, rights, and skills of fellow birders, as well as those of people participating in other legitimate outdoor activities. Freely share your knowledge and experience, except where code 1(c) applies. Be especially helpful to beginning birders.

4(b) If you witness unethical birding behavior, assess the situation and intervene if you think it prudent. When interceding, inform the person(s) of the inappropriate action and attempt, within reason, to have it stopped. If the behavior continues, document it and notify appropriate individuals or organizations.

Group Leader Responsibilities [amateur and professional trips and tours].

4(c) Be an exemplary ethical role model for the group. Teach through word and example.

4(d) Keep groups to a size that limits impact on the environment and does not interfere with others using the same area.

4(e) Ensure everyone in the group knows of and practices this code.

4(f) Learn and inform the group of any special circumstances applicable to the areas being visited (e.g., no tape recorders allowed).

4(g) Acknowledge that professional tour companies bear a special responsibility to place the welfare of birds and the benefits of public knowledge ahead of the company's commercial interests. Ideally, leaders should keep track of tour sightings, document unusual occurrences, and submit records to appropriate organizations.

PLEASE FOLLOW THIS CODE— DISTRIBUTE IT AND TEACH IT TO OTHERS.

Additional copies of the Code of Birding Ethics can be obtained from: ABA, PO Box 6599, Colorado Springs, CO 80934-6599, (800) 850-2473 or (719) 578-1614; fax: (800) 247-3329 or (719) 578-1480; e-mail: member@aba.org

7/1/

NOTES

Index

Note: City/chapter names (in italics) follow
the name of each birding site.

Belle Isle *Detroit* 144
Belleplain State Forest *Philadelphia* 316
Big Branch National Wildlife Refuge *New Orleans* 279
Big Cottonwood Canyon *Salt Lake City* 367
Big Creek Greenway *Atlanta* 31
Big Creek National Wildlife Area *Toronto* 430
Big Cypress National Preserve *Miami* 233
Big Marsh *Chicago* 85
Big Sycamore Canyon *Los Angeles* 209
Bill Baggs Cape Florida State Recreation Area *Miami* 227
Birch Cove Park *Halifax* 156
Bird Island Pier *Buffalo/Niagara Falls* 55
Bird Islands Seabird Sanctuary *Halifax* 161
Bird Sanctuary
    Addison Street *Chicago* 77
    Bolivar Flats *Houston* 170
    High Island *Houston* 172
    Inglewood *Calgary* 61
    Lincoln Park *Chicago* 77
    Quintana Neotropical *Houston* 174
    Reifel Migratory *Vancouver* 436-437
    T. S. Roberts *Minneapolis/St. Paul* 241-242
Birds Hill Provincial Park *Winnipeg* 475
Bishop, Orange 207
Bittern
    American 57, 106, 129, 140, 161, 217, 236, 309, 312, 334, 365, 426, 436, 447, 459, 475
    Least 16, 57, 83, 85, 106, 140, 149, 199, 206, 217, 228, 236, 243, 246, 262, 266-268, 301, 312, 315, 459-461, 475
Blackbird
    Brewer's 57, 69, 82-83, 186, 330
    Red-winged 283
    Rusty 62, 153, 259
    Tricolored 206, 208-209, 217, 395, 397, 399
    Yellow-headed 57, 85, 128, 140, 186, 217, 243, 246, 283, 299, 334, 361, 363, 365, 439
Blackwater National Wildlife Refuge *Washington, D.C.* 463
Bluebird
    Eastern 104, 173, 234, 258, 279, 301, 307, 350, 426, 456, 469
    Mountain 69, 121, 131, 158, 195-196, 211, 339, 371, 408
    Western 13, 131, 196, 208, 323, 327, 330, 381, 395, 399, 408
Bobolink 90-91, 102, 107, 146, 161, 217, 283, 301, 456, 461
Bobwhite, Northern 89-90, 107, 146
Bolivar Flats *Houston* 170
Bolsa Chica Preserve *Los Angeles* 209
Bombay Hook National Wildlife Refuge
    Philadelphia 317
    Washington, D.C. 463
Bonnet Carre Spillway *New Orleans* 281
Booby
    Brown 237
    Masked 237
Bosque del Apache National Wildlife Refuge *Albuquerque* 16
Botanic Gardens
    Chicago 83
    Fort Worth 115
Botanical Garden
    Missouri *Saint Louis* 351

Royal *Toronto* 426
Botanical Gardens
    Desert *Phoenix* 321
    Montréal 259
    Niagara Parks 48
Boulder Bird Club 126
Boulder City *Las Vegas* 193
Bountiful Landfill *Salt Lake City* 361
Bowen Park *Chicago* 81
Bowman Reservoir *Las Vegas* 199
Boy Scout Woods *Houston* 172
Boyce-Thompson Arboretum *Phoenix* 322
Brant 36, 55, 206, 294, 296, 300, 312, 378-379, 410-411, 445
Brasstown Bald *Atlanta* 33
Brazos Bend State Park *Houston* 173-174
Brecksville Reservation *Cleveland* 104
Brier Island *Halifax* 161
Brigantine National Wildlife Refuge *Philadelphia* 312-313
Brookline Bird Club 36
Brooklyn Bird Club 288
Buckeye *Phoenix* 323
Buckhorn Island State Park *Buffalo/Niagara Falls* 55
Bufflehead 26, 28, 40, 50, 62, 81-82, 115, 278, 296, 419
Bulbul, Red-whiskered 226, 230
Bunting
    Indigo 24, 86, 111-112, 153, 173, 198, 246, 279, 307, 469